HESS

Peter Padfield is an established biographer and naval historian. His interest in German history stemmed from a book he wrote on the Anglo-German naval rivalry prior to the First World War, *The Great Naval Race*, since when he has written three major biographies of leaders of the Third Reich, Grand Admiral Karl Dönitz, the Reichsführer-SS, Heinrich Himmler, and this book on Rudolf Hess. All three are published by Cassell.

By the same author:

BIOGRAPHY

Dönitz: The Last Führer
Himmler: Reichsführer-SS

NAVAL AND MARITIME HISTORY

The Sea is a Magic Carpet
The *Titanic* and the *Californian*
An Agony of Collisions
Aim Straight: A Biography of Admiral Sir Percy Scott
Broke and the *Shannon*: A Biography of Admiral Sir Philip Broke
The Battleship Era
(*Revised edition:* Battleship)
Guns at Sea: A History of Naval Gunnery
The Great Naval Race: Anglo-German Naval Rivalry 1900-1914
Nelson's War
Tide of Empires: Decisive Naval Campaigns in the Rise of the West
Volume I: 1481-1654
Volume II: 1654-1763
Rule Britannia: The Victorian and Edwardian Navy
Beneath the Houseflag of the P&O: A Social History
Armada: A Celebration of the 400th Anniversary of the Defeat of the Spanish Armada
War Beneath the Sea: Submarine Conflict 1939-1945
Maritime Supremacy and the Opening of the Western Mind

NOVELS

The Lion's Claw
The Unquiet Gods
Gold Chains of Empire
Salt and Steel

HESS

THE FÜHRER'S DISCIPLE

PETER PADFIELD

CASSELL&CO

Cassell & Co
Wellington House, 125 Strand
London WC2R 0BB

A catalogue record for this book is available from the British Library

ISBN 0-304-35843-6

Printed and bound in Great Britain by MPG Books,
Bodmin, Cornwall

CONTENTS

List of Illustrations   vii
Acknowledgements   ix
Introduction to the new edition   xii
Prologue   xx

PART ONE: HESS

 1 Hess   3
 2 Hitler   12
 3 *Mein Kampf*   22
 4 The Secretary   31
 5 The Brown House   43
 6 Power   52
 7 Night of the Long Knives   59
 8 The Deputy   71
 9 The England Game   85
10 War   96

PART TWO: FLIGHT

11 Peace Feelers   107
12 Churchill   116
13 Hubris   122
14 Turn East   129
15 Flight Plan   134
16 The Double Game   147
17 Sam Hoare   161
18 The Duke of Hamilton   170
19 Final Preparations   184
20 Flight   192

PART THREE: CAPTIVITY

21   Prisoner of War   205
22   The Peace Plan   218
23   The Propaganda War   229
24   Mytchett Place   242
25   Lord Simon   253
26   Psychosis   268
27   Disinformation   285
28   Nuremberg   298
29   Spandau   317
30   Post-Mortem   334

Postscript   346
Afterword   352
Notes   381
Bibliography   393
Index   396

ILLUSTRATIONS

Between pages 98 and 99

Hitler and Hess in 1924 (Spooner/Gamma)
With his wife Ilse in 1929 (Rex Features/SIPA)
Hitler with Nazi chiefs in Berlin 1931, with Hess behind (Hulton-Deutsch Collection)
Hess with Hitler, Munich (Hulton-Deutsch Collection)
Hitler and Hess at the Berghof, his Alpine retreat (Hulton-Deutsch Collection)
In the cockpit of his Messerschmitt, 1934 (Popperfoto)
Hess and Ernst Röhm, Chief of the SA, (Hulton-Deutsch Collection)
Hess with Martin Bormann (Hulton-Deutsch Collection)
Goebbels, Himmler, Hess, Hitler and General Blomberg at the Sportpalast, Berlin, 1937 (Hulton-Deutsch Collection)
A Nazi rally in 1938 (Hulton-Deutsch Collection)
Ilse, Hitler and Hess in the grounds of Hess's Munich villa (Rex Features/SIPA)
Professor Karl Haushofer (second left) and his son Albrecht (inset) who were largely responsible for Hess's flight to Scotland in 1941 (Ullstein)

Between pages 162 and 163

Hess deputizing for the Führer in 1938 (Hulton-Deutsch Collection)
At home with his son 'Buz', Wolf Rüdiger Hess (Rex Features/SIPA)
Sir Samuel Hoare leaving for Spain, May 1940 (Hulton-Deutsch Collection)
The Duke of Hamilton (Hulton-Deutsch Collection)
The wreckage of the ME 110 (Hulton-Deutsch Collection)
Mytchett Place where Hess was detained for a year (*After The Battle* Magazine)

The Defendants at Nuremberg, 1945 (Hulton-Deutsch Collection)
Eating from a tin, Nuremberg (Hulton-Deutsch Collection)
A 1961 'Free Hess' leaflet (Rex Features/SIPA)
In his cell aged 92 at Spandau (Rex Features/SIPA)
Alone in the prison garden (Spooner/Gamma)
Hess's last letter to his daughter-in-law Andrea (Rex Features/SIPA)
Wolf Rüdiger, Andrea and Ilse Hess leave Spandau after a visit (RexFeatures/SIPA)
The 'suicide note' (by permission of Wolf Rüdiger Hess)
Wolf Rüdiger Hess with the body of his father (Rex Features/SIPA)
The post-mortem (by permission of Wolf Rüdiger Hess)

ACKNOWLEDGEMENTS

My thanks to the very many people who have given their time to help in this enquiry: my agent, Andrew Lownie, produced several of the contacts and was always a mine of suggestions; the Duc de Grantmesnil-Lorraine, formerly Kenneth de Courcy, was prodigal with his first-hand knowledge of the British political scene and personalities of the 1930s and 1940s, likewise Robert Cecil with his first-hand knowledge of the Foreign Office and secret service scene at that time, and from his researches into the Nazi era and ideology; Dr Eduard Calic was as prolific with first-hand information on the Nazi political scene and gave warm encouragement. Adrian Liddell Hart was generous with the results of his own researches into Hess's mission, as was the pioneer in the field, James Leasor; Roy C. Nesbit helped enormously with air technicalities, the British air defence system and records; Ian Sayer produced a wealth of documents and press cuttings from his archive, and Mike Tregenza produced evidence of Hess's connection with the 'Euthanasia' programme. Peter C. Hansen, who knew Canaris, provided valuable background colour besides translating an indecipherable document in old German script. Lindsay Charlton and Alan Patient, both of whom were involved in television programmes exploring aspects of Hess's flight, provided valuable leads and assessments. Donald McCormick advised on secret service personalities, as indeed did former officers of the SIS. And from the other side of the Second World War intelligence divide Drs Wilhelm Höttl and Otto John provided valuable information. Dr Scott Newton of Cardiff University provided insights into the motives and personalities of those known as 'appeasers' in the 1930s and 1940s, as did Richard Lamb, author of *Ghosts of Peace 1939–1945*. Hugh Thomas, who has argued so persuasively that the 'Hess' in Spandau jail was not Hess, provided early help and leads. His very successful books provide an amusing commentary on just how counterproductive is the British fetish for official secrecy.

The Dowager Duchess of Hamilton and the present Duke of Hamilton provided information about the 14th Duke – more than I have been able to include – and the present Duke's brother, Lord James Douglas-Hamilton, whose *Motive for a Mission* pioneered avenues covered here, has granted permission to quote from letters he published from his father's papers, for all of which I am most grateful. Lord Sherfield, as Roger Makins in charge of the Foreign Office end of the 'Hess affair' under Sir Alexander Cadogan, gave me his recollections as did his former FO colleague, Sir Frank Roberts; Lord Gladwyn, then Gladwyn Jebb, provided valuable background information. Felicity Ashbee and Moira Pearson, who played parts in plotting Hess's aircraft in towards the English coast, recalled that night in some detail, as did Maurice Pocock, who was 'scrambled' in a Spitfire, but too late to intercept. His former companion in Spitfires during the Battle of Britain, Bob Beardsley provided much background 'gen'. Lieutenant Colonel John McCowen provided first-hand information about the SS team dropped into England to assassinate Hess and – especially interesting – the source of the warning that they were coming.

Professors W. Eisenmenger and W. Spann of the Institut für Rechtsmedizin, Munich University, spent much time and trouble answering queries about the autopsy they conducted on Hess, for which I am most grateful, as indeed to Hess's son, Herr W. R. Hess, who commissioned this second autopsy and released the pathologists from their oath of silence; I am grateful too for W. R. Hess's permission to quote his father's 'suicide note' from his latest book, *Mord an Rudolf Hess?*, and to use my translations of poems his father wrote. Colonel D. C. Robson, Director of Army Pathology, spent much time helping me to understand the pathologists' reports and comments, and introducing me to forensic medical textbooks and procedures, for which I am most grateful. Any conclusions I have drawn are mine, not his.

Professor Robert Waite, whose superb exploration of Hitler's psyche, *The Psychopathic God*, provided the most valuable background, helped greatly with insights from his researches. I should also like to thank Lord (formerly David) Eccles, Anthony and Jeremy Pilcher, the late Group Captain Frederick Winterbotham, Dr Kurt Gossweiler, Martin Gilbert, Lieutenant Colonel Anthony Le Tissier, G. Etherington-Smith, and R. C. Langdon, John A. Chambers, Jack R. Busby, James Douglas, T. W. Dobson, Squadron Leader R. G. Woodman, Nancy Goodall and the scores who replied to my letter in the *Sunday Telegraph* with valuable background information about the RAF reaction on 10 May 1941. I am most grateful to Mrs Cope of *Who's Who*, who provided the lead to the Haushofer's 'Mrs Roberts', and Neil Flanagan, archivist of Eton College and Alan Kucia, archivist of Trinity College, Cambridge, for their help in following it up. Christine Wilson and her predecessor at the Foreign and Colonial Office foreign documents archive were enormously helpful, as were Dr Henke of the Bundesarchiv, Koblenz, Dr Maria Keipert of the Auswärtiges Amt Politischen Archiv, Bonn, Dr Hermann Weiss of the Institut für Zeitgeschicht, Munich, Dr Tuchel of the Stauffenberg Memorial Museum, Berlin, and the staff of the German Historical Institute Library in London. Philip Reed of the Imperial War Museum, London, was as ever immensely helpful, as were Dick Bright of the Museum's Duxford archive and Christina Harris of the BBC Written Archives Centre.

My son, Guy, read French books on Hess for me, typed out much of the typescript, assisted with letters and enquiries in Germany, and was an invaluable source of help and sound comment. Ulla Payne helped with medical correspondence in German

Finally, I should like to thank the following authors, editors and publishers for permission to quote from published works: Druffel Verlag for Ilse Hess's *Ein Schicksal in Briefen*, and *Gefangener des Friedens*; Dedo Graf Schwerin von Krosigk for his father's *Es geschah in Deutschland*; Kohlhammer Verlag for General Halder's *Kriegstagebuch*; Dr Heinz Boberach for his magnificent series *Meldungen aus dem Reich*; Klett-Cotta Verlag for Ursula Laack-Michel's *Albrecht Haushofer und der National-sozialismus*; Propyläen Verlag for *Die Weizsäcker Papiere*, edited by E. Hill; Ullstein Langen Müller Verlag for *Rudolf Hess: Briefe 1908-1933*, edited by W. R. Hess; Hodder & Stoughton for John Colville's *The Fringes of Power*; Harper Collins for Harold Nicolson's *Diaries and Letters*; The Bodley Head for David Eccles's *By Safe Hand*; Times Newspapers for Cecil King's *Malice Towards None*; David Higham Associates for Sir Alexander Cadogan's diary; Eugene Bird for *The*

Loneliest Man in the World; Weidenfeld & Nicolson for Dusko Popov's *Spy, Counterspy*. I have been unable to trace the copyright holders in Lieutenant Colonel A. M. Scott's 'Camp Z' diary at the Imperial War Museum, or Hans Frank's *Im Angesicht des Galgens*.

INTRODUCTION
TO THE NEW EDITION

This is a biography of Hitler's most loyal follower whose devotion to his Führer never wavered. It is also by necessity an enquiry into the extraordinary solo flight he made from Germany to Great Britain in May 1941, perhaps the most bizarre mystery of the Second World War. In that respect it is an ever-changing story, for fresh facts continue to seep from under the official cover-up. I use the word advisedly.

After the first edition came out files previously listed as 'closed until 2017' were released to the Public Record Office; at the same time many people who had been involved with one or other aspect of Hess's mission to this country wrote to me with their accounts, which prompted further investigation. In sum these new sources allowed me to solve the main riddle posed by the flight, so I believe. I incorporated much of the new material and my conclusion in an 'Afterword' to the second edition. Unfortunately the key informant on whom the solution hung would neither allow publication of his name or details of his position and responsibilities during the war, and the vital document he revealed was missing from the recently released files. Hence the case could not be proved.

Since that second edition much more information has emerged: it derives from further releases of previously closed files, notably the MI5 papers on the case, and from the indefatigable detective work of John Harris, who first published his findings under the pseudonym John McBlain in a booklet entitled *Rudolf Hess: the British Conspiracy* in 1994.[1] He later expanded this with M.J. Trow into a book, *Hess: the British Conspiracy*[2], and added more material in a paperback edition in 2000.

The new facts Harris has brought to the table do not prove clandestine British involvement in Hess's flight beyond reasonable doubt but, taken with all the other evidence and the conspicuous anomalies in the stories of the main participants, the coincidences he has uncovered are so suggestive as to make the existence of a British deception, in my view, a practical certainty. They concern the 'old lady', Mrs Violet Roberts, whose note to Karl Haushofer in August 1940 via a post-box number in Lisbon (see pages 136ff below) appears to have started the chain of events leading to Hess's flight to Scotland. Far from being just an old friend of the Haushofers – Hess's political advisers on foreign affairs, particularly England – Harris has discovered that she was the aunt of Walter Stewart Roberts, a contemporary at Eton of Sir Stewart Menzies – head of the Secret Intelligence Service (SIS or MI6) – and with him in the prestigious Eton prefectorial society 'Pop', who was recruited in 1940 to the black propaganda branch of the Special Operations Executive (SOE) known as SO1, soon to become the Political Warfare Executive (PWE). From there he emerged in 1946 as Deputy Director General of Political Intelligence. Not only was he the nephew of Mrs Violet Roberts, he was evidently close to her: she was a widow, and after her only son, Patrick Maxwell Roberts, was killed in a car crash outside Athens in 1937, she stayed with Walter at his home at 36 Queen's Gate, London SW7 during probate proceedings.

I had assumed in the first edition of this book that Major T.A. Roberston of MI5 'B' Division responsible for internal security and double agents – the famous 'Double Cross' Committee – was the controlling figure in the deception that resulted in Hess's flight. However, I managed to contact him after publication, and discovered I was wrong: he had advised against following up Albrecht Haushofer's reply to Violet Roberts' note after it was intercepted by mail censorship. I corrected this in the 'Afterword' to the second edition (see page 362 below). John Harris has now, I believe, pointed to the secret organisation which *was* responsible for following up Haushofer's letter, namely SO1/PWE, whose members included such flamboyant hoaxers as Sefton Delmer and Leonard Ingrams – not to mention their contact in Naval Intelligence, Ian Fleming. For it is a fact I have not seen mentioned in any account of the Hess affair that Ivone Kirkpatrick, the man Churchill sent up to

Scotland immediately after Hess's arrival, ostensibly to check his identity, was a member of the SO1/PWE Committee.[3]

It is also a fact, discovered by Harris in the SO1 files, that on the morning of the day Hess arrived in Scotland, 10 May 1941, the customary Saturday meeting of the SO1/PWE Committee at its headquarters in Woburn Abbey was attended, most unusually, by two cabinet ministers, Anthony Eden, Foreign Secretary, and Hugh Dalton, Minister of Economic Warfare and head of SOE. The Director General of Political Warfare, Robert Bruce Lockhart, was also there; his diary reads:

> Sat. 10th May 1941. Back to Woburn Abbey for meeting with Eden...[who] talked about appeasers in Conservative Party, plenty of them...Dalton nearly gave away one of our biggest secrets at luncheon.[4]

The number of appeasers in the Conservative Party – and their high social and financial standing – is one of the keys to the whole deception since it enabled the plotters to paint an entirely plausible picture of a high-powered 'Peace Party' composed of leading politicians, city financiers, grandees like the Duke of Buccleuch, up to members of the Royal Family, the Duke of Kent and the ex-King Edward VIII, then Duke of Windsor, ready to topple the Churchill government and sign a compromise peace with Germany. This was a picture propagated by all arms of British disinformation, including Major T.A. Robertson's 'Double Cross' agents, not simply by SO1/PWE; the aim was to convince Hitler he need not defeat Great Britain militarily, but could neutralize her at the peace table while he turned east against his real enemy, Soviet Russia.

Another remarkable discovery made by John Harris is an envelope addressed by Violet Roberts to Karl Haushofer dated 10 May 1941. This is in the Haushofer papers in the Bundesarchiv, Koblenz. Unfortunately the letter it once contained is missing – like her original note of August 1940. Nonetheless it provides proof that the correspondence did not end with the seizure of Haushofer's reply to her original note by British mail censorship in November 1940, thus tends to support the accounts of Eduard Benes, head of the Czech government in exile in England, and his intelligence chief, Frantisek Moravetz, that British Intelligence used Haushofer's reply to Violet Roberts to open a clandestine correspondence with Hess (see pages 181 and 292 below). And it is perhaps significant that the liaison officer to the Czech government in exile was the Director General of Political Warfare, Bruce Lockhart.

The envelope also adds to the number of messages sent on the day of Hess's flight to or from key personalities in the story: thus the Duke of Hamilton, whom Hess flew over to see, wrote to Captain Stammers of Air Intelligence on that day to say he was prepared to travel to Lisbon to meet Albrecht Haushofer (see page 183 below); the same evening Haushofer's confidant in Madrid, Heinrich Stahmer, sent a strangely-worded wire to Berlin informing Haushofer he was due to give a lecture in Madrid in two days time; now it appears that Violet Roberts wrote to Karl Haushofer on the same day. Can all these messages on the day of the flight be simple coincidence, or were they conveying a meaning which had little to do with the content? That is a question that cannot at present be answered.

Turning now to the recently released MI5 files on Hess, they confirm T.A. Robertson's denial of his involvement in the Hess deception: a report he wrote on 13 May 1941 shows that he was called to the Air Ministry on the afternoon of 12 May – before news of Hess's arrival had been broadcast – and asked what he knew of Haushofer. He gave a brief outline of Haushofer's reply to Violet Roberts which had asked her to forward a letter to the Duke of Hamilton; after which he was asked if he knew of the latest development. He replied, 'No', and was told that 'an Me110 had landed in Scotland' and the pilot had asked to see the Duke of Hamilton since he had a message for him from Haushofer. There is probably no significance in the description of the Messerscmitt landing, rather than the pilot baling out, since it could easily have been a misunderstanding at that early stage. Robertson said he would make enquiries through the MI5 regional office in Edinburgh. It was only later that evening that he heard on the 9 o'clock news of a German announcement of Hess's disappearance, and not until next morning, 13 May, that he learned from the newspapers that the pilot he had been asked to investigate was Rudolf Hess.[5]

The report of the investigation he initiated through Major Peter Perfect, Regional Security Liaison Officer – MI5 'B' Division representative – in Edinburgh, was dated 19 May. It detailed all the service and Home Guard personnel who had been interviewed about Hess's arrival and detention by an officer named Buyers whom Perfect had delegated for the task – a list which did not include the Duke of Hamilton, his Intelligence officer or any RAF personnel – and gave an account of Hess's capture in all respects similar to that represented in this book. However, the last page or pages of the report are missing from the file. This is indisputable since by the convention of the day the first word of a continuation sheet was typed on the bottom left corner of the preceding page, and this practice was followed for the first three pages of the report. At the bottom left of page three is the word 'As/'. Yet that is where the report ends. However, there is a clear indication of some of the content of the last page or pages in the covering letter, a portion of which runs:

> ...I had not heard of the picking up, through censorship, of a photostat of a letter which Hess had in his possession at the time of the landing, but as Buyers concludes in his report, there is the possibility that some articles may have fallen from the 'plane at some distance from where it crashed. I do not know whether you think the documents which were recovered from a ditch in the field where Hess landed, could have got there in such a way, or were as you think, planted there by someone who had pilfered them earlier...[6]

This is of extraordinary significance: it is the only document in any open file confirming that Hess had a 'letter in his possession at the time of landing' or that 'documents...were recovered from a ditch in the field where Hess had landed'. Roy Nesbit and Georges van Acker claim in their book *The Flight of Rudolf Hess* that an inventory of his possessions on landing is included in the recently released Foreign Office file 1093/10 at the Public Record Office.[7] This is not so. That list, dated 27 May, is part of a Medical Research Council 'Report on the Collection of Drugs etc. belonging to German Airman Prisoner, Captain Horn' – Horn being the psuedonym Hess chose for his flight. It is not and does not claim to be an inventory of articles taken from Hess when he landed on 10 May.

At least three such inventories or receipts from officers successively responsible for Hess from his arrest to his final detention on the night of 10-11 May are missing from the files containing these officers' reports, although it is stated in the reports that they are attached or enclosed (see pages 207 and 353 below). And there is nowhere in any open file in this country or abroad a single copy of the letter or documents Hess brought with him. Can it possibly be coincidence that the documents themselves, three inventories of Hess's belongings when he landed and the page or pages of the MI5 report referring to the letter and documents have disappeared from the files? To calculate the odds against this being coincidence one would need to know how many other documents have disappeared from the files, and this is plainly impossible; yet it would require a clerical regime of extreme sloppiness to render the absence of so many crucial documents on a single aspect of the affair statistically insignificant.

The sensational finding, however, is that there is, at last, incontrovertible documentary evidence that Hess brought a letter addressed to Hamilton and other documents with him when he landed in Scotland. Since the existence of such documents is at the heart of the solution to the riddle posed by his flight and the subsequent official cover-up (see 'Afterword, pages 377ff below) this MI5 letter provides the strongest support – short of the missing letter and documents themselves – for the elucidation of the puzzle presented in the 'Afterword'.

Further support comes from another MI5 file which details a portion of the post-war interrogation of H. Bohle, half brother to Gauleiter Ernst Bohle, head of Hess's *Auslands Organisation*.[8] Ernst Bohle, according to his own post-war interrogation, did 'all the translation work for this [Hess's] trip to England. I didn't know he was going to England, I thought he was going to Switzerland' (see page 144 below). The work had lasted intermittently from October 1940 until January or February 1941. Significantly January 1941 is the month in which Hess seems to have made his first attempt to fly to Scotland, only to be defeated by bad weather.[9] The interrogation of his half brother, H. Bohle, in the MI5 files reveals that he was called in to help with the translation:

> In 1941, as my record shows, I was translator (German-English) in the *Sprachdienst* [Language Service] of the German Foreign Ministry. One day I was called to my brother's office and was thunderstruck to find that my help was solicited to translate certain passages of a letter or letters from Hess to the Duke of Hamilton. This I was called upon to do on more than one occasion. I was sworn to secrecy.[10]

The letters the two half-brothers helped turn into good English for Hess may have been in reply to letters from Hamilton fabricated by SO1/PWE – with or without the Duke's knowledge – to lure Hess with the bait of a strong 'Peace Party' in Britain, as well as the letter and documents Hess brought with him on his flight. The probability is that it was for the latter work that Ernst Bohle called in his half-brother from the Language Service of the Foreign Ministry. For my informant who cannot be named is quite clear that the documents Hess brought with him were drafted in the German Foreign Ministry in official diplomatic German with an English translation attached (see 'Afterword' pages 369ff below). The informant was one of those deputed by Ivone Kirkpatrick to elucidate those German phrases which had not been adequately or totally unambiguously translated into English. The first two of the 14 or so pages concerned Germany's claims in eastern Europe and made her aims of conquest in Russia absolutely clear; until recently the informant could quote clauses from memory.

Another aspect of the story on which the covering letter to the MI5 report sheds light is the Duke of Hamilton's extraordinary delay in either interrogating Hess when he was told the latter had a message for him, or in reporting the Deputy Führer's arrival. Although he finally saw Hess on the morning after his arrival, it was not until about 5.30 that afternoon, Sunday 11 May, after visiting the crash site of Hess's Messerschmitt, that, according to his report, he rang the Foreign Office (see page 214 below). It beggars belief that a serving RAF Wing Commander, as the Duke was, should have waited the best part of a day to report such an extraordinary event as the arrival by air of the Deputy Führer of Nazi Germany with a message for him; just as it is inconceivable that Churchill's secretary 'Jock' Colville, who fielded Hamilton's call at the Foreign Office, should have been sent over there by Churchill on a Sunday afternoon, as he claimed, unless the Prime Minister already knew of Hess's arrival (see page 215 below). However, if the documents Hess brought with him were recovered from a ditch in the field where he – or his aircraft – landed, the sequence of events becomes more understandable: Hamilton must have learned of the missing documents when he interviewed Hess that morning, and after reporting the Deputy Führer's arrival and the extremely serious possibility of the missing documents getting into the wrong hands, must have set out to try and recover them from the crash site; and it was only after the search that he rang the Foreign Office with the news he had 'some interesting information' – or a similar phrasing. Churchill then sent for him at his weekend retreat, Ditchley Park, as is well known, and Hamilton flew down to deliver Hess's letter and documents in person; these made crystal clear what Churchill had already learned from Intelligence sources: Hitler was about to attack Russia.

The documents Hess brought with him were first mentioned in the open MI5 files in a letter dated 17 May 1941 from Major Peter Perfect in Edinburgh to Alan MacIver, overall commander of all MI5's Regional Security Liaison Officers in the country.[11] This reveals that Perfect had been informed by a Flight Lieutenant Muirhead that:

> ...various pieces of paper, presumably belonging to Hess, were in the hands of unknown persons. A photograph of one of these pieces of paper has been submitted to the Air Ministry by Censorship...[12]

A postscript runs:

> Would you confirm to Senter that it now appears that Pilot Officer Randolph received the information regarding the photostat copy of the letter, which I have referred to, from Group Captain Blackford, and that Randolph passed it to Muirhead.

It is interesting that although the mail censor's interception of the 23 September 1940 letter from Albrecht Haushofer to Violet Roberts – enclosing a letter to the Duke of Hamilton – is to be found in two files at the Public Record Office, there is no record in the open files of 'this piece of paper...presumably belonging to Hess'.[13] It is also of interest that Group Captain Blackford was the officer who had asked Hamilton in late April if he was prepared to travel to Lisbon to contact Haushofer.

Returning to Peter Perfect's letter dated 17 May, he enclosed notes taken from Inspector Hyslop of the Giffnock Constabulary, 'which give you an idea of the complete mess everything was in regarding Hess's arrival.' Among other things, the Inspector's notes reveal that the man originally asked to interpret during Hess's interrogation was a fluent German speaker named Fairweather, of Newton Mearns nearby. However, he was ill in bed and his Polish lodger, Roman Battaglia, who worked at the Polish Consulate in Glasgow, offered his services instead (see pages 353-55 below). Battaglia's examination of Hess, according to the Inspector, lasted about two hours.

The confusion evidently caused by Hess's arrival throws serious doubt on the contentions of those who suggest that his Messerschmitt was deliberately allowed through British air space and that a reception committee awaited him on the ground near Dungavel – unless of course he flew in through the wrong air space. The sector he actually arrived in was controlled from RAF Ouston, near Newcastle – who vectored altogether three Spitfires to attack him (see page 355 below). He did not enter the sector controlled by the Duke of Hamilton from RAF Turnhouse, near Edinburgh, until he approached the west coast (see map page 197 below), and he was still in the Turnhouse sector when he baled out near the Duke's home, Dungavel House. If a reception committee was waiting, the welcome was badly bungled. But again, he might have come down in the wrong place. However, if there was a real 'Peace Party' ready to greet him, 'B' Division of MI5, responsible for counter-subversion, appears from the papers to have been blissfully unaware. On the other hand, the chaos provides ample cause for the Duke of Hamilton's alarm that night, to which many have testified; and, as suggested earlier, it provides a plausible alternative to the narrative of his official statement.

Turning now to other 'conspiracy theories': Hess's son, Wolf Rüdiger Hess, remains convinced that his father was murdered in Spandau Prison, Berlin, in August 1987 to prevent him revealing secrets of his peace mission which the British government was anxious should remain secret. I pointed to the suspicious circumstances of Hess's death in the first edition (see pages 338ff below): chiefly the extremely uninformative report by the British pathologist, Professor J.M. Cameron, the implication that he had been strangled – rather than hanged himself – in the report of the two German pathologists who examined his body subsequently, and particularly his suicide note, which made no sense whatever (see pages 335-36 below).

The British governor of Spandau at the time, Tony Le Tissier, has since published his account in *Farewell to Spandau*, which clarifies the manner of his suicide.[14] Apparently the light flex in which Hess tied a noose was permanently knotted to the window handle inside the so-called 'summer house' in the garden; consequently he did not have to fasten it. He merely 'looped the loose end of the cable round his neck and tied it there with a simple once-over slip knot', then slid his back down the wall with his legs sticking out in front.[15] This might account for the unusual course of the ligature marks found by the German pathologists, and it is certainly possible to commit suicide in this way from a relatively low attachment point. The description also fits Hess's character and his numerous previous suicide attempts. I have also had it from a source I cannot identify – but is certainly A1 – that the German government, anxious about Hess becoming a totem for Neo-Nazi movements, asked the British government to clarify the circumstances of his death, whereupon all the files – bar the Military Police investigations – were examined by a Foreign Office official. He found the verdict of suicide unassailable and stated that no suspicion fell on either the warder, Jordan, or any other persons. The German government was satisfied with the assurance.

Despite this, the suicide note remains a mystery. From the content, it is inconceivable that Hess penned it in 1987, the year he took his life; yet it is written on the back of a letter written by his daughter-in-law, Andrea Hess, dated 20 July 1987. Therefore it must have been forged from a much earlier suicide note retained by the prison authorities. But why? Was it an attempt to forestall the inevitable suspicions which would be aroused by the manner of his death? If so it was badly bungled and only gives sustenance to Wolf Rüdiger's allegations of murder. Tony Le Tissier states that a handwriting expert was called in from the Laboratory of the Government Chemist in London, who before starting his examination pointed out that he was 'not operating under laboratory conditions, nor was he familiar with either the German language or the kind of script used by the prisoner'.[16] Nevertheless he established the authenticity of the note. Wolf Rüdiger is surely entitled to retort, 'He would, wouldn't he.'

Of other conspiracy theories, the more extreme have only helped prolong the life of the official account, firstly by confusing the issues with red herrings, chiefly by tending to bring anyone who questions the received version into disrepute as a 'conspiracy theorist'. Nesbit and van Acker have rightly rejected many myths in *The Flight of*

Rudolf Hess, particularly that an Me110 could not have reached Scotland from south Germany, that the RAF allowed Hess's aircraft through British air defences[17] and, most absurd of all, that the man who arrived in Scotland and subsequently served 46 years in captivity was not Hess, but a double. But in proceeding from technically-based arguments to debunk alternative theories in general, they have given unfounded comfort to the guardians of the authorized version.

The persisting stories of British Intelligence involvement they put down to Russian suspicions, which they refute by stating, correctly, that Hess never mentioned being lured across. It is probable he never knew. He assumed and stated frequently that he had fallen into the hands of the British Secret Service acting on Churchill's orders to drug and silence him and prevent him meeting those representatives of the 'Peace Party' he had come over to parley with. And, of course, he was right. His sense of failure led to his first suicide attempt. He seemed to regard Hamilton as a friendly figure powerless against Churchill and the Secret Service, and in a note written on 15 June, just before that first suicide attempt, he left his uniform to the Duke, 'who may be good enough to send it to my family in peace time.'[18] As my 'Afterword' to the second edition makes clear, I believe the British traitor, Kim Philby, and the Czech Intelligence chief, who were most responsible for Russian suspicions, knew more of the true story of Hess's flight than the majority of Churchill's cabinet or the Foreign Office officials supposedly handling the case, or even MI5. This is the secret that is still being hushed up. My unnamed informant on the documents Hess brought with him was willing to go public until he contacted his former authorities; then he fell silent. Sixty years after the event 'they' still pull the strings.

Nesbit and van Acker also adhere to the authorized German version: Hitler knew nothing of his Deputy's mission. Again they rely much on Hess's statements, repeated often enough to the end of his life, that he had flown entirely on his own initiative. If he did he was truly mad. His adjutants and others who assisted with his flight preparations have stated he was not mad, and could not have made his flight if he was. The simple fact is that his mission was unattributable and had to be for very obvious political reasons. Hitler's play-acting when he 'learned' the news – which conspicuously failed to impress some of those present at Führer Headquarters – the arrests of astrologers, adjutants, Haushofer and anyone connected with the flight, the entire SS investigation, and Goebbels' diary entries were all part of a charade designed to convince the world that Hess had indeed gone mad and flown off on his own. In the upper echelons of the Third Reich nothing can be taken at documentary value – least of all the recently published diaries of the Propaganda Minister.

In this affair, as in others, the British Prime Minister proved the abler gamesman; and the British documents presently on public record lay the more deceptive trail. It had to be so: Churchill had to prevent his cabinet, his Party and the country from splitting; above all he had to convince the United States that Great Britain would never give in.

The charade over which Churchill presided is, like Hitler's, so replete with inconsistencies and preposterous anomalies it cannot be believed; nor, however, can it be fully understood until copies of the documents that Hess brought with him are brought to light, or more actors in the drama are prepared after sixty years publicly to reveal what they know. Until then, the recently released MI5 files which prove beyond peradventure what has hitherto never been officially conceded, but has instead been weeded from the files – that Hess *did* bring documents with him – and the revelation that the 76-year old widow whose note to the Haushofers started the correspondence to the Duke of Hamilton was a close relative of Walter Roberts of SO1/PWE open giant cracks in the official version of events which can never now be papered over.

The evidence for a cover-up rests on documents that should be in the open files but are not. Nevertheless, the view through the breaches which have appeared in the public record confirm the account given here in the 'Afterword'. All searchers after historical truth are invited, when they reach the end of the book, to return for verification to this new beginning.

Peter Padfield, London, 2000

REFERENCES

[1] John McBlain, *Rudolf Hess: the British Conspiracy*, (Northampton: Jema Publications, 1994).

[2] John Harris and M.J. Trow, *Hess: the British Conspiracy*, (London: André Deutsch, 1999).

[3] See Ellic Howe, *The Black Game: British Subversive Operations against the Germans during the Second World War*, (London: Michael Joseph, 1982), p.159.

[4] Kenneth Young (ed.), *The Diaries of Sir Robert Bruce Lockhart*, (London: Macmillan, 1980), p.98.

[5] P.R.O. KV 2/34.

[6] *ibid.*

[7] Roy Nesbit and Georges van Acker, *The Flight of Rudolf Hess* (Stroud: Sutton Publishing, 1999).

[8] P.R.O. KV 2/38

[9] See Nesbit and van Acker, *op. cit.*, pp.152-53

[10] Interrogation 10 July 1945, in P.R.O. KV 2/38

[11] See Nigel West, *M.I.5*, (London: Bodley Head, 1981), pp.147,171

[12] P.R.O. KV 2/34

[13] P.R.O. INF 1/912; DEFE 1/134

[14] Tony Le Tissier, *Farewell to Spandau*, (Leatherhead: Ashford, Buchan & Enright, 1994).

[15] *ibid.*, p.73

[16] *ibid.*, p.78

[17] Nesbit and van Acker, *op. cit.*, pp.131-34. However, despite the evidence that Hess's aircraft was not deliberately allowed through British east coast air defences, a question mark hangs over his reception when he reached the west coast. This derives from the testimony and personal flying logs of two Czech Hurricane pilots serving in 245 Squadron RAF, based at Aldergrove, Northern Ireland; both were vectored on to a single bandit that evening, which proved to be an Me110, but just as they approached for the kill they were ordered to break off action and return to base. The details are in a book by two Czech military archivists, Jiří Sehnal and Jiří Rajlich, called *Stíhací Pilot (Fighter Pilot)*, published by Naşe Vojsko, Prague, in 1991. The gist of their account was reported in the *Sunday Telegraph*, 21 February 1999, 'RAF hid secret of how Czech pilots nearly killed Hess.' Nesbit and van Acker point out that the Operations Record Book of 245 Squadron records only one of the pilots in the air that evening, and he landed at 22.40, over quarter of an hour before Hess reached the west coast. However, ORBs are notoriously fallible. They were often written up by officers as a punishment and some time after the events recorded. Both

Czech pilots are now dead, but there is sufficient supporting evidence for their story to persuade air historian, Tony Marçam, to continue an already considerable research effort into this story.

[18] P.R.O. FO 1093/10

PROLOGUE

Hess loved Hitler. This is the essential; without this he becomes merely incomprehensible, the wild adventure that brought him notoriety as inexplicable as his silence afterwards to the grave and his refusal to recant. He adored Hitler. Whatever faults he may have discerned in him and however his rational, sensitive, soft side may have recoiled from the abominations associated with his idol's name, like a woman who knows her man is guilty yet loves him despite all, so Hess loved Hitler.

It is impossible to read Hess's letters from Landsberg, where he and Hitler were locked up in fortress detention after the failed *putsch* of November 1923, without concluding that these must have been the happiest months of his life. They are breathless with young love; seldom is the subject other than Hitler, referred to as 'the Tribune' – the tribune of the people. Even those to his faithful girl-friend and hiking companion, Ilse Pröhl, are transparent:

The Tribune looks radiant. His face is no longer so thin. The forced rest is doing him good. He does gymnastics vvvv [the Hess family laugh sign in correspondence], bathes, does not smoke, drinks scarcely any alcohol apart from a little beer; here indeed he *must* be healthy without the former stress, with plentiful sleep, fresh air a[nd] a moral state that is far from depressed.[1]

In the fine spring mornings of 1924 he and Hitler 'wandered between the blossoming fruit bushes in the garden' discussing everything under the sun. He was enthralled by Hitler's power of anecdote, continually surprised by the range of his 'knowledge and understanding of subjects not really his own', amused or moved by his extraordinary talent for mimicry. From his letters one would scarcely know that others were in detention with the two of them. Sitting writing at the desk in his bedroom one day, Hess described hearing Hitler from the adjacent communal living- and dining-room performing one of his wartime experiences, simulating exploding grenades and machine-gun fire, 'springing ferociously around the room, quite carried away by his imagination'.[2]

On another occasion, as Hess brought Hitler his afternoon tea, Hitler asked him to stay and listen to the latest passage from the memoirs he was writing. It concerned the outbreak of war, his entry as a volunteer in the Bavarian Infantry, departure for the front, Flanders and the whistle of the first heralds of death as his unit was ordered to charge; then softly at first, increasing in volume, the sound of *Deutschland Deutschland über alles ...*' rising from the throats of these young men until it rolled along the entire front. Men were mown down by fire, but the singing never ceased. As he read, Hitler's voice became slower, the pauses between his phrases longer until suddenly he let the page drop, lowered his head into his hand and sobbed.

'That my composure also dissolved, I need not tell you,' Hess wrote to Ilse Pröhl.[3]

Pulling himself together, Hitler referred to the passage that had moved him so, and opened his heart. He had been mortally afraid; he had felt his chest constricting and his legs falter with feelings of self-preservation: '... "and it was only cowardice. I slowly overcame it all; winter [19]15, [19]16 I was completely free of it." He admitted it quite openly, without shame that he had more sensitive nerves than the others ..."[4]

As Hess took his leave afterwards, they squeezed each other's hands at length. 'I am more devoted to him than ever!' Hess wrote. 'I love him!'

A visitor to Landsberg who testified to Hitler's talent for acting and mimicry was the Munich art publisher 'Putzi' Hanfstaengl, one of his earliest admirers from the educated classes who had become virtually his social secretary. He described the repertoire of sounds Hitler deployed in his anecdotes concerning the front, from the single crack of a French, British or German howitzer or mortar to the whole battlefield din with 'the hammering tack-tack of machine-guns'.[5] As a dangerous rival for Hitler's favour, Hanfstaengl was made aware of Hess's jealousy. Approaching the two of them seated together to speak to Hitler one day, he found Hess rising with bad grace, only to take another chair near by and start performing gym exercises with it to distract attention.

Whether Hess's intimacy with 'the Tribune' in Landsberg was homosexual in any physical sense may be doubted. Hanfstaengl seemed to discount it in his published account of his years with Hitler, suggesting that on Hitler's part the relationship was another manifestation of what he called 'the unclear orientation of his [Hitler's] emotional drives, which lay outside every sexual norm and could not be classified'.[6] Earlier, during the war, Hanfstaengl had told American interrogators that Hess was known among the Party homosexuals as 'Fräulein Anna', and he suspected that his relationship with Hitler 'may have bordered on this type'.[7]

Over twenty years later, speaking to one of the most percipient of Hitler's biographers, Robert Waite, Hanfstaengl was more catagorical about the relationship and, although Waite found him 'personally unsavoury', he tended to believe him: 'He basked in his Doctorate in history and prided himself on the accuracy of his statements. I might also add that his own homo-erotic inclinations made him rather knowledgeable in these matters and may lend credence to his assertion that Hess was a homosexual.'[8]

A curious support for this statement is to be found among the papers of the British lawyer Walter Monckton. In his capacity as Director General of the Press and Censorship Bureau in 1940, he interviewed a woman internee in London named Kell-Pfeffer, who claimed to be the sister of Hess's aide and intelligence chief, Franz Pfeffer von Salomon, hence to know intimate details of the Nazi leaders; certainly she appears to have known more about Himmler than was available to the public. Of Hess she said: '. . . the complete Yes-man and has no personality of his own. His attitude to Hitler is that of a faithful dog . . . He is a homosexual. Röhm used to call him "*die schwarze Paula*" (the black Paula).'[9]

Hess was known by a number of such derisive names during his years of power. The Berlin Jewish columnist Bella Fromm recorded in her diary in December 1933 that he was dubbed by his comrades '*die schwarze Grete*',[10] and she wondered if there were any truth in the rumour that he painted his toenails red. One of the comrades, Kurt Ludecke, wrote that the disrespectful called him '*Fräulein Hess*';[11] but whether this was because of his self-effacing character and submissive devotion to the Führer – attributes which in the all-male cameraderie of the Nazis were deemed womanly – or whether he was thought to be actively homosexual is impossible to determine. It is scarcely important. What is not in doubt is that he and Hitler were intimates in Landsberg and remained very close. Hanfstaengl recorded Hitler after his release lamenting that Hess was still locked up inside: '*Mein Rudi, mein Hesserl!*' he wailed to him.[12] Later, one of Hitler's valets, Willie Schneider, noted with surprise that, whenever Hitler received a present he liked or drew an architectural sketch which pleased him, he would 'run to Hess as a little boy would run to his mother to show his prize to her'.[13]

The testimony to Hess's absolute devotion is unanimous. Hanfstaengl went so far as to say that his whole relationship to the world was embraced in one name – Hitler.[14] Hess's personal adjutant, Alfred Leitgen, described his chief as having only one ambition, 'to be the loyalest interpreter of Hitler'.[15] The Finance Minister, Count Schwerin von Krosigk, wrote in similar vein, describing Hess's devotion to Hitler as 'boundless': 'He perceived himself as the herald of the Führer and therefore obliged to allow his own personality to shrink behind his [master's] figure.'[16]

PART ONE

HESS

1
Hess

Rudolf Hess was born into the house of a prosperous German import-export merchant in the Egyptian seaport of Alexandria in 1894. The firm, Hess & Co., had been founded almost thirty years earlier by his grandfather, a self-made man who had married well. His father, Fritz Hess, ran the business and his family with the punctilious formality and sternness natural to the age. The household revolved around his convenience. For Rudolf and his brother, Alfred, born three years after him in 1897, he was an inhibiting, frightening presence who seldom showed affection; it was only later that Rudolf Hess discovered his father's real fondness for them. Fritz's circle of acquaintance and his outlook were narrowly German and business-orientated; Hanfstaengl, meeting him in later years, described his conversation as banal, his mentality that of a bowling club member,[1] an estimate that seems borne out by the few anecdotes Rudolf Hess told about his father. So Rudolf was sent first to a one-room school serving the small German community, and then, from the age of twelve, taught at home by his mother and tutors. It was accepted that he would follow his father into the family firm.

All the pleasantest memories of childhood which returned to him in later years were connected with his mother and the beauty of sky and sea, garden and desert shared with her. When he read the names of stars, they evoked her image under the shining Egyptian night as she pointed them out and identified them. Exceptionally beautiful sunsets recalled the blazing colours he had watched with her from the roof garden of their substantial villa in the coastal suburb of Ibrahimieh.[2] 'What a paradise it was in our garden at the edge of the desert,' he reminded her in 1951. 'Do you remember how we would gather violets together, and how glorious they smelled ...?'[3] From confinement in Landsberg he wrote to Ilse Pröhl: 'One's whole youth is incorporated in one's mother. She is part of one's being, one's own original essence – even today ... without her one would have become someone else.'[4]

Every summer from 1900 Fritz Hess took his family 'home' to Germany to holiday in a large house he had had built in Art Nouveau style below the hamlet of Reicholdsgrün in the Fichtel mountains of northern Bavaria. It was not far form the village of Wunsiedel, where his father's forbears had been master shoemakers. No doubt this and the isolated position in hilly country so different from the low coastal plain of Egypt recommended the place; it could not have been desire for society, nor it seems for culture. It was not until Rudolf was fourteen and placed in a boarding school in Bad Godesberg on the Rhine that he developed a love of music, particularly Beethoven, which lasted throughout his life. Hanfstaengl recalled that the only time he ever established brief personal, as opposed to professional, contact with Rudolf Hess was during a social get-together at Hess's house in 1933: Hess asked him to play Beethoven and told him how he had discovered his love for the great man's works while a pupil at the Evangelical School at Godesberg.[5]

As a man, Hess was withdrawn and difficult to know;[6] his adjutant Leitgen described him as coming out of his shell only in the small circle of his brother and parents.[7] His wife Ilse said that he had difficulty in opening up to others.[8] He was also highly sensitive. Projecting these traits back to his schooldays and remembering the sheltered life he had lived until then in the restricted family circle, it can be assumed that things were not easy for him as a boarder at Bad Godesberg. He was known there as 'the Egyptian', partly perhaps because of his dark hair and complexion; it was an epithet which stuck to him throughout his years in the Nazi Party. In class he proved well above average in maths and the sciences, and his teachers suggested he should study engineering or physics at university. This accorded with his own inclinations and lack of any desire to follow his father into the family business, but Fritz Hess would not hear of it. As the future head of the firm, he was to have a commercial training. Thus, after three years at Bad Godesberg, the seventeen-year-old was sent to the Ecole Supérieur de Commerce at Neuchâtel, Switzerland, and, after a disinterested year there, he was apprenticed to a firm in Hamburg to learn the practical side of trading.

War came as a personal, emotional release for him. Strong as he was in mathematical and practical abilities, he was also a dreaming idealist with fervent emotional drives which became visible on occasions in his deep-set greenish eyes. The coming of war at the end of July 1914 was surely one such. It found him at the villa at Reicholdsgrün on holiday with his family – now augmented by a little sister, Margarete (Grete), born long after the boys in 1908.

For years, like all Germans, he had been exposed to an insistent chorus of triumphal expansionist aspiration. It was proclaimed from every organ of Government and State, from press and lectern, led by the Kaiser, Wilhelm II himself, who called for a German 'place in the sun' alongside (more practically at the expense of) the older colonial empires as metaphorically he brandished the 'mailed fist' that would assure this world power. 'Weltpolitik' was the name of the exercise – 'world policy' as opposed to the traditional Prusso-German continental policy. It was supported by big business and finance and more reluctantly by the Prussian ruling class of soldiers and officials who leant their agreement in the hope that it would divert internal social and, as it was believed, pre-revolutionary pressures caused by the rapid industrialisation of the country, thus enabling them to preserve their power and status beside the Kaiser at the head of the empire. The policy was also supported by the Navy, a parvenu service which had hardly existed in the previous century and then only as the coastal arm of the Prussian Army. The means used to bring the claims of the Navy before an essentially land-orientated nation gathered terrific momentum until the inspiration and creator of the new German fleet, Admiral Tirpitz, had become a major political force.

Rudolf Hess was one of the thousands enthused by the naval propaganda. Whether this was because he was working in the commercial port of Hamburg, whether it had something to do with his Egyptian background, childhood glimpses of British battle squadrons or the ever-present impression of the power of the sea empire which held this cross-roads between east and west, or whether perhaps it was simply caused by his need to find something more inspiring to feed his idealism than trade and ledgers is unclear. Whatever the reasons, he had developed an interest in warships and naval history which he was never to lose. Some years later he told his brother that it started while he was working in Hamburg: he had learnt Köhler's Fleet Calendar by heart and knew the vital statistics of all the principal German warships.[9]

It was also during this time immediately prior to the war that the German architects of Weltpolitik in the Foreign Ministry and in the Kaiser's cabinets, and powerful backers like the shipping magnate Albert Ballin were confronted with the contradictions inherent from the first, namely that the propaganda needed to awaken the German people to their world mission and the huge naval building programmes required to support it first alarmed Great Britain, whose world position rested on her unchallengeable fleet, then forced her into a hostile alliance with France and Russia. The German Chancellor, Bethmann-Hollweg, and his Foreign Minister made great efforts to curb Tirpitz and smooth British feathers; indeed, they were sufficiently successful that, by July 1914, when they provoked what they believed to be the inevitable showdown with Russia and France, they still hoped that the pacifist wing of the British Government would prevail and keep the island empire out of their continental war.

As the crisis broke, Bethmann sent Albert Ballin to London to sound out the reaction. Returning to Berlin, he reported that no British cabinet minister had stated unequivocally that the British Government would support France if she were attacked; and, misled by the strong pacifist sentiment of several ministers and a general feeling in the country that what happened in the Balkans – seat of the Austro-German pretext for war – was none of their concern, Ballin was able to conclude that the British decision would turn on Germany's intentions towards France. Thereupon Bethmann called in the British Ambassador: Germany had no desire to 'crush' France in any conflict which might arise and, 'provided that the neutrality of Britain were certain, every assurance would be given to the British Government that the Imperial [German] Government aimed at no territorial expansion at the expense of France'.[10] The British Foreign Secretary, Sir Edward Grey, read this note of the conversation with despair: that anyone should propose a bargain which would reflect such discredit not only on Great Britain's honour but also on her common sense and instinct for self-preservation ... He replied that His Majesty's Government could not entertain the proposal; it would be a disgrace from which the good name of the country would never recover.

Rudolf Hess could not have known of these exchanges or the delusions prevailing among the Kaiser's ministers as they braced themselves for the leap into the dark of European war, but twenty-five years later, as Hitler's deputy, preparing to follow his Führer into a second European war, he was animated by the same illusions about the exigencies of Britain's honour and self-preservation – illusions which continued to shimmer in his imagination long after England had once again been forced into the hostile camp.

At the end of July 1914 the young Hess, a few months past his twentieth birthday, was concerned only with enlisting for the front. A skilfully managed press campaign had convinced Germans that they were encircled by an envious coalition jealous of their success and determined to invade and crush the Fatherland. Even the Socialists, who had been appealing the previous week for international workers' solidarity and 'Down with War', were swept up in ardent nationalism. When the Kaiser proclaimed, 'I no longer know parties – only Germans,' they rallied behind him. 'Brilliant mood,' the chief of his naval cabinet wrote in his diary, 'the Government has succeeded very well in making us appear the attacked.'[11]

Everywhere the call to arms was greeted with enthusiasm. In Munich, Adolf Hitler, living a lonely, rootless existence as a view-card painter and copier joined the cheering multitudes in the Odeonsplatz and, eyes shining, waved his hat high to '*deliverance*' from the aimlessness and frustration, 'from the vexatious moods of my youth'.[12]

Similar emotions gripped Rudolf Hess in Reicholdsgrün. Rebelling openly for the first time against his father's determination to make him a businessman, he sped off to Munich to volunteer as a trooper in the cavalry, 'firmly resolved', as he wrote to his parents on 3 August, 'to play my part in giving these barbarians and international criminals the thrashing they deserve'. He added that he had just read that enemy aircraft had been buzzing across the borders before the outbreak of war and that the French in Metz had attempted to sow cholera bacilli in the wells. 'It makes one's hair stand on end just to think of it.'[13]

Both his parents replied with their blessing, his father ending his letter, 'now farewell, dear Rudi, acquit yourself well, we all embrace you heartily and send you most affectionate greetings and kisses. Your Papa.'[14]

The regiment Hess applied to join was over-subscribed, but on 20 August he enrolled as a private in the 7th Bavarian Field Artillery, then transferred for some reason a month later to the 1st Reserve Battalion of the élite 1st Bavarian Foot; 'Rejoice with me,' he wrote home, 'I am an infantryman.'[15] On 4 November, after initial training, the Reserves were moved up to the line in Flanders and Hess received his baptism of fire before Ypres. Five days later, according to his service record drawn up in November 1937, he was honoured by a transfer to the 1st Company of the 1st Bavarian Foot[16] serving on the Somme. He was brave and fully committed, and in April 1915 was promoted Gefreiter (Lance Corporal) and awarded the Iron Cross, 2nd Class; a month later he was promoted Unteroffizier (Corporal), and at the end of August was posted to the Army Training School at Münster for a ten-week course for Reserve officer applicants; there in October he was promoted Vizefeldwebel (literally Vice-Sergeant).

Returning to the front with the 1st Company of the 1st Foot in November, he was engaged in more trench warfare in the Artois sector, and early the following year, 1916, took part in the battles for Neuville St Vaast. Then, struck by a throat infection in February, he spent most of March and April in various hospitals with acute laryngal catarrh. Years later he could recall his pleasure as the only patient at St Quentin to beat a Berlin chess master who took on twelve opponents at once.[17] He had been introduced to the game by his mother when he was twelve while he and his brother, Alfred, had been in quarantine for scarlet fever.

After barely two weeks' leave at Reicholdsgrün at the end of May, he returned on 2 June to his battalion, which was transferred to the murderous battle for the French strongpoint at Verdun. The horrors he witnessed here struck as deep as anything he experienced at the front

and it was this 'gruesome massacre' which he addressed later in a poem **he wrote** as a memorial to his fallen comrades, 'Before Verdun':[18]

For months the battle
had raged in the semi-circle around Verdun.
Along the whole front a savage fire stormed,
or rather,
howled like a supernatural hurricane
in which individual blows were scarcely heard.

Easterly from Douaumont, northerly from Thiaumont
the First Battalion of the First Regiment
for the second time already
has entered the fearful struggle.

Pitch-black night
and cold rain without intermission.
In their sunken, mud-filled trenches
the hard-boiled old fighters squat.
Between them smooth, milk-white faces – lads
who a few days before,
garlanded with flowers and singing,
marched away through the streets of home.
By the glaring light of rockets,
the youngsters gaze
bemused at their comrades
lying so uncannily still in the trench
and on the ledge as if thrown down,
so waxen-colourless.
Blood traces on the shabby, mud-gold tunics.
Scents of putrefaction
mixed with acrid clouds of gas and high explosive
streak the chilly forms.

One or another,
leaning on his friend, sinks,
despite exploding shells,
into a dead sleep . . .

It was a sensitive memorial, not overstated nor overly heroic, rather fatalistic.

On 12 June near Fort Douaumont he was so severely wounded by shrapnel from an exploding shell – in his left hand and upper arm according to his later service record – that he was sent back to hospital at Bad Homburg and afterwards on convalescent leave. It was apparently while in hospital that he was fired by stories of the German air aces – and no doubt by memories of the flying machines he had seen glinting above the lines – to apply for flying training. He was turned down.

In early December he was posted to the Bavarian Reserve Infantry Regiment 18 on the south-eastern front, fighting Romanian forces in the mountains of Transylvania. On Christmas day he was appointed a Platoon Leader in the 10th Company and from then on, through January 1917, he was engaged in the battle of Rimnicul-Sarat and in subsequent pursuit of the enemy until the latter regrouped with their Russian ally.

In July, while leading his platoon between the lines, he received a second wound, a small shell splinter in his left arm close to the splinters he had received at Verdun; it was not serious enough to keep him from duty, however, and the following morning his colonel called him personally to express his appreciation.[19] Next month he received a third, near fatal wound. As he described it to his parents in unsteady writing from his clearing station bed, it was 'a clean through-shot, in under the left shoulder, out at the back. No bones broken . . . ' and he added a postscript: 'The shot was from a Russian Inf[antry] rifle, very small calibre. Appetite splendid.'[20]

He gave more details of this brush with death in a subsequent letter. He was moving towards an enemy trench which had been reported as occupied by Austrian troops when he found himself suddenly confronted by a Romanian at thirty paces, who shot him and the soldier with him, before running off.[21] Some twenty-five years later he recalled the moment in a letter from captivity in England to a friend, Dr Gerl. The incident occurred in woodland in bright daylight. He was ten paces from the trench when he became aware of a Romanian sentry aiming at him quite calmly and, before he could think, the man had fired:

As you well know, the shot went right through between the aorta and heart so that the latter was almost grazed. And on the other side it came within a finger's breadth of a spinal-column shot. Therefore, for the copper alloy lump – which is exactly what it is as you know better than I – there was every chance on its way through the body of carrying me off into the unknown, hopefully pleasanter regions. Obviously, however, it was ordained that I should hang around here for some time.[22]

Asked by his parents about his feelings as he was shot, he wrote: 'As the bullet hit I was simply surprised, and it passed through my mind that it had probably been intended for me beforehand.' He called out to the man with him, 'rather as one imparts an interesting fact, indeed I believe I laughed'. Then, almost blacking out, he realised he ought to get down and take cover. He did so, only to find that the stretcher bearers had run off and left him, or so it appeared. He clutched his pistol, sprang up and made a curving run back to the gap in his own wire through which he had set out, 'curious as to where the next shot would strike and surprised I wasn't hit and that I felt no anxiety'. He described his emotions then as like the expectation during a game of *Deutschball* when one had lost sight of the ball and did not know when or from what direction it might be thrown. 'The whole thing seemed to me just like sport.'[23]

He made light of the incident to reassure his anxious mother, and succeeded. Although it was a serious wound needing blood transfusions, which kept him in various hospitals until December, she wrote back pleased that he had come through so well again and was only lightly wounded. A passage in her letter is interesting as a reminder of how the patterns of the Second World War echoed this opening round. Referring to a vain bid by the Pope to negotiate peace, she pronounced that ultimately the people would realise that it was the *Entente* powers, Great Britain, France and Russia, who were conducting a rapacious war, not as they (the enemy) maintained, the German *Reich*; and she added, in reference to the United States' declaration of war on 6 April that year, 'The *Entente* appears to be hoping for military help from America in the spring. Before that our U-boats and armies will, with God's help, have won peace . . .'[24]

Meanwhile, he made another application to join the Flying Corps. The air arm was being expanded fast and this time he was accepted, subject to passing fitness and suitability tests when he was well. The news came as a shock to his parents. His mother wrote to say that, while they could not pretend to be pleased, they were unselfish enough to be glad for him now that 'his most fervent wish' was fulfilled. She added that, because he possessed 'strength, great presence of mind and the requisite sang-froid [*Kaltblutigkeit*]', he seemed well suited to such a difficult and dangerous occupation.[25]

While still in hospital, he heard he had been commissioned a Lieutenant in the Reserve, and on 21 October he was delighted to receive official confirmation; the appointment was dated 8 October.[26]

He was finally discharged from hospital on 10 December and spent the rest of the month convalescing at Reicholdsgrün, before going to Munich for the medical tests for the Flying Corps: 'Nerves, lungs, heart all perfect', he wrote home happily on 3 January 1918. 'Eyes extraordinarily good.' The following month, after escorting a Reserve battalion to the western front, he learnt from an acquaintance from his time in the 18th Infantry that he had been recommended for the Iron Cross, 1st Class, but that none had been available for the regiment. In mid-March he started a two-month course to probe his aptitude as a pilot, and on

15 May entered Flying School 4 at Camp Lechfeld, near Augsburg, for intensive training on Fokker D-VIIs.[27]

Meanwhile, an unrestricted U-boat campaign, on which the High Command had staked all to force Great Britain to her knees before the manpower and industrial strength of the United States could become effective on the continent of Europe, had been defeated by the general introduction of convoys. Fresh US troops and war materiel had flooded in to France. Moreover, the Allied 'hunger blockade' of the central powers was biting into civilian morale, making industrial workers ripe for Communist subversion. By the time Hess completed his Flying School training in October and transferred to Fighter Squadron School 1 at Nivelles, Belgium, it was clear that both internally and externally the *Kaiserreich* had lost the gamble. The mood among the flyers was somewhat depressed, he wrote home.[28] Every day they saw thousands of refugees trailing by with pitiful possessions on wagons and hand-carts. 'It is unspeakable misery. Savage hate lights the eyes of the people, naturally as even now they regard us as the guilty party for the world catastrophe.'[29] He flew in 'very active' aerial combat without either hitting or being hit by the enemy, then on 1 November, he was posted to Jagdstaffel (Fighter Squadron) 35 on the Valenciennes sector of the front. Here he took part in the last air battles of the war.

By this time the German fleet had mutinied; parties of revolutionary sailors fanned inland raising the red flag of insurrection in industrial centres. The Kaiser abdicated and fled to exile, and a hastily convened Socialist Government was advised by the military high command that there was no alternative to accepting armistice terms dictated by the western powers. The 'brilliant mood' of August 1914 and the glorious prospect of world power held out to Germans in the two preceding decades had turned sour. Hess felt the humiliation deeply and beneath the bitterness, a rankling, vengeful sense that the blood and pain, the host of young lives cut short could not all have been in vain, a feeling expressed succinctly by the commander of his fighter wing, Hermann Göring, at a farewell party on the dissolution of the squadrons: 'Our time will come again!'[30]

2
HITLER

Ilse Pröhl saw Rudolf Hess for the first time on a sunny April morning in 1920. She had arrived in Munich on the night train from Berlin and was on the ground-floor verandah of the *pension* where she was to stay while she took her *Abitur* – university entrance examination – surveying the minute garden. Suddenly a young man in field-grey uniform with the bronze lion of the Freikorps Epp on his arm appeared from a back way and took the steps up to the house three at a time. Surprised by her presence, he stopped, clicked his heels together and bowed briefly; she had the impression of a grim, unfriendly look from beneath bushy brows, then he was away. Recalling the encounter twenty-five years later, she wrote that she knew with an unforgettable clarity that her life had been directed towards this young man, that 'the almost gloomy apparition' represented what she sought.[1]

She had been raised in an upper-middle-class milieu by her mother, a wealthy woman in her own right who had attended to her cultural education from an early age, and her father, a medical officer in what had been the Kaiser's swaggering 1st Regiment of Guards at Potsdam. Her world, like Hess's, had been broken in Germany's defeat and the bloody revolutionary and counter-revolutionary aftermath. Her father was dead, and recently she had lost two of her friends, bright young men, members of the romantic, back-to-nature *'Wandervögel'* movement before the war, front-line officers in the war and afterwards volunteers in one of the loyalist ex-servicemen's Freikorps, which the Republican Government used to supplement the regular forces to put down the Communist rebellions breaking out intermittently in industrial areas. Both young men had been killed in the wake of a rightist, monarchical insurrection, the Kapp *putsch*, and, as she described it, literally torn to pieces, like animals by the Berlin mob.[2]

When she first saw Hess, he had just returned from a mission flying aircraft to reinforce a squadron engaged in crushing a Communist 'Spartakist' uprising in the Ruhr – hence his field grey. He had joined the Freikorps Epp the previous May after Communists had taken power in Munich and established a *Räte* (soviet) republic there. Three Russian Bolshevik emissaries, all Jews, had taken over this soviet government and begun a reign of terror until overthrown by central Government forces augmented by Hess's Freikorps led by the Bavarian Colonel Ritter von Epp. It was a crucial experience for Hess. He was already a member of the extreme nationalist, anti-Marxist, anti-Semitic secret society, the Thule *Gesellschaft* (Society), whose motto was 'Remember you are German. Keep your blood pure' and whose symbol was the swastika. The murderous activities of the three Bolshevik Jews in the *Räte* government confirmed every prejudice on which the Thule was founded, and, if Jews and Bolshevism were not already linked in his mind, they were now joined inextricably in his emotions. So it was for Hitler, Himmler, Röhm and other future leaders of the Nazi movement in Munich. Thus, in ruthlessness and contempt for all ethical restraint, Bolshevism evoked its natural counter-force and mirror image.

The Pension von Schildberg, where he and Ilse Pröhl found themselves occupying adjacent rooms was in Schwabing, the intellectual and artistic quarter of Munich, cultural capital of southern Germany. The occupants of the *pension*, all young or youngish people from the educated middle class, formed congenial groups, going to concerts or theatres together, cycling or hiking in the mountains. Hess remained somewhat aloof. By nature earnest and reserved, deeply affected by his experiences at the front and by Germany's humiliation, he took life very seriously; as Ilse recalled, 'He laughed seldom, did not smoke, despised alcohol and simply could not understand how after a lost war young people could enjoy dancing and social life.'[3]

His consuming interest was politics. After demobilisation, he had enrolled as a student at Munich University to study political economy; since then he had met and been befriended by Karl Haushofer, an army general and expert on Far Eastern affairs with an intellectual bent, who was founding a university department for 'geopolitics' – the study of the interaction between peoples and the land they inhabited. Haushofer was a man of unusual charm; in the words of one of Hess's later adjutants, he had 'a bewitching way of handling people and an outstanding, fingertip feeling for human relationships'.[4] Hess fell under his spell. In addition to Haushofer's knowledge of the world, his wide reading, erudition and intuitive approach, so different in every respect to the father who had tried to force Hess against his will into the mould of businessman, the General had a positive message about Germany's place in the world which met Hess's deepest needs. For his part, Haushofer took a fatherly interest in the quiet, ardent young man with a first-class war record who so obviously idolised him.

'He is a capital fellow (*famoser Mensch*)', Hess wrote to his parents in June 1920. In good weather, he continued, Haushofer always collected him from work before lunch or dinner for a walk together; recently they had been for an early morning stroll through the English Garden in Munich from seven to eight-thirty. In the same letter he described having family dinner alone with the Professor, his wife – 'who is also very nice' – and their two sons, Heinz and Albrecht; the latter 'has a good English accent, I sometimes take a stroll and speak English with him'.[5]

Twenty-five years later, after a second lost war, Haushofer was questioned by an American colonel about Hess in his university days. 'He was a very attentive student,' Haushofer replied, 'but you see his strong side was not intelligence but heart and character I should say. He was not very intelligent.'

'Did you find that he evinced great interest in the subject matter that you taught?'

'He had great interest, and he worked very hard, but you see at that time there were all those students' and officers' associations and a very strong political movement and so the young men were always drawn away from their work.'[6]

Two other older men who had great influence on Hess at this time were Dietrich Eckart and Captain Ernst Röhm, the former a rabid racist, anti-Semitic writer, poet and wit, who held forth at a regular table at the Brennessel beerhouse in Schwabing, the latter a regular army officer of combative, swashbuckling spirit serving on the staff of the district Army commander, now General Ritter von Epp. It was probably from one or both that Hess first heard of Hitler.

Eckart, a member of the Thule Society, had discerned Hitler's remarkable gift for street oratory and had taken it upon himself to groom him as the charismatic leader who had borne his part in the ranks during the war, above all who spoke the language of ordinary people, who might wean them from Bolshevism and lead them on the *völkisch*, national-racial crusade he desired. One of the early supporters of the movement, Kurt Ludecke, described Eckart as 'something of a genius, and to a great degree the spiritual father of Hitler'.[7]

If Eckart was the intellectual mentor who polished Hitler's raw talent, Röhm was the decisive influence on the growth of the infant German Workers' Party, which Hitler joined in 1919 after attending one of its meetings as an agent for the propaganda department of the local Army command. The Party had been backed originally by the Thule Society to win workers for its *völkisch* cause. By diverting secret Army funds and arms, and encouraging ex-service and Freikorps freebooters to form a paramilitary wing, the Sturmabteilung or SA, Röhm converted it into a hammer of the opposing Socialist and Communist organisations. He, too, personally supported and befriended Hitler, signally honouring the former Corporal with the familiar '*Du*' when they talked.

Whoever it was that first alerted Hess to this mesmeric new hope for the *völkisch* cause, it was in the spring of 1920, soon after making his devastating first impression on Ilse Pröhl, that he persuaded the General, as he called Haushofer, to accompany him to a meeting of the Party, now renamed the National Socialist German Workers Party (NSDAP) – in shortened form, 'Nazi' Party. The headquarters were in an old, shabby quarter of Munich, in the small back room of a beerhouse called the Sterneckerbräu. Furnishings were of the simplest, the atmosphere smoky and few, if any, of those sitting in upright wooden chairs around a bare table were from the social milieu of the General or his favourite student. Yet, after Adolf Hitler rose and began to speak, Hess was enraptured. One of those who went through a similar experience two years later, Kurt Ludecke, described it: Hitler stood silent for a moment, an unremarkable, limp man of the people with pale face and sloping shoulders, dark brown hair, small moustache and strange, slightly protruding blue eyes – perhaps with one hand like a shield before his crutch as later newsreels show him doing while holding his audience's attention by his stillness and his piercing, almost mesmeric gaze. 'Then he began to speak, quietly and ingratiatingly at first. Before long his voice had risen to a hoarse shriek that gave an extraordinary effect of intensity of feeling. There were many high-pitched, rasping notes, but despite its strident tone, his diction had a distinctly Austrian turn, softer and pleasanter then the German . . .'[8]

Hitler urged the revival of German honour, indicted the leaders in Berlin as the 'November criminals' who had signed away German honour at Versailles – no doubt he also indicted the international conspiracy of Jews which sought to undermine all states through capitalism and Bolshevism, political intrigue, conspiracy, deception and manipulation of the mind of the mob, for he had been introduced recently to *The Protocols of the Wise Men of Zion*.[9] Ludecke found his critical faculties being swept away by the sheer force of Hitler's conviction, and it was clear that Hitler himself responded to the emotional commitment he evoked in his audience. 'His voice rising to passionate climaxes, he finished his speech with an anthem of hate against the "Novemberlings" and a pledge of undying love for the Fatherland. "Germany must be free!" was his final, defiant slogan. Then two last words that were like the sting of a lash: "*Deutschland erwache!*"'[10]

'Germany awake!' Ludecke felt sure that no one who had heard Hitler speaking could doubt that he was the man of destiny, 'the vitalising force in the future of Germany'. This was precisely Hess's response.

Ilse Pröhl was working at her school books when he returned from the evening, 'a new man, lively, radiant, no longer gloomy, nor grief-stricken.'[11]

'You must come with me the day after tomorrow,' he burst out, 'to a meeting of the National Socialist Party. I have just been there with the General. An unknown man spoke, I don't remember his name. But if anyone will free us from Versailles, this is the man – this unknown will restore our honour.'[12]

Ilse Pröhl – jumping at the chance of a whole evening with Rudolf Hess, then little more to her than an attractive symbol of concerned, idealistic, battle-seasoned young manhood, just what she wanted, hoping only that he would emerge from his shell and grant her a little conversation – agreed to go. Whether she, too, fell immediately under Hitler's spell or whether it was sufficient for her that Rudolf Hess was captivated is not clear. The evening marked the beginning of a companionship between the two which became ever closer, but for her part she must surely have realised that she could never claim all her man; she had to share him with Adolf Hitler.

'Idealist' was a word used about Hess throughout his career. Much of the charm Hitler exerted on him was the result of his message keying in with the ideals Hess had drawn from the Thule Society, from the Freikorps and his old 'front comrades', from the very air of his circle in Munich, heavy with disillusioned nationalism and horror of Bolshevism. Hitler appeared as the realisation of Hess's dreams. A letter he wrote to his parents after the failure of the Kapp *putsch* in March that year, thus before he had even heard the name of Hitler, illustrates this. 'A great part of the people cry for a strong government, for a dictator who will create order, oppose the Jewish economy, put an end to graft and profiteering', he wrote; yet, when such a man appeared, the alarm was raised against 'disturbers of the peace' and scarcely anyone rallied round. Referring to a successful change to a rightist government in Munich even as Kapp failed in Berlin, he went on, the Jewish press was doing its utmost to brand the new people as '*Junkers*', 'reactionaries', 'Monarchists' and raising the alarm against '*Alldeutsche*' – meaning pan-Germans, who called for a strengthening of national consciousness and foreign expansion. He asked rhetorically how Britain conducted her successful policy and answered, because every Briton was what in Germany would be called an *Alldeutschen*; the Government could, therefore, conduct a strong policy, knowing it was supported by the masses. 'Yet a strong German policy does not suit our Jewish rabble (*Judenpack*) and therefore they exert the power of their press in the corresponding direction.' He went on to say that he, his brother Alfred and some others, all dressed like workers, had been distributing leaflets against pan-Jewry (*Alljuda*) in working-class areas of Munich, 'some 3,000 posted up by night in the workers' quarter of Giesing or shoved under the doors'.[13]

Hitler had emerged from precisely this spiritual, intellectual milieu of the 'front fighters' of the lost war; for Hess he was the strong man they needed, the future dictator and saviour of Germany. Despite the General's doubts about the unkempt rabble-rouser – and Haushofer's charming wife, Martha, was the daughter of an influential Jewish businessman – Hess joined the Party the following month, in June. His membership number was recorded later as 16, an obvious exaggeration of his status as an early entrant. From then on he took more and more time off from his studies to attend meetings at the Sterneckerbräu, to listen in admiration to 'the Tribune' holding forth to his circle of like-minded colleagues at coffee houses, prepare and post up notices, write letters, distribute leaflets – in which activities Ilse Pröhl also took time off from her studies to help. He wrote home saying he was in well nigh daily contact with Hitler – 'this splendid fellow'.[14]

Twenty-five years later, in June 1945, after millions had perished, Germany had been overrun and divided between the war victors, and Hitler had died in the rubble that had once been Berlin, Hess wrote to Ilse from captivity in England. She could imagine, he said, how often his thoughts had returned to the past quarter century, concentrated for them in one name full of the most wonderful human experiences: 'It has been granted to few to take part as we have from the outset in the development of a unique personality in joy and sorrow, cares and hopes, hates and loves and all the marks of greatness – and also in all the little signs of human weakness which alone make a man wholly lovable.'[15]

The first test of the Tribune's stature in his self-appointed task came in Autumn 1923. Germany appeared ripe for take-over or dissolution by Bolshevism. Inflation was running out of control, the savings of the middle class were wiped out, unemployment was rising, and real hunger was spreading in urban streets and, with it, Communist insurrection, both real and potential.

To Hitler's supporters and the thousands of ex-service and Freikorps men lured to Bavaria by the more congenial political climate since the take-over there by the Right, the situation was ripe for a *putsch* to oust the Social Democratic Government of the Republic – Hitler's 'Jewish traitors' and 'Novemberlings' – and set up in its place a Nationalist regime under a strong man. Powerful elements in the Bavarian Government under the Generalstaatskommissar Gustav von Kahr were under equal pressure from their supporters to declare an autonomous Bavaria led

17

by a restored monarchy, either within a confederation of German states or within a south German and Austrian Catholic union – in that case leaving the Protestant north to stew in its own anarchy. Since separation was anathema to the *völkisch* nationalists who followed Hitler and Röhm – now retired from the Army to lead his own paramilitary organisation, *Reichskriegsflagge* – the Right was split. The preponderant power factor, however, was the Army, commanded from the War Ministry in Berlin, and there the decision had been taken that in order to prevent the break-up of the country in civil war, insurrections must be put down whether from the Left or from the Right.

In this infinitely tangled situation Hitler was unable to do more than act as a sounding board for his followers, thus increasing expectations he could not fulfil without persuading the regional Army commander, von Lossow, and the police chief, von Seisser, to his side. There is evidence that both were prepared to assist a Nationalist 'march on Berlin' in October, but by early November they had either been warned off or had thought better of it. Von Kahr, meanwhile, organised a mass meeting of Nationalist leaders from Bavaria and throughout Germany for the evening of 8 November to mark the fifth anniversary of the armistice talks to end the war. Convincing himself that Kahr would use the demonstration to declare Bavarian independence under a restored monarchy, Hitler determined to pre-empt him and seize the initiative; probably he knew he could not delay action further without losing his followers.

His principal lieutenant for the coup was the former Air Force Captain Hermann Göring, whom he had appointed leader of the Party Stürmabteilung (SA) the previous November; he was to provide the assault troops to take over the hall of the Bürgerbräukeller, where the meeting was to be held. Rudolf Hess came under Göring's overall command, as he had formed and led the student detachment of the SA, but it was Hitler who gave him his orders on the morning of the operation 'clearly and succinctly', as Hess described it in a letter to his parents begun the same day. He was to seize all the Bavarian Government ministers in the hall and confine them under house arrest. 'With a solemn handclasp I promised unconditional silence, and we parted until evening.'[16]

Came the evening and Hess, 'in the old uniform, with pistol strapped under my greatcoat'[17] made his way to Party headquarters, thence by car to the Bürgerbräukeller on the other side of the River Isar. The hall was full to overflowing and he was refused entry, but managed to bluff his way in 'as a kind of adjutant' to a general in full uniform, the leader of the Thule Society paramilitary organisation, Oberland, who happened to be going in then. Following his instructions, he found a room off the lobby and installed some of his troops inside. Shortly afterwards Hitler appeared in the lobby, incongruous in an ill-cut black tail coat with Iron Cross, accompanied by Göring and one or two others. Pacing 'somewhat nervously' by the entrance, he beckoned Hess to his side. In the hall von Kahr had begun reading his speech. Suddenly there was a disturbance at the outer doorway, the guards were thrust aside and steel-helmeted men of Göring's shock troops burst in with machine pistols, threw open the inner doors to the hall and forced a passage for Hitler through the packed audience towards the speaker's lectern. Hess went in on Hitler's left. Near the platform where Kahr was staring with an expression 'like a child slapped in innocence', Hitler jumped on a chair and called for quiet, seconded by his bodyguard, Hess and the others with them. They could not be heard above the commotion; Hitler raised his revolver and fired into the ceiling. There was stunned silence.

'The national revolution in Munich has just broken out,' he shouted. 'The whole city is at this moment occupied by our troops. This hall is surrounded by 600 men.'[18]

Turning to the platform, he asked von Kahr, von Lossow and von Seisser to accompany him outside, and took them to the room Hess had prepared. While he harangued them to join in the new 'provisional national government' and his car was sent to fetch Field Marshall Ludendorff, victor of Tannenberg, to be the figurehead and command the loyalty of the Army, Hess went back to the hall with his men to arrest the ministers. He called them from their seats by name, starting with the Minister President, von Knilling, placing them under guard in the landlord's living-room before despatching the most senior members separately in cars under escort to the house of a sympathetic publisher. There he held them overnight.

Hess was not present, therefore, to witness the rest of this extraordinary evening of bluster, passion and finally bathos. Von Kahr, von Lossow and von Seisser were persuaded to give their support to Hitler – whether genuinely or as a tactical ploy because of Hitler's revolver remains debatable – and they returned to the hall to make short speeches of affirmation. Ludendorff arrived, was greeted with a standing ovation and, as Hitler clasped each of the great men emotionally by the hand, the words of the national anthem broke out spontaneously from the throats of the massed audience. Hitler snapped to attention and stood beaming with joy; a historian present described his 'childlike, frank expression of happiness I shall never forget'.[19]

After this moving climax everything fell apart. Hitler allowed the reigns to slip from his hands. Professor Waite has pointed out that 'the first ten or twelve hours of any *coup d'état* are of crucial importance to its success. During these hours [of 9 November] . . . no order at all came from the Putschist high command.'[20] No key buildings in the city were occupied. Röhm led his *Reichskriegsflagge* – Heinrich Himmler bearing the colour – to the War Ministry, but could not gain entrance. He threw a barbed wire and machine-gun cordon round the building, and was then surrounded in his turn by the police. Apart from Hitler's disastrous lapse into apathy, Göring made the major blunder when he accepted the words of von Kahr, von Lossow and von Seisser as officers and gentlemen, and allowed them to return to their ministries. Whether or not their original conversion was genuine, they were soon brought back to reality. Von Lossow's adjutant had left the hall early and alerted the High Command in Berlin, and von Lossow was now told that either he suppressed the *putsch* or other forces would. He had no option but to obey. With the Army committed, von Kahr and von Seisser had no option but to follow suit. Hess believed their original conversions genuine – 'it was a change of mind, not theatre from the beginning',[21] he wrote. How he knew he did not say; he was not there.

The following morning the chief conspirators were still at the Bürger-bräu, Hitler in a state of exhaustion, 'a little man in an old waterproof coat with a revolver at his hip', as *The Times* correspondent found him, 'unshaven with disorderly hair, and so hoarse that he could hardly speak'.[22] It was plain by then that von Kahr and the others had gone back on their word; the situation seemed hopeless, but Ludendorff proposed a march on the centre of Munich to show what they were made of. Hitler and Göring agreed, and so began the march of the SA and other paramilitary formations which had converged on the area overnight, whose end under the guns of a police cordon across the narrow funnel of the Residenzstrasse near the centre of Munich entered Nazi mythology. Ludendorff escaped unscathed, Hitler's left shoulder was dislocated as he was pulled violently to the ground, Göring was wounded by a bullet in the groin; fourteen martyrs died in the fusilade.

Hess heard of the collapse of the *putsch* that afternoon at the publisher's villa. He decided to hide two of his hostages, the Interior and Agricultural Ministers, in ski huts in the mountains; bundling them into a car with two of his student SA men, he climbed in himself and told the chauffeur to take the road to Bad Tölz. His decision stemmed less from calculation than from his mood which, to judge from his actions, was bitter and vengeful; he played macabre jokes on the two hostages, repeatedly having the chauffeur stop the car by woods and point the headlights into the trees while he ostensibly searched for a suitable tree from which to hang them.[23] Sadistic as this appears, it was not untoward for a young man schooled in Freikorps hate and violence. Arriving at Tölz, it became evident that snow and darkness would prevent them reaching the huts, so he left the car to persuade the occupant of a secluded villa to put them up for the night. The parley lasted longer than expected and by the time he returned to the car, it had gone – so he wrote in a letter home. The chauffeur had driven back towards Munich, the young SA men playing out the same cruel game with the ministers on the way. 'Maybe it was the best solution,' Hess wrote the following month. 'Nothing more was to be saved by holding the ministers any longer.'[24]

He walked the mountain paths which he knew from hikes with Ilse, sheltered on the way by members of the Oberland fraternity, and reached safety in Austria. There he learned that Hitler had been arrested and confined in the fortress of Landsberg until his trial. He assumed Hitler would receive good treatment there; he would be low in spirit, Hess suggested in a letter to his parents, but would recover from that; 'he has elasticity enough'.[25]

Hess had never lost the interest in the stars awakened at his mother's side in Egypt; at his boarding school at Bad Godesberg he had bought and borrowed books on astronomy.[26] By 1923 he had acquired an interest in astrology too, perhaps through Karl Haushofer, who was also a student of the occult.[27] Hanfstaengl and many others found the later Hess inclined to mystical and astrological speculation;[28] von Krosigk wrote that often when he spoke to Hess it was as if he had just returned from another planet and only with difficulty adjusted himself to this world; he 'lived in unreality, he believed in dream-readings, prophecies and astrology'.[29] Certainly there are indications of this in the letters Hess wrote from self-imposed exile in Austria. At the end of November he wrote to Ilse to say that, astrologically speaking, the next weeks would be decisive for him; the aspect was marvellous; the high point would be in the next month, and he would treat this case as a touchstone.[30] To his mother he wrote in fatalistic tones of steering a course in the stream of fate, powerless to affect the trend and final goal. Maybe one had presentiments of the direction, of fortune and misfortune, he went on, but although many others in his situation would with reason tear their hair over lack of career, status, home and children, he had no anxiety about his future; 'we [outlaws] who are sought, have the certainty that we are cleaving a course in the stream [of fate] in rhythm with the Führer.'[31]

3

*M*EIN *K*AMPF

Hess's confidence in 'the Tribune', whom he regarded as the *Führer* (leader) seemed to be vindicated by the use Hitler made of the trial of several leaders of the *putsch* beginning at the end of February 1924. The proceedings were a charade played out largely for Berlin, because the Bavarian judiciary, from the Minister of Justice down, was sympathetic to the *putschists* and Hitler's biting interjections, and his final impassioned speech left them even more on his side. He became a national figure. On 1 April sentences were passed: Ludendorff was acquitted, Röhm given fifteen months and released at once on his own recognisance, Hitler and three others were given five years' fortress detention, but were to be released after six months. *The Times* correspondent noted, 'The trial at any rate proved that to plot against the constitution of the Reich is not considered a serious crime in Bavaria.'[1]

Hess read the reports in the Austrian press and decided to return and give himself up. As he wrote from a skiing break later that month, they really could not deal more harshly with him than with 'the master. vvvv.'[2] He returned to Munich, writing to his mother – his father had gone to Egypt to reactivate his company – to say that, had he not done so, the authorities would have caught up with him later at a less opportune moment. Besides, if he were sent to Landsberg for a while, he would have 'peace to study, interesting company, good fare, a common living-room, individual bedroom, garden, lovely view, so! vvvv.'[3]

And thus it proved, although the unique boon was proximity to the Tribune. 'So, happily, I've landed here,' he wrote to his mother on 16 May after being sentenced to eighteen months' fortress detention, to be released after six months, 'and can be with the splendid fellow, Hitler, every day ... I told you before I would certainly not be in bad humour if it came to this.'[4] He described the fortress as consisting of several large buildings, modern and stylish, surrounded by a garden. Their rooms were furnished magnificently; they had a modern bathroom for their sole use and continuous hot water. Their treatment was perfect, indeed honourable. Everything was shining clean. They were allowed in the garden six hours every day, and there was no lack of visitors; that day they had drunk wine brought for them by Ludendorff. As for the Tribune, he was 'well and lively, in no way downcast – quite the contrary.'[5]

A few days later he wrote to Ilse to tell her of the Tribune's architectural ideas: Hitler felt that the cupola form had not been developed as it could have been with modern materials and technology, and had shown him a design he had sketched for a great building for national festivals surmounted by a huge 100-metre dome, and surrounded by other buildings housing a national museum to commemorate the First World War, a theatre, a national library and so on. He also showed him pen and paint sketches of stage designs for operas, *Tristan*, *Lohengrin* and *Turandot*, which had amazed him; he had never seen this side of Hitler before. The Tribune also told him of his ideas for an advisory parliament for political and economic matters with the task of considering law emanating from a senate and the head of State in combination, or making proposals to them; they had discussed the composition of such a senate. Next day they were discussing, in view of the recent loans made to Germany under the US Dawes Plan designed to cure her economic woes and enable her to pay war reparations, whether they would ever be able to break free from the grip of international capital. Hitler was putting his hopes in this respect on Britain, Hess reported.[6] The following week Hitler told him of his ideas for mass-produced prefabricated family homes; he did not want this talked about, though, lest someone took them up for personal profit. Hess told Ilse he was writing about these things because of a long-cherished intention to record the ideas and sayings of the Tribune, and preserve them for the future – 'regardless of what his destiny may be'.[7]

In daily intimacy Hess grew ever more certain of that destiny: at the beginning of June he told Ilse he had the firm conviction 'as indeed the Tribune has – rock-like – that he will not be stopped and at the right time will stand where he must stand' regardless of whether his followers split apart – as indeed they were doing in his absence. He did not need them. He went his way regardless, 'in his heart burning love for his *Volk* and high esteem for the masses, from which outwardly he himself comes, but to which, like every great man, he has certainly never belonged inwardly'.[8]

Karl Haushofer was one of Hess's regular visitors, bringing books and advising him on points brought up in his discussions with the Tribune. At the end of the Second World War he was asked about the influence he had exerted on Hitler through Hess, particularly in the

23

fields of philosophy and geopolitics; he replied that Hitler, who was only semi-educated, had noticed that Hess was far more educated in these fields than himself.

'Don't you think that Hitler was influenced a great deal by Hess?'

Since Hess was about to stand trial as a war criminal, Haushofer's answers were cautious. 'Hitler knew just as little about these things as Hess,' he replied. Pressed, he admitted that Hitler was certainly told about these subjects by Hess, 'but I received the impression, and I am utterly convinced that Hitler never understood these things and did not have the right outlook for understanding them'.

'But Hitler, being an uneducated man, would talk at great length on the subjects of *Lebensraum* [living space] and geopolitics. Don't you believe he got these ideas from Hess?'

'Yes,' Haushofer replied. 'Those ideas come to Hitler from Hess, but he never really understood them, and he never really read about them from the original books. He never read those books.'

'Did you ever talk to Hitler?'

'Very seldom, because you see, my visits to Landsberg always were meant for Hess, he being my pupil. It wasn't really allowed that one visited more than one person and I was only interested in visiting Rudolf Hess.'

'Isn't it true that Hess collaborated with Hitler in writing *Mein Kampf*?'

'As far as I know Hess actually dictated many chapters of that book.'

'Then do I understand that you would discuss these matters with Hess and then Hess in turn would discuss them with Hitler, and that is how they got the book?'

'In matters where I saw that neither Hitler nor Hess had any geographical ideas, I tried to visit Hess and tried to explain to him the basis of Ratsel's book dealing with political geography.'

Pressed as to whether Hitler had adopted these ideas, he admitted that he had sometimes tried to. 'But you see I remember quite well whenever Hess understood such a thing and tried to explain it to Hitler, Hitler usually came out with one of his new ideas about an *Autobahn* or anything else which had nothing to do with it, while Hess just stood there and did not say any more about it.'9

In view of the belief in the West that Hitler's plans for conquest stemmed from Haushofer's teachings, notably the concepts of *Lebensraum* for the German peoples in eastern Europe and an alliance with Japan – the Prussia of the East – and since his friend and former pupil, Rudolf Hess, was about to stand trial for his life, it is natural that Haushofer refused to admit that Hitler understood his geopolitical teachings. Nevertheless, there is confirmation in Hess's letters from Landsberg that

Haushofer was far from enthusiastic about Hitler. Thus in June Hess wrote to Haushofer beseeching him to re-examine his estimate of the Tribune, assuring him that Hitler held him (Haushofer) in extraordinarily high regard. 'Your calm and intellectual way of speaking have made a great impression on him.'[10] Haushofer told his interrogator after the war that he always had the impression that Hitler felt a certain distrust for him, 'the distrust of a semi-educated person towards a scientifically educated person'.[11] In his letter Hess touched on the point that perhaps concerned Haushofer most about Hitler: the Tribune had not reached his present standpoint on the Jewish question without 'hard inner struggle', he wrote. He had been beset by doubts about whether he was not doing the Jews an injustice. 'And to this day he speaks in a small circle of educated people differently from the way he speaks to the masses; before these he can only represent the most radical viewpoint.'[12]

The same day Hess wrote to Ilse Pröhl that he would like to see Haushofer's face when he received his letter. 'Am curious as to whether I will succeed in turning the General into a Tribune follower, or at least in bringing him to a recognition of his personality as such.'[13]

The advisers who had done most to form Hitler's views on the Jewish question were undoubtedly Dietrich Eckart, the writer and poet who had spotted Hitler's talent and taken it upon himself to groom it, and Alfred Rosenberg, an Estonian with German forbears and a romantic enthusiasm for all things German, who had felt so emotional about Germany's defeat in the war that he had travelled to Berlin – in his own words 'to acquire a Fatherland' – then at the beginning of 1919 gravitated to Munich; there he had joined the Thule Society and had met Dietrich Eckart. He came with first-hand knowledge of the Bolshevik Revolution, and simple, unshakeable analyses of its cause and significance: it had been brought about by a subterranean conspiracy organised by international Jewry – which had caused the outbreak of world war in the first place; the revolution signified 'defeat for Nordic [Germanic] blood in its struggle for the soul of Russia', which country had now regressed into racial chaos. Should the same thing happen in Germany, it would be the end for her and for western civilisation.[14]

Rosenberg drew his certainty about the real, if concealed, puppet masters behind the Russian revolution from *The Protocols of the Wise Men of Zion*, a forgery produced originally by the Tsar's secret police, the Okhrana, purporting to be extracts from the minutes of the first Zionist Congress at Basel in 1897; the Okhrana used them to foment and justify pogroms around the turn of the century. The *Protocols* had been amplified and, in 1905, published as an appendix to an anti-Semitic book by a Russian, Serge Nilus; it was in this form that Rosenberg first read them while studying architecture in Moscow in the summer of 1917. He was already strongly under the influence of the works of Houston Stewart Chamberlain, an Englishman who had adopted Germany as his spiritual home and viewed European history as the outcome of the struggle between the German peoples and the subversive influences of Judaism and the Roman Catholic Church. Now the *Protocols* provided textual proof of the international plot by which Jewry, 'through treachery and cunning', aimed to 'undermine society, overthrow governments, plunge mankind into war and seize power throughout the world'.[15] Rosenberg swallowed it whole and brought it with him in his intellectual baggage to Munich, where Eckart and other anti-Semitic publishers – including J. F. Lehmann, in whose villa Hess held his ministerial hostages during the 1923 *putsch* – employed him as a researcher and writer. Also through Eckart, Rosenberg met Hitler. They made a profound impression on one another. Ludecke described Rosenberg as having read much 'and when he spoke he revealed himself at once as a thinker, expressing original thoughts in a fine form with the inner assurance that marks a high intellect.'[16] How much more it must have appeared to Hitler, who lacked Ludecke's formal education and, although he liked to cite authors and books he had read, completely lacked patience to do more than skim through a few pages to find ideas which matched his own. Above all, of course, Rosenberg's belief in the underlying racial explanation of world history keyed in precisely with his own. Rosenberg, moreover, could provide the historical proofs. So, besides becoming assistant editor, then editor of the Nazi Party newspaper, *Völkischer Beobachter*, he became, in Ludecke's words, 'Hitler's closest co-thinker, and more than anybody else, in his later writings, shaped the Nazi *Weltanschauung*' (world view or philosophy).[17] This estimate of his intellectual influence is confirmed by others close to Hitler at the time, Hanfstaengl, for instance, found Hitler 'deeply under the spell of Rosenberg'[18] and Otto Strasser went so far as to write that Hitler was known for years as Rosenberg's mouthpiece.[19]

Rosenberg marched in the 1923 *putsch*, then went into hiding; he did not visit Landsberg, therefore, to contribute in person to Hitler's book, later published as *Mein Kampf*, but his views on the Jew as, on the one hand, the originator of anarchism and Bolshevism, and, on the other hand, of materialism and democracy – equally subversive of society – and his belief that the Roman Catholic Church and international Freemasonry were tools of the Jewish world conspiracy seeking to undermine all states and finally to inherit the Earth, were already stamped on Hitler's thinking. Undoubtedly many advisers contributed to specialist areas touched in *Mein Kampf*, but for the core of ideological, racial, geopolitical and foreign policy objectives, Alfred Rosenberg and Rudolf Hess, as conduit for Karl Haushofer, played the chief roles. While it is apparent from Hess's letters from Landsberg that Hitler wrote some chapters and read them out to him, if Haushofer was correct in his statements to his American interrogator, Hess wrote much of the book himself. There is no doubt he discussed points arising from Hitler's own readings,[20] drew up notes of these discussions,[21] consulted Haushofer and other experts in different fields, and finally typed the manuscript for publication. How much he acted as co-author, reordering and rewriting Hitler's undisciplined monologues and adding sections of his own, how much he was merely the faithful disciple taking down and making corrections to the thoughts of the master, will probably never be known. But to judge by Hitler's *louche* habits, complete lack of work discipline, incapacity to synthesise the products of his powerful memory and his subsequent failure to write the intended sequel to the two volumes of *Mein Kampf*, it is extremely probable that Hess's position was closer to co-author than faithful servant.[22]

However this may be, and however much Hess failed to bring clarity or felicity to great swathes of the book – or even sound grammar, according to one indomitable German researcher who counted over 164,000 errors in syntax[23] – there can be no question that he was a party to those passages about race which give the lie to the assertion in his letter to Haushofer that Hitler, when talking about Jews in small circles of the educated, used a different voice to that which he used before the masses. There is, for instance, that section dealing with the Marxists in the homeland who, the book alleged, caused the German defeat in 1918 by fomenting revolution behind the fighting fronts:

If at the beginning of the war or during the war one had held twelve or fifteen thousand of these Hebrew *Volk*-corrupters under poison gas such as hundreds of thousands of our very best German workers ... had to endure in the field then the millionfold sacrifices of the front would not have been in vain.[24]

This can be matched precisely to a letter Hess wrote to Ilse Pröhl from Landsberg on 29 June. It described the occasion Hitler broke down in tears while reading Hess an account of his early experiences at the front, afterwards confessing how frightened he had been himself. After some further description of his battles and injuries, Hitler had come to the treachery at home – by Marxists and Parliamentarians in 1918: 'Oh, I will take a merciless and fearful revenge on the day I am able to do so! I will avenge in the name of the dead whom I saw before me then!'[25]

It was after this, as Hess was leaving, that the two clasped hands in a long, firm grasp and Hess realised he was more devoted to Hitler than ever – that indeed he loved him.[26]

The question of Hess's contribution to *Mein Kampf* is important for any estimate of his character and responsibility for what came after, for embedded in the turgid, often impenetrable prose is the plan to make Germany master of Europe, then the world – not of course the detailed tracts or timetable, but the grand strategic outline. Central to this was race; and central to the racial question was, on the one hand, the weeding out of the mentally, genetically and racially unfit from the body of the *Volk*, and on the other hand, the preservation and reproduction of the most valuable (Germanic) racial elements. Eugenics or 'racial hygiene' were established concepts with a long tradition; in *Mein Kampf* they were pressed to the ultimate – nothing less than the selective breeding of a 'master race' of Aryans to usher in the German millennium. 'The *völkisch* state has to perform the most gigantic rearing task here. One day, however, it will appear as a deed greater than the most victorious wars of our present bourgeois era.'[27]

This suggests that the breeding of the master race took predominance even over the coming battles for *Lebensraum* in the east, although both were essential and complementary. The vision was so audacious it is little wonder that Hess, having found in Hitler what he needed to fill his yearning for an ideal way and a star, felt bound to his *Führer* in admiration and awe. He could scarcely have foreseen the depth of horrors to which such a policy must lead, but he was aware that at the least it meant mass sterilisation, for this was almost spelled out in the book: the wishes and egos of individuals had to yield before the *völkisch* State, which would 'place the most modern medical means in the service of this [racial hygenic] perception.'[28] It would be unjust to hold the passage about subjecting Hebrew *Volk*-corrupters to poison gas as proof that Hitler and Hess planned such a method of exterminating the Jews; for one thing it was by no means obvious that this would prove the most efficient means of mass liquidation; many experiments would be necessary before it was adopted. The passage probably has more to do with Hitler's emotional response to the horrors of the trenches.

The coarsening or deranging effects of such long periods in the trenches as Hitler, Hess and others of their generation suffered have not been investigated sufficiently in the context of their attitudes. To suggest one aspect: throughout history terror societies have bound their members and made them capable of atrocity with initiation ceremonies requiring them to perform monstrous, bloody acts running counter to conscience and human feeling. Trench warfare provided a similar initiation on the grand scale for those who took part; such sensitive characters as Hitler and Hess cannot have escaped unscathed or at least unchanged.[29]

Besides typing out *Mein Kampf* chapter by chapter in Landsberg, Hess performed the functions of Hitler's private secretary, Ilse Pröhl acting as his assistant and courier outside. He took it upon himself to convey his leader's views to outside sympathisers, concerned that the movement was breaking up in faction while Hitler did nothing. Thus, in July, he wrote in reply to a letter from his judicial and economic adviser, Heinrich Heim, that he had been unable to elicit an answer from Hitler to the points raised:

Now indeed, he [Hitler] has withdrawn publicly from the management [*Leitung*]. Reason is he does not wish to take responsibility for that which occurs outside without his knowledge and in some cases against his will. Even less is he in a position to settle the eternal quarrelling, at least from inside here. He feels it unnecessary for him to grapple with all the little unpleasantnesses.

On the other hand he is convinced that soon after he has attained his freedom he will be able to direct everything on to the right track again. Above all he will then very quickly bring to an end everything which leads in any way to confessional [Church] opposition and will concentrate forces for the struggle against Communism, [which is] the more dangerous as it is always conspiring to prepare a great blow.

I believe that the moment is coming only too soon when everyone will stand behind Hitler in a battle of desperation against the Bolshevik pestilence . . .[30]

He hoped that Hitler would be freed early enough to lead the fight. If Hitler's book came out in the autumn, he went on, it would give the public a picture of him not only as politician but also as a man.

A week after this letter he wrote to Ilse Pröhl rejoicing that, by being with Hitler continually, he had come to know him completely in every direction; what was more, he had gained so very much 'not only of sentimental value in respect to the man who will one day stand at the head of the newly sound Germany he has created, but also in respect to the further development of my mind, stimulation and study'. Regularly when Hitler had finished a chapter of his book, Hess continued, he came and read it aloud to him and explained it, after which they discussed this or that point.[31]

In another letter that month, July, he described the effect on him of Hitler's readings: the blood hammered through his veins as he listened and at the end he breathed a deep sigh of relief as at a release of tension; it was exactly the effect produced by Hitler's best speeches, not the result of words alone, but of his whole personality as expressed in delivery and gesture. He would never forget the picture of him sitting in a wicker chair in his (Hess's) room: 'Nor will I ever forget how he beams and shows the joy of a young boy if he sees his own conviction of the excellence of his handiwork confirmed by its effect on another, and if one says a couple of words of appreciation.'[32]

For his part, Hitler looked on this time in Landsberg as of particular

29

value in his own development, referring to it later as his 'college education at State expense'.[33]

Hess's intimacy with Hitler did not exclude Ilse Pröhl; rather it was as if he wanted to share his delight and admiration for *their* paragon with her, his trusted love. The frequency and content of his letters show how close he was to her. In September he wrote her a charming little poem;[34] it began:

> Cooling wind blow
> in dark of the night
> thither to swirl,
> thither to storm,
> greeting the sweetheart,
> seeking her out,
> gently to fan
> her, softly so soft,
> caress her,
> cherish her,
> kiss her from me!

Hitler was due to be released from Landsberg on parole on 1 October, and was looking forward to it, in Hess's words, as keenly as a child; but the authorities were anxious about his colleague, Röhm, then building up a nationalist paramilitary organisation called Frontbann, and kept him inside. It was not until December, after elections revealed a collapse in the *völkisch* vote, which fell to under a million, that it was felt safe to allow him his freedom. Hess, who was not released, wrote to Ilse that on purely personal and egotistic grounds he was naturally very sorry to lose '*his* company'.[35]

At the end of December 1924 Hess, too, was released. Ilse Pröhl was outside the gates with a car, as she had been when Hitler walked free, and she drove him to the small Italian café Hitler patronised, the Osteria Bavaria, opposite the offices of the now banned *Völkischer Beobachter* in Schellingstrasse, in the Schwabing district of Munich. There the Tribune was waiting to greet him.

4
THE SECRETARY

Hitler soon fulfilled his prediction that after his release he would restore the movement to the right track. That meant, in the first place, asserting his own undisputed leadership. In this respect Hess's influence can hardly be overstated. His absolute belief in Hitler as the *Führer* who would one day 'stand where he must stand', his eagerness to submerge himself in the great task of ensuring that he would stand there, his transparent devotion, fed Hitler's belief in himself. In Landsberg the two had used the familiar '*Du*' mode of speech; now, at least when others were present, Hess reverted to the formal mode and referred to Hitler as leader – *Führer*. Thus he began the mythologising process which was to lead eventually to 'the Führer' acquiring semi-divine status as the earthly representative of the very soul of the German people, whose will was the highest law; this even became true in a legal sense; as put by one of the leading judicial figures of the Third Reich: 'Our Constitution is the will of the Führer.'[1] Undoubtedly this is how Hess viewed Hitler's rightful position virtually from the time he first met him, certainly from the Landsberg interlude. On both their parts it was a remarkable act of faith, an extraordinary self-fulfilling prophecy.

The fact that Hess's vision came to be realised so perfectly suggests that he was a paradigm of the German masses who wanted to believe and soon came to believe in the figure of the strong father, warlord, god that Hitler acted out for them. Just why they wanted to believe is debatable; one percipient German wrote:

He absolved the weary, the desperate and the down-trodden from the heaviest burdens of their souls. He allowed them . . . to gather hope and to feel superior. He released them from the loads of reason, responsibility and morality . . . [and] let them relax into a pre-civilised, pre-social, infantile stage. He allowed them to hate and believe, to strike and obey [2]

Recalling Ilse Pröhl's description of the heavily burdened, desperate young Freikorps officer she encountered on her first day at the Pension Schildberg in Schwabing who was changed into a 'new man, lively, radiant, no longer gloomy' after first hearing Hitler speak, remembering the fatalism and recourse to astrological speculation revealed in this newly-born man's letter from hiding in Austria, it is apparent that the analysis provides at least a partial explanation of Hess's faith. A full explanation of his devotion, his failure to bring critical faculties to bear and his desire to surrender himself wholly to a man and a creed beyond reason must, of course, take into account his childhood experience of a frightening father, a loving mother, the trauma of the trenches, the humiliation of the Fatherland and not least the characteristics he inherited in his genes.

Hitler's most influential rival for the leadership of the *völkisch* movement was Gregor Strasser: a straightforward, even naive, emotional bear of a man, as bluff as Hitler was intuitive and receptive. The son of a lower official who could not afford to put him through the doctor's training he aspired to, he had become a chemist and had entered the war with vague Socialist ideas and dissatisfactions. These were crystallised by the comradeship of the trenches, where he proved a fearless and inspiring leader, gaining the Iron Cross 1st and 2nd Class and, like Hess, promotion to Lieutenant of Reserves. He was no thinker; his ideas never progressed beyond the slogans of nationalist and *völkisch* propaganda, and sentimental nostalgia for the equality of the front line, where men were valued for what they were, not for money or class. Despite – more probably because of – this, he was an effective public speaker. Above all, he was an enthusiastic and capable organiser. He had been sent to join Hitler and the others in Landsberg for a short time after the *putsch* for recruiting for the banned Nazi Party, but had been released when elected to the State Parliament. Since then he had reorganised the Party and sa groups in his district or *Gau* of Lower Bavaria under a new banner, the National Socialist Freiheitsbewegung (freedom movement). He had also travelled extensively in northern Germany, making speeches recruiting and forming groups, leaving a newly acquired secretary, Heinrich Himmler to nurse the Bavarian *Gau*.

Strasser was the man Hitler had to come to terms with if he was to lead a reformed Party. He took the first step at a private meeting in February, allowing Strasser freedom to organise the Party in the north, while he himself took responsibility for the stronghold in the south. In agreeing, Strasser made it clear he was prepared to serve with Hitler as a colleague, not under him as a follower. He was one of the first among many who completely misjudged Hitler's psychic need to be predominant, first and only.

Having squared Strasser and prevailed on the authorities to unban the Nazi Party, Hitler called a mass meeting of the movement – as an inspired touch, choosing the scene of his recent failure, the Bürgerbräukeller. The most important leaders of factions, Ludendorff, Röhm and Strasser kept away; so did Alfred Rosenberg because, he told Ludecke, he knew the kind of 'brother kissing' Hitler intended.[3] This was true, since of course Hitler knew his powers of mass suggestion; in another sense, though, Hitler acted as a medium, divining the deepest subconscious desires of his audiences and amplifying them.[4] So it was in this instance. By the time he told the packed gathering in the Bürgerbräukeller that he was forming the Party anew and they must forget their quarrels and shake hands again with one another, his listeners were wallowing in mass emotion. Former faction opponents came to the platform together, many unable to restrain their tears, and vowed their undivided loyalty. Ludecke likened the scene to a revivalist meeting. It was an apt observation.

Since Hess's release from Landsberg, Hitler had wanted to renew the association they had enjoyed inside and repeatedly asked him to become his private secretary on a permanent, salaried basis. Haushofer had already suggested Hess become his assistant at the Geopolitical Institute, the Deutsche Akademie, promising him an academic career leading to a professorship. Hess had accepted, but in April he decided to take up Hitler's offer instead. It was a fateful decision; he gave up a secure post with status and prospects under a man who was both friend and respected counsellor to work for the leader of a Party recently riven by faction, whose constituency appeared to have shrunk to the very fringe of politics, whose membership consisted almost entirely of inarticulate, little-educated artisans, small shopkeepers and lower rank officials. Hess's only point of contact with most was the shared 'front' experience and, of course, enthusiasm for the Führer. But given his relationship to Hitler and his faith, he surely had no choice; his decision was visceral, only the preliminary hesitations rational.

To his parents, now both re-established in Alexandria, naturally he rationalised his decision: it was much better paid than the Akademie post, at first twice as much and, when the Party had been refinanced, it would be considerably more. His time was his own; he could, therefore, continue his studies. This seemed to be belied by his description of his duties – representing Hitler in many matters, receiving visitors for him, attending to his correspondence, travelling and acting on his behalf. He left out of account one of Hitler's major preoccupations at this period, the completion of *Mein Kampf*, which took up a great deal of time and energy. However, there are some passages in his letter which hint at the real explanation for his choice: 'Here I remain on the course I have trod for years ... I acknowledge the Tribune as *Führer*'. And later, explaining that since he had been in the movement from the days it could count less than a hundred members, he knew it through and through: 'In the same way I know the inner thoughts of the Tribune, his attitude on every conceivable question, his whole mode of behaviour (*Art*). He knows me; the mutual confidence to the last, the understanding is there.'[5]

Owing to his studies, he continued, he was well suited to act as a bridge between educated circles and the mass movement, after which he made the interesting admission: he was much too convinced of the necessity 'for often unpleasant means and forms of the struggle – in respect of the psychology of the masses' to be deterred from the work as so many other educated people were, including, of course, although he did not say so, the General. He had the feeling he could exert a favourable influence in many directions towards '*the* position'. He added in a post-script that the Tribune had an unshakeable belief in his prospects, and not simply because certain astrologers had predicted his star in the ascendant for the autumn of that year.[6]

An example of Hitler's remarkable belief in himself – or simply perhaps his abiding passion for designing buildings – occurs in a letter Hess wrote to his parents that July; he had just visited Berlin with Hitler, touring the city in the inevitable Mercedes. Hitler, he wrote, loved the architecture, but dreamed nevertheless of extending it some day.[7]

Apart from travels to inspire the faithful, Hitler and Hess spent much of the summer of 1925 in the Bavarian Alps at Berchtesgaden, first at a *pension*, then at the Hotel Deutsches Haus, working on *Mein Kampf*. Hitler, subsidised by a few wealthy patrons, women prominent among them, lived an idle, self-indulgent life, much as he had as a view-card painter, much as he always would, rising late, talking a great deal, but quite unable to listen, ever restless if something exciting were not happening, diverting himself by touring in the supercharged Mercedes he had bought soon after coming out of Landsberg, taking picnics by the roadside, cream cakes and sweet tea or lemonade at cafés, exhibiting in everything he did and wore what Ludecke called 'typical Austrian *Schlamperei* ... a lackadaisical casualness ... an all-embracing disorderliness'.[8] It was left to Hess to provide the working discipline, order and organisation to hold the fissile Party together. He was hardly ideal. He did, however, enable Hitler to complete *Mein Kampf*, which was published that autumn. He coached him in gesture, expression and turns of phrase for his speeches or before meeting important individuals; he fed his ego. But, while dedicated and, in the words of his later adjutant, Leitgen, 'cautious and painstaking', he was 'in no way a systematic person'.[9] He was, moreover – Leitgen again – 'a burning idealist who avoided reality'.[10] It was not the best combination for the higher direction of a political movement and soon the Party began to divide again into local factions.

The most fundamental challenge came, once more, from Strasser, not simply because he led a north German grouping becoming impatient of Munich, but because he and more particularly his brother Otto adhered to the 'Socialist' as much as to the 'National' in the Party title. Hitler did not; he equated Socialism with Marxism, hence Jews. Moreover, he had learned from his failed *putsch* or from the Landsberg seminars, most probably from the example of Mussolini, whom he admired hugely, that courting the rich and influential was a surer way to power than attempting to seize the government by force; just as Mussolini's Fascist Party had been subsidised to power by the Italian propertied classes fearful of revolution, so Hitler aimed to solicit 'protection' money from Germany's rich industrialists. To do this he needed firstly to convince them of and, if possible, exacerbate the Bolshevik threat and secondly to deliver a mass movement of workers obedient to his leadership who might otherwise be seduced by Bolshevism. Simple, like all great ideas, it needed the utmost deception in practice lest it become obvious that the 'Socialist ... Workers' Party was actually the tool of big business. The trick, similar to the policy tried by the Kaiser's Governments before 1914, was to beat the nationalist, expansionist, militarist drum which evoked such stirring echoes in the mass psyche, at the same time conjuring enemies to hate. Of course the groundwork had been laid in the anti-Semitic literature, *The Protocols of the Wise Men of Zion*, and the slogans of his own speeches about the 'November criminals' who had signed the 'Shame Treaty' which chained Germans with 'the shackles of Versailles'. He did not have to alter his style; he had always been a reactionary nationalist; he merely had to focus and polish the message, and ensure it carried no dangers for the industrialists he intended to milk to pay his way to power by 'legal' means.

Hess was a willing, indeed convinced, accomplice in this intended double deception of the masses and of the industrialists, an attitude which gives added meaning to those passages in his letter to his parents which speak of 'knowing the inner thoughts of the Tribune, his attitude on every question, his whole mode of behaviour',[11] especially his confession that he would not be deterred, like so many other educated people, from the 'often unpleasant means and forms of the struggle – in respect to the psychology of the masses'. The first editions of *Mein Kampf* carried the sentence, deleted just before the Party came to power, 'The German has not the slightest notion how a people must be misled if the adherence of the masses is sought.'[12] This does not mean that Hess set out with his Führer on a programme of deliberate deception for the sake of personal power; it is far more likely from all that is known of him that he did it for his Führer and for Germany, which had become synonymous in his mind. He was a burning idealist. If he was naive or ignorant of the effects of power on personality, he shared this failing with millions of his countrymen raised on Wagnerian and Bismarckian myth.

By the end of 1925 Gregor Strasser posed a direct threat to this strategy; he was advocating the nationalisation of heavy industry and large estates, and supporting a Socialist-Communist bill in the Reichstag which demanded the expropriation of the property of the German monarchs deposed in the 1918 revolution. It was obvious that such policies must frighten the propertied classes Hitler intended wooing. He met the threat and other local dissatisfactions early in 1926 by convening a meeting of Party leaders from all areas in Bamberg, northern Bavaria. By packing the venue with his own supporters and staging it like a Party rally with banners, an SA band and swastika-bedecked cars to ferry the delegates from the station to the hall past lines of uniformed SA, he forced his rivals into his own strong suit, the mass meeting. Probably it was the aura of power as much as his own oratory which broke the potential opposition. It certainly caused Strasser's principal lieutenant and propagandist in the north, the club-footed little Doctor Goebbels, to renege on his chief and throw in his lot with Hitler – to be rewarded later that year by appointment as Gauleiter (*Gau* leader) of Berlin. Strasser bowed to the decision of the meeting which went Hitler's way, dropped his support for the princely expropriation bill, and accepted Hitler's leadership of a united Führer Party.

With another major internal crisis staved off, Hitler and Hess were able to return to the higher, visionary spheres of leadership. They were an extraordinary pair: Hitler in worn trench coat and trilby, carrying a riding whip, beating it against his thigh or open palm, or in an ill-cut blue suit spotted with dandruff, increasingly betraying in his face and podgy body his sweet tooth and distaste for exercise, was a coquette in company, delighting his circle of admirers with prophetic monologues interspersed with wicked take-offs of public figures, a chameleon suiting his character to the company, although far less successfully in more elevated society where his gaucheness was an embarrassment, less successfully too among professional men with educated minds, but compelled wherever he was to be the centre of attention; Hess, taller, well set-up and virile with a strong-boned, ascetic face, deep-set grey-green eyes betraying glints of fanaticism beneath bushy brows, addicted to mountain hikes and skiing, and reticent to the point of coldness, impossible to know, deferring obviously to his Führer, always at his side, jealous of those who drew too much of his attention, yet never conspicuous, deliberately it seemed sinking his personality like his person behind Hitler. Despite his athletic appearance, despite his war record and a reputation he had won leading the SA in a famous tavern brawl, it is small wonder that Party wits started referring to him as Fräulein Hess.

Had anyone outside the ranks of the faithful or fanatic predicted that these two had a realistic strategy which would take them to supreme power inside ten years, he would have been judged mad.

Hess had not lost his enthusiasm for flying. When, in May 1927, Charles Lindbergh made the first transatlantic flight from America to Europe, he was fired to be the first to repeat the exploit in the other direction, east to west. Apart from his own ambition, it would provide splendid publicity for the Party. Whether Hitler saw it in this light or as a dangerous adventure which might cost him his trusted right hand is unclear. The Party was poor, still on the margin of politics and existing chiefly on the modest subscriptions of members, so Hess sought financial sponsorship from the Detroit car manufacturer Henry Ford. It is a measure of just how poor the Party was that he instructed Ilse Pröhl to wire the request to Ford in German or English, whichever was shorter since 'one word costs approximately 1 M[ark]'.[13]

Henry Ford had the same attitude to Jews and the worldwide menace of Bolshevism as Hitler and Hess; anti-Semitic articles from a newspaper he owned, reprinted in four volumes under the title *The International Jew* and translated and published in German and most other languages round the word, are credited with inspiring some of *Mein Kampf*; a few passages are so similar it has been suggested Hitler actually copied them.[14] Central to both Ford's and Hitler's view was the Jewish world conspiracy by which Jewish-run capital on the one hand and Jewish-led Bolshevism on the other subverted, then took over gentile firms, economies and finally states on their plotted path to world domination. Besides publishing his views, Ford used his wealth to subsidise anti-Semitic organisations around the world; one of these was the infant Nazi Party, hence Hess's wire which asked for 200,000 Marks to fund the attempt in a single-engine plane. Evidently the millionaire did not oblige. Hess abandoned the plan.

His own views of the Jewish-Bolshevik menace were heightened by a book about Russia he was reading around this time. To judge by comments he made in a letter to a cousin, he was roused to fury by a chapter describing the activities of the Cheka, Stalin's secret police. His reaction helps to explain how, a little over a decade later, he was a party to Hitler's policy in the east, for it was the mirror image of Stalin's. The Cheka, he wrote, 'almost throughout Jews and ... Jewesses', had the task of eliminating the former ruling strata in Russia and liquidating the intelligentsia who might rise against Bolshevik rule. They carried out mass executions as a kind of sport, he went on, testing for the most effective methods, providing descriptions of which blood orgies were more gruesome than the wildest flights of imagination.[15]

He also talked about the chapter to Pfeffer von Salomon, appointed chief of the SA in the reformed Party after Röhm had refused to serve on Hitler's terms. Pfeffer told him of his personal experience of finding Cheka victims in the Baltic area. Hess declined to set down the details in his letter; one could not believe, he wrote, 'how perversely inventive people are in satisfying their bloodlust'.[16]

His letter was in reply to one which must have asked why he did not stand on a more healthy platform than the Nazi Party; he gave an impassioned defence: should his experiences 'in the filth and mud, in the hells of Verdun and Artois', shaken day after day by continuous barrages, sleeping in a dug-out in which half a Frenchman lay, should all his and his comrades' suffering have been in vain? The armistice he described as like a bullet through his brain. Then he had met the *one* man whom he knew after once hearing him speak was the only man who could raise Germany again to power and prestige. One of the indispensable preconditions for this was to inspire the masses with nationalism; only with such a nationalistic *Volks* mass would they be able to break the chains of Versailles and achieve living conditions for the nation:

... obtain space for our *Volk*, space! Air for development, prosperity, the conditions for further cultural development ... Why do you write to me therefore about the 'healthier base' you want for me. I stand on the healthiest base possible for me today under the given conditions. Because understand: all of us who have the doubtful honour today of belonging to the German *Volk* are on an unhealthy base ...[17]

He concluded his excited defence by saying that they must strive to awaken in the hearts of their contemporaries a new ideal of growth, completely clear and logical, and at the same time ardent, imperative, 'endowed with all the enchanting power of yearning'.

It was in the summer of 1927 that the other pole of the strategy, the advance towards big business, showed the first signs of germination. Hitler had begun the campaign the previous year by speaking to groups of businessmen in various parts of the country. Now one of his earliest patrons, Frau Elsa Bruckmann, wife of the Munich publisher of Houston Stewart Chamberlain and other nationalist authors, wrote to the Director of the Rhenish-Westphalian Coal Syndicate, Emil Kirdorf, inviting him to meet Hitler. She explained that 'as an enthusiastic follower of the Führer', she sought a way of bringing him together with leaders of industry.[18] Besides representing a group of labour-intensive industries whose owners were becoming desperate about the crippling social and welfare costs imposed by the Government, Kirdorf was by nature an aggressive nationalist and reactionary of the most extreme persuasion. He was already interested in Hitler; he had heard one of his addresses to business-men the previous year, and he agreed to a meeting at the Bruckmann home on 4 July. Here, during a long and searching discussion, Hitler succeeded in enthusing him to such an extent he suggested that if Hitler would set his ideas down on paper then he would circulate them to leading industrialists. Undoubtedly Hess worked on the paper; indeed its main thrust was that of the letter to his cousin earlier that year – the vital necessity of creating a 'nationalistic *Volks* mass' to win the workers from Marxism. It was printed as a pamphlet by the Bruckmann Press under the title *Der Weg zum Wiederaufstieg (The Road to Revival).* Kirdorf circulated it to top industrialists privately and, because of its explosive message about the means of 'pacifying' the workforce to prevent a transformation of society, very secretly.[19]

The economy was still riding a tide of prosperity generated by US loans under the Dawes Plan, and the pamphlet had limited impact in terms of immediate donations to the Party treasury. Nevertheless, the capture of such a powerful figure as Emil Kirdorf was a big step which was to pay dividends. Kirdorf not only joined the Party that August, he also infiltrated an agent of influence, Josef Terboven, who soon became Gauleiter of the heavy industrial city of Essen. While Kirdorf himself resigned from the Party the following year, there is every reason to sup-pose that this was a tactical move, and he remained an enthusiastic sup-porter.[20]

That winter, 1927, Hess married Ilse Pröhl. It was over seven years since they had first met. Since then they had been constantly in one another's company, working for the Party, on walking tours – although recently he had been too busy to take vacations – sharing the excitements and hopes, setbacks and vexations of their visionary friend and leader whom they still referred to as 'the Tribune'. Whether Hess had felt his prospects too uncertain to suggest marriage earlier, whether he had been too committed to his task and his leader, or whether he had thought of her more as good companion than wife, '*kleines Kerlchen*' (little chap-kin) as he addressed her in a letter at this time, is unclear. Her feelings are probably easier to guess.

By her account, she was considering leaving Munich, where she was working in a second-hand bookshop, to go to live in Italy, but, when she mentioned this one evening at the Osteria Bavaria, Hitler took her hand, placed it in Hess's and said, 'Haven't you ever thought of marrying this man?'[21] The story rings true. Hitler idealised marriage and, indeed, women in the role he cast them as wives and mothers; he is known to have made similar suggestions to other Party leaders. There was also propriety. Whatever the nature of his relationship with Hess, it was important that the Führer should not be touched by any hint of homosexuality. If wits were already referring to Fräulein Hess, it was important that speculation and gossip be killed; there was no better way than if he or Hess took a wife.

When forty-four years later as a prisoner in Spandau, Hess was confronted with Ilse's account of Hitler suggesting they marry, he denied it hotly. 'It has been said before and it is a lie.' It was possible, he went on, that Hitler had agreed Ilse would make a fine wife, but that was quite different. 'Love is not suggested by anybody. We have had a long and lasting love, my wife and I; she has been loyal and true to me for all these years ... Something like this could not be built on [another's] suggestion.'[22]

By this date Hess had covered himself with so many layers of protection against memory and against the outside that little he said can be trusted. The facts suggest he was deceiving himself: he had been close to Ilse, indeed loved her for seven years without proposing marriage. Ilse herself told his first biographers, Roger Manvell and Heinrich Fraenkel, that she had been thinking of leaving Munich when the subject was first raised – obviously leaving him, too, because his place was beside his Führer. She, therefore, provoked the suggestion, whether intentionally or not. After their marriage, it was ten years before a child was born. This might happen to any couple, but Hanfstaengl reported Ilse complaining once that she had about as much from her marriage as a confirmee.[23] It is a question of whether the unsavoury Hanfstaengl can be believed. One thing is not in doubt: from their letters it is evident they were close.

They were married in a brief civil ceremony in the old *Rathaus* in Munich on 20 December, rejecting a church service, since as true National Socialists neither believed in any current religion; as Hess wrote to his parents, they intended coming to terms with their Master in their own way. It was a brilliant sunny winter's morning. Hitler collected them in his Mercedes driven by his chauffeur, Emil Maurice, Professor Karl Haushofer with him. Haushofer and Hess were back on their old footing after a break in their relationship when Hess rejected the Akademie post for service with Hitler; now these two most powerful influences in Hess's adult life, the general and the Tribune, were to be the witnesses at his wedding.

The registrar was evidently overcome by Hitler's presence and passed over the usual address, contenting himself with verifying their identity, then quickly joining them in marriage. 'Painless, as the General thought', Hess reported to his mother later. 'We were extremely delighted. The Tribune was pale and trembling with excitement ...'[24]

Afterwards they drove Haushofer back to his home, from thence to Hitler's small apartment above a chemist's shop in the Thierschstrasse to admire a new bedroom suite the Bruckmanns had donated, and finally back to Ilse's apartment in the Ainmillerstrasse. Her two sisters were waiting; they had decorated the room with flowers and greenery, and candles lit the wedding presents on the table which had as centrepiece a large silver fruit bowl from Hitler, engraved with a dedication in his own hand-writing. They drank a toast, then all sat down to a snack lunch. Hitler worried about eating too much, for the Bruckmanns had prepared a lavish wedding dinner for the evening; he did not want it to appear that he did not appreciate their table.

It is evident that even in this description of his wedding day Hess had far more to say about the Tribune than about Ilse; indeed, in the published version of his letter to his mother describing the day, his *aller-liebste* is present only by implication.

The attitude revealed was not peculiar to Hess. A recent study by Klaus Thewelweit of the letters, memoirs and novels of seven Freikorps officers suggests that it was typical among these soldiers of fortune. Their wives appear to have been marginal to their interests, little more than social assets, child-bearers, supporters, almost symbolic figures without a perceived life of their own, scarcely even mentioned by name.[25] Thewelweit found that these Freikorps men claimed to love the German people, the Fatherland, the native soil, their town or village, the uniform, other men – comrades, superiors or subordinates – the community of blood among fellow countrymen, weapons, fighting and animals, especially horses.[26] Women were never described in the terms used for these, which Thewelweit defined as the very things which protected these men from 'real love-object relations'.[27] It is apparent that other men were so described, which led Thewelweit to wonder whether he were dealing with homosexuality or latent homosexuality. He concluded that there was insufficient understanding of what these terms implied.

If Hess therefore loved, claimed or thought he loved his Führer more than his new wife, he conformed to the type of his Freikorps comrades, as of course he did in his proclaimed love for the Fatherland, the *Volk*, the German blood community.

After taking the leave he had postponed for two years for a honeymoon, he and Ilse settled in a small apartment on the northern outskirts of Munich, and he plunged back into his work, soon accompanying Hitler on another round of addresses to groups of businessmen. He found himself astonished by his chief's improvement as a speaker in these critical gatherings; in a letter to Ilse from Essen he described his performance as 'of *unsurpassable clarity and precision*', underscoring the words in his enthusiasm.[28]

The masses, though, were not yet ready for the message addressed to them; national elections revealed the Party still on the political fringe with under 1 million votes – a mere 2.6 per cent, entitling them to only twelve seats in the Reichstag. Hess took comfort from the fact that their *völkisch* rivals had been practically eliminated. 'Now the battle has been decided', he wrote to his parents in June. 'The better, stronger, more battle-worthy has won through on the path of natural selection' – Hitler's fundamental maxim – 'and continues as the only Party of *völkisch* orientation, united in leadership, united in its whole construction.'[29] While not entirely true, since Otto Strasser and elements in the north were still pulling in a 'Socialist' direction, Gregor Strasser had been won over to Hitler's line, or so it appeared from his speeches, which now appealed to emotional nationalism rather than anti-capitalism. Strasser had also taken over Party organisation in Hitler's inflated style as Reich Organisation Leader. This was as shrewd an appointment as Hitler made; it not only tied his rival to the '*Führer* principle' of his own leadership, but harnessed Strasser's real talents as leader and administrator. He fulfilled as far as was practical Hess's rhetorical flourish 'united in leadership, united in its whole construction', and built the tightest organisation of any political Party in time for the next election, which responded immediately, without question to every touch of the leader on the helm. Such was the *Führer Prinzip*.

Meanwhile, in the summer of 1928, Hess was at his Führer's side in the Alps. Hitler now rented a villa called Haus Wachenfeld in the heady air above Berchtesgaden, commanding wide views of the Obersalzberg, shining alpine peaks, woods and sloping meadows. Here they worked on another book, which came to be known as the 'Secret Book' since it was not published in Hitler's lifetime. It dealt chiefly with foreign policy, mapping out the steps towards world domination. The content at this time, when the Party was represented by twelve out of 491 deputies in the Reichstag and counted less than 100,000 members, is as revealing as Hitler's plans for remodelling Berlin with epic buildings as the imperial capital. Hess told his parents towards the end of that year how they often laughed 'for all that with a serious undertone' when driving through Berlin as Hitler waved his hand to signify the demolition of old and unlovely buildings.[30]

5

THE BROWN HOUSE

German politics was in crisis before the Wall Street Crash at the end of 1929 and the onset of the 'great depression'. Nationalist Parties which had never accepted the Republican, democratic Government, the disarmament forced on Germany by Versailles, or the loss of overseas colonies had become more radical and vocally intolerant of the horse-trading that passed for politics in the 'chattering shop', the Reichstag. Communists had moved further to the Left, even indicting their Socialist allies as 'social Fascists'. Polarisation and extremism were symptoms of profound social and economic sickness. The established ruling groups of *junker* landholders, Army, heavy industrialists, the very grouping which had unleashed the First World War largely in defence of their own power position, felt their interests, their whole tradition and way of life in mortal danger. They were threatened now not simply by potential social revolution but, in the case of the industrialists especially, by a real profit and investment crisis created on the one hand by the high wage and welfare costs forced by the militant labour movement in the Reichstag, and on the other hand by a drastic reduction in demand for coal, iron, steel, ships and armaments both at home and from their former export markets as a direct result of the limitations imposed by Versailles. They were also threatened by Socialist and Communist calls for nationalisation of heavy industry and large estates.

A yet more insidious threat came from the light industries of the second industrial revolution, chiefly chemicals and electrics, which were more in demand, less labour intensive, and more profitable and exportable. The owners of these dynamic new industries, notably the huge IG Farben chemical complex, generally favoured an American-style mass-production, mass-consumption economy within the framework of the world economy now dominated by the United States; they were thus prepared to work with the moderate trade union leaders for better wages and conditions – which of course neither heavy industrialists nor large

43

landowners could afford. And implicit in their outlook was a radical modernisation of agriculture to provide cheaper food for the workforce. They were as hostile as the Socialists to the great landowners, who used feudal, hugely inefficient, labour-intensive methods unchanged in centuries, and the mass of small, equally inefficient peasant farmers, who also called for protection and higher food prices.

It was towards these threatened groups that Hitler directed his message. His whole platform and initial successes had been created by the Army and the Navy with secret funds, secret arms and ex-officers and men to provide the cadre of the paramilitary arm. The Party's membership and electoral successes, such as they were, derived chiefly from small businessmen ruined by inflation and peasant farmers; now heavy industry under mortal threat from every side stepped in to provide the funds for expansion. Hitler's message was tailored for them. One of the key arguments of the secret pamphlet, *Der Weg zum Wiederaufstieg*, circulated for him by Emil Kirdorf in 1927, was the need for armaments. Hemmed in as they were by the industrial powers of the United States, Great Britain and France, threatened particularly by American economic imperialism, they must remember 'the decisive factor in economic conflict in this world has never yet rested in the skill and know-how of the various competitors, but rather in the might of the sword they could wield to tip the scales for their businesses and hence their lives'.[1] Naturally this struck chords with heavy industrialists: rearmament for which they had been preparing in secret with the full knowledge and connivance of successive German governments under the noses of the Allied Control Commission policing Versailles, meant reinvestment and expansion; further, if Hitler should succeed in building a racially aware, national *Volks* mass they could expand within the context of an obedient, indeed inspired workforce opposed to revolutionary Marxism. Beyond and above rational, economic and self-interested arguments were the necessities of pride savagely humiliated, of the militarism and autocracy which dominated the national psyche, and of the romantic vision of a third *Reich* led by a warlord – all of which inspired the nationalists and none more than the worried masters of heavy industry. With hindsight, it hardly seems a question of whether these barons who abominated democracy and the Republic would rise to Hitler's fly, but who would be first and with how much.[2]

Mystification still surrounds the precise amount of funds donated to the Party. A few things seem clear: Hess, who believed his chief contribution to be the ability to mediate between educated circles and the mass movement, and who had been trained as a businessman, made the approaches. He saw Emil Kirdorf as early as autumn 1928 with a request for funds to enable the Party to move from its cramped offices alongside the *Völkischer Beobachter* in Schellingstrasse to a more prestigious central headquarters suitable for a national movement. Kirdorf put him in touch with Fritz Thyssen, Chairman of Germany's largest steel trust, the United Steel Works, and one of the wealthiest men in the country. Thyssen had experienced at first hand the revolutionary terror after the war, only narrowly escaping with his life after being arrested by a 'Red' posse as a 'capitalist pig' and traitor. The memory of those days and subsequent uprisings after the Kapp *putsch* and after the French occupation of the Ruhr had left their indelible mark; Hitler's anti-Bolshevik message touched a personal nightmare. Hess must have put the case with skill, none the less, for Thyssen agreed to a huge loan; he never admitted the size or the repayment terms (which were, in any case, never met), but the transformation in the Party's assets suggest well over 1 million Marks. Thus, in the course of 1929, Hitler moved from his minute apartment over the chemist's shop into a spacious nine-room flat in the highly fashionable Prinzregentenstrasse, meanwhile acquiring a palace for the Party in the equally high-tone Briennerstrasse. It was the conversion of this elegant three-storey building under Hitler's personal direction into a modern, sumptuous combined headquarters and projection of National Socialist symbolism that reveals the scale of the funding Hess had tapped. Everything from the bronze Party standards outside to the wood-panelled 'beer cellar' mess in the basement bore the unmistakeable aura of expensive materials, craftsmanship and wealth.

Christened 'the Brown House' after the colour of the Party uniform, it was a tangible example of Hitler's extraordinary faith in his destiny; this was revealed particularly in the great 'Senators' Hall on the second floor. Approached from a grand staircase from the foyer and next door to Hitler's own room, the entrance was flanked by marble memorial tablets to martyrs who had fallen for the movement. Inside, the walls were panelled in curl-grained walnut above a deep-pile carpet woven with swastikas, but the dominant impression was provided by bright red leather upholstered chairs for the 'leaders', flanked by forty-two more for the 'Senators'. One is reminded of Hess's description from Landsberg of Hitler outlining his plans for laws enacted by a senate and head of State in combination. Above the Führer's central red chair was a mosaic of a golden eagle on a bright red ground with important dates in the Party's history picked out below. 'The reception rooms, including the Führer's room, are so *wunderschön*', Hess wrote to his parents, 'that representatives of foreign States can be received here at any time.' His own room, 'very lovely, light and airy'[3] with a window overlooking the Briennerstrasse, was next to Hitler's; on the other side was his office, where a 'bureau chief' and two female typists worked – not that 'office' was a term he used officially; even at the cramped headquarters at

45

Schellingstrasse, his paper was headed 'ADOLF HITLER *Kanzlei*' – Chancellery.

By coincidence or prophetic insight on the part of Thyssen and the other industrial backers who had made it possible, no less than Hitler and Hess themselves, the Brown House was fashioned just as the Party emerged from the margin of politics. By the time the building was inaugurated officially on 1 January 1931, what appears extravagant pretension when the plans were first drafted expressed new reality.

The Party's rise started in the summer of 1929, when Hitler joined an extreme Right grouping organised to denounce a new schedule for war reparations drawn up by a committee of the former Allies under the chairmanship of an American banker named Young – the so-called 'Young Plan' to replace the 'Dawes Plan'. The leader of the movement against the plan, and particularly the 'war guilt' clause on which war reparations rested, was Alfred Hugenberg, head of the conservative Deutschnational Party, a virulent pan-German anti-Semite who represented the *junker* landlords and the extreme wing of the heavy industrialists like Kirdorf and Thyssen. He controlled a huge media complex of newspapers, new agencies, publishing houses, film companies and cinemas, and it was this which attracted Hitler. While Hugenberg intended to exploit Hitler's pull with the masses, Hitler – against the protests of the Strasser brothers, who believed he would simply become a puppet of the powerful reactionary forces behind the campaign – intended to exploit Hugenberg's media. He was proved right. Day after day, as the campaign gathered impetus, the 'respectable' press carried his name, his picture and his message nationwide.

Came the Wall Street Crash in October that year, and the subsequent slump was exported to Germany as US loans which had supported her post-war growth ceased or were called in. Unemployment rose and with it the social frustration and anger on which Hitler had always thrived by providing simple scapegoats and facile solutions. Party membership grew apace, as did subscriptions and donations to the Party treasury. On the other side of the balance, the sight of Hitler so obviously in bed with the most reactionary elements in the nation was too much for Otto Strasser and his supporters in north Germany. The dispute came into the open in the spring of 1930, when Strasser publicly supported a strike by the trade unions in Saxony. Hitler had to move. Strasser asserted later that Hitler had made a formal pact with Kirdorf in 1929 that, in return for 'lots of money', Kirdorf and his associates could dictate the Party line in so far as it affected them and their property.[4] Whether this was so or not, Strasser's 'Socialist' wing obviously had to be called to order or the industrial backers Hitler had wooed so assiduously would take fright.

He arrived in Berlin unannounced on 21 May, and Hess, with him as always, called Otto Strasser to invite him to their hotel, the Sanssouci on the Linkstrasse; Hitler wished to speak to him urgently. Strasser came and in a lengthy discussion face to face accused Hitler of throwing in his lot with the stock exchange capitalists and betraying Socialism.

'What you call Socialism is pure Marxism,' Hitler responded. 'Your whole system is theory which has nothing to do with real life.'[5] He went on in decidedly mystical terms to outline his own theory. The principle or 'idea' of the movement was embodied in the Leader; he alone knew the ultimate goal, and every Party member had to do what the Leader ordered. He described the masses with Nietzschian contempt as having absolutely no understanding of ideas, desiring only bread and circuses. And the revolution he intended, he depicted in terms of Nietzsche's 'superman' as purveyed fifth-hand in the social Darwinian, 'race hygiene' and *völkisch* theories which impregnated his thinking. It was the creation of a classless society from which the fittest would rise to the top irrespective of privileges of birth or wealth, simply by virtue of their blood; 'a new dominating class', he told Strasser, 'not moved as you are by the ethic of pity, but quite clear in its own mind that it has the right to dominate others because it represents a better race. This caste ruthlessly maintains and assures its dominance over the masses.'[6]

When Strasser changed the discussion to economics and argued against the profit motive and association in the world market, Hitler accused him of the 'most wicked dilettantism'. On the contrary, he asserted, their task to take in hand on a grand scale the organisation of the entire world economy so that each country produced what was best suited to it under the control of the white, Nordic race. Warming to his theme, 'Believe me, the whole of National Socialism would be worth nothing if it were limited to Germany and failed to seal for one to two thousand years the world mastery of the high-value race.' He added that the leadership of the world had to be exercised in co-operation with the Anglo-Saxons.[7] It was a view from which neither he nor Hess ever departed.

The following day the debate was resumed with Hess and Max Amann, Hitler's sergeant in the war, now Party business manager, together with one of Otto's supporters and his brother, Gregor. There could be no meeting of minds. Otto was an idealist; he would neither be bribed by a national position Hitler offered him – *Reich* press chief – nor submit to the discipline of the Führer principle. The following month Hitler unleashed Goebbels against him and early in July Otto led his supporters from the Party under the banner 'The Socialists leave the NSDAP' to establish what became known as the 'Black Front' of 'Revolutionary National Socialists'. Gregor Strasser disassociated himself from his brother, calling him a 'theorist', taking the lead in purging the Party of anyone suspected of supporting his aims in secret, constantly proclaiming his own loyalty to the Führer.

Little in the Nazi Party can be taken at face value. The two brothers remained in touch on a personal level and it may be that Gregor remained in the Party deliberately to provide, when the time came, a more acceptable 'Socialist' alternative to Hitler's leadership. It may be that he was already supported by IG Farben and others in the electro-chemical grouping. They would have been strangely remiss if they had not sought to gain agents of influence within a Party which appeared to be under the control of the heavy industrial and landholding establishment. The Marxist historian Kurt Gossweiler believes IG Farben supported agents within the Party at least as early as the heavy-industrial, landholding groups, but better camouflaged; he cites Gregor Strasser, Robert Ley, Wilhelm Keppler and Heinrich Gattineau among the most prominent; the last had studied under Karl Haushofer and knew Hess. It is interesting that during the long discussions at the Sanssouci both Otto and Gregor Strasser argued for an economic strategy soon to be advocated publicly by the head of IG Farben, namely secession from the US-led world economy and the construction of an autonomous, German-led economic bloc which would stretch 'from Bordeaux to Sofia'.[8]

Shortly after Otto Strasser's departure from the Party, the Government found itself without a majority for new taxes designed to meet the terms of the Young Plan for reparations. After a brief experiment in ruling by emergency decree, the Chancellor, Brüning, dissolved the Reichstag and called new elections for September. Hitler ordered his SA into battle – literally. The intention was not simply to prove he had the forces to combat the Communists, but to provoke street battles and so enhance perceptions of the threat Bolshevism represented, meanwhile talking up the danger in extreme terms. The Communists were as belligerent: at street level in industrial areas the campaign was conducted with marching men, bands, battle songs, shouted slogans, fists, clubs and set-piece tavern fights.

Hess took a personal hand in one lawless exploit. He obviously relished it hugely, although it was scarcely important save as an illustration of the scale of funding the Party now enjoyed and the ineffectual or sympathetic attitude of the Bavarian authorities towards the Nazis. It was on the morning of 10 August; the Munich branch of the Socialist Reichsbanner League of Republican War Veterans was holding a rally on the exhibition ground in Munich. Hess donned his pilot's gear and took off in a small aeroplane bearing the legend '*Völkischer Beobachter*' on the underside of the wings and a swastika painted under the fuselage. He flew towards the ground at approximately 1,500 feet, coming down to around 500 feet as he approached the rally soon after it started at about 9.45. He overflew the gathering at low altitude, turned and came back and continued circling back and forth low over the crowd for the next two and a half hours. As described in the Reichsbanner's formal complaint to the police:

The aircraft's intention to disrupt the rally with the roar of the propeller was obvious. By flying at low altitude the noise was so strong and had such a disturbing effect that the singing and the address of the Reichstag deputy Vogel was from time to time completely drowned by the sound of the propeller.[9]

At the end of the rally the veterans formed up and marched into the city, where their leader, Wimmer, took the salute. Hess followed low overhead, and it was not until the marchers had dispersed from Mozart-strasse, complaining angrily 'that such a crude public nuisance could continue for three hours without one of the relevant public authorities taking action', that Hess flew off.[10]

With the complaints from the Reichsbanner, the police filed one from a flying club: 'Sporting aviation will be profoundly retarded by the irres-ponsible behaviour of such reckless pilots and every serious aviation body must condemn the behaviour of this pilot in the sharpest terms and request his punishment.'[11]

Questioned by the police, Hess said innocently that he had merely been on a propaganda flight to win subscribers to the *Völkischer Beo-bachter*; he agreed, however, that this was an unlikely result in view of the anger he had caused the veterans.[12] There the matter rested.

The September elections turned into an overwhelming vindication of Hitler's strategy. The Party polled almost 6½ million votes – nearly one-fifth of the electorate – moving in one stride into second position in the Reichstag, only just behind the Social Democrats. The Communists also increased their vote, polling 4½ million, which of course helped Hitler's cause. His position as leader was strengthened immeasurably; so was the pressure felt by the leaders of the electro-chemical groupings to influence the Party in their desired direction. If Gregor Strasser was not already IG Farben's man, he became so now, as did Ernst Röhm, whom Hitler cajoled back to lead the SA. Thus the struggle for control of the economic direction of Germany and with it the position of the established power groupings moved inside the Nazi Party.

Here Hess played a key part, both as one of the main links with indus-trialists and as guardian of Hitler's position as *Führer*. In this role he sifted reports from the various intelligence agencies of the Party, the most important of which in terms of quality probably came from Heinrich Himmler, chief (or *Reichsführer*) of the SS, which had been formed speci-fically as the élite guard of the Führer; it's leaders had standing instruc-tions to report 'in urgent cases immediately' if they believed anything was not in order in the Party political leadership or SA spheres.[13]

Himmler had the same psychological need as Hess for a strong leader and a cause in which to immerse himself; like Hess, he believed Hitler had been sent by divine providence to restore Germany to spiritual and material health. In addition, he believed absolutely in the Party creed: the international conspiracy of Jews, Freemasons, the Catholic Church, aiming to subvert the world through Bolshevism, democracy, liberalism, the ethic of 'humanity', and on the other hand the mission of the superior value Nordic race to overcome this poison in the *Volks*' body – all were as real to him as his unsatisfactory physique and physiognomy and dark hair, none of which conformed in any way to the Nordic ideal; he surrounded himself with tall, blond men with blue eyes. Alike as he and Hess were in burning idealism and devotion to the Führer, Himmler was the more practical and guileful political animal with a more plausible tongue and never averse, as Hess was, to pushing himself forward. '*Der Heini macht es schon*' – 'Heini will see to it' was a phrase that had followed him from his days studying agriculture at Munich University. At this stage of their relationship, though, Himmler was junior partner to the rather unworldly secretary who had the ear of the Führer and jealously guarded the rights of access.

This did not prevent 'Heini' carrying Hess in the SS books – SS number 50 – as 'Adjutant to the Reichsführer SS' and 'Personal Adjutant to Adolf Hitler', both backdated to 1 April 1925, without apparently granting him SS rank.[14]

Formally Himmler was directly subordinate to Ernst Röhm, from 1 January 1931 executive chief of staff of the SA, but he was also Hess's man and it is very probable that Hess did not approve of Röhm; apart from the more or less open scandal of his homosexual activities, he was too much of a freebooting, independent-minded soldier of fortune. Earlier, at the refounding of the Party, he had refused to toe the Führer's line, and within a year or two of his reinstatement Hess was certainly suspicious, in the words of his adjutant, Leitgen, that Röhm 'would in no way act as a loyal custodian of Hitler, but go his own way'.

However that may be, Hess, Röhm and Himmler worked together on a major internal challenge from the SA that spring 1931. Captain Walter Stennes, SA chief for north-east Germany with his headquarters in Berlin, had challenged the Munich leadership the previous August just before the elections. On that occasion Himmler's SS chief in Berlin, Kurt Daluege, had remained loyal. Now Stennes, who had been an adherent of Otto Strasser and like many of his men disliked Hitler's 'legal' way to power through the ballot box in collaboration with the 'reactionaries' – and who it seems was financed by at least one of the leaders of the new, light industries, Herman Bücher of the German General Electric

Company (AEG), struck again, this time in earnest. He captured the Berlin Party headquarters and launched trucks full of his men to SA taverns to intimidate Hitler loyalists into joining him. Gun battles took place on the streets. As before, the SS remained the focus for loyalty and provided the intelligence – there is even a suspicion that Himmler may have lured Stennes to commit himself. After Hitler and Röhm had restored the situation with SA formations from Munich, and expelled Stennes and his lieutenants from the Party, Hitler sent Kurt Daluege a letter containing the phrase '*SS-Mann, Deine Ehre heisst Treue*' – 'SS man, your honour signifies loyalty' – which became the motto of the SS.

Hess received a letter from his mother rejoicing with him in the downfall of the 'Judas'. She took her son's view of Hitler; how could Stennes have imagined that he, a former officer, could win over the masses, she wrote; 'They know that Hitler is one of them, would sacrifice body and life for them. With Stennes it is certainly only ambition, not love for the *Volk*.'[15]

6
POWER

The struggle of the landed and industrial-financial power groupings for dominance within the Nazi Party came to a head towards the end of 1932. Over the past two years the Party had swollen, drawing recruits from those thrown out of work by the deepening depression and those too young to have known regular work, and at the upper end of the social spectrum from sons of the landed nobility and young professional men jumping on the escalator of Germany's and their own future. Most of the latter joined the ss because of the élite status carefully fostered by Himmler, and drawn perhaps by the elegance of the black uniform with silver flashes. Many joined from national idealism, many from the landed classes to preserve their caste inheritance. The great Brandenburg landowner, Prince Eulenburg-Hertefeld, had sent a circular to his peers in February 1931 stressing the need for men of their class with leadership qualities to enter 'the Party, which despite many socialistic ideas is the opposite pole to Marxism and Bolshevism'.[1]

In elections in July 1932 the Party, greatly changed in its upper tiers from the rump of embittered 'small men' and disillusioned soldiers of fortune of 'the days of struggle', polled 13.7 million votes, more than the Communists and Socialists combined, but insufficient to gain an over-all majority in the Reichstag. The old President, von Hindenburg, who alone possessed constitutional authority to appoint a Chancellor, but who distrusted the 'Bohemian Corporal' and his sA street hoodlums, called on von Papen – representative of those very landholding and industrial power groups who supported, but intended also to control, Hitler – to attempt another essay in government by presidential decree. It was short-lived; new elections were called for November.

The deadlock in the Reichstag was matched by a deadlock between the forces battling for control of the Nazi movement. The group that has left the most obvious trace is the circle of bankers and industrialists gathered by Hitler's economics adviser, Wilhelm Keppler, in the spring of 1932. Later this circle was to broaden its representation and become the Freundeskreis RFSS (Circle of Friends of the Reichsführer SS), Heinrich Himmler, to whom it donated large sums annually to aid him in his 'special tasks'. The first twelve members in 1932 appeared to represent the most significant groups of monopoly capital and one member of the Prussian landholding nobility. The leading spirits were the Cologne banker, Kurt von Schröder, personally an extreme nationalist, connected to both American and British Schroeder banks, and Hjalmar Schacht, former President of the Reichsbank, who had powerful connections in US and British banking circles. During the period when the United States had been injecting capital into the German economy, Schacht had been the principal German agent of the American John Pierpont Morgan financial empire, and it is significant that another member of the Circle represented the Dresdner Bank, which was intimately linked with Morgan. There seems little reason to doubt Gossweiler's conclusion about the strategic consensus reached by this Circle led by von Schröder and Schacht : to pursue Germany's expansionist and colonial claims so rudely checked in the Great War and to build German hegemony in Europe at the expense of Russia – thus, of course, of Bolshevism – in partnership with US capital.

Significantly absent from the original Circle of advisers were open representatives of the largest, most dynamic of the 'new' industrial complexes, IG Farben, or of the Deutsche Bank, which had a large stake in the group. The strategists of IG Farben, besides being hostile to the 'Kraut' junkers and unrestructured heavy industrialists who supported and appeared to control Hitler, were averse to further penetration by American capital ; and wanting to break free of the US-led world market, they looked to build hegemony with the aid of French capital in a closed European economic bloc – again at the expense of Russia and Bolshevism. They appear to have worked through Gregor Strasser and Ernst Röhm, who had built up the SA with the aid of their massive subventions into a superbly organised force far larger than the regular Army and imbued with revolutionary fervour. Outside the Party, the self-appointed political power-broker, Kurt von Schleicher, War Minister in von Papen's Government, but an untypical soldier with a dislike of the landed caste, pursued the IG Farben line by trying to unite Strasser and Röhm with the moderate trade union leaders. Such a return to Socialism and parliamentary democracy was not only outside the horizons of the reactionary landed and industrial groups but it also posed clear, imminent threats of nationalisation on the one hand and ruinously higher wages and social welfare on the other ; it was simply out of the question.

Obviously the response of individual industrialists and bankers was, in the words of the American economic historian David Walters, 'various,

53

inconsistent and contradictory', and, as always in such confused and impossible situations, most must have supported trends rather than absolute policies and changed their minds often. None the less, the role of monopoly capital groupings was crucial. German industry had always been State-centred, as befited the Prussian warrior ethos; it was marshalled by State legislation and the banks into huge syndicates and cartels designed to serve the national economy and penetrate export markets – at the expense of the German consumer, who paid in higher prices for the inevitable distortions and inefficiencies. It was the reverse of the Anglo-American market ethos, where consumer choice was maximised and prices minimised by encouraging free competition and outlawing price-fixing cartels.

The banks also played a different role. In Germany they were active partners in the concerns they supported, with representatives on the boards who took a role in strategic planning. Thus comparatively few bankers and directors of giant trusts decided the direction of the national economy; and, since Germany was a capitalist democracy, it was *their* logic, the inexorable logic of capital which had to prevail ultimately.[2] This logic had been upset by the success of the trade unions and Socialist administrations since the war and a consensus had formed among the great men of finance and industry that the unions would have to be smashed – together with parliamentary democracy in the view of the heavy industrialists – or incorporated into the State structure. There was also a consensus about shaking off the burden of war reparations and the other 'shackles of Versailles' which limited the armed forces, the merchant marine and ability to compete in world markets. There was consensus about the need to expand eastwards, subjugating Russia and destroying Bolshevism. There was consensus about bringing Germanic order to a messy continent – then to the world. There was consensus that these things could only be accomplished and the internal threat of Bolshevism overcome by working with the Nationalist mass movement created by the Nazis. But, on the equally vital question of restructuring the economy in the direction IG Farben and the associated wing of the Deutsche Bank believed necessary, there could be no concensus.

For Hitler the economic arguments were simply tools to gain power. It is here, inside this brain which had absorbed and exemplified consciously and unconsciously all the yearnings imprinted on the national psyche by the *kaiserlichen* grab for world power, all the humiliation and vengefulness of defeat, that the logic of capital dissolved. Here the ultimate logic was the *Weltanschauung*, which recognised only one main enemy, the Jew, one means to salvation through the pure blood of the superior value Nordic race. The rational men of finance and sound practical sense believed, on the whole, that all this was no more than a useful way of gaining the masses – and for some gaining Jewish businesses cheaply – for what had impressed them most about Hitler's addresses to select business groups was his *logic*. They thought that, even if he did believe these things, he could be manipulated. Schacht wanted him as Chancellor for this reason above all.

Hess, the idealist who only seven years before had thrown up a respectable career to work on the fringes with the Tribune, now propelled into the eye of the German and world financial storm, is less easy to gauge. To those who met him for the first time he appeared an impenetrable figure. The public did not know his name. Undoubtedly he revered the Führer but his attitude to the conflicting demands of the business groupings is as unclear as the view he adopted when discussing them with his Führer. Gossweiler puts him on the Strasser wing with Himmler and Hitler's economic adviser Wilhelm Keppler, as cleverly camouflaged agents of IG Farben, in position if the first-line Strasser-Röhm axis should fail. Both Himmler and Keppler were very much Hess's men.

There is no doubt that Carl Bosch, one of the founders of the IG made an approach to Hitler at about this time via Karl Haushofer and Hess to ascertain his line on synthetic petrol, which had obvious importance inside a closed economic bloc, and on which the concern had already expended some ten millions. At the subsequent meeting with the technical director, Dr Bütefisch, Hitler more than satisfied the company with his eloquence about building *Autobahns* and motorising Germany.[3] Nor is there any doubt that after the Party achieved power IG Farben set up a department which became virtually a research institute for Germany's war plans. None the less, in the absence of trustworthy evidence from bankers and industrialists who consorted with the Nazi Party, it appears more probable that at the end of 1932 Hess and Himmler played their parts less as agents of any grouping than as fanatical supporters of Hitler, who could reassure all groups that with the backing of the SS it would be Hitler's will, not Strasser's or Röhm's, that would prevail. This is no doubt the key to understanding why it was Hess and Himmler, not Göring, Strasser, Röhm, Goebbels or other leading figures who now appear to have played the key roles in mediating a compromise between the power groupings.

The elections held on 6 November 1932 resulted in a drop of 2 million in the Nazi vote and a rise in the Communist vote. Evidently the peak of the Party's electoral fortune was behind. Meanwhile, the heavy industrialists, fearful of Strasser's 'Socialism' and alarmed by the open revolutionary spirit of Röhm's SA, indicated who held the reigns by withholding funds; after the heavy election expenses, the Party faced bankruptcy. It was in this crisis, four days after the results, that Hess and Himmler made their first known appearance with Keppler in a meeting with the banker von Schröder.[4] Afterwards a petition was drawn up and presented to Hindenburg calling for the appointment of Hitler as Chancellor; it was signed by Schacht, von Schröder, Fritz Thyssen and numerous members of the Keppler circle, Ruhr heavy industry, great landowners, Hamburg shipping and trading interests and the banks, although no open representatives of IG Farben or the Deutsche Bank. Subsequently Hindenburg had two meetings with Hitler, but was not persuaded to appoint him; instead, at the beginning of December, he called on von Schleicher, who immediately asked Strasser to enter his cabinet as Vice-Chancellor.

This did not break the deadlock, since Strasser could not deliver a united Party without Hitler, and Hitler – after initial wobbling – was held firm to the line of no compromise. After a furious argument, during which he accused Strasser of negotiating behind his back and Strasser, like his brother earlier, accused Hitler of betraying all the ideals of the Party, Strasser resigned in fury; possibly he intended to bring pressure on Hitler, possibly he did not wish to split the Party, or possibly he simply lacked the will and killer instinct to take up this ultimate challenge. Hitler split his Party organisation office between Dr Ley, the Gauleiter of Cologne, Goebbels and Hess, to whom he gave the resounding title Political Central Commissioner of the NSDAP, a further indication of Hess's key contribution in this political crisis.[5]

How much Hess was the schemer, how much the intermediary and co-ordinator of the strategy that now evolved is impossible to know. It was a two-pronged campaign, on the one hand to win over the former Chancellor, von Papen, to serve as Vice-Chancellor in an administration led by Hitler, on the other hand to suborn Hindenburg's son and adviser, Oskar, by promising him rank and additional land while hinting that abuses in the subsidy system for east Prussian landowners would be exposed if his father did not withdraw his opposition to Hitler. Himmler's recently acquired secret service chief, Reinhard Heydrich, was entrusted with this task together with the preparation of disinformation about an imminent Army revolt and a plot to assassinate Schleicher. The other task was to bring IG Farben into the agreement. Traces of this policy are discernible within a day of Hess's appointment. On 11 December Schacht, Keppler, Himmler and von Papen met to discuss the latter's possible participation in a Hitler administration, and scarcely over a week later Keppler was able to report that von Papen had agreed to discuss it with Hitler.[6] On 24 December Himmler appointed Hess ss-Gruppen-führer – equivalent to Lieutenant General – a curious Christmas present, the significance of which is unclear.

Such was the background to the well-known meeting between Hitler and von Papen at von Schröder's Cologne villa on 3 January 1933. Hess,

Himmler and Keppler accompanied Hitler, but did not take part in the lengthy discussion that ensued; only the host was present for some of the time. Hitler opened with a lengthy exposition of how he would radically alter the present situation by removing all Social Democrats, Communists and Jews from leading positions and by re-establishing public order. They came on to the question of industry; this was the reason for von Schröder's presence, and it is evident from the minute he drew up afterwards that he had mediated a compromise with IG Farben beforehand. Hitler agreed to the formation of national industrial cartels with greater influence than hitherto, and to the general stimulation of industry through state contracts:

Hitler promised to increase the armed forces from 100,000 to 300,000 men, to take in hand the construction of *Autobahns*, and to make credit available to state and local authorities for road-building, and Government credit for the aircraft and automobile industries and their ancillary firms.[7]

This is reminiscent of Hitler's promise to Dr Bütefisch of IG Farben, and was clearly a programme to suit the new light industrialists since it was they, not heavy industry, who were promised the cream of State subsidy.

Finally Hitler promised 'the liquidation of the Versailles Treaty, the restoration of a militarily strong, economically independent Germany . . .' – the order of precedence is psychologically revealing – after which von Papen assured him his appointment as Chancellor would follow in a short time. It was agreed that both von Papen and the ultra-Nationalist press baron Hugenberg would be included in the cabinet, whereupon Hitler reminded von Papen of the difficult financial position of the Party, which had to be rectified if they were to become partners in government.[8]

Von Schröder took it upon himself to form a consortium to underwrite Nazi Party debts. Prominent in this group was a leading representative of the giant Deutsche Bank – to which von Schröder's own bank was affiliated – which had a large stake in IG Farben, Siemens (electrics), Daimler-Benz and other of the modern, dynamic section of industry. Here, as in Hitler's promise to von Papen to promote automobiles and aeroplanes, the hidden hand of the light industries is revealed. Meanwhile, the members of Keppler's original Circle contributed 1 million Marks to Himmler for the ss, a plain indication of the role of the Führer's praetorian guard during this crisis mediation.[9]

At the end of the month President von Hindenburg, stampeded by Heydrich's fabrication of an Army plot to remove von Schleicher, called on Hitler to form a government. Oskar Hindenburg received his rewards later. So Hitler, by adjusting his platform to the point where it harmonised with all industrial, financial and landed groupings – save Jewish banking and industry – at street level by offering 'protection' from Bolshevism, achieved power legally through the democratic system. Emotionally it was a concensus of Prusso-Germany's old ruling caste and the bankers and industrialists of the new wave to restore German pride, avenge Versailles and continue the interrupted march to world power. Those in the know perceived it, correctly, as a pact for war.

Rudolf Hess, who had provided the steady moral backing Hitler needed in alternating moods of elation and depression, and, at the height of the crisis with Strasser, profound despair, who had acted as chief of staff in the campaign to woo the industrialists, guard against the machinations of von Schleicher and suborn the President's advisers, surely felt elated. Equally surely he felt no qualms about the methods; from the start, from his Freikorps time before the beginning, he had been fighting an insidious enemy for the restoration of the Fatherland; it had been a civil war against the 'Reds'; the most brutal means had been used on both sides, political murder and extortion had been commonplace. Now the Führer 'stood where he had to stand' and they were in sight of the ultimate victory. At the end it had been an extraordinarily close-run thing. It was a miracle.

Hess was one of the first to congratulate Hitler when he returned from the President's Palace to the Kaiserhof Hotel on 30 January as Chancellor. It is not difficult to imagine some of his feelings as the two clasped hands in silence.

7

NIGHT OF THE LONG KNIVES

It was now necessary to fulfil the commitment to the Party's backers – and the *Weltanschauung* – to smash democracy and Marxism. Hitler's proposal, seconded by Göring at the first cabinet meeting on 30 January 1933, was to call fresh elections, ostensibly to increase the combined Nazi-Conservative representation in the Reichstag to the two-thirds necessary to alter the constitution. Behind the proposal were schemes to seize dictatorial power by provoking or simulating the signs of a Communist uprising.

First Communist Party headquarters were raided for evidence which might be used to outlaw the Party. Finding nothing, the evidence had to be manufactured. It was apparently Goebbels who suggested that the Reichstag, symbol of democracy, should be burnt down.[1] Göring, Himmler and Heydrich attended to the details, and on the evening of 27 February an ss team trained in arson made it's way from Göring's Palace as President of the Reichstag through an underground passage to the cellars beneath the Reichstag, laid fires in the main chamber and departed the way they had come, leaving a half-crazed Dutch Communist youth to be caught.[2]

On the strength of this outrage Hitler persuaded Hindenburg to grant him emergency powers suspending all civil liberty. The sa and ss, empowered as auxiliary police, were unleashed to round up Communist and Socialist leaders listed beforehand by Heydrich's Security Service, the sd, and then individual Communist Party members anywhere. All were thrown into jail or *wild* (extemporised) camps, where they were brutally treated, often tortured or murdered. With the Communists and many Socialists locked up, and others terrorised or demoralised by open intimidation, Hitler was able to gain the majority he needed to pass a law enabling him to govern without further parliamentary restraint.

Hess's part in what has been called the provocation of the century is as little documented as that of the other conspirators and State hijackers, as the ss arsonists called themselves. It emerges briefly in a letter he wrote to the sa leadership that September asking whether there were former Communists in the sa 'in a position and prepared to testify' that arson was a weapon in the Communist Party arsenal.[3] He sought such people for the forthcoming 'show trial' of Communist leaders who were to be put up before the court with the Dutch youth on a charge of conspiring to burn down the Reichstag. The letter appears to confirm what the historian, Eduard Calic, was told after the war by a trade unionist named Joseph Schepp, that Hess was responsible for gathering false witnesses for the trial.[4] No doubt, as in the run-up to the election, his office was the co-ordinating *Zentrale*. In the event, the prosecution failed to establish the necessary link between the Dutch youth and the Communist leaders and, to silence the youth, he was executed – illegally since the conspiracy charge had failed. There is no doubt Hess was an accessory to this judicial murder.

In April Hess was raised dizzily to Stellvertreter or Deputy to the Führer, nominally second man in the Party, although still without a ministerial post in Government. He was working closely with Göring, real second man in terms of personality and executive control in Prussia, who helped him gain offices for a liaison staff – *Verbindungsstab* – in the Wilhelmstrasse, Berlin. Twelve years later Hess was in captivity feigning amnesia when his us interrogator called in his former colleagues one by one to try and spark some flash of memory.

'Do you remember the beginning of the year 1933?' Göring asked him.

'No,' Hess replied blankly.

'You told me that you wanted to become a member of the Government,' Göring went on, 'and I told you that I would try to help you. Do you remember that you moved into the Wilhelmstrasse, into the palace which really belonged to me as the Prime Minister of Prussia? But I enabled you to live there.'

'I don't know.'

'I visited you many times. I handed it to you so you would have a house to live in. I turned the house over to you for your benefit.'

'I have been told,' said Hess, 'that everything will come back at some time by a shock.'[5]

Ludecke called on Hess in his elegant Wilhelmstrasse office shortly after he had moved in. 'There sat a man not easy to read,' he recalled afterwards. He could not imagine why he was known as 'Fräulein' since he seemed manliness itself: 'Luxurious dark hair crowned a strong, angular face; he had grey-green eyes under heavy, bushy brows; a fleshy nose, a firm mouth, and a square, determined jaw. Slender and lean-limbed, he was good-looking and rather Irish in appearance.'[6] Ludecke noted a restrained fanaticism in Hess's eyes, but his manner was cool; he was altogether 'a commanding presence, a compliment one can pay to only a few of the higher Nazi chiefs'.[7] Later Ludecke was talking to Hitler's photographer friend, Heinrich Hoffmann, and a woman friend of Hoffmann's; she told him to beware of Hess: 'I'm a woman – I understand men's eyes.'[8]

Significantly perhaps, Bella Fromm, the Jewish society columnist remarked in similar vein on Hess's eyes when she met him for the first time that December at a reception given by the Foreign Minister, von Neurath. Hess was without Ilse, who did not like going out in society; nor did he. Bella Fromm saw him sitting 'gloomy and morose' in a deep armchair apart from everyone, his glance flitting over the chattering groups. Then he rose and came up to her, clicking his heels. She thought of the name he was known by in the Party, 'Black Grete' as she studied him:

Tall, slender, well-built, somewhat effeminate looking. Not much poise. Unsteady, vague, sly eyes, bushy brows that meet in an almost straight line at the ridge of his nose. His nose is certainly not his best feature. It is fleshy, ill-shaped, and ends in a knob. His large, almost lipless mouth gives him the look of something cruel and obstinate.[9]

Bella Fromm was a hostile witness; she detected an intimidatory air about him. Perhaps this was a symptom of his unease in company making small talk, particularly in the company of women. Moreover, she was a Jewess working for the Jewish publishing house of Ullstein; he was still, underneath, a Freikorps man, a dedicated enemy of Jewesses and all 'Red' women.

She was wondering if the rumour were true that he painted his toenails red when Göring came up and insisted on having his photograph taken with them. After the flamboyant had gone, Hess turned to her and said in a rude, bullying manner that, if the picture included him, he forbad publication. Then he left abruptly 'to continue his eavesdropping'.[10]

Here Bella Fromm was right in more senses than she probably realised. While Hess's *Verbindungsstab* in Berlin was officially the mediating agency between State and Party functionaries, it was also the highest intelligence *Zentrale*, where Hess kept overall surveillance on a bewildering network of overt and covert agencies. Besides Göring's two main agencies, the Prussian Secret State Police (Gestapo) – soon to fall into Himmler's hands – and a telephone-tapping and signals intercept service covernamed the Research Office (*Forschungsamt*), he received intelligence from Himmler's Bavarian and other secret State political police services, from Heydrich's Security Service (SD), from Admiral Canaris's Military Intelligence and Counter-intelligence (Abwehr), from his own agents and organisations of Germans living abroad, and from a diplomatic intelligence network run for him by the former SA chief, deposed after the Stennes *putsch*, Captain Franz Pfeffer von Salomon. This service was a relic of Imperial German armed forces intelligence which had continued functioning after the war as an arm of the underground service struggle against both the Weimar Republic and the Versailles powers. The former Freikorps officer and dedicated Nazi supporter Colonel von Reichenau had managed to hide the funding in the service budget in a way that maintained security and continuity. According to von Salomon his service had penetrated the British, French, US and Russian Embassies in London, Paris and Moscow, and had acquired knowledge of these powers' policies from their internal correspondence; new, interesting or conclusive insights into political or economic policy behind the scenes were passed directly up to Hitler.[11]

While all leaders in a position to do so were spying on all others in the jostle for advantage around the Führer and it is doubtful, therefore, if Göring, Himmler or Röhm, who had his own SA intelligence service, passed all significant information to Hess's office, there is every reason to believe that in these early years of power Göring and Himmler did work closely with Hess; on Göring's part this was as much for self-protection as loyalty, on Himmler's part because he was still Hess's man, very ambitious, and Hess had the ear of the Führer. In any case co-operation was necessary as the old splits between left and right of the Party had reappeared in more dangerous form.

This time schism was to end in a blood purge. It is possible to see with this murderous resolution on 30 June 1934 a change in Hess's devotion to Hitler: before it he was the enthusiastic disciple; after it the determined follower beset by mental and spiritual strains manifesting themselves as griping stomach pains which forced him to bed for days at a time.

There are other explanations. The scope of his task as representative of the Führer settling quarrels between Party chiefs and Government officials in an administrative system mirroring Hitler's chaotic and suspicious nature was beyond anyone, and he was not suited to it. Alternatively, possibly the sight of more thrusting rivals beginning to usurp his position at the Führer's side preyed on him. He was not unique among the Nazi leaders in suffering what must have been psychosomatic symptoms: Himmler was often crippled with pain; Göring came to depend on drugs and outlandish costumery, Hitler himself on amphetamines. No doubt the Führer principle was to blame with its apparently rock-like pyramid of command concealing a fluid struggle for influence through intrigue. It is possible that those who selected themselves because of their emotional needs were especially vulnerable to this form of sustained psychic torture. Hitler only suffered those who needed a god and a faith, who submitted unconditionally.

It is interesting that the way Hess signed his name changed around this time. What had been, especially in his Landsberg days, a confident, flowing signature tending slightly upwards in a straight line towards the right, now drooped at the end to form, an arc. Even his short signature, 'R. Hess', which had risen, also dipped despondently at the end.

By mid-December 1933, when Bella Fromm found him 'gloomy and morose' the internal Party schism had become a national crisis. The most obvious sign was an open, leftward, revolutionary spirit in the SA, whose ranks had been swollen by thousands of former Communists turning into Nazis almost overnight after Hitler's triumph; scarcely concealed beneath their cries for a second revolution to get rid of the 'reactionaries' was Röhm's ambition to become Minister of War and transform the Army with his men into a Peoples' Army. The SA was well armed and organised, and numerically far stronger than the regular forces. The threat to all those landed, financial and industrial groups who had backed Hitler to sustain their own position against Socialism was very real.

In deeper layers beneath Röhm's ambitions, and so cunningly concealed it is not possible to this day to be specific, were the financial-industrial and international groupings also opposed to the landed élites and to US economic imperialism who had been forced to accept compromise rather than victory at the 4 January meeting at von Schröder's villa; outside the Party their chief political exponents remained von Schleicher and Gregor Strasser.

Precisely when Hitler decided to act against Röhm, von Schleicher and Strasser rather than with them against his own backers, the 'reactionaries' and exactly why remains unclear. Whether Röhm had detailed plans for the take-over of Army and State by the SA, or whether, as often alleged, Himmler and Heydrich manufactured evidence against them to convince Hitler is equally muddy. Even David Irving, whose knowledge of the archival sources is second to none, and who has written a detailed description of Göring's *Forschungsamt*, which had phone taps on all the SA and political 'conspirators' from an early date, is vague about what these revealed and what Röhm's alleged treason really amounted to.[12]

One thing is clear: to complete the *Machtergreifung* and make himself absolute dictator of Germany, which was his undoubted aim, Hitler had either to rid himself of the President of the Republic or assume the office himself. Using Röhm's SA to 'complete the revolution' was the obvious way, if he chose the first alternative, but it implied civil war with the regular forces opposed to him. Making a deal with the 'reactionaries' was the sole way to the second alternative; it had the advantages that, like his appointment as Chancellor, it could be arranged to appear legal and, instead of civil war, all the forces of the State could be used to 'restore order' while the SA was rendered leaderless by an internal Party coup. Most of the signs suggest that this 'legal' path was chosen early, certainly before the end of 1933.

No doubt Hess again had a central co-ordinating role, although it is impossible to say how much he contributed to ideas and strategic planning. There are only indications that he was not the straightforward 'idealist' he is usually painted: they come from Heinrich Hoffmann's lady friend as reported by Ludecke, and Bella Fromm's perception of the vague, sly look in his eyes – both hostile witnesses – but as revealing are the character studies of him in confinement in England and the games he played with 'amnesia' which took in nearly all the doctors and psychiatrists assigned to look after him. These marks of deviousness in his personality and his known closeness at this period to Göring and Himmler – once again the front men in the *coup* – taken together with the statement of his adjutant, Leitgen, that there was a long-standing antagonism between Hess and Röhm, 'because Hess saw in Röhm a man ruled by ambition who could become dangerous to the chief, Hitler',[13] suggest Hess may have played a strategic as well as a co-ordinating role.

Most accounts of the affair give prominence to Göring and Himmler colluding to get rid of Röhm, and Hitler wavering until the last moment, when he was brought into line with their plan either by Himmler's manufactured evidence of an SA plot or by the 'brown pages' of transcripts from Göring's telephone-tapping service. Yet Hitler always wavered before large or even small decisions. His 'unalterable will' was in part propaganda myth, in part the hard cover of a chronic vaccilator, an aspect of the extraordinary 'duality' in his character noted by Robert Waite.[14] It is far more likely, far more in keeping with the strategy of combined deception and 'protection' by which Hitler had risen that it was the intention from the beginning to frighten the conservative élites with the SA and force them into a position where they had to choose between a 'second revolution' spearheaded by Röhm's organised hoodlums or hand over the State Presidency to Hitler. Was Hess the strategist who brought order and held Hitler steady to this plan? To ask the question casts a strange light over the whole history of Hitler's rise to power illuminating Hess, deep-set eyes glowing with other-worldly fanaticism, still standing behind his Führer, but managing and manipulating his genius.

Leitgen stated in 1952 that the example of Hitler's personal brutality on 30 June was one of the hardest blows Hess suffered, which 'deeply wounded his marked, almost feminine, sensitivities' and aged him by years.[15] If true, and it is not entirely supported by other testimony, it does not necessarily mean that the whole affair came as a shock to him, simply that he envisaged most of the victims being thrown into concentration camps like the Communist and Socialist enemies of the State until they had repented of their ways – not murdered. That was the shock.

The campaign of deception, and surely it was such, began on 1 December, when both Röhm and Hess were called into government, Hess as Minister without portfolio. Early in the New Year, 1934, while Heydrich's agents spread disinformation about SA plans against the Army, Göring met the Army Commander in Chief, von Fritsch, to urge Army support for action against the SA. In February the armed services adopted the swastika eagle as an element of uniform and ensigns; but the final pact by which they agreed to aid the SS against the SA and to support Hitler's appointment as President on the death of von Hindenburg is generally believed to have been sealed between Hitler and the pro-Nazi Minister of War, von Blomberg, aboard the warship *Deutschland* on 12 April.

Meanwhile Himmler and Heydrich, intent on creating a unified Reich Secret Political Police, battered at the gates of Göring's Prussian Gestapo, the last of the State Political Police departments to fall. When Hitler signalled support for Himmler's aspirations, Göring broke down, realising suddenly that, for all his apparent power, without Hitler he was nothing. Himmler was Hess's man; it is possible to see this defeat for Göring in Prussia as another victory for the Munich *camarilla*. In any case Himmler and Heydrich formally took over Gestapo headquarters at 8 Prinz Albrecht Strasse in Berlin the week after Hitler's meeting with von Blomberg aboard the *Deutschland*. All was now prepared for Röhm's downfall, a unified political police force under the Reichsführer SS, a guarantee of Army – SS co-operation in the strike.

The same month Hess opened secret talks with Gregor Strasser designed apparently to pave the way for Strasser's entry into Hitler's cabinet in the autumn.[16] Hitler, meanwhile, led Röhm to believe that he would back his plans to take over the War Ministry directly the foreign political position had stabilised – probably in the autumn – and encouraged Röhm's lines to the French Government. To reinforce the impression, Goebbels began a virulent propaganda campaign against 'reactionaries'.[17]

At the same time, however, Hess's new 'England expert', von Ribbentrop, was appointed Special Commissioner for Disarmament and instructed to canvass support in London for an increase in the strength of the regular Army permitted Germany under the Versailles agreement by 300,000 men, to be compensated by a decrease of more than double that number in the paramilitary SA. The Commander in Chief of the Navy, Admiral Raeder, was instructed to prepare plans for naval building up to a third the strength of the British Royal Navy – a proportion calculated specifically not to alarm England. Earlier, the head of British Air Intelligence, Group Captain Frederick Winterbotham, had visited Germany on the invitation of Alfred Rosenberg and been introduced to Hitler, Hess and officers of the General Staff who had told him of their plans for conquest of Russian space by tank columns supported by air strikes. One of these officers was Hess's secret political intelligence collaborator, von Reichenau.

In May Hjalmar Schacht had a secret meeting with the Governor of the Bank of England, Sir Montagu Norman – a pronounced anti-French, anti-Roman Catholic anti-Semite – and again the following month, when he is supposed to have assured Norman there would be no 'second revolution' in Germany; on the contrary the SA would be reduced.[18]

After the war Hess's adjutant, Alfred Leitgen, commented on the affair:

Undoubtedly Röhm's inclination was to have the SA granted a place within the armed services, thereby obtaining great political and military power [for himself]. At the same time Röhm's foreign political conception had a bearing since he wanted to co-operate with France, while Hitler had his sights on the Anglo-Saxons.[19]

The British connections are significant since, of course, friendship with England was the foundation of Hitler's plans for conquest, and here it is evident that Hess's political intelligence service under von Salomon, funded by Reichenau, played its part.

Whether or not Hitler had ever wavered between the alternatives, there can be no question that by May the decision had been cast against Röhm; Göring and Himmler had begun preparing a list of enemies who should disappear headed in grandiloquent style the 'Reich List of Unwanted Persons'. Detailed preparations for the action began on about 20 June, when Himmler and Colonel von Reichenau drew up plans for Army support for the ss. On 21 June Hitler visited von Hindenburg to assure him his part of the bargain would be fulfilled within the next few days. On 25 June Himmler summoned his ss regional and district commanders to a meeting in Berlin, and told them of an expected SA *putsch*, after which he outlined plans for a pre-emptive strike in co-operation with the Army and police. On the same day Hess gave what sounded like an even-handed warning to both 'reactionaries' and 'revolutionaries' in a nationwide radio broadcast. It was carefully equivocal: some day the Führer might drive matters forward by revolutionary methods, but he alone had to decide the timing. The Führer was the great strategist of the revolution who alone knew the limits of the possible at any given moment:

He acts after close and ice-cold appraisal of the situation, often seeming only to serve the moment, yet always pursuing the ultimate aims of the revolution ... Woe to him who breaks faith, and thinks to serve the revolution through rebellion! Woe to him who clumsily tramples the Führer's plans in the hope of quicker results![20]

It is probably significant that this 'warning' was delivered on the day Himmler initiated his ss leaders, serving to reinforce the message to them. Röhm, on the other hand, would not have read it as a warning; he had been assured by Hitler that his time would come in the autumn. He had publicly ordered the majority of the sa to take their leave in July, ending his announcement with the threat that, if their enemies deluded themselves that the sa would not report back for duty after the summer, they would receive 'a fitting answer at the time and in the form which appears necessary. The sa is and will remain Germany's destiny.'[21]

In the final days before the strike an air of studied normality prevailed in the higher levels of the Party. Hitler and Göring went to Essen as witnesses at the marriage of Gauleiter Josef Terboven; that evening, 28 June, Hitler telephoned Röhm, who was convalescing at the Tegernsee resort of Bad Wiessee, and instructed him to convene a meeting of all sa leaders, Gruppenführer upwards, at Wiessee for noon, 30 June. The same day Hess was in Berlin meeting representatives of the German Chamber of Foreign Commerce. His speech held no reference to the internal situation; it was concerned chiefly with a foreign boycott of German goods organised in answer to German anti-Jewish measures. The attack was directed against their *Weltanschauung*, Hess said; 'The rest of the world feels that a new *Weltanschauung* has been born in Germany which shakes the fundamental thinking of our time.'[22]

Afterwards he returned to Munich. Göring returned to Berlin the same day. Himmler, already in Berlin, placed the ss and police on alert, and ordered his adjutant, Karl Wolff, to Göring's palace on the Leipzigerstrasse with an overnight bag. At Gestapo headquarters in Prinz Albrecht Strasse. Heydrich briefed eighteen crack shots from the élite ss-Leibstandarte Adolf Hitler on their targets. Hitler, after a scheduled inspection of a labour camp, drove to his favourite Hotel Dreesen at Bad Godesberg; that evening he was pale, tense and withdrawn. Much later he left and drove to Bonn airport, where a Junkers Ju-52 was waiting to fly him to Munich; it was two in the morning of 30 June. Two companies of the Leibstandarte were on their way to a small station near Landsberg, southern Bavaria, to rendezvous with a detachment of concentration camp guards from Dachau and drive in personnel carriers provided by the Army to Bad Wiessee.

Hitler, accompanied by Viktor Lutze, an informant of Hess's inside the SA and earmarked to succeed Röhm as SA chief, together with several carloads of detectives collected in Munich, arrived before the SS units. Disarming the SA guards by his presence alone, Hitler strode to Röhm's room and walked in, pistol drawn, to tell him he was under arrest. Röhm's few companions at the *pension* were arrested by the detectives and all were driven back to Munich at speed. Hess was waiting in the Brown House, which was heavily guarded by SS. Whatever Hitler and Hess may have said to Röhm on this last occasion they were together will never be known, but, after interrogation, Röhm and the other SA officers were driven to Stadelheim prison to await execution.

Hitler's personal mission heralded the opening of the operation nationwide. SA leaders were rounded up in all major cities; in Berlin the listed victims were picked up by police or squads of SS men in lorries and taken to the Leibstandarte barracks at Lichterfelde to stand before a firing squad; in some cases they were murdered where they were found at home or in their office. Göring, Himmler and Heydrich controlled the operation from the Leipzigerstrasse Palace.

In the Brown House, Munich, Hitler and Hess were closeted alone, wrestling, according to Leitgen, who was in an adjacent office, in 'protracted and heated' argument over the death list.[23] 'Hess fought passionately with Hitler over individual names, not allowing himself to be intimidated even by Hitler's strongest outbursts. There were many, it will never be known how many, he saved.'[24]

Hans Frank, leader of the Party disciplinary court and Bavarian Minister of Justice, wrote an account with a somewhat different emphasis while awaiting sentence of death at Nuremberg after the war. Sepp Dietrich, commander of the Leibstandarte Adolf Hitler, and Prince Waldeck, one of the earliest sons of the nobility attracted to the SS, who had served as Himmler's personal adjutant in 1930, appeared in Frank's office late that afternoon with a list of SA leaders, some 110 of whose names had been crossed through with a pencil. These were the 'death candidates', Dietrich told him; he had orders from the Führer personally to shoot them at once. Frank immediately rang Hitler; Hess answered the phone and Frank told him he could not sign the death warrants. There was a pause, then Hitler himself came on the line.

'You refuse to obey an order from me? Do you sympathise with these criminal *Lumpen*? I will eradicate these fellows root and branch!'

Frank said he had no written authority, only a list of names, to which Hitler replied hotly that he was *Reich* Chancellor and this was a *Reich* matter. Suddenly Hess came on the phone again and said the order must be executed. Frank now tried to persuade Hess, 'who was much calmer, more objective, anyhow more refined than Hitler', that most of the SA leaders in Stadelheim had been pulled off the train, the others out of their beds unarmed, without plans or knowledge of any *putsch*, and many were highly decorated officers of the First World War. Hess told him to wait; he wanted to speak to the Führer again. This was, perhaps, the period Leitgen described, for the wait was prolonged into the evening.

Finally the telephone rang. Hitler refused to speak to me personally. Hess told me that, in agreement with the Reich President, Hitler had full powers to carry out all measures necessary to prevent the threatened *putsch* without reservation. the chief culprits were by his instructions to be shot. I then asked, 'Which?' And, with the list in my hand I heard down the telephone nineteen names. I marked them with a red pencil. After the last there was a pause. I asked, 'And the others who are not marked down?' Hess said, 'The Führer has checked the list and will limit it to these names.' Röhm was not on the list. Hess said to me, 'About Röhm, further advice will follow. For the time being all are to remain in jail.'[25]

Hitler, Hess and Goebbels flew to Berlin, stepping out of the plane against a blood-red sunset; Hitler's white, unshaven face seemed 'gaunt and puffed out at the same time'; Hess was enveloped in deeper gloom than usual. Later, at the Chancellery, Hitler told Göring he intended sparing Röhm for the sake of their long association. Whether he was trying to salve his conscience, knowing Röhm to be innocent, whether he was vaccilating again before a decision, or whether he felt genuinely sentimental, it was hardly an option to spare the head in the midst of the bloodbath of his subordinates. The debate continued in Hitler's close circle the following day, while around the country the killing and private vendettas continued. In his diary Rosenberg recorded Hitler saying to Amann that Röhm had stood beside him in court after the November *putsch*.

'The biggest swine must go,' was all Amann replied, and turning to Hess, 'I'll shoot Röhm myself!'

'No,' Hess said, 'that's my duty, even if I should be shot afterwards myself.'[26]

The same day Himmler's Inspector of Concentration Camps, Theodor Eicke, entered Röhm's cell and handed him a Browning revolver loaded with one bullet. Röhm asked to speak to Hitler. The request was refused; he was told he had ten minutes. In the stipulated time Eicke returned to find Röhm standing, facing the cell door with bared chest. Eicke ordered his escort to shoot. Röhm collapsed with the words, '*Mein Führer!*'

Von Schleicher and his wife had been murdered in their home the previous day, and Gregor Strasser in a cell at Gestapo headquarters. How many others were eliminated before Hitler called off the action at four in the morning of the next day, 2 July, will never be established. Hitler admitted to seventy-six; the real number is probably nearer 250.

The glimpses of Hess emerging from behind his Führer and the more obvious strong men of the Party throughout the action, his known close connection to von Reichenau, chief exponent of Army co-operation, and his control of all intelligence input give the clearest indication of the role he played and had played since Landsberg. It may perhaps be compared to that of those wives of great men who provide counsel, resolution, contacts and support. Hitler, of course, had no wife and his mistress, Eva Braun – 'Evi' to Hess – lacked the intellectual capacity to play such a part. Hess could. How much he actually determined policy is impossible to say.

In a speech at Königsberg on 8 July explaining the 'Night of the Long Knives', which had shocked the world – although not the old and ailing President, von Hindenburg, or the Army and landed élites who had showered Hitler with praise for his resolution – Hess said that 'in those hours when it was a question of to be or not to be for the German people', it had not been possible to weigh the precise guilt of individuals; there was, he continued, profound meaning in the principle by which mutinies were quelled in the Army, 'shooting every tenth man out of hand without raising the slightest question as to whether he was individually guilty or not'.[27]

Five days later Hitler told the Reichstag that the destiny of the nation stood high above that of the individual; and he referred to warnings he had received about Röhm, 'especially from my Deputy, Rudolf Hess', which he had been unable to ignore.[28]

A week later, at the beginning of August, von Hindenburg died. The Army fulfilled its side of the pact, supporting Hitler's appointment as President and reaffirming the loyal oath as 'unconditional obedience to Adolf Hitler, Führer of the Reich and of the German people, Supreme Commander of the Armed Forces . . .'

8

THE DEPUTY

Hess's position as Deputy to the Führer combined the role he had played since 1925 as Hitler's secretary and organiser with part of Gregor Strasser's former function as chief of Party organisation. His duties were defined as ensuring that the Party carried out the tasks placed on it by the Führer, representing the Party position to the organs of the State, and in the area of law-making seeing that 'the demands of the National Socialist *Weltanschauung* were brought more and more to realisation'.[1] In addition to thus guiding and representing the Party on behalf of the Führer and the *Weltanschauung*, he acted as a super ombudsman to whom 'every German *Volk* comrade has the right to turn with his concerns [*Sorgen*]. He can expect his advice and help.'[2]

For these tasks Hess built an organisation which paralleled the State Ministries in Berlin and in some cases performed functions outside those of any Ministry. Thus in the 'Ribbentrop Bureau' in Berlin he had a shadow Foreign Ministry in direct competition with the diplomats of the old school under von Neurath, but he also had a 'Foreign Organisation' in Berlin under a thrusting English-born, South-African-educated thirty-one-year-old named Ernst Bohle, whom he had appointed in 1933. Bohle was a rival of both Ribbentrop and the old-school diplomats of the Foreign Ministry, and it was felt destined one day to become Reichsaussenminister (Foreign Minister) himself. Outwardly Bohle's Foreign Organisation was to keep Germans living abroad in touch with affairs in the Reich and assist their sense of being part of the German community; beneath, it was a propaganda, fifth column and intelligence service. Under interrogation in 1945 Bohle admitted that he had a good reporting system.

'And you were able to get these reports to Hess, Bormann and Himmler even before other people knew about it?'

'In some cases . . . yes.'[3]

Hess took particular interest in the Foreign Organisation both because of its intelligence function and because of his own origins as a German abroad. In his speech to the Chamber of Foreign Commerce two days before the 'Night of the Long Knives', he had reminded them he was himself an *Auslanddeutscher*:

I still keep in touch in a personal way with Germandom abroad so that I feel quite justified in saying I know exactly the concerns of my German *Volk* comrades in foreign lands ...

You know and I know that the former [German] State neglected to maintain and freshen up the ties of blood that bind Germans at home to Germans abroad or to make full political use of both parts of Germandom to obtain tangible results. Making good this neglect and facilitating the common task I see as special duties of the National Socialist State.

The new Germany needed and expected their co-operation, he continued, and their readiness for spiritual and material sacrifice for the 'greater German *Volk* community'.[4]

Hess had Karl Haushofer appointed President of yet another foreign organisation, the *Volks* Alliance for Germandom Abroad (VDA), which under the usual cultural cover established Nazi 'bases' among the minority groups of Germans in neighbouring countries; these were activated to foment internal strife when necessary to complement German foreign policy. This plethora of competing foreign and intelligence organisations within his control, none knowing what the others were doing, all competing for influence, suggest that Hess aped Hitler's methods of ruling by division.

For internal affairs Hess had an office for public law, one for art and culture, one for the press under his adjutant, Alfred Leitgen, one for education, another for high schools, one for employment, finance and Tax Policy, one for 'all questions of technology and organisation' under Dr Fritz Todt in Berlin – the so-called Todt Organisation, which became famous for constructing Germany's *Autobahns* and static defences, and had tentacles stretching into all areas of German industry – another for 'practical technical questions' under Theo Croneiss, a director of the Messerschmitt Aircraft Company whom Hess had known since his flying days in the war; and he had an important office for *Volks* health with two tributary offices for 'race policy' and 'kinship investigation' – chiefly research into ancestry to discover Jewish blood. There were several other offices, well over twenty by 1939, the most important of which was the liaison and intelligence *Zentrale*, the *Verbindungsstab* at 64 Wilhelmstrasse in Berlin.

To run this vast empire he had a most industrious, businesslike 'fixer', Martin Bormann, as chief of staff. On the other hand he also had party rivals with their own empires who sought to expand their influence in the same areas. Chief among these was Robert Ley, head of both the

'Labour Front', supposedly representing the interests of the German workers since the unions had been dissolved, and the 'Political Organisation', which had subsumed and expanded Gregor Strasser's administrative structure. The Party ideologist, Alfred Rosenberg, was another, although less powerful, rival. His influence had waned since the early days; nevertheless he was charged with 'the entire intellectual and ideological education and training of the Party and all affiliated organisations', and he had a foreign policy organisation called the Foreign Political Office in direct rivalry with both the Ribbentrop Bureau and Bohle's Foreign Organisation, and whose aim was identical – the cultivation of friendship with Great Britain. There were also the major Party figures holding public office, Göring, Goebbels and Hess's own protégé, Himmler, now as both Reichsführer ss and head of the political police beginning to build his own secret state within the State.

Hitler himself had a Chancellery headed by the thirty-four-year-old Philipp Bouhler, another front fighter during the war, subsequently a reporter on the *Völkischer Beobachter* who had entered Hitler's closest circle of confidants when appointed Party Business Manager. His chief of staff as head of Department 1 at the Chancellery was Martin Bormann's brother, Albert. The official task of the Chancellery was to keep Hitler in contact with his movement and preserve close connections with Hess's organisation, but, since in the *Führer* system 'contact' or 'liaison' were frequently euphemisms for parallel lines of command by-passing regular channels, some of the Chancellery's most important tasks were to pursue Hitler's personal or secret policies.

As Minister without portfolio, Hess was a member of Hitler's cabinet, theoretically the highest council of State; as Stellvertreter, he was second in the *Oberste Reichsleitung* or highest Party council. Yet formal structures counted for nothing; ultimate decisions were Hitler's and increasingly, as power and sycophancy worked their inevitable decay, he was guided only by genius, by the ideas of State or Party leaders or by Chancellery officials who would carry out his 'wish', which was also the highest *Reich* law. In such a system it was inevitably the power seekers and political manipulators like Himmler and Martin Bormann who increased their influence.

Hess was neither. In Leitgen's words, he had only one ambition: 'to be the loyalist interpreter of Hitler'.[5] He lacked the qualities of vivid leadership or showmanship, or the aptitude for faction of other paladins vieing for Hitler's favour; knowing this, it almost seems as though he exaggerated his natural tendencies in the opposite direction towards reticence, humility, asceticism, mysticism and, to offset the ostentation of so many of the new élite, he made virtues of his idealism and incorruptibility. He turned himself into 'the conscience of the Party'. In his burning devotion and jealousy, he rationalised his feelings by convincing himself – again in Leitgen's words – 'no one could realise Hitler's innermost aspirations to make the Party his personal battle instrument so well as he [Hess]'.[6]

This was not how it appeared. Outside his personal staff he was regarded as characterless and too weak. The Minister of Finance, von Krosigk, described him as the 'most colourless apparition in Hitler's immediate circle', who as herald of the Führer felt it his duty to hide his own personality behind that great image:

Therefore even at Party rallies he always wore only the brown shirt without orders and decorations, thereby making a double impression beside Göring's bird-of-paradise hues. In Hess Hitler had appointed his loyalest follower. He may have believed that at the head of his unruly and wayward guard belonged a man who was immaculate in his personal life and to whom intrigue was as foreign as ambition. But he also placed in a position which should have directed and held his followers together, not a centre of gravity, but a vacuum.[7]

Party wits parodied St Matthew's Gospel for Hess: 'Come unto me all ye that labour and are heavy laden, and I will – do nothing!' Poor Hess, Hanfstaengl wrote, 'what could he do against a chief like Hitler?'[8] Hans Frank wrote in the same vein:

In his views and attitude Hess was fundamentally clean, but seized with jealousy he looked enviously at Göring, whose shining star as the real 'second man' in Reich and Party began to outshine the nominal *Stellvertreter* ... Like a pallid and unpretentious private secretary, Hess waited, a sufferer in the shadows, for the Führer to recognise his reserve and to distinguish him with preference over the loud, publicity-seeking 'Iron Hermann'.[9]

By 1936, when an Australian academic, Stephen Roberts, took a sabbatical to study the Nazi regime at close quarters, Hess gave the impression of being 'washed out and lifeless'; he was 'not very impressive personally', indeed he appeared to Roberts 'curiously negative, almost anaemic, and has high moral character, apparently without any personal ambitions ... Content to give out the reflected brilliance of his Führer, he has drawn all light from himself and has really become a substitute – a *Stellvertreter* – for his Leader.'[10]

Hess's own man, Bohle, gave a similar impression under interrogation in 1945: 'Well, he was only regarded over here as a soft man, that is to say the man to whom anybody could apply, who had an ear for everybody, looked after everything and was deadly against the die-hards in the Party.'

'Was he a sincere Nazi?'

'He was sincere as an idealist, in my opinion the biggest idealist we

THE DEPUTY

have had in Germany, a man of very soft nature, no uniforms with him or that sort of stuff, he very seldom went into the public field.'[11]

Analysts and commentators since the war have also seen lack of business sense in so many of the new leaders, especially Hess in his pivotal role between Party and State, as chiefly responsible for the disorder permeating the higher levels of the Third Reich.[12] But it was the *Führer* system itself which created disorder and duality – Hitler's need to create power rivalries to safeguard his own position as arbiter, his chronically suspicious nature, his distrust of professional men, his sure nose for those who would surrender all critical faculties before his genius, the very nature of his profligate mind and the ideology which alone gave it cohesion. The high gearing of the system arising from these personal traits had been ideal for the shifts and turns necessary in fighting a guerrilla war against democracy; it was not suited to the rational government of a great industrial nation; nor was the *Weltanschauung* which rested on eternal struggle. Hess had been instrumental in creating the Führer and the system; the very qualities and psychological needs which suited him for that role now made it impossible for him to take firm action against Hitler's very nature.

Leitgen cited practical examples of Hess's difficulties, as when he attempted to act against Julius Streicher, editor of the pornographically anti-Semite paper *Der Stürmer*. He succeeded in firing Hitler to the point of promising to draft Streicher to a punishment battalion as a private on the morrow. Came the morrow and he had changed his mind, and Streicher was back in the old familiar circle. Hess told Leitgen he knew he was called too weak, but, like Bormann, he had to avoid pressing his case so far as to isolate himself from Hitler.[13] Leitgen explained the dilemma:

As *Stellvertreter* of the Führer Hess had the problem of either playing the strong man and enforcing his will, or, as he often explained to us, of making allowance for the fact that he could not go against all Reichsleiters and Gauleiters, thereby conjuring up a guerilla war. Hess was of the opinion he could not expose Hitler to such a situation and that it was better in his view to carry through his ideas step by step in certain areas of special interest.[14]

These confessions were Hess's rationalisation of impotence. With the objective part of his mind he had perceived the worm in the apple. Yet his devotion and idealism were too strong, indeed unconditional because a part of him, the positive part rescued from the 'hell of Verdun' and black despair at the aftermath, was forged in the comradeship of the Freikorps men; and that comradeship, too, sealed the negative part, the hatred of 'Reds' who had conspired to defeat Germany behind the fighting front. 'To be sure', Leitgen said, 'Hess was stamped with an almost pathological aversion to the Asiatic-Bolshevik *Weltanschauung*.'[15]

It was in the ideological sphere that Hess concentrated his 'step by step' drive to realise Hitler's goals – according to Leitgen 'most conspicuously in the Church question, the Jewish question and the HJ'[16] – Hitler Youth. But the first, most obvious symptom was described by Hans Frank: more and more lawyers were drawn into the Stellvertreter's office for public law which, 'covered by the total authority of Hess ... took over all *Reich* legal work'.[17] Frank seemed to lay most of the blame on Martin Bormann, abetted by Himmler, Heydrich and Ley. Yet apart from Ley, all were Hess's men, Bormann his most loyal organisation man at this stage. It was the concept of 'revolutionary justice' emanating from Hess's legal office overwhelming the traditional law of the State authorities – however that may have been compromised since the war – which allowed Himmler to create the secret terror state founded on a closed triangle, political police-concentration camps-ss, by-passing all legal processes. It was this system which enabled Hitler to wreak the terrible revenge he had vowed on his enemies from Landsberg in 1924 – 'Oh, I will take a merciless and fearful revenge on the day I am able to do so.'[18] It was the spirit in which Himmler administered the camps. Rudolf Höss, later commandant of Auschwitz, described his initiation at Dachau by Himmler's Inspector of Concentration Camps, Theodor Eicke, in repeated lectures, admonitions and orders that the inmates were dangerous enemies of the State: 'Through his continual influence in this direction, he generated a hate, an antipathy against the prisoners which is inconceivable to those outside.'[19] Thus were the Communists, Socialists, trade union leaders and other political and religious dissidents taken out of circulation for as long as Himmler chose, their would-be adherents and sympathisers terrorised into conformity. The camps were not simply cages for incorrigible enemies of the State; the undefined, therefore limitless sense of terror they inspired was a standing threat to every *Reich* citizen who might think of stepping out of line or even criticising the regime. Ultimately Himmler's authority rested on Hitler's wish, but it was Hess's legal officers interpreting the law in the sense of the *Weltanschauung* who enabled him to realise the system.

It was the same with the 'Jewish question', which Leitgen recorded as one of Hess's particular concerns. It was by legal process that the Jews were gradually inched out of German life, starting in March 1933, barely six weeks after Hitler had taken power, with a decree removing their right to sue for compensation for damages caused by pogroms. The following month a law debarred Jews from the Civil Service; legal prohibition from other professions followed 'step by step'. In September 1935 the notorious 'Nuremberg Laws' for 'the protection of German blood and German honour' prohibited marriage or extra-marital relations between Jews and citizens of German or kindred (*Artverwandten*) blood. The preamble ran: 'Imbued with the perception that the purity of German blood is the precondition for the survival of the German *Volk*, and impelled by the inflexible determination to secure the German nation for all time, the Reichstag has passed the following law unanimously ...'[20] It was signed by Hitler as Führer, the Reichsministers of the Interior and of Justice, and the '*Stellvertreter des Führers*, Rudolf Hess, Reichsminister without portfolio'. It was not something to which he appended his signature as a matter of duty. He was actively engaged in the Jewish question at the time, as indicated by a letter he sent Hitler twelve days before the law was promulgated. Starting as always '*Mein Führer*', it concerned an analysis by his brother, Alfred – Bohle's Deputy in the Foreign Organisation – of the effects of 'the Jewish incited boycott' of German goods abroad. The surprising conclusion was that the decrease in exports to most of the countries where such incitement had occurred was less than the average decline in exports generally. He ended the letter:

on the assumption that [the analysis] will be of value to you if need be against those who raise the reproach that the economic and foreign exchange difficulties are a consequence of the treatment of the Jews in Germany.
Heil! Ever your
Rudolf Hess[21]

The Jewish question was really the nub of the *Weltanschauung*, both because the Jewish world conspiracy lay behind and beneath all evils, and of even more importance emotionally because of the necessity to purify German blood of all 'inferior value' admixtures – of which the Jews provided by far the largest portion. Whatever Hess had understood Hitler to mean when he had written to Karl Haushofer from Landsberg that in educated circles Hitler spoke about the Jews in a different manner to that which he used before the masses,[22] he had collaborated in *Mein Kampf* and knew Hitler's mind intimately. He knew that the Jewish question was not a bogey raised to focus frustration on a scapegoat, but lay at the very root of all Hitler's thinking. And he knew that at the opposite, positive pole of the blood question was the concept of the 'master race', the pure Aryan superspecies; it was written in *Mein Kampf*: 'The *völkisch* state has to perform the most gigantic rearing task here. One day, however, it will appear as a deed greater than the most victorious wars of our present bourgeois era.'[23]

The theme had been elaborated since. Two key works of Nazi philosophy published in Munich in 1930, Alfred Rosenberg's *The Myth of the Twentieth Century* and Himmler's colleague, Walther Darré's *New*

Nobility from Blood and Soil, both stressed the need for laws to protect endangered Nordic blood by culling inferior value specimens and promoting the selective breeding of the 'ideal type' inside a 'closed blood source'.[24] Himmler had begun with the ss even before Hitler came to power; candidates for his élite formation – which was also to become the racial core of the new Germany – were chosen for their Nordic appearance and both they and, when they sought permission to marry, their intended wives were required to prove pure blood for several previous generations. In a 1934 booklet for schools entitled *Race Policy* Himmler described the Nordic type he sought: tall and slender, the beautifully articulated frame 'a refined instrument of movement and bearing', and inside it the 'Nordic soul' of 'startling clarity and brightness, coolness and level-headedness', which fulfilled itself 'only through eternal striving, inquiry and organisation, thereby never at peace, lost to the world as it seeks the unending and unattainable'.[25] The inferior type to be culled had been described the previous year by one of Walther Darré's colleagues, Dr Gauch, in *New Fundamentals of Race Research*: the type belonged to a 'between stage' linking anthropoid apes with Nordic man, and Gauch had suggested the designation '*Untermensch*' – 'sub-human'.[26] Himmler adopted the term and used it in a booklet entitled *The ss as Anti-Bolshevik Battle Organisation*:

Many believe that this Bolshevism, this battle of the *Untermenschen* organised and led by Jews, is completely new in world history … We hold it right to state in this respect that so long as there have been men on this earth, the struggle between men and *Untermenschen* has been the rule, that this battle against people conducted by Jews has belonged … to the natural course of life on our planet.[27]

The question of Jews and pure blood was thus intimately linked at the deep heart of the Nazi *Weltanschauung* with the battle against Bolshevism. Hess believed it as firmly as his Führer's philosophical colleagues, Rosenberg and Darré, and his idealistic executors, Himmler and Heydrich. He made this plain in a speech to a mass rally in 1934, when he described National Socialism as 'nothing but applied biology'.[28]

One of those who heard the speech, described in Professor Robert Jay Lifton's recent study, *The Nazi Doctors*, for reasons of anonymity as 'Dr S', was so inspired he 'felt himself merged not only with Hess, but with the Führer himself'. He explained to Lifton that 'Hess knew exactly what Hitler thought … He was the only one closely involved with him all the time.'[29] After the speech Dr S joined the Party and became an sa doctor, a member of the National Socialist German Doctors' League and an energetic campaigner for the Nazification of German medicine. In this field he worked closely with Dr Gerhard Wagner, Hess's protégé and head of his Office for *Volks* Health. Wagner, a former Bavarian infantry officer and Freikorps fighter, was notorious for his public advocacy of anti-Jewish racial laws, and had the two offices for 'race policy' and 'kinship investigation' as tributaries of his main office in Munich. Dr S said that both Wagner and Hess regarded National Socialism as a movement rather than a Party, a living organism which grew and changed 'according to the health requirements of the *Volks* body: just as a body may succumb to illness, the *Volks* body could do the same.'[30]

Himmler expressed the same concept in more extreme form in his booklet on the ss battle against Bolshevism: the life and death struggle between men and *Untermenschen* led by the Jews was 'quite as much a law of nature as man's struggle against some epidemic, as the struggle of the plague bacillus against the healthy body'.[31]

The bio-medical concept of Jews and others of 'inferior blood' as a bacillus in the *Volks* body could lead in only three directions: forced mass emigration, forced mass sterilisation or mass liquidation. There were no other options if the problem were to be tacked as rigorously as the Nazis certainly intended. There is little doubt Hitler had liquidation in mind. It was the only certain and clean solution; the emigration of the millions of Jews and other *Untermenschen* who would be caught in the drive for eastern *Lebensraum* was not practical; forced sterilisation would be difficult to handle and, besides provoking a storm of feeling around the world, would leave a large, vengeful fifth column working against the *Reich* from within.

It is doubtful if these considerations played any part in Hitler's thinking; his attitude was emotional; it may have stemmed from a suspicion that his grandmother had given birth to his father after being seduced by her Jewish employer, a story Hans Frank recorded in his death cell memoirs.[32] Prodigious research has not revealed this Jew. None the less Robert Waite has produced telling evidence from Hitler's speeches, conversations and habits to suggest he did suspect his own blood might be tainted from his father.[33] He had written in *Mein Kampf* – and presumably Hess had typed it – 'the black-haired Jew-boy lurks for hours, his face set in a satanic leer, waiting for the blissfully innocent girl whom he defiles with his blood'. It is suggestive that he checked every word of the 1935 'Nuremberg Laws' prohibiting marriage or sexual relations between Jews and Germans, and made a point of emphasising paragraph three, which prohibited Jews from employing female household staff of German or kindred blood under forty-five years old.[34] Of course Jewish lust for pure Aryan maidenhood was a cliché of anti-Semitic tracts and the very stuff of Julius Streicher's odious *Der Stürmer*. It may be that Hitler had simply fallen victim to his own propaganda. Yet his association with Streicher, whom many supporters of the movement regarded with distaste, if not shame, speaks for his compulsion to share these sexual nightmares; as Leitgen revealed, Hess tried his utmost, without success, to remove Streicher from Hitler's circle.

Whatever the root of Hitler's hatred of Jews, there is no doubt it was all-consuming, and that from the early 1920s he gave vent in public and private to the most blood-curdling promises to eradicate them, root and branch[35] – 'mit Stumpf und Stiel aus(zu)rotten' – a phrase which suggests wiping out completely, obliterating from the map. In conversation he talked of having gallows erected in Munich directly he had power: 'Then the Jews will be hanged one after another, and they will stay hanging until they stink ... Exactly the same procedure will be followed in other cities until Germany is cleansed of the last Jew.'[36] The word 'cleansed' is psychologically significant too. In 1936 the Australian Stephen Roberts was shown around a collection of Nazi Party memorabilia in Munich by the curator, an old man of 'the academic class'; as the pièce de resistance he produced 'a small sculptured wooden gibbet from which was suspended a brutally realistic figure of a dangling Jew'. It had, he said, decorated the table at which Adolf Hitler had founded the Party: 'Is it not funny?' Roberts replied that it was very, very tragic.[37]

Albert Speer was to reflect on Hitler's 'insane hatred of Jews' in his cell in Spandau long after the war, and to conclude that it had been his central conviction; it even seemed to him that everything else had been mere camouflage for this 'real motivating factor'. Hess, who prided himself on knowing Hitler's 'inner thoughts',[38] his attitude on every conceivable question, his whole mode of behaviour', could not have been unaware of this hatred rooted in his Führer's soul. Yet Hitler played many parts for many different people; possibly with his more educated and other-worldly disciple, his 'Hesserl', he showed a more rational face. The difficulty is to imagine what rational solution there could have been to the Jewish 'blood problem' as it existed in the Weltanschauung which did not end in mass liquidation. It seems that Hitler explained a solution to Hess in the spring of 1928, at the time he was wooing the industrialists – unless possibly the 'he' Hess referred to in a letter to Ilse was not Hitler but an industrialist he described as marvelling at Hitler's ability to fit his boundless imagination to present realities: 'He gave me a lecture on the solution of the Jewish problem which inwardly astounded me.'[39] Tantalisingly, that was all Hess wrote about it.

The problem of whether Hess understood the ultimate destination of the 'step-by-step' sequence of the anti-Jewish laws of the mid-1930s is complicated by his close relationship with the Haushofer family. There is no doubt about his fond friendship-discipleship with 'the General',

Professor Karl Haushofer. At Nuremberg after the war Haushofer was one of those the Americans produced unexpectedly to try and revive Hess's memory.

Rudolf, don't you know me any more … we have called each other by our first names for twenty years … If you are patient, your memory will come back and then you will remember your old friends and also your youth and how we circled around the mountains in the Fichtelgebirge with an aero-plane when we flew from Berlin to Munich. Don't you remember how you made the aeroplane circle in the Fichtelgebirge because the landscape was so beautiful . . .[40]

Haushofer's eldest son, Albrecht, was one of Hess's best-connected roving agents. He had served him well in Berlin in the critical months before Hitler took power.[41] He had established high-level contacts in British political and landed circles, and travelled extensively in England, America and the Far East, reporting regularly on developments in Great Britain and the USA for the *Zeitschrift für Geopolitik*, edited by his father. He also held a post teaching geography and geopolitics at the High School for Politics in Berlin. The Jewish blood he had inherited from his mother should have debarred him and his brother from any official posts, but they and their mother were protected by Hess. It was a complex relation-ship; the geopolitical outlook of the Haushofers, father and sons, coin-cided in so many respects with Hess's goals, indeed virtually drove Nazi thinking on foreign policy,[42] but both had strong reservations about Hitler and the methods used. Thus Albrecht, while serving Hess, was also in covert opposition, rationalising his impossible situation like so many of the traditional élite by convincing himself that he could serve his country best by being in a position of influence, educating his masters and preventing the worst mistakes in foreign policy, while waiting for an alignment of anti-Nazi forces to topple the regime. His personal feel-ings towards his protector were expressed in a letter he wrote towards the end of 1933:

For the fact that we have not been swept on to the rubbish heap as Germans of inferior value, we – my brother and I – have to thank exclusively your inter-cession. You will understand if I say that it is very difficult for an inwardly proud and direct person to owe so much thanks that he examines himself minutely before he asks or makes a request for himself. I would not have been able to accept this [post] . . . if I did not feel certain that in case of need I would be capable of full personal commitment to you as a person . . .[43]

The phrase 'commitment to you as a person' seems carefully chosen; certainly by the autumn of the following year Albrecht Haushofer was telling one of his students in Berlin about a small, close circle who were watching developments with a view to overthrowing the regime; among the names he mentioned were the Prussian Minister of Finance, Johannes Popitz, and the Chief of the General Staff, Ludwig Beck; later he mentioned the diplomat Ulrich von Hassell, a lynchpin in the undercover opposition to Hitler.[44]

Yet on the Jewish question his views were not clear cut. In a letter to his father in October 1933 congratulating him on finding a suitable way of co-operating with Hess in supreme control of questions of 'Germandom' – as President of the VDA (*Volksbund* for Germans Abroad) – he described a recent Polish journey: 'The whole Jewish question is fearfully difficult; from Kattowitz I went to Bendzin and Sosnowiec – pure Eastern Jewish towns – and have truly spent enough time with the Chosen People. Obviously they are a foreign body which can only be digested in selected specimens.'[45]

Albrecht Haushofer revealed his true sense of inner schism in a letter to his parents towards the end of July 1934, directly after the murder of the Austrian Chancellor, Dollfuss, by Austrian Nazis masterminded by Hess, Himmler and Heydrich from Munich; the plan, which proved premature, was to install a government which would bring Austria into the German Reich. Albrecht Haushofer, who could scarcely have been unaware of his protector's involvement, wrote: 'At times I ask myself how long we can continue to carry the responsibility which we bear, and which starts little by little to turn into historic guilt or at least complicity ... however, we are all indeed in the position of "conflicting obligations" ... and must carry on even if the task has become completely hopeless.'[46]

He had continued in prescient vein: 'There will be many violent deaths and no one knows when the lightning will strike in his own home.'[47]

The following month he wrote even more pessimistically and prophetically to his mother about his father's birthday: he was wondering whether he should not really wish him 'something which no one may wish a man, before he has to experience things which are best left unspoken. That says basically all that I expect and do not expect of the future.'[48]

A scholar of precocious talent, Albrecht Haushofer was also a gifted poet and playwright; the combination of sensitivity and historical perspective made him acutely aware of the knife-edge of conscience on which he and his father balanced.

There are no similar documentary proofs of Hess's doubts. Yet beneath the Freikorps-Nazi carapace with which he protected himself was, to judge by his poetry and letters and by the testimony of those closest to him, a 'very soft' (Ernst Bohle), 'almost feminine' (Alfred Leitgen) and sensitive nature. His relationship to the Haushofers, mother and sons, who were 'tainted' with 'inferior value blood', yet were models of intellect and wit, charm and worldly poise, which he lacked and admired, could not have failed to introduce conscious and subconscious doubt. He was, in any case, not a balanced character; Hans Frank described him as an 'unstable (*haltlos*) dreamy weakling',[49] Leitgen as 'very unstable (*labilen*)' and 'nervously sensitive and pensive'.[50] It is probable that the misgivings he surely had were expressed in the ever more frequent bouts of illness and resort to astrology and alternative medicine which all who knew him noted. Thus Alfred Rosenberg, interrogated in 1945:

He suffered from stomach spasms. He suffered from severe pains and was often yellow in the face. He could not always fulfil his official duty. He had consulted a good many doctors to remedy this inner illness, but he had obtained no improvement of his condition ... he told us that a doctor had thought he had some infection below his teeth and consequently the teeth were extracted, but this did not help his constitution at all.[51]

Whether his illnesses were a consequence of psychological conflict about the ultimate destination of the racial policy or chiefly a response to the impossible demands of serving as chief liaison for a Führer to whom rational and unitary administration were unnatural – or whether he felt himself slipping away from his former position at Hitler's side – in his public and official character Hess remained fanatically committed to the racial-biological core of the *Weltanschauung*.

The initial stage in the 'step-by-step' bio-medical policy had been initiated in the first months of power with a law 'for the prevention of hereditarily diseased offspring'. It was argued on the alarming proposition that harsh and far-reaching methods were imperative if the nation were to be saved from '*Volks* death', and it introduced compulsory surgical sterilisation for all the 'hereditarily ill', defined as congenitally feebleminded (mentally deficient), schizophrenics, manic depressives, the insane, epileptics, the hereditarily blind or deaf, those suffering grave physical malformation and even 'hereditary alcoholics'. This law, extended the same year and again in October 1935 after the 'Nuremberg Laws', began the process of practical 'race hygiene' (eugenics), creating the structures, gaining the enthusiasts like Dr S, who heard Hess speak about National Socialism as 'applied biology' in 1934, above all removing medical inhibitions by gradually transferring the doctor's ethical responsibility for the patient to the State. It marked the beginning of totalitarian medicine and, as such, the start of a process that was to end at Auschwitz, Treblinka and other purpose-built factory death camps.[52]

Whether Hess either knew or foresaw this ultimate goal is a secret he carried with him in death. That his officials set up the 'hereditary health courts', which adjudicated in secret on those to be compulsorily sterilised, that he was privy to all the medical arguments over methods and procedures is proved by the papers of Dr Wagner's head office for *Volks* Health.[53] It is also not in doubt that he played a leading role in a 'step-by-step' policy to emasculate the Churches, who would provide the chief ideological resistance to the biological goal of Nazi policy. For this task he employed Franz Pfeffer von Salomon, the head of his political intelligence service, who had his offices in the *Verbindungsstab* in Berlin.[54]

Whatever qualms Hess may have suffered before the awesome bio-medical vision to which he was committed, it is apparent that his over-riding ambition remained simply 'to be the loyalest interpreter of Hitler'.[55]

9

THE ENGLAND GAME

In foreign policy Hess's paramount idea, which accorded with Hitler's strategy from the beginning, was friendship with Britain to secure Germany's back and to neutralise France, while German armies thrust east for *Lebensraum* and the extirpation of Bolshevism at source. Like the General Staff officers, who had revealed their plans for *Blitzkrieg* into Russia to Group Captain Winterbotham in 1934, he believed that if only the English could be convinced that Hitler had no designs on their world empire, they would welcome such an agreement to remove the Russian Bolshevik threat to India and the Middle East. He took English lessons specifically to enable him to play his part in the task of winning over influential Britons. One of the earliest he tried to persuade was the MP and Under-Secretary at the Ministry of Health, Geoffrey Shakespeare. He met him in 1933, when Shakespeare's son was receiving treatment from a Bavarian Doctor Gerl, one of his own intimates. He invited the Englishman on stalking expeditions after chamois and over the next two years, when Shakespeare spent his holidays in Bavaria, the two came to know each other quite well.

During the war Shakespeare reported his impressions of his one-time stalking and social acquaintance: 'a man of some charm and a likeable creature' of 'superb personal courage', but 'no great intellectual gifts'; quite the reverse, 'he is the simplest of souls and incapable of acting a part'. Shakespeare could not help but realise he was 'entirely devoted to Hitler, who is his god', but it is interesting that, despite Hess's halting English, he also perceived the 'queer streak of mysticism in his make-up, and his glance and countenance gave me the impression of an unbalanced mind'.[1] Karl Haushofer made similar remarks to Erika Mann after the war: his friend, he said, had never been quite normal; he showed suicidal tendencies as early as 1919, and a lack of balance. 'I recall having sent him to our family physician, Dr Bock, who discovered traces of infantilism.'[2] However that may be – for Haushofer committed suicide together with his wife not long afterwards – Shakespeare found Hess 'a complete amateur in politics and diplomacy' who had 'no knowledge of government', an extraordinary verdict on the second man in the *Reich*.

His fixed idea when I met him was that there was no reason why Germany could not exercise supreme power in Europe without lessening the power of the British Empire in the world. England and Germany between them could govern the world. I do not think he liked England, but he admired the English in many ways . . . He hated Russia and all it stood for . . .[3]

The crowning year for 'England *Politik*' was 1935. Until then Alfred Rosenberg and Göring had made the running with successful overtures to the British Air Ministry under Lord Londonderry; now Ribbentrop, one of whose advisers on British affairs was Albrecht Haushofer, brought home a bi-lateral Anglo-German Naval Agreement. Besides being a tacit repudiation of Versailles and of the collective security covenant of the League of Nations, it was a slap in the face for Great Britain's ally, France; it was, indeed, one of the chief German aims to drive a wedge between the two. That the British Government and the Royal Navy fell for it was due chiefly to a complete misunderstanding of Hitler and National Socialism. The Foreign Secretary, Sir John Simon, who had given Rosenberg a rough time over the treatment of Jews only two years before, believed that the practical choice was between a Germany which continued to re-arm without any limiting agreement and a Germany which could be brought 'into the comity of nations' by being granted recognition of its rights. The British naval staff believed Ribbentrop's threat that, if they failed to close with Hitler's offer of building up to a third of the Royal Navy's strength, there would be no check on German naval expansion.

Contributing to these naive ideas concerning the aims of the New Germany were feelings of sympathy for the former enemy in the highest quarters: the Royal Family, landed and banking interests especially saw Russia and Communism as a greater danger to the Empire and their established position, indeed they were coming to regard Germany, as Hitler intended, as the bastion against Communism, and it was felt that a war between her and the western allies could only be to Russia's advantage. In the Royal Air Force it was recognised that the development of the bombing aeroplane had fundamentally altered imperial strategy by removing the island invulnerability of the homeland; in the Royal Navy there was a hankering after a blue ocean policy to defend the Empire without Continental entanglements such as had resulted in the appalling blood-bath of the Great War; there was also concern on the one hand about American naval rivalry, which appeared to be driven by anti-

(British-) imperial sentiment, and on the other hand about a possible German-Italian-Japanese coalition against the British Empire. On all these counts the friendship Germany offered was enticing. In addition, beneath the practical, strategic considerations, the notorious British sense of fair play and a certain wilful forgetfulness or innocence about the methods by which the Empire had been won played their part.

At the Berlin Olympic Games in the following summer of 1936, seduction continued. The capital was transformed. Even the lime trees which gave Unter den Linden its name were uprooted to make way for forty-five-foot high swastika banners. 'Everything is colossal', Bella Fromm noted in her diary. 'The swastika is everywhere, and so are the black (SS) and brown (SA) uniforms.[4] As remarkable were the cosmetic changes to remove all signs of anti-Semitism and concentration camps. Notices and graffiti abusing Jews were removed; *Der Stürmer* disappeared from the reading boxes at street corners; works of writers banned since 1933 reappeared in book-shops; political prisoners doing forced labour on the land were kept from the vicinity of roads. Hess appeared at the grand opening ceremony on 1 August at the right of his Führer.

Among the British guests of honour that day was a good-looking young MP, the Marquis of Clydesdale, heir to the Duke of Hamilton and Brandon. Clydesdale was an enthusiastic and highly professional aviator, a flying instructor in the Royal Auxiliary Air force – a reserve for the Royal Air Force – and commanding officer of 602 City of Glasgow Squadron. He was referred to in the popular press as 'the Flying Marquis', sometimes as 'the Boxing Marquis'. As a schoolboy he had boxed for Eton, subsequently for Oxford University, and had gone on to become amateur middleweight boxing champion of Scotland. He had even toured the world giving exhibition bouts to raise money for charity. Now he was known chiefly as a flyer. Three years earlier he had led a team charting by air the unmapped regions of the Himalayas and as such had been the first man to fly over Mount Everest. He was always modest about the achievement which he chronicled jointly with Wing Commander MacIntyre in *The Pilot's Book of Everest*, ascribing his feat to the development of the super-charger and the large propeller.[5]

He represented the Scottish constituency of East Renfrew, and on his return from the Himalayas he had been honoured with a celebration dinner given by the House of Commons. Winston Churchill had sat next to him.[6] At one time Clydesdale had been among Churchill's younger friends and supports, but he had fallen out with him since over his 'English' attitude to Scottish affairs.[7]

Hess was, of course, an equally enthusiastic aviator. He had failed to gain the backing to rival Lindbergh by flying the Atlantic east to west in 1927, but in 1932 he had come second in the 'Round the Zugspitze' air race, and in 1934 had won that famous race. He was fascinated by flying and everything connected with it. It is curious, therefore, that, despite the opportunities provided by the official functions to which the distinguished British guests were invited during the Olympics, he did not meet Clydesdale – so he and the Duke of Hamilton (as Clydesdale was to become) later maintained. Their claims are backed by Hamilton's wife, the Dowager Duchess of Hamilton, and her eldest son, the present Duke, and by Ilse Hess.

There was at least one function at which both Hess and Clydesdale were undeniably present. This was a dinner Hitler gave at the Reichs Chancellery in honour of Sir Robert Vansittart on 12 August. It is difficult to believe that Hess did not have himself introduced to the famous aviator on this occasion, especially as Clydesdale was a member of the Anglo-German Fellowship, precisely the type of influential Britisher whom Hess needed to know and impress with his convictions about British-German solidarity against the common Bolshevik foe. If he did not do so, it could only have been because of his natural reticence or embarrassment perhaps at his lack of fluent English.

The first full German explanation of Hess's 1941 flight to Scotland stated that the two had met during this time in Berlin. Of course this was put out by Dr Goebbels's propaganda ministry which might have sought to cause dissension in Britain by suggesting a more personal connection between Hess and Hamilton than actually existed. Yet the British Ministry of Information put out a similar statement at that time, which they denied almost immediately. The most convincing evidence for a meeting between the two was provided by Karl Haushofer just before the Nuremberg trials in 1945 – as will appear. Also the Duke's brother, Lord Malcolm Douglas-Hamilton, believed the two met in Berlin. A discussion he had on 24 May 1945 with the (German) Duke of Brunswick concerning Hess's mission left no doubts on that score in the mind of his navigator, R. C. Langdon, who was present.[8]

Whatever the truth, there is no doubt that Clydesdale met Albrecht Haushofer during the Olympics. In the course of a long talk which Albrecht was to refer to later as 'perhaps the most pleasant of all my "Olympic visitors'" memories',[9] Clydesdale expressed a wish to see the Luftwaffe Göring had built in secret under cover of amateur flying clubs and civil aviation. Albrecht introduced him to Göring at an extravagant party the great man laid on at his Carinhall estate outside Berlin on 13 August. Clydesdale was impressed by his personality, as indeed were many leading British politicians. Now Göring called over his chief lieutenant in the construction of the Luftwaffe, Erhard Milch, who told Clydesdale he would be very happy to arrange for him to be shown round Staaken and Doberitz airfields next day; in the meantime he discussed Luftwaffe questions with him apparently quite openly since, he told him, 'we have a common enemy in Bolshevism'.[10]

Both Albrecht Haushofer and Clydesdale saw to it that their acquaintance begun at Berlin was refreshed. Thus at the end of the year Albrecht sent season's greetings to Clydesdale in Scotland, while Clydesdale, who was on a skiing holiday in Austria at the time, called in on Albrecht on his way home. Albrecht took him to visit his parents at their Hartschimmelhof estate. Geopolitics was not discussed apparently. Afterwards Clydesdale sent Karl Haushofer a copy of *The Pilot's Book of Everest*, and wrote to Albrecht to say he had put his name before the Royal Institute of International Affairs, Chatham House. Albrecht replied that he would be happy to speak at the Institute; he would in any case be in London in March (1937) and hoped to see Clydesdale then.[11]

Meanwhile Ribbentrop had been appointed German Ambassador to London with instructions to follow up his naval treaty success with a more far-reaching agreement with Great Britain. A man of surpassing arrogance and insensitivity, with the face of 'a very distinguished female novelist' (the travel writer Robert Byron) and 'the eyes of a fish' (Bella Fromm), he was a disastrous choice; contemptuous of the British for having allowed him to threaten them into Hitler's poisoned treaty, he now tried much the same tactics with the threat of Bolshevism. The names coined for him by more discerning Englishmen, 'Ribbensnob' or 'von Brick and Drop', tell their own story. It appears that Hess sent Albrecht Haushofer to London to retrieve some of his mistakes; that at all events is what Albrecht told Clydesdale when he arrived in London in the spring of 1937.[12]

From the course of events it is at least possible that Clydesdale was acting as an honorary agent of the British Secret Intelligence Service (SIS) or perhaps Group Captain Winterbotham's Air Intelligence when he sought out Albrecht Haushofer after the Olympic Games. Hess was a prime target for British intelligence; his letters to his parents in Alexandria were being opened and read; Karl Haushofer was known in London as Hess's mentor and Hitler's geopolitical expert, while Albrecht made no secret of the fact that he was one of Hess's most trusted agents. For his part, Albrecht – and indeed Hess – must have suspected that Clydesdale was acting for British intelligence, apart from anything else because it was accepted in Germany that every upper-class Englishman or Scotsman might be co-opted as an unpaid agent when abroad. Whatever either knew or suspected about the other, there can be little doubt that both aimed for much the same goal: an understanding between Great Britain and Germany which, unlike the Nazi understanding, would not lead to European war. It also appears from their correspondence that they became personal friends; by the summer of 1937 they were calling one another 'Albrecht' and 'Douglo' – short for Douglas – and Albrecht had stayed as a guest at Douglo's Scottish seat, Dungavel House, south of Glasgow.[13]

Beneath the pomp of the Berlin Olympics, the unequalled triumphalism of the annual Nuremberg Party Rally which followed in September, behind the apparent successes of the 'England *Politik*', the revolutionary process Hitler sought to direct was directing him, as perhaps it always had; now the course was set irreversibly towards the two-front war he was committed to avoiding. Internally, concentration on armaments at the expense of exports had sucked in raw materials and produced recurrent foreign exchange crises. Hitler met them head on in the summer of 1936 by appointing Göring supremo of a 'Four-Year Plan', which initiated a war economy, increasing armaments and attempting to save imports by producing synthetic oil and rubber. It was seen as an interim measure only; the 'final solution', as Hitler expressed it in his memorandum, lay as ever 'in an expansion of *Lebensraum*' to provide a sufficient 'raw materials and foodstuffs base'.[14]

The plan shifted influence decisively from Schacht, Minister of Economics, and the advocates of the world market to the IG Farben-led economists looking towards a closed European market decoupled from the world economy. IG Farben was chief beneficiary of the synthetics programme Göring was committed to driving forward; the IG was also enmeshed in the war economy through a liaison office with the War Ministry, *Vermittlungsstelle W*, and had already become virtually a research and development institute for the armed services' procurements departments, conducting officially designated 'war games' to test the effects of new munitions.[15] It appears that the original group of industrialists Wilhelm Keppler had gathered to advise Hitler, now the Circle of Friends of the Reichsführer-SS, had reached a concensus in favour of economic autarchy supported by a rapid take-over of the industries and raw materials of Austria, Czechoslovakia and the Danube basin, for Keppler was the adviser whom Hitler heeded against Schacht's arguments. In any case, the decisive shift away from the world economy marked by the Four-Year Plan signified a shift away from the economic world powers, America and Great Britain.

The same shift occurred in foreign affairs. The outbreak of the Spanish Civil War in August polarised the ideological issues in western Europe: France was caught between the pincers of a Nazi Germany and either a Fascist or Communist Spain, depending on the outcome. Great Britain faced a Fascist Italy and either a Fascist or Communist Spain poised over her imperial lifeline through the Mediterranean. In October 1936

Hitler came to an agreement with Mussolini about German-Italian co-operation over Austria and the Balkans, and a number of other issues, chief among them the principle of 'anti-Bolshevism'. In November Mussolini made the first public reference to the German-Italian 'Axis' of Europe. The same month Ribbentrop absented himself from London to close an 'Anti-Comintern Pact' with Japan designed to defeat 'the Communist world conspiracy' and binding both parties to sign no political treaties with the Soviet Union. While loosely phrased, the pact marked the beginning of military co-operation between Germany and Japan in the anti-Russian sense desired by Karl Haushofer.

To the master planners – and no doubt the experts of the Circle of Friends of the Reichsführer-ss – all seemed set fair for the drive eastward within the time-scale of the Four-Year Plan or its successor. Only two issues clouded the view: externally the uncertain attitude of Britain, internally the regrouping of a conservative opposition in the upper levels of the diplomatic and government bureaucracy, upper levels of the Army, and the economists and industrialists of Schacht's persuasion – collectively the *'Reaktion'*, who had supported Hitler against Röhm; they had seen the ss take the place of the sa and now perceived all too clearly where the *Reich* was being driven. They were not, in most cases, against the general aims of the eastern strategy, rather appalled at the haste and economic and political recklessness with which it was being conducted. Many foresaw probably not the ultimate abyss, but certainly the moral bog into which the country had been drawn.

To Hess they were enemies. For him the Führer remained the great strategist who saw far into the future;[16] 'for him', in Leitgen's words, 'the so-called Führer decision was sacrosanct'.[17] This is evident from the speech he made to the *Gau* – and *Kreisleiters* – (Party regional and district leaders) at the end of the Nuremberg Party Rally in September 1937. It was not a public speech, so he could say mostly what he thought – not that he ever enjoyed speech-making. Ilse revealed that he 'sweated blood' before every one and, although he seldom drank alcohol, he always had a small bottle of pink champagne before a speech; only then could he summon up the strength to go to the podium.[18]

On this occasion he began by reminding his 'old battle comrades' how the Nuremberg Party Days now attracted the eyes of the whole world and how the speeches, especially the Führer's speech, gained from year to year in significance for the world. 'Each Party Day becomes a new milestone in the history of the battle against Bolshevism. And this battle decides the history of our world.'[19]

Each one of them, he continued, stood under the searchlight of publicity. If they had criticisms about ministries or public authorities, they should direct them to those responsible. Referring to his own role as 'the wailing wall of the movement', he told them that for those who off-loaded their frustrations on to him, 'it must suffice for you to know that I know about it, you must have confidence in me that I am trying to find a remedy'.

He reminded them that they could not carry on as in the good old days of struggle, letting rip against the Government and throwing down demands: *they* were the Government now and ultimately the Führer might have to grant their demands to the prejudice of his own measures. In this respect, as a soldierly movement, they had to maintain discipline. And he urged them always to put the true facts before the people. It was astonishing what could be done if reason and self-sacrifice were mobilised, astonishing what could be done if one had the *will*. He proceeded to illustrate this with an example from foreign trade.

There were, he told them, a considerable number of German firms who still employed Jews as their representatives abroad. If one queried it, one was told it *had* to be on economic grounds; trade would be injured otherwise and so on. There were cases, however, where these supposedly indispensable Jews also represented foreign rivals and took part in the boycott of German goods. The Party had not been idle here. The Party foreign trade office had worked on these firms, achieving successes here and there, and the result had not been a diminution of sales:

On the contrary, the AEG, for example, wrote to the Party that the replacement of Jewish representatives by Germans had given 'a huge stimulus', and the higher costs associated with the change had not only been recovered, but had resulted 'above that in sales and financial advantages which are already of considerable significance'.[20]

This proved, he asserted, that despite the initial scepticism of economists, National Socialist fundamentals could be applied successfully to trade. He went on to discuss German-Spanish trade in the light of the Spanish Civil War and the difficulties raised by 'all the forces of liberalism and Freemasonry'; he cited examples of Jews or half-Jews and Freemasons working against German interests in the Spanish peninsula:

What does it signify if some Jews here or there become saucy again? It serves above all as a reminder of the Jewish question, which otherwise we could too easily forget: because in large areas today the Jew appears so little that there is a danger it will be forgotten what a role he once played. And it has already been suggested to me by those who have returned from journeys to Vienna and Budapest that the leadership of the Party should be sent to these beautiful cities of the Danube from time to time; every one of them would certainly come home newly armed with pitilessness and hate.

What did it signify, he went on, if Freemasons considered it necessary now and then to repeat their old assertions? And what 'in comparison to the great development' – the Nazi movement – was the significance of Freemasons, Jews and other enemies in what was perhaps their last manifestation? They should not neglect these people; on the contrary they must watch everything, report everything – 'only do not get annoyed by taking them too seriously'. He turned to the priests.

The less we give them occasion to divert the attention of the *Volk* on to them and their Churches, the more we can attend to the great work in peace and demonstrate ever new achievements, the more the religious concept will pale into insignificance. Until the time comes when the next generation who have passed through the Hitler Youth, the League of German Girls, the Labour Service, the Party becomes the true bearer of the life of our *Volk*; then the last footing of those who sow unrest will have been removed – the *Volk* however will stand ever more reverentially before God, who is with them.

Here we have all Hess's chief concerns as Leitgen itemised them: 'the Church question, the Jewish question and the HJ'.[21] After which he soon returned to his main obsession, 'the greatest world enemy, Bolshevism ... *the* destroyer of the peace of the world'. He attacked 'the repulsive Jew Finkelstein-Litvinov', the Soviet Foreign Minister, who, he said, was seeking to destroy world peace at 'a so-called Mediterranean Conference with his Old Testament abuse of Italy and Germany', but so stupidly 'as the Jew usually acts when he really draws near the danger zone' that even British and French newspapers not suspected of anti-Semitism or Fascist leanings were casting doubt on his manoeuvres.

The danger that Bolshevism represented for the world, he stated, was increased by the fact that this 'power instrument of Jewry' was not bound territorially. It had its exponents in most countries and it was only if one considered how in those countries Freemasons and Jews exerted their effect – usually in the background – that one could understand much which would otherwise be incomprehensible, for instance, England's practical support of Bolshevism. Britain had every reason to extirpate the epidemic root and branch – he used Hitler's phrase '*mit Stumpf und Stiel auszurotten*' – since she had within her world Empire hundreds of millions of coloured subjects who were not exactly blessed with earthly goods, who could all too easily threaten the fundamentals of the Empire.

But England's attitude is determined by the loathing of her pig-headed democrats for the National Socialist and Fascist regimes – through Freemasonry and Jewish forces who make their influence felt in favour of Bolshevism – naturally under clever camouflage.

The same went for France. The purpose of the Franco-Soviet alliance was to attack Germany between them as soon as the string-pullers considered it appropriate. In consequence it was the common goal of Italy and Germany to prevent the 'Bolshevisation' of Spain as well.

The world had to thank the historical personalities of Hitler and Mussolini that it can still be called a culture-world. Without these two men Jewish-Asiatic barbarism would reign in the one-time centre of culture. A higher providence gave these men to this world to save its culture. We are permitted to hope that this higher providence will hold them side by side to fulfil their mission.

The determining factor in their relations with other countries, he went on, was their attitude to the world danger of Bolshevism. This was the key to their relationship with Japan, whose impulse to Continental expansion must lead to lasting conflict with Soviet Russia. So he dealt with the previous year's German-Japanese anti-Comintern Treaty.

Like Hitler, Goebbels, Himmler and the other Nazi speakers, Hess characterised the country and the forces Germany was arming to attack – or in the case of the internal 'Jewish-Bolshevik conspiracy' had already attacked – as threats, not as victims. It was a remarkable reversal of roles, known to psychologists as 'projection', which shows through his speech time and again.

Germany is the antipode of Bolshevism. But how small is the basis of this antipode. One looks at the globe and recognises with a shudder the little speck in the middle of oceans and continents that is called Germany!

He finished with an appeal to make 'comradeship' the first rule of their creed and to be a 'battle ready, loyal and thereby true comradeship for Adolf Hitler!'

He led the customary 'Sieg Heil!'

It was an important speech, revealing Hess as fanatical as his Führer; and, while not so extreme in expression as Himmler in his secret speeches to his higher ss officers, Hess expressed precisely the same world view of the conspiracy of Jews, Freemasons and Bolshevism in the same terms of 'pitilessness and hate'. But it is also interesting for reflecting the decisive turn Germany had taken away from the western democracies some weeks before Hitler drew the consequences of this to the attention of his Foreign Minister, von Neurath, his War Minister, von Blomberg, and his service chiefs, von Fritsch, Raeder and Göring. During this conference on 5 November 1937 – usually known as the Hossbach Conference after the adjutant who wrote up the unofficial minutes, Colonel Hossbach – Hitler outlined his strategy for the two-phase assault on world power: firstly, the incorporation into the *Reich* of Austria and Czechoslovakia, and the drive east for *Lebensraum*; and secondly the acquisition of overseas colonies. He referred to Britain, whom he had wooed so recently, and France as their two 'hate enemies' who would not welcome a German colossus in the middle of Europe; but, despite the risks, and he reminded them of the risks Frederick the Great and Bismarck had had to run, he would begin the first stage at the latest by 1943–45, when their rearmament would have peaked and before the other powers could catch up. However, if the foreign political situation appeared favourable before then, he would seize the opportunity – possibly as early as next year, 1938.

Raeder, bribed by a huge increase in the Navy's steel allocation and the vision of a fantastic oceanic fleet, and Göring, master of the Four-Year Plan, bowed to their Führer's genius. Von Neurath, von Blomberg and von Fritsch, convinced that Britain and France would intervene, and knowing that German forces were not yet equal to a major war, raised objections. Within a few months all three had gone. First, at the end of November, von Neurath was replaced as Foreign Minister by von Ribbentrop; at the same time diplomats of the old school serving as ambassadors in Vienna, Rome and Tokyo were replaced by men more attuned to the Party; also Schacht, who had wanted to resign when he lost the economic argument to Keppler and Göring that summer, was replaced by Walther Funk, representative of the views of Himmler's Freundeskreis and the IG. Early the following year von Blomberg and von Fritsch both found themselves enmeshed in sexual scandals and resigned. In Blomberg's place Hitler appointed himself Supreme Commander of the Armed Forces (Wehrmacht); in von Fritsch's place as Army Commander in Chief, he appointed the more malleable von Brauchitsch. Of more significance was a change in the Army command structure whereby the *Wehrmachtamt*, a germ cell of younger, Nazified officers in the War Ministry introduced to co-ordinate the three fighting services, was raised in status to *Oberkommando der Wehrmacht* (OKW) – Armed Service High Command – and provided with a completely pliable chief, General Keitel. Thus Hitler formed one of his wonted parallel lines of command to rival and by-pass the Army General Staff in the heart of the *Reaktion*'s power structure.

10
WAR

The wild card in 'England *Politik*' was the Duke of Windsor. As Prince of Wales and during his brief reign as King Edward VIII he had made no secret of his belief that the peace of Europe depended on an alliance between Great Britain and Germany, nor had he disguised his admiration for Hitler. When he was forced to abdicate because of his determination to marry the American divorcee Wallace Simpson, Ribbentrop lost all hope in the success of his mission to London. He reported that Britain would fight to prevent Germany becoming paramount in Europe; he also reported that the abdication had been arranged because the British Government could not be certain that Edward would co-operate in an anti-German policy.

In October 1937, the former King of England and his wife made a visit to Germany described as 'for the purpose of studying housing and working conditions'.[1] He had been advised against going; his inspection of Hitler's achievements in housing and employment was bound to be used for propaganda, as of course it was; that was the purpose of the invitation. The trip was hosted by the alcoholic leader of the Labour Front, Dr Ley, and included meetings with Hitler and the top echelon of the regime in their own homes. Hess's turn came towards the end of the month. Ilse was at this time heavily pregnant with their first child; she felt daunted by the thought of receiving 'the most elegant and *mondaine* woman of the century', as she described the Duchess of Windsor in a letter to Hess's mother in Egypt; 'you can imagine how hugely *mondaine* I look at present! vvvv.'[2] Her apprehensions proved groundless. In her next letter she described the Duchess as 'a very lovable, charming, warm and clever person', whose affection for the Duke, 'which she did not attempt to conceal even before us strangers', captivated them all.

Ernst Bohle, Hess's chief of the Foreign Organisation, interpreted on this occasion. It is probably the dinner he described having attended at Hess's house in Munich-Harlaching when he was interrogated in 1945:

'We all talked about Germany and England. During the whole talk there was nothing but an understanding between Germany and England, and not in the diplomatic and political way, but coming from the depths of his [Hess's] heart. That was his opinion; there is no doubt about that.'[3]

During the course of their talk Hess took the Duke up to his attic study to show him his collection of model warships and to refight the Battle of Jutland. As for Ilse, she and the Duke were talking together 'so brilliantly' by the end of dinner, as she put it in her letter, that the others were simply listening and they forgot to leave the table.

Both Hess and Ilse were hoping their child would be a boy;[4] on 18 November their wish was granted. At the time Hess was staying with Hitler at the sumptuous residence and headquarters complex he had constructed around the villa high above Berchtesgaden, which the two of them had shared in the early 'time of struggle'. Now it was called the Berghof, which might be translated appropriately as 'Mountain Court'. From a letter Hess wrote to his mother in January 1938 describing life there, it is evident that he was not a frequent visitor. It is as breathless with new detail as his letters about 'the Tribune' from Landsberg: the Führer, it appeared, was more nocturnal here than in Berlin; he liked to watch a film in the evening, then sit talking through the night, not retiring until morning. He was not woken until one or two in the afternoon. After lunch with adjutants and house guests, the party usually strolled up to a tea pavilion he had had built with magnificent views over Salzburg. Afterwards they were driven back to the house, where Hitler devoted himself to plans for rebuilding Berlin and other cities drawn up by professionals to his own sketches. One of the courtiers Hess mentioned in his letter, although he did not describe him as such, was the architect Albert Speer.[5]

Speer's recollections confirm the impression that Hess was an infrequent guest. He described Hess arriving for dinner at the Chancellery in Berlin every two weeks or so followed by an adjutant bearing a container of his special diet food to be heated in the Chancellery kitchen, until Hitler tired of the performance and told him if he could not eat the meals prepared by his own 'first-class diet cook' he would have to eat at home. 'After that Hess seldom appeared at the meals.'[6] On the other hand Hanfstaengl's memoirs suggest that Hess had never been a frequent member of Hitler's lunch or dinner circle.[7]

Whether he was slipping away from his Führer, as most memoirs and accounts of the period suggest, there can be little doubt that was how Hess perceived it. He had always been jealous of rivals for Hitler's favour, even in the closed confines of Landsberg. Now the men whom he had raised, particularly Himmler, Ribbentrop, even his own chief of staff,

Martin Bormann, had direct access to the Führer and might be given instructions which by the law of the Führer's system and the 'Führer's decision' or the 'Führer's wish' might not be revealed outside the chain of command of their own empire. According to Bohle after the war, Bormann controlled Hess's personal office and was always with Hitler; 'He saw Hitler ten times as much as Hess did.'[8] Hans Frank's death cell memoirs lend authority to Bohle's statement, which might otherwise be regarded as an effort to exculpate Hess from the war crimes with which he was charged. Bormann, wrote Frank, used his position in Hess's staff to usurp the influence of all other Party leaders 'always under the skilful pretext of securing Party unity'; Hess not only suffered this, but actively promoted it, believing he was thereby promoting his own influence at the Führer's court:[9]

From about 1937 Bormann was in the truest sense of the word 'near the Führer', a cringing, dissembling, power-hungry figure who obstructed all the good and, by calculating exploitation, realised all the bad. What Himmler did for the State by systematically and hysterically building up the despot-state, Bormann did for the movement.[10]

Here Frank was probably unburdening his own sense of guilt at having followed the Führer: Bormann's and Himmler's success was surely built on adaptation to Hitler's will. Nevertheless, it was the fact of their influence which preyed on Hess's mind. His doctor, Ludwig Schmitt, recalled after the war that Hess had told him of his anxieties about Bormann and Dr Ley usurping his own position with the Führer; he had also broken down and wept over Röhm's death, according to Doctor Schmitt, blaming himself for insisting on the execution when Hitler had wanted to spare their old comrade.[11]

Whether from conscience and surely not over Röhm's death alone, or from a sense of losing to others his intimate position with the Führer who was so apt to overrule his recommendations on Party affairs, there is no doubt that the earlier signs of imbalance in Hess's character had become marked. His frequent bouts of illness, chiefly griping pains in the abdomen, forced him to bed sometimes for fourteen days at a time. Leitgen thought this 'possibly an expression of the very unstable character of a nervously sensitive and pensive man', but he also perceived that Hess was 'continually tormented with doubts as to whether the course steered was correct, for which he compensated with his belief in the Führer's genius'.[12]

Von Krosigk expressed the same idea: 'He [Hess] had recognised that the conflict between good and evil which ran through the whole development of the NSDAP played itself out in the person of the Führer and had to be decided there. But his loyalty to the Führer prevented him

'The Tribune', as Hess called Hitler during their detention together in Landsberg fortress in 1924, when *Mein Kampf* was born

Hess and his faithful girlfriend, Ilse Pröhl, who took the photo in Landsberg, seen here shortly after their marriage in 1927; both enjoyed hiking, skiing and the open-air life in the Bavarian Alps

The 'Time of Struggle': (above) Hitler arriving in Berlin to campaign with his principle adherents in December 1931; Hess is just behind him and Ernst Röhm second from left; (below) in Munich with Hermann Göring on his left, Hess seated at his right

After the 'Seizure of Power': the Führer in characteristic stance with hands protecting his groin, and his most fervent disciple at his Alpine eyrie, the Berghof on the Obersalzberg

In the cockpit of his Messerschmitt in March 1934, when he won the 'Round the Zugspitze' air race

Ernst Röhm, Chief of the SA, and Hess in the uniform of an SS-Obergruppenführer six months before the SA leadership was cut down by the SS in 'the Night of the Long Knives'

With his Chief of Staff, Martin Bormann, who usurped
his position to become chief power broker of the Reich

Propaganda Minister Dr Goebbels, Reichsführer-SS Himmler,
Hess in SS-Obergruppenführer uniform, Hitler and General
Blomberg at the Sportpalast, Berlin in 1937

Hitler taking the salute at a torchlight rally in 1938 (after
Blomberg had been removed), with his Deputy behind

Ilse, Hitler and Hess in the extensive grounds of the Hess's Munich-Harlaching villa

Hess's mentor and friend, Professor Karl Haushofer (second from left), and his son (inset) Albrecht, who served Hess as his 'England-expert'

Hess represents his Führer at a dedication to Austrian Nazis in 1938

interfering in the process. He suffered from this, but found no way out.'[13]

As Leitgen suggested, his way out was probably through psychosomatic illness, but also in resort to astrology and ever more bizarre forms of fringe medicine, faith healers, hypnotists, magnetists and dieticians. According to Hanfstaengl, it went so far that he could not go to bed without first checking the direction of the underlying water with a divining rod.[14] Obviously this was hyperbole, but Hess did suffer from sleeplessness; he mentioned it in at least one speech, and his secretary, Hildegard Fath, described him trying out one cure he had been recommended by going to bed at five in the afternoon and rising for a walk in the early hours of the morning.[15]

There was a more positive side to his interest in fringe medicine. Germany had a tradition of healers – *Heilpraktiker* or *Heilkundiger* – who advocated outdoor living, natural foods and a complete reorientation away from urban habits of life, which keyed in with that strand of the Nazi *Weltanschauung* springing from the desire to return to the simple life close to the soil enjoyed by their Germanic forbears. Himmler shared all Hess's interests in natural cures, collected old *Volk* recipes and grew herbs in extensive plantations worked by concentration camp labour; Hitler took pills made up from the faeces of Bulgarian peasants. 'Natural' medicine also keyed in with the mystical biological core of the *Weltanschauung* which saw all history as determined by natural biological and racial laws. Hess's Party Office for *Volks* Health under Gerhard Wagner, which was involved in the preservation of the genetic health of the *Volk* through the sterilisation laws, also strove to bring 'natural' medicine into use with or alongside conventional medicine and so to synthesise a truly National Socialist form of medicine. Wagner was as enthusiastic as Hess, but, against the organised opposition of conventionally trained doctors, he had eventually to admit defeat.[16]

While Hess's anxiety over his position with the Führer was natural in view of his reclusiveness and the ambitions of his thrustful, intriguing rivals and subordinates, there is no evidence that he was pushed to the margins of influence or that Hitler ever lost his trust and affection for him, rather the reverse. Hitler was a sponsor or, in Christian terms, godfather to Hess's son, together with Karl Haushofer; the boy was name 'Wolf' according to Ilse's contemporary letter to her parents-in-law because that was what Hitler was called during the 'time of struggle',[17] 'Rüdiger' because he was 'one of the finest figures of German saga', 'Adolf' after the Führer and 'Karl' after 'the General'. Of course this proves little more than Hess's continuing devotion to Hitler and Haushofer.

On 4 February 1938, however, Hess was appointed a member of Hitler's secret Cabinet Council. Again it could be argued this was a hollow gesture since cabinets and councils had no place in the Führer's system, and there are no records of this one having met. Yet the date of the appointment is suggestive, a day before the announcement of the changes in the Army command structure which marked the end of the General Staff as an effective bastion of conservative opposition. Was the appointment in recognition of Hess's contribution to the downfall of von Blomberg and von Fritsch, in which case he was still at the very centre of affairs, or merely to placate him on Göring's promotion to Reichsmarschall for his part in the affair?

The action against the Generals was prepared in conjunction with the take-over of Austria; here Hess's intelligence and fifth column organisation of Germans abroad played a crucial role, and he and Himmler were the first Nazi leaders into Vienna on the day of the *Anschluss*. Could it be that the Cabinet Council did meet informally somewhat as the Ministerial Council for the Defence of the Reich, to which Hess was appointed on 30 August 1939 (the day before the onslaught on Poland which triggered the Second World War) in order to provide data on which the Führer took decisions on the *Anschluss* – March 12th 1938 – then the incorporation of the Sudetenland after the Munich agreement – September 29th 1938 – the annexation of the rump of Czechoslovakia – March 15th 1939 – and finally the assault on Poland on September 1st 1939? If not it is difficult to understand why the Council was established in the first place. Even if it did not meet as a Council there can be no question of the vital importance of Hess's lines of intelligence from the western capitals, especially from London where the issue of European war was ultimately to be decided; nor is there any doubt that until the final move into Poland Hitler received the right advice from that quarter. He did incorporate Austria and Czechoslovakia as he had said he would at the 'Hossbach' meeting of November 1937, and Britain and France did not intervene. The strong presumption must be that Hess and his secret diplomatic intelligence chief, Pfeffer von Salomon, were at the very centre of these events.

It appears Albrecht Haushofer was also involved; there is an atlas passed down to the present Duke of Hamilton in which an area of Czechoslovakia has been marked, and a note hand-written by his father states that Albrecht Haushofer drew this to show the portion of the country Hitler wanted.[18] Whether or not Hamilton was reporting directly to the SIS, he must surely have passed this news to Halifax or Chamberlain.

As for Hess's frequent bouts of sickness and sleeplessness at this period, the presumption must be that Alfred Leitgen perceived the true cause, namely that he was 'continually tormented with doubts as to whether the course steered was correct'.[19] There is support for this in the diary of Ulrich von Hassell. In December 1938 he recorded Hess's old friends, the Bruckmanns telling him of Hess's despair over the nationwide pogrom in November known as *Reichskristallnacht* when mobs were incited to go on the rampage against Jewish shops and businesses. Hess had been depressed 'as never before' and had left the Bruckmanns in no doubt he 'thoroughly disapproved'. He had beseeched the Führer to refrain, but without success; Goebbels, he said, had been the real instigator of the action.[20]

In August 1939, as Ribbentrop brought home a deal with the enemy, Soviet Russia, and Hitler gave orders for the assault on Poland whom Great Britain was committed by treaty to defend, Hess, his world turned on its head, had no recourse but to believe, desperately, in the Führer's genius.

That he did so is revealed in a speech he made at the seventh Annual Congress of Foreign Germans at Graz in the evening of 25 August. A few hours before Hitler had ordered 'Case White', the assault on Poland, to begin in the early hours of the following morning. He postponed this as the British government showed it intended to honour its obligations and Mussolini declined to honour his, but it is doubtful if Hess knew of the postponement as he rose to speak.

He began by stressing Germany's forbearance in the face of Polish incitements to war and mistreatment of Germans living within Poland, and he invited the British Prime Minister, Chamberlain, to come and inspect the German refugee camps, see with his own eyes and hear with his own ears the cruel reality of Polish outrages. To storms of applause he said:

There is bloodshed, Herr Chamberlain! There are dead! Innocent people have died . . .

The responsibility for this, however, lies with England, which talks of peace and fans the flames of war. England that has pointblank refused all the Führer's proposals for peace throughout the years. She not only refused these proposals, but before and after the Munich agreement threatened Germany by arming Czechoslovakia. As the Führer extinguished this blaze, England incited Poland to refuse the Führer's peace proposals and to make her appearance as the new threat to Germany from the east.[21]

The reason, he went on, was that Jews and Freemasons wanted the war against Germany, 'against this Germany in which they have lost their power'. Despite all, however, they had failed to bring in Russia to complete the circle of aggressors. 'Germany and Russia have made their contribution to the peace of the world with their non-aggression and consultation pact'. He concluded with an affirmation of faith that providence was with Germany, 'because we have faith that providence sent the Führer as our deliverance from deepest necessity. In standing by the Führer we fulfil the will of that which sent us the Führer. We Germans – we stand by the colours of the Führer – come what may !'

Chamberlain and his Foreign Secretary, Lord Halifax, like their counterparts in July 1914, were attempting to divert war by convening talks. Their line corresponded to suggestions Albrecht Haushofer had made in a letter to his friend 'Douglo' Clydesdale on 16 July. He had warned then that 'any date after the middle of August may prove to be the fatal one', and had suggested that as 'the terrific forms of modern war' would make a reasonable peace impossible, they simply had to prevent one starting. He had suggested a compromise: 'some sort of change in the Polish Corridor' through east Prussia, and a long-term settlement between Germany and Poland 'based upon considerable territorial changes *combined* with population changes on the Greek-Turkish model . . .'[22]

Haushofer did not post the letter from Berlin, but while cruising on the Norwegian coast, and he instructed Clydesdale to destroy it when he had read it 'and destroy it most carefully'. Then he added that he could show it *'personally'* either to Lord Halifax or to his Under-Secretary, Butler, 'if *you* see fit of course'; however, no notes should be taken, his name should never be mentioned and the letter should be destroyed immediately afterwards. He signed himself: 'Yours ever sincerely A'.

In fact, Clydesdale had shown the letter to Winston Churchill as well and, instead of destroying it, had deposited it in his bank. However, the conspiratorial sound of Albrecht's instructions suggest either that he sent the letter in his 'opposition' hat or that he intended Clydesdale to assume this. Certainly the 'appeasement' policy he had suggested bore similarities to the messages which had been reaching the British Government from the civilian leaders of the German Conservative opposition,[23] although he had gone further in suggesting 'territorial changes' and he had made no mention of the chief point in the other opposition messages, that the British Government should give Hitler unequivocal warning that resort to force would be met by force. Indeed, examined closely, there was little in his message that Hess might not have wanted to convey to Halifax as he saw friendship with Britain, the cornerstone of the *Lebensraum* policy, slipping away and Ribbentrop's agent negotiating a pact with the real enemy in Moscow. Shortly after the date of this letter, a leading member of the civilian opposition, Ulrich von Hassell, had noted in his diary from inside information that the regime was in disarray and wavering for the first time: Ribbentrop was conducting himself like a 'lunatic madman, unbearable in office, has no friends', and was no longer even on good terms with Hess.[24] It is possible, therefore, that Albrecht Haushofer's letter to Douglo Clydesdale was an attempt by Hess – which implies with Hitler's consent – to achieve another 'Munich' settlement over the question of Danzig, the Polish Corridor and the German inhabitants of Poland. However, having been cheated before, the British Government was not prepared to grant Hitler major concessions 'in return for the debased currency of mere undertakings'.[25]

So, finally, the 'England *Politik*' had failed. To prevent the two-front war, a pact had been struck with the devil. Hess was in Berlin as the crisis unfolded; there is a glimpse of him on 28 August in a surviving fragment of Himmler's diary. The British Ambassador had been received by Hitler at the Chancellery that evening. He had brought with him a note reiterating Great Britain's determination to honour her agreement to Poland and concluding that, while a just settlement of the differences between Germany and Poland might open the way to world peace, 'Failure . . . would ruin the hopes of better understanding between Germany and Great Britain, would bring the two countries into conflict, and might well plunge the whole world into war.'[26]

Hitler said he would give his reply next day. After the Ambassador had gone, Himmler noted that Göring, Hess, Bodenschatz and he (Himmler) joined Hitler and Ribbentrop in the conservatory; Hitler appeared to be in a very good mood, mimicking the Ambassador's 'thick English accent'. Despite the clear warning, he was determined to advance, for he told the small group that it was necessary now 'to aim a document at the British (or Poles) that is little less than a masterpiece of diplomacy'.[27] It is a powerful image of the Führer system at the turning point. Probably it was too late to reverse; probably the real turning point had been in the summer of 1936, or in 1934 or in 1933. Now the Führer pretended confidence with his closest advisers on foreign policy and his two principal lieutenants, his Stellvertreter, Hess, and Göring, perceived as the real number two man; but neither of these wanted war with England. Göring was conducting shuttle diplomacy with London through the Swedish businessman Birger Dahlerus and he continued to do so up to and past the morning of 1 September, when German armies launched across the Polish borders; he even offered to fly personally to London – an initiative which was perhaps not lost on Hess – but, so far as is known, neither he nor Hess felt equal to disputing the genius of the Führer. According to Himmler's diary entry, they were content for Hitler to sleep on the problem because, as he told them, he got most of his best ideas in the small hours between five and six a.m.[28]

Yet Hitler was as much a prisoner of the system and the situation he had created. There are striking parallels with the inexorable course of events in the last days of July 1914, when in London the British Government wrestled with its repugnance for war against the arguments of honour and self-preservation, and in Berlin the Kaiser's agitated, over-strained Chancellor, Bethmann Hollweg, answered Admiral Tirpitz, appalled at his strategy, by 'raising his arms to heaven' and saying, 'It is necessary because the Army want to send troops across the frontier'.

PART TWO
FLIGHT

11
PEACE FEELERS

On 3 September, two days after the German armies erupted across the Polish borders, Chamberlain, with the utmost reluctance, fulfilled his pledge to Poland, and France followed suit. Hess's state of mind at this juncture may be gauged from a request he made to Hitler for permission to enter the Luftwaffe to serve as a pilot at the front. Hitler knew his man; he demanded a promise that Hess would not fly an aeroplane for the duration. Hess managed to limit the prohibition to one year.

Behind the advancing thrusts into Poland specially prepared SS Einsatz-kommandos rounded up the leading and intellectual classes and Jews, and hanged or shot them, or used them for murderous sport. The campaign for racial and political health foreshadowed in *Mein Kampf* had begun in earnest. There is little doubt that Hitler had always intended to begin it under the cloak of war. During the 1935 Nuremberg Party Rally he had told Hess's *Volks* Health chief, Gerhard Wagner, that the demands and upheavals of war would smother religious opposition to killing the incurably ill.[1] Secret discussions about methods and procedures for liquidating these unfortunates and the mentally and genetically ill – aggregated as *'lebensunwerte Leben'* (beings unworthy of life) – had continued up to the summer of 1939, when Hitler instructed Gerhard Wagner's successor, Dr Leonardo Conti, to set up such a programme. Conti had refused without formal authority, which Hitler declined to give. Instead Hitler had turned to the head of his Chancellery, Philipp Bouhler, commissioning him and the extreme National Socialist doctor, Karl Brandt, to organise a 'euthanasia' programme for the *'lebensunwerte Leben'*. It was evident, as Martin Bormann remarked, that Hitler did not intend stopping at the mentally ill and incurable; for one thing the instruction sheets produced for the doctors who would have to report patients for the programme listed, after the mentally and genetically ill, the permanently institutionalised and the criminally insane, those 'who do not possess German citizenship or are not of German or kindred

107

blood'. A note explained this: 'Jew, Jewish *Mischling* (cross-breed), 1st or 2nd class, Negro, Negro *Mischling*, Gypsy, Gypsy *Mischling* etc.'[2] This programme could not have been realised without Hess's knowledge and approval; as he had stated in 1934, National Socialism was 'nothing but applied biology',[3] and Gerhard Wagner had been his instrument.

At about the same time that Bouhler had begun setting up this programme in July 1939, the head of his Chancellery Section 2, Viktor Brack, commissioned the chief of Heydrich's criminal police, Arthur Nebe, to develop a suitable killing method. Nebe turned to the head of the chemistry and physics department of his Criminal Technical Institute, Dr Albert Widmann, who advised the use of carbon monoxide gas; shortly afterwards, work was started on prototype gas chambers, the first of which were completed that winter.

That these plans were set in motion just before the onslaught on Poland is a clear indication that the racial vision at the core of the *Weltanschauung* was a main driving force behind the war; indeed Robert Jay Lifton concludes from his study of Nazi doctors that it was the prime driving force: 'the deepest impulses behind the war had to do with the sequence of sterilisation, direct medical killing and genocide'.[4] If this is true, it is difficult to imagine how Hess, so intimate with Hitler and Gerhard Wagner, could have failed to understand the fate planned for European Jewry.

Nor could he have been ignorant of the design for Poland. As Heydrich explained it to his departmental heads and the commanders of his ss Einsatzkommandos on 21 September, the Polish nation was to be expunged from the map and the Poles themselves, whose leaders and intellectuals were all to be liquidated, were to become a migrant workforce for the *Reich*. Again, this was not a policy produced hurriedly after the outmatched Polish forces had been overrun by *Blitzkrieg*; it emerged from the fundamental 'master race' principle of *Weltanschauung*. After the brief campaign was over, on 8 October 1939, and the Russians had advanced into eastern Poland as agreed in the secret protocol of Ribbentrop's pact with Stalin in August, Hess added his signature after Hitler, Göring and the Interior Minister, Dr Frick, to a decree announcing the dismemberment of the German-occupied western half of the country: it was divided into new German *Gaus* and a rump in the south named the '*General Gouvernement Polen*'; here all Jews were to be concentrated for the first 'short-term' stage before what Heydrich termed 'the ultimate solution' to the Jewish problem.

Great Britain and France had made no effort to save Poland. There had been no military plans to do so and no political will in either country; indeed Chamberlain and his political adviser, Horace Wilson, had been seeking ways out of their pledge long after the German assault had begun. Moreover Chamberlain, Horace Wilson and the Foreign Secretary, Lord Halifax, known not simply for his Christian piety and love of hunting as 'the Holy Fox', still hoped to escape from the war without serious fighting. In this they reflected powerful groups from the Royal Family and court circles, the great landed houses, the Governor of the Bank of England, City financiers, leading industrialists, press lords, service chiefs and influential military historians, notably J. F. C. Fuller and Basil Liddell Hart, to humanitarian intellectuals and, strangely at this stage, 'peace' groups who took their instructions from Moscow.

At the political end of this spectrum were the considerations that war with Germany must entail ruinous expenditure and a scale of state intervention which would destroy liberal democracy.[5] More accurately, it might destroy the existing order; as A. L. Rowse, an aspiring Labour candidate during the period of appeasement, described it: 'The Tories connived at sacrificing their country's interests for their class interests.'[6] Like the power élites in Germany, they had played the Nazi's game long past the hour they could call a halt. Now that hard choices had to be made Chamberlain especially believed that, if they continued the war, the British Empire must end up dependent on the United States. It was, in any case, widely believed among the landed and propertied classes that American hostility to the British Empire was grounded on US economic imperial ambitions. Dependence on America applied as much in grand strategic terms. After two decades of disarmament, Great Britain was in no position to defend her far Eastern possessions and trading interests against Japan, while facing Germany on the Continent and Italy in the Mediterranean. With vivid memories of the terrible casualties in the trenches in the First World War, service thinking had returned to what appeared to be the traditional certainties of a British 'blue water' policy, withdrawing from Continental entanglement to use all resources on a fleet and air force capable of defending the homeland and Empire. They had to play for time. After time wasted, policy had shrunk to 'gaining the time needed to rebuild British military power'.[7]

The financial arguments were as powerful as the military and political: German and British banks had collaborated for decades. The Governor of the Bank of England, Montagu Norman, City and big business circles had looked to resist US finance and reassert Great Britain's former banking predominance on the basis of extending the Anglo-German partnership.[8] Hitler's economic policies pulled in the opposite direction, but, should Hitler be removed, there were rational German economists in the wings.

The threat of international Bolshevism was another prime factor with all circles opposed to the war. A strong and prosperous Germany was seen as the best antidote to the spread of the contagion. The young Jock Colville, just appointed one of Chamberlain's private secretaries, noted a talk he had with the Prime Minister's Principal Private Secretary, Arthur Rucker, on 13 October: Rucker believed that Communism was now a greater danger than Nazi Germany; it was a plague that did not stop at national boundaries, and with the advance of the Soviet Union into half of Poland, the eastern European countries would find themselves exposed to the danger: 'It is thus vital that we should play our hand very carefully with Russia, and not destroy the possibility of uniting, if necessary, with a new German Government against the common danger. What is needed is a moderate conservative reaction in Germany; the overthrow of the present regime by the Army chiefs.'[9]

This was Chamberlain's policy precisely. At that moment two secret service heads of station in Holland, Major Stevens and Captain Payne Best, were attempting to establish contact with the German opposition group around the former Chief of the General Staff, Beck, known to be planning a generals' revolt against Hitler. The group was penetrated by double agents and the intermediary whom Stevens and Best finally met was Walther Schellenberg, chief of Heydrich's foreign counter-intelligence service, now disguised as 'Captain Schaemmel' of the transport division. They discussed peace terms, the British officers relaying Chamberlain's desire to deal with a 'reasonable' Germany – with Hitler removed – and to create a league of European states under the leadership of Great Britain to provide a front against militant Communism.[10] Schellenberg promised to report back to his superiors, then, so he told his American interrogator in 1948, meet the British again furnished with details of the arrangements to depose Hitler by force. He went on: 'Furthermore it was agreed that possibly, and this was a possibility I did have to anticipate, I would have to report to Lord Halifax and go there by aeroplane to see him. Due to the necessity of maintaining contact we exchanged modern radio equipment and we arranged for special secret codes and so on.'[11]

At the same time a Sudeten German aristocrat, Prinz Max zu Hohenlowe, was talking to Britons in Switzerland about the possibility of removing Hitler so that peace talks could be started with Göring;[12] Hohenlowe was a member of the financial-industrial Circle of Friends of the Reichsführer ss and his approaches were, unbeknown to the British, also on behalf of Himmler – possibly Ribbentrop too. Göring's Swedish friend Birger Dahlerus was making similar approaches to the British Government,[13] and Alfred Rosenberg had previously despatched an agent to Switzerland to contact Baron de Ropp, his go-between to Group Captain Winterbotham of British Air Intelligence. All these approaches stressed that the only beneficiary of war between Germany and Great

Britain would be Russia, the only result the 'Bolshevisation' of Europe, including England.[14] It was a massive 'peace offensive' deception orchestrated by Hitler, buoyed up now with his lightning victory in Poland and determined to move against the western alliance to ensure it could never again interfere with his plans.[15]

The approaches were taken by Chamberlain and Halifax as signs of genuine dissent within Germany; they were so confident of the results promised by the secret channel through Holland that on 1 November Chamberlain reported it to the war cabinet. The response was not as he had expected. Winston Churchill, First Lord of the Admiralty, was particularly unhappy and warned Halifax privately of the great danger that the Germans might use the talks to undermine French confidence in Britain 'with possibly fatal effects'.[16]

Nevertheless the intelligence play continued. 'Schaemmel' promised to bring the 'General' leading the revolt against Hitler into Holland to meet the two British officers on 8 November. At the last moment he postponed the meeting, arranging another rendezvous for the following day, at the Café Bacchus in Venlo close by the customs post just inside the Dutch-German border. That night German radio broadcast news of an unsuccessful bomb attempt on Hitler's life after his annual speech at the Bürgerbräukeller in Munich to commemorate the 1923 *putsch*. It seemed to Stevens and Payne Best as they drove to Venlo in Best's Rolls Royce that their 'General' might have tried to move already. However, as they approached the Café Bacchus an armoured car holding an ss snatch squad crashed the border barrier from Germany and, after a brief exchange of fire mortally wounding a Dutch agent with the two Englishmen, both were seized and carried into Germany.

Debate continues about the real purpose of the 'Venlo incident' – since Schellenberg was a compulsive liar and his post-war account is patently false. The simplest explanation is that it was engineered in tandem with the Bürgerbräu bomb as a deception or provocation in the manner of the Reichstag fire. As with the fire, tactical control was exercised by Reinhard Heydrich; Schellenberg/Schaemmel was his man; so was the leader of the ss snatch squad, ss Sturmbannführer Alfred Naujocks. No proof has been found to link Heydrich with the lone former Communist named Georg Elser arrested for placing the bomb in the Bürgerbräukeller, but the whole affair bears his hallmark, and it is significant that no one in the security service was charged with negligence. Elser himself was neither tortured nor executed, like those connected with the 20 July 1944 attempt on Hitler's life, but was shut away in comparatively easy conditions in a concentration camp for the rest of the war. Finally, just before the camp was liberated in 1945, he was shot on Gestapo orders.[17]

The Bürgerbräu/Venlo provocation served many purposes. Since

Stevens and Payne Best had operated from the Hague with Dutch and Belgian connivance, it could have been used as a pretext for launching the blow against the West through Holland and Belgium or, as seems to have happened, to reinforce disinformation about the imminence of such a blow to cause doubts about the reliability of certain sources. Probably the main purpose, however, was to cow those generals who were against the winter offensive in the west and were tentatively dusting off earlier plans to arrest Hitler – for the Führer's apparently narrow escape attributed by all organs of propaganda to 'Divine Providence' had created a surge of sentiment and loyalty for him throughout the *Reich*. When, on 21 November, Himmler released the findings of an inquiry he had commissioned into the bomb plot, he confirmed officially inspired allegations that Elser had been a tool of British intelligence, operating from the 'British terror and revolution *Zentrale* in the Hague'.[18]

As for Hess's role in this double provocation, it may be significant that he was originally scheduled to make the Bürgerbräu address in place of Hitler. Since he was identified with the efforts to achieve conciliation with Britain, there was speculation in diplomatic circles that his appearance in the leading role at this major festival of the 'old fighters' in the capital of the movement might be another sign that Hitler wanted peace. Possibly it was only after Schellenberg's intelligence game made it certain Chamberlain was not prepared to make peace on any terms so long as the present German regime remained in power that Hitler gave vent to his anger and derision by sanctioning the plot to implicate the British Secret Service in the 'assassination' attempt. 'And behind them', the official release stated, 'stand the British war agitators and their criminal satellites, the Jews.'[19]

The head of the British Special Intelligence Service – SIS or outside the organisation MI6 – Admiral Sinclair, had died shortly before the Venlo incident. On 29 November his deputy, Sir Stewart Menzies, was confirmed as his successor, traditionally known as 'C'. Churchill had argued against Menzies's appointment, preferring a sailor, the Director of Naval Intelligence, chiefly because he felt that Menzies was identified with those circles who still thought in terms of a compromise peace with Germany. As these included the most powerful members of Chamberlain's war cabinet, Halifax, Sir Samuel Hoare and Sir John Simon, his was a minority view.

Menzies was to prove a remarkable 'C', who has been compared to that paragon of spymasters Sir Francis Walsyngham. He had been born into the very centre of British power. It was rumoured that he was the illegitimate son of the Prince of Wales, later Edward VII, but it is fairly certain his real father was Sir George Holford, a grandee at Edward's Court, who later married Menzies's mother, a great beauty and Court favourite. In *Who's Who* Stewart Menzies described himself as the son of Lady Holford.

He had received his baptism of fire in the First World War, like Hitler and Hess, outside Ypres, and had served through 1914 and 1915 with great distinction and *sang froid*, inwardly detesting the slaughter which cut down all his group from Eton and all the regimental officers with whom he had gone to war. At the end of 1915 he had been posted to the intelligence section of the staff of the Commander-in-Chief in France; there he found his niche in life. He was soon recognised as a brilliant intelligence officer and after the war was invited to join a department established to counter Communist subversion in England, from where he moved into the Secret Intelligence Service – SIS.

To the outside world Menzies appeared a very private man devoted to his regiment, the Life Guards, and the Beaufort Hunt. He might have been a model for a Buchan hero, known for what he was only to that charmed inner circle which, behind the front of 'liberal democracy' still held ultimate power in the country, the Empire and the world, and who consequently looked at the United States, now flexing its economic strength worldwide with as much suspicion as it regarded international Communism. Menzies dealt with the regular business of the service at SIS headquarters, 54 Broadway, off St James's Park, but used his club, White's, to initiate unofficial agents drawn from the rich and well-connected – his 'honourable correspondents' – for special tasks in the Great Game.[20]

Churchill had every reason to oppose his appointment as 'C'. Menzies had been deeply implicated in the recent failed SIS attempt to by-pass Hitler and negotiate with the German opposition; apart from the possible danger for the Anglo-French alliance, Churchill did not believe in a 'reasonable' Germany; for him German military expansionism, with or without Hitler, was the greatest danger. Judging by the attitudes of the German military, the demands of the German opposition and the aims of big business as since revealed, he was right. He also knew that to defeat Germany they needed the active involvement of the United States; he realised that Menzies was, at the least, cool about America. Above all Menzies was a lynchpin at the concentric hub of those high Tory, Court, City and Service circles which saw *rapprochement* with Germany and even a tacit alliance with her against Communism as the sole means of preserving the Empire. To judge by post-war history, they too were right.

One of the most articulate lobbyists for this view immediately before the outbreak of war was Kenneth de Courcy, secretary and intelligence officer of the Imperial Policy Group. Because of his social and political connections, which extended to the Court and the great landowners, de Courcy had been contacted from as early as 1935 by Army officers anxious about the disparity between Great Britain's imperial commitments and her reduced forces after years of disarmament. The first and most prescient of these was Lieutenant Colonel W. S. Pilcher, Grenadier Guards, a close friend of Stewart Menzies, who, like Menzies, had suffered the loss of most of his contemporaries in the war. Afterwards he had served in eastern Europe, witnessing Bolshevik atrocities at first hand. He had also come to know France well and, forseeing her collapse, had regarded it as folly to be drawn into a Continental alliance with her. De Courcy had become convinced of the soundness of these views from his own travels abroad, and had represented them in reports to Menzies, who had forwarded them to Halifax and Chamberlain. Subsequently Chamberlain had asked for de Courcy's reports to be sent to him direct.[21]

De Courcy also made these views known to leading circles in the Continental capitals, namely that Great Britain's true interest lay in keeping out of Continental entanglements and allowing Hitler and Mussolini a free hand against the Soviet Union. While this was not the policy of the permanent officials of the Foreign Office, who sought ways of reimposing Britain's traditional balancing role on the new Continental realities, it was what Chamberlain's efforts really amounted to. De Courcy – now the Duc de Grantmesnil-Lorraine – has confirmed that it was certainly the view of Menzies and his close circle;[22] it was also the view of the most prestigious military writer of the day, Basil Liddell Hart, and found echo in all three services. Obviously Hess had been keenly aware of this powerful consensus through his diplomatic intelligence service run by Pfeffer von Salomon and from his own contacts: in the summer of 1939, for instance, General Sir Ian Hamilton had invited Hess to stay with him in Scotland, where he hoped he might see Liddell Hart.[23] It helps to explain why Hitler had been so confident in August 1939 that Chamberlain would find some way out of his pledge to Poland.

The view had not only survived the outbreak of war, but the SIS embarrassment at Venlo as well. On 8 January 1940 Lord Halifax saw an agent of the pro-German Lord Brockett named Lonsdale Bryans and gave him official sanction to meet Ulrich von Hassell of the civilian opposition to Hitler in Switzerland. The meeting took place in Arosa on 22 February, Bryans in the guise of a doctor treating von Hassell's son. He delivered the message that, in the event of an alteration of the present regime in Germany, the British Government would not exploit the internal confusion, but would do all in their power to bring about an armistice and negotiate a lasting peace. For his part von Hassell wrote out a memo in English for Bryans to take to Halifax stating that all 'serious-minded people in Germany' considered it important 'to stop this mad war as soon as possible'. He proposed leaving Austria and the Sudeten area within the *Reich*, but re-establishing independent Czech and Polish states with borders approximating those before 1914; what he proposed to do about the Soviet-occupied half of Poland was not stated in the memo.[24] On his return to England on 24 February Bryans reported to the Permanent Under-Secretary – or non-political head – of the Foreign Office, Sir Alexander Cadogan, who granted him facilities for another visit to Switzerland in April.

Meanwhile the *Express* newspaper group's owner, Lord Beaverbrook, friend and First World War colleague of Churchill, decided to back a peace campaign initiated by the Right-wing Labour Member of Parliament for Ipswich R.R. ('Dick') Stokes. Beaverbrook published articles by Liddell Hart in both his *Sunday Express* and *Evening Standard*, and confessed himself one of his 'disciples'.[25] Liddell Hart's private views at this time could not have been more pessimistic: asked by the editor of the *Sunday Pictorial* what was to be done, he replied, 'Come to the best possible terms [with Germany] as soon as possible.' He appraised the situation from the standpoint of a student of war, he went on, and, barring a leader of Napoleon's stature – which he could not see – Great Britain had no chance of avoiding defeat. Liddell Hart also wrote unofficial reports on the strategic situation for Lloyd George, the Liberal Prime Minister who had led the country to victory in the First World War. Lloyd George believed he might be called upon again, this time to negotiate peace, and he feared from a position of weakness, for he too could see no prospect of victory.

Besides these two voices of doom Beaverbrook was, in the words of Sir Robert Vansittart, 'a buddy of Mr Kennedy [the notorious defeatist US Ambassador in London] and most of the "Money-in-our-time" brigade – a detachment of the Fifth Column'.[26] Vansittart, while head of the Foreign Office before the war, had been as vocal as Churchill in warning and trying to rouse successive administrations to positive action about the threat posed by Hitler's Germany. Chamberlain had pushed him into the shadowy post of Chief Diplomatic Adviser – taking private counsel from the wholly unrealistic Horace Wilson. In March 1940 Vansittart advised that Beaverbrook would do a great deal of damage with his peace campaign: '(1) here, (2) in France, (3) in the USA where there is anyhow considerable distrust of us and, (4) he will be a great gift to German propaganda. He should, therefore, be stopped ... For the peace he has in mind would only result without fail in our all having our throats cut in a couple of years ...'[27]

This was Churchill's attitude.

12

CHURCHILL

In April the 'real' war started in the west as German forces invaded Norway. Dissatisfaction with Chamberlain's leadership was brought to a head by deficiencies revealed in the campaign and he resigned, reluctantly. The need was for a 'national' coalition to unite the nation in crisis and, since the Labour Party refused to serve under the conventional Conservative choice, Lord Halifax, Churchill was called to form a Government. By chance on the day he took office, 10 May, Hitler launched his *Blitzkrieg* in the west with a feint through Holland and Belgium.

In Churchill Great Britain had found a leader guided – like Hitler – by instinct, emotion and imagination. Like Hitler, he lacked formal academic training, like him he tended to oversimplify complex issues and extemporise solutions – 'a mind not judicial in any sense, not logical, not analytical' his doctor, Lord Moran, diagnosed;[1] and Jock Colville, whom Churchill took over as private secretary from Chamberlain, observed that 'his mind did not operate in predetermined grooves ... a sudden whim or unexpected judgement caught his family or staff unawares no less frequently than the Cabinet or Defence Committee'.[2] In more conventional Conservative circles he was distrusted as a reckless personal adventurer who lacked judgement. Yet he was a student of war no less than Liddell Hart, and his intuition was informed by the broad sweep of Great Britain's history. He revelled in the strategy of war, seeing his role in the light of his ancestor, John Churchill, first Duke of Marlborough, judging the present struggle by the standards of the long series of wars in which Great Britain had thrown her Navy and her trading power into the scales against Continental tyrants. His historical vision thus transcended the present balance which so hypnotised Liddell Hart and Lloyd George; he divined that Hitler and Stalin must in the long or short term come into collision; in the meantime the priority was to hold on and somehow draw the United States into the struggle. On his mother's side he was American and perhaps this contributed to his view; in the words of Sir Ian Jacob, he 'had a vision of the ultimate conjunction of the English-speaking peoples, whose history he had nearly finished writing'.[3]

Here the Jewish question assumed significance. Churchill held the conventional view that the Balfour Declaration of 1917, by which Great Britain had assured the Jews a permanent home in Palestine, had mobilised Jewish and importantly American Jewish support for the western Allies in the First World War and at the least tipped the balance for the United States' entry on the Allied side. The Nazi treatment of Jews since 1933 had made the American Jewish lobby a natural ally of anti-German forces, and was an obvious instrument for exerting influence on the present United States President, Roosevelt. For their part, Jewish associations had courted Churchill from the mid-1930s as the most prominent anti-Nazi politician in Great Britain. In this sense Hitler and Hess had good grounds for their paranoia about an international Jewish conspiracy against Germany; they had called it down upon themselves; it could not be expected that a proud race would consent to be ostracised, humiliated, driven out and robbed without organising against the perpetrators. The financial stakes alone were monstrous, since under the cloak of the *Weltanschauung* Göring and his collaborators in German finance and industry had taken over Jewish banking and industrial interests, and had made it clear their aim was to 'Aryanise' the economy of the entire Continent.

Churchill had close family connections with the British line of the international Jewish banking house of Rothschild: the first Baron Rothschild had been his father Randolph's intimate adviser at the Treasury, entrusted with cabinet secrets and relied upon for personal loans. When Lord Randolph Churchill died, he had owed Rothschild the then enormous sum of £66,000.[4] Winston Churchill knew the family socially as a guest at their country seat at Tring in Hertfordshire. Despite or in part because of his father's association, Churchill had not been entirely free of some of the current prejudices about Jews that Hitler and Hess had taken to extremes. He had supported Zionism at first because he believed that the Bolshevik revolution had been fomented by Jews and that Jews with a national home in Palestine could be used to counter Jewish Bolsheviks, then because he believed that Jews in Palestine could serve as a British imperial bastion to defend the Suez Canal, and after 1933 because the Jews became natural allies in his struggle to warn of the dangers of Nazism.

In the summer of 1936 he had lent his backing to the World Anti-Nazi Non-Sectarian Council – whose name was changed to 'The Focus' on his recommendation for something less political – established by Jews with the trade unions for the fight against Nazism. The chief financial support came from British Jews, the main sources of intelligence from Jewish banking connections and the German-Jewish emigrés who had fled from Hitler. Beaverbrook was, no doubt, near the truth when he wrote in 1938 that there were 20,000 German Jews in Britain working against *rapprochement* with Germany.[5] The same year Beaverbrook had cancelled a contract Churchill had to write for his *Evening Standard*, as a result of which Churchill, already deep in debt, had been forced to put his home, Chartwell, on the market; he was rescued by Sir Henry Strakosch, born a Moravian Jew, who paid the then substantial sum of £18,162 to clear his debts. Chartwell was withdrawn from sale.[6]

It would be mistaken to draw the conclusion either that Churchill felt beholden to or was bribed by the Jewish interest or, on the other hand, that Churchill used the Zionists quite cynically for his own ends; one of the paradoxes of his character was that, despite his frequently overbearing, insensitive treatment of colleagues and family, he felt genuine British compassion for underdogs; and the plight of the Jews in Germany and, since the outbreak of war, in Poland moved him deeply. The Labour Party leader, Clement Attlee, recounted how in the House of Commons one day Churchill had tears pouring down his cheeks as he described to him what was being done to the Jews in Germany.[7] That he played the Zionist card for all it was worth in his attempt to tip the United States into the war is not in doubt, however. Nor, sadly, is it in doubt that throughout the war he did as little to ameliorate the horrors suffered by Jews in German hands as Chamberlain had done for the Poles.

Churchill's second card was Soviet Russia. Long before the war he had foreseen that the only way to counter German military expansionism was to weld the European nations, including Russia, into a ring around Germany. It had been the failure of successive Conservative Governments even to contemplate bringing the Soviet Union into a defensive alliance which had finally projected Stalin into Hitler's arms and set the scene for war. Both security services, MI6 and the internal counter-espionage service, MI5, were stamped with similar anti-Soviet feeling for the good reason that international Communism had represented the main threat to security until Hitler's rise to power; and still under Chamberlain, both counter-espionage services were directed against Communism as the main enemy intent on embroiling Great Britain in war with Germany.[8] Stewart Menzies and his circle were described, as Churchill himself had been once, as 'terrific anti-Bolsheviks'.[9] Churchill could scarcely sack Menzies so soon after he had been confirmed as 'C'; instead he appointed his personal assistant and intelligence officer from the inter-war years, Major Desmond Morton, as his liaison and filter to Menzies and the Foreign Office, to which SIS was subordinated. He did, however, sack the head and founding father of the internal security service, MI5,

Sir Vernon Kell, almost immediately.

There have been many theories seeking to account for this. Kell was sixty-five and an asthmatic; however, as one MI5 officer of the time recalled, he had been sick for many years 'and had still run an efficient service ... To get rid of a man like Kell at a moment's notice was a Churchillian blunder.'[10] Possibly it was. It is also possible it was a determined move to eradicate the anti-Communist stance of the service and turn it into a basically anti-Nazi organisation.

This is undoubtedly what happened: the first outward sign was on 22 May, when Churchill ordered the arrest and internment without trial of the right-wing, anti-Semitic Member of Parliament Archibald Maule Ramsay, the leader of the British Union of Fascists, Sir Oswald Mosley, Admiral Sir Barry Domvile, who headed another organisation devoted to co-operation with Germany called 'The Link', together with most members of the organisations they led. Three days later Kell was sacked.

Meanwhile MI5 had been penetrated by Soviet agents. In the post-war speculation about how many and who they were suspicion has fallen on Roger Hollis, in 1940 Assistant Director of 'F' division, monitoring extremist political parties, chiefly the Communist Party of Great Britain; Graham Mitchell, who worked under him monitoring Fascist extremists; Guy Liddell, director of 'B' – counter-espionage – division, under whose auspices the known traitors Anthony Blunt and Guy Burgess entered the service; Maxwell Knight, head of B5(b), who worked in tandem with 'F' division monitoring and infiltrating agents into potentially subversive groups, including the Oxford – and presumably Cambridge – University Communist Society; and a host of others.[11] In the view of de Courcy it is not a question of which of these were guilty; all were.

The Imperial Policy Group, whose views de Courcy had represented before the war, had been dissolved, but he retained his close connections with its extraordinarily influential former members, who were still, for the most part, strongly opposed to the German war on imperial grounds – not the pro-German, anti-Semitic grounds of the organisations Churchill had moved against. De Courcy worked on an editorial board publishing a *Review of World Affairs*, later *Intelligence Digest*, which broadly reflected these views. He alleges that the patron of the 'Russian group' of spies was the late Victor Rothschild, the third Baron. Rothschild, who had joined MI5 on the outbreak of war, knew Churchill socially, not only through the family connection, but because he and his first wife had been part of Churchill's pre-war 'counter-appeasement' set. He was then a brilliant and flamboyant undergraduate, afterwards a Fellow of Trinity College, Cambridge, and associated with several of those notorious members of the secret aesthetic, anti-moral establishment society, the Apostles, who were recruited then as Soviet agents. De

Courcy has no doubt he was their sponsor:

Rothschild saw these brilliant young men at Cambridge, all of whom had a weakness, and he spotted it and put it to advantage, thinking they would get into higher levels of affairs. He saw the Nazis as the greatest threat to the Jewish race ever and was determined to back the Russians. He encouraged these men, helped them financially, succoured them and stood back.[12]

De Courcy was a prime target for the 'Russian group'; a Soviet booklet entitled *Russia's Enemies in Britain* devoted 39 of its 70 pages to attacking him.[13] And there is no question that he was in a position and possessed the contacts to know *his* enemies in Britain; thus his allegation about Rothschild – not that he passed information, but that he sponsored those who did – carries great weight, as too his allegations about Hollis, Mitchell, Guy Liddell, Maxwell Knight and others.

This is not so far-fetched as it might appear; indeed it seems to explain the otherwise inexplicable: first the entry of so many former Communists and/or homosexuals, often with *louche* habits, into the *security* services of the state in wartime; second as Peter Wright has demonstrated convincingly, the extraordinary obstacles that were later placed in the way of those investigating Soviet penetration of MI5 and MI6, and the enormous length of time it took to winkle out a few traitors, by no means all; the investigation has not been concluded satisfactorily to this day. The climate of intellectual opinion in the inter-war years also has to be taken into account: the intelligentsia, disillusioned by the Great War and its aftermath, contemptuous of the system which had given rise to it and which condemned the working classes to a grey life and unemployment, arrogant in their own powers of reason against older certainties of religion, conventional morality or simple love of country, forgetful or ignorant of the practical results of all former essays in utopian politics, fell easy prey to Marxist propaganda and really believed Soviet Communism heralded a new dawn for mankind. It was fertile soil for Stalin's recruiters and they succeeded to an extent which has not yet been admitted.

Possibly Vernon Kell's dismissal can be seen in the light of Churchill's support for the 'Russian group'. However that may be, there is no question that after he became Prime Minister MI5 redirected its efforts against the enemies on the Right and anyone suspected of favouring a compromise peace with Germany for whatever reasons, leaving the enemies on the Left relatively undisturbed.[14]

Churchill was not, of course, a fellow traveller of the Left. He was as realistic as Hitler or Hess about international Communism and the murderous barbarity of Stalin which the Nazi's aped. He made no moral choice between them, simply an imperial choice, for he was as dedicated as the high Tory, Court and Service circles to the maintenance and glory of the British Empire. But, in truth, whichever choice was taken, it was too late; the Empire was doomed. Playing the German card would open the way to Hitler's domination of the Continent, after which Great Britain would have to fall into line with the 'new order', no doubt preserving the trappings of power, the Royal Family and dominion over large parts of the world, but politically and socially *gleichgeschaltet* – liberal democracy expiring with British Jews and all others of 'inferior value' blood or radical left-wing views. On the other hand, if the American and Russian cards were played, the Empire would be placed in pawn to the United States and be obliged to fall into line with American economic and political/social aims while leaving at least eastern Europe, possibly the entire Continent, dominated by Soviet Communism. Playing for time with a compromise peace would only defer the choice.

Churchill had made his choice before the war. In power he followed it through ruthlessly to its logical conclusion. He had a boyish spirit and a strong heart schooled in adversity. Aspects of his childhood had been shaped, like Hitler's, by trauma, in his case parental neglect. He had known despair and continued to experience that darkest pit which he called his 'black dog'.[15] Probably only such a man, neither analytical nor stable, but touched with the spark of folly necessary to overcome the highest obstacles could have pulled the country through the crisis which now unfolded as German *Panzer* columns sliced through the French armies, dividing them from the British Expeditionary Force, and the French Government evacuated Paris and Mussolini threw in his lot with Hitler. On 22 June France formally capitulated.

Churchill wavered once when he agreed to a plea from Halifax, whom he had retained as Foreign Secretary, that a message might be sent to Mussolini suggesting a peace conference, but the impulse was rejected the same day. After the evacuation of the greater part of the British Expeditionary Force from the beaches of Dunkirk he told the country and Hitler 'we shall go on to the end ... we shall never surrender', but fight on 'until in God's good time, the new world, with all its power and might, steps forth to the rescue and liberation of the old'.[16]

The nation responded. As Lord Gladwyn, formerly Gladwyn Jebb, has described it, 'We knew what we were fighting for. No doubts any longer about how the war could possibly be won; it just had to be won, and that was that. Churchill, I believe, was really the symbol of this collective instinct.'[17]

13
HUBRIS

In Germany all sections of the administration were seized with euphoria some weeks before Hitler hopped a tight little jig of triumph at that spot in the forest of Compiègne where the armistice had been signed ending the First World War.

On 23 May, with the complete collapse of the western armies imminent, the Secretary of State at the Foreign Ministry, Baron Ernst von Weizsäcker, had noted they might well offer Great Britain an easy way out by keeping out of Continental affairs and letting Germany take over. 'Peace would perhaps appear advantageous for the English,' he had added, 'but shameful.'[1]

Von Weizsäcker had been one of those from the traditional official class who had decided to remain in office to restrain the Nazis and prevent them filling all important posts. Like Haushofer, he was in inner opposition to the regime he served. He liked to discuss with Beck, Canaris, von Hassell and others how Hitler could be removed. However, there was no organisation and, without the wholehearted backing of Hitler's generals, no possibility of effecting such a change. Whether he ever suffered such a crisis of conscience as Albrecht Haushofer is not clear; outwardly he remained a faithful servant of the regime to the end. His note on this occasion, 23 May 1940, appears to confirm Churchill's judgement that there was scant difference between Hitler's ultimate territorial – as opposed to racial – aims and those of the German oppositionalists like von Weizsäcker. On the assumption of overwhelming victory in the west he wrote that, whether England gave up now or whether she had to be persuaded with bombs, 'there remains a further settlement of accounts in the east'.[2]

Towards the end of May von Hassell had found the triumphal mood in Berlin ruling circles accompanied by 'plans for the partition of the world in grand style'.[3] It was no exaggeration. On 31 May, for instance, the Society for European Economic Planning and Extended Area

Economy, which had been called into being on 21 October the previous year, produced a memo:

A continental European extended-area economy under German leadership must as its final peace goal include all the peoples of the continent from Gibraltar to the Urals and from the North Cape [of Norway] to the island of Cyprus, together with their natural colonial radiations into the Siberian area and across the Mediterranean into Africa.[4]

Meanwhile, in the *Reich* Security head office Heydrich had started planning security services for the colonies,[5] and in Munich Hess's Race Policy Bureau was working out guidelines for colonial racial policy; as laid out in a paper, 'Colonial Question and Race Idea', these were concerned chiefly with the 'psychologically and practically correct leadership of the [indigenous] peoples'. The most important task of the white race was 'to practise a *Herren* [master] role and form their own way of life in conformity'.[6] A rigorous *apartheid* was to be practised: masters and natives were to live in separate areas, communication between them not allowed except with formal permission, sexual contact absolutely prohibited and enforced with the death penalty for the African partner.[7]

The excitement of victory and preparations for the new world order proved too much for Hess, who went down with severe stomach pains and gall bladder trouble. Himmler asked his private masseur, Felix Kersten, to examine him. After the Armistice ceremony on 22 June Kersten recorded Hess returning from the Forest of Compiègne 'charged with tension' to the hotel rooms in Bad Godesberg where he was treating him. After recounting the superlative events he had been party to, Hess told Kersten he was certain they would make peace with Britain as they had with France; only a few weeks earlier the Führer had told him again about the great value of the British Empire in the world. Germany and France had to stand together with Great Britain against the enemy of Europe, Bolshevism.

'I can't imagine that cool, calculating England will run her neck into a Soviet noose,' he went on, 'instead of saving it by coming to an understanding with us.'[8]

Despite Churchill's accession to power, this was an accurate reflection of the view of the British Foreign Secretary, Lord Halifax, and his Under-Secretary of State, the young R. A. ('Rab') Butler. Kenneth de Courcy recalls Butler arranging a private meeting with him at the Belgrave Square house of his private secretary, the wealthy café society socialite 'Chips' Channon, on 7 June, shortly before the French armistice. Butler told him they were working for an arrangement with Hitler through the Vatican; the problem was to persuade Hitler. De Courcy had asked what terms he had in mind; Germany should be given the mouth of the Rhine,

123

Butler had replied. De Courcy could not agree to that and suggested that the US Ambassador, Joseph Kennedy, be asked to press for an American initiative similar to the 'House memorandum' of the First World War with an American commitment to guarantee the outcome and to enter the war if Germany refused to attend or dismissed the proposals. Butler authorised him to put this to Kennedy, who had appeared surprisingly receptive.

Next day, at the Carlton Club, Butler had beckoned de Courcy over. Congratulating him on his talk with Kennedy, who, he said, had already spoken to his chief, Halifax, who was very happy, he wanted him to see Kennedy again to jolly him along. Shortly afterwards de Courcy received an urgent phone call instructing him to meet 'Chips' Channon on the bridge in St James's Park. He was to express surprise; Channon would express surprise, and it must appear a chance meeting.

De Courcy did as instructed and met Channon, who said, 'My master is in deep trouble over this Kennedy business. I want you to go back and destroy your file of letters with my master, then go to Scotland for a couple of weeks and don't see any diplomats.'

De Courcy assumed Churchill had wind of what Butler and Halifax were up to. He did not destroy the file, nor did he go to Scotland, but he took care not to see Kennedy or any other diplomats for a while.[9]

Butler was also working through a member of the Committee of the International Red Cross in Geneva, Carl Burckhardt, to establish connections with Prinz Max zu Hohenlowe of Himmler's Circle of Friends. As Hohenlowe reported his conversation with Burckhardt to von Weizsäcker at the Foreign Ministry, influential British circles had realised after the Norwegian and French campaigns how widely they had underestimated the power of the German armed forces and economy, 'and those who had spoken out against Churchill and his circle about intervention on the Continent are beginning to point out how right they were. Butler especially, who is overflowing with pessimism, belongs to this group and is feverishly searching for a way out.'[10] He added that the Spanish Ambassador in Berne, who had met Butler recently, had confirmed this. The British view, he went on, was that Germany could have no interest in causing the downfall of the British Empire: she was not in a position to replace British influence in India, Australia and Canada, and it could not be in her interests either to weaken the status of the white race in these areas or, on the other hand, to help the United States take them over.[11]

Hohenlowe offered his own opinion – reflecting the general *hubris* – that it came down to a question of whether Hitler wanted to smash the British Empire or not. Finally, he reported, he had asked Burckhardt what would happen to Churchill and companions if England were to come to an agreement with Germany. 'This was dismissed with a wave of the hand and he explained that Churchill had only succeeded to his present position by chance. He would have to stand down if other situations emerged.'[12]

This is remarkably similar to Butler's comments to the Swedish envoy to London, Bjorn Prytz, during a now notorious interview on 17 June. According to his own account, Butler had chanced upon Prytz while returning from lunch across St James's Park, and had asked him to go back to his room for a talk. Since the Swedish Government was under great pressure from Germany on the questions of iron exports and troop transfers through Sweden to Norway, there is no doubt that Prytz wanted an interview to ascertain London's position after the collapse of France, and the 'chance' encounter was arranged much as de Courcy's had been.[13] Prytz reported Butler as saying that 'no opportunity would be neglected for concluding a compromise peace if the chance was offered on reasonable conditions', and adding, 'No diehards would be allowed to stand in the way.' Butler then received an urgent summons to Lord Halifax and left the room, returning minutes later with a message from the Foreign Minister: 'Common sense and not bravado would dictate the British Government's policy'. Obviously Halifax had known of the meeting. Churchill did not. Halifax later instructed the British envoy in Stockholm to make soundings about the German and Italian attitudes to peace talks.

When Churchill found out a few days later about Butler's talk with Prytz, he wrote to Halifax saying that it was quite clear his Under-Secretary had used 'odd language' and given the Swedish envoy 'a strong impression of defeatism'. Halifax covered up, making no mention of his own input and expressing complete satisfaction with Butler's discretion and loyalty to Government policy. Butler's own written account for Halifax stated that he 'happened to meet him [Prytz] in the park and he came into the office for only a few minutes; not being an arranged interview, I did not keep a record'.[14] Here, in what appeared to be a private letter, Butler was evidently covering his chief, who must have called Butler from his meeting with Prytz specifically to add the weight of his own authority to his Under-Secretary's remarks. The impression left by this affair and the records of the cabinet meetings from 24 May onwards is that Halifax, strongly supported by Butler, was still running an appeasement policy in direct contravention of Churchill's agreed public policy.

The British Ambassador in Switzerland, Sir David Kelly, was putting out similar peace feelers. In July Hohenlowe reported to Ribbentrop that Kelly had taken him aside at a reception in the Spanish Ambassador's residence, saying he wanted to speak to him about the situation. Hohenlowe said that, if he was a postman for Churchill, there was no point, at which Kelly replied, 'Our mutual friends in England, Butler, Vansittart and Halifax, have a following.' He went on to agree with Hohenlowe that Britain's position was serious and they scarcely had any choice but to continue fighting for the honour of the Empire until they were in a position to make a reasonable peace. The conversation turned to Churchill; Hohenlowe could not believe that such an unserious person so frequently under the influence of alcohol really embodied the nation. Kelly, he reported, 'agreed my criticism insofar as he said Churchill was a bull running his head into a wall, but the attitude of Butler and Halifax and also Vansittart was not the same'.[15]

Hohenlowe soon ended the conversation, he reported, because of the obvious suspicion that Kelly, 'who spoke with much passion and gesture', was simply talking to gain time. Hohenlowe was probably correct; the more Hitler could be convinced that underneath the bluster, Great Britain was prepared to make peace on reasonable terms, the less urgently he would press plans for invasion and instead turn his gaze eastwards towards the real enemy. Churchill was not a simple bulldog; he believed war to be a combination of plausible fiction and maximum force against a narrow front. Vansittart was his ally, and the fact that Kelly linked Vansittart's name with Butler and Halifax suggests that he had been instructed to keep open the channels to the enemy – in short that his feelers were essentially disinformation to gain time and intelligence about Hitler's real objectives.[16]

This cannot be said of remarks made that same month by the Duke of Windsor to various Spanish go-betweens in Lisbon. The Duke had always been convinced of the necessity for an agreement with Hitler. After the fall of France, where he had been serving with the British Military Mission, he had made his way into Spain, thence to Lisbon in Portugal, making so little attempt to disguise his feelings about the war that Churchill had decided to remove him as far away as possible with an appointment as Governor of the Bahamas. The German Minister in Lisbon soon learned of this and wired Berlin that the Duke was being sent away from England, where his return would provide the strongest encouragement to 'English friends of peace'. He added that the Duke intended to delay his departure from Portugal as long as possible 'in the hope of a change in his favour soon'.[17]

Hitler had similar hopes of a change in British opinion. He had put off sealing his triumph in the west with a public offer of peace, as von Weizsäcker noted, 'to give time for internal developments in England'.[18] As these did not occur he made a speech on 19 July appealing, as he had after the Polish campaign, to 'reason and commonsense in Great Britain' to end the war. By chance on the same day, the British Ambassador in Washington, Lord Lothian, who before the war had been a leading member of the 'Cliveden set' which had argued for an agreement with Germany, wired London that the German Chargé d'Affaires in Washington had informed him that, if desired, he could obtain Berlin's peace terms. In fact, Lothian had initiated the sounding by asking an American Quaker, Malcolm R. Lovell, then negotiating for the release of German Jews, to try and find out what Hitler's terms were from the German Chargé d'Affaires. This is proved by von Weizsäcker's note of 'a curious peace feeler from the British Ambassador in Washington. Lord Lothian made advances through a Quaker, Lovell, for which, if he were a normal British Ambassador, he must have been authorised'.[19] The wire on which von Weizsäcker based this note is missing from the German documents; no doubt it revealed that Lothian had been authorised by Lord Halifax; it could not have been Churchill since, as soon as he heard of it, he instructed Halifax that Lothian should on no account pursue the matter.[20]

Confirmation of the division at the highest level of British politics arrived in Berlin the same day *via* Switzerland. The Swiss Ambassador in London reported that Churchill was meeting ever fiercer opposition from Court and financial circles and from a part of the Conservative Party:

These circles are no longer inclined to follow Churchill and Eden [War Minister] unconditionally. The Prime Minister therefore sees his following limited to Conservative diehards and the Labour Party, which wishes to continue the war on ideological grounds.[21]

This was a fair assessment of the political situation. Churchill was aware that a group of his own party in Parliament was demanding a moderate response to Hitler's public appeal to reason. On the other hand, the people as a whole, largely unaware of the horrendous economic and military stakes, were undoubtedly behind Churchill – as Lord Gladwyn expressed it, Churchill was the symbol of their collective instinct.[22] With such solid support in the country Churchill was able to ensure that Halifax broadcast a firm rejection of Hitler's appeal to reason.

The following day, 23 July, von Weizsäcker noted that the Führer, who wished to come to a friendly understanding with England, was always asking himself what Churchill was banking on in continuing the war. Since it could not be England's own strength, it was evident he was waiting for America or Russia to join in. Von Weizsäcker himself concluded that Churchill's resistance was 'not a logical, but a psychological question'.[23]

In the sense of present realities von Weizsäcker was correct. In another sense Churchill's historical intuition and his assessment of his opponent were more reliable than Weizsäcker's reason. This was proved at the end of the month. Admiral Raeder presented an account of naval planning for the invasion of Britain to Hitler at the Berghof. Afterwards, as the Chief of the General Staff, Franz Halder, noted in his dairy, Hitler expressed extreme scepticism about the 'technical possibilities', stressing the effects of weather and the overwhelming numerical superiority of the Royal Navy. He believed that the U-boat and air offensive could prove decisive against England, but that would take one to two years. He went on – in Halder's shorthand:

England's hope is Russia and America. If hope of Russia falls away, so too America because falling away of Russia means huge increase in value of *Japan* in Far East.

   Russia Far Eastern sword of England and America against Japan.

   ... Russia factor on which England banks most.

   ... If however Russia is smashed, then England's last hope is eradicated. The master of Europe and the Balkans is then Germany.[24]

Russia had to be finished off, Hitler concluded. His first idea had been to turn east that autumn, but there was insufficient time to prepare and winter would close down the operation halfway – for he anticipated a five-month campaign. He decided to wait until the following spring, until 'May 1941'.

In deciding to turn east, he did not call off the projected invasion of England, codenamed 'Sealion'; this remained an option should Göring's pilots succeed in establishing air superiority. The following day, 1 August, he issued a directive to the Luftwaffe to subdue the Royal Air Force in the shortest possible time, then to bomb harbours and warehouses. Together with the U-boat campaign against merchant shipping, he could hope to starve the British into submission.

The same day the Windsors sailed from Lisbon for the Bahamas. This did not mean a final break, the Duke explained to his Portuguese host and go-between to the Germans, since he could return again in twenty-four hours by aeroplane from Florida;[25] he arranged a code word by which he could be recalled when sentiment in Great Britain changed and he was required to take his part in peace negotiations.[26]

———— 14 ————
TURN EAST

Preliminary planning for the assault on Russia began in early August 1940 in the Army General Staff and Hitler's own vehicle, the Armed Forces High Command (OKW). Himmler instructed Heydrich to begin planning the operations of the *Einsatz* groups who would follow the advancing fronts to carry out the racial and political goals of the *Weltanschauung* by liquidating Bolshevik functionaries, Jews and the intelligentsia as a preliminary to settling the conquered areas with racial Germans. Towards the end of the month the Chief of the general Staff, Halder, noted in his diary after a discussion with Admiral Canaris, head of the Abwehr: 'In the East measures for removing the intelligentsia and the Jews begin again.'[1]

Canaris had once been a convinced supporter of National Socialism and Hitler personally. The abominations practised by the SS Einsatzkommandos in the Polish campaign had shocked him profoundly however, provoking a crisis of conscience; he had instructed his agents in the field to submit detailed reports of SS activities and used them to alert Army commanders to what was being done in the name of Germany. In private, with those he could trust, he lamented, 'Our children's children will have to bear the blame for this.'[2]

Whether the pessimism which drained him inwardly from that time on, leaving little but the white-haired, rather shabby-looking outer shell of a spy master, led him to betray his country remains a matter for debate. There is no doubt that he used numerous channels of communication with Great Britain; of those that are known, one led through the Vatican, and was used for peace soundings with Lord Halifax; another through the British Ambassador in Madrid, Sir Samuel Hoare, for the same purpose;[3] another through Madame Synanska, wife of the former Polish Military Attaché in Berlin. Madame Synanska's husband had been taken prisoner of war; some time in the late summer or autumn of 1940 Canaris sent an agent to arrange for her to travel through Germany to

Switzerland. Afterwards he visited her from time to time; it is often said that she was his mistress; she denies it. After Canaris had departed, the local SIS unit chief would call on her and she would tell him what Canaris had said. This was then encyphered and sent by wireless to 'C''s deputy in London.

It was in this way that Churchill obtained probably the first firm confirmation of his predictions that Hitler would turn east. On this occasion Canaris revealed that every member of the Communist Party in Russia was to be shot and described a meeting at which people had remonstrated in vain that this would provoke resistance among the Russians.[4] The date of the revelation is unclear; so is the motive. Canaris abominated Bolshevism and he knew, of course, that the feeling was shared in the highest circles in Britain. Much later, on 9 June 1941, Göring was to send a similar message to England via Birger Dahlerus which gave the actual date of Hitler's assault on Russia a fortnight later.[5]

It is possible to interpret both messages as pleas to Britain to settle the differences between them and join the crusade against Bolshevism – or even as a part of an elaborate deception. Kenneth de Courcy, however, is convinced that Canaris viewed the war with Britain as a tragedy and believed that until peace could be negotiated it was imperative for the preservation of Christian values that Great Britain was not defeated; Canaris considered this such a high duty he was prepared to betray his country, and did so, according to de Courcy, passing information directly to 'C' by some more regular channel than Madame Synanska. De Courcy is convinced that Canaris's intelligence was delivered personally by 'C' to Churchill together with the 'Ultra' material gained from breaking the German Enigma cyphers in orange-buff boxes to which Churchill and he alone held the keys.[6]

The purpose of the SS programme in Poland, begun again in August 1940, was to liquidate the entire Polish intelligentsia and leadership classes after the Soviet pattern, separate the population into ethnic components so that the people would lose all 'Polish' national consciousness, draw out those of German bloodstock to be re-educated in German values and used to settle the four new German *Gaus*, while collecting what Himmler termed the 'inferior value population' in the *General Gouvernement Polen* 'as a leaderless work *Volk* of annual itinerant labourers ... to be called upon to co-operate on the Germans' eternal cultural exploits and building works'.[7] To prevent a new leadership class arising, no education was to be permitted the children of these people except for four-year primary schools where they could learn to count up to 500, write their name and learn that it was 'a Divine Commandment to obey

Germans and to be honest, industrious and trustworthy'. Himmler did not consider reading necessary for them. They were to be helots – slaves for the German *Reich*.

Himmler had outlined this programme to Hitler in a six-page memorandum towards the end of May; 'The Führer',[8] he noted afterwards, 'found [it] very good and correct.' Among those to whom copies were sent was Hess's Chief of Staff, Martin Bormann. Apart from the fact that Himmler was still, at least formally, Hess's man, it was essential for Hess to know the plan in his role as liaison between Party and State. It was essential in his task of ensuring that the demands of the National Socialist *Weltanschauung* were realised in the area of law-making – as it was put in the Party Year Book.[9] It was essential in his role as super-ombudsman, to whom every German *Volk* comrade could turn; it was essential for those offices in his organisation which dealt with race, schooling and especially perhaps public law. Many queries and petitions addressed to him which arose from the occupation of Poland were simply redirected to Himmler, whom Hitler had made responsible for 'Germanising' the area with the title Commissar for the Consolidation of German Nationhood. However, it is evident from other letters that Hess took a personal interest in the eastern plan. In correspondence with the Minister of Justice about ordinances denying Jews and Poles legal rights and making them subject to special penal sanctions, including forced heavy labour, he expressed the opinion that 'the Pole is less susceptible [than the German] to the infliction of ordinary imprisonment'.[10]

Himmler devoted remarkably scant space in his memorandum to the fate of the Jews, merely hoping that 'the concept of "Jews" will be completely eliminated through the possibility of a great exodus of all the Jews to Africa or otherwise into a colony'. This was an agreed deception. After the fall of France, it had been worked up in a department of the Foreign Ministry as a plan to ship all Jews to the island of Madagascar, off the coast of East Africa, and Heydrich adopted this 'Madagascar Plan' as camouflage for his 'ultimate solution' to the Jewish problem.[11] It was especially necessary for American consumption. Ribbentrop was as anxious to prevent the Jewish lobby from tipping America into the war on Great Britain's side as Churchill was to promote it. He had a section monitoring activities in former Poland for incidents damaging to Germany's standing in American eyes, while Himmler was fostering the emigration of Jews – in exchange for hard currency – through the good offices of an American-based Jewish committee. Camouflage was also necessary internally: for the Church leaders, who might otherwise speak out against planned deportation from the *Reich* and all occupied countries and not least for the Jews themselves, who were to be persuaded peacefully to leave for the east with the promise of 'resettlement'. The

Madagascar Plan was also in all probability designed to show German good intentions with regard to the Jews in the peace settlement it was hoped to conclude with Great Britain.[12]

The clue to the real plan for the Jews was that section of the 'euthanasia' programme questionnaire requiring doctors to discriminate on the grounds of race, and the gas chamber experiments ordered by Heydrich at the same time, ostensibly for the same purpose, on the instructions of Hitler's Chancellery. The first demonstration gassing of mental patients for Philipp Bouhler, Brack and other Chancellery officials had taken place in January 1940 in a disused prison at Brandenburg-on-Havel.[13] Subsequently six euthanasia 'killing centres' had been established with their gas chambers disguised as shower-rooms – apparently a refinement suggested by Bouhler himself – and in June the first gassings of Jewish mental patients had taken place at one of these, Castle Grafeneck in Brandenburg. The Inspector of the Euthanasia Killing Centres, Criminal Commissar Christian Wirth, was later to become Inspector of the first purpose-built death camps in the east, employing gas chambers disguised as showers for the planned extermination of the Jews. The other death camp commandants, police officers like him, also graduated from the euthanasia killing centres. Of equal importance in these death camp operations were the doctors who were inured to killing in the euthanasia programme. Robert Jay Lifton has pointed out that this 'destruction of the boundary between healing and killing' was crucial for the medical men who took part in systematised genocide, who killed in the name of racial purity.[14]

Hess was well aware of the euthanasia programme. In his role as conscience of the Party, he received letters from those who suspected that patients were being liquidated. One such was the deputy head of an institution at Stetten, Jakob Friedrich Rupp, who had written to him at the end of May. The only reply Rupp received was that his letter had been forwarded to the responsible office in Himmler's organisation. 'After receiving this,' Rupp recalled after the war, 'it was clear to me that all was lost for our patients because even before the war I saw Himmler as Hitler's evil spirit.'[15]

Hess was also aware of the atrocities against Jews in Poland since, as arbiter between Party and State, he had received complaints from the Army Commander-in-Chief East from at least as early as the winter of 1939–40, about the damage to morale caused by ss activities. As with the euthanasia petitions, Hess appears simply to have passed the matter to Himmler to deal with. Complaints resumed as the killings started again in August, coming to a head the following February 1941 to judge by Halder's diary, when Hess demanded the removal of General Mieth, who had spoken out against the ss actions in front of his officers.[16]

Everyone in the know in Berlin was aware of the atrocities in Poland.[17] Albrecht Haushofer had written an anguished letter to his mother the previous December attempting to describe the confusion of his feelings and his impotence in face of the terrible events he had long foreseen: 'An example: I sit at a table with a man whose task it will be to cause a great part of the Jews transported to the Jews' Ghetto in Lublin to freeze and starve to death according to programme . . .'[18]

It is inconceivable that Hess was unaware of these ss actions, and equally inconceivable he was unaware that the Madagascar Plan was a huge deception. With his conviction of the racial-biological goal of National Socialism and his intimate knowledge of Hitler's inner mind, it is difficult to believe he was unaware of the link between the 'ultimate solution' to the Jewish problem and the euthanasia programme, which also was run largely by the ss, although controlled from Hitler's Chancellery office. Those who have argued that Hitler neither ordered nor even knew of the plans for liquidating the Jews on the ground that there is no documentary evidence linking him with the programme can argue the same for Hess. Yet Himmler explained to many top-level groups that he was acting on Hitler's commission and bore the responsibility on behalf of Hitler. In the same way, it must be assumed, Hess, the conscience of the Party, had to be kept clear of public involvement.

It is impossible to determine Hess's private thoughts about the 'necessary' horrors on the way to the goals he believed in. According to von Krosigk, he was aware that the conflict between good and evil in the development of National Socialism was played out in the person of Hitler. His adjutant, Leitgen, subscribed to this view and believed the resulting inner struggle caused Hess's frequent bouts of ill health.

15
FLIGHT PLAN

Hess first conceived the idea of flying to Great Britain to make peace in June 1940, when he was with Hitler during the later stages of the French campaign – so he told Sir John Simon in England a few weeks after his arrival.[1]

Part of this rings true. A dramatic gesture such as a peace flight to Britain must have appealed to Hess's unstable, romantic nature. Chamberlain's flight to Munich to avert war in September 1938 had made as much of an impression in Germany as in England. Göring's offer to fly to London in September 1939 to prevent general war had impressed Hess. In September 1940 he would be released from his pledge to Hitler not to fly an aeroplane for a year. It can be imagined how he indulged in day-dreams of outshining Göring and his other rivals by cutting through diplomatic flummery and piloting himself to London. He must have visualised the headlines around the world.

In July, after Churchill had rejected Hitler's public appeal to reason, the fanciful idea acquired substance. Hitler's new strategy of forcing Britain to terms by knocking out Russia, her hoped-for Continental sword, promised the two-front war he had always determined to avoid. Moreover, Hess was aware from his intelligence sources that Roosevelt was preparing to trade destroyers in return for British Empire naval and air bases to protect the western hemisphere, and was generally preparing the United States to become Great Britain's armaments supply base and ally. Albrecht Haushofer, Hess's expert on the Anglo-Saxon nations, had always been clear that at bottom the United States' interests coincided with Great Britain's and she would always, in the last resort, side with her. New realities in the Far East made this certain. Japan's military expansionism threatened supplies of tin, rubber and other strategic materials on which the United States was as dependent as Britain; yet Britain, with her hands fully tied in Europe, was quite incapable of protecting them. Their defence had devolved entirely upon America.[2] The shadow loomed of global war in which Germany would be faced not only by the population resources and vast spaces of Soviet Russia but also with the economic and industrial potential of the United States. In recognition of this, Ribbentrop was sending his chief Far Eastern expert to Japan to attempt to gain a pledge of alliance from her should America enter the war.[3]

On the other hand, intelligence also revealed that Churchill was not so firmly in the saddle as the British press and radio maintained. The Prytz episode in June and the Lothian feeler from Washington in July had revealed that there was at least one dissident in the war cabinet, Lord Halifax. It could easily be imagined that he was supported by Chamberlain, whom Churchill had also retained in the war cabinet, and behind these two were powerful sections of the Conservative Party and landed interests.

Other suggestive despatches came from a variety of sources: from Berne it was reported on 5 August: 'certain circles around the Court, the banking world and trade would be happy if a warlike dispute with Germany could be avoided.'[4] The same report from Berne stated that the view in these circles did not extend to the British people as a whole. But the conclusion was that a great air offensive which showed up the vulnerability of the Royal Air Force might allow these people, who were already prepared for negotiations, to express their view and perhaps gain the upper hand. The situation, from Hess's point of view, was precisely analogous to the situation in Germany seen from Chamberlain's and Halifax's standpoint; that is, while the leader was supported by the mass of the people, powerful groups were waiting in the wings prepared to topple him and make peace.

At the beginning of August Hess asked Albrecht Haushofer about the possibility of contacting such people, and on the 15th he summoned him again and instructed him to begin preparations for the 'special task' of opening a way to these circles.[5]

Haushofer was by now a spiritually broken man. He had been devastated by the events of the spring and summer, and had jettisoned all hope of ever being able to work under conditions in which he could 'halfway inwardly say yes' – as he had described it in a letter to his mother on 4 August – together with almost all human relations outside his family.

He fooled himself on occasions, he wrote, that he could do something in the name of reason, but it did not alter the fact that he had lost all hope. There were few people he could even talk to: 'Worst of all are those one knows well and "friends" who believe they can claim more than a detached [business] share [of one]'.[6] Outwardly he remained the expert adviser on geopolitics, the Anglo-Saxons and the Far East;

inwardly he observed himself playing the part.

By contrast, Hess, his patron, was experiencing a new meaning to life, which he had probably not felt since the early years of the Party. That weekend, 31 August, he went to see his old friend and mentor, Karl Haushofer, at Hartschimmelhof in such animated mood that they talked until two in the morning. Karl Haushofer described part of their discussion in a letter to Albrecht three days later:

Everything is prepared, as you well know, for a very hard and sharp action against the known island so that the top man only needs to press a button and everything goes off. However, before this perhaps unavoidable decision, the thought arises again whether there is really no way of preventing the infinitely grave consequences. In this context there is a line of thought which I absolutely have to pass on to you since it has obviously been imparted to me with this intention. Can you see no way at all by which one could speak about such possibilities at a third place with a middleman such as the old Ian Hamilton or the other Hamilton?[7]

The phrasing of this sentence suggests that, in his talks with Hess, Albrecht had been extremely pessimistic about the possibilities – as he remained. The 'old Ian Hamilton' referred to General Sir Ian Hamilton, who had invited Hess to stay with him in Scotland in the summer of 1939. The 'other Hamilton' referred to Albrecht's friend Douglo Clydesdale, now Wing Commander the Duke of Hamilton.

Karl Haushofer replied to these suggestions that coming centenary celebrations in Lisbon would provide especially good cover for such a meeting, and he went on:

In this connection it seems to me a sign of fate that our old friend Missis [sic] V R has evidently found a way, even if only after a long time, of sending a card with kind and cordial good wishes not only for your mother, but also for Heinz [Albrecht's brother] and me, and added the address: [in English] 'Address your reply to: – Miss V. Roberts, c/o Post Box 506, Lisbon, Portugal.' I have the feeling one should pass up no good possibility, at least one has to consider it.[8]

The Haushofers' old friend was Mrs – not Miss – Mary Violet Roberts, widow of Herbert Ainslie Roberts of Cambridge, and mother of Patrick Maxwell Roberts, one time Second Secretary at the Berlin Embassy, who had been killed in a motor accident in 1937.[9] It remains a mystery why his mother should have contacted the Haushofers with all the difficulties involved at this stage of the war and arranged a post office box number in Lisbon for them to maintain the contact; even more of a mystery why Hess, who had excellent contacts through his foreign organisations, should have seized upon this apparently fortuitous message from an old lady in his attempt to change the course of world history. To judge by the correspondence, that is what he did. He must have believed there was more than remembrance of old times behind the card, for the next Sunday, 8 September, he summoned Albrecht to discuss the details of sending a message through Lisbon, writing afterwards to Karl Haushofer:

We must not disregard the contact or allow it to fizzle out. I consider it best for you or Albrecht to write to the old lady of your acquaintance [to say] she might like to ask Albrecht's friend whether he would perhaps be prepared to come to the neutral country in which she lives or has her forwarding address, in order to talk to Albrecht some time. If he is unable to do this immediately, might he nevertheless communicate via her where he expects to be in the near future. Possibly a neutral acquaintance, who has something to do over there could seek him out and arrange something, referring to you or Albrecht. This person might not be happy to go over there to find out where he is living or have to make a journey in vain ... The basic requirement is naturally that the inquiry and the reply do not go through official channels, because you would certainly not want to get your friend over there into trouble.[10]

'Albrecht's friend' was, of course, the Duke of Hamilton. Why Hess should have been so anxious to contact him is another mystery. By comparison with the real grandees of the Tory Party who were known to favour compromise peace, men such as the Duke of Buccleuch or Lord Londonderry, Hamilton had neither political nor social influence, nor indeed a political brain. He was a rather reserved, modest, thoroughly decent Scottish peer with a practical, non-scheming, indeed non-intellectual mind, all of whose energies and great professional skill and experience were presently devoted to the Royal Air Force. He was almost the last person in the kingdom to turn to in an attempt to unseat Winston Churchill, which is what compromise peace amounted to. It is true that *The Times* had printed a letter from him in early October 1939 in which he had agreed injustices had been done to the German people after the First World War, and concluded:

We shall, I trust, live to see the day when such a healing peace is negotiated between honourable men, and the bitter memories of twenty-five years of unhappy tension between Germany and the Western democracies are wiped away in their responsible co-operation for building a better Europe.[11]

It is true that this letter was quoted on German radio at the time. It is also true that Hamilton had been appointed Lord Steward of the Royal Household after Churchill had had Lord Buccleuch removed from that office for his lobbying activities in favour of peace. Hess believed Churchill had placed Buccleuch under house arrest in his Scottish castle.[12] Whether true or not, reports to this effect had come in during August.

There seems no doubt that Hess believed that as Lord Steward, in fact a purely ceremonial title, Hamilton had influence and immediate access to the King. Hess knew, of course, of the Duke of Windsor's views. By coincidence, the Duke had wired his message *via* his Lisbon intermediary asking to be informed as soon as he was required to act on the very day, 15 August, that Hess had initiated Albrecht Haushofer into the 'special task'. Hess believed that the Queen Mother, Queen Mary, the Duke of Kent and other members of the Royal Family, who had not forgiven the Bolsheviks for the murder of their Royal cousins, the Tsar's family, shared the Duke of Windsor's views about the senselessness of the war.

It may be thought that Hess chose Hamilton as his go-between because of the friendship between Albrecht and the Duke or because he believed Hamilton had been acting as an agent for Stewart Menzies – in which case he was a direct channel into the secret establishment at the heart of Tory England – or simply because of what Albrecht told him about his friend. Advisers naturally inflate the value of their own contacts. Yet Albrecht's report for his father on the two-hour discussion he had with Hess on 8 September makes clear his prime recommendation was not Hamilton; it was the British Ambassador in Washington, Lord Lothian, whom he said he had been 'in close contact with for many years', and who, 'as a member of the highest aristocracy and simultaneously an intellectually very independent personality', would be able to make a robust move at the earliest moment, provided only that he was convinced that 'a bad and uncertain peace' was better than a continuation of the war. This would only be the case, he went on, if Halifax came to the conclusion from his experience in Washington 'that the English hopes of America were not realisable'.[13]

Albrecht Haushofer also mentioned the British Minister in Budapest, O'Malley, and the British Ambassador in Madrid, Sir Samuel Hoare, whom he described interestingly as 'half side-lined [by Churchill], half lying in wait'; he did not know Hoare personally, he said, but could 'open a personal way to him at any time'. According to his report to his father, it was only afterwards that he mentioned Hamilton:

As a last possibility I then suggested a personal meeting with the closest of my English friends on neutral ground: with the young Duke of Hamilton, who had access at any time to all important personalities in London, even to Churchill and the King.

He stressed the difficulty of making such contact and his conviction, which he had made plain already, that the chances of success were remote.

Hess said he would think it over. He was clearly acting on Hitler's instructions; the distinction he attempted to make later between Hitler's

138

commission and his wishes as he (Hess) knew them to be did not apply in the *Führer* State. Hitler's wishes *were* instructions and, of course, the highest law. Hess had said at the start of the interview that it was Hitler's 'earnest wish' to make peace with Great Britain. The continuation of the war was suicidal for the white race; Germany was not in a position, even after the most complete success, to take over the British Empire – which Hitler had never wanted to destroy in any case. Was there no one in England prepared to make peace? Albrecht replied that no one in England believed in Hitler's word. The circles most ready for peace were those who had most to lose, but even they would regard peace as only a temporary truce. For the British of all classes Hitler was the incarnation of all they hated, all they had defended themselves against for centuries, and 'in the worst case the English would rather sign away their whole empire piece by piece to the Americans than subscribe to a peace which ceded mastery in Europe to National Socialist Germany'.[14]

Throughout the interview Haushofer gained the strong impression that 'it was not conducted without the foreknowledge of the Führer, and that I would doubtless hear no more of the matter, unless there was a new agreement between him and his Deputy'.[15] If Albrecht was correct – and he had observed his patron over the years with the shrewd eyes of a poet and dramatist – Hess made his decision to contact the Duke of Hamilton after further discussion with Hitler. In that case it was only one of many feelers which Hitler was extending, after his invariable custom, through many different channels. These further appeals to reason were accompanied, again after his invariable custom, by blows. During August Göring had endeavoured to knock out the Royal Air Force. In early September he switched the attack to London and other cities to soften up civilian morale prior to the peace offensive.

After the interview with Albrecht, Hess wrote to Karl Haushofer to say that the contact with the 'old lady' must not be allowed to fizzle out; he or Albrecht should write to Albrecht's friend, and it would be best if an agent of the Foreign Organisation delivered the letter to Lisbon *via* the post box number:

To this end Albrecht must speak with Bohle [Chief of the Foreign Organisation] or my brother [his deputy]. At the same time the lady must be given the address of this agent in L. – or if he is not permanently resident there of another agent of the Foreign Organisation who is a permanent resident – to whom in turn the answer can be delivered.[16]

Although part of a general peace offensive, Hess's initiative was unique since he was planning to fly across himself as the emissary; this is virtually proved by the statements of both his secretaries after the war – unless both lied to plan, as his adjutant, Karl-Heinz Pintsch, certainly did.

139

His Berlin *Verbindungsstab* secretary, Ingeborg Sperr, said that she was ordered to obtain weather reports over the Channel, North Sea and the British Isles 'beginning in the late summer of 1940, I cannot give the exact period of time any more.'[17] His Munich secretary, Hildegard Fath, stated:

Beginning in summer 1940, I cannot remember the exact time, by order of Hess I had to procure secret weather reports about climatic conditions over the British Isles and over the North Sea, and forward them to Hess.[18]

It was at about this time, too, that Hess began flying again. First he asked Göring for a plane, but he refused and Hess turned to Professor Willi Messerschmitt, whom he knew and whose technical director, Theo Croneiss, he had known since his flying time in the First World War. That it happened this way is shown by one of Göring's attempts to revive Hess's apparent loss of memory at Nuremberg after the war:

Do you remember Mr Messerschmitt? You were well acquainted with him. He constructed all our fighter planes, and he also gave you the plane which I refused to give you – the plane with which you flew to England. Mr Messerschmitt gave that to you behind my back.[19]

Here, possibly, is the clue to why the Duke of Hamilton was chosen. It must be assumed Hess knew Hamilton had a private landing strip at Dungavel House; Albrecht Haushofer, after all, had stayed there as a guest. It seems possible, therefore, that Hamilton was chosen because he was believed to have influence in the circles that counted, right up to the Palace, and because he had a private landing strip – where one might drop in under cover of darkness, unseen and unbeknown to the authorities, and, with luck and additional fuel provided by the host, fly off again after parleying. If this was Hess's idea, it was badly misconceived. The grass strip at Dungavel was on a slight incline and, apart from the impossibility of locating it in darkness, was quite unsuitable for the modern fighter-bomber Hess contemplated flying.[20] Hamilton had used it for Tiger Moths and similar very light aircraft with landing speeds no higher than some 80 miles an hour; to attempt a night landing with a Messerschmitt 110 would have been suicidal. Yet that, apparently, is what Hess did intend for, according to his later account for Ilse, he never practised a parachute jump, nor even found out how to make one – and thereby nearly killed himself anyway. Also it is difficult to account for the weather reports he required, not simply of the Channel, but of the North Sea and British Isles at the very time he initiated the approach to Hamilton, unless he was intent then on flying to see him in Scotland.

Such an idea fitted his psychological needs: in place of the compromises and humiliations of his Party liaison post, he would be acting positively, spectacularly in a practical field, flying, which he had mastered and loved. And success, besides fulfilling his Führer's long-term strategy would ensure his own position at his Führer's right hand.

The idea must also have appealed to Hitler. He had been sure right up to Halifax's rejection of his public 'appeal to reason' in July that the 'reasonable' elements in Britain would prevail over the 'die-hards'.[21] Reports were coming in all the time to suggest they still might; on 19 August the Spanish Foreign Minister, after a discussion with the British Minister at Madrid, had stated his impression that it was possible England was prepared for negotiations.[22] At the beginning of September it was reported again *via* Madrid that the Spanish Ambassador in London had described English capitalists wanting an end to the war and the City as 'the stronghold of pacifism and pessimism'.[23] From Lisbon on 10 September came a report that, since the start of the air attack, the opposition to Churchill had come to life again; it did not constitute a serious movement yet, since it was not compact; 'the most united [are] among the Conservatives themselves and in the country the industrialists of Leeds, Birmingham.'[24] The same report described clear preparations for the flight of the cabinet across the Atlantic and the relegation of Churchill to Roosevelt's adviser; 'it appears established that preparations are far advanced for the transfer of the Royal Family to Canada.'[25] On 17 September came a far more dramatic despatch from Lisbon, reporting the 'organisation of London completely destroyed' by the air raids, looting sabotage and social tension:

Anxious capitalists fear internal disorders. Growth of opposition against cabinet is plain. Churchill, Halifax are blamed for sacrificing England to destruction instead of seeking a compromise with Germany, for which it is still not too late.[26]

At the end of the month came a report from Washington of the latest piece of pessimism from the US Ambassador in London: 'England', Kennedy had wired Roosevelt, 'is finished' (*erledigt*).[27] The diaries of Harold Nicolson and Jock Colville, both close to the centre of affairs in London, reveal these reports were not far wide of the mark: in August Nicolson had noted his wife asking 'the unspoken question which is in all of our minds, "How can we possibly win?"' He imagined the heavy bombing to come and a great German peace propaganda drive representing Churchill as responsible for the tremendous suffering by holding out obstinately; and he imagined the fifth column setting to work in the country:

... the extreme Left taking orders from Moscow ... the extreme Right, angry at the humiliation by Churchill of the Conservative Party ... the lower middle-classes frightened of the bombs ... and then there will be the Pacifists and the Oxford Group people who will say that material defeat means nothing and that we can find in moral rearmament that strength that is greater than the riches of this world ...[28]

He foresaw Lloyd George or Beaverbrook emerging as prophet of this mood. In September, after ten days of bombing in London, he noted concern about the feeling in London's East End, 'where there is much bitterness'; and at the back of everyone's mind lay the question: if Hitl· continued the attack twenty-four hours a day, would they be able to stand it?[29]

Hitler had every reason to suppose he could break the morale of the British people and Government. The idea of his deputy flying to England to crown the peace offensive as Chamberlain had flown to Munich must have appealed to his sense of theatre; he was the great simplifier and, since his victory in the west, everything appeared possible. This must be how the plan was conceived; for both Hitler and Hess it was, to paraphrase von Weizsäcker on Churchill, not a logical but a psychological necessity.

The Haushofers were not informed of Hess's intention to fly to Great Britain, but, as Albrecht told his parents on 19 September, he thought even that part of the mission with which he had been entrusted 'a fool's errand'. His latest information, he went on, was that the British Empire and the United States were on the point of signing an alliance.[30] Nevertheless, there was nothing he could say to dissuade Hess and he drafted a letter to Hamilton to be enclosed with a few lines to Mrs Roberts, both so phrased as to appear harmless to British censors and not endanger either the recipient or the old lady. He sent a copy to Hess and explained:

H [Hamilton] ... cannot fly to Lisbon without obtaining leave ... that is, without at least the Air Minister, Sinclair, and the Foreign Minister, Halifax, knowing of it. If he receives permission, however, to answer or to travel, then there is no need for a statement of his whereabouts in England; if he does not receive it then an attempt through neutral middlemen will also have little success.[31]

In any case, he continued, the technicality of finding out the whereabouts of the first peer in Scotland would be no problem for the neutral middleman Hess intended sending to Britain. This must have been just as obvious to Hess, suggesting again that there was to be no middleman; he was to fly there himself. Albrecht concluded:

That – and why – the possibilities of success of attempts to reach a compromise between the Führer and the British upper classes appear – to my own great sorrow – so infinitely small, I have already attempted to argue recently. Despite that I should not like to conclude this letter without pointing out again that even now I rate the chances via the Ambassador Lothian in Washington or Sir Samuel Hoare in Madrid as somewhat better than via my friend H.

Nothing in Nazi Germany can be taken at face value. How much Albrecht's pessimism was genuine, how much he was covering himself against being accused later of originating the scheme is difficult to determine. He wrote to his father, 'I have now established clearly enough that it was a matter in which I did not take the initiative'.[32] The draft letter to Hamilton was in English; the substantive paragraph runs:

Of [sic] you remember some of my last communications before the war started you will realise that there is a certain significance in the fact that I am, at present, able to ask you wether [sic] there is the slightest chance of our meeting and having a talk somewhere on the outskirts of Europe, perhaps in Portugal. There are some things I could tell you, that might make it worth while for you to try a short trip to Lisbon – if you could make your authorities understand so much that they would give you leave. As to myself – I could reach Lisbon any time (without any kind of difficulty) within a few days after receiving news from you. If there is an answer to this letter, please address it to . . .[33]

Hess approved the draft, and Albrecht, after conferring with Hess's brother, Alfred, wrote out a fair copy with a few alterations, adding the address of a firm in Lisbon whose owner was a member of the Foreign Organisation and to which a reply could be sent. He dated it 'Sept. 23rd', and for his own address at the top simply put 'B' for Berlin, in itself enough to alert the censor. After adding good wishes from his 'father and mother' to his own, he signed with the stylised 'A' he used in letters to those he knew well. He folded the three sheets and placed them in an envelope, addressing it to 'His Grace the Duke of Hamilton & Brandon, House of Lords, London'. He then wrote a note to Mrs Roberts asking her to forward the letter to the Duke of Hamilton, whom he had known, he said, as Lord Clydesdale. It might be of significance for him and his friends in high office, he declared; he was 'sincerely convinced' that it could do no harm and it was conceivable it might be 'useful for all of us'.[34] Addressing the whole package to 'Mrs V. Roberts, Lisbon, Caixa Postal 506', he handed it to Hess's brother for delivery. Afterwards he wrote a brief note to Hess: 'The letter you wished was written early this morning [23rd] and has gone off.'[35]

The same day he wrote to his father reiterating his conviction that there was not the slightest prospect of a peace, but he could not refuse his patron any longer:

You know that I see for myself no satisfactory possibility of action in future. If there is the 'total victory' for our wild people from Glasgow to Capetown that is envisaged, then the drunken sergeants and the corrupt profiteers will set the tone anyway; experts with quiet manners will not be needed then. If there is not, if the English succeed in absorbing the first push and then create a long-term war equilibrium with American help and use of the Bolshevik insecurity factor, then of course there will be a need for such as us – in circumstances, however, in which little enough will remain to salvage. If therefore I am now called in it only means I am in danger of a senseless wear and tear – which I can only face if I make it completely plain beforehand how small the prospects of success of any attempt. That I have tried to do. If despite it I am ordered, I can do no more . . .[36]

He had, he went on, spoken on the same theme with von Weizsäcker, who was in a similar position. Von Weizsäcker had agreed that they would only be able to affect events when circumstances changed to vindicate their known pessimism. Should it not come to that, Albrecht concluded, the ss types would have the higher historical law on their side.

In October Hess started on another line. He summoned Ernst Bohle, the South African-educated chief of his Foreign Organisation, gave him a letter he had drafted to Hamilton and asked him to translate it into English. Again he did not reveal his intention of delivering the letter himself.

After the war Bohle told his interrogator: 'I did all the translation work for this trip to England, I didn't know he was going to England, I thought he was going to Switzerland . . .'[37]

What Bohle described as 'translation work' lasted intermittently from October 'until January or February' the following year, 1941. Hess's son, Wolf, claims that Bohle did not work on the letter after 7 January.[38] From all the talks Bohle had with Hess during this time he knew that the object was to stop the war, but he had no idea Hess intended flying to England.

It was suggested by Professor Haushofer . . . that I would meet in a neutral country, possibly Switzerland, and it was my firm opinion at the time, which I cannot prove today, that Hitler knew all about it because it seemed impossible to me that Hess would do anything of such importance without asking Hitler . . . It was my opinion that only three people in Germany knew anything about it, Hitler, Hess and myself. It was kept away from them. I had orders to speak to nobody, not even to his [Hess's] own brother, who was in my own office, not even to his secretary.[39]

Later, when Bohle was called in as one of those trying to revive Hess's memory before the Nuremberg trial, Göring said, 'Remind him that it was you who translated his letter.'

'Don't you remember', Bohle said to Hess, 'that I translated your letter to the Duke of Hamilton?'

'No.'

'Don't you remember that you took this letter to the Duke of Hamilton, that it was I who translated it?'[40]

It seems strange that Bohle was occupied on translation work for a single letter for some three or four months, yet he was not probed. Whether Hess was updating and adding to the letter he eventually took to Hamilton or whether there were other letters in between remains unclear from his testimony.

Bohle also testified to a complete change in Hess's health and spirits from this time on; 'From the moment he had that idea ... there was such an enormous difference in him, no more doubt, [he] was fresh and seemed to be enthusiastic about the whole affair, [it] made him a perfectly, absolutely quiet man, well spirited'.[41] Bohle assumed, no doubt correctly, that this was due to his new-found sense of purpose. Release from the flying prohibition probably played its part too. The Messerschmitt works at Augsburg were a little over forty miles from his house in Harlaching and once or twice a week he drove out there to practise on the twin-engined, two-seater, Me-110D fighter-bomber – works number 3869, radio code vJ+oQ – that Professor Messerschmitt had made available for his personal use.[42] On his initial flights he was accompanied by Hitler's pilot, Hans Baur. After most flights he would relax in the canteen with the test pilots, discussing technical points or modifications which he required. By the beginning of November, to judge by a brief note he wrote for his wife and small son, Wolf, he felt ready:

My dears,

I firmly believe that I will return from the flight I am about to undertake in the next few days and that the flight will be crowned with success. If not, however, the goal I set myself was worth going all out for. I know that you know me: you know I could not do otherwise.

Your Rudolf[43]

As an insight into his character, this note may be compared with a letter he wrote from imprisonment in Britain in January 1945:

I have only one wish for my son: that he is able to be 'obsessed' by something, irrespective of whether a machine design, a new medical idea or a drama – even if no one builds the machine, no one reads the drama or even wants to perform it or doctors of all persuasions unite to fall upon him and tear him to pieces intellectually ...[44]

However, as a piece of evidence about his immediate purpose, the farewell note is puzzling because, so far as is known, there had been no reply to Albrecht's letter to Hamilton, indeed, it was at that date lying in the 'Terminal Mails (Private Branch)' of the British censorship headquarters adjacent to MI5, Wormwood Scrubs, London. It had arrived at table II, Department PR4, on 2 November; examiner 1021 had noted:

Cook's Mail – letter forwarded from Cook's office in Lisbon, Mrs V. Roberts address being filed in Cook's office, Berkeley St., London. Writer possibly a German & possibly writing from Berlin ('B') requests addressee to forward a letter to the Duke of Hamilton . . . He gives the name and address of an intermediary in Lisbon through whom letters may be transmitted with a minimum of delay.[45]

It appears that it was submitted to MI12 for MI5 and it was decided to send the original to the Foreign Office. That was changed, however, and on 6 November the original was sent to MI12 for MI5, photostats to the Foreign Office and the IRB.[46] Albrecht had signally failed to keep either Hamilton or his family's elderly lady from possibly serious trouble.

Wing Commander the Duke of Hamilton and Brandon was serving as station commander at RAF Turnhouse, just outside Edinburgh; he had been there since the end of July. On Tuesday 12 November, six days after Albrecht's letter went to MI5, he handed over to his second-in-command, Wing Commander Pinkerton, and took ten days' leave,[47] it is not known where since his papers are unavailable.

By coincidence, on the same day, Albrecht Haushofer wrote to his mother: 'From L. [Lisbon] nothing. It will doubtless come to nothing.'[48]

─────16─────
THE DOUBLE GAME

Hess's active interest in a settlement with Great Britain was not confined to the Haushofers and Bohle; if the memoirs of a remarkable double agent, Dusko Popov, are to be believed, Admiral Canaris was in the picture. Popov was an upper-class Yugoslav, educated in France and at Freiburg University, Germany, who worked for a Yugoslav banking consortium in Lisbon. In 1940, while Canaris was attempting to increase his sparse coverage of agents in Britain, Popov was recruited into the Abwehr and attached to the Lisbon office. In December he was sent to London, where it was felt his social and financial connections would give him assured entrée to the best society. They did, but it was chiefly because he had already informed the British secret service of his recruitment; he travelled over as a double agent working for Stewart Menzies.[1]

Before leaving, he was briefed by a friend from his university days, Johann Jebsen, born into a wealthy Hamburg shipping family, now an Abwehr agent in Division 1 – foreign intelligence – and on friendly terms with the head of the division, Colonel Hans Pieckenbrock, who in turn was close to Canaris. During the course of the briefing, Jebsen told him that Hess was aware, he assumed through his *Verbindungsstab* intelligence, of 'high personalities' in Great Britain who were seeking contact with Germany.[2] He also told him that the Abwehr was in touch with Welsh Nationalist groups who were talking of Lloyd George returning as Prime Minister and negotiating peace. Probably these rumours had been planted on the Abwehr by two of the earliest double agents controlled by the British, codenamed 'Snow' and 'Biscuit', whose ostensible sources included a man said to be in the Welsh Nationalist Party, codenamed 'GW'.[3]

This was the work of a special section of MI5 established that summer and designated 'W' branch – later B1a – specifically to control German agents who had been 'turned' and who, while pretending to work for their Abwehr masters, were in reality sending intelligence to the instructions of their case officers in 'W' branch. Those agents caught on arrival in Britain who could not be 'turned' were executed. A 'W' board had been formed at the end of September consisting of 'C', the three heads of the service intelligence departments and the head of 'B' Division MI5 – of which 'W' branch was a part – in order to co-ordinate the mixture of false and true intelligence the double agents were to spread. By the time Popov arrived in England, therefore, the basic structure of the 'double-cross system', which came to control the entire German espionage net in Great Britain for the duration of the war, was in place.[4] All that was lacking was a lower-level board to supervise the day-to-day work of the agents; before the end of the year this was established as the 'xx' for 'Double-Cross' or 'Twenty Committee'.

Popov arrived from Lisbon in Bristol and was driven by an MI5 officer to London, where he booked in to the Savoy. There he was interviewed by the head of 'W' branch, Major T. A. ('Tar') Robertson, 'looking like the Hollywood concept of a dashing British military type';[5] and afterwards he was grilled for four days by a series of intelligence officers including the Oxford don, international-class sportsman and writer of mystery novels J. C. Masterman, who worked for MI5 and was to head the xx Committee. Popov impressed his interrogators and was given the code name for double work of 'Scout', later changed to 'Tricycle'. He was given a case officer, who took him to visit places he was required to report on for the Abwehr, chiefly in connection with British defences against invasion, and was set up with a bogus export-import company with an office near Piccadilly.

He was also invited to a New Year house party by Stewart Menzies, who told him he required information on Canaris and everyone close to him. Menzies believed, rightly, that Canaris was a catalyst for anti-Hitler elements, and he wanted to be able to assess their strength. Apart from this special information, which he was to report directly to Menzies without intermediaries, Popov's task for Masterman and the Double-Cross Committee was on the one hand, to impress his German masters with the strength of the defences against invasion and, on the other, to give the impression from his social contacts that there were elements in Britain ready to make peace with Germany.[6] With both propositions he was working with a grain of truth and, at the same time, providing Hitler and of course Hess – of whose active interest in 'high personalities' wishing for peace he had undoubtedly informed his interrogators – with what they most wanted to hear, that an invasion was too risky and that Churchill could be toppled.

Many reports from the German Minister in Lisbon to the Foreign Ministry in Berlin attest to the stories planted by the xx Committee, and some can be ascribed to Popov. One sent by wire on 4 January

1941, the day after Popov returned to Lisbon, referred to 'the demoralising effects of the bombing', which made it seem impossible that British resistance could be maintained. It described Beaverbrook taking a pessimistic view in the cabinet, and continued: 'Halifax has been kicked out because, even though loyal to the Government externally, in the Cabinet he continually represented certain policies of "appeasement".'[7]

All this was close to the truth. Beaverbrook, who was obtaining superhuman results as Minister of Aircraft Production, had evinced signs of extreme pessimism that autumn and in October had urged Lloyd George to meet him in London to save the country 'from the doom into which it is heading with its accustomed blind fury'.[8] Lloyd George had been equally pessimistic; throughout the autumn his 'military adviser', Basil Liddell Hart, had been producing memoranda urging compromise peace since the most that could be hoped for in the military field was stalemate, which would bring economic ruin, cultural devastation and epidemic disease to both sides; the only beneficiaries would be Soviet Russia and perhaps the United States.[9]

In December Lord Lothian died suddenly. Via Beaverbrook, Churchill had asked Lloyd George to go to Washington as British Ambassador in his place, but he had declined, pleading age and his doctor's advice; in reality he believed Churchill was heading for disaster and wanted to hold himself in readiness to take over and negotiate a settlement with Germany.[10] Churchill had then asked Halifax to take up the Washington post; reluctantly and sadly he had agreed, confiding to Rab Butler that he thought it was because Churchill wished to get rid of all the gentlemen.[11] In Halifax's place as Foreign Secretary Churchill had appointed Anthony Eden as his own liege man.

The wire from Lisbon on 4 January cannot be ascribed to Popov, but a despatch later that month can be. It was again from the German Minister in Lisbon to the Foreign Ministry, Berlin, and was dated the 23rd. It enclosed a report from an 'agent of the local Abwehr about the present position in England'.[12] The agent had been in England from 10 December to 3 January 1941. While this arrival date does not match exactly that given for Popov in Masterman's book, *The Double-Cross System*, practically everything else in the report matches Popov's account in his memoirs. Thus, the agent in the report visited Bristol – where Popov had arrived – and cities which Popov in his memoirs describes visiting with his case officer. The agent reported on the defences against invasion – 'All harbours from Hunstanton to Portsmouth have concrete defence installations' – and stated the strength of the Army as twenty-seven to thirty divisions with some new divisions being formed. In his memoirs Popov wrote: 'The Germans, to our knowledge, estimated that fifteen of the known twenty-seven British Divisions were fully equipped

... Actually hardly six Divisions were ready to take the field ...'.[13] The agent spent the night of 29 December in London under a great air attack, describing the three hours it lasted as 'the most horrifying of his life ... a hell of fire, explosions and splinters ...'. In his memoirs Popov described a bomb on the Savoy which caused splinters of glass from a mirror to cut his face. These scratches 'spoke more than a thousand words' when he arrived in Lisbon properly bandaged and plastered, 'and they made my stories of unbearable bombing effects more credible to the Germans'.[14] There can be little doubt that this report from Lisbon emanated from Popov in his double-cross role; this makes the concluding section especially interesting:

As friendly towards peace the agent specifies:
   (1) Lord Brocket
   (2) Lord Londonderry
   (3) Lord Lymington
If one gave these three men the power they strive for, they would agree to any conditions.[15]

What Lord Lymington's real views were at the time is not known; he was not a man of power, rather an eccentric. Lord Londonderry, however, had been Air Minister at the time of the expansion of Göring's air force and he had given it his blessing in the sense that John Simon and the Admiralty gave their blessing to the expansion of the German fleet. Before the war he had been dubbed 'the pro-Nazi Lord Londonderry' by Beaverbrook's columnists and in the House of Commons he was regarded with suspicion as the leader of the compromise peace lobby in the Lords. Like Buccleuch, Liddell Hart and others, his arguments were strategic rather than pro-Nazi. However, Lord Brocket, probably the most active of the peace lobby, was said to hold pro-Nazi views. In his case Popov's report of willingness 'to agree to any conditions' was no doubt true.[16] Brocket was the sponsor of Lonsdale Bryans, who had met von Hassell in Switzerland with Lord Halifax's approval in February 1940 and again in April with Sir Alexander Cadogan's approval – by which time his mission had been overtaken by events. In early 1941 he was in Lisbon making a nuisance of himself at the British Embassy and claiming he was acting for Lord Halifax, while attempting to arrange another meeting with von Hassell in Switzerland.[17] It may be that his activities were condoned, since they fitted the deception campaign on which the 'W' board and the Double-Cross Committee had embarked.

Hess is supposed to have made two or three false starts before his successful flight to Scotland. Helmut Kaden, one of the Messerschmitt test pilots who was responsible for the preparation of Hess's plane at Augsburg, has stated that Hess made his first attempt on 21 December 1940, and a second on 18 January 1941.[18] Hess's farewell letter dated 4 November suggests he was ready by this time. His son Wolf, however, rules out the December date and states that his father made his first attempt on 10 January.[19] This was the date that Hess's adjutant, Karl-Heinz Pintsch, gave the author James Leasor, when Leasor was writing his book on the Hess mission in 1969.[20] Hess himself told Sir John Simon in June 1941, four weeks after his flight, that he had made his first attempt on 7 January, but had not been able to carry it through 'on several grounds, weather situation, etc., and difficulties cropping up with the plane at the works'.[21]

Hess also told Simon that he had postponed his plan from the beginning of January until shortly before he made the flight in May 'on the grounds that English successes in North Africa and the Greek successes against the Italians made the situation unfavourable for England to yield'.[22]

However, this political situation applied to all the suggested dates, 21 December, 7, 10 and 18 January. The first spectacular British success against the Italians had been the Fleet Air Arm attack on the Italian fleet at Taranto on 11 November. On 9 December General Wavell had launched an offensive against the Italian Army in North Africa, winning the first major victory at Sidi Barrani on the 12th; by the 15th the Italians had been driven from Egypt and were in full retreat, leaving thousands of prisoners behind them.

The 21st of December was, therefore, not a propitious date to fly to Britain with peace terms. Even if Hess did take off on that date, it is scarcely conceivable he would have revealed to Kaden what must surely have been the closest secret in the *Reich*. The situation in North Africa was even worse, from the Axis point of view, by 7 January, when Hess himself claimed he had made his first attempt, while Karl-Heinz Pintsch's story about the 'first attempt' on 10 January is simply unbelievable in every detail. The flight has been surrounded by deliberate mystification on both sides; without contemporary documentary evidence there is no reason to believe in these early unsuccessful flights. On the other hand, it is easy to see that Hess would have wanted to suggest earlier attempts in order to remove the suspicion that he was coming over to settle things with Britain just before Hitler attacked Russia – which, of course, is what he was doing. Karl-Heinz Pintsch was presumably trying to back Hess's story, but, since he did not know what Hess had told Sir John Simon, none of the details tallied.

It is apparent, in any case, from the continuing conversations between Hess and Haushofer and between Haushofer and various neutrals through the early months of 1941 and the astonishing number of British Foreign

Office files for this period closed until 2017 either that Hess was not ready to fly by January or that his original plan was being modified.

The world power situation in early 1941 was critically poised. Japan had signed a tripartite pact with the two Axis powers at the end of September 1940. In November Roosevelt had been re-elected President of the United States, beating his isolationist rival. His commitment to aid Great Britain as the first line in the defence of America itself was well known and ascribed in Germany to the Jews in his *entourage* and administration. Nevertheless, the sheer scale of British orders in the United States for munitions, the cost of which far exceeded British gold and currency reserves, created problems for Churchill. It proved the point being made by the City magnates, Conservative grandees, Lloyd George, Liddell Hart and the rest that the only outcome of the war would be ruin and finally the dependence of the British Empire on America – thus the end of the Empire – while the apparent avidity of the Americans to demand payment for what was seen as a common cause to defeat the evil of Nazism confirmed the anti-American prejudices in these circles. The situation was only eased by Roosevelt's bill announced in December to 'lend and lease' war materials under a gentleman's agreement for repayment in kind after the war. This was not passed until March, but it cast its shadow over German strategic thought, implying as it did a virtual alliance between the two Anglo-Saxon powers and the vast potential of American industrial strength harnessed for the destruction of National Socialist Germany.

Hitler's decision to knock out Great Britain *via* Russia had hardened, meanwhile, into an *idée fixe*. In November the Russian Foreign Minister, Molotov, had been invited to Berlin ostensibly to discuss her entry into the Tripartite Pact to create a great anti-British alliance whose partners would carve up the British Empire between them after England's fall. Hess was one of those who met Molotov. It was a simple deception, as the sphere of interest allotted to the Soviet Union in Ribbentrop's draft protocol makes clear. Less than a week after Molotov had left and before the Soviet Government had replied to the proposals, von Weizsäcker noted that it was being said 'unless we liquidate Russia no order can be created in Europe',[23] and at the end of November General Paulus of the General Staff had begun the first phase of a war game to prove the proposed eastern offensive. In early December he started the second phase of the game 'up to gaining the line Minsk-Kiev', and on the 18th, after the completion of the final phase to the capture of Moscow, Hitler had issued Directive 21, code-named 'Barbarossa': the armed services were to be prepared by 15 May 1941 to smash Russia in a lightning campaign.[24]

Hitler laid bare his thinking before the Generals early in January 1941: after repeating his earlier justification that Britain placed her hopes on Russia and America, he explained that Eden was the man for an alliance with Russia. This was true; Halifax had been such a terrific anti-Bolshevik that he had made a point of never even seeing the Russian Ambassador unless it was unavoidable.[25] Since Britain could not be knocked out by the Luftwaffe and u-boats, Hitler continued, the Germans must establish themselves so firmly on the continent of Europe during the course of 1941 that they could face the continuation of the war against England and America. Japan was prepared to co-operate, and, by tackling the Russian question, they would give her a free hand against Great Britain in the Far East. 'Decision for a radical settlement of the continental situation. As early as possible!'[26] Meanwhile Operation 'Sealion', the invasion of Britain, was definitively postponed, pretended preparations to be continued only as a deception.

Hitler presumably used the same arguments to Hess, who would, in any case, have been instructed at every stage of the ripening plans by his liaison staff with the armed services. On ideological grounds he would have welcomed the decision finally to proceed against the real enemy; and, since he would not have questioned his Führer's strategic genius, he could only have been spurred in his decision to try to avert the fratricidal blood-letting with the British beforehand. It can hardly be doubted, therefore, that he was in the most receptive frame of mind to be taken in by the subtle deception Stewart Menzies, Masterman and Tar Robertson were weaving with the double-cross system.

Sir David Kelly, the British Ambassador in Berne, was another arm of the deception. Whether this was intentional or whether he was simply acting on instructions to keep up contacts with the Germans for intelligence purposes is not clear; the result was the same. Thus Himmler's and Ribbentrop's agent, Prince Hohenlowe, had reported in December 1940 that Kelly had taken him aside and asked if he had passed on the gist of their last discussion in July to the German authorities. When Hohenlowe replied non-committally, Kelly, a tall, patrician diplomat of the old school, said he had now come round to the opinion that an understanding between Britain and National Socialist Germany was not beyond the bounds of possibility. He could not imagine, however, that the British Government would enter negotiations simply on German promises; it would depend on what guarantees Germany was prepared to give in regard to the evacuation of conquests. Hohenlowe, according to his own report, said there was no question of German troops withdrawing from conquests before the conclusion of a peace, at which Kelly was silent.[27] According to Kelly's report of the conversation, Hohenlowe expressed interest that the British Government might even consider a settlement with Hitler and said that Germany would give up everything except Poland and Czechoslovakia.[28] However, the overall impression Hohenlowe derived from the talk confirmed many other reports coming in to Ribbentrop's ministry:

I assumed ... Kelly spoke out of concern that the development of the war could lead to great, perhaps decisive injuries to the internal political and power position of the propertied class in England. Kelly himself belongs to this class and appears to me to incline towards a compromise with Germany.[29]

Shortly after this meeting in Berne another of the go-betweens who had taken part in Hitler's initial peace offensive in late 1939 began a further round of soundings. This was Baron Knut Bonde, a retired Swedish diplomat brought back for the war to serve in the Swedish Legation in Berne. He was married to the daughter of a former Scottish colonel of Stewart Menzies's regiment, the 2nd Life Guards, a niece of Lord Rennell, and had a home and business interests in Scotland. On the Swedish side he was close to Count Eric Rosen, the brother of Göring's Swedish first wife, Karin, hence his earlier attempts at conciliation had been on behalf of Göring. He was an ardent Christian and was regarded at the Foreign Office in Whitehall as a man of the highest integrity and sincerity, and a considerable nuisance. Shortly before Christmas 1940 he had received a telegram from one of his oldest and closest English friends, Lady Barlow. As with Violet Roberts's card to the Haushofers, the contents are not known, but it impelled him to return to Sweden to try and set up another meeting with Göring. He succeeded in gaining an interview with the great man on 14 January 1941 and the manner in which he was received convinced him that, if he had only had some positive proposal from the British side, Göring would have shown his hand and they might have found some ground on which to start negotiations. Instead Göring said, 'We have offered England peace twice. If I send any message now, it will be taken as a sign of weakness.'[30]

Bonde returned to Berne and told Kelly, who wired the Foreign Office that the meeting suggested Göring was 'at least sufficiently uncertain of future as to welcome any personal message from our side'. Bonde then wrote to Lady Barlow telling her of his reception by Göring and concluding:

If I could go to London I would try to see Mr Lloyd George and tell him that my conviction is that a peace negotiation undoubtedly could be started through my intermediary and I think it would be extremely wrong not to try this channel before worse things have happened. If you get this letter and if Mr Lloyd George thinks he can induce the Government to do something on the lines I suggest, will you send me a telegram? I can see Göring again at any time and nobody outside will know of it. A message could reach me through the British Legation here.[31]

The letter reached Lady Barlow and was forwarded in February to Sir Alexander Cadogan at the Foreign Office by Colonel Scovell, who had arranged a meeting between Bonde and Halifax in December 1939. In an accompanying note to Cadogan, Scovell wrote:

... I should perhaps explain that Halifax asked me to come straight to you should anything of interest arise from this direction ... Unless you tell me to the contrary, I think I can undertake to prevent anything going to Lloyd George, whom both Lady Barlow and I know well.[32]

Long before this reached Cadogan, Churchill had stepped in to prevent further contacts of this kind. The message from Kelly about Bonde's effort had not been the first intimation that Göring would be responsive to peace overtures. Sir Samuel Hoare, British Ambassador in Madrid, had sent two messages to that effect, the first on 4 January, citing the Hungarian Minister in Madrid as his source,[33] the second on 11 January, citing information from Vichy France.[34] On 20 January Churchill wrote a note to Anthony Eden:

I presume you are keeping your eye upon all this. Your predecessor was entirely misled in December 1939. Our attitude towards all such inquiries or suggestions should be absolute silence. It may well be that a new peace offensive will open upon us as an alternative to threats of invasion and poison gas.[35]

The reference to Eden's predecessor being misled referred to the negotiation Halifax had attempted through Baron Bonde. The following week Cadogan wrote a minute on the Bonde file: 'Note that Göring would "welcome any possible message from our side". I have no doubt he would. He wants us to sue for peace. It is just what he won't get ... I think the PM's decree of "absolute silence" meets all purposes.'[36]

Eden asked Cadogan to speak to him on this point, as a result of which instructions were wired to Kelly in Berne, Mallet in Stockholm and Hoare in Madrid, the three neutral capitals from which most peace feelers had come: the attitude to be adopted to all peace soundings and suggestions should be absolute silence – nevertheless any indication of German inclinations to negotiate should still be reported fully.[37]

Meanwhile, yet another channel had been opened through Carl Burckhardt of the Red Cross in Geneva, who it will be recalled had acted as go-between for Rab Butler, Under-Secretary of State at the Foreign Office, to Hohenlowe at about the time of the fall of France. Burckhardt, described by Harold Nicolson, who had met him at the beginning of the war, as 'rather a dapper, smart, fresh-coloured Swiss aristocrat',[38] had no illusions about National Socialism. He had known all the top Nazis for some years and had discerned Hitler's main source of energy as hatred. But it was plain to him that, unless the war could be stopped, America and Russia must be drawn in; like Bonde, he believed it essential to avert such a world catastrophe. On 30 January he looked up von Hassell in Arosa. Von Hassell was there to visit his son, hoping also to arrange another meeting with 'the Doctor', Lonsdale Bryans, who had just wired him from Lisbon. Burckhardt told him that he had been approached very recently by the Finnish art historian, Professor Borenius, who had lived in London for many years and had come to him 'on behalf of the English authorities', as von Hassell put it in his diary, to say that a reasonable peace could still be concluded. Borenius had told him he was convinced this was the mood in the English Cabinet although Eden's entry in place of Halifax created difficulties.[39]

Either Borenius was mistaken about the mood in the cabinet or he was being used deliberately to propagate disinformation, for probably the only members of the cabinet or Defence Committee holding these views were Lords Hankey and Beaverbrook, who was still not entirely certain that Lloyd George and Liddell Hart were not right about the war. There were, of course, many outside the cabinet who held the view Borenius described, but, without knowing the name of the confidant, left blank in von Hassell's diary, it is idle to speculate.

On 2 February, shortly after Burckhardt electrified von Hassell with this news, Albrecht Haushofer travelled to Sweden; what his business was and whom he talked to are not known. His visit lasted until the 5th. The Duke of Hamilton, meanwhile, who had taken ten days' leave shortly after Albrecht's letter had been passed to MI5 in November, was on leave again from 26 January to 4 February.[40] Once more it is impossible, without access to his papers, to know where he was and whether Albrecht's visit to Sweden towards the end of this period was anything more than coincidence.

Immediately after this there are a remarkable number of Foreign Office files closed until 2017; the first two can be dated to 4 or 5 February and 5 or 6 February and are without doubt papers to or from Sir Samuel Hoare in Madrid.[41] The next three can be dated to 12 or 13 February, 20–22 February and 28 February.[42] From the references to these latter three in open files it is certain that all have some connection with the Baron Bonde-Göring-Lady Barlow-Lloyd George peace feelers. There are no less than eight more closed files up to the date of Hess's flight to Scotland and a further six afterwards to June, three of which are concerned directly with the flight.[43] There may be others.

Although Hess later told Sir John Simon that he made no attempt to fly to Great Britain between early January and the end of April because of British military successes, there was another way of looking at it. Britain was proving she could win campaigns and was by no means defeated. The sea blockade of the Axis powers was holding; Wavell's army had won a string of victories against the Italians in North Africa; and British forces were in the process of overrunning the Italian East African Empire. In the light of all this, a compromise peace would no longer be seen as shameful, as von Weizsäcker had once termed it, but could be negotiated on the basis of a German 'free hand' in Europe in return for a British 'free hand' overseas without loss of prestige.[44]

This was not how it was perceived at the Foreign Office. Anthony Eden and the permanent officials were right behind Churchill in his uncompromising attitude; thus on a wire from Madrid on 12 February, which reported the Spanish Air Minister expressing the view that the British Empire had recovered enough prestige to negotiate a reasonable peace, F.H. (now Sir Frank) Roberts minuted: '. . . the Germans would be ready to end the war tomorrow on their own terms . . . It is we who are, for excellent reasons, responsible for the continuation of the war . . .'[45]

Cadogan agreed. But despite this clear line and Churchill's rhetoric, despite the British victories in North Africa, those circles concentrated in the City of London and the House of Lords who knew the war could not be won without American and probably Russian help, and who did not relish either, were becoming increasingly dissatisfied. Lloyd George still saw himself as their champion. On 24 February he wrote to Beaverbrook suggesting that the time was approaching 'when I think it will be urgent that I should have another talk with you'.[46] Beaverbrook agreed to a meeting because, he wrote, 'I would like so much to hear your views on the immense issues which now impend'.[47] Lloyd George's views, as expounded to others, remained that the war was a blunder, and they were still blundering and the war cabinet was giving no real direction. He believed that time was on Hitler's side and, if Great Britain managed to hold out for another year, she would be weaker, Germany stronger. When he tried to tackle Churchill about peace negotiations, however, Churchill simply grew excited and shouted, 'Never, never, never!' He concluded, 'Winston likes the war.'[48]

It was in these circumstances that Hess developed his plan to outflank the peace soundings *via* the usual sources in the neutral capitals directed at Churchill's Government, and instead to appeal to the 'opposition' directly by flying to Great Britain. It seems probable that he regarded Lloyd George as leader of the political side of this 'opposition'. Since he summoned Albrecht Haushofer to him from 21 to 24 February, it seems probable that this was the subject of their talks.

Meanwhile, the 'W' board developed their deception, for at the end of the month the Duke of Hamilton received a letter from Group Captain F. G. ('Freddie') Stammers of Air Intelligence dated 26 February asking him if he would be in London in the near future; he was anxious to see him about a certain matter.[49] On 8 March Hamilton handed over to his second in command at RAF Turnhouse and took ten days' leave – his third ten days in the past four months – during the course of which he travelled to London and saw Stammers. According to his own account of the interview as given by his son, James Douglas-Hamilton in *Motive for a Mission*, Stammers asked him what he had done with the letter Albrecht Haushofer had written to him. Thinking he meant the July 1939 letter, Hamilton said he had deposited it with his bank. It then became apparent they were talking of different letter and Stammers pushed a photocopy of the 23 September 1940 letter across the table to him. This surprised Hamilton as 'it had never occurred to him that Albrecht Haushofer would attempt to make contact with him during the war'.[50]

This story suggests astonishing incompetence in the intelligence services. Either MI5 had passed the original of this letter to Hamilton, in which case he could hardly have been surprised by it, or MI5 had retained the original, in which case they should have informed Stammers of this when they passed him the photocopy. It is difficult to conceive circumstances in which MI5 would have passed on a photocopied letter from an enemy subject to another intelligence department in such casual fashion that they omitted to explain the action taken and the reasons. On the other hand, the Duke of Hamilton's account was probably written after the war, after his attempts to distance himself from the whole Hess mission by denying that he had met Hess in Berlin at the time of the Olympic Games. It is likely that this was another attempt to distance himself from his part in the affair by placing it on record that he had not received Albrecht's letter.

In any case, Stammers asked him if he would go to Lisbon to meet Haushofer 'and see what it's all about'. Hamilton, according to the account he gave James Leasor, did not show much enthusiasm. Nevertheless, he received a command to report to Group Captain D. L. Blackford at the Air Ministry the following month. At that meeting he found Major Tar Robinson, head of the B1a, 'double-cross' section of MI5, and was asked again if he would go out to Portugal.[51]

In parallel to the MI5 B1a deception, there was a curious deception emanating from Hitler's own personal pilot, Hans Baur. Since it is inconceivable in the Führer's system that Baur would have initiated anything so dangerously ambiguous on his own, and since it is hard to think of a reason for him doing so, it must be assumed that he was acting, like Hess, on Hitler's authority. Baur flew with Hess on his early training flights and it may be that his deception was connected with Hess's mission; it seems more likely, however, that it was conceived as an alternative should Churchill be toppled before Hess flew or should the Churchill Government rise to the bait of the peace feelers.

It began in late December 1940; a Bulgarian peasant farmer named Kiroff approached the British Military Attaché in Sofia claiming that his daughter was married to Hitler's pilot, and producing photographs of the Baur family to prove it. Baur had become disillusioned with the war, he said; he had lost two brothers already, and was prepared to aid the cause of world peace by attempting a forced landing in England with Hitler and *entourage* aboard his plane.[52] The Attaché called in the Air Attaché, Squadron Leader Aidan Crawley, who contacted his chief in London and the Ambassador, who wired Cadogan. Both the Air Ministry and the Foreign Office approved continuing the contact and Kiroff was handed instructions for Baur detailing signals he should fire when approaching the British coast. After that the two British Attachés lost contact with Kiroff, who failed to arrive at an arranged meeting in Belgrade.[53] Baur, however, maintained contact with the Air Ministry in London, since on 7 March Air Vice-Marshal Sir Arthur ('Bomber') Harris wrote to the Fighter Command chief, Air Marshal Sir W.S. ('Sholto') Douglas, to describe changes Baur had made in the recognition signals he proposed making over Lympne aerodrome in Kent, which had in the meantime been prepared for his reception.[54] Fantastic as the idea was that Hitler's private aircraft with fighter escort should stray into British airspace and land at Lympne, it was evidently taken seriously at the Air Ministry. On 18 March Bomber Harris arranged for a Ford v8 box-body touring car with motorcycle escort to be sent to the aerodrome in order to bring Hitler to London.[55]

It is possible that Baur's channel to the Air Ministry was Baron de Ropp, Alfred Rosenberg's contact in Switzerland. De Ropp, a Balt deprived of his estates, was both a double agent acting for Fred Winterbotham of Air Intelligence and an opponent of Bolshevism whose aim almost certainly coincided with Rosenberg's, that is, an Anglo-German alliance or British neutrality allowing Germany to overrun Soviet Russia. His last known communication with Rosenberg had been in October 1939, when he had said the British Air Ministry was of the same view as Rosenberg's emissary and 'by no means wished to be a party to the present policy of England of waging war to the finish . . .'[56] In the changed circumstances of 1941 it is not impossible that Air Intelligence – who were called in on the Haushofer letter at the latest by 26 February, when Stammers wrote to Hamilton – were working with the xx Committee to depict an influential 'opposition' to Churchill, perhaps including the Air Ministry and its political chief. If so, it is likely the channel of communication went through de Ropp and Rosenberg, in which case it would certainly have reached Hess as well as Baur. This, however, is pure speculation. All that seems certain is that Bomber Harris was thoroughly convinced Baur was about to bring Hitler and possibly other top-level Nazis across to England in a four-engined Condor aircraft at some date towards the end of March.

17
SAM HOARE

At some time in late 1940 or early 1941 Hess authorised Albrecht Haus-hofer to open a channel to Sir Samuel Hoare in Madrid; Albrecht had recommended this line in September when sending Hess the draft of his letter to Hamilton; it may have been the subject of their discussion when he and Hess were together between 21 and 24 February. For the purpose Albrecht used a former student of his named Heinrich Stahmer, whom he had helped to a position in the German Embassy in Madrid. Stahmer made his approaches through the Swedish Embassy there, as a result of which, according to a note Stahmer made in 1959, Haushofer and Hoare came to an agreement that an armistice in the west must depend on the removal of both Hitler and Churchill.[1]

There is no contemporary documentary evidence of this agreement or of the meetings which made it possible; nor is there any documentary evidence that Hess authorised them; indeed, it has often been asserted that Albrecht made the approach on behalf of von Hassell's circle of opposition to Hitler. This is to mistake Albrecht's attitude to the war 'between the two white master races', the delicacy of his position in the Führer state, and the ubiquity of Himmler's agents. If he were putting out feelers on behalf of the 'opposition' through an official of the German Embassy, he would not have done so without first covering himself with explicit instructions for the approach from Hess. This is virtually con-firmed by Stahmer's 1959 note, which went on to state that a meeting between Hoare and Halifax on the one side and Hess and Haushofer on the other was proposed for February or March 1941 at the Spanish Escorial or in Portugal.[2] There is no trace of such a proposal in Hoare's reports to the Foreign Office, and it is certain that none is contained in any of the closed files covering this period, since in April 1941 a permanent official of the Foreign Office, P. Grey, drew up a summary of all German peace feelers to date and neither Hess nor Haushofer is mentioned in it.[3]

161

Stahmer was either wrong about the months – and there is evidence that a meeting of some kind was arranged later – or Hoare was not reporting all peace feelers to the Foreign Office; the only reasons for this could be if he were conspiring with the enemy behind Churchill's back or if he had been initiated into the Double-Cross deception to play a part as a leader of the British 'opposition' to Churchill, possibly the part of Churchill's successor. This was, of course, something which he could have made very convincing to the German side. He was well known as a leading former 'appeaser' and one of the 'guilty men' forming the subjects of a book on the lead up to the war recently published in English. Jock Colville, who was of course close to Churchill at this time, wrote later of Hoare's 'natural bent for intrigue ... It was not without justification that he was called "Slippery Sam".'[4]

Hoare was a superbly intelligent man, a consummate politician who had held a succession of the highest cabinet posts for the past eighteen years, Secretary of State for Air, for India, for Foreign Affairs, First Lord of the Admiralty and Lord Privy Seal, who might have succeeded Chamberlain as Prime Minister in 1939. In May 1940 Churchill had cleverly relieved himself of his presence in the war cabinet and made use of his diplomatic skills by sending him as Ambassador with a special mission to Madrid to keep the Spanish dictator, Franco, from entering the war on the Axis side.

David Eccles, who held a roving commission for economic and intelligence affairs in the peninsula, was in Lisbon when Sir Samuel and Lady Maud Hoare, 'suitably dressed for a garden party at Buckingham Palace',[5] had arrived there on their way to Madrid. When the wretched conditions in Spain were explained to Hoare together with the latest intelligence that Hitler was on the point of drawing Franco into the war, he had turned pale, said his mission was useless, he had been deceived and would return to London in the morning. Eccles wrote: 'This was the first of many times when I was to see him panic. Selby [the British Minister] and I rallied him as best we could, but when he reached Madrid he kept his private aircraft waiting ready to take him home and he had to be persuaded to unpack.'[6]

Later Eccles came to know Hoare well and to admire him for his knowledge of the world, his social gifts, extraordinary talent for administration and high powers of negotiation. Writing to his wife in September 1940, he had described the Spaniards liking Hoare very much, 'quite undisturbed by that element of Jesuitism in his character, which is so often found in their own'.[7] His weaknesses, he added, lay in his politician's training to be all things to all men and a lack of physical courage, which failings produced 'bouts of hesitation and compromise that mark the limits of a highly gifted nature'.

At home in Harlaching with his three-year-old son, 'Buz'
(Wolf Rüdiger Hess), shortly before his flight to Scotland

Wing Commander, the Duke of Hamilton, whom Hess flew over to see

'Sam' Hoare, British Ambassador in Madrid: did his 'special mission' include a leading part in Churchill's grand deception campaign?

The remains of the fuselage of Hess's ME 110 (VJ + OQ)
now at the Imperial War Museum, Duxford

Mytchett Place, the manor house near Aldershot where
Hess was held under maximum security during his first
year in Britain

Odd man out at the Nuremberg trials of the major war criminals; while his co-defendants, Göring (left), Ribbentrop (third from left) and behind them the Grand Admirals, Dönitz and Raeder, listen to the translation, Hess sits vacantly

Eating from a mess tin at the Nuremberg trials

A 1961 plea for commuting Hess's 'life' sentence

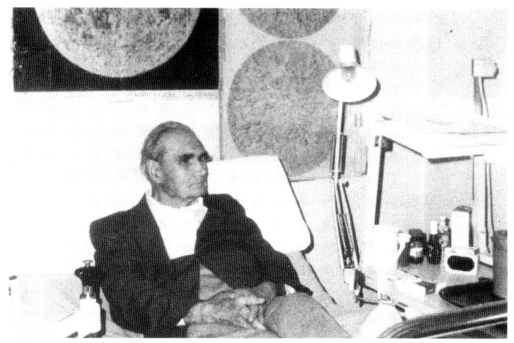

Aged 92 (above) in his final cell in Spandau a year before his death, and (below) his lone walk in the garden at the rear

In his last letter (to his daughter-in-law) three days before his death, Hess displays his old wry humour: 'Dear Andrea, I have received your letter of 20 July. With it was a picture of a pretty young lady, but you do not say who she is. Presumably, however, one of the grandchildren, who else?' Compare the handwriting with that of his 'suicide note'

Why was it considered necessary to forge this 'suicide note'?

Ilse supported by Wolf Rüdiger Hess and his wife, Andrea, in May 1987

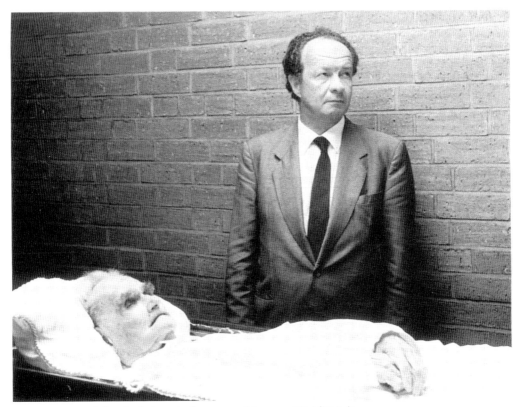

Hess's body is handed over to his son, Wolf Rüdiger, after the British post mortem conducted by Professor J. M. 'Taffy' Cameron

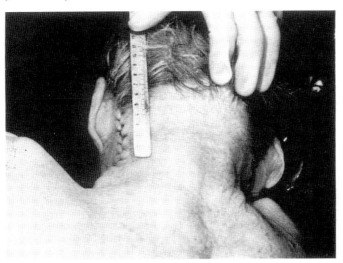

The horizontal discoloration around Hess's neck photographed during the second (German) post mortem. Professor Cameron's stitches can be seen behind the left ear

Although it had often seemed Franco might join Hitler for a share in the spoils of victory, his country was devastated by the recent civil war, his people literally starving, and he had no desire to engage in real war. The British were attempting to stiffen his will to remain neutral through their ability to ship in wheat and other foodstuffs; the Germans were using the doctrine of the 'inevitability' of their victory and of the German 'New Order' in Europe to persuade him to the 'winning side'. In October they had gained a victory when Franco replaced the pro-British Foreign Minister, Juan Beigbeder, with his own aggressively ambitious, pro-German brother-in-law, Serrano Suñer. Through Suñer Hitler had increased the pressure on Franco, if not to join the Axis, at least to allow German troops through the country to take Gibraltar, the British fortress holding the western gate of the Mediterranean. To a great extent this was part of his deception campaign to cloak the design against Russia; it was also a serious strategy to keep British forces fully occupied in the west – should it prove impossible to come to a settlement with Britain – while he turned east.

From the British Embassy in Madrid the pressure was not perceived as deception, but as an increasingly real threat – hence Hoare's fits of panic. In February 1941 the position appeared particularly dangerous. At a meeting early in the month Franco told Hoare that Europe was committing suicide: the longer the war continued the more complete the destruction of Europe would be. What else he said may be in one of the Foreign Office files dealing with German pressure on Spain dated 5th and 6th, which are closed until 2017. It may be that he offered to act as a mediator between the Axis and Churchill; he had acted as go-between for the French armistice negotiations. It may be he threatened that, if his offer were rejected, he would be obliged to enter the war on the Axis side. That is speculation.

On 20 February, after the leading Spanish General, Aranda, had told Hoare the military were unanimous in wanting to keep Spain out of the war and that Franco was determined to resist both pressure from Hitler and from his brother-in-law, Suñer, Hoare wired Churchill personally to urge more economic aid for Spain and suggesting a co-ordinated pro-gramme of economic help worked out with the United States, including US credits and US shipping, and announced in a personal message to Franco by Churchill and Roosevelt jointly.[8] In a further long and nervy wire sent the same day he suggested that, as economic help became more effec-tive, the German pressure would increase and it might become necessary, in order to strengthen Spain's powers of resistance, to allow 'certain quan-tities of carefully selected goods to pass through for sale to Germany by pre-arrangement' – in short, to allow goods through the naval blockade of the Axis *via* Spain to increase Franco's bargaining power with Hitler.[9]

163

Towards the end of the month, after a discussion with President Roosevelt's special envoy, Colonel William Donovan, Hoare wired Churchill again:

It is my considered opinion that crisis here will come in two months. Minister for Foreign Affairs [Suñer] is obviously counting upon a British defeat in the Near East and chance of forcing Spain against its will into the Axis. Every day he is showing more openly his hostility to us. I none the less believe that if there is no British calamity [and] we can quickly develop a policy on the lines of ... my telegram No 320 [above], we have a good chance of side-tracking his machinations ... If however we are to succeed we must act very quickly.[10]

On 2 March Hoare sent another long, repetitive, nervy wire for Churchill's immediate attention, starting: 'I feel sure that if we are to avoid a repetition of our Norwegian failure in Spain and Morocco we must take very swift decisions on our military and economic policy ...'[11]

Roger Makins (now Lord Sherfield) of the Foreign Office minuted:

These telegrams from Sir Samuel Hoare ... seem to me both excitable and confused. There has evidently been an increase in the tension in Madrid which is leading the Ambassador both to revise his estimate of the situation and to make rather impractical proposals ...[12]

Cadogan, too, was puzzled by Hoare's wires, and annoyed that he insisted on communicating directly with Churchill instead of with the Foreign Office in the normal way.[13] So far as economic help for Spain was concerned, Hoare already had authority to sign a loan agreement on behalf of the British Government.

The following morning Cadogan spoke to Colonel Donovan, who had arrived in London. Donovan's view was that Spain should be supplied with foodstuffs 'on a scale insufficient to enable her to build up stocks'; but, if they wanted US help, Britain must also agree to the supply of unoccupied France – something the British Government was against.[14]

The Governor of Gibraltar, General Mason MacFarlane, was also in London at this period discussing military aid for Spain. After a meeting of the chiefs of staff on 1 March the Foreign Office had been informed of the composition of a British Liaison Delegation to the Spanish Government proposed by General MacFarlane, not if, but 'on the outbreak of hostilities in that country'.[15]

There seems little doubt, therefore, that, viewed from London, Gibraltar and the British Embassy in Madrid, Hitler was set to coerce Franco into declaring for the Axis or, failing Franco's agreement, marching into the country. Planning for military assistance to Spain, including irregular operations by the Special Operations Executive (SOE), was at an advanced stage.

Such was the situation when Prince zu Hohenlowe appeared in Madrid. It will be recalled that Hohenlowe, although reporting to the German Foreign Ministry and no doubt to Himmler, had begun his peace feelers in Switzerland in late October 1939 by suggesting that Chamberlain's Government negotiate with Göring rather than Hitler. The following June Hohenlowe had reported to Ribbentrop that Rab Butler, Under-Secretary at the Foreign Office, was attempting to contact him through Carl Burckhardt, and in July he had reported Kelly, the British Minister in Berne, telling him that Halifax, Butler and Vansittart had a following and that their view of the war was not the same as Churchill's. In December 1940 Kelly had taken him aside again and said he believed peace with Nazi Germany was not beyond the bounds of possibility. Hohenlowe knew Hoare and had met him in London from time to time in the months immediately before the outbreak of war, but not, according to Hoare, since. On 5 March Hoare saw him and sent a long memorandum of their talk to Cadogan the next day together with an accompanying note:

In the ordinary course of things I would have telegraphed to you before seeing him. As, however, he may be leaving Madrid at any moment it was a case of seeing him yesterday or not at all and I only heard of his desire to see me the night before. I hope you will approve of my decision to see him and of the line that I took in the discussion.[16]

The inference to be drawn from this note is that after Churchill's instruction for 'absolute silence' Hoare knew the Foreign Office would not authorise a meeting with Hohenlowe. If so, he was right. This is made clear by the minutes on the file and Cadogan's reply:

Dear Sam, ... We quite understand that you had to make a quick decision whether or not to see Hohenlowe. You would be quite right in surmising that as a general rule we are not much in favour of meetings of this sort, which run a risk of disclosure and misinterpretation.[17]

Hoare's memorandum of the conversation began:

Prince Max Hohenlowe, who has large properties in Spain, arrived in Madrid a few days ago. He subsequently met Brigadier Torr [British Military Attaché], an old friend of his, at a party, and said to him that he would like to have a talk with me. I considered carefully whether I should see him and I should naturally have preferred to have consulted London before agreeing. I had, however, to decide at once as the Prince was liable to leave Madrid at any moment. I accordingly saw him in Brigadier Torr's flat with the Brigadier present in order that there should be no subsequent misrepresentation of the talk. The place of meeting was absolutely secure as the flat in which I saw him is in the same building as the flat of one of his personal friends whom he had frequently been meeting.[18]

Hohenlowe appeared ill at ease at the beginning of the talk, Hoare went on, as a result of which he and Brigadier Torr gained the impression the Prince must have come 'with some kind of a special mission from Göring'. The explanation for this remark is presumably that Hoare remembered Hohenlowe's soundings, ostensibly on behalf of Göring, in October 1939; Torr, as an old friend of Hohenlowe's, presumably also knew that he had acted for Göring earlier. In any case, after Hoare had left the flat, Hohenlowe continued talking with Torr, telling him that he had been staying with Göring recently and that the Reichsmarschall had been 'full of praises for the British character and British pluck'.[19]

Hohenlowe's message for Hoare was that the war was a calamity; Hitler had been ready to make peace the previous July after his great success in the west; why was Great Britain not prepared to make peace now after her successes in North Africa? Germany could never be defeated; the only result of continuing the war would be the end of European civilisation and the 'Communisation' or 'Americanisation' of the world, whereas, if peace were made now, Hitler would be very reasonable; he had never wanted to fight Great Britain.

I pressed him as to what he meant by Hitler's reasonableness. The answer was that Hitler wanted eastern Europe and China. As to western Europe and the rest of the world he wanted little or nothing. He must however have Poland and Czechoslovakia and the predominant influence in the Balkans. Having obtained this answer, I said to him as definitely as I could that for two reasons I could see no possibility of any peace. In the first place no one in England believed Hitler's word ... In the second place, the specific terms that he had suggested meant the German domination of Europe, and we were not prepared to accept any European dictatorship ...[20]

Hohenlowe replied that, if Britain would not make peace with Hitler, she would not be able to make peace at all: 'Hitler was the only man who counted in Germany'; he would carry the nation with him. Göring could not, nor could anyone else. After this the discussion got no further, although Hohenlowe was 'very frank about Russia', saying that 'sooner or later, in his view the sooner the better, Germany would have to absorb the Ukraine and the Russian oilfields'. This passage of Hoare's memorandum was scored in pencil in the margin, presumably at the Foreign Office. On parting, Hoare made it clear once again that he saw 'not the least chance of finding any basis for a peace discussion'.

Such, in essence, was Hoare's report of the conversation. The account

Hohenlowe must have made is missing from the archives of the German Foreign Ministry. It is possible that he reported to Hess *via* Pfeffer von Salomon – if he had been commissioned by Hess – and it seems probable that von Salomon's file on Hess's mission to Great Britain was destroyed by Ilse Hess after her husband's flight.

However, the Italian Ambassador at Madrid sent a report of a conversation between Hoare and Hohenlowe of about this date which has been published in the Italian diplomatic documents. It gives a remarkably different story. Hoare, according to the Italian account, stated that the position of the British Government could not remain secure; Churchill could 'no longer rely on a majority' and sooner or later he (Hoare) would be 'called back to London to take over the Government with the precise task of concluding a compromise peace'. He went on to say that he would have to remove Eden as Foreign Secretary and replace him with R. A. Butler.[21]

This account was sent on 14 March, thus nine days after the meeting referred to in Hoare's message: since it is scarcely conceivable that Hoare would have uttered such sentiments in the presence of Brigadier Torr, it may refer to a second clandestine meeting between Hoare and Hohenlowe. Alternatively, it may have been a rumour consequent on the meeting of 5 March, exaggerated in the feverish atmosphere of Madrid, or deliberate disinformation by the Germans. German propaganda had spread similar stories about Hoare at the time of the Duke of Windsor's stay in Madrid the previous summer.[22]

If, however, it was more or less accurate, it might suggest either that Hoare was establishing his credentials with the Germans as a future leader of a pro-German Britain or that he panicked in the face of what appeared an imminent German descent on Spain. In 1983 David Eccles wrote of him:

On another occasion when rumours reached him that German troops were about to cross the Pyrenees he invented an offer of a place in the War Cabinet which it was his duty at once to go home and consider. We knew that this story was pure fantasy but we saw how much he needed the pretence of going back into government as a tranquilliser for his nerves ... It was pitiable to see such cowardice in a potentially great man.[23]

The simplest explanation was that Hoare did tell Hohenlowe what the Italian Ambassador reported, and it was for the purpose of the deception on which the 'W' board and the Double-Cross Committee were engaged – that there *was* a substantial opposition in Great Britain prepared to negotiate with Germany and Churchill's position was not secure. This would tie in with Stahmer's notes and the later known German contacts with Hoare.

It is also possible, of course, that Hoare was playing both sides, much as it seems Beaverbrook was at this time in his association with Lloyd George. Beaverbrook was also close to Hoare. He appears to have supported him financially and had agreed to be responsible for the substantial sum of £6,000, which Hoare had owed to Lloyds at the time he left for Madrid in May 1940.[24] The two exchanged 'Dear Max' and 'Dear Sam' letters every week during Hoare's time in Madrid – Hoare saying how well Beaverbrook was producing aeroplanes, Beaverbrook saying how well Hoare was doing in Spain.

It will be recalled that at this period Lloyd George was making no secret of his dissatisfaction with Churchill's leadership, and it is significant that Harold Nicolson in the Ministry of Information wrote in his diary on 2 March that, while he felt the country could resist the worst Hitler could throw at them, the people would become so exhausted that it would be difficult to reject an offer of an honourable peace, should Hitler make one. When things got very bad, he went on, there might be 'a movement to attribute the whole disaster to the "war mongers", and to replace Churchill by Sam Hoare or some appeaser. That will be the end of England.'[25]

It may also be significant in view of the disquiet in City circles that another peace feeler at this time suggested a secret meeting in Sweden between Montagu Norman, Governor of the Bank of England, and his German banking friend, Dr Hjalmar Schacht. This proposal came from 'the highest officials' in Berlin, but not Hitler himself – thus presumably Göring or Ribbentrop, possibly Hess, although that appears unlikely for an overt sounding – *via* the US Minister in Stockholm and his 'Swedish informant who . . . is a distant relative of Göring's' – thus possibly Baron Bonde's friend, Count Rosen. Certainly it was in much the same terms as Göring's messages *via* Bonde and Hohenlowe: Germany was anxious to extend the hand of friendship and if the first move came from Britain, Germany would go at least halfway to meet it.[26]

The German peace offensive was co-ordinated with powerful threats. Besides the deception to suggest an imminent descent on Spain to take Gibraltar and a similar pretence of preparations for the invasion of England – now that it was a deception, codenamed 'Haifisch' (shark) – German troop and Luftwaffe movements into the Balkans and across to North Africa to stiffen the Italians promised an attack on Britain's whole Middle Eastern position and the Suez Canal. Hitler was also urging the Japanese to attack Singapore, the bastion of Britain's Far Eastern position, believing such an attack must finally convince England there was no point in continuing the war. The stakes for the British Empire were immense.

Whether Hoare, occupying one of the hottest seats of intrigue, who could see the dangers better than most and whose nerves were not as steady as his ambition, was actually playing a double game of his own or whether he was engaging in a subtle deception ordered at the highest level, by Churchill himself, or whether possibly the Italian Ambassador in Madrid was retailing mere rumour/disinformation is unclear. All that can be certain is that Hoare's messages were unnecessarily long-winded and confused, and his actions becoming unusual. Besides meeting Hohen-lowe himself, when it was quite evident this was against Churchill's express instructions, and Brigadier Torr might have obtained the same information himself, he next wired the Foreign Office that he was going to Lisbon with three service attachés to meet General Mason MacFarlane on his way back to Gibraltar. Cadogan sent an immediate reply: 'Is not a visit by yourself and your three service chiefs to Lisbon a rather spectacular step and likely to provoke undesirable speculation ... could not some more discreet method of establishing the necessary contacts be devised?'[27]

Hoare thought better of it; instead, in the second week in April, he travelled to Seville and Gibraltar for a week, stirring up a barrage of speculation about his purpose, which extended to the Foreign Office. Roger Makins minuted:

It should be on the record that the Ambassador went to Gibraltar in spite of categorical instructions that he was not to do so. He did not inform us of his movements, nor has he given any explanation why it was necessary for him to spend a week at Gibraltar. As we feared, he has laid himself open both to speculation and to attack.[28]

18
THE DUKE OF
HAMILTON

On 10 March, five days after the meeting between Hoare and Hohenlowe in Madrid, von Hassell met Albrecht Haushofer in Berlin at the house of a fellow opposition member, Dr Johannes Popitz. It seems that this may have been the first time the two had met as von Hassell's diary entry refers to Albrecht as 'E's friend H', who, the entry continued, was still employed by Hess and told them of 'the urgent wish from above to make peace'.[1]

Albrecht Haushofer had now come round to their point of view, von Hassell recorded; they discussed how von Hassell's connections in Switzerland might be used to enable Albrecht to obtain confirmation of the view that negotiations with Britain were possible providing there were a change of regime in Germany.[2]

On the following day von Hassell talked with other members of the opposition – Albrecht was not present – about whether another attempt should be made to win over the Army Commander-in-Chief, von Brauchitsch, to the proposition of an Army *putsch* against the regime. The history of the German opposition is filled with such ultimately vain discussions; on this occasion they concluded that in the present triumphal atmosphere it would be useless.

Himmler and Heydrich, meanwhile, were preparing the ss role in the conquest and subjugation of Russia. Himmler had visited his concentration camp at Auschwitz in the *General Gouvernement Polen* at the beginning of the month, instructing the Kommandant, Höss, to commence construction of a vast new compound to take 100,000 prisoners of war. In his retinue were senior executives of IG Farben, there to inspect the site of what was to become a giant complex for production of synthetic oil and rubber. Himmler had instructed Höss to make 10,000 of his prisoners available for the construction of the works, which, when complete, was to employ camp inmates; IG Farben had agreed to pay four Marks per man per day to the ss for this slave labour. Now Himmler's attention was concentrated on the ss *Einsatz* groups who would follow in the wake of the advancing Army groups to eradicate Communism with its 'carriers', the Party functionaries and Jews. He was suffering crippling headaches and stomach spasms at this time, and was told by his masseur, Kersten, that he was trying his nervous system too severely.[3]

On 13 March special instructions were issued by the Armed Forces High Command (OKW) to be attached to Directive 21, 'Barbarossa', stating that in the Army's operational area the 'Führer had commissioned the Reichsführer–ss with special tasks, resulting from the 'final settlement' of the struggle between the two opposed political systems.'[4]

Hitler initiated the General Staff into these tasks on 17 March: 'Stalin-free Republics' had to be created behind the front. The Communist intelligentsia had to be eradicated. Heydrich's orders to the Commanders of the *Einsatz* groups made it clear that 'eradicated' meant, as in Poland, physical liquidation, and that all Jews, whether Party members or not, were also to be liquidated since Judaism was the source of Bolshevism, therefore had to be wiped out 'in accordance with the Führer's orders'.[5] Himmler called his senior commanders together at Wewelsburg Castle, which he had been refurbishing as the seat of his Knightly Order of the ss, to initiate them into the secret plans for the east later that month, and, on the 30th Hitler gave the senior commanders of the armed services and their staffs a two-and-a-half-hour lecture on the grand strategic situation and the task before them in Russia. Towards the end of this monologue he explained the requirements of ideological war. Communism was equivalent to asocial criminality, a colossal danger for the future, and in the fighting in the east they must disassociate themselves from their soldierly ideals; it was a battle of annihilation. 'Leaders must demand of themselves the sacrifice of overcoming their scruples.'[6]

None of the generals and admirals present raised a word in protest or question. When Hitler finished speaking, they trooped out to lunch with him. Hess was not present at this gathering, nor, so far as is known, were his departments involved as the concept of ideological war was formulated by the military staff into the so-called 'Commissar Order' for the summary execution of all Communist Party functionaries. But again it was necessary for him to be informed, and for his legal and political department chiefs to know precisely what the orders were to be behind the fronts in the east. At the very least it would be his task again, as in Poland, to adjudicate between the conflicting interests of the Army, ss, Party and civil authorities, and to uphold the ideological line against those with complaints against the mass barbarities involved.

Karl Haushofer suggested at his interrogation after the war that Hess flew to Great Britain because of 'his own sense of honour and his desperation about the murders going on in Germany. It was his firm belief that, if he sacrificed himself and went to England, he might be able to do something to stop it.'[7] It may be that this was how Hess represented the situation to him within the *Reich*. Since the reason for his flight was to make peace in the west to allow a concentration of all resources against Russia, it is evident that, whatever his sense of honour about the murders in Germany, the consequences of his mission, if successful, would ease the path to mass murder in the east. This was the necessary outcome of the *Weltanschauung* and of his own 'almost pathological aversion to the Asiatic-Bolshevik *Weltanschauung*'; like Hitler, he knew Bolshevism as a system of criminality steeped in blood and the torture of millions.

Unlike Himmler, suffering from the awesome demands of the coming campaign, Hess appears to have remained in good spirits. Some time that spring he and Hitler visited their old patron, Frau Else Bruckmann, where the talk turned to flying. On leaving, Hitler signed the visitors' book, 'In the year of completion of victory'; Hess wrote, 'The era of adventure is not yet over.'[8]

The thought of his great adventure never left him. Taking tea with Schwerin von Krosigk one Sunday in April, he told him of his despair that the two Germanic nations should be tearing themselves apart while Bolshevism looked on laughing. There had to be a possibility of bringing the madness to an end. The British had shown no interest in the Führer's peace proposals unfortunately; yet, if one could only speak to influential Englishmen oneself, show them the danger threatening western culture, and could make them believe that Germany – above all Hitler – wanted nothing from England, an agreement must be possible. He dismissed von Krosigk's objection that British statesmen would find it difficult to negotiate with Hitler after all his broken promises; the point was to bring Hitler's entire conception and the danger of Bolshevism to the attention of the British.[9]

Looking back on it after the war, von Krosigk thought that Hess's decision was also rooted in a desire to prove himself as a soldier. 'He only felt at home in the soldierly world ... He had taken it hard when Hitler had refused him permission to take part in the war as a Luftwaffe pilot and finally prohibited him from flying.' Nevertheless, during that Sunday talk between the two of them, Hess gave no indication that he intended to try to heal the rift between the Germanic races himself.[10]

From his prison cell nine years later Hess confessed in a letter to Ilse that he had probably been no longer entirely normal during that spring. Life had become nothing but instruments, fuel tanks, radio direction finders, Scottish mountain altitudes.[11] At night he fixed a map of the area of the border country and southern Scotland to the wall of his separate bedroom at Harlaching, the highest peaks circled in red, and committed to memory his planned route across to Dungavel House. A large new radio he had installed in his study was tuned to the Danish station of Kalundborg, to whose beams he would set his radio compass on his flight; the station lay on the same latitude as his intended landfall on the north-east coast of England.

He had even less desire than usual for his official duties. Ilse was astonished by the amount of time he spent at home with their three-and-a-half-year-old son, whom they called 'Buz', taking him for long walks along the river Isar, which ran along the bottom of their back garden, and playing games with him behind the closed doors of the study. As Ilse reflected afterwards, he must have been very aware that he might never have the chance again.[12]

In early April war in the Mediterranean theatre took an ominous turn for Churchill. He had weakened the Army in North Africa by sending an expeditionary force to support Greece against Italian invasion. Now the troops Hitler had sent to North Africa under Rommel to stiffen the Italians and hold Mussolini in the war began a spectacular advance, driving the British back; at the same time German forces in Bulgaria descended on Greece in overwhelming strength in an operation designed originally as camouflage for 'Barbarossa'. By 11 April Rommel had recaptured the whole of Cyrenaica except for the fortress of Tobruk, while the British involvement in Greece promised a debacle to equal the Norwegian failure; inside a week it had become evident that Greece was lost and the British force, not yet up to designed strength, would have to be evacuated.

It was at this time that Hess summoned Albrecht Haushofer to another extended period of talks – from 12 to 15 April. As with the previous session in March, there is neither documentary nor oral testimony about what they discussed. It can be assumed that one topic was a meeting with von Hassell's contact, Carl Burckhardt, for Albrecht travelled to Geneva to see him towards the end of the month. The preparations were made by von Hassell's wife, Ilse, who told Burckhardt that Albrecht was coming with a double face – 'outwardly for Hess, *de facto*, however, for the resistance movement'.[13] Albrecht could not have made the journey, though, without Hess's express instructions. After Hess's flight he wrote a long explanation for Hitler stating that in April he had received a message from Burckhardt conveying greetings from his (Albrecht's) old English circle of friends, and suggesting he might like to visit him some time in Geneva. Shown this document after the war, Burckhardt said it was possible someone had mentioned Albrecht Haushofer and he had said 'please give him my best wishes', but he could not possibly have sent him greetings from his old English circle of friends since he did not know any of them.[14] It appears, from von Hassell's diary entry of his talk with Albrecht on 10 March, that he or Ilse or Albrecht himself fabricated the message from Burckhardt about his English friends and the invitation to meet him in Geneva so that he could persuade Hess to authorise the journey. But it is also possible that Burckhardt was indeed used by those circles in England desiring a compromise peace or alternatively as a witting or unwitting middleman for the 'W' Board and the Double-Cross Committee, and he had to deny it because of the strict rule that the Red Cross did not involve itself in political matters. Albrecht, in his statement for Hitler, wrote that Burckhardt showed great anxiety lest his name become known publicly in this context of peace negotiations.[15]

That Burckhardt was not telling the whole truth emerges from his own denial taken against the evidence in von Hassell's diary and Karl Haushofer's post-war interrogation. Following the meeting von Hassell recorded that Albrecht and Burckhardt had agreed to a second meeting in a few weeks' time after Burckhardt had been in touch with the English again;[16] Karl Haushofer said the same, adding that at the second meeting Albrecht would be flown to Madrid for a conference with Sir Samuel Hoare.[17]

The question arises, therefore, whether the approach to Hoare was one of the topics Hess and Albrecht Haushofer discussed between 12 and 15 April. Hoare was acting unpredictably at this time, away in Seville and Gibraltar against Foreign Office instructions from about 6 April to at least the 13th, Easter Sunday.[18] The next week German sources launched a propaganda drive that Rommel would be in Alexandria by 1 May; the Spanish Ambassador in London called on Rab Butler on the 16th 'in a state of considerable perturbation', telling him that, if this were so, the Germans would certainly invade Spain to take Gibraltar as well. Butler calmed him by saying that Tobruk, where the British were still holding out, had been very heavily fortified.[19]

Towards the end of the week came a spate of reports that Franco was about to be forced into the pact with the Axis, and after the weekend of the 19th-20th intelligence from a variety of sources suggested that Hess had flown to Madrid to deliver Hitler's ultimatum personally to Franco.[20] This is the first occasion that Hess's name appears in the British Foreign Office files concerned either with Spain or with peace feelers. A file dealing with German pressure on Spain dated between 20 and 22 April is one of those closed until 2017. Since the next file on the subject is in the series on the British Liaison Delegation to Spain in the event of war, it must be assumed that the reports about Franco joining the Axis or the Germans invading Spain were taken very seriously and instructions sent to Hoare involving the Liaison Delegation, the chief members of which were his three service attaches. That Monday the

21st Harold Nicolson wrote in his diary of the news from Spain: 'Hitler is evidently determined to turn us out of the Mediterranean',[21] and at the end of the week Frank Roberts minuted on a cable from Hoare: 'The scare of last weekend has turned out to be at least premature.'[22] The extent of the scare is indicated by the fact that on that Monday the 21st Churchill's Defence Committee took the desperate step of sending a convoy loaded with tanks and aircraft for Tobruk through the hazardous narrows of the Mediterranean rather than round the longer, safer Cape route.[23]

David Eccles wrote to his wife from Washington: 'The war has come to the point of absolute crisis. We can't win if the US doesn't come in. They won't come in if we suffer more reverses. They are essentially commercial, their money must go on a horse that has a reasonable chance...'[24]

On Tuesday 22 April Hoare wired the Foreign Office to say that he had learned from a personal friend of Suñer's that Franco had agreed to sign the pact with the Axis powers when the Germans took Suez and that the Pact would include the right of passage of German troops through Spain with the object of taking Gibraltar. Until Suez was taken, however, Franco would maintain his present policy.[25] From Washington Halifax reported hearing from Vichy French sources that German troops would soon be moving through unoccupied France into Spain with or without Spanish consent.[26]

Hoare, meanwhile, had been asked to comment on the reports about Hess flying to Spain to deliver an ultimatum to Franco. German radio had already broadcast a report denying that the Stellvertreter had been in Spain and on Friday the 25th, Hoare wired the Foreign Office in the same sense: all his information inclined him to discredit the story.[27] The 'next paper' referred to in this file repeats the pattern of 'the last weekend' since it is in the series concerning the British Delegation to Spain; it is closed until 2017, the only closed file in this series.

On Saturday 26 April both Albrecht and Karl Haushofer were with Hess; it is certain they must have discussed Albrecht's forthcoming visit to Burckhardt in Geneva, which Ilse von Hassell had fixed for two days later, Monday the 28th.

In Britain, as might be imagined, all the separate forces for peace had taken new heart. As early as 7 April the right-wing Labour MP Dick Stokes had written to Liddell Hart asking him to address a meeting of MPs about the war situation with the object of creating 'a really well-supported alternative to the "bitter end" policy' of the Government.[28] The day before this the Australian Prime Minister, Robert Menzies, on an extended trip to England, had visited Beaverbrook at his country house in Surrey; another guest, Bruce Lockhart, had noted that both Beaverbrook and Menzies had debunked Churchill's Greek adventure.[29]

Menzies, who had been sitting in at war cabinet meetings, had formed an opinion of Churchill's leadership and the 'Yes-men' who surrounded him as devastating as Lloyd George's. On 14 April he cabled home a request to prolong his stay in London. Australian troops were fighting in North Africa and in Greece, and he was worried about looming disasters in both areas, intensely concerned about Churchill's total dominance of the war cabinet and his uncompromising policy towards Germany. Whether he had conceived an ambition to succeed Churchill, as the Australian historian David Day has argued recently – although it is difficult to see how this could have happened in the British parliamentary system – he certainly saw himself as an important moderating figure and was the darling of sections of the British press who were putting down markers in various coded ways in favour of a war cabinet including representatives from the Dominions – an Imperial as opposed to a British war cabinet.[30] In addition, it could not have escaped Menzies that if the military disasters he foresaw were sufficiently serious, they could destroy Churchill's Government. Lloyd George certainly foresaw disaster. On 16 April he told Cecil King, editor of the *Daily Mirror*, that in the resulting shake-up, he thought Churchill would remain Premier, but would have to accept the guidance of a cabinet of five or so members without portfolio. King noted in his diary, 'He clearly expects to be in such a cabinet'; Lloyd George thought Beaverbrook would be another member.[31]

On 17 April Oliver Harvey, soon to become Anthony Eden's Principle Private Secretary, noted in his diary 'much criticism of Winston, I hear, in City circles, for bad judgement – it is an attack which really cloaks defeatism among the rich and wet of course'.[32] The following day he again recorded criticism of Churchill's Government as 'the dishonest cloak for defeatism – at the end of that road lies L.G. [Lloyd George], who, abetted by that ass Liddell Hart would readily be a Pétain to us, with the support of the Press Barons and City Magnates.'[33] Harold Nicolson also noted the stirrings of dissatisfaction; the people, he saw, wanted some assurance of how victory was to be achieved. They were bored by talks about the rightness of the cause and eventual triumph. They wanted facts indicating how the Germans were to be beaten. He had no idea how to give them those facts: 'as in last July, I wake up with terror in the dawn.'[34]

Churchill could have provided the facts, but did not; they were too secret. From Canaris, from the 'Ultra' decrypts concerning German troop movements that Stewart Menzies brought him every morning before he started the day's work, Churchill knew and, indeed, had long known that Hitler would attack Russia in early summer. On 16 April Eden had proposed an Anglo-Soviet pact to the Soviet Ambassador in London whom Halifax had shunned. Stalin remained suspicious, seeing another ploy by the western capitalists to embroil him in war with Germany. Besides, Hitler had woven two more skilful double bluffs into 'Barbarossa': the movement of German forces eastwards was, on the one hand, a part of the 'greatest deception operation in the history of warfare', designed to make the British believe he had called off the invasion of England, and, on the other hand, to back up demands he intended putting to Stalin. Stalin was prepared to make practically any concession to avoid war.[35] That was not the point. The idea had been implanted in his mind that Hitler would make demands. Stalin prepared to accommodate them to buy more time to build his armaments.

Churchill's other secrets concerned the United States. While Roosevelt could not pull his nation into the war against its wishes, he had moved it into undeclared alliance. In Washington secret Anglo-American staff talks initiated by the Americans had concluded with the 'ABC-1' agreement: should the two powers be involved in war in both Europe and the Far East, their principal effort would be made in Europe. This was of particular significance since the British chiefs of staff were not only agreed that the defence of British and Empire interests in the East was beyond their resources and had to be entrusted to the Americans but also that it was acceptable to risk war with Japan if that pulled the United States in.[36] At the beginning of April an Anglo-American conference on secret intelligence resulted in an agreement for the 'full and prompt exchange of information' between the intelligence and cryptographic services of the two countries; the British began to pass 'Ultra' decrypts of German Enigma transmissions to the Americans, receiving in return US 'Magic' decrypts of Japanese cyphers. Long messages to Tokyo from the Japanese Ambassador in Berlin revealed Hitler outlining his plans to attack Russia and urging Japan to attack Singapore and British and Dutch Far Eastern possessions.[37] Meanwhile, in the vital Atlantic battle against German U-boats, Roosevelt had thrown off all pretence of neutrality and moved a so-called 'US Security Zone' patrolled by escort groups of the US Navy progressively further east into mid-ocean some 2,000 miles from America's eastern seaboard. It was plain he was angling for an incident to draw the United States into a formal declaration of war.

From Churchill's viewpoint the strategy was clear; he only had to hang on until the date Hitler had set to attack Russia, until a Japanese attack in the far East or until loss of American life in the Atlantic battle allowed Roosevelt to harness the full power of the United States for the defeat of Nazi Germany. Churchill could not, however, fully reveal his hand. Moreover, he had blundered in Greece and could not survive if Rommel reached Suez – hence the desperate decision to send tanks and aircraft for Tobruk through the Mediterranean. His position – and, with it, history – would turn on events in North Africa in the next few weeks, for outside the merest handful of those who knew his ultimate secrets there was little to rely on but faith, pride and the determination never to give in; and naturally those who were against the war in any case were poised to strike. Hugh Dalton, chief of SOE, noted in his diary at the beginning of May that a titanic struggle was about to break out between those who wanted a premature peace and those who intended to fight to the finish.[38]

These were the circumstances in Britain when, on 28 April, Albrecht Haushofer met Carl Burckhardt in Geneva. Precisely what was said may never be known. Only hints have surfaced so far. Ilse von Hassell met Albrecht and had a long talk with him in Arosa after the meeting, from which it emerged that Burckhardt, on the grounds of discussions with British diplomats and the art historian Borenius believed England was still prepared to make peace on a 'reasonable basis', but, as von Hassell put it in his diary, '(1) not with our present ruler and (2) not for much longer'.[39] Von Hassell noted that in a few weeks Albrecht was to make another trip to see Burckhardt, 'who wanted in the meantime to take further soundings', after which they would evaluate the total picture.

Albrecht Haushofer's account of his meeting written for Hitler after Hess had flown – thus at a time of considerable personal danger – stated that Burckhardt had told him he had been approached in Geneva some weeks before by a person 'known and respected in London, who was closely connected with leading Conservative – and City [of London] – circles', and this person, whose seriousness Burckhardt had vouched for without naming him, had told him of the desire of 'important English circles' to test the possibilities of peace. His (Albrecht's) name had cropped up in the exploration of suitable channels.[40]

For his part Albrecht had told Burckhardt that, if his confidant were prepared to make another journey to Switzerland and to reveal his identity through confidential channels so that his seriousness and that of his mission could be investigated in Germany, he believed he could promise to make another journey to Geneva. His statement continued:

Herr Professor Burckhardt said he was prepared to act as mediator in this, merely passing to England through a completely secure channel the fact that there was a prospect of the confidential agent from London, after he had given his name, meeting a German in Geneva, also well-known in England, who was in a position to bring such information as there was to the attention of the responsible German authorities.

Albrecht went on to describe the view of 'the more moderate groups in England' about a settlement as they had emerged from his talk with Burckhardt: English interest in east and south-east Europe, apart from Greece, was nominal, but no English government capable of acting would be able to abandon western Europe. However, Albrecht stressed, nothing could be done on these lines unless a 'general basis of confidence' were established between Berlin and London, and this, since the mass of British people regarded the conflict with 'Hitlerism' as a religious war, would be 'as difficult to find as in the Crusades or the Thirty-Years' War'.

If anyone in London is prepared for peace it is the native portion of the plutocracy which could calculate when it, together with the native, British tradition would be annihilated [vertilgt], while the alien, above all Jewish, element has already, for the most part, made the leap to America and the overseas Dominions. Burckhardt's own deepest anxiety was that if the war continued for a longer period all possibility of the reasonable forces in England compelling Churchill to make peace would disappear because the entire power of decision would have been taken over by the Americans.[41]

Here Albrecht was obviously putting views into Burckhardt's mouth which he knew coincided with Hitler's: that Churchill was acting for Roosevelt and playing into the hands of American finance and industry. However simplified the concept, it was not without foundation.

Albrecht's report was written on 12 May, von Hassell's diary entry on 18 May. Neither mentioned the future meeting with Hoare in Madrid, which Karl Haushofer was so specific about when interrogated after the war:

May I perhaps add something more important about which I don't know if you are informed. At that time Hess initiated peace feelers and the responsible man in dealing with these peace feelers was my murdered son [Albrecht]. He was in Switzerland and talked with Burckhardt and Burckhardt told him to come back again to Switzerland and there he would be flown to Madrid and would there have a conference with Lord Templewood [Hoare]. When my son returned from Switzerland Hess spoke to him again and it was after that that he flew to England. I don't know what he spoke to him about at this discussion.[42]

In an interview with Erika Mann in Munich, Karl Haushofer gave more details: Burckhardt had agreed to act as the contact man between Hess and the British at some time during the second half of May. Hess was to meet Hoare on an abandoned tennis court near Madrid. Albrecht had reported this to Hess, who seemed pleased with the success of the meeting, but, 'feeling utterly unhappy about much that happened in Germany and from a mixture of depression, romanticism and impatience', he decided to fly to Britain instead of waiting for the meeting in Spain.[43]

If this was the case, it is a puzzle that Albrecht did not mention it in his report for Hitler. He assumed Hitler was behind Hess's flight; knowing Hess as he did, he could not have believed he had taken off on his own without at least the Führer's approval, hence, if a meeting had been arranged in Spain, Hitler would surely have known about it and Albrecht would have mentioned it in the report. It is also apparent from von Hassell's diary that Albrecht did not tell Ilse von Hassell of the arrangement with Hoare, since by that account Burckhardt was merely going to take further soundings in England, after which they could evaluate the position.

There can be little doubt that, of the three, only von Hassell's account can be taken at face value. As for Karl Haushofer, it is evident from the phrases he used that at this time, when his favourite student was standing trial for his life as a war criminal, his aim was to separate him from Hitler and the regime, and to give the impression that he had taken off on his own initiative in a desperate bid to end the war.

There is, however, equally no doubt that Hoare was the prime target for German peace feelers at this period. Stahmer of the German Embassy was still acting for Albrecht Haushofer, as will appear; and one of Ribbentrop's senior agents, Gardemann, was in Madrid attempting to contact Hoare through the pro-British former Spanish Minister for Foreign Affairs, Juan Beigbeder.[44] Meanwhile, the pressure of rumour about Franco joining the Axis and German troops massing on the Spanish border was maintained. Hoare was obviously affected. On 1 May he wrote a letter to Eden extraordinary even by the standards of his long and circuitous despatches. During the course of it he summed up the position:

Spain is shaking under the shocks of the past few weeks. A bad catastrophe to British arms in the eastern Mediterranean would probably mean an almost complete Spanish surrender to the doctrine of the inevitability of German victory. If Suez fell into German hands there would be few in Spain who would not believe that the British Empire was breaking up, and that it was urgently necessary for Spain to seize its spoils in Gibraltar and North Africa before she was forestalled by the Germans and Italians. If, on the other hand, we can manage to hold the position in Africa and the Battle of the Atlantic does not go in favour of Germany, I believe that the unstable inertia of the present position will continue . . .[45]

Hoare's letter is puzzling; it contained nothing new apart from a wild proposal to harness Latin America to the cause of Spain's neutrality. It is as if he wrote it to calm his nerves with a justification of his stewardship. There is one passage near the beginning, however, which suggests some inner knowledge of the secrets on which Churchill was banking, possibly communicated to him by Eden when he stopped in Gibraltar during his Mediterranean tour:

For months past I have been telling Spaniards that the spring and summer of 1941 were the grand climacteric of the war, that during this period we must expect heavy blows, but at the end of it we shall be emerging into safer and more open country. I have believed what I have said and they have also believed me.

It is difficult to understand how such a superbly intelligent, informed realist as Hoare could have believed at this time, when the German pincers appeared to be closing, that they could soon emerge into 'safer and more open country' – the sub-Churchillian phrase is striking, or is this perhaps a metaphor for the plains of Russia? – unless he had been initiated into Churchill's highest secrets.

It is possible that the signs of stress in the letter had their origin in reports contained in two of the Foreign Office files closed until 2017,[46] which deal with German pressure on Spain and are dated 30 April to 1 May. It is possible these concerned a 30 April meeting in Munich between Hess and the leader of the Spanish Falange (extreme pro-Fascist) syndicates which was reported by German radio.

In Britain the Double-Cross Committee continued the deception, merging ever closer with reality, that a powerful 'opposition' was prepared to make peace. Whether they were now targeting Hess specifically is not altogether clear. Much later Eduard Benes, leader of the Czech Government in exile in London, learned from intelligence sources that Albrecht Haushofer's letter to the Duke of Hamilton had been answered by British intelligence.[47] Benes certainly had close contacts with MI6 since the exiled Czech intelligence service ran a star agent in occupied Europe codenamed A-54 jointly with the SIS. However, it seems clear that, if Hess did receive a reply, he did not show it to Albrecht Haushofer, who wrote in his statement for Hitler on 12 May: 'Whether the letter [of September 23rd] reached the addressee is unknown to me. The possibilities of loss on the way from Lisbon to England are certainly not small.'[48] Albrecht would not have written this if it was untrue, since he must have assumed that Hess had kept Hitler fully informed of the progress of his mission. This does not rule out Benes's information; it simply means that, if the letter was answered, the answer was not shown to Albrecht.

The Double-Cross Committee were, of course, interested in Hamilton. It will be recalled that the Duke had taken ten days' leave only a week after Albrecht's letter had been handed to MI5 by the censor in November the previous year; and a further ten days from 26 January to 4 February 1941 coinciding with Albrecht Haushofer's visit to Sweden and Carl Burckhardt's approach to von Hassell in Switzerland about the art historian, Borenius, sent by British circles who still believed in a reasonable peace; at the same time von Hassell had received a message from Lord Brocket's emissary, Lonsdale Bryans, in Lisbon. In March Hamilton had taken a further ten days' leave, during which he had seen Group Captain Stammers, who had asked if he was interested in going to Lisbon to see Albrecht Haushofer. This was a few days after von Hassell had met Albrecht in Berlin and discussed how he might use his Swiss connections, Carl Burckhardt and Borenius. Towards the end of March Hamilton had taken a further two days off, and on 25 April another two days when he travelled to London and saw Group Captain D.L. Blackford, Major Tar Robertson and other intelligence officers at the Air Ministry.[49] Here, according to the account he gave James Leasor, it was suggested to him that he write to Haushofer to say he was willing to meet him in Lisbon. He hesitated and was asked whether he was prepared to do it. 'If I am ordered to,' he replied.

'We don't like to order people to do these sort of jobs,' he was told. 'We like volunteers.'[50] So it was left.

Two days later, after seeking advice from Lord Eustace Percy, a former cabinet minister, Hamilton wrote to Blackford agreeing to go on the conditions that he was allowed to explain his mission to the British Ambassador – actually Minister – at Lisbon and to Sir Alexander Cadogan at the Foreign Office. He also raised the question of how he was to explain to Albrecht Haushofer why he was answering his letter after a delay of seven months. It might, he suggested, 'give the impression that the authorities here had "got the wind up" now and want to talk peace'. He concluded by asking for an explanation of the circumstances in which the letter had been withheld from him the previous autumn.[51]

Blackford replied on 3 May, apologising for 'not having been here when you came to London'. The wording provides a small puzzle because, according to the account Hamilton gave James Leasor, followed by James Douglas-Hamilton, the Group Captain was at the meeting at the Air Ministry on 25 April; since Hamilton reassumed command at RAF Turnhouse on the 27th, the day after seeing Lord Percy, and wrote his letter to Blackford on the 28th, there hardly seems time for him to have 'come to London' twice. Blackford went on to say he had discussed Hamilton's letter with Air Commodore Boyle, chief of Air Intelligence, 'and he agrees with you that this may not be the right time to open up a discussion, the nature of which might well be misinterpreted'. Blackford had also put Hamilton's views to 'the department concerned' – obviously MI5 B1a. He went on:

In my own view the delay which has occurred makes it extremely difficult to find a watertight excuse for action at the present time, and although quite a good one has been suggested on the lines of an enquiry from you as to why your previous letters have not been answered, it might not carry conviction and so have undesirable political consequences.[52]

This suggests that, if B1a had replied to Albrecht Haushofer's letter of 23 September, Hamilton was not informed at either of his meetings in London. It would seem that Albrecht had not answered any such reply since, if one arrived, it had not been shown to him. It is possible, therefore, that B1a, having waited for some months for an answer to their forged reply, decided to bring Hamilton into the game by sending him to Lisbon, hence the delay between 6 November, when Albrecht's letter was handed to MI5, and 26 February, when Stammers asked Hamilton to see him in London. It is also possible that the delay was due, as Blackford put it in his letter, to 'another department having mislaid the papers'; certainly it seems there was considerable confusion in MI5 from October 1940 onwards due to a move from Wormwood Scrubs to Oxford.[53]

Blackford ended his letter by asking Hamilton to regard the matter as in abeyance.

Hamilton replied on 10 May. His opening paragraph repeated what Blackford had said rather in the manner of a formal response to an invitation: he would regard the matter as in abeyance until he heard that it had come forward again; he realised the Air Ministry was in no way concerned with the policy question involved and that it was the fault of another department that the papers had been mislaid. 'If the proposition materialises', he went on, it might be best for him to write to 'x' to say he had not replied to the letter because he had 'seen no opportunity of leaving the country at that time', but it now appeared there would be a chance 'of arranging a meeting abroad with you at some time in the next month or two'. He added what seems to be superfluous unless the original proposal from Tar Robertson had been for him to go out to Lisbon without writing beforehand: 'I would then wait for a reply before starting, so that I would only have to leave my service duties for the minimum time and avoid the appearance of waiting anxiously on his doorstep.'[54]

To add to the coincidences which seem to dog his involvement, on the same day Hess took off from Augsburg to visit him.

19

FINAL PREPARATIONS

On 26 April Rudolf Hess was forty-seven. The following day the papers celebrated the event together with the eighth anniversary of his appointment as Stellvertreter des Führers. 'A long time ago – even before the outbreak of this war – Rudolf Hess was dubbed "the conscience of the Party" ', the *National Zeitung* commented – the reason being, it went on, that there was no area of public life with which he was not concerned.[1] It is interesting that in the brief review of his career the *Zeitung*, no doubt following the guidance of Goebbels's Ministry of Propaganda and Public Enlightenment, omitted his infantry service in the First World War: 'he took part in the war as a flyer, receiving a series of high decorations'.

The notices appear to be part of a drive to strengthen his standing prior to his flight, for on the Labour Day holiday on 1 May, when the Führer by custom addressed his *Volk*, Hess stood in for him. He gave the speech at a ceremony at Messerschmitt's Augsburg works, so familiar to him from his practice sorties, which he was to honour with the Award of the Golden Flag and the title 'National Socialist model enterprise' for its outstanding contribution to armaments. At the same time he was to bestow the accolade of 'Pioneer of Labour' on the Reichsleiter for the press, Max Amann, the Reichspostminister, Dr Wilhelm Ohnesorge and Professor Willi Messerschmitt.

His speech contained the mixture of patriotic and Party propaganda to be expected on such an occasion. He referred to the unique quality and abundance of weapons the German soldier enjoyed thanks 'to the indefatigable effort of Adolf Hitler over many years', for whose reliability, however, he had to thank the German production workers.

At the end of his speech he addressed the three new Pioneers of Labour individually, before conferring on each a gold medal; the last was Messerschmitt:

You, Party comrade Professor Dr Messerschmitt, are the designer of the best fighter aircraft in the world. I know, partly from personal experience, what difficulties you had to contend with in forcing your new ideas through. You held out despite everything to gain victory for your brilliant designs, thanks to which the German Luftwaffe enjoys its present undisputed superiority over its enemies in the field of aerial combat. That speaks for itself as it speaks for you.

Finally he awarded the Golden Flag for the model enterprise and dedicated the annual 'performance battle' of 1941–2 to 'the military decision' and the achievement by German industry of its highest production. The ceremony ended with a roll of drums and the singing of '*Brüder in Zechen und Gruben*' – which might loosely be translated 'Drinking companions in the mineshaft'.[2]

Afterwards he took Willi Messerschmitt aside and discussed additional modifications to his personal Me-110, which he needed by the following Monday 5 May, according to a works memorandum signed by Messerschmitt the following day.

On 4 May Hess was in Berlin for Hitler's speech in the Kroll Opera House, still doing duty as the Reichstag. He and Göring, Himmler and the Minister of the Interior, Dr Frick, entered with Hitler, while the loyal deputies rose to their feet and roared approval. Hitler spoke, as he had after the fall of France, as the conqueror, referring to Churchill with ironic scorn. Hess's mixed feelings of pride, frustration and suppressed excitement, the sudden catch at his heart when he thought of what he was about to undertake, may be imagined.

The target of his emotions, Churchill, was enjoying warm spring sunshine at the Prime Minister's country seat, Chequers. The clocks had gone forward an hour the previous night to double British summer time. While the rest of the weekend houseparty, which included Captain Hillgarth, Naval Attaché at Madrid – 'and a fervent disciple of Sam Hoare', Jock Colville noted – took tea inside, Churchill sat in a chair on the lawn working at the special buff boxes.[3]

Next morning, Monday 5 May, in the *Reichs* Chancellery, Berlin, Hess had what was to prove his last meeting with Hitler. It was an extended talk lasting some four hours. What was said will never be known for there were no witnesses, but from the length of the meeting and the report of an aide waiting in the ante-room outside, who heard their voices raised at times – although not what was said – it is evident that weighty matters were discussed; almost certainly they concerned his mission to Great Britain. When the doors of the study finally opened and the two emerged, Hitler put his arm around Hess's shoulders in what the same aide described as an almost cheerful leave-taking. His last words were apparently, 'Hess, you are and always were thoroughly pig-headed' ('*ein entsetzlicher Dickkopf*').[4]

From Berlin Hess drove to Augsburg, presumably to inspect the modifications to his Messerschmitt, afterwards returning home and summoning Albrecht Haushofer to report on his mission to Geneva. There is no record of this discussion either. Albrecht had phoned his mother on Saturday, after which she entered in her diary that his mission was 'not completely unsuccessful',[5] and on Monday she wrote again that his discussion with Burckhardt in Geneva had 'turned out not entirely fruitless, which is more than we had expected'.[6]

Two months later Karl Haushofer was to write to Hans Lammers at Hitler's Chancellery that the news Albrecht had brought from Switzerland had appeared so promising Hess had instructed him to make immediate arrangements for a second visit,[7] and after the war he was to tell Erika Mann that 'Hess seemed pleased' with what Albrecht told him about the trip.[8] However, it will be recalled he was to tell his US interrogator that he did not know what was said between Hess and his son on this their last meeting before Hess's flight.[9] None of this supports his post-war assertions that Burckhardt had agreed to act as a go-between with Hoare in Madrid and that a meeting had actually been arranged for the second half of May. Probably Albrecht's report sounded to Hess like the outcome of so many other feelers – yes, there were circles in England desiring peace, but the great obstacle was Hitler himself . . .

It must have been about this time that Ribbentrop's agent, Gardemann, went to Madrid and asked Don Joachim Boa, a close personal friend of the pro-British former Spanish Minister for Foreign Affairs, Juan Beigbeder, to speak to Beigbeder and ask if he would approach Hoare on his behalf to ascertain what ideas the British had about peace and to find out their general state of mind. It would be understood, naturally, that the Germans were certain of victory, but as they wanted to reconstruct the world they wanted to know what the English thought; this presumably referred to the British Empire. Although Gardemann made the approach before Hess's flight, it is uncertain when Beigbeder saw Hoare, who did not report the sounding until 20 May by diplomatic bag, referring to it then as 'a curious and very secret note that has just been sent me from Beigbeder'.[10]

It seems evident that, whatever cause Hoare may have given Hohenlowe, Albrecht's former pupil Stahmer, or Gardemann *via* Beigbeder to think he might be sympathetic to peace, it had not gone further than preliminary soundings. It is also evident that Hess made up his mind – at the latest by 1 May, when he ordered the final modifications to his personal Messerschmitt – to fly to Scotland to meet the Duke of Hamilton. Since he could not have known that the Duke, a serving RAF officer, would be in Scotland, it is equally evident that Major Robertson's Double-Cross Committee had got word to him somehow, possibly through a forged reply to Albrecht's letter. If so, Albrecht had not been told. That does not rule it out, for Hess did not reveal his intention to fly either to Albrecht or Karl Haushofer, and it appears from a letter Ilse Hess wrote to Himmler towards the end of the war that Hess never liked Albrecht. In a passage about Albrecht, who had disappeared after the failed 20 July 1944 plot against Hitler's life, she confided to the Reichsführer that she was filled with deep mistrust for him for he had never had her sympathy: she knew moreover from the papers left behind in her husband's armoured safe when he flew to Scotland that Albrecht had played a middle-man role. 'I tremble at the thought of what Albrecht [if now abroad] can do, so little did my husband ever care for him personally . . .'[11]

Apart from the question of how Hess learned that Hamilton was in Scotland, to find the reason behind his resolve it is necessary to know what Hitler was thinking, because ultimately, regardless of his personal motives, he always acted for his Führer.

What appears to be an accurate glimpse into Hitler's mind is contained in the contemporary notes of von Weizsäcker at the Foreign Ministry. Von Weizsäcker had been against turning east from the start 'so long as the more important England' remained in contention.[12] Hitler's view, on the other hand, as explained to him on 1 May was that Russia could be finished off, as it were, by the way without affecting the issue against England, which would fall that year with or without Russia. Then the British Empire would have to be sustained; Russia, however, would have to be 'rendered harmless'.[13]

The same day von Weizsäcker gained further insights into Hitler's mind from another source. The Führer had been airing his views on the French as an inferior race, declaring that the time had come to consolidate Europe, forcing the Latins back to their proper place. This had led him on to his beloved building plans for Berlin; for there could be only one central city for Europe, 'not Berlin *and* London *and* Paris, but only Berlin'. He would make Berlin into the mightiest and finest city in the world, 'the centre of gravity of Europe and thereby its capital'.[14]

Such were the Führer's expectations on the eve of Hess's flight; such were Hess's expectations. There was another factor, however, which gave his mission urgency: as General Jodl, the brains in the OKW staff had put it in December: 'We must have solved all continental European plans in 1941 since from 1942 the USA will be in a position to step in . . .'[15]

Hitler foresaw in 1942 the start of the gigantic final struggle for world mastery between German-dominated continental Europe and the United

States of America. For this he wanted control over London and the Empire, since the only alternative he perceived was the flight of the British Government, the Royal Family and Royal Navy to Canada to continue the struggle under the control of Washington. The British would not deal with him, but those powerful groups in opposition to Churchill might be prepared to deal with his Stellvertreter, 'the conscience of the Party'. This, is presumably, what the Double-Cross Committee had fed Hess when informing him of the whereabouts of the Duke of Hamilton. This, then, is why Hitler sent Hess to Britain.

There are other possible or contingency reasons. Hess was known for his hostility towards Bolshevism and his advocacy of friendship with Great Britain. It could be supposed, if he flew to Britain, that this cleared the way for a closer coming together of Germany and Russia, or indeed that he had taken the desperate step because those elements who wished for a closer German-Soviet alliance were gaining the upper hand – in short, a deception. More persuasively, perhaps, if it were assumed he had flown to make peace with Britain, and if he failed, Stalin could be expected to draw the conclusion that Hitler would not risk attacking Russia. On 30 April Hitler had put back the date of 'Barbarossa' from 15 May to 22 June, but Stalin's gaze, like that of the world's intelligence services, would be fixed on May. Even the German public believed there would be a showdown in May and that it would be provoked by their own Government. Thus an SD secret public opinion report gathered in the week Hess was preparing for his flight summarised the current talking points:

Since Germany has to feed practically all Europe in the coming winter it sees itself forced to secure the Ukraine and the Russian oilfields. Another version runs in similar vein: the German grain stock is declining; not much is expected from the coming harvest, Germany must therefore gain possession of the Ukraine. The attack must however begin in May since in June the harvest will be gathered in the Ukraine and then there will be a danger that the grain will be destroyed by burning it.[16]

Most of the 'numerous rumours' concerned coming war with Russia; 'the date for the start of the Russian offensive is named overwhelmingly as 20 May.'[17]

These public opinion reports are significant because they were compiled by agents of Reinhard Heydrich's *Reich* Security main office and were to a certain extent manipulated. Heydrich had played a key role in all the major Nazi deceptions and it is probable he played a role in Hess's flight. He was himself a skilled pilot and was detached for special flying duty during the week preceding Hess's flight, probably to make reconnaissance sorties over Britain.[18] That his secret opinion reports were indicating 20 May suggests a deception campaign.

Whether Hitler sent Hess in the belief that peace with Britain was possible, whether he sacrificed him for a deception against Stalin or whether he sent him because either way he gained will probably never be known. It depends largely on the information Hess had been fed by the Double-Cross Committee, because those who were not initiated into his plans, yet were privy to much intelligence from England, like Albrecht Haushofer and von Weizsäcker, thought the chances of an understanding remote.

Another item in the SD secret public opinion reports for this week is interesting in view of what Hess was to say when he arrived in Scotland; it was a report of a new enemy propaganda leaflet which had been dropped over various areas, including Augsburg, and was entitled 'Not Your Child'. It had a picture of a severely wounded, dead child, under which the text read:

This is not your child, but one of the countless children caught by German air raids: in Warsaw, in Rotterdam, in Belgrade . . . How much grief and misery, how many burnt-out houses, destroyed churches and villages throughout Europe today indict the man who preached war for seven years and on 1 September 1939 started it.[19]

On 7 May opposition to Churchill's direction of the war was expressed in the House of Commons by the former Secretary of State for War, Hore-Belisha, and by Lloyd George, supplied with the gloomiest predictions by Liddell Hart and criticism of the Prime Minister's dictatorial style in the war cabinet by Robert Menzies, among others. Churchill had the advantage over his critics that he had been reading 'Ultra' decrypts of the German Army and Luftwaffe orders; he knew that in North Africa Rommel was running short of supplies and had been instructed not to make further attacks on Tobruk, nor to advance into Egypt, and that in the Balkans Hitler was moving his *Panzer* divisions to jumping-off points for the Russian campaign. In his reply he conveyed the true confidence he felt. Harold Nicolson entered the House as he held the floor after lunch:

He stands there in his black conventional suit with the huge watch-chain. He is very amusing. He is very frank. At moments I have a nasty feeling that he is being a trifle too optimistic. He is very strong, for instance, about Egypt and our position in the Mediterranean . . .[20]

After pointing to Hitler's problems Churchill ended, 'I feel sure we have no need to fear the tempest. Let it roar, and let it rage. We shall come through.'[21] He was rewarded in the division that followed by a

189

vote of confidence of 447 to 3, and as he left the chamber a spontaneous burst of cheering broke out and was taken up outside. 'He looks pleased', Harold Nicolson noted; later Jock Colville recorded: 'He went early to bed elated by his forensic success.'

If the recently published Goebbels diaries are taken at face value, Goebbels discussed Churchill's speech with Hitler the next day, 8 May, judging it the product of despair. Churchill was relying on America, but, they concluded, Roosevelt only wanted to extend the war because he wished to inherit the British Empire.[22] Undoubtedly Hitler believed this: Churchill would be the ruin of the Empire.

Whether Hitler and Hess discussed the speech and the vote is not known; if they did, they must have disregarded it, assuming perhaps that the Commons operated like the Reichstag as a rubber stamp for the leader. Certainly behind the emotion in the House doubt remained. Harold Nicolson noted in his diary that day, 8 May, that he feared people would jump at any escape which made cowardice appear respectable. 'Morale is good – but it is rather like the Emperor's clothes.'[23]

Barring bad weather, Hess's mission was now fixed for Saturday 10 May; the message he carried was to be reinforced by the heaviest air-raid yet on central London. On Friday the 9th the top echelon of the leadership initiated into the plot began to disperse from Berlin, Hitler himself *via* Munich, where he was met by Göring, to his Alpine retreat above Berchtesgaden, Göring – after Munich – to his castle Veldenstein, near Nuremberg, Ribbentrop to his castle Fuschl, near Salzburg, Himmler apparently to Sofia. Hess remained in Munich, and Rosenberg in Berlin.[24]

Rosenberg's role is obscure. It will be recalled that, like Hess, he believed profoundly in union with Great Britain against Bolshevism and retained contact with British Air Intelligence through his fellow Balt and dedicated anti-Communist, Baron de Ropp, in Switzerland. Since 1933 he had been eclipsed almost completely by Ribbentrop, Ley and Himmler, although he retained his shadow Foreign Political Office (APA) and various departments concerned with ideological, ecclesiastical, educational and cultural questions, also an office for Jewish and Freemasonry questions, with a recent addition, the Institute for Research into the Jewish Question, at Frankfurt-am-Main. Here, in March, he had made the inaugural speech at a so-called 'International conference' on the Jewish question and had referred to 'the solution of the Jewish question presently entering its decisive phase'. He had been advised by Martin Bormann to make no mention of Madagascar.[25] The Jews, he had said would have to be removed to a reservation where they could work under police supervision.[26]

On 20 April Hitler had appointed him as his delegate for Central Planning for Questions of the East European Area, a post which would be upgraded after the start of the Russian offensive to Reichsminister for the Occupied East in direct rivalry to Himmler in his role as Commissar for the Consolidation of German Nationhood [in the east].

On 9 May, according to a recent statement by his adjutant at that time, Rosenberg in Berlin was called by Hess and told he must come to Munich at once.[27] He replied that it was impossible. If true, this suggests he may not have been initiated into Hess's mission, hence that de Ropp and British Air Intelligence were not the channel by which Hess had been informed of the Duke of Hamilton's whereabouts and whatever else he had been fed. This would support Group Captain Winterbotham, who always claimed he was not initiated into the British side of the operation.[28] In any case, Hess told Rosenberg he had laid on a plane; he must fly down that night, which he did; the next morning, 10 May, he drove to Hess's home at Harlaching at midday for an early lunch.

Apparently Hess also called a legal officer on Bormann's staff on 9 May and asked him the position of the King of England,[29] a strange request at that stage of the planning. And the same evening he tried three times to get through to Walther Darré, Minister of Agriculture, but, failing to do so, wrote him a short note postponing a conference he had previously agreed to arrange in mid-May: 'I am making a long trip and don't know when I shall be back ...' but, he ended, he would contact him when he returned.[30]

20
FLIGHT

Saturday morning, 10 May, was fine and sunny. Hess took his little son's hand and they went for a walk along the river with their German shepherd dog and its three puppies.[1] Obviously he knew it might be for the last time; he could not have guessed the circumstances that would make it so. He saw himself as a peace envoy and expected that, if he arrived safely at his destination, whatever the outcome he would be granted safe passage home. That is what he suggested afterwards. But it is certain that Churchill, however much he knew of or encouraged the secret service game Stewart Menzies and the Double-Cross Committee were playing, could not have given official sanction to a peace emissary, and on the other side Hess had to pretend he came without his Führer's knowledge or permission. Neither the Führer nor any other member of the regime could be connected in any way with his mission lest it betoken weakness. It had to appear that he came entirely on his own initiative simply to convince the British that the Führer meant them no harm. To further the deception, he had written a long letter to the Führer explaining his mission and the reasons for it, which his adjutant, Karl-Heinz Pintsch, was to carry personally to the Berghof after he had taken off. He had also written letters which he would leave for Ilse, for his parents and brother Alfred, for Albrecht Haushofer and for Himmler, the latter stating that none of his staff had known what he intended and requesting that no action be taken against them, so Ilse maintained after the war. None of these letters have come to light. However, Ilse found a copy of her husband's letter to Hitler with her farewell note and claimed later that she could remember its final passage word-perfectly: ' . . . And should, *mein Führer*, my project, which I must confess has very little chance of profit, fail, it can have no evil consequence for you or for Germany; you can always distance yourself from me – declare me mad.'[2]

Hess knew he was on his own; if he expected to be allowed home, it could only be after success or because he believed in the British sporting instinct. If so, it was of a piece with his misjudgement of the character and state of mind of his opponents and their view of him as a Nazi.

Rosenberg arrived at noon. The butler opened the door and showed him in to Hess. Ilse did not join them; she had been unwell for some days, she stated afterwards, and stayed in bed that morning. So the two went into the dining-room, whose French windows looked out on to the lawn and trees behind the house. A light lunch of cold meats, German sausage and salad had been laid out, and they ate alone; Hess had given instructions they were not to be disturbed by the household staff. There is no record of what they discussed and both were careful after the war to reveal nothing. Nor were either probed by their interrogators. Rosenberg was asked if he had noticed anything unusual about Hess on that last occasion.

No. I was in Munich and he had invited me for dinner. We had spoken very calmly and we remained together after dinner for some time and it only seemed queer that after his son had gone to bed directly after dinner he took him down again, and then on the following day we were informed he had flown to England ... He was rather quiet during the dinner, but nothing peculiar had struck me in regard to his behaviour.[3]

That was all Rosenberg had to say and he was not pressed. According to Rosenberg's adjutant, who accompanied him to Munich, Rosenberg drove straight to Hitler at the Berghof after leaving Hess.[4] Since he left at about one o'clock and the distance from Munich to Berchtesgaden is a little over 150 kilometres (110 miles), much of it along a fast road, it is probable he arrived before Hess took off on his flight.

Hess, meanwhile, had a short rest, so Ilse recalled later, then at about 2.30 he came to have a cup of tea with her in her bedroom to say goodbye. She was apparently surprised at what he was wearing: bluish-grey breeches tucked inside high, fur-lined flying boots, a light blue shirt and a dark blue tie. Later, among his papers she found a bill from a Munich military tailor for a Luftwaffe captain's uniform.[5]

Ilse Hess has always maintained she knew nothing of her husband's destination or purpose, and this appears to be borne out by one of Hess's letters from captivity recalling how he had gone 'hot and cold' when he thought she had divined his real intention at this last leave-taking.[6] He never discussed his official business with her and it may be thought he would have kept this hazardous enterprise from her to spare her anxiety. On the other hand, she had seen his chart of Scotland – saying afterwards she thought it was the Baltic coast – and on this parting day in bed she was apparently reading *The Pilot's Book of Everest* by the

Marquess of Clydesdale – as the Duke of Hamilton had been – and Wing Commander D. F. McIntyre. It had been given to them by English friends two years before the war, she told James Leasor. It will be recalled that Clydesdale had sent a copy to Karl Haushofer in early 1937. That morning Hess had asked her what she was reading, and she had handed him the book. He had looked at the inscription inside: 'With all good wishes and the hope that out of personal friendships a real and lasting understanding may grow between our two countries'.[7] He had turned to a picture of Clydesdale, gazing at it for a moment presumably, before handing the book back open at this page. 'He's very good looking.'

Ilse had agreed, puzzled, she recalled.

If this occurred and she really had no idea where he was going, it was a truly remarkable coincidence. As for his recollection of going 'hot and cold' when he thought she had guessed his destination, he wrote this in a letter from Nuremberg when he was still maintaining – as he continued to do for the rest of his life – that no one else had known of his intention. Probably it was a hint to her to maintain the pretence.

After taking tea with her in her bedroom, Hess leant over, took her hand and kissed it, then walked to the connecting door to his son's room, turning to look at her. 'I still see my husband before me as if it were yesterday', Ilse wrote twelve years later, '. . . suddenly remarkably serious, pensive, almost hesitating.'

'When will you be back?' she asked.

He looked away for a moment. 'I don't know exactly – perhaps tomorrow, perhaps not, but I'll certainly be home again by Monday evening.'[8]

She did not believe him; in the circumstances it was understandable. 'Come back as soon as you can. Buz will miss you.'

'I'll miss him too.'

He turned quickly and went to make his farewell to his young 'Buz'. So they parted.

Some minutes later, after pulling on a trench coat, he joined his adjutant, Pintsch, and his personal detective outside by his Mercedes. A small suitcase containing little but a flat box of homoeopathic medicines, Ilse's camera, a letter to the Duke of Hamilton, charts of his route, and probably a wallet containing family photographs and Karl and Albrecht Haushofer's visiting cards had already been placed in the boot. He climbed in to the front seat beside his driver, the other two in the back, and they started off, driving through Munich and on to the *Autobahn* towards Augsburg.[9]

They were ahead of schedule. He had planned the flight so that he would make his landfall on the northern English coast soon after sunset. Shortly before the turning to Augsburg, so Pintsch told James Leasor many years after the war, they came to a wooded stretch, and Hess told the driver to pull in to the side. He and Pintsch climbed out in the sunshine and walked among the crocuses and spring shoots for half an hour or so before resuming the journey.

Since it was Saturday, the Messerschmitt works were deserted when they arrived save for the sentries and a small reception party, but Hess's plane, a pale blue-grey below with mottled grey-green camouflage above and the black Luftwaffe cross on the fuselage flanked by the code 'VJ + OQ', was standing ready on the runway. Hess entered the administration building, Pintsch following with the small suitcase. Inside he donned his Luftwaffe captain's jacket and a fur-lined flying suit, transferred the contents of the suitcase to various pockets and hung the camera round his neck. Pintsch folded the discarded trench coat inside the empty case and accompanied him out to the runway, where Hess shook hands with the works group and his staff before climbing into the cockpit of the plane and going through the starting rituals. It was about six o'clock – according to a chart he marked later while a prisoner in Britain, a quarter to six. Soon afterwards he was taxiing away up-wind and rising into the sunlit evening.

The chart of his route, which he drew up afterwards, showed a track north-westerly from Augsburg following the Rhine over occupied Holland to the Texel, where he altered course ninety degrees to head easterly over the Dutch islands until off the mouth of the Ems, thence resuming his original north-westerly course to fly up the North Sea some 125 miles from the English east coast. The former Messerschmitt test pilot, Helmut Kaden, who was responsible for technical preparations for Hess's flight, believes that he may have described such a dog-leg in order to deceive his British interrogators about German advances in navigation by radio beam.[10] Kaden assumes that he probably flew a northerly course passing over Hanover and Hamburg, since this would have enabled him to use the secret navigation aid he had, and would have avoided the heavily defended air-space over the industrial areas of the Rhine. He would then have continued northerly over the Frisian Islands to Jutland, tuning in to the directional beams which interspersed classical music from the Danish radio station, Kalundborg, until he arrived at the latitude of the station and turned due west across the North Sea towards his landfall on the coast of Northumberland. This must have been what he did for the final leg of the journey, otherwise there would have been little point in carrying a radio compass. The course he followed prior to that depends on whether he truly flew the solo mission he always claimed, or whether he was escorted over the North Sea by Me-109 fighters commanded by Reinhard Heydrich and, if so, where he made the rendezvous with Heydrich. Long after the war, while in captivity in Spandau, he told the US Director of the prison that, when booking in his flight to Augsburg on 10 May, he had entered his destination as 'Norway'. This implies the northerly course Helmut Kaden suggests.[11]

Naturally, if he was escorted, he and everyone in the know had to deny it, otherwise his story that he acted entirely on his own initiative would have lacked any credibility. Yet there are two clues that Heydrich was involved. Firstly, Heydrich's widow, Lina, wrote a memoir long after the war in which she claimed that her husband learnt of the Hess episode 'while he was "residing" on the Channel [coast] and likewise piloting Me-109s towards England'.[12] It is hard to imagine why Himmler's chief of security should be flying fighter missions to Britain at this time, before the offensive against Russia, in which his *Einsatz* groups were to play the key role exterminating Bolsheviks and Jews behind the lines, unless he was involved in such a vital mission as protecting the Stellvertreter. The second clue comes from Hans-Bernd Gisevius, an informer for the German opposition and later for US intelligence in Switzerland; he was close to Heydrich's chief of Criminal Police – also an informer for the opposition – Arthur Nebe, who told him that Heydrich was flying over the North Sea on the day of Hess's flight. Nebe also told him that he had asked Heydrich on his return to head office whether it could have happened that he might have shot down the Deputy Führer. Unusually Heydrich was lost for words for a moment, then he replied shortly that, if he had done so, it would have been a historic coincidence – so Gisevius told Heydrich's biographer, Eduard Calic, after the war.[13]

The distance from Augsburg north on a more or less direct route to the Jutland coast, then due west to the coast of Northumberland is approximately 900 miles. The time Hess took, assuming he left at six and made his landfall soon after ten was rather over four hours, implying a speed of something under 225 mph. This is less than the Me-110 D's normal cruising speed of 280 mph, but 200 mph was the economical cruising speed. Moreover, Hess told the Duke of Hamilton afterwards that he had underestimated the length of twilight in northern latitudes, and consequently turned back and circled a while before finally coming in.[14] If he added forty minutes to his flight time in this way – as implied in his subsequent sketch track chart – it would have brought his cruising speed over the whole distance to approximately 270 mph. Helmut Kaden's hypothesis is eminently possible. Nevertheless, until it can be established whether he made a rendezvous with Heydrich and, if so, where, his flight plan cannot be reconstructed with any certainty. All that can be said is that, if Hitler did not order fighter protection for his 'Rudi', his 'Hesserl', on this vital, sensitive and dangerous intrusion into British air-space, he was acting out of character.

Flying over the North Sea was supremely grand and lonely, Hess

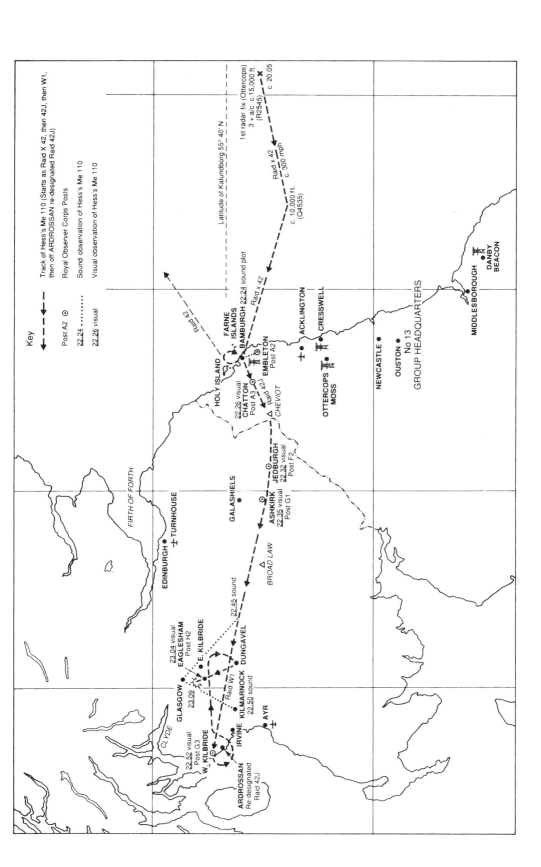

Key

- – – ▶ Track of Hess's Me 110 (Starts as Raid X 42, then 42J, then W1, then off ARDROSSAN re-designated Raid 42J)
- Post A2 ⊙ Royal Observer Corps Posts
- <u>22.24</u> .... Sound observation of Hess's Me 110
- <u>22.26</u> visual Visual observation of Hess's Me 110

1st radar fix (Ottercops)
3 + a/c c.15,000 ft.
(RZ545)
c. 20.05

Latitude of Kalundborg 55° 40′ N

Raid x 42
c. 300 mph

c. 10,000 ft.
(Q4535)

Raid x 42

FARNE ISLANDS
BAMBURGH <u>22.24</u> sound plot

Raid 42

ACKLINGTON
CRESSWELL

HOLY ISLAND

Raid 42

<u>22.26</u> visual
CHATTON
Post A3

EMBLETON
Post A2

Raid 42J
CHEVIOT

OTTERCOPS
MOSS

NEWCASTLE

OUSTON
No 13
GROUP HEADQUARTERS

MIDDLESBOROUGH
DANBY BEACON

FIRTH OF FORTH

EDINBURGH
TURNHOUSE

GALASHIELS

ASHKIRK ⊙ JEDBURGH ⊙
22.35 visual   22.32 visual
Post G1   Post F2

BROAD LAW

<u>23.04</u> visual
EAGLESHAM
Post H2

GLASGOW
23.09

<u>22.45</u> sound

E. KILBRIDE
DUNGAVEL

Raid W1
KILMARNOCK
<u>22.50</u> sound

AYR

CLYDE

<u>22.52</u> visual
Post G3

W. KILBRIDE
IRVINE

ARDROSSAN
Re-designated
Raid 42J

recalled later in letters to Ilse from Nuremberg, the evening light 'magically beautiful'. A myriad of small clouds far below gave the effect of ice-floes on the sea, all tinged with red. Further and the clouds disappeared leaving him no cover at all. For a moment he considered turning back, then he thought of the night landing involved: even if he managed it without irreparable damage to the plane, it would be impossible to keep it secret; it would be reported 'above', so he wrote to Ilse, 'and then it would be at an end, all over, finished for ever!' 'See it through', he told himself, 'come what may!'[15] Once again the assumption must be that he was indicating to Ilse the line she must take; his mission had not been known 'above'. Otherwise it is nonsense. Flying a fighter-bomber through several different German air defence zones could not possibly have been kept secret; moreover, he was contemplating a hazardous landing at an unknown grass strip outside a private house in Scotland.

Fortunately, he wrote, he saw over Britain a haze reflected in the evening light and dived from several thousand feet at full throttle to hide beneath it, attaining 'a tremendous speed' as he crossed the coast. He had to thank this dive, he wrote, for the fact that he was not shot down by a Spitfire on his tail, which he had not seen. Since he never saw the Spitfire, he must have been told this by the Duke of Hamilton after he landed. Whether there were any Spitfires on patrol here at the time seems doubtful, as will appear.

He had been picked up first at 10.10 p.m., when some seventy miles out to sea by the Chain Home RDF – high, fixed array radar – at Ottercops Moss, north-west of Newcastle-on-Tyne.[16] This was comparatively early days for radar and Ottercops had an unfortunate reputation for reporting false echoes from atmospherics, so much so that one of the 'tellers' on duty in the filter room at Fighter Headquarters, near Stanmore, recently recalled that 'a just audible ripple of mirth' went round the WAAFs at the plotting table when it was noticed that Ottercops had reported the signal.[17] It is clear from a secret investigation carried out by the RAF in the week following Hess's arrival that Ottercops reported 'three plus aircraft' at approximately 15,000 feet and, as the reports continued, the course of the group, now designated 'Raid X [unidentified] 42', was due west, speed 'approximately 300 mph'. As it approached the coast, Raid X42 was reported by two more Chain Home stations in the area, Danby Beacon and Douglas Wood, and two Chain Home Low – directional aerial radars – at Cresswell and Bamburgh, the latter just south of the Farne Islands and practically in the track of the raid. All four new stations estimated the echo as a single aircraft. The later investigators, therefore, 'thought that the Ottercops Moss estimate should be waived in favour of the estimate of the other four stations'.[18]

The picture was confused by another echo or echoes, stated in the Operations Record Book (ORB) of 13 Group Headquarters, RAF Ouston, near Newcastle-on-Tyne, as possibly from '72 White [two Spitfires of 72 Squadron] who were detailed to raid and were searching off Farne and Holy Islands.'[19] However, the ORB of 72 Squadron shows without a shadow of doubt that '72 White' took off on patrol at 6 p.m. and landed at 6.30, and the next patrol, 72 Blue, took off at 7.29 and landed at 9.10 – an hour before Hess appeared – and there were no patrols in the air at 10 p.m.[20] It is, in any case, hard to see how the echoes could have been from a Spitfire on Hess's tail as he dived from some 10,000 feet to roar across the coast near the Farne Islands at fifty feet, skimming over the roofs of the village of Belford, since the radar stations continued to plot the echo moving out to sea north-easterly of Holy Island. Hess, at his low level, had disappeared from the radars, which were directed seawards, and the filter room plot of Raid 42 was continued on the echo moving eastwards – that at least is the conclusion of the secret investigation, which assumed this echo was from 'a fighter aircraft despatched to intercept Raid 42'.[21]

Without the raw information on which the RAF investigators based their report it is not possible to speculate on why this 'fighter' was not given an 'F' (friendly fighter) designation from its Identification Friend or Foe equipment, nor why RAF Ouston recorded 72 White as detailed to Raid 42 when it is clear from the ORB of 72 Squadron that there were no Spitfire patrols in the air at the time. Nor is it possible to analyse the alternative, namely that the Ottercops Moss original estimate of 'three plus aircraft' coming in was correct and that the echoes turning east and fading as Hess sped inland over the coast were Heydrich's Me-109 escorts.

The British air defence system relied on the radar chain detecting incoming enemy aircraft over the sea. Once over land, reporting was taken up by the Royal Observer Corps, trained in aircraft identification and organised in posts reporting to group centres, where the observations were plotted on a table similar to the tables in the control rooms at the RAF fighter stations. At 10.23 observer post A2 at Embleton, on the coast some ten miles south of the Farne Islands, reported a sound bearing of Hess's plane coming in,[22] and two minutes later A3 at Chatton, some ten miles south-west of Belford, reported seeing the aircraft at fifty feet, identifying it as an Me-110. Hess, in his letters to Ilse, allowed himself some licence for this period, describing how he was at 'perhaps five metres [15 feet] and less', skimming 'trees, houses, cattle and people' in what 'the English pilots call "hedge-hopping"'; he added that the English had been impressed, according to 'Lord Hamilton and a very respectful review in an English Flying Journal'.[23] For himself, he was enjoying it hugely as he aimed directly for the first of the landmarks he had committed to memory, the Cheviot, and 'literally climbed the slope a few metres above the ground', both throttles open. Then, making a small alteration of course to the right, he dropped down the other side, hopping houses and trees, waving to people – so he wrote in happy recollection. At 10.30 he was reported by observer post F2 at Jedburgh and moments later by G1 at Ashkirk, both identifying his plane as an Me-110.

The RAF controller at Ouston disbelieved the reports since an Me-110 would not have sufficient fuel to return home; he thought it was probably a Dornier, as did the controller at Fighter Command Headquarters, where the aircraft was being plotted as 'Raid 42J' – 'J' for a split raid as the main Raid 42 was being plotted heading easterly out to sea.

Hess had the chart of his route to Hamilton's seat, Dungavel House, in a transparent envelope strapped to his right thigh, but he did not have to concern himself with it, he wrote, since every landmark was etched in his mind. He passed between the peaks of Broad Law and Pikestone, inclining right again and descending in gathering dark lit by a full moon through clouds, until he saw what he took to be his destination ahead; he decided to fly on to the west coast to make certain. It was about 10.45. The Royal Observer Corps had lost him west of Ashkirk, where there were no posts, but a Dornier 215 heading west had been passed to No 34 Observer Group Centre, Pitt Street, Glasgow, and they picked him up by the sound of his engines to the south as he roared across at what they estimated as 300 mph. They started to plot him as 'Raid W1', reporting the aircraft from the speed alone as probably an Me-110.[24]

In the meantime, a Spitfire from 72 Squadron at Acklington on the east coast had been scrambled to intercept, but, by the time the pilot reached 8,000 feet, Hess had streaked away to his north-west over the border hills and he never saw him.[25] However, a Defiant from a new RAF station on the west coast at Ayr on the Firth of Clyde had taken off on a night patrol at 10.35, and this was ordered to intercept.[26] The Defiant's engine was heard from the Observer Group Centre in Glasgow as the sound of the Me-110 faded westwards.

Observers at post G3 on a hill at West Kilbride on the Firth of Clyde some twenty-five miles south-west of Glasgow heard Hess's plane approaching – they had already been alerted by Glasgow – then saw it flying low and actually below the level of the post. They were able to make out every detail of the twin-engined, twin-tailed aircraft as it shot past them and swung round over the Firth in the moonlight.

Hess recalled the water flat as a mirror under the rising moon and ahead, as he crossed the west coast, a hill rising sheer to some 500 metres, lit with a magnificent reddish glow – no doubt Little Cumbrae Island.

He turned southwards along the coast until he saw a spur of land curving in to the sea at Ardrossan, exactly as he had memorised it on the map. He swung in across the coast again and picked up the silver ribbon of railway line leading north-easterly to Glasgow,[27] and flew on to the line from Kilmarnock until he saw the bow it made by Dungavel and the hill and the lake glinting to the south of the estate.

Surely his original intention was to land there. In the darkness it must have appeared strange and far too hazardous. Determining on a parachute jump – something he had never practised – he pulled the control column towards him and circled while he gained height. At about 2,000 metres, (6,500 feet) he shut off the engines, feathered the propellers, pushed back the cockpit canopy and tried to get out. The plane was still moving at speed and he found himself glued to the back of the seat by the wind pressure. It was impossible to move. Suddenly he remembered having heard that the way to jump was to turn the plane on its back and fall out. He had never been instructed in this; instead of a half roll, he pulled the column back for a half loop so violently that he blacked out momentarily as the nose swung up. Coming to, he saw the speed gauge was at zero. He had stalled. The plane was hanging upright in the sky on its tail. Desperately he flung himself out, hitting a part of one of the tail planes hard with his right foot as he fell, then he pulled the ripcord. The parachute opened and held him, 'an indescribably marvellous and triumphant feeling in this situation,' he recalled later.[28]

Observers at post H2 on the edge of Eaglesham Moor, some twelve miles north-west of Dungavel House, saw him bale out and the parachute open as the aeroplane fell away and dived out of control. Moments later they heard the sound of the crash and saw a bright glare of flame. It was nine minutes past eleven.

Hess floated down into a grassy field, white in the moonlight, stumbling and falling as his bruised foot hit the ground, and once more he blacked out.

201

PART THREE

CAPTIVITY

21
PRISONER OF WAR

The field in which Hess landed was a pasture just north of Eaglesham village behind Floors Farm; the nearest of the farm buildings was a cottage in which the ploughman, David McLean – or M'Lean to the local press – lived with his mother and sister, and it was he who greeted Hess as, coming to, he rolled on his back trying to extricate himself from the parachute harness.[1]

'Who are ye?' McLean demanded. 'British or German?'[2]

Hess replied in what the ploughman later described as 'almost perfect English' and 'without any sign of fright or anxiety to escape' that he was German – *Hauptmann* [Captain] Alfred Horn, and he had an important message for the Duke of Hamilton.[3]

He unfastened the harness, but had difficulty in standing on his injured foot and McLean assisted him the short distance through the field gate to the door of his cottage – as Hess put it in a letter to Ilse, he 'helped me very pleasantly into the house to the fireside and a cup of tea'.[4] It was McLean's mother who asked if he would like tea. 'We knew when he came into the cottage and spoke to us that he was a man of some standing and used to command,' she told reporters after it was discovered who their guest had been. She was particularly struck by the quality of his fur-lined flying-boots, which seemed to be made of glove leather.

'I do not drink tea at night, thank you,' Hess replied, and asked for water instead.

McLean went out to fetch someone of authority, returning presently with Lieutenant Clarke of the local Home Guard unit, together with two men from the Royal Artillery Clarke had collected from a nearby camp and a part-time or 'Special' Constable. Having seen a parachutist coming down near the farm, they and two other Home Guard officers were doing 'a converging manoeuvre' on the farm buildings. Clarke was brandishing a Webley pistol of First World War officers' issue, and by

Hess's later account staggering, reeking of whisky. This may be what Mrs McLean meant when she told reporters that there was 'some excitement in the kitchen when the military people came to take him away, but he [Hess] was the coolest man of the whole lot'.[5]

Clarke, having ascertained that his prisoner was Hauptmann Alfred Horn and unarmed, prodded him in the back with 'his huge revolver' and marched him out to a car, 'belching merrily and continuously and stumbling' in the dark. 'God's finger was truly between his unsteady finger and the trigger!' as Hess recalled it later for Ilse.[6] They drove to 'C' Company, 3rd Battalion Renfrewshire Home Guard headquarters in a scout hut in the next village of Busby, and Hess was escorted in with more pistol-prodding from the belligerent Clarke and ordered to a side room. It was bare and he lay down flat on his back in a relaxation posture he often practised; he was weary now and needed all his resources for this extravagant anti-climax to his great effort. His spirits were revived somewhat by 'a really nice little "Tommy"' who brought him a bottle of milk; he had probably provided it for his own night watch, Hess thought.

The time was about 11.45.[7] Battalion Headquarters at the Scout Hall, Florence Road, Giffnock, about a mile up the road, were alerted by telephone and in turn attempted to report the incident to the Argylle and Sutherland Highlanders headquarters at Paisley, west of Glasgow, to request a military escort for the prisoner. The lines were so busy they could not get through until after midnight; in the meantime they sent a squad to collect the airman from the scout hut in Busby and shortly before 12.15 Hess, protesting vainly that he had an urgent message for the Duke of Hamilton, was brought in to the scout hall at Giffnock. By then the duty officer of the Argylls had been informed and had reported to Clyde Sub-Area Military Command, who said the prisoner should be put in police cells for the night. Whilst the Argylls' duty officer conveyed this to the Home Guard at Giffnock, Clyde Sub-Area called Glasgow Area Command; the duty officer at Area then tried to call Giffnock. The line was engaged continuously and he had to have a conversation interrupted before he could get through. He was told that the airman held was claiming he had flown across to call on the Duke of Hamilton, whom he knew very well. He gave instructions that the man was to be held in the scout hall until he had arranged for the nearest military unit to collect him.[8].

In the meantime the Home Guard battalion commander, not satisfied that his airman should be lodged in a prison cell for the night, had already called the Argylls back and told them the prisoner was 'an officer of some importance and might require medical attention' – further that the man had a message for the Duke of Hamilton and it seemed essential

206

he should be interrogated at once as he was apparently prepared to talk to the right party. The impression gained by the Argylls' duty officer was that the prisoner, 'a personal friend of the Duke of Hamilton', was 'seriously injured and would require immediate medical attention', and he passed this on to Clyde Sub-Area together with the suggestion that the prisoner should be interrogated as soon as possible; he added that there was a possibility that the 'prisoner might not last out the night'. Clyde Sub-Area passed this up to Area, as a result of which the night duty officer at Area gave instructions that the airman was to be taken to Maryhill Barracks in north-west Glasgow, which had proper medical facilities. He then called RAF Turnhouse to alert the interrogating officer, Flight Lieutenant Benson. It is not clear from his report whether he knew that the Duke of Hamilton was commanding officer at Turnhouse – although very probable – nor whether he knew that the far closer RAF Abbotsinch, near Glasgow, had been alerted a short time before by the Argylls' duty officer; he had asked whether they wanted the airman for interrogation. The reply had been a firm 'No, put him in the police cells for the night.'[9]

In the scout hall, meanwhile, Hess was the centre of a growing number of curious police and Home Guard officers. He had been searched and required to turn out the contents of his pockets on to a table, and an inventory had been made. This inventory and two others made later as his few possessions were passed on to different authorities are missing from the reports to which they were attached originally in the file WO 199/3288A; no doubt they are in the companion file 3288B, which remains closed until 2017. The reason for the secrecy is presumably because one of the items was Hess's letter to the Duke of Hamilton.[10] While there is no doubt from the open reports that Hess came over specifically to see the Duke, the fact that he brought a letter is not apparent. The only possible hint is in the report of the Home Guard commanding officer, who advised the Argylls 'that this officer [the prisoner] had a message for the Duke of Hamilton'. It may be that the inventories are held back in order to conceal the existence of a letter whose contents belie the official story – in short, to conceal the fact that the letter itself is being withheld. It is difficult to think why the inventories should otherwise have been detached from the report and placed in the 'closed file'.

At some time the Polish Consul arrived at the scout hall to interpret for the police, and later the Assistant Group Officer of the Royal Observer Corps, Major Graham Donald, with some RAF officers. Major Donald had watched Hess's plane being plotted across his table at Group Centre, Glasgow, and after the report that it had crashed had set out for the scene. There he had found wreckage scattered over an acre and a half, but the fire had not been extensive and he had been able to identify the aircraft from the twin rudders and remains of the fuselage as an Me-110. Finding no trace of guns or bomb-racks – he probably meant cannon, since the official report later stated that three machine-guns were found 'still covered in protective grease'[11] – and curious about the pilot, he had driven to the scout hall in company with two officers of RAF Ayr whom he met at the site.

The atmosphere was rather tense when they arrived. Hess was being quizzed by the Polish Consul about 'the other parachutists'; he was insisting he had been entirely alone and was refusing to speak English. Donald had spent some time in Munich before the war, knew some German and probably formed a suspicion about the identity of the prisoner as soon as he saw him; he decided to help with the questioning. It was well after 12.30 by this time, possibly after 1 a.m. and Hess must have begun to despair; he told Donald he had a vital secret message for the Duke of Hamilton and must see him at once. According to Donald, this produced mirth all round. Hess was obviously not amused. Donald studied him closely, then said, 'You look exactly like Hess.'[12]

'That is nothing new to me,' Hess replied coolly. 'It's a fact which has embarrassed me often enough.'[13]

Seeking to catch him off guard, Donald sheafed through his aircraft identification cards and producing an Me-110 asked Hess to sign it.

Hess obliged.

Donald saw that he had written 'Alfred Horn'. It seems, too, that an envelope addressed to Hauptmann Alfred Horn bearing a Munich postmark was on the table with the flat box of homoeopathic medicines, hypodermic syringe, the wallet containing family photographs, the envelope addressed to the Duke of Hamilton, and the visiting cards of the Haushofers that Hess had turned out of his pockets for the police. Finally Donald told him that he would see his message was conveyed to the Duke. 'I shall also tell him that your name is Rudolf Hess.' This was greeted with another roar of laughter by his account, while Hess himself gave an 'exceedingly forced laugh'. Hess did not mention it in his letters to Ilse; perhaps it had been embarrassing. Donald assured the officers grouped around that he was in earnest.

A week later he wrote to a friend in London that he had been the first and only person to identify the prisoner as Rudolf Hess: 'This was easy. My difficulty lay in getting one sensible individual up here with enough eyesight to bear out my identification! Fortunately I was able to contact the Duke of Hamilton about 2 a.m.'[14]

Donald's call to Hamilton was one of at least three that night. The first was probably made by Squadron Leader Hector MacLean, controller for Prestwick and Ayr on the west coast. By his account he was called by a police sergeant from Eaglesham police station about an hour after the Me-110 crashed – thus some time after midnight – and was told they had a German captain who said he wanted to see the Duke of Hamilton. MacLean immediately phoned Turnhouse, but met a certain amount of opposition when he asked to speak to the Duke; he had gone for the night.

'Where?'

'He has a house on the station.'

MacLean insisted he must be put through, then met more opposition from a retainer who answered the phone in the Duke's house; he finally admitted that the Duke had gone to bed. MacLean insisted he must be fetched. A few minutes later he heard the Duke's voice asking him rather tetchily what it was all about. MacLean told him.

'Good heavens!' the Duke replied. 'What does he want to see me about?'

'I don't know, he won't say any more.'

'What d'you think I should do about it?'

MacLean told him he thought he ought to go and see the pilot. Hamilton agreed; he thought he would.[15]

The next call came from the Observer Corps, possibly this was Major Donald, but if so he was a long way out when describing the time of his call as 'about 2 a.m.' in his subsequent letter, for the call to Flight Lieutenant Benson at Turnhouse by the night duty officer, Glasgow Area, was made well before 1.30, and by that time Turnhouse had already been alerted by someone from the Observer Corps.[16] The duty officer at Turnhouse took the call from Area and said that Flight Lieutenant Benson was not available. When told that the captured airman was asking to see the Duke of Hamilton and was evidently prepared to talk, he replied that they had heard the story before, 'both from the Observer Corps and from Ayr Aerodrome'; he added that Flight Lieutenant Benson had been informed and would leave for Glasgow at 8.30 the following morning.[17]

If Major Donald was approximately right in his timing, he called Turnhouse about half an hour afterwards to say that not only was the captured airman asking for the Duke of Hamilton but he was Rudolf Hess. According to James Douglas-Hamilton, the Duty Pilot did not pass on the message in this form, 'possibly because it appeared incredible'.[18]

He gives no source for the assertion, which appears to be partly contradicted in a passage of one of Hess's own letters to Ilse. The Duke of Hamilton, he wrote, was also informed of the 'strange similarity' to Hess.[19]

The oddest and most significant fact arising from the reports in the open files of Hess's capture is the behaviour of the Duke of Hamilton;

like Sherlock Holmes's dog that did not bark in the night, he did nothing.

The point was made at the end of the month by Colonel Firebrace, head of the intelligence section of the General Staff, Scottish Command:

If it is true that the RAF authorities were informed before 0100/11th that an important prisoner was anxious to make a statement to them, their laxity is most unfortunate as the prisoner might have had urgent operational information to divulge. It can only be assumed that the decision to do nothing until the morning was taken by Wing Commander the Duke of Hamilton and that in consequence Flt/Lt Benson could not go post haste to the spot as he should normally have done.[20]

It will be recalled that Hamilton had sent a letter to Group Captain Blackford of Air Intelligence that Saturday, 10 May, about the possibility of his going to Lisbon to contact Albrecht Haushofer. The same afternoon he had flown a Hurricane from Turnhouse to Drem aerodrome, near North Berwick, at the entrance to the Firth of Forth, and by James Leasor's account, which he must have got from the Duke, practised a dog fight over the Firth with his second in command. No details of the patrols have survived in the records of RAF Turnhouse, but the Operations Record Book (ORB) of 603 Squadron shows 'B' flight moving from Turnhouse to Drem on 10 May, 'A' flight from Drem to Turnhouse.[21]

That evening Hamilton was on duty in the operations room at Turnhouse as controller when Raid 42 was picked up out to sea in the sector below his. He had no responsibility, therefore, for the action taken. It is not possible to discover what action was taken at the responsible station, RAF Acklington, since their ORB is a scanty document; no patrols or sorties were entered. It will be recalled that the ORB of No 13 Group Headquarters, RAF Ouston, suggested that '72 White [two Spitfires] . . . were detailed to raid and were searching off Farne and Holy Islands', but 72 Squadron ORB makes it clear there were no Spitfires in the air at the time. However, as the raid appeared to split, a single Spitfire was scrambled from Acklington to intercept '42J' – only one since the sun had gone down and two Spitfires would not have been able to stay together during an extended sortie in the dark. 42J only entered the sector as it crossed the Scottish hills, but, since it was heading for Glasgow, it was Hector MacLean, controller for Prestwick and Ayr on the west coast who vectored a Defiant from Ayr on to it. The later statement from Turnhouse that 'normal action' was taken 'to intercept and shoot down the enemy aircraft' is thus borne out by the record, fragmentary as it is, and also by the accounts of those who took part; for instance, the pilot of the Spitfire scrambled from Acklington at 10.20, Maurice Pocock, is in no doubt that he was sent up to intercept and shoot down the intruder.[22] The statement from Turnhouse is only misleading in so much as it came from Turnhouse, which had no hand at all in the affair. If something had been arranged between Hess and Hamilton on the lines of the arrangements made at RAF Lympne for the reception of Baur's Condor with Hitler aboard – arrangements which were still in force on 10 May – Hess made his landfall in the wrong sector. Hamilton could only look on as others tried to intercept. It has been suggested that Hamilton's sortie over the mouth of the Forth that afternoon together with the fact that he was on duty in the operations room that evening might have significance; he may have been on the look-out for Hess. That is conjecture.

What is not conjectural is his refusal later to see the strange airman or even, it must be inferred, to allow his interrogating officer, Benson, to see him, despite many reports that the airman wanted to talk and had a message for him. This was not only contrary to guidelines for interrogating aircrew before they could recover from initial shock, it was contrary to common sense. Even if Hamilton himself was exhausted after some days of activity over his sector, he could have sent Benson or requested RAF Abbotsinch or Ayr to try and find out what it was all about. By the time he left the operations room for his house on the base, central London was under heavy air attack, which was to prove the most damaging raid to date. The lone airman might have had vital information. Undoubtedly Hamilton's failure to respond to the reports was deliberate and the probability must be that he had informed Sholto Douglas at Fighter Command Headquarters and had been instructed to do nothing until morning. This might also account for RAF Abbotsinch not sending an officer when alerted by Glasgow Area at some time after 12.15.

There is not much doubt that Churchill, Cadogan and, it must be inferred, Stewart Menzies, Tar Robertson, Boyle of Air Intelligence and Sholto Douglas were expecting someone that night. This is apparent from what happened the next day. And if a remarkable story by the then Yorkshire Area Secretary of the Transport and General Workers' Union, Albert James Heal, is to be believed, they were expecting Hess. Heal's account was published in the *Yorkshire Post* in 1969.[23] He claimed that at about midday on 9 May he was phoned by Ernest Bevin, Minister of Labour in Churchill's Government, who asked him to go to the Civic Hall, Sheffield, that evening at about 6.30; he (Bevin) was due to address a regional conference there and he needed to speak to Heal urgently. When Heal arrived, Bevin took him into a private room and produced a coded message which, he said, he had just received from one of his industrial contacts inside Germany. The code was one that Heal had devised when Secretary of the South Wales 'No More War' movement;

211

he had taught it to a London girl, now the 'industrial contact' Bevin referred to. Decoded, the message appeared to say that Hess was to fly to Britain to meet the Duke of Hamilton, but Heal asked for more time to make sure. So it was not until later, after Bevin had finished his speech to the conference and they had adjourned to a hotel room in Leeds, that Heal confirmed Hess was about to fly to Hamilton with peace proposals. Bevin immediately telephoned Churchill. Heal, who overheard a part of the conversation, thought Churchill treated it as a joke.

The following morning at 9.30 Heal met Bevin again and was told that Hess had landed in Scotland; he was under no circumstances to divulge the information. Of course, on that morning, 10 May, Hess had *not* landed in Scotland. However, it is probable Heal mistook the date; he was remembering the event almost thirty years on. Probably he simply worked back one day from the date Hess was known to have landed, 10 May,[24] and assumed he must have been called to decode the message on the previous day, 9 May. In fact, Bevin spoke in Leeds on the evening of Saturday, 10 May, asking for over-age men to volunteer for agricultural drainage work to win the Battle of the Atlantic by putting a million more acres into agricultural production. Thus, if Heal's dates are moved forward one day, as it appears they should be, the account becomes wholly plausible – paradoxically because it is hard to think why a trade union official should invent such a basically preposterous story.

If the account is accepted, it means not only that Churchill expected Hess but also that the Duke of Hamilton knew it was Hess who had arrived in the lone Me-110, for at 9.30 in the morning of Sunday, 11 May, when (by moving Heal's story forward one day) he was told by Bevin that Hess had landed in Scotland, Hamilton had not yet visited Maryhill Barracks in Glasgow to see Hess.

As for the London girl who was Bevin's 'industrial contact' inside Germany or more probably the go-between to his industrial contact, it seems astonishing that she or her source was able to discover one of the two closest secrets in Nazi Germany – the other being the actual date for launching 'Barbarossa'. The most plausible explanations are that the source was inside Messerschmitt's works at Augsburg, possibly Professor Willi Messerschmitt himself or very close to Göring. Both Messerschmitt and Göring were quite as anxious for peace with Great Britain as Hess; both had to know the timing of the attempt; both are believed to have passed messages to the British later – Messerschmitt to warn of ss assassins parachuting in to find Hess, and Göring to pass the warning that 'Barbarossa' was imminent.[25]

✽

The Duke of Hamilton arrived at Maryhill Barracks with his interrogating officer, Flight Lieutenant Benson, at ten in the morning of Sunday, 11 May. The officer of the guard showed them the articles from the prisoner's pockets, which had been lodged in the safe. According to the Duke's personal account, these included 'a Leica camera, photographs of [Hess] himself and a small boy and some medicines, also visiting cards of Dr Karl Haushofer and his son, Dr Albrecht Haushofer';[26] he made no mention of a letter addressed to himself. Perhaps this had been forwarded to RAF Turnhouse during the night and he had it with him. That is conjecture; it does not seem unreasonable conjecture, although later, in the House of Commons, the Air Minister, Sinclair, denied categorically that Hamilton had ever received any communication from Hess.

Next the officer of the guard showed them a small side room of the barracks' hospital which had been furnished with a bed for Hess after he had been brought in at 2.30 that morning. He was in bed when they entered. Immediately he told Hamilton he would like to speak to him alone, and the Duke dismissed the other two. Consequently his own account is the only report of what passed between them. According to Hamilton, Hess opened by saying he had seen him at the Berlin Olympics in 1936 when the Duke had lunched at his house; he wondered if he recognised him and introduced himself: 'Rudolf Hess.' In his report Hamilton claimed he had no recollection of having seen Hess before.[27]

The same inference might possibly be drawn from a passage in one of Hess's letters to Ilse. Hamilton, he wrote, had not believed it could be Hess when he came to visit him, but as they talked and he gradually had to believe it, he said, astonished, 'Sind Sie es wirklich?'[28] – literally, 'Are you really it [the Hess]?' This could as easily be taken to mean that Hamilton had not at first believed that Hess had come over, but as they talked realised it was indeed him. His astonishment may be imagined. Add to that, Hess may not fully have understood his English. The main point is, however, that it is difficult to understand how he could have come to the conclusion that it really was Hess during their talk unless he had met Hess and remembered a certain amount of private detail from the meeting or meetings.

Hess, speaking in English, told Hamilton he was on a mission of humanity. The Führer did not want to defeat England and wished to stop the fighting. Albrecht Haushofer had told him that he (the Duke) was an Englishman who would understand this point of view, he thought, and he had tried to arrange a meeting in Lisbon. Of his own mission he said this was his fourth attempt to fly to Dungavel; the first had been in December, but he had been turned back by bad weather then and on the other occasions. While Britain was gaining victories in Libya he had made no attempts, as his mission might have been interpreted as weakness; now that Germany had gained successes in North Africa and Greece he was glad to come, and the fact that he came in person showed his sincerity and Germany's willingness for peace. The Führer was convinced that Germany would win the war in the long or the short term and he wanted to stop the unnecessary slaughter.

Hess then asked Hamilton if he could assemble leading members of his party 'to talk over things with a view to making peace proposals'. Hamilton replied that there was only one party now in the country, at which Hess told him what Hitler's peace terms would be: first he would insist on an arrangement whereby the two nations could never go to war again. When Hamilton asked how this could be done Hess said that Britain would have to give up her traditional policy of always opposing the strongest power in Europe. Hamilton replied that, if such an agreement were possible, it would have been made before the war started, but, as Germany had chosen war when Great Britain was anxious to preserve peace, he could see no hope of an agreement now.

This apparently was how the discussion was left. Although Hess had been able to express himself in English, Hamilton gained the impression he had not understood all that he (Hamilton) said, and told him, therefore, that he would return for a further conversation with an interpreter. No doubt he wanted to report and obtain instructions; otherwise he could have called Benson in as interpreter. Before he left, Hess asked him to request parole for him from the King; he also asked him to keep his identity from the press and to send a telegram to Rothacker, Hertzog Strasse 17, Zurich, stating that Alfred Horn was in good health. Frau Rothacker was one of two elderly aunts of his living in Switzerland.

Hamilton appears to have been in little doubt about Hess's identity when he left the room. He reported to the garrison commander that the prisoner was 'an important person and should be removed out of danger of bombing and put under close guard'.[29] According to James Douglas-Hamilton, Hess himself had asked to be moved out of Glasgow because he was anxious not to be killed by a German bomb. This statement does not appear in Hamilton's report. In any case the garrison commander acted promptly on the advice: soon after lunch Hess was taken by ambulance under escort to Drymen Military Hospital in Buchanan Castle by Loch Lomond and held under strong guard.[30]

Hamilton, meanwhile, took the photographs Hess had brought with him, then drove to the site where Hess's Me-110 had crashed, returning afterwards to Turnhouse and according to his 'Additional Notes on the Hess incident', written probably in 1945, reporting by telephone to his Air Officer Commanding that he had an important matter to communicate to the Foreign Office. His 'notes' continue:

I then tried to get in touch, by telephone, to report the matter to the Permanent Secretary, Sir Alexander Cadogan. I got through to his secretary and asked for an interview with Sir Alexander himself. I was informed that Sir Alexander was an extremely busy man and he might be able to see me the following morning if he could fit me in between engagements. I got involved in a tremendous argument with the Secretary [sic] . . .

Suddenly in the midst of this rather acrimonious discussion a strange voice said, 'This is the Prime Minister's secretary speaking. The Prime Minister sent me over to the Foreign Office as he is informed that you have some interesting information. I have just arrived and I would like to know what you propose to do.'[31]

It is clear from this that Churchill had been informed before Hamilton phoned the Foreign Office. The secretary whom the Prime Minister had sent to the Foreign Office was Jock Colville. The stories Colville cooked up long afterwards to account for his presence are proof, if more is needed, that the inner truth about Hess's arrival differs from the official version; indeed it is notable that all main participants, Churchill, Eden, Hamilton, were at such pains to suppress parts of the truth in their accounts that they contradict one another. The story Colville gave James Douglas-Hamilton in 1969 was that he had experienced a vivid dream that early morning combining elements from a book by Peter Fleming called *Flying Visit* – a fantasy about Hitler arriving in England by parachute – and recent reports that Göring had been overflying London to survey the results of the bombing. The impression left by the dream was so strong that he was still thinking of it later that morning when he spoke to Hamilton on the phone. Hamilton told him that something extraordinary had happened, 'like something out of an E. Phillips Oppenheim novel', although he could not reveal exactly what. Colville, the dream in his mind, said, 'Has somebody arrived?'[32]

'Yes', Hamilton said after a pause. Upon this Colville rang the Prime Minister and received instructions to have Hamilton brought to Ditchley Park, the country house outside Oxford where Churchill was spending the weekend. In 1985, in the published edition of his diaries, Colville gave the account more detail: he had walked over to the Foreign Office during the morning to gossip with Anthony Eden's Second Private Secretary, Nicholas Lawford, who was on duty over the weekend. As he entered, Lawford was on the telephone; seeing Colville, he said to the person he was speaking to, 'Hold on a minute. I think this is your man.' He took the phone and Hamilton told him about the incident involving 'a crashed Nazi plane' which could only be compared to an E. Phillips Oppenheim novel.[33]

Colville did have a vivid dream about the *Flying Visit* that morning which he described in his diary, but it is evident that Hamilton's call was made late in the afternoon, not the morning as Colville described in both post-war accounts. James Douglas-Hamilton states that his father, the Duke, drove back to Turnhouse 'in the afternoon, when he collected the letter which Albrecht Haushofer had written in July 1939'; he also collected the copy of Albrecht's September 1940 letter which he had been given by Air Intelligence; perhaps his first impression was that Hess was indeed the herald of a workable peace. It was after this that he rang his Air Officer Commanding. However, the diary of Sir Alexander Cadogan gives a more positive timing for the call to the Foreign Office:

5.30 Addis [duty clerk] rang me up with this story: a German pilot landed near Glasgow, asked for the Duke of Hamilton. Latter so impressed that he is flying to London and wants to see me at No 10 tonight. Said I shouldn't be in London before 8. Fixed meeting for 9.15. Half an hour later, heard PM was sending to meet His Grace at airfield & wd. bring him to Chequers – so I needn't be tr-r-r-oubled!

Left about 6. Home 7.50. London awfully knocked about last night . . .[34]

Cadogan, burdened with the heightened wartime business of the Foreign Office, was relaxing at his country cottage, yet he made an appointment to see a wing commander from Edinburgh that evening in London on the strength of a story about a German pilot landing near Glasgow. Churchill, relaxing outside Oxford, first sent Colville to the Foreign Office, then, after Colville had taken the expected call from Hamilton, had him arrange for a car to be at the nearest airfield, Kidlington, to fetch the Duke to Dytchley Park – Cadogan was mistaken when he wrote Chequers. Although the Duke had social status, so far as his duties were concerned he was a wing commander from a rather remote aerodrome; it is simply incredible that either Churchill or Cadogan would have made such arrangements had they not known someone was expected. As Colville admitted asking, 'Has somebody arrived?'

On the telephone Hamilton had told Colville he would fly to Northolt; he immediately jumped into a Hurricane and did so. Arriving, he found instructions to proceed to Kidlington, but, while he was working out his route, someone primed the Hurricane's engine and he could not restart it. By the time he had requested another aircraft, he had wasted an hour or so and it was dark when he flew in to Kidlington – thus ten or after. He found an official car waiting and was driven to Dytchley Hall, a sixteenth-century mansion near Churchill's birthplace, Blenheim Palace. After he had washed and tried to make himself somewhat presentable after the exhausting day, the 'very pompous and smart butler' asked whether he wanted to be shown to the ladies or the gentlemen. 'The gentlemen,' he replied, and was taken to the dining-room, where the men were sitting with cigars after dinner listening to Churchill in best form. The Prime Minister looked up as he entered, and called, 'Now tell us this funny story of yours!'

Hamilton said he thought he had better speak to him in private, but Churchill evidently felt he ought to eat first for he was ushered to a place and served dinner. Churchill continued to hold forth 'in tremendous form', as Hamilton described it, 'cracking jokes the whole time', until eventually 'all the gentlemen withdrew except the Prime Minister and the Secretary of State for Air who happened to be one of the guests'.

He then told his story. The Prime Minister, he wrote, 'was rather taken aback'. According to James Douglas-Hamilton, Churchill asked the Duke very deliberately and with much emphasis, 'Do you mean to tell me that the Deputy Führer of Germany is in our hands?' Hamilton undoubtedly said that was his impression, and produced the photographs he had taken from Hess's wallet. After examining them, both Churchill and Sir Archibald Sinclair agreed that it looked 'rather like Hess'. Churchill was showing signs of impatience by now. A film had been scheduled for the evening.

'Well, Hess or no Hess,' he said, 'I am going to see the Marx brothers!'[35]

The detailed discussion was adjourned until afterwards.

22
THE PEACE PLAN

Churchill left Dytchley at 9.15 next morning, Monday the 12th, taking Hamilton with him, and was driven 'very rapidly', ignoring all speed restrictions, to 10 Downing Street.[1] Police, firemen and Civil Defence teams were working amid the débris and smouldering ruins left by the raid on the night that Hess had arrived. In the near vicinity Westminster Hall, Westminster Abbey and Parliament had been hit; Big Ben continued to tell the time and sound its reassuring peal, but its face was scarred and pocked with splinters. Further afield the devastation spread across central London, down Fleet Street to the City and East End; many priceless monuments to English history and architecture had been turned into gutted shells. It was a picture Göring had contrived deliberately to illustrate the message Hess carried.

Hamilton was shown into an ante-room at No 10 together with the service ministers while Churchill talked to Eden. Jock Colville managed to snatch a word with the Duke and learned, as he noted in his diary, that 'the occupant of the Nazi plane was Rudolph Hess. There never has been such a fantastic occurrence.'[2] Eden was with Churchill when Hamilton was called in. Churchill told him he wanted the airman identified with all possible speed; he meant that Hess's identity had to be checked in case a 'double' had been sent. Hamilton then accompanied Eden to the Foreign Office, where they were joined for a discussion by Cadogan, who noted in his diary afterwards, 'Talk with A & Duke of Hamilton, who says it is Hess!'[3]

Afterwards Cadogan sent for Stewart Menzies to consult him about sending Ivone Kirkpatrick up to Glasgow, as he put it, 'to "vet" Hess'. Kirkpatrick, who had been First Secretary at the British Embassy in Berlin from 1933 to 1938, was an obvious choice; not only had he met Hess as often as most Englishmen, he had taken the measure of the Nazis and become a convinced opponent of the policy of 'appeasement'. The fact that Cadogan called in 'C' is no proof that the secret service was already involved with Hess since intelligence of the kind the Deputy Führer might provide was naturally of the utmost interest to Menzies; obviously, though, it does not rule it out. Menzies agreed Kirkpatrick should be sent.

Meanwhile Beaverbrook had called at No 10 to see Churchill. According to his account to James Leasor, Churchill handed him a photograph of a man and a small boy and asked, 'Who is he?' Beaverbrook, who had met Hess in Berlin and discussed international politics with him, replied immediately, 'Hess.'[4]

Ivone Kirkpatrick did not arrive at the Foreign Office until after three that afternoon; he went in to see Eden with Cadogan, and at four Hamilton was shown in. Where the Duke had been in the interim is not clear from his account. It is not impossible that Churchill had agreed to him seeing the King; there is no indication when the King was first told the news. It is more probable that he was busy drafting a report for Churchill of the circumstances of Hess's arrival. Certainly he gave Churchill such a report that day. However, he and Kirkpatrick were soon driving to Hendon aerodrome, north of London, and at 5.30 they took off in a De Havilland Rapide for Scotland.

At the Berghof it must be assumed Hitler had received news of Hess's imminent departure from Rosenberg during the afternoon of Saturday 10 May. That evening Karl-Heinz Pintsch or another member of Hess's personal staff had arrived with a packet containing Hess's no doubt pre-arranged letter and explanatory briefing together with the news that the Stellvertreter had taken off successfully from Augsburg at 1800 hours.[5]

Long after the war Pintsch spun an extraordinary story about waiting in Hess's special carriage at Munich station until it was hitched to the midnight train for Freilassing, thence to Berchtesgaden, where he arrived at seven in the morning of Sunday the 11th and phoned through to the Berghof for a car.[6] Most other points in Pintsch's account of Hess's flight are demonstrably absurd, intended to back the official version, that Hess flew entirely on his own initiative and Hitler knew nothing. It is not clear how the story of the midnight train served this purpose. However, it is backed by a diary entry of Ribbentrop's liaison officer to Hitler, Walther Hewel, for 11 May; this noted Pintsch's arrival at the Berghof 'in the morning' with a letter for Hitler; 'Great excitement'.[7] It is possible, therefore, that Hess's senior adjutant, Leitgen, drove to the Berghof to bring the first news of Hess's take-off to Hitler in the evening of 10 May, Pintsch arriving with another letter in a carefully stage-managed manoeuvre the following morning before more independent witnesses. Pintsch's story is so bizarre it might be true.

After the war, when Hess was a prisoner in Spandau, Leitgen and Pintsch stuck to the official line that Hitler had known nothing of the flight in order, it must be assumed, not to prejudice their former chief's chances of release. Anything implicating him with Hitler's plan for eastern conquest and the great deception before 'Barbarossa' would have been especially damaging in Russian eyes.

In any case it is clear Hitler knew of Hess's flight long before Sunday morning. Adolf Galland, the air ace commanding a fighter group on the Channel coast, described in his memoirs being called by Göring early in the evening of 10 May and ordered to take off immediately to intercept the Deputy Führer, who had gone mad and was flying to England in an Me-110.[8] Galland asked for details and was told that Hess had flown off from Augsburg. The light was failing, Galland recalled, 'there were about ten minutes left to darkness'. If he meant civil twilight, this places the call at about ten o'clock, just as Hess was approaching the Northumbrian coast. As a token Galland ordered each of his wing commanders to send up two aircraft; naturally they found nothing. It is possible to interpret this episode as part of the deception that Hess took off on his own initiative without permission. It is difficult to imagine why Galland should have made the story up.

Another pointer to Hitler's knowledge of the flight before Pintsch's arrival on the morning of the 11th comes from a recent statement by Hess's driver, Lippert. He and the security man who had escorted Hess to Augsburg were arrested at 5.30 that Sunday morning, the 11th, in the village of Gallspach, Austria.[9] This agrees with Pintsch's story in one respect: Pintsch claimed he had sent them there in a small, inconspicuous DKW car to stay with a homoeopath friend of Hess's until the situation had cleared.[10] In doing so he had probably been acting on the instructions of Hess, who feared widespread arrests would be made – and were made – to preserve the deception that Hitler knew nothing. Nevertheless, for the two of them to have been picked up in the early hours, shortly after the time Hitler normally retired for the night, means that both Hess's flight and their whereabouts were known long before Pintsch, by his own account, pulled in to Berchtesgaden in the overnight train. Also, the fact that Lippert took a DKW, left the powerful Mercedes for Pintsch or Leitgen.

In addition to Rosenberg's, Pintsch's and Leitgen's reports – and perhaps a phone call from the Messerschmitt works at Augsburg with a coded phrase for 'successful take-off' – by the late morning of Sunday 11 May Hitler had probably heard from Heydrich that Hess had completed the penultimate leg of the flight across the North Sea. Heydrich's biographer, Eduard Calic, asserts that, having escorted Hess towards the English coast, Heydrich broke off the flight to report to Hitler at

Obersalzberg;[11] Calic gives no source, and no accounts of Heydrich's appearance at the Berghof have surfaced. Nevertheless, if Heydrich escorted Hess across the North Sea, he would undoubtedly have reported the successful completion of his mission either to Himmler or 'in the highest quarter'.

No doubt Hitler was now waiting for a call from Hess's aunt, Frau Emma Rothacker in Zurich, to the effect that 'Alfred Horn was in good health', or an announcement from the BBC. Neither came. Lunch was served. Pintsch sat down, according to his account, with Hitler, Eva Braun, Martin Bormann, Fritz Todt, chief of the Todt Organisation, Otto Dietrich, the *Reich* press chief, and Walther Hewel and General Karl Bodenschatz, respectively Ribbentrop's and Göring's liaison officers. To judge by Hewel's diary entry and later comments by Bodenschatz, Hitler played the astonished, maddened and uncomprehending innocent. Bodenschatz at least was not deceived.[12]

By the end of lunch there was still no word. Pintsch found himself under arrest, and Hewel and Bodenschatz were ordered to summon their chiefs post haste from their weekend castles. Ribbentrop arrived at some time in the afternoon, Göring not until 8.45 that evening according to his own diary, nine according to Hewel's diary.[13] Hewel added that there followed a long and very heated discussion in the hall between Hitler, Ribbentrop, Göring and Bormann; 'a lot of speculation'.[14] No doubt there was. Still no news had broken in Great Britain. Hess was under guard in Buchanan Castle simply as 'an important person' and the Duke of Hamilton was still on his way to Kidlington aerodrome.

It was perhaps as a result of this discussion that it was decided to send for Albrecht Haushofer. His mother, Martha, noted in her diary with some concern: 'Evening call from the *Reichs* Chancellery in Berchtesgaden asking for Albrecht's telephone number in B[erlin], which made us think [*denken*]'.[15] The previous night of 10–11 May, after Hess had flown, Albrecht's former pupil, Stahmer, now at the Madrid Embassy, had wired the Foreign Ministry in Berlin with a message for him to the effect that he (Albrecht) had to give his lecture to the Academy of Science in Madrid on 12 May.[16] Since Albrecht had charged Stahmer with the task of opening a line to Sir Samuel Hoare, it is usually assumed this message may have been a coded signal that a meeting had been arranged with Hoare for that date. However, Stahmer himself said after the war that he had sent the wire to warn Albrecht after he had heard a Reuter flash that Hess had landed in England.[17]

Since no news broke until two days after this, Stahmer's account, like so many on both sides in the affair, is patently fabricated. It will be recalled that Stahmer also wrote a note after the war to say that he had established contact with Hoare through the Swedish Embassy in Madrid some time before Hess's flight, and Albrecht Haushofer and Hoare had come to an understanding that the removal of both Hitler and Churchill was the necessary precondition for an armistice. If this was the case, it opens up the possibility that Hoare or someone else in Madrid, perhaps in the Swedish Embassy, was privy to the fact that Hess had taken off for Scotland that afternoon and Stahmer did indeed wire Albrecht Haushofer to warn him of his danger. This is no more far-fetched than Albert Heal's story of Bevin's 'industrial contact' inside Berlin sending the message about Hess, particularly if Hoare had been initiated into the Double-Cross Committee deception.

It is reasonably certain from Martha Haushofer's subsequent diary entries that Albrecht had apparently known nothing of Hess's intention to fly on 10 May,[18] although Karl Haushofer knew in a general way that Hess was preparing a mission. On one of their last walks together he had tried to find out more and perhaps dissuade him from a too reckless attempt by describing a dream in which he had seen Hess striding through the tapestried walls of English castles, so he had said, bringing peace to the two great Nordic nations. Hess had not risen, and it is certain that Haushofer knew nothing of the details. On 9 May, when Hess had been making final preparations for the flight, Haushofer had been composing a letter to him.[19] It was a plea for two families of his acquaintance who had run foul of the Nuremberg Laws against non-Aryans. One request concerned a girl whose mother came from a noble Bavarian family and whose late father had been a much-decorated Austrian officer. He had Jewish blood and had shot himself so that he would not stand in the way of his children inheriting his property. Now the girl wished to marry an Aryan. The other request concerned two boys orphaned by the First World War and adopted by an industrialist who had not realised that on their mother's side they inherited Jewish *Mischling* (half-caste) blood. Now one was applying for officer entry and wanted to become engaged to a pure Aryan girl.[20]

Why Albrecht Haushofer apparently made no response to Stahmer's wire from Madrid is as unclear as the meaning of the message itself, but, after his Berlin telephone number had been obtained, he was called and ordered to fly to Berchtesgaden on the morrow, 12 May. He arrived late that Monday morning. By then the presumption must have been forming in Hitler's mind that Hess had crashed or been shot down over Britain. He did not interview Albrecht; he knew in any case that he had not been involved in Hess's flight. Instead he had him provided with paper and pen, and ordered to write an account of his British contacts and the possibilities of using them. Believing Hess must have failed, Hitler was picking his English expert's brains.

Albrecht, unaware of his patron's flight, sat down to write, first describing the Englishmen he had known 'for years from close personal contact'; these included the former Parliamentary Private Secretary of Neville Chamberlain, Lord Dunglas (*sic*) (now Lord Home), the Under Secretary of State at the Foreign Office, Rab Butler – who was 'despite many of his public statements no follower of Churchill or Eden' – and, of course, the Duke of Hamilton. He exaggerated the close connection of this group to the Court by citing Hamilton's younger brother, who was related to the Queen through his wife, and his mother-in-law, the Dowager Duchess of Northumberland, who was Mistress of the Robes in the Royal Household, and also pointed to close contacts between his group and older conservatives, the Stanleys, Derbys and Astors. 'The young Astor . . . was Parliamentary Private Secretary to the former Foreign and Interior Minister, Sir Samuel Hoare, presently English Ambassador in Madrid'.[21] He knew, of course, that Hitler was fully informed about most of these personalities and their pre-war desire for an accommodation with Germany. He moved on to describe his attempt to contact Hamilton, again assuming Hitler was fully informed.

What he did not mention – as discussed – was his attempt to contact Hoare through Stahmer at the Madrid Embassy nor anything about Stahmer's wire to him on the night of the 10th–11th. This is odd, suggesting that this approach, although surely covered by permission from Hess, was also behind Hess's back on behalf of the conservative opposition; if so, he had not informed von Hassell or von Hassell had not noted it in his diary, or nothing had come of it until, perhaps, Stahmer's wire the night before. It will be recalled that Ribbentrop was also trying to contact Hoare at this time through his agent Gardemann and Juan Beigbeder.

As Monday wore on without news, Hitler's fears for Hess must have turned to near certainty. He had his press chief, Dietrich, draft an announcement and, after several changes, for it was not an easy thing to explain rationally, at 8 p.m., more than forty-eight hours after Hess had taken off, a communiqué was broadcast to German home stations:

The Party authorities state: Party member Hess, who has been expressly forbidden by the Führer to use an aeroplane because of a disease which has been becoming worse for years, was in contradiction of this order able to get hold of a plane recently. Hess started on Saturday 10th May at about 1800 hours from Augsburg on a flight from which he has not yet returned. A letter which he left behind unfortunately showed traces of mental disturbance which justifies the fear that Hess was the victim of hallucinations. The Führer at once ordered the arrest of Hess's adjutants who alone knew of his flight and who, in contradiction to the Führer's ban, of which they were aware, did not prevent the flight nor report it at once. The National Socialist movement has unfortunately in these circumstances to assume that Party Comrade Hess has crashed or met with a similar accident.[22]

Hamilton and Kirkpatrick were still in the air on their way to Scotland when the announcement was broadcast. It was picked up in England and reported by the BBC on the nine o'clock news. Eden immediately called Cadogan, who sent for the text of the German communiqué, 'paraded "C"', then met Eden at the Foreign Office, and the three of them went to see Churchill in the underground cabinet war room. By then it was nearly eleven.[23] Churchill had drafted an announcement based chiefly on the report Hamilton had made, together with a brief biographical note about Hess prepared by his personal intelligence liaison, Major Desmond Morton; this last included the remark, 'He [Hess] has a rather feeble personality, and his moral character is doubtful (in ribald circles he is known as the "First Lady in the Land").'[24] Churchill's draft, which he probably read out, began, 'Rudolf Hess, the Deputy Führer of Germany and Party Leader of the National Socialist Party has landed in Scotland in the following circumstances . . .' After describing the Me-110 crashing near Glasgow and a German officer being found in the neighbourhood suffering a broken ankle, it continued: 'he at first gave his name as Horn, but later on declared that he was Rudolf Hess and that he had come to England in the name of humanity hoping that a peace might be made between Great Britain and Germany . . .'[25]

Cadogan winced, probably Eden too. Only that weekend Eden had been talking to Robert Bruce Lockhart of the Political Intelligence department lodged in Woburn Abbey about the appeasers in the Conservative Party, 'plenty of them', he had said.[26] He was right: that very day, Saturday 10 May, Woburn's owner, the Duke of Bedford, was writing to the Labour MP Dick Stokes proposing that Lloyd George, 'so obviously the one man who could save the country', should make a public statement indicating peace terms to which Germany could respond.[27] And two days later, even as they sat discussing Churchill's proposed communiqué, Hugh Dalton noted in his diary that some peers had begun to lack resolve and were openly suggesting suing for peace in the autumn.[28] Eden and Cadogan managed to persuade Churchill to cut the explanation for Hess's visit and the announcement was made to the press at 11.20 without the offending passage.[29]

Afterwards Cadogan got away and went to bed, too tired even to write up his diary. When he did so the following night he noted Churchill had had the text of an announcement stating that Hess had come 'in the name of humanity'. This would not do, he wrote; it sounded like a peace offer, whereas they might want to suggest Hess had quarrelled with Hitler.[30]

By this time Hamilton and Kirkpatrick had landed at Turnhouse to be met with the news of the German announcement and instructions from Sir Archibald Sinclair, Secretary of State for Air, that they were to proceed without delay to identify the prisoner. With scarcely a pause they had set off by car through the blacked out streets, but it was after midnight before they arrived at Buchanan Castle and were shown to the prisoner's room.[31] Hess was sound asleep and had to be woken by the guard. At first he did not recognise Kirkpatrick, but, as the former First Secretary at the Berlin Embassy reminded him of various incidents they had witnessed together, it became obvious 'there could be no doubt whatever about his identity'. Hess had been busy most of the day writing pages of notes, and he now began to read them to Kirkpatrick, beginning by saying it was necessary to go back a long way to explain the circumstances which led to his visit. He started in 1904, the date of the Anglo-French *Entente* promoted by King Edward VII, he alleged, 'in the certain knowledge that this would lead to a conflict with Germany', and cited *England's Foreign Policy under Edward VII* by the British historian Farrar to back this assertion. Thus, he claimed, England was responsible for the world war. Coming to the Treaty of Versailles, he repeated the usual German arguments about its vindictive nature and the subsequent failure of the British Government to make concessions which would have allowed the Democratic Government of Weimar to retain support, 'hence the rise of Hitler and National Socialism'. In 1938 Hitler had been compelled to annex Austria in accordance with the wishes of the Austrian people and subsequently, because the French had been determined to make Czechoslovakia an air base against Germany, the Sudetenland. Britain and France had then attempted to arm the remaining State of Czechoslovakia and Hitler, who could not stand this, had acted as any British Government would have done. The Polish crisis had been caused by Britain's determination to oppose the strongest power on the Continent, Germany; captured Polish documents had shown that the Polish Government would have accepted Hitler's proposals had it not been for the efforts of the British Government to prevent a solution on these lines. Hamilton, who had sufficient German to understand the trend of the lecture before he nodded off from sheer tiredness, and who doubtless had it explained to him by Kirkpatrick afterwards, described it as 'one long eulogy of Hitler'; naturally, with Hess it could not have been otherwise.

At about 1 a.m., while Hess was still in full flow, Kirkpatrick and Hamilton were called away to the telephone; it was Eden, still closeted with Churchill and impatient to know whether identity had been established and, if so, what the prisoner was saying. Kirkpatrick replied that there was no doubt about his identity, but he was only halfway through

225

his speech – presumably the bundle of manuscript pages Hess was reading from – and so far there was no explanation of why he had come. They returned, and Hess continued for another hour and a half, 'talking rapidly all the time' according to Hamilton's later notes, while Kirkpatrick listened with admirable patience and 'never batted an eyelid'.

The second part of Hess's exposition was designed to prove that Germany would inevitably win the war. German aircraft production was enormous, far larger than that of Great Britain and America combined, and whatever efforts Britain made she could never alter the present relationship of British to German aircraft. When Britain had started bombing Germany the previous May, Hitler had believed it a momentary aberration; he had waited with exemplary patience 'partly so as to spare the world the horrors of unrestricted air warfare and partly out of a sentimental regard for English culture and English monuments', as Kirkpatrick summarised Hess's words. 'It is only with great reluctance that after many weeks of waiting he had given the order to bomb England.' As for the Battle of the Atlantic, U-boats were now being constructed in large numbers all over Germany and occupied Europe, and the waterways used to transport parts to the coast for assembly. Britain would soon see vastly increased numbers of U-boats working in co-operation with aircraft against shipping. Finally there was not the least hope of bringing about a revolution in Germany since Hitler had the blind confidence of the masses.

At last Hess turned to the reason he had come; as summarised by Kirkpatrick:

He said that, horrified at the prospect of the prolongation of the struggle, he had come here without the knowledge of Hitler to convince responsible persons that, since England could not win the war, the wisest course was to make peace now. From a long and intimate knowledge of the Führer which had begun eighteen years ago in the Fortress of Landsberg he could give his word of honour that the Führer had never entertained any designs against the British Empire, nor had he ever aspired to world domination. He believed that Germany's sphere of interest was Europe and that any dissipation of Germany's strength beyond Europe's frontiers would be a weakness and would carry with it the seeds of Germany's destruction. Hitler would sincerely regret the collapse of the British Empire. At this point Hess tried to make my flesh creep by emphasising that the avaricious Americans had fell designs on the British Empire. Canada would certainly be incorporated into the United States . . .

Hess then made the old proposal that Great Britain should give Germany a free hand in Europe and Germany would give Britain a completely free hand in the Empire – apart from the former German colonies, which she required as a source of raw materials. Kirkpatrick cast a fly by asking if he included Russia in Europe or Asia. 'Asia,' he replied. In that case, Kirkpatrick went on, since Germany was only claiming a free hand in Europe, she would not be free to attack Russia. Hess reacted quickly: Germany had certain demands to make of Russia which would have to be satisfied either by negotiation or war; there was, however, no foundation for the rumours that Hitler was contemplating an early attack on Russia. Kirkpatrick asked him about Italy's claims; Hess brushed them aside, they would not be excessive.

By then the interview had lasted about two and a quarter hours; Kirk-patrick roused Hamilton and rose to leave. He explained in his report that he had allowed even Hess's most outrageous remarks to pass unchal-lenged 'since I realised that argument would be quite fruitless and would certainly have deprived us of our breakfast'. At the door Hess delivered a parting shot: he had forgotten to emphasise that his proposal could only be considered on the understanding that it was negotiated with a British Government other than the present one. Churchill, who had planned the war since 1936, and his colleagues who supported him were not persons with whom the Führer could negotiate.[32]

Hamilton and Kirkpatrick were given breakfast at the hospital, the first meal since lunch the day before, then drove back to Turnhouse and went to bed. Kirkpatrick was up again in a few hours and rang Cadogan before eleven with a short report on the interview, after which Cadogan told him to wait where he was for further instructions. Cadogan then dictated a summary for Churchill incorporating a suggestion from Kirkpatrick that Hess might open up more freely if he thought he was talking to a member of the Conservative Party who gave the impression of being tempted by the idea of turning out Churchill's Government:

... Mr Kirkpatrick suggested that it might be best if the Duke of Hamilton could move him [Hess] to his own house, which is now a hospital, and he further suggested that the Duke of Hamilton's brother, who speaks German well, might eventually be put in touch with him together with some other indivi-dual who might play the role of member of the Conservative Party indicated above ...

Mr Kirkpatrick said that Hess appeared to be quite calm, but slightly off his balance. He maintained that he had come of his own initiative and Mr Kirk-patrick judged that he had been turning it over and over in his mind until it had become a kind of monomania. He had made up his mind that Germany must win the war, but saw that it would last a long time with all the destruction and bloodshed of modern warfare. He felt that if only he could persuade the people in this country that there was a basis for a settlement it might bring the war to an end and avert unnecessary suffering ...[33]

To judge by Hess's descriptions of the dreams he experienced in these

227

first days of captivity, Kirkpatrick was correct about his mania. He dreamed he was at home and had not managed to complete preparations for the flight or that he had returned home without success – nightmares during which he did everything he could to achieve his goal, yet sank into frightful despair at the prospect of failure. When he awoke to find he was in Scotland, his first sensation was relief without any clear realisation of the true situation, 'so deeply had my goal, peace, taken root in my subconscious'.[34] While this had evidently come through clearly to Kirkpatrick, Hess had misled him very successfully in other directions – as he continued to do with all British observers – for Kirkpatrick gained the impression that he was ill informed on German strategy and production, and had indeed come on his own initiative, not on his Führer's commission.

Cadogan took his summary of Kirkpatrick's report to Churchill at noon, noting later in his diary : 'Undoubtedly it is Hess. But can't say why he's come unless he's mad'. The doctors had reported he was not.[35]

Churchill did not bite on the suggestion that someone should impersonate one of the 'opposition' group whom Hess had come over to persuade, for he had already discussed with 'C' how Hess was to be isolated in quarters wired to pick up his every word and sigh; he wrote a note to Eden that day saying that Hess was to be treated as a prisoner of war under War Office, not Home Office, supervision :

... This man, like other Nazi leaders, is potentially a war criminal and he and his confederates may well be declared outlaws at the end of the war. In this case his repentance would stand him in good stead.

2. In the meanwhile he should be strictly isolated in a convenient house not too far from London, fitted by 'C' with the necessary appliances, and every endeavour should be made to study his mentality and get anything worthwhile out of him.

3. His health and comfort should be ensured ; food and books, writing materials and recreation being provided for him. He should not have any contact with the outer world or visitors ... Special guardians should be appointed. He should see no newspapers and hear no wireless ; he should be treated with dignity as if he were an important general who had fallen into our hands. W.S.C. 13.5.1941[36]

228

23
THE PROPAGANDA WAR

Directly Hitler heard that the British communiqué about Hess's landing in Scotland had been issued from 10 Downing Street – and he had no word from Frau Rothacker in Switzerland – he knew that Hess's mission had misfired and he would be kept in Britain for the duration of the war. The exasperation and anger, indeed grief noted by so many at the Berghof on that Monday 13 May were genuine, only the bewilderment was feigned.

He had already decided to appoint Martin Bormann as Hess's successor in control of the Party machine; it was implicit in the text of the communiqué he had broadcast the previous evening announcing the disappearance of the Stellvertreter; there could be no return for a man suffering 'a disease which has been becoming worse for years', whose correspondence 'showed traces of mental disturbance' and who was 'the victim of hallucinations'. His ever faithful, close companion from Landsberg and the 'years of struggle' was finished. Hess himself did not know it, but there was no longer a place for him in the Führer's *Reich*. Undoubtedly Hitler was stricken. It was, as his interpreter Paul Schmidt recalled, 'as though a bomb had hit the Berghof'.[1] The decree was broadcast early that same Monday morning: 'The office of the Führer's Deputy will from now on be termed the "Party Chancellery"; it will be under my personal jurisdiction. As heretofore, Reichsleiter Martin Bormann will be its head. Adolf Hitler, 12 May 1941.'[2]

In retrospect many Nazi leaders saw Hess's flight as marking the fatal turning point between the triumphs of Hitler's early years and the catastrophes to come; many saw Bormann's appointment as a turning point for Hitler himself, and Hess's evil legacy. Hans Frank wrote that Hess's chief guilt lay not so much in bad intentions as in allowing such a *Lumpen* creature as Bormann to rise to power.[3] In truth this was an attempt to evade responsibility. Bormann simply moulded himself to Hitler's will, a *Lump* indeed, working, toadying and intriguing tirelessly for power in a way that Hess could never do with a whole heart. Viewed from this contrast between their characters, it is possible to see Hess's flight, stripped of rationalisation and the moral gloss Karl Haushofer tried to put on it later, as pure psychological necessity: an escape from the trap of his Führer's will by doing his Führer's will.

Following the announcement from London, which had become an instant sensation around the world, it was necessary to issue another communiqué. Goebbels, who had been summoned the previous evening, arrived at the Berghof to work on the problem. According to his diaries, published recently, he was taken completely by surprise by the news; but since his diary entries reveal him surprised before every Nazi theatre coup this is evidence only of what he wished to purvey to posterity. Hitler showed him the documents Hess had left: 'an incoherent jumble of sixth-form dilettantism', he noted. 'What a buffoon the man next to the Führer was.'⁴ The explanations bristled with rudimentary occultism, his entry went on, leading to the conclusion that Professor Haushofer and his wife had been the evil spirits: 'A thoroughly pathological affair. One wants to beat his wife, his adjutants and his doctors into jelly.'

These diary notes follow the line Goebbels took in the communiqué broadcast at 2 p.m.:

On the basis of a preliminary examination of the papers which Hess left behind him it would appear that Hess was living under the hallucination that by undertaking a personal step in connection with the Englishmen with whom he was formerly acquainted it might be possible to bring about an understanding between Germany and Great Britain. As has since been confirmed by a report from London, Hess parachuted from his plane near the place in Scotland which he had selected as his destination . . .

As is well known in Party circles Hess has undergone severe physical suffering for some years. Recently he had sought relief to an increasing extent in various methods practised by mesmerists and astrologers, etc. An attempt is also being made to determine to what extent these persons are responsible for bringing about the condition of mental distraction which led him to take this step.

It is also conceivable that Hess was deliberately lured into a trap by a British party. The whole manner of his action, however, confirms the fact, as stated in the first announcement, that he was suffering under hallucinations . . .⁵

The statement went on to say that Hess was better acquainted with the Führer's various peace proposals than anyone, and had apparently deluded himself into thinking that, by making a personal sacrifice, he could prevent 'developments which in his eyes could only end with the complete destruction of the [British] Empire'. The Party regretted that 'this idealist fell prey to tragic hallucinations'; nevertheless, it concluded, it did not affect the Führer's determination to prosecute the war until the men in power in Britain had been overthrown or were ready to make peace.

All Party regional and district leaders had been summoned to the Berghof to hear an explanation for their chief's sudden disappearance at source; that afternoon they were given a similar explanation. First Bormann read out to them the letters and papers Hess had left, then Hitler rose to comment. Hans Frank, who had not seen him for some time, was shocked by his shattered appearance. 'He spoke to us in a very low, halting voice expressing an underlying depression beyond words'.[6]

He described the flight as pure insanity.

Hess is above all a deserter, and if I ever get hold of him he will pay for it as a common traitor. For the rest it appears to me that this step was most strongly induced by the astrological clique whose influence Hess has surrounded himself with. It is time, therefore, to make a radical clean sweep of this astrological rabble.[7]

It is a remarkable fact that not only was the moon nearly full on 10 May – with obvious practical advantages for night navigation – but there were no fewer than six planets in Taurus.[8] What significance, if any, this may have had for Hess is impossible to determine without the letters he left behind for Hitler, Ilse and Karl Haushofer. But nothing he said or wrote subsequently suggests any astrological input into his choice of a date for flying – only the tainted pages of Goebbels's diaries and the hearsay evidence of those who gathered at the Berghof and listened to Bormann reading Hess's letters and Hitler's devastating commentary.[9] Hess was well-known in the Party as a crank with an inclination for astrology, homoeopathy and every kind of non-conventional medicine. The strong probability is that Hitler, Goebbels and Bormann used this obvious tool to brand him crazy and laid the blame on astrologers for sending him to Britain. Many astrologers and clairvoyants were rounded up apparently, but how long they were kept under arrest or in concentration camps is not known. One who was brought to the Berghof at the same time as Albrecht Haushofer after the flight was the Swiss astrologer Karl Krafft.[10]

The official explanation which the Reichsleiters and Gauleiters carried away with them from the Berghof and which was provided for the General Staff later was that Hess had been under strain because of his inclinations towards Britain and his anxiety about the two Germanic peoples tearing each other to pieces, also because he had wanted to serve as a pilot at the front but had been refused permission a second time.[11]

The full purpose of his mission, as revealed to the Gauleiters from the papers he had left was broadcast to the German people and the world the following day, Wednesday 14 May:

Hess embarked on his flight with the intention of proceeding to the estate of the Duke of Hamilton and Brandon in Lanarkshire ... Hess had made the acquaintance of the Duke at the Olympic Games, Berlin, in 1936, and believed that the Duke belonged to the British group in opposition to Churchill as representative of the clique of warmongers. Hess further believed that the Duke possessed sufficient influence to be able to wage an effective fight against the Churchill clique ... The object of his journey was to explain to these circles [around the Duke], which he believed possible [sic] by reasonable arguments, the real position of England and also the position of Germany. Rudolf Hess viewed the German-British struggle as a struggle between the two great Nordic people, which, if it was continued, could in the long run have only one outcome, the complete destruction of Great Britain. Rudolf Hess therefore flew to Great Britain in order to explain to the circles with which he hoped to get in touch the completely hopeless situation of Great Britain in the long run and to show them the unassailably strong opposition of Germany ...[12]

He had believed that his personal intervention would make it possible for these circles to enlighten the British public, the broadcast continued, and to prepare the soil for a German-British understanding. It had certainly not been his intention to contact Winston Churchill – on the contrary, he had sought the internal opposition against Churchill 'as becomes unmistakably clear from his notes which have been found'; he had, moreover, 'the absurd idea that he could return again to Germany after a short while' for 'in his *idée fixe*' he had been almost a hundred per cent certain of success; this was clear from his notes, the broadcast concluded.

Since Kirkpatrick had reported Hess's mission in precisely similar terms, it is certain this was the truth. Kirkpatrick had phoned his report through before this explanation was broadcast in Germany and Goebbels could not possibly have known what he said. The two statements from opposite sides prove each other, therefore, and there can be no doubt that, for whatever reason, Hess believed Hamilton was a member of the conservative opposition to Churchill and had flown across to persuade him of the necessity of toppling Churchill's Government.

For the rest, though, the earlier broadcasts about hallucinations, mesmerists and astrologers, the references to strain and ill health, there is no confirmatory evidence apart from Hess's known interest in astrology and distrust of conventional medicine. The testimony from Bohle suggests rather that he had recovered health and spirits remarkably since beginning his preparations, and, according to Cadogan's report in the morning of 13 May, Kirkpatrick said Hess 'appeared in the best of health and was able almost at once to plunge into the reading of a huge statement which he had prepared'. This had caused Kirkpatrick to discount the suspicion that he was taking drugs 'and the Doctors had said that there was no trace of that'.[13]

As for the astrologers, Karl Krafft was released after being brought to the Berghof; so indeed was Albrecht Haushofer. Martha Haushofer recorded a call from him in the morning of Monday the 13th, and he arrived at her home at four that afternoon, still unable to tell her anything of Hess's whereabouts.[14] He stayed until Thursday the 16th, when there was a call from the Berghof to say he was 'discharged' and could return to Berlin, which he did. Some days later he was taken into Gestapo custody, but, as he told his mother, was treated 'in thoroughly honourable form',[15] and he was released at the end of July. Nor were Professor Karl Haushofer or Ilse Hess, in Goebbels's diary 'the evil spirits' of Hess's enterprise, arrested, let alone 'beaten into jelly'. Ilse was able to keep her splendid house in Harlaching and was granted a pension equivalent to that of a government minister. Pintsch and those who had accompanied Hess to Augsburg were held for a while, as they had to be for appearances, but the real accomplices, Willi Messerschmitt, Theo Croneis, the test pilots at the works and Hitler's personal pilot, Baur, were not touched. In view of Hitler's real grief at the loss of his 'Hesserl' and his uncontrollable vindictiveness when crossed, this can only be explained by the supposition that he sent Hess himself. The astrologers, the strain and the Haushofers' influence were simply blinds to mask the real influence under which Hess had flown – the Führer's will. In April 1945, as the *Reich* was collapsing, Karl Wolff, then Himmler's plenipotentiary in northern Italy, reported to Hitler that he had succeeded in opening a channel to the White House in Washington. Hitler told him to follow it up. 'Should you fail,' he added, 'I shall have to drop you exactly like Hess.'[16]

Von Hassell characterised the impact of Hess's flight inside Germany as 'indescribable', the first communiqué with its suggestion that the *Volk* had been saddled 'for months, indeed years, with a half or completely crazy Stellvertreter – and what is more destined successor to the Führer' was particularly foolish.[17] The impression conveyed to Hitler and the top leadership by Heydrich's SD public opinion report was subtly different: 'great consternation' certainly in every part of the *Reich*, and the Party comrades felt 'deep despondency', indeed because of the great trust the people had in Hess the news had not been believed at first; yet all reports showed the 'extraordinary and deeply felt concern of every section of the German *Volk* at the blow which has struck above all at the Führer'; and 'together with this sympathy each and every *Volk* comrade has heightened belief and faith in the Führer . . .'[18]

There is no doubt Germans were bewildered. They had been waiting for the final settlement with Britain, retaliation for the bombing of their cities; instead the Stellvertreter had flown across to propose *peace*. The shock was plainly discernible in conversations between prisoners of war monitored by British Intelligence. Together with the apparent ineptitude and confusion displayed in the German official broadcasts, this suggested that Hess's story, bizarre though it seemed, might actually be true; he might have come over on his own initiative.

More interesting in retrospect than the official broadcasts were the rumours: from Stockholm, a potent thoroughfare for German disinformation, came the story that 'Hess was disquieted over the tendency of German-Soviet relations'.[19] And it is interesting that Count Eric von Rosen, Baron Bonde's liaison with Göring, was one of the first to send a wire of 'kindest regards of good wishes' to Hess in Scotland.[20] By the 14th Ministry of Information officials in London had discerned a pattern of stories suggesting Hess had quarrelled with Hitler and Ribbentrop over their Russian policy, and had fled Germany because he was not prepared to be a party to the spread of Communism. It was noted that this was a dangerous line which played into the hands of 'those in many countries who want to try and stop the war because of the fear of the spread of Communism'.[21]

Significantly, the SD public opinion reports, often an indicator of rumours spread deliberately by Heydrich's agents, soon reported a change of attitude among the people towards the prospect of war with Russia. Contrary to the long-held view that conflict was unavoidable, it was now believed in all parts of the *Reich*, particularly in the eastern areas, 'that a war with Russia is not at present imminent'. It was being said that 'Russia will shortly join the Three-Power pact' and 'Ribbentrop is staying on in Moscow'.[22]

In London there was as yet no clear line on how the story of the Deputy Führer's arrival should be treated and, since Churchill had been persuaded to cut the phrase from the original communiqué about Hess having 'come to England in the name of humanity', no official explanation had been offered, despite the clamour of the press. After Goebbels's broadcast on Wednesday the 14th confirming that Hess had flown over in the interests of an Anglo-German understanding, Churchill decided he must make a statement to the House of Commons. That evening Eden and Cadogan went round to No 10 with Stewart Menzies and the Minister of Information, Duff Cooper, to discuss what he proposed to say. Eden left after a while and the other three had to wait while Churchill dictated. Cadogan was already exasperated by the extra work Hess was causing him. '*How* slow he [Churchill] is,' he wrote afterwards in his diary: again he felt Churchill's proposed statement quite wrong as it corresponded to the broadcast the Germans had put out that afternoon. He suggested the German people should be led to think Hess a traitor, not an emissary of peace, but was brushed aside by both Churchill and Duff Cooper.[23]

The fact was, as Harold Nicolson put it two days later, it was not possible to extract maximum propaganda from the incident both at home and abroad.[24] However, it is remarkable that so far as the home front was concerned and especially that influential section who wanted a compromise peace, neither Churchill, Cadogan nor Duff Cooper appeared to worry about the effect of announcing that Hess had come over because Hitler wanted peace. Thus Cadogan's concern seems to have been for the effect on the *German* public, while, as he noted, the statement Churchill dictated told the same story as Goebbels's latest broadcast, dismissing the earlier allusions to Hess's ill-health and 'hallucinations'. It stated that Kirkpatrick had visited Hess twice – the second time that day – and Hess had volunteered other statements to doctors, nurses and 'guardians' – Menzies's officers – continuing, with later additions in brackets:

He is reported to be perfectly sane and, apart from the injury to his ankle, in good health, as indeed seemed probable from the remarkable flight which he made. It is abundantly clear from the disclosures on the German wireless that he had no mission to this country from the German Government (and that he came here without their knowledge and against their will). From his statements it would seem that he had the idea that there was a strong peace or defeatist feeling (movement) in Great Britain with which he might negotiate, and that by convincing the British public of the overwhelming power of Germany to win the war, he might bring about a peace on the basis that Great Britain and the British Empire should be left intact, apart from the return of the German colonies, and that Germany under Herr Hitler should become unquestioned master of Europe.[25]

Either Churchill thought it so self-evidently bad if Germany were master of Europe that he could make such an honest statement, or he was unaware of the growing opposition searching for an opportunity to promote a compromise peace which exercised other members of his Government, including his close colleague Beaverbrook, who was in touch with these circles. He even went on to list Hess's reasons for asserting that Germany was bound to win, and American help would arrive too late: 'He appears to hold these views sincerely and he represented himself as undertaking a (self-imposed) mission to save the British nation from destruction while time remained.'[26] Here he virtually allied Hess with Lloyd George and Liddell Hart. Churchill did go some way to satisfying Cadogan's desire for propaganda, though, by saying that there was no information about 'the dissensions or state of tension prevailing in high

German circles' and that Hess's outlook was a 'proof of the ignorance of the actual facts prevailing among those who at the head of Germany have access to all the information at the disposal of the German Government' – suggesting that he discounted the idea of a 'strong peace or defeatist movement' in Britain. However, it is evident that the propaganda, or properly the truth, which interested him far more, welled from his deep detestation of Nazi barbarism:

It must not be forgotten that the Deputy Führer, Rudolf Hess, has been the confederate and accomplice of Herr Hitler in all the murders, treacheries and cruelties by which the Nazi regime imposed itself first on Germany, as it now seeks to impose itself on Europe . . .[27]

The statement went on to list the blood purge of June 1934, the 'horrors of the German concentration camps, the brutal persecution of the Jews' and the 'unspeakable, incredible brutalities and bestialities of the German invasion and conquest of Poland'. Hess, it continued, was being held as a prisoner of war and also 'in the character of a war criminal whose ultimate fate must be reserved for the decision of the Allied nations when victory has been won'.

Next the statement touched on the Duke of Hamilton, whose name had been brought in by the German broadcast that afternoon. Churchill was at pains to point out that the Duke's conduct had been 'in every respect honourable and proper'; he had been 'ordered to go to the hospital' to receive the prisoner's statement, and had reported it at once. Churchill accepted that Hess had met Hamilton before, since he had been advised that 'the Duke had met Hess on one or two occasions before the war in connection with matters of sport in which they were both interested'.

Finally Churchill summed up:

I feel sure that the House, the country and our friends all over the world will have been both entertained and cheered by this remarkable episode, and it is certain that the action taken by the Deputy Führer in quitting Germany and his chief at this juncture will be the cause of deep-seated bewilderment and consternation throughout the ranks of the German armed forces and throughout the Nazi Party and the German people.

Beaverbrook dined with Churchill that night and backed up Cadogan's arguments against making the statement, after which Churchill, furious, called Eden to another meeting. Eden, wearied by his chief's nocturnal habits, said he had not slept well enough that afternoon and a heated discussion was carried on by phone instead, Eden finally prevailing on Churchill to make no statement.[28] It appears from a brief note initialled by one of the Prime Minister's private secretaries that he had already decided not to do so.[29]

There is a curious handwritten addition in the margin of one typed copy of this statement that Churchill never made which is hard to interpret: 'He [Hess] has also made other statements which it would not be in the public interest to disclose'.[30] The published copies of Kirkpatrick's reports of his first two interviews with Hess provide no indication of what these 'other statements' might have been about; it may be significant that the originals of the reports are missing from the open files.

The published version of Kirkpatrick's second interview with Hess at Buchanan Castle that Wednesday reveals little new, merely that Hitler would not leave Iraq in the lurch since she was fighting on the German side, and secondly that British and German nationals whose property had been appropriated as a result of war should be indemnified – no doubt Hess was thinking of his father's firm in Alexandria. He also asked for three books: '*Sea Power* by Grenfell; *Dynamic Defence* by Liddell Hart; *Three Men in a Boat* by Jerome K. Jerome'.[31] The request was refused by the commanding officer. The first two titles are interesting as they advocated a strategy of non-involvement in Continental affairs which, reading between the lines, pointed to a compromise peace with Germany precisely on the lines of Hess's proposals. *Sea Power* had been published under the pseudonym 'T-124'; that Hess knew it was by the serving naval officer, Commander Russell Grenfell, testified to the depth of his knowledge of British strategists – or possibly what he had been fed by the Double-Cross Committee; the same went for *Dynamic Defence*, a collection of Liddell Hart's recent articles which had only been published in October 1940. For the rest Hess had attempted to add to the effect of his dire promises of what was in store for the British Isles from the vast number of u-boats and new types of aircraft Hitler was preparing;[32] yet all this was fully covered in Churchill's proposed statement:

... he [Hess] states that the German production of u-boats and aircraft was such that, apart altogether from invasion, the British Isles would soon be starved out and that American aid would be cut off or arrive too late. He further stated that if, after the surrender of Britain, the British Empire and the United States endeavoured to continue the war, this would be of no avail because Herr Hitler would continue the blockade by u-boat and aircraft until either a general peace was made or the last Englishman had starved to death.[33]

This was a precise summary of Hess's threats, and if it was not damaging to the public interest there are no 'other statements' in Kirkpatrick's reports which qualify. It is, of course, possible that Hess made these other statements to 'C's' officers, whom Churchill called 'the guardians'.

Hamilton had accompanied Kirkpatrick on his second journey to Buchanan Castle; the next day, Thursday the 15th, Kirkpatrick went on his own to interview Hess for the third and, as it turned out, last time. He had instructions to probe Hess on German intentions towards America. Roosevelt had suggested this in the hope that the Deputy Führer might let slip something which could be used to wake the American people to the Nazi threat: 'infiltration, military domination, encirclement of the United States, etc'.[34] Hess did not oblige. 'Germany had no designs on America. The so-called German peril was a ludicrous figment of imagination'. Hitler, however, reckoned on American intervention and was not afraid of it since Germany could outbuild America and Great Britain combined in aircraft. America, Hess went on, would be furious if Britain made peace now since she wanted to inherit the British Empire and he (Hess) had flown over to provide a chance for opening such talks. If Britain were to reject the chance, it would be clear proof she desired no understanding with Germany; Hitler would then be entitled, indeed it would be his duty, to destroy Britain utterly and keep her in permanent subjection. Finally Hess named two German prisoners of war whom he would like to assist him if talks were opened.[35]

Hamilton, meanwhile, had handed over to his second in command at Turnhouse once again and returned to London. Although a ban had been imposed on press or broadcasters mentioning his name, rumour was rife in Scotland linking him with Hess's visit and suggesting that the Deputy Führer had been allowed to fly across Britain unopposed. It is probably significant that Turnhouse Station orders that day carried an unusual reminder headed *Discipline – Disclosure of Information*: 'All personnel are forbidden to communicate any service information which might directly or indirectly assist the enemy . . .'[36] Attention was also drawn to the King's Regulations, and qualified barristers or solicitors among the officers were instructed to report to the Adjutant.

Hamilton's first call in London appears to have been at the Foreign Office, where he handed Cadogan 'full written reports' of Kirkpatrick's first two interviews with Hess – now missing from the open files[37] – and told him he personally wanted to see the King. Cadogan advised him to see the Prime Minister first. Presumably he did, and probably Churchill suggested he see Duff Cooper, for he called on him that evening. As Minister of Information, Duff Cooper was honourable and incompetent. Both qualities had been shown up by Hess's arrival, and his Director General, Sir Walter Monckton, had been reduced by the lack of direction and lack of outside confidence in the ministry to the point of imminent resignation.[38] A great deal of the trouble had been caused by Churchill's indecision about how to handle the affair and the consequent loss of the initiative to Goebbels. This was augmented by Duff

Cooper's failure to suggest any clear line or even to let Monckton see the initial reports of what Hess was saying. Meanwhile Goebbels's broadcasts about Hess's peace proposals and the Duke of Hamilton together with the complete silence from the Ministry of Information had roused the American and British press corps to what Monckton described as 'a state of fury such as neither I nor Ridsdale, the Head of the Foreign News Department, had seen before or during the war'.[39] Monckton consequently took it upon himself to leak the fact that Hess had attempted to contact the Duke of Hamilton indirectly the previous September; this, he told Duff Cooper on 27 May, when he finally did hand in his resignation, 'served to calm the press, to exonerate the Duke and also to keep the Hess matter on the front page, as we wished'.

The question arises: how did Walter Monckton know about Albrecht Haushofer's letter to the Duke and why did he connect it with Hess's arrival? There is no mention of this or any other letter in Kirkpatrick's published reports, Cadogan's report to Churchill, Churchill's proposed statement to the House or any of the memos and minutes connected with these in the open files, nor in any German broadcast. The answer may be that he was told by J.C. Masterman, head of the Double-Cross Committee. Masterman, Guy Liddell and Dick Butler of MI5 (section B19 dealing with rumours) were regular visitors to his office;[40] another whose name appears in his appointments diary in the early months of 1941 was Lord Swinton, head of the Security Co-ordination Committee, set up, as the name implies, to co-ordinate the activities of the SIS, MI5 and the service agencies. There is no doubt that Swinton was involved in the question of Albrecht Haushofer's letter a few days later and it is interesting that Monckton lunched with him on 9 May – the day before Hess's arrival – and Monckton's first appointment after lunch that day was with Masterman. On Tuesday 13 May it appears from scrawled initials in his diary that he saw Masterman at 6.30 in the evening after a talk about Hess with a name that looks like 'Vance' – possibly Sir Robert Vansittart; later that evening he saw Alec Hardinge, King George VI's private secretary. With this range of contacts it is not surprising that Monckton knew about Albrecht's letter to Hamilton.

The first press reports that Hamilton had received a letter from Hess – not Haushofer – appeared that Thursday, 15 May.[41] To judge from the diary of Cecil King of the *Daily Mirror*, Duff Cooper himself started the story that day during a lunch Beaverbrook threw for editors and lobby correspondents at Claridge's. Beaverbrook explained after the meal that he wanted to help Duff Cooper to create a greater flow of news and Hess's arrival provided an opportunity. King noted:

Beaverbrook then suggested that what was wanted at the moment was as much speculation, rumour and discussion about Hess as possible. The Prime Minister would make no statement as that would put an end to the discussion. Would we, therefore, do on our own initiative all we could to make the most of this episode to the detriment of Germany ?[42]

The editors were unhappy about speculating without a clear line since a later Government announcement might make them look foolish. Moreover, the most damaging stories for the enemy, that Hess was a traitor or that there were splits within the Nazi hierarchy and he had fled for his life, had been virtually ruled out by the German broadcasts about his peace bid and the recent admissions from the British side that he had corresponded with the Duke of Hamilton. King summed up the conference as 'a pathetic exhibition – Duff Cooper believing that truth is the best propaganda and yet there must be some other ingredient somewhere'[43] and Beaverbrook wanting to help, but 'both hamstrung by the Prime Minister'.

When Hamilton came to see him that evening anxious to clear his name from the rumours of traffic with Hess, Duff Cooper suggested either an official statement by Churchill in the House or a reply to an inspired question. Next morning Hamilton saw Cadogan again briefly, then went to Buckingham Palace and lunched with the King, who was naturally agog for his personal impressions of Hess.[44] They also discussed means of clearing Hamilton's name; afterwards Hamilton told Duff Cooper that His Majesty preferred the second of the alternatives he had suggested, and Duff Cooper promised to draft out a reply to a question in the House and put the matter to Churchill.[45]

Churchill, meanwhile, had 'got over his tantrum', as Cadogan put it, at not being allowed to make his statement and at the midday cabinet meeting he admitted that the Foreign Office view had been correct. He had instructed Duff Cooper to lead the press on the line that Hess was 'one of the "War criminals" whose fate must be decided by the Allied governments after the war'.[46]

The War Office had now selected a country house called Mytchett Place, near the Army town of Aldershot in Surrey, as being suitable for Hess's accommodation, following Churchill's decree regarding his treatment. A suite of rooms and a defensive perimeter in the grounds were being prepared, and sound engineers were wiring up the entire suite so that 'C's' 'guardians' could listen in. In the meantime Churchill agreed that Hess could be brought down and lodged in the Tower of London; he used the move as an excuse to thwart Duff Cooper's latest plea for permission to 'send a photographer to Scotland to take some pictures of the Deputy Führer'. Churchill minuted: 'Wait a few days. He is on the move.'[47]

The 'few days' would turn into years. Since the opportunity actively to exploit the sensation had been lost by excessive secrecy, caution and especially by Churchill's extraordinary disregard for the dangers of a full and honest statement[48] – which resulted in no statement at all – the initial curtain of secrecy was drawn tighter and speculation, strictly unauthorised, was given reign, while in secret the 'guardians' were to probe Hess's mind for intelligence he might not even know he possessed.

Cadogan drafted a 'Most Secret' circular to explain the policy to the British representatives in neutral capitals:

No indication of Hess's statements or views should on any account be given to anyone except your immediate diplomatic staff. Our intention is to remain in constant contact with him and try to draw him. We do not know what will emerge, but we might eventually obtain information from him. For the time being we propose to say nothing officially about any results of interrogation, but to try to keep Germans guessing. It may be possible however that by way of 'whispers' or gently inspired speculation in the press we may be able to cause embarrassment to the Germans . . .[49]

This last sentence was cut out before the wire was sent early in the morning of Saturday 17 May; instead:

. . . Their own official statements show the confusion that has been caused by Hess's escapade and we hope to make the most of this, so as to instil doubt and fear into the German government and people. Hess will be branded a war criminal and any attempt to sentimentalise over him discouraged.[50]

24

MYTCHETT PLACE

If Hess had any suspicion that his mission had failed and both his Government and Churchill's were seeking to erase his name from public memory, the news that he was to be transferred dispelled it immediately. Major Shephard, the officer sent up to supervise his travel, reported that 'he seemed somewhat elated at the news and assumed an air of great importance'.[1] He tried to find out his destination and, when told he was going by train, assumed it must be to London. The commanding officer of the hospital came to see him just before he left; Hess thanked him for his kindness and the treatment he had received and said he felt much better.[2] 'Was resigned and calm during his journey to the station', Shephard reported:

In the train he became very restive and objected to having any lighting in the compartment and wanted the guard officers withdrawn – these requests were naturally refused, whereupon he raised his voice in temper, saying he would not make any attempt to sleep if under observation. Finding his demands very ineffective he appeared to sulk for the greater part of the night.[3]

From the London terminus, he was taken by ambulance to the Tower of London and lodged in officers' quarters in the Governor's House – 'charming' he recalled years later.[4] In the days that followed from his window he watched the guards drilling to drums and bagpipes with a precision and stamina which, he wrote, 'would have done credit to Prussians'. He asked to see the Duke of Hamilton and Ivone Kirkpatrick. The request was not granted.

Churchill was still, in Cadogan's words, 'hankering after his stupid statement about Hess'.[5] On Monday the 19th he read it to the cabinet with great gusto, but there too all were unanimous against it. 'I think he has dropped the idea' Cadogan noted with relief. Afterwards Kirkpatrick reported personally on his interviews with Hess, and Churchill agreed to the proposal that pretence negotiations should be started to try and draw more information from him; Cadogan suggested Sir John Simon, strongly associated, like Sam Hoare, with pre-war appeasement politics, and Churchill adopted the idea. Eden was given the delicate task of seeing if Simon would play.

The alterations and wiring to Mytchett Place were completed by the following day, Tuesday the 20th, and that afternoon Hess was driven there by ambulance, escorted by two cars carrying armed officers of the Scots and Coldstream Guards who had been picked to serve as both his jailors and officers of the guard protecting Mytchett Place. Hess was designated 'Z', the house and grounds 'Camp Z'. The small convoy arrived at 5.30 p.m. and Hess was taken straight up the staircase and through a newly erected metal grille to his suite on the first floor. He went to bed immediately. It was while in bed that General Sir Alan Hunter, Director of Prisoners of War, introduced him to Camp Z's commandant, Colonel A. Malcolm Scott, the young officers of the guard and three intelligence officers who were to be his 'personal companions', 'Colonel Wallace', Major Foley, and 'Captain Barnes'. Finally Hunter told him that Colonel Scott was responsible to him (Hunter) and would forward any requests. Hess replied that he was comfortable, but he wished to see the Duke of Hamilton and Ivone Kirkpatrick.[6]

Major Shephard, whose duties were completed now that Hess was installed in permanent quarters, had probably seen more of Hess than anyone since his arrival in Scotland. Churchill had requested that he put his impressions down on paper and forward them to him.[7] He did so the next day. At first, he wrote, Hess had appeared a little shaken and suffering from his recent adventure, but had conversed freely with officers guarding him and had 'seemed to derive considerable pleasure in relating the details of his flight'. His nights had been rather restless and he had always asked for a sedative. After this preamble, Shephard, who was described by General Hunter as 'a first-class type of shall I say a temporary but emphatically natural gentleman' – a reference to his social class – no doubt flattered by the Prime Minister's interest, plunged into psychoanalysis:

At times I have been doubtful of his [Hess's] mental stability and I have formed the impression that he is controlled in some degree by some form of mental influence. To instance this, I have observed that when a conversation is started in small talk and suddenly developed to call for a considered opinion he immediately averts his gaze and his eyes take on a strange and distant look, and he is then very cautious in his replies. He is cunning, shrewd and self-entred ... very temperamental and will need careful handling if he is to be outwitted ...[8]

This assessment seems in many ways more accurate than that of the

243

psychiatrists who reported on Hess later. Yet in his concluding paragraph Shephard, who appears to have made no allowance for the very uncertain situation in which Hess found himself or for his sudden fall from great power, treated him less as a subject for study than as a projection of his own hatred of the Nazi enemy, or so it reads, for he provided no observations to back his impressions. Despite this, there are astonishing echoes of Hess's slavish dependence on Hitler remarked by all on the German side:

I believe by the very nature of his make-up, which reflects cruelty, bestiality, deceit, arrogance and a yellow streak, that he has lost his soul and has willingly permitted himself to become plastic in the hands of a more powerful and compelling personality. My personal view is that he has lost favour and in order to rehabilitate himself he has cunningly conceived the idea of appearing as a peace envoy to enable him to justify his action both here and in Germany ...[9]

It is interesting that this was written before any authoritative British statement that he had come as a peace envoy. Finally Shephard summed up Hess as 'a man lacking in personality which is only offset by the power invested in him by his master and used ruthlessly without regard for the finer instincts of humanity'.

The doctor at the military hospital at Buchanan Castle, Lt Colonel Gibson Graham, who looked after Hess and who had accompanied him down to Mytchett Place, where he continued to attend him, had written a more sympathetic description in a letter to a relative or friend on the 15th:

I found him surprisingly ordinary – neither so ruthless-looking nor so handsome, nor so beetle-browed as the newspapers would have us believe. Quite sane, certainly not a drug-taker, a little concerned about his health and rather faddy about his diet, quite ready to chat (to one of our junior officers) even about the origin of the war ...[10]

When he wrote, Gibson Graham had no idea of why Hess had come; it is not clear how Shephard had found out or whether his was a guess inspired by the rumours circulating round Glasgow.

In Berlin von Weizsäcker had been kept almost as busy with Hess as had Cadogan, but he was not privy to the higher secrets of the affair and actually knew less than his London counterpart. On the 19th he recorded the conclusions he had reached: he recalled that he had always had the impression the Führer would not be unhappy with a settlement with Britain on the lines that the British Empire remained intact but Britain had no say on the continent of Europe. He also seemed to recall that Hess had talked to him in social gatherings about peace rumours, and it was said he ran them all to ground as thoroughly as he could. It seemed, therefore, as though he had indeed staked his own person in an attempt at a settlement between the 'two white nations', as stated in the communiqué of the 13th. He refused to believe other stories, and deplored Hess's old friends, now suddenly prepared to credit him with evil character defects.

Hess always appeared to me as a fanatic, not however as abnormal. I consider it quite out of the question that he would be disloyal to the Führer or betray military or political secrets. Certainly the method of his peace action is more unworldly than I had believed him capable of.[11]

He assumed that Hess had acted in good faith in conformity with the Führer's line in seeking an agreement with England, further that Hitler and Ribbentrop were also in agreement on this. It is symptomatic of the *Führer* system that von Weizsäcker did not know, but had to assume the policy of his Foreign Minister. This note and von Hassell's diary entry cited earlier both indicate that conservative opposition circles were quite as surprised by Hess's flight as the rest of the population, confirming the supposition that Albrecht Haushofer knew nothing about Hess's final preparations and hence was not involved in them.

On the day von Weizsäcker recorded his impressions, Monday the 19th, the British Minister in Stockholm heard a very different story from the US Military Attaché in Bonn, who had been in Berlin at the time of Hess's flight. He said that the flight had been preceded by several days of 'tense expectation that all was not well'. The reasons:

Hess was known to disagree with Ribbentrop's pro-Soviet policy and hatred of England. It is believed that at the last meeting of the Party chiefs on a date between May 1st and May 4th, Hess spoke out against Ribbentrop's policy, but Hitler supported Ribbentrop. It was remarked at the Kroll Opera [Reichstag] meeting on May 4th that Hess practically turned his back on Ribbentrop ...[12]

Since the disagreement between Hitler and Ribbentrop, on the one hand, and Hess, on the other, was not known to the permanent head of the Foreign Ministry in Berlin, even by rumour, and since the idea of dissension over the policy of friendship towards Russia had appeared in earlier, probably inspired, stories it is reasonable to suppose that the US Attaché was unwittingly spreading disinformation which had been planted on him. If, as the wording suggests, he had been made aware of the schism at the top *before* Hess's flight it might be assumed that disinformation also started before the flight, and the flight itself was simply an extension of the campaign – no doubt unbeknown to Hess. If so, Hitler must have despatched his deputy not so much in the serious hope of peace as for a spectacular deception on Stalin.

That, of course, is speculation. Meanwhile Gardemann, Ribbentrop's principal agent seeking a channel to Hoare, had been telephoning his contact in Madrid, Don Joachim Boa, frequently and anxiously to find out whether *his* contact, Juan Beigbeder, had approached Hoare on the British attitude to Hess's mission. On 20 May Hoare sent a memo to Eden about Gardemann's approaches with a cryptic accompanying letter marked 'Personal and Secret':

Dear Anthony

... I have just written Winston a short personal note in view of the fact that he took so much interest last year in agreeing to our secret plans. I thought that he would like to know that during the last two or three weeks they have worked out very much as we hoped.

I am enclosing a curious and very secret note that has just been sent me from Beigbeder. The suggestions in it bear a remarkable resemblance to what I imagine Hess has been saying in England. You will therefore no doubt wish to take it into account in connexion with anything that you get out of Hess. I feel sure that in each case our reply will be a very definite negative . . .[13]

The question is, what secret plans had Hoare and Eden concocted and Churchill agreed to at some date in 1940? Almost certainly they concerned Spain; yet nothing of note had happened in Spain in 'the last two or three weeks' during which Hoare suggested the plans had worked out 'very much as we hoped'. It will be recalled that the weeks immediately preceding these 'last two or three weeks' from 20 May when Hoare wrote had been heavy with German threat and reports that Franco was about to be forced into the Axis or that German troops would march through Spain to take Gibraltar. After the weekend of 19–20 April reports from a variety of sources had suggested Hess had flown to Madrid to deliver Hitler's ultimatum personally to Franco. A Foreign Office file about this date concerned with German pressure on Spain is closed until 2017. Might it be that the 'secret plans' involved Hoare playing the appeaser to deflect the German threat to the peninsula and particularly to the vital base at Gibraltar? Could it be that Hoare had said – as the Italian Ambassador had reported him suggesting to Prinz Max zu Hohenlowe – that Churchill's Government could not last long and he (Hoare) would be recalled to London shortly to take over? Was Hoare working with the grain of the Double-Cross Committee deception that powerful voices in England wanted peace? Stewart Menzies's double agent Dusko Popov wrote in his memoirs that after Hess's arrival he couldn't help wondering 'how much our planted reports of low British morale might have influenced Hess – and even Hitler'.[14] It would be interesting, he had speculated, 'if British Intelligence had unwittingly inspired the Hess incident'.

If this is what the 'secret plans' amounted to, could it be that Hess did fly to Madrid during or after the weekend of 19–20 April where he contacted Hoare through the agency of Albrecht Haushofer's former pupil, Stahmer, or perhaps Beigbeder? Here speculation runs ahead of evidence. Nevertheless, someone from the British side convinced Hess that there was a powerful opposition in Britain anxious to topple Churchill and make peace; from what he said in Britain there is no doubt of that. Moreover, several of the files 'closed until 2017' point to Hoare. Further, the second paragraph of Hoare's 20 May letter to Eden supposed that Beigbeder's remarks to him (Hoare) bore 'a remarkable resemblance to what I imagine Hess has been saying in England'. The wording might be construed to mean that Hoare knew what Hess was likely to be saying in England. In fact, Boa's message *via* Beigbeder did bear a remarkable resemblance to what Hess was saying; it concerned the certainty of German victory; the Germans did not wish to destroy the British Empire however, hence wanted to ascertain the British attitude to peace talks.[15]

At the end of the month Beigbeder called on Hoare again to tell him that Gardemann had arrived in Madrid from Paris and had asked Don Joachim Boa whether he (Beigbeder) had agreed to make discreet contact with Hoare, and if Hoare thought the moment opportune for an interview between English and German representatives. Boa had told Gardemann he must regard his offer of mediation as having fallen through, upon which Gardemann said he regretted this since Hitler did not want to destroy England and still desired a friendly arrangement, the more so at this time when the Germans would like to liberate Great Britain from slavery to America:

He also said that Englishmen and Germans are racial brothers and can understand each other, that he could not understand the blindness of England, which would be attacked between 15th June and 15th July with new destruction methods so terrible and deadly that everything done hitherto will seem mere child's play and that it was Germany herself who wished to avoid this cruelty, but she finds herself compelled to undertake it before the US help becomes effective . . .[16]

Although Gardemann's message promised an attack on Britain between 15 June and 15 July with deadly new destructive methods – a warning which Hoare might have been expected to report by wire – and although he asked that his instructions as to how to reply should be sent by 'urgent telegram', he did not send the memo to Eden until 4 June and then by diplomatic bag so that it did not reach London until 20 June, five days after the beginning of the period of 'deadly destruction'.

From the other side, this and other messages from Madrid about Gardemann suggest that Ribbentrop was attempting to use Hoare as one arm of the grand deception for Stalin which Hitler was preparing to fall on Great Britain that June to force her to terms – this at a time when Heydrich's SD public opinion reports and von Weizsäcker's notes reveal on the one hand a massive spread of rumours about an impending treaty between Berlin and Moscow whereby Stalin would purchase peace, and on the other hand the brimming confidence of the German military that their campaign against Russia would be over in four to eight weeks, 'at the most ten weeks'. Hitler himself took a hand in this deception. At a meeting with Mussolini at the Brenner Pass on 2 June, he told the Duce privately that England was on the point of giving in – due to the sea and air blockade; Churchill would be replaced by Lloyd George. Then he spoke about Hess and wept.[17]

By the time he was installed in his suite at Mytchett Place Hess realised his mission had misfired. His repeated requests to see the Duke of Hamilton had met with no response; he was still not allowed to see newspapers or hear the wireless. He guessed he had been abducted and was being kept hidden from the world by the secret services, and it appears he imagined they would quietly get rid of him.[18] When on his first morning there, Wednesday 21 May, his breakfast was brought up to his bedroom, he ate little since, he said, he feared it might be poisoned. He had recovered his spirits by one o'clock, when he was escorted downstairs to have lunch with his doctor, Colonel Gibson Graham, and his three 'companions', and he apologised to the doctor for his earlier suspicions. He did not lose them though; indeed, they appeared to grow; over the following days he made it clear that the doctor was the only person he trusted and he was convinced the young Guards officers planned to murder him. It is not apparent whether he really feared this or whether it was play-acting of the kind he indulged in later most successfully – intended perhaps to bear out the Führer when it became necessary for Hitler to distance himself from the mission by declaring him insane. Six weeks later he wrote a long deposition claiming that after arriving at Mytchett Place he was 'given in food and medicines a substance which has a strong effect on brain and nerves', and he described it thus:

... a short time after taking it a curious development of warmth rising over the nape of the neck to the head. In the head feelings which are similar to headache pains but which are not the same. There followed during many hours a feeling of extraordinary well-being, physical and mental energy, *joie de vivre*, optimism. During the night little sleep which did not in the least destroy my happy feeling. If no new quantities of the substance were added to change the feeling to the contrary, when the period had expired especially, pessimism bordering on a nervous breakdown without any cause and ... extraordinary fatigue

248

of the brain. After the first taking of this substance the negative reaction to the initial well feeling was so strong in me that I should become insane if they succeeded in giving me further quantities . . . [and] the negative reaction would cause me to lose my nerves completely . . . [19]

This reads like the effects of an amphetamine followed by withdrawal symptoms. Hess was not a drug-taker, but Göring was and Hitler almost certainly boosted himself with amphetamines during the day ; Hess might easily have learnt the effects. On the other hand he might in these early days simply have been describing the ups and downs of his own nervously unstable character exaggerated by his sense of failure, extreme frustration and bewilderment. The symptoms changed later – as will appear.

When, years afterwards, in Spandau prison in Berlin he set down his impressions of Mytchett Place for Ilse, he made no mention of substances in his food ; what stuck in his mind were the fragrant glycineas and rhododendrons in the grounds where he walked with his 'companions', and evenings during which he heard 'wonderfully sensitive Mozart' played (on the gramophone) in the music-room below by the commandant – 'in peacetime a professional artist, with a true artist's nature ; outside were warm summer nights, and my heart was aching so'.[20]

The devastating impression of Hess's character formed by Major Shephard before his arrival at Mytchett Place, his 'very temperamental' nature and the sulks Shephard described, together with the fact that he declared his suspicion of poison after only one meal at Mytchett – dinner in his room on the first evening – suggest that his behaviour and his later accusations about drugs in his food were his response to failure and imprisonment, and perhaps the realisation that he had been made to look a fool. At all events he lost the respect of the British officers ; on the first Saturday, 24 May, Gibson Graham remarked that 'Z' was daily decreasing in stature ; he estimated his worth at not more than £2 0s 0d a week.[21]

His behaviour became increasingly bizarre. He confessed to being afraid that a member of the secret service would creep into his room while he was asleep and cut an artery to fake his suicide ;[22] to pre-empt this he told Gibson Graham that he had given his word to the Führer that he would not commit suicide. At meals he swapped plates or, when a dish of food was passed for him to help himself, chose not the next or nearest portion, but a further one. His moods swung, rather as he described them in his later deposition about the effects of the substances placed in his food and medicine, from cheerfulness to extreme depression, and he made no attempt to disguise either. The Guards officers, bred in a stiff school to shun emotion as unbefitting an officer and a gentleman, were not impressed. Lieutenant W.B. Malone, who kept a diary, noted on Wednesday 28 May difficulty in imagining 'that this rather broken man who slouches into his chair careless as to his dress' could have been the Deputy Führer. 'He is such a *second-rater*, with none of the dignity, the bearing of a great man.'[23] The same day the 'companion', 'Colonel Wallace', rated him worth thirty-five shillings a week, 'no more'.[24]

Hess suffered his usual sleeplessness that night, but appeared more distressed than usual. This probably stemmed from news of the loss of the great new battleship *Bismarck*, which had been given to him suddenly at lunch that day, presumably with the intention of knocking him off balance – which it had. At 2.20 a.m. he walked through to the duty officer just inside the grille, who was Malone, and asked for a small whisky to help him sleep. Malone gave him one, but he was back inside half an hour, saying he still could not sleep. Then in a stage whisper he told the young lieutenant his reasons for coming to Great Britain to see the Duke of Hamilton, and asked him to get in touch with the Duke and request him to arrange an audience for him with the King. If he would do that, he assured him, he would receive the thanks of the monarch for a great service to humanity. Malone said it was impossible and 'this sort of thing put the Duke in a most unfortunate position', at which Hess told him he believed the secret service had hidden him here at the behest of a clique of warmongers so that the Duke could not find him. They were trying to drive him to insanity or suicide by preventing him from sleeping at night or resting during the day : doors were opened and shut loudly, people ran up and down uncarpeted stairs, motorbikes were stationed near by with engines running and special aeroplanes sent overhead. Malone explained that there was an army camp close by. 'This seemed to have no effect', Malone reported :

> He shook his head and flapped his hands about on the arms of his chair listlessly. He then went to bed. A few minutes later he got up again and asked me to excuse him for what he had said, saying that he was in a very nervous condition and perhaps did not mean all he said . . .[25]

In his diary Malone described his impressions of Hess that night : slumped in his chair in a white dressing-gown with red facings, he had looked suddenly old and almost wizened – 'shaggy eyebrows, deep animal sad eyes, a look of anguish and torture on his face'.[26]

The 'companions' could not get a word out of him next day and after lunch Dr Graham told Colonel Scott that in his opinion 'Z' was 'definitely over the border that lies between mental instability and insanity'. Scott thereupon rang the Deputy Director of Prisoners of War, Colonel Coates, and explained the situation. Coates rang back some two and a half hours later to say that a psychiatrist would be sent down to relieve Colonel

Graham at the weekend, 'which', Scott noted in his diary, 'is all to the good'.[27] After dinner that evening Hess told Colonel Scott he wished to speak to him privately. Scott called his 'companion', Major Foley, to interpret and Hess put a number of requests; these included the right to walk in the garden whenever he wished, and the provision of at least a summary of the news – obviously a reaction to the *Bismarck* provocation. He gave his word of honour not to escape, and argued that he was entitled to put these requests 'in view of the fact that he had come here of his own free will and thrown himself on the chivalry of His Majesty the King'.[28]

From Scott's diary entry it appears that the idea of Hess becoming insane – for Gibson Graham had reported him absolutely sane after he landed in Scotland – originated inside Camp Z, specifically with Dr Graham. Lord Beaverbrook, however, told the author, James Leasor, that he had suggested the idea to Churchill while walking through St James's Park discussing how to prevent the spread of rumour that Hess had come to Great Britain with a genuine peace plan. Beaverbrook, a Canadian, had said that he believed that in Britain anyone who came under the care of a psychiatrist was written off as mad and this might provide a quick way to discredit Hess.[29] If true, it appears from Colonel Scott's addendum, 'which is all to the good', that he at least was not privy to the plot; in which case it must have been suggested to Gibson Graham, perhaps by 'C's' men, probably on the instructions of 'C' himself, who had visited Camp Z and spent an hour and a half with the 'companions' in the early evening of the previous Sunday, 25 May.

The origin of the call for a psychiatrist is not without significance since it was Beaverbrook who first suggested to James Leasor that he write a book about Hess – subsequently assisting him – and Leasor gained the impression this was because he had a guilty conscience about his suggestion that Hess should be declared mad. If, however, Beaverbrook had another reason for guilt, if for instance he knew that Hess had been lured over, if he himself had played a part, the reason he gave Leasor might have been invented as a cover, for it has been suggested that it was Beaverbrook whom Hess came over to see – the friend of Lloyd George and constant correspondent with Sam Hoare, at the same time in Churchill's innermost councils, and yet in the earlier stages of the war he had had a foot in the peace camp.[30]

The night before Hess's temporary breakdown, German parachutists had been dropped in England to assassinate him. It appears to have been a wild and amateurish attempt, provoking the suspicion that the assassins were expended simply to back Hitler's claim that Hess came over without his knowledge. No official files on the affair are open, nor will they be since the parachutists were wearing civilian clothes and were treated as spies and executed. The attempt was revealed in 1979 by Colonel John McCowen, in 1941 a Major on the staff of Air Vice-Marshal Leigh Mallory, commanding 11 Fighter Group.[31]

In the night of 27–28 May Leigh Mallory summoned Major McCowen and told him that a coded message had been intercepted indicating parachutists would be dropped in the early hours of the 28th under cover of a bombing raid on Luton. Their aim would be to assassinate Hess. Luton, in Bedfordshire, north-west of London, was under twenty miles from the RAF interrogation centre at Cockfosters, where the Germans must have assumed Hess was being held. McCowen was ordered to move a mixed brigade of anti-aircraft guns and searchlights to the area. He did so, and alerted the local Home Guard battalion commander, so that all was ready for the reception of the assassins when the enemy planes appeared shortly before 3 a.m. and dropped their 'covering' bombs on and around Newlands Farm, off the London Road, near Luton Hoo. However, the chief interest of the story is that McCowen gained the impression that the warning message which had been picked up by 'Y Service', who monitored enemy signals traffic, had been addressed to Leigh Mallory personally by Willi Messerschmitt.[32] If so, this raises the possibility that Messerschmitt alerted Leigh Mallory in the same way before Hess's flight on 10 May – in short that he was fully initiated into the plot and, like Göring, wanted peace with Great Britain as much as Hess.

25

LORD SIMON

The move to clear the Duke of Hamilton's name with an inspired question in the House of Commons had failed to damp speculation. The question had been put by a Conservative Member of Parliament on 22 May. Sir Archibald Sinclair, Secretary of State for Air, had replied, saying that the Duke had not recognised Hess when he had visited him in hospital the morning after his landing in Scotland, and 'contrary to reports which have appeared in some newspapers, the Duke has not been in correspondence with the Deputy Führer'. It would seem, Sinclair had concluded, 'that the conduct of the Duke of Hamilton has been in every respect honourable and proper'.[1]

Pressed, he had said, 'I cannot speak as to whether or not Hess wrote a letter to the Duke of Hamilton; I can only say that no letter from Hess to the Duke of Hamilton has reached the Duke or any responsible authority in this country.'

The press statements led to an acrimonious exchange of letters between Sinclair and Duff Cooper about how the Ministry of Information had come to suggest that Hamilton had been in correspondence with Hess in the first place; the chosen scapegoat was Walter Monckton and he offered his resignation on 27 May;[2] it was not accepted. The files reveal that Lord Swinton, head of the Security Co-ordination Committee, had intervened and had a hand in framing Sinclair's replies in the House, and in a note on 29 May Sinclair's private secretary stated: 'Certain secret papers on this aspect of the case are held in the private office.'[3] It is also apparent from the exchange of letters that Sinclair was assured personally by Hamilton that he had never received a letter from Hess and that he did not remember ever having met Hess before. The Duke held to this story for the rest of his life.[4]

It is understandable that Hamilton should have sought to protect his name from speculation and rumour that he had invited the Deputy Führer across, but a puzzle as to why the security services, as represented by

Lord Swinton, should have been so exercised about whether Hamilton had known Hess before the war and whether he had received a letter. Monckton's original 'leak' to the press had stated merely that Hess had 'made an attempt to communicate with the Duke by letter some months previously. The Duke immediately placed the letter in the hands of our security services and Hess got no reply.'[5] This form of words had been agreed with the Foreign Office, presumably Cadogan; it referred not to any letter Hess might have brought with him, but to Albrecht Haushofer's letter of 23 September and 'departed from the truth', as it was put at the ministry, by saying that the Duke received the letter and passed it to the security services – whereas, of course, it had happened the other way round. Either Lord Swinton and his committee were anxious to protect Hamilton's name because they had involved him in the affair in the first place, or they were attempting to protect Albrecht Haushofer inside Germany – in which case Albrecht was their man, one of 'C's' strategically placed agents – or, of course, they were protecting both these two friends.

The solution to the puzzle is no doubt contained in one of four files on Hess dated between 17 and 27 May which are closed until 2017.[6] One open file in this series on Hess is a wire from Hoare in Madrid dated 22 May; it refers to the second paragraph of a wire he had sent on the 17th which ran: 'Several of the Nazi Party officials in Spain, nominees of Hess who have organised a German colony, have suddenly been recalled to Berlin.'[7] These were presumably members of Bohle's 'Foreign Organisation'. Hoare's wire of the 22nd stated that these officials had not yet left Madrid; 'they seem to have sent a temporising reply and are still very worried'.[8] While this wire does not appear to be connected with any of the closed files in the Hess series, it indicates that Hoare had a source inside or close to this group of 'Hess nominees'.

Far from stilling speculation, Sinclair's vindication of Hamilton's honour in the House smelt so obviously of fudge that rumour gained wing. At the beginning of June the Communist Party of Great Britain took a hand, producing a pamphlet referring to the Duke of Hamilton's 'enjoyment of the close personal friendship of Rudolf Hess' and alleging a plot between British industrialists, bankers and aristocrats with Fascist tendencies to patch up a deal with the German Government and regime.[9] This was the usual Communist provocation based on a sub-stratum of truth; for what they alleged was precisely what Hess was angling for and there were of course British bankers, industrialists and landed aristocrats who wanted a patched-up peace – not usually because they were Fascists. Nevertheless, the Communist Party did have superb sources of information inside the British security services. James Leasor, after serialisation of his book on Hess's mission, received a letter from a former

MI6 or MI5 officer who had fought in the First World War and had the rank of captain – Leasor cannot recall his name, and the letter, which came from the Manchester area, has not survived – who claimed he had given information about Hess to the Communist Party headquarters. This episode occurred later, in the early autumn of 1941, when Hess was visited by Lord Beaverbrook. 'Captain X' was stationed with a stenographer in the adjoining, wired-up room transcribing the conversation; afterwards he made a copy of the transcript and took it straight round to Communist Party headquarters. Not only was the tone of his letter to James Leasor unrepentant, but he thought he had done a good thing.[10] It is possible, therefore, that the communists had exact information on Hess's earlier conversations with the 'companions'.

Of the three 'companions', the chief so far as Hess's interrogation was concerned was Major Frank Foley. Like Sir Stewart Menzies, Foley had transferred to intelligence after being wounded in the First World War. He was a first-class linguist and during the Twenties he had been posted to the British Embassy in Berlin as passport control officer, the invariable and transparent cover for SIS agents in foreign capitals. After the Nazi seizure of power Foley had concerned himself on personal, not professional grounds, with the plight of the Jews and had done all he could to assist them to leave Germany – today he is remembered in Israel by a grove of trees planted in Kibbutz Harel. In the early part of the war he served in Oslo, then returned to England and was posted to the counter-espionage Section V of the SIS. He was also co-opted as senior adviser on Masterman's Double-Cross Committee, because the fifteen years he had spent in Berlin before the war gave him unrivalled knowledge of Abwehr methods and personalities.[11] If, as seems probable, the Double-Cross Committee had played a part in deceiving Hess, Foley must have had a hand in the operation himself. He was, in any case, an obvious choice to head the team of 'companions'.

Foley was an intelligence officer with a remarkable record and cannot be suspected of leaking information to the Communists. The same cannot be said of the 'companion' who went by the pseudonym 'Captain Barnes', since his real name is not known. Like the other companion, 'Colonel Wallace' – probably Lieutenant Colonel Thomas Kendrick, who had been station chief in Vienna before the war – 'Barnes' left Mytchett Place during June, thus before the Beaverbrook interview. However, he may well have been recalled when someone was required to record the Beaverbrook conversation. That is speculation.

However the Communist Party obtained their information, Hamilton, who was handed a copy of their pamphlet by a stranger, immediately took out an injunction. Proceedings dragged on through the summer with Churchill himself involved when it appeared the Communists intended calling Hess as a witness.[12] Early the following year the case was settled out of court.

Hess, meanwhile, sank into deeper depression. The arrival of a psychiatrist, Major Henry V. Dicks, in place of his doctor, Gibson Graham, had done nothing and obviously could do nothing to relieve his sense of failure, nor his suspicions of those about him. On the afternoon of Wednesday 4 June he sat under a tree in the garden, in the words of Colonel Scott 'in the most uncomfortable position, refused to speak to anyone, was morose and in a fit of the deepest depression'.[13] After dinner he went out and, again refusing company, 'walked up and down in an agitated way' until ten o'clock. Half an hour later 'Colonel Wallace', Major Foley and Dicks told Scott that they feared he might attempt suicide that night. Their reasons were that for the first time he had written a letter to his wife and it contained a significant fatalistic quotation from Goethe; then he had wished the 'companions', 'Good night,' something he had never done before, and he had been heard to mutter to himself, 'I can't stand this any more.' Lieutenant Malone was instructed to watch him closely.

Lord Simon had by now agreed to Eden's proposal that he should assume the role of a sympathetic negotiator with Hess,[14] and next day, 5 June, Hess was told a high representative of the Foreign Office was to visit him the following Monday.[15] At first the news seemed to calm him, and he spent some time in his room writing notes as he had before his initial interview with Hamilton and Kirkpatrick. As the date of the appointment drew nearer, he grew more agitated and difficult. On the day before Simon was due he rose late after a bad night, refused to have soup or fish at lunch and, when the meat dish came round, instead of serving himself, snatched 'Colonel Wallace's' plate from him. He would not speak to anyone. Later he refused to take tea or dinner and finally retired to his room, as Colonel Scott put it, 'like a spoilt child in a towering rage'.[16]

Simon, meanwhile, briefed himself on all the previous interviews with Hess; besides Hamilton's and Kirkpatrick's initial reports, there were four records of conversations Hess had had with his 'companions' at Mytchett Place. None of these are in the open files, only the briefest of summaries which Cadogan made for Churchill on 6 June:

Generally speaking Hess has stuck to the line which he took in his original interviews ... namely the insistence on the certainty of German victory and the senselessness of continuing the struggle. He still maintains that it was his own personal idea to come to England and that he was not sent by the Führer. He still professes anxiety to get in touch with the leaders of the opposition in this country who, he supposes, represent a strong peace party ...[17]

It is evident from the summary that Hess had fooled even such experts as Frank Foley about the extent of his knowledge of military affairs. However, Cadogan believed that with the right questions 'a certain amount of information on political matters might be obtained by inference', and in particular whether he had been sent by Hitler. He suggested that Simon might point out to him that he had been disavowed by Hitler and negotiations could not be conducted until the Government was satisfied on this point – whether or not he had the Führer's authority. 'Hess's reactions might be violent or he might be led to confess that he is on a mission from Hitler – if indeed that is the case.'[18]

In fact this suggestion had come from Kirkpatrick, who a few days earlier had given Simon his views on how to draw Hess out. One of the questions he had suggested putting to Hess proves beyond doubt that Hess had revealed nothing about 'Barbarossa': *'Russia*: What is the use of [Great Britain] concluding a peace of understanding with Germany if Germany is going to sign up with Russia and bring Bolshevism into Europe?'[19] From this it appears that Hess had not merely been silent on 'Barbarossa', but threatened, in line with current German propaganda, that Hitler was about to make a closer, probably military, alliance with Russia.

Simon arrived at Mytchett Place at one o'clock on Monday 9 June accompanied by Kirkpatrick as his 'witness'. To preserve secrecy and anonymity, both carried special passes countersigned by Cadogan in the names of Dr Guthrie and Dr Mackenzie, although Hess himself – designated 'Jonathan' in the subsequent transcript of the interview – had insisted on being told who was coming and knew their real names. While they had lunch with Colonel Scott, Hess, who had dressed with some care in his Luftwaffe uniform that morning, remained in his room with 'Captain Barnes', refusing all food in case the secret service should make a last attempt to poison him; instead he took glucose tablets.

At two o'clock, Scott recorded in his diary, three MI5 officers arrived with a German 'witness' named Kurt Maass, whom Hess had requested specifically from internment to strengthen his side, and at 2.30 Simon, Kirkpatrick, a stenographer and Maass walked upstairs and through the grille to where Hess waited to receive them in his drawing-room. 'Captain Barnes' was to interpret. Whether Simon gave Hess his hand is not recorded. What is quite clear from the papers is that Simon was acting a part specifically to draw Hess, and his instructions from Churchill stated that 'His Majesty's Government are of course not prepared to enter into negotiations for peace either with Hess or any other representative of Hitler',[20] while Hess himself believed Simon had come in good faith.

'Herr Reichsminister', Simon started after introductions, 'I was informed that you had come here feeling charged with a mission and

that you wished to speak of it to someone who would be able to receive it with Government authority. You know I am [Dr Guthrie] and therefore I come with the authority of the Government, and I shall be very willing to listen and discuss with you as far as seems good anything you would wish to state for the information of the Government.'[21]

'*Ich bin ausserordentlich dankbar . . .*' Hess [Jonathan] began.

'He is extremely grateful,' 'Barnes' translated, 'that [Dr Guthrie] has come out here. He realises that his arrival here has not been understood by anyone – because it was such a very extraordinary step to take he can't expect us to.'

Hess then launched into an explanation of the genesis of his idea the previous June during the French campaign, of how the Führer, ever since he had known him, had always said there must be an understanding between Germany and Great Britain and how he (Hess) then had the idea that if only people in England knew this, they might perhaps be prepared to come to an agreement. When, after the French campaign, England had turned down the Führer's offer of peace, he (Hess) had become all the more determined to realise his plan.

After 'Barnes' had translated this, Hess paused for a long time. When he resumed, he spoke of the air-raids and the heavy damage and losses caused. He had gained the impression, he said, that England could not give way without losing prestige and he had therefore said to himself, if he went over to England they could use that as an occasion for negotiat-ing . . .

Kirkpatrick interrupted 'Barnes's' translation : 'What he really said was "*Anlass nehmen*" – his arrival here would be a peg, a ground for starting negotiations, without a loss of prestige.'

'I must admit', Hess continued in German, 'that I faced a very difficult decision, the most difficult of my life obviously. And I believe I was able to take it by keeping ever before my eyes an endless row of children's coffins, on the German as much as the English side, with the crying mothers behind them – and conversely the coffins of mothers with chil-dren behind.'

No doubt Hess was sincere ; he had been disturbed by the scenes of devastation he witnessed during the French campaign.[22] But it will also be recalled that one of the propaganda leaflets dropped over Augsburg in the days immediately preceding his flight carried a picture of a badly wounded, dead child with the caption, 'This is not your child, but one of the countless children caught by German air-raids . . .'[23]

After the humanitarian, Hess addressed what he called 'the psychologi-cal aspects'. This involved taking Simon back through the review of his-tory to which he had subjected Kirkpatrick at his first interview, starting with the machinations of King Edward VII at the turn of the century, coming finally to the valid point that Britain's policy was always to form a coalition against the strongest power on the Continent and in the short or long term attack it.

He proceeded to the charge levelled against Germany of breaking international treaties, which he could match, he said, with an endless series of broken treaties and violations of international law in British history.

'Certain it is that Germany has not treated any nations like the Boers, the Indians, the Irish [have been treated]. We have had no Amritsar episode. Nor have we created concentration camps for women and children as was the case with the Boers . . .'

All this was the standard Nazi version of history. Hess explained his reason for going into it: so they could lay mutual reproaches aside and 'speak to one another frankly as men'. Nevertheless, he returned at once to the British bombing of the civilian population of German towns. The Führer had continually put off retaliation, and when forced to act had great difficulty in giving the orders for bombing; his heart had ached.

It is not impossible this is how Hitler had presented his decision to Hess, whom he knew had a soft heart and deplored the fight against the wrong foe. There can be little doubt, however, that Hess was aware that the most devastating of all the Luftwaffe attacks on the population of London had been timed to coincide with his own arrival in Scotland. This, indeed, was implicit in his next remarks after Simon, unable to restrain his impatience, for Hess had been talking for the best part of an hour, said he wished to hear his proposals.

'My flight was influenced essentially,' Hess replied, 'the decision to make this flight, by the fact that those around the Führer are absolutely convinced that England's position is hopeless . . .'

They had asked themselves on what grounds Britain was continuing the war, he went on. Their own production of aircraft was so enormous that they had been hard pressed during the winter to find space for all the machines, and the Luftwaffe personnel was equal to the entire British expeditionary force to France. Simon tried to pin him down to numbers, but he would say only that the flying personnel was numbered not in tens but hundreds of thousands.

What had happened to Britain in previous air-raids would be a mere curtain raiser in comparison to what would come. And that was the reason, he wanted to stress it, why he had come over here. It would be unimaginably horrible, an air war of this type in the dimensions it would assume . . .

'Something quite inconceivable, the forms such aerial warfare will take . . .', 'Barnes' translated.

'I hold myself, so to speak, duty-bound as a person to appear here with a timely warning and make the offer I have brought over.'

Hess must have known that the defenceless condition of London and other British cities against air attack and the dire predictions of the Air Staff about the results of bombing had been probably the major factor behind Chamberlain's policy of appeasement in 1938.

Simon asked why, if Germany had something which would defeat Britain straight away, she went on losing men in Crete and Iraq, and other fields. Hess could only reply that he had not said they had these things in their hands already, but they would come. Simon asked him again for his proposals. Hess said he had one more point he would like to make first about the U-boat war; instead he returned to the air war and the losses among the civilian population, stressing that the Germans were as tough as the British. This had been demonstrated in the last war, he said, when the German collapse had come not from the front line but the home front – 'and this internal enemy we have basically eliminated [*ausgeschaltet*]'.

'And this enemy behind the lines has been liquidated,' 'Barnes' translated.[24]

Simon made no response. Perhaps he was merely exasperated by Hess's interminable explanations; perhaps the treatment of Jews and Communists inside the *Reich* was not a question he had been asked to probe. It seems surprising, none the less, after Hess's previous remarks about British concentration camps for Boer women and children and with the knowledge Simon had of what had happened to Jews in the Polish campaign, especially in view of his pre-war distaste for the German treatment of Jews, that he let the remark pass. But that, according to the record, is what he did and Hess went on talking.

'On the contrary, love for the Führer has never been so great among the German *Volk* as it is now.'

After he had been talking for some minutes Simon interrupted again; he had been waiting for two hours, he said, yet he still had not heard a word about the mission he had come down here to learn of. Hess laughed; he would quickly mention the U-boat war. That was the point. Around the Führer they were convinced this was the decisive point for Britain. As he had done for aircraft production he proceeded to describe the vast output of U-boats and the way production had been decentralised; some factories did not even know the parts they were producing were for U-boats. Assembly plants had been moved up rivers far inland. Simon attempted to probe him, as he had been asked, on the damage done by air-raids to the U-boat yards at Kiel and Bremen, but Hess simply countered by saying that aerial photographs did not give an accurate picture of damage and as for reports from agents, they had their own experiences on that score. He went on to point out that the U-boat war had brought the British Isles very close to catastrophe in 1917, when

Germany had only the narrow base of the Heligoland Bight from which to conduct operations; now they had the entire Atlantic coast of France. Moreover, they were convinced that American ship-building capacity could not change the picture; it was not sufficient to make up the British losses. Mention of America led him to point out that the idea that the British could carry on the war from the Empire was false; in such a case Germany would continue the blockade of the British Isles and starve the population; they would not occupy the island since that would mean feeding the people; evidently feeling he might have given something away, Hess added quickly 'presupposing it had not already been occupied'.

Simon asked him again to explain his mission.

'The conditions under which Germany would be ready to come to an understanding with England,' Hess replied, 'I have learned from the Führer during a number of discussions with him . . .', after which he wandered off the point, saying he had deferred putting his plan into effect from the beginning of January until shortly before he had made the flight on account of British successes in North Africa and Greek successes against the Italians.

Simon interrupted him to point to his earlier statement that he had formed the plan during the French campaign the year before.

Without waiting for 'Barnes', Hess agreed, 'Yes, *das ist ganz wahr*' (quite true). He had conceived the plan that June and had attempted to execute it on 17 January this year, but had been unable to do so on account of a series of reasons, weather conditions and so on.

Simon asked him if he came with or without his Führer's knowledge.

'Without his knowledge,' Hess replied in English. '*Absolut!*' and he laughed.

Pressed by Simon as to why he had not come earlier, he described his difficulties in getting hold of an aeroplane and then training on it; his official tasks had not left him much time and there had been the added complication that he had to prevent Messerschmitt knowing what it was about. Ivone Kirkpatrick interrupted to say May had really been the first opportunity. No, Hess replied, it had been possible from December on, but the weather had always been against him. Kirkpatrick said, 'So, what with the postponement because of the weather and the postponement because of Wavell's victories, May really was – '

Hess agreed, 'On May 10th I made the first attempt.'

This is an interesting admission, especially so as an 'Amended Version' of the Simon interview prepared for the legal officers at the Nuremberg trials has this phrase as: 'On January 10th I made my first attempt.'

Why should the British Foreign Office – presumably where this 'amendment' was made – have wished to put the date back four months? Was it on account of the Russian belief that Hess had come over to

261

seek British aid in attacking Russia, or to deflect attention from the date of the negotiations or deceptions that obviously preceded the flight?

Finally, after parrying further probes about whether he had really been sent by the Führer, Hess handed to Kirkpatrick two half-pages of notes he had prepared and gave his word of honour that they represented what the Führer had told him in several talks.

Kirkpatrick read them out in translation: 'Basis for an understanding. One – in order to hinder, to prevent future wars between England and Germany there should be a definition of spheres of interest. Germany's sphere of interest is Europe. England's sphere of interest is her Empire –'

'Europe then means continental Europe?' Simon interrupted.

Hess agreed, 'Continental Europe, yes.'

'Does it include any portion of Russia?'

'European Russia interests us obviously if we, for example, conclude a treaty with Russia, then England should not intervene in any way.'

'Russia which is not Asia – Russia which is west of the Urals?'

'Russia does not interest us –'

'Moscow and all that part, one wants to know, is that part of the European zone?'

'No, not at all.'

Eventually Kirkpatrick was able to move on to the next points, which were much as Hess had expressed them in his first interview – return of German colonies, indemnity for war losses suffered by individuals, and now peace with Italy to be concluded simultaneously – also that the Führer could not leave Iraq in the lurch. Simon pressed for detail – what, for instance, would happen to Holland, Norway, Greece – to all of which Hess replied that the Führer had not pronounced. He returned to the basic point that England should interfere in continental affairs as little as Germany should interfere with the British Empire.

They were able to get no further. Simon, who had concluded by now that Hess was, as he was to put it in his report for Churchill, 'quite outside the inner circle which directs the war' and knew nothing of strategic plans, wound up the interview. Hess made one final attempt to convince him that if Britain did not come to an arrangement now she would be forced to do so later, but Simon took this as a threat and told him they were not very fond of threats in Britain. Hess replied that it was not intended as a threat, but as his personal opinion; that was indeed how he had phrased it.

As his visitors rose to leave he asked Simon if he could have a word in private. Simon agreed and, when the others had gone, Hess began addressing him very earnestly in English; his words were picked up by the microphones concealed in the room and transcribed by a stenographer in the adjoining secret recording-room.

'I have come here, you know, and I appealed to the gallantry of the King of England and the gallantry of the British people here and I thought that the King and the Duke of Hamilton would take me under their protection. I have been very well treated in the hospital and in the barracks in London. I came here and I seemed to be treated well. But not behind me. I have been asked things since I am here if I am sensitive to noises. And I am, because I am bothered by my journey. I had "Oropax" against noise.'

'You mean stoppers in your ears?'

'Yes. The second or third night began in the corridor to my room, my bedroom, noise after noise. I could not sleep the whole night. The following day began noise by motorcycles on the road here and noise by aeroplane continually. When I went to my bedroom to sleep an hour you get noises in the house through doors banging and upstairs, downstairs, upstairs, downstairs, I can't sleep . . .'

Simon assured him very solemnly that his idea of something intentional about the noise was absolutely unfounded, as was his idea that his food was being interfered with, and indeed the notion that the secret service had infiltrated the officers somehow. That sort of thing was simply not done in Great Britain. The delusions were 'childish, idiotic you know'.

'If you will not believe me, I will go off my head and be dead,' Hess said desperately, and after more dismissive remarks by Simon, 'Then I don't eat more in the house.'

'That is very silly of you.'

'I would prefer to die by hunger than because my nerves, my brains distracted – '

'It is perfectly absurd of you – '

'I don't know who. I have no proof, but I know it – '

His English became more excited and ungrammatical as he tried to convince Simon that, if he died here, if he was found with his veins cut, the German people would be convinced he had been killed by the secret service and it would be the definite end of understanding.

He took out the pictures of his son and wife he had brought with him and handed them across. 'Please save me for them. Save me for peace and save me for them.'

He did not trust the new doctor, he went on. Simon revealed that Dicks had only been brought in because it looked as if he (Hess) had some 'nervous psychology' and the new man was a specialist in that branch. He advised Hess to behave like a soldier and a brave man.

'I am a soldier and I have been a brave man, but I have my experiences . . .'

Simon left after a further admonition to show courage; but, as Hess pointed out, he had proved his courage by flying over in the first place.

Dr Dicks found him totally exhausted after the interview and also very hungry. Hess asked Dicks to assure him that no one intended to poison him and got him to shake hands on it, after which, despite having just told Simon he would prefer to die by hunger than go mad, he demolished a dish of cake and asked for more. Colonel Scott recorded in his diary: 'For the rest of the evening he seemed relieved, was somewhat arrogant and truculent and strutted about the lawn after dinner with Major Foley.'[25]

This entry accords with Shephard's report about his behaviour when told he was about to be transferred from Buchanan Castle, suggesting he was not play-acting with Simon so much as exhibiting the egocentricity of a spoiled and not quite balanced child; this ties in with what Karl Haushofer said of him just after the war: 'He has never been quite normal. As early as 1919 he showed suicidal tendencies and a lack of balance. I recall having him sent to our family physician, Dr Bock, who discovered traces of infantilism.'[26] Naive and childish as Hess appeared, he had yet been shrewd enough to deceive the Lord Chancellor as he had already deceived Kirkpatrick and Frank Foley. In his report of the conversation drawn up the next day, 10 June, Simon concluded:

(1) Hess has come on his own initiative. He has not flown over on the orders or with the permission or previous knowledge of Hitler. It is a venture of his own ... When he contemplates the failure of his mission, he becomes emotionally dejected and fears he has made a fool of himself ...[27]

Simon reiterated this later. It was clear that 'Hess's plan is his genuine effort to reproduce Hitler's own mind as expressed to him in many conversations.' More interesting was Simon's second conclusion, which seems to be derived as much from his study of the previous conversations as from his own:

Hess arrived under the impression that the prospects of success of his mission were much greater than he now realises they are. He imagined that there was a strong peace party in this country and that he would have the opportunity of getting in touch with leading politicians who wanted the war to end now. At first he asked constantly to see leaders of opposition and even imagined himself as likely to negotiate with a new government. He is profoundly ignorant of our constitutional system and of the unity of our country. He has constantly asked to have a further meeting with the Duke of Hamilton under the delusion that der Herzog – perhaps because of his rank! – would be the means of getting in contact with people of a different view to the clique who are holding Hess prisoner – i.e. the Churchill Government. His confusion of mind on all this is extreme.[28]

This is surely the clearest indication that Hess was the victim of Masterman's Double-Cross Committee. Simon was almost an impartial observer, certainly outside the inner circle of Churchill's Government and the secret service. This was his objective report from what he had read and heard from Hess's own mouth. Undoubtedly Hess believed that the Duke of Hamilton would be his contact with a powerful opposition grouping, yet he could not have believed it unless fed it by double-cross agents. Albrecht Haushofer had not told him; von Weizsäcker, who saw the ordinary intelligence reports, did not believe in a British capitulation. Only Hess and presumably the other leading members he had initiated into the scheme knew. Hitler had told Mussolini at the Brenner that Churchill would be succeeded by Lloyd George; the following January Hitler was to tell his lunch guests at his East Prussian headquarters, Wolfschanze, 'If Sir Samuel Hoare were now to come to power, as is to be hoped, he needs only to free the Fascists,'[29]

The bare, indeed naive, terms of Hess's proposals are another sure indication that he came not to open talks with a British government capable of negotiation, but to spell out Hitler's mastery of the Continent and indicate to those in Britain who already believed the war lost how Britain might escape the further consequences of her decision to oppose the Führer – he came to talk to the defeatists. His immediate request for Liddell Hart's recent book of essays is an indication of the kind of disinformation with a sub-stratum of truth he must have been fed. All other peace feelers in the files have some discussion of the sort of terms which a British government might be able to accept with regard to Poland, Czechoslovakia, the Low Countries, France. Hess told Simon merely that the Führer had not pronounced on these matters and he himself had not racked his brains over them. Even given the view of his former British hunting companion, Geoffrey Shakespeare, that he was 'a complete amateur' in politics and diplomacy, he would not have risked his life to bring such crass proposals to Britain unless he had been led to believe that a strong body of influential people already advocated such a view – that Great Britain was Germany's natural ally and that her natural role was on the oceans worldwide, leaving the Continent to the continentals, as advocated by Liddell Hart and Russell Grenfell, whose book Hess had also requested.

One of those privy to what Hess had said since his arrival – it is not clear how – was the Lord Provost of Glasgow, Sir Patrick Dollan. The week that Simon visited Hess Dollan decided, apparently on his own initiative, to reveal to the British public the true reason Hess had flown across, and he did so in a series of talks in the Glasgow area – for which he was condemned and ridiculed afterwards by spokesmen put up by the Ministry of Information. He stated Hess had come in the belief that he could stay in Scotland for two days, discuss peace proposals 'with a certain group', and then return to Germany with petrol supplied by his hosts to report on his conversations. One of the threats Hess made, Dollan revealed, was that unless Britain accepted his terms Germany would enter into a military alliance with Russia.[30] Since this is virtually confirmed by Kirkpatrick's suggestion to Simon about drawing Hess on Russia – 'What is the use of conducting a peace of understanding with Germany if Germany is going to sign up with Russia ...?' – it is apparent that Dollan knew what he was talking about. It is interesting, therefore, that after the war he stated that Hess's Me-110 was 'trailed by a New Zealand pilot' as he entered the country, 'who, following instructions, kept him in sight but refrained from attack'.[31]

From everything that is known of Hess, it is virtually inconceivable that he did not tell the Führer the precise information he had and the arrangements he had made. From everything that is known of Hitler, he exacted vengeance after setbacks – usually on the Jews. It may not be coincidence, therefore, that on 20 May, by which date it must have been apparent that Hess had failed, Göring issued a circular – undoubtedly on Hitler's authority, although this cannot be documentarily proved – banning all further Jewish emigration from the Reich and occupied areas, including France; the reason was 'the doubtless approaching final solution [Endlösung]'[32] – the first use of this euphemism for the mass liquidation of the Jewish race in Europe. Later that month Heydrich's right-hand man, Walter Schellenberg, circulated the security police departments in precisely the same terms, the 'zweifellos kommende Endlösung', and on 2 June a decree ordered the internment of all Jews in France.

As for Hess and Simon, if there is a passage omitted from the transcript after Hess referred to the 'elimination' or, as it was translated, 'liquidation' of the internal enemy, and if in this passage Simon asked Hess what he meant by the term, Hess would undoubtedly have explained it away as 'resettling' the Jews in Poland; if pressed, he would have referred to the 'Madagascar Plan' for their ultimate settlement in that island. This was the deception current when he took off from Augsburg; it was the explanation he was to give Lieutenant Malone during July: 'Hitler had decided to banish all Jews from Europe at the end of the war. Their probable destination was Madagascar';[33] it was the story he was able to hide behind for the rest of his life. However, there is no hint in the open files that he so much as mentioned the word 'Jew' during his various 'conversations'. This in itself is strange. It is difficult to believe that Frank Foley at least did not bring up the topic.

When Churchill received the transcripts of 'Jonathan's' harangues to 'Dr

Guthrie', he minuted Eden that they appeared to be 'the outpourings of a disordered mind', and went on: 'They are like a conversation with a mentally defective child who has been guilty of murder or arson. Nevertheless I think it might be well to send them by air in a sure hand to President Roosevelt . . .'[34]

─────── 26 ───────
PSYCHOSIS

Hess's satisfaction evaporated when nothing came of his talk with Simon, and all his suspicions and truculence came back. At the end of the week Colonel Scott recorded him pacing the terrace like a caged lion and refusing to answer when spoken to.[1] That night Hess woke the duty office at a quarter to one in the morning in a very agitated state to ask for Lieutenant Malone. Malone was on guard duty outside, so Dr Dicks went in to see him instead. Hess, who had convinced himself that Dicks was one of the secret service plants out to kill him, confronted him with eyes glowering, fists clenched, shouting, 'I am being undone, and you know it!'[2]

Like Gibson Graham earlier, Dicks formed the definite opinion that his patient had crossed the borderline to insanity.[3] Hess asked to see Colonel Scott. Instead, Scott's adjutant, Lieutenant the Hon. S.J. Smith, who spoke German, went in to see him. He found him 'very drawn and pale, eyes sunk deep in his head . . . in a state of extreme nervousness'.[4]

Hess told Smith he had come to trust Lieutenant Malone and wished to give him certain last letters he had written, as he feared he might not live through the night. Smith replied that Malone was on duty outside, but he could trust him (Smith). Hess said he trusted all members of the guard, but he was in the hands of the secret service and was being poisoned – specifically, the whisky Dicks had brought him the previous night was poisoned. Smith sent the duty officer to get a new bottle, meanwhile drinking from Hess's bottle 'in spite of his clinging to my arm and begging me not to risk my life', he reported.

The new bottle arrived. I opened it and he poured out some for himself and drank it. By this time he was appreciably less nervous. He then went to his bedroom and produced a medicine bottle, on the label of which he had drawn a skull and crossbones, as on all poison bottles in Germany. He said this was a sample of the poisoned whisky. Would I have it analysed privately without the knowledge of the Doctor. I agreed, but again in spite of his protests had a drink from this bottle, after which we had a long and muddled argument centring about the certainty on his part that he was being got at in every way ...[5]

Smith finished the whisky in the medicine bottle and the remainder of the bottle from which it had come, but as Hess continued to insist that he was in the hands of the secret service, and to contradict Smith's assertions that the Guards officers were in full control of all that happened in the house, he adopted 'German parade ground tones', barking he would not be called a liar, *'verstehen Sie!'* Hess jumped to his feet, apologised and shook his hand, and Smith was able to get him to go back to bed. Half an hour later he was snoring.

Smith told Malone afterwards that Hess had 'the mentality of a poorly educated, cheap little clerk' and he was convinced he was mad.[6]

Hess rose late that morning, dressed in his uniform and again asked for Lieutenant Malone; this time Malone was relieved of his perimeter guard duty and went up to him. Hess rose when he appeared and greeted him with a warm handshake – something he had never done before – then launched into a repetition of his allegations about being poisoned to the instructions of a small clique of warmongers who wanted to prevent him bringing about peace; he knew the Guards officers were being hood-winked, he said. When Malone tried to answer his points, he elaborated: after drinking some milk four days before his interview with Dr Guthrie, his head had felt as though clamped in a vice and, when he had tried to write, he found words appearing on the paper he never intended. He believed they were administering a drug of Indian origin to kill him or drive him insane – he thought one of the cooks was involved.[7]

He then handed Malone two letters with envelopes unsealed addressed in pencil to *'Mein Führer'* and Ilse, and asked him to despatch them through official channels as soon as he was dead. Since, he said, he did not believe they would be forwarded, he gave Malone two duplicates to deliver personally at the end of the war. He also handed him his wallet, which contained 'a large number of photographs of his son'. Malone said he would have to report the duplicates and Hess begged him 'in the name of humanity' to keep them secret. He could not do that, Malone replied, but he would ask permission to retain them and, if this were not granted, he would hand them back. Hess thumped his foot on the floor and flapped his arms on the chair arm as he resigned himself to the compromise, but, as Malone left, retrieved the letters from him.

Malone saw him again later that morning and Hess asked him to go to Germany after the war and inform his wife and family he had 'died the death of a brave man'. Malone promised that in the unlikely event of his fears being realised, he would do so. What he did not know was that Hess had decided to commit suicide. Hess explained the decision in a later deposition. If, in spite of all his precautions in eating only from common dishes, the secret service succeeded in administering further quantities of poison, he might lose his nerve completely:

I thought that in view of my position in Germany I could not offer this picture to foreigners, especially I wished to avoid being shown to journalists as an insane person. I decided therefore ... to depart this life of my own free will. I wrote relevant farewell letters in complete calm.[8]

According to Dr Dicks, his letter to Hitler stated the conviction that his 'final mission' would bear fruit and that, 'perhaps despite my death or even because of my death, my flight will have brought about peace and a reconciliation with Britain'.[9]

In the early hours of the next morning he woke the duty officer and told him we was not sleeping well and had taken some whisky. He was in pyjamas. He then returned to his bedroom. Five minutes later he called out from his room to the warder outside the grille, asking him to fetch the doctor as he couldn't sleep. The warder walked the thirty odd feet across the landing to the door of Dicks's room, roused him with the message, then returned to his post by the grille. As Dicks came out in his dressing-gown, holding a bottle of sleeping tablets and approached the grille, the warder slid the bolts back and swung the door out towards him to let Dicks pass. Hess appeared at that moment from the shadows of his bedroom, in full uniform with flying boots, wild despair on his face, 'eyes staring, his hair dishevelled' and charged the opening. Dicks thought for an instant he was about to be attacked, but Hess side-stepped, brushed him away, and rushing to the bannister surrounding the stairwell, vaulted over. As he fell, his left leg caught the stair rail below, taking the force of his descent; there was a heavy thud as his body struck the stone floor of the hall. A warder mounting the stairs with a cup of tea dropped it and drew his revolver. Dicks shouted, 'Don't fire!' Hess lay groaning in extreme pain as Dicks and the others dashed down the stairs to him.[10]

He was fully conscious, pointing to his left thigh and calling for morphia as Dicks took his pulse. A quick examination revealed he was not badly shocked; his thigh was fractured, but he appeared not to have suffered internally. Nevertheless, Dicks did not administer the morphia he was demanding lest it mask signs of abdominal injury; instead he injected distilled water. Hess was not fooled and, in a later deposition, used this as evidence of the plot against him. By this time the other occupants of the house, officers, 'companions' and domestic staff had crowded on the scene, offering pillows, blankets and hot tea. Hess, when not crying out for morphia, took great interest in what was being done for him, according to Dicks's account 'supervising arrangements in a very businesslike manner. His reactions were a curious mixture of schoolboy interest with annoyance at having failed in his attempt and a certain desire to manage other people.'[11]

Foley, meanwhile, called 'C' in London and obtained permission for a surgeon from the nearby military hospital to be called in. The surgeon arrived at five, almost exactly an hour after Hess had taken the flying vault over the bannister and diagnosed an uncomplicated fracture of the left upper femur with no abdominal injury. Dicks recorded Hess's reactions at this point as 'chagrin at having his beautiful breeches cut open with scissors' and 'docile childlike trust in and co-operation with the surgeon'. His leg was put into a temporary splint and he was carried back up to his bedroom, where he was given an injection of morphia.[12]

At ten the next morning Lieutenant Malone relieved the duty officer. Hess was lying in semi-darkness, the curtains drawn, but he was awake and after a short silence he told Malone he had written to his family the day before telling them what he was about to do. He could not be mad in England, he explained. Malone reported:

I said surely you did not intend to kill yourself. He said that he certainly had tried to kill himself and still intended to do so. He could not face madness. It would be too terrible a thing for himself to bear and too terrible for others to witness. In killing himself he would be acting like a man. He knew that recently he had been behaving like a woman. When he first came here he had behaved as a man. 'I got up at eight o'clock in the morning, but then came a period of no sleep, no sleep' and he had begun to go to pieces under the influence of wine and drugs . . .[13]

Malone reminded him that he had promised the Führer he would not take his life. Hess denied it; he had only written that in a letter to the Duke of Hamilton, he said, because he knew that it would be seen and would stop anyone who planned to kill him.

Dicks's chief, Colonel J. R. Rees, Consultant in Psychological Medicine to the Army, came down to see him that evening, after which the surgeon anaesthetised Hess and set the fractured femur. Rees came to see him again two days later, reporting afterwards:

Hess's condition has deteriorated markedly since my first visit [on 30 May]. The delusional tendency which I then noticed has become more marked and more definitely organised so that he now has a delusional idea of poisoning and of a plot against his life and against his sanity which no one can argue him out of. He told me that his suicidal attempt was because he would rather be dead than mad in this country. As is usually the case his delusional ideas are centred on different people at different times. I gather that on Sunday last it was the officers of the guard whom he suspected, whereas on Monday when I talked to him the intelligence officers and Major Dicks constituted the gang who were driving him into insanity . . .[14]

Rees was clear that Hess's condition, which had been 'somewhat masked', had 'now declared itself as a true psychosis' (insanity). He felt there was no form of treatment promising good prospects of success, and thought the outlook rather gloomy for the disease tended towards spontaneous remission, so that a patient appeared perfectly normal for a while until some new stress occurred, 'when he breaks down again into his deluded, mentally hunted condition'. Rees believed that Hess must have had similar attacks previously and concluded that they might have him on their hands as a mental patient permanently.[15]

With Hess's physical injury and the diagnosis of 'a true psychosis' the regime at Mytchett Place changed significantly. He was now super-vised by medical orderlies with mental nursing qualifications rather than the young Guards officers;[16] two of the 'companions' were returned to their duties, 'Captain Barnes' to MI6, 'Colonel Wallace' to the RAF interrogation centre at Cockfosters – leaving Frank Foley as 'C's' only direct representative – and Hess was allowed *The Times* every day. Until then he had been permitted no news unless the 'companions' decided to tell him something. How much these last two changes were consequent on his suicide attempt is not clear. Possibly Cadogan and Stewart Menzies had concluded there was little more information to be squeezed out of him anyway; what, if any, information they already had apart from his slip to Lord Simon in discounting the invasion of the British Isles is not clear. Possibly, however, knowing 'Barbarossa' was about to be launched, Foley wanted to study Hess's reaction. Hess himself had not breathed a word of it. It is possible, indeed, to interpret his delusions as a mask to conceal the information he knew the 'secret service' was trying to extract; if so, it had worked.[17]

Meanwhile, on 9 June, the day he had assured Simon that the Führer had no interest in Russia, Göring had informed both British and US representatives in Stockholm *via* his go-between, Birger Dahlerus, that Germany would attack Russia 'by about June 15th'.[18] Four days later Eden conveyed the warning to the Soviet Ambassador in London – it was only the most recent of scores of warnings Stalin refused to believe.

Churchill had the idea of announcing Hess's broken thigh, but once again Cadogan and Eden dissuaded him, and, as Cadogan put it in his diary, he 'agreed that in regard to H[ess] "Mum's the word"'.[19]

So it remained when the rumours about the whole affair were aired in the adjournment debate in the House on 19 June. Churchill had answered questions about Hess on the 10th: 'I have no statement to make . . .' and to a supplementary, 'I have nothing to add to the answer I have given . . .'[20] Now Rab Butler played an equally dead bat for the Government. When Dollan's statements were raised, that 'Hess arrived in this country expecting to make contact with certain individuals or groups whom he does not venture to name and to be able to go back in two days' time', Butler denied that the Government had authorised the Lord Provost to say this.[21] When Dick Stokes, the Labour member for Ipswich, in favour of a compromise peace, said that he had heard from people who had belonged to various flying clubs on the Continent that 'there is no doubt whatsoever that the Duke of Hamilton knew Hess well to speak to and certainly by sight', Butler said he had nothing to add to the statement made by the Secretary of State for Air.

One interesting rumour was raised by the Labour member for Nelson and Colne, Mr Silverman; it concerned a diplomatic mission Hess had made to Madrid, when it was said he had 'telephoned to someone he knew in Gibraltar to inquire what would happen to him if he were to fly from Madrid to Gibraltar. Apparently according to this report, he was told that if he did try he would be shot down, and for that or for some other reason he evidently decided not to make the venture.' Silverman asked whether Hess had come to propose peace and, if so, whether the Government was afraid that the morale of the people would be affected by knowing it.

While Butler refused to be drawn, Churchill's case was made unofficially from the backbenches by Major Adams, Conservative MP for Leeds West. He set about Dick Stokes, accusing him of identifying himself with the opinions of Lord Londonderry – the former Air Minister popularly believed to be a friend of Göring – whereas, he said, people generally were more favourable to the hawkish views of Lord Vansittart.

'This country is resolute for victory,' he went on.

They know perfectly well that if we allow a strong unitary Germany to emerge in the centre of Europe after the war we are certain within a measurable time to have to face another war. The people of this country are not so stupid as to wish to annihilate the German people, but they wish to obliterate the present German state for the sake of the security of their descendants.

I believe that Hess came to this country under the fond delusion that he could debauch our aristocracy by saying to them, 'Join us or we join Russia'. It seems that he came having in his pocket proposals which might attract the mentality which now wants peace at any cost. There is such a mentality and it is mainly to be found here and there in corners among the well-to-do. Those who have more money than sense, those who whisper the dangerous fallacy, better defeat with our possessions than victory with Bolshevism, which is exactly what Hitler wants them to say. Such an outlook is to be found only half-ashamed in the corners of another place [the Lords]. Appeasement is not dead among those whom I may call for the purpose of rough convenience the Cliveden [Lord Astor's house] set, an expression as historically convenient and geographically inaccurate as the Holy Roman Empire . . .

He went on to berate *The Times*, Astor's newspaper, which, he alleged, would quickly make surrender or compromise appear acceptable, and he advised the Government to examine the records of all those who in the past had treated Germany as some kind of bulwark against Bolshevism. Finally he warned against the two clichés which could still be heard, 'You cannot keep Germany down' and 'The German is not a bad fellow'; 'It is a most unfortunate fact that the majority of Germans at present are rather worse than bad fellows, they are filthy fellows and Hess is one of the filthiest.'[22] These were, of course, Churchill's sentiments.

In the early hours of the following Sunday morning, 22 June, the first anniversary of the French armistice in the Forest of Compiègne, the German armies and Luftwaffe fleets deployed on the eastern front from Poland to the Balkans launched the invasion of Russia. The Red Army and Air Force were caught by surprise, their planes destroyed on the ground, their positions overrun after fearful artillery bombardments. Stalin became paralysed with indecision.

Major Dicks brought the news to Hess's bedroom that morning. 'So,' Hess said with an inscrutable smile, 'they have started after all.'[23]

Whether from the discomfort of his injury or the excessive heat of that midsummer day, or whether he was thinking of his Führer, now embarked on the final stroke for the mastery of Europe and the consummation of all their plans, Hess could neither sleep nor concentrate on reading or writing that day. In the evening the medical orderly in attendance reported him 'not so restless', but sitting 'with a far-away look in his eyes'.[24]

If his mission to remove the pressure from the western front had failed, no doubt he could reflect that the German armies would be in Moscow by late summer or early autumn, after which the 'warmongers' who were hiding him away must see reason or be toppled before US aid could become effective.

For Churchill, and behind him Roosevelt, Hitler's attack was the long-expected, hoped-for deliverance and the fatal mistake. Even if he succeeded in defeating the Red Army and taking Moscow, which the British general staff expected in shorter time than the German generals, he would still become bogged down in the effort of administering the vast regions he had overrun and containing guerrillas, who were bound to take over from the Red Army the defence of Mother Russia. The prime feeling was relief. Churchill had told Jock Colville the evening before that his life was much simplified by having only one purpose – the destruction of Hitler – 'if Hitler invaded Hell he [Churchill] would at least make a favourable reference to the Devil!'[25]

At nine that evening of the 22nd Churchill broadcast to the nation, aligning himself and the Government firmly, not with the Communists whom he abhorred, but with the Russian people defending their homes. He did not conceal his view that Russia might be beaten quickly, but left the impression none the less that Britain's eventual victory was certain. Going to bed that night, he kept on repeating to Colville how wonderful it was that Russia had come in.

In the following weeks, as the *Panzer* spearheads advanced rapidly eastwards and Heydrich's *Einsatzgruppen* of mixed Gestapo, criminal police, uniformed police and SD followed behind executing the political tasks of liquidating Communist functionaries and Jews, Churchill was able to monitor the scale of murder through the 'Ultra' decrypts of their summaries to headquarters. Reports from the Polish underground and other sources fleshed out the statistics in grisly detail, but he and the Ministry of Information remained as silent about the atrocities as about Hess's arrival. He was engaged in a tortuous balancing act: on the one hand he encouraged the Zionists with promises which he could not fulfil for fear of an Arab reaction which would endanger the whole British Middle-Eastern position, and on the other hand, in order to counter the almost universal pro-Axis sentiment of the Arabs, he encouraged Arabs to believe that Britain would support Arab unity. His prime concern was, of course, to ensure that the compact Jewish lobby in the United States worked for American entry into the war, but so delicate was the Middle-Eastern position and so effective was German propaganda in the Arab world that he could not even allow the Jews to raise a division for action against Germany, nor afford to raise the pre-war quotas for Jewish immigrants to Palestine.[26] Although the way was still open through south-east Europe and the Black Sea for thousands of refugees, the British officials in Palestine stuck rigidly to the cardinal principles laid down early in the war that there would be no co-operation with the Germans to enable the emigration of German Jews, no acceptance of Jewish refugees from German-occupied territories; and so effective was their control that Jewish immigration was restricted to about half the agreed schedule.[27]

In pursuit of his single-minded aim to destroy Hitler, and its necessary precondition to bring the United States into the war, Churchill had to woo both Jews and Arabs, but he could neither make his courtship too public nor ever consummate a union. This, too, affected his response to the news of the round-ups and exterminations behind the German armies in eastern Europe. It is a measure of his sensitivity that he instructed Brendan Bracken, his intimate who was to succeed Duff Cooper as Minister for Information, that he was not to bring him news of the slaughter of European Jewry and he gave Eden full authority to determine the Government's policy on this subject.[28]

On 20 July a number of ministerial changes were announced. The chief talking point was Duff Cooper's replacement as Minister for Information by Brendan Bracken; the Hess affair had proved the last straw in Cooper's unhappy time in the post. More interesting perhaps for the background to Hess's mission was Rab Butler's move from Under-Secretary of State for Foreign Affairs to President of the Board of Education. He had been tipped for the post early in the New Year, immediately after Eden had succeeded Halifax as Foreign Secretary. Butler's ideas on foreign policy and on Germany had been absolutely in line with those of his former master, Halifax, whereas Eden was a disciple of Churchill; and, in fact, Butler was never able to take Eden quite seriously.[29] The feeling seems to have been mutual since during Butler's last months at the Foreign Office – after Eden's return from his Mediterranean tour – he had been consigned to the outer periphery of affairs, performing the most clerkish of almost routine tasks and others which were not routine but equally trivial like solving the problem the Spanish Ambassador had with insufficient clothing coupons.[30]

Butler had known about his coming move to education since at least early June; he had recorded thinking about it on 6 June. Churchill had told him, 'I think you can leave your mark there. It is true this will be outside the mainstream of the war, but you will be independent . . .'[31] But why had Churchill left him, as it were, 'in the mainstream' at the Foreign Office for so long ? His performance in the Prytz affair had marked him as unreliable on the vital issue of war or peace; his Personal Private Secretary, Chips Channon was spectacularly unreliable, a notorious pro-German who, on Churchill's accession to power on 10 May 1940, had drunk a toast to 'the King over the water' – Chamberlain – as Jock Colville recorded it in his diary.[32] He is also said to have described Churchill as a 'half-breed American' and 'the greatest political adventurer of modern times'.[33] It is a puzzle, therefore, why Butler with his odd secretary, both of them so obviously incompatible with Anthony Eden and Government foreign policy were not transferred from the Foreign Office immediately after Halifax left, when indeed the first press speculation about such a move appeared. Might it be that Churchill and Eden kept Butler at the Foreign Office as a part of the deception being conducted by Masterman's Double-Cross Committee, aided perhaps by Hoare in Madrid, to suggest that not all Churchill's men were 'diehards'? By early June, when Butler knew he was to be moved, Hess had arrived to propose a settlement; by July, when the move was announced, Hitler had struck east and there was no pressing need to suggest an influential opposition prepared to come to terms. That, of course, is pure speculation.

On the same day, 20 July, that Rab Butler's move was made official, at Mytchett Place Colonel Scott took a new adjutant, Captain Ashworth, Grenadier Guards, up to introduce him to 'Z' as he lay in bed with his leg still encased in plaster and strapped to a 'Balkan frame'. 'He seems to improve every day', he noted afterwards in his diary, 'and one begins to wonder if Colonel Rees and Major Dicks were right in their diagnosis that he is permanently insane.'[34]

Lieutenant Malone, who enjoyed Hess's fullest confidence, noted that 'superficially' he appeared much better and would seem quite normal to anyone unaware of the events of the past weeks; underneath, however, were 'jagged thoughts and treacherous suspicions'. Apart from these signs of paranoia, if such they were, he was obviously not insane. This is clear from Malone's summary of the impressions he had gained over a series of long conversations:

Z's references to relatively unimportant English names, his understanding of background evidenced in conversation, demonstrate that his sources of information about England must have been considerable, that his memory and grasp of detail are excellent, and that he has made a close study of the English scene for a considerable time. He says that his English was only learnt at school but it is far too good and colloquial for this to be true: and his use of peculiarly English phrases indicates recent coaching.[35]

On 26 July the duty officer, Lieutenant Percival, reported that Hess had contradicted his previous statements about his flight and now said that 'members of the government' had known of it. While noting this in his diary, Scott added that it 'appears to have been a misunderstanding on the part of the duty officer'.[36]

Meanwhile, Malone had left Mytchett Place for another posting. Hess, impressed with a new young Guards officer, Lieutenant Loftus, transferred his confidence to him; on the 27th he told him he was the only one in the house he could trust and he had something of momentous importance about his flight to divulge if he would give his word that he would tell no one there. Loftus, acting on Foley's instructions, said he could not do that until he had consulted his father, who was a Member of Parliament and, he stressed, 'a friend of Germany'. This did not please Hess. He had been working for some days on writing a long submission revising his previous statements in the light of Hitler's attack on Russia; he intended to give it to Loftus for secret transmission to his father. Balked by Loftus's refusal to keep quiet, he resumed his previous demands to see the Duke of Hamilton.

Loftus, for his part, had formed an impression of Hess strikingly similar to Geoffrey Shakespeare's: 'I don't think he is a subtle man or a liar. I think he is one of the simplest people you could meet.' He was incredibly vain, he added, and flattery, for instance about his flight, put him in a good humour. His report continued:

Obsessed as he is with his own mission he is incapable of seeing things as they are. I should say his mind is about as virginal as Robespierre's and given the chance he might be as dangerous an idealist, though I doubt whether he has personality enough or eloquence to put it across. He is very courteous in his manners, has a disarming smile and laughs easily. His appearance is slightly spoilt by the teeth of his upper jaw which tend to stick out. He is chiefly remarkable for his eyes which are astonishingly deep-set under pronounced brows and of striking intensity. He speaks passable English but understands everything that is said to him.[37]

On 1 August Hess spent the whole day writing out a fifteen-page 'deposition' detailing the attempts to drug or poison him since he had been at Mytchett Place. It began with the description of the effects of the substance he alleged had been administered in his food and medicines – as quoted previously – 'a curious development of warmth rising over the nape of the neck to the head' followed by many hours of 'an extraordinary feeling of well-being, physical and mental energy, *joie de vivre*, optimism', but leading, if no more of the substance were administered, to 'pessimism bordering on a nervous breakdown'.[38]

The description suggests the effects of the drug LSD. In tests for the CIA in the 1950s changes from exhilaration to the blackest depression, fear of insanity or death were noted in experimental subjects. One biochemist whose after-dinner Cointreau was laced, unbeknown to him, with LSD was soon exhibiting 'psychotic behaviour'; his emotions became unstable 'with abrupt swings from pointless euphoria to equally inappropriate anger or weeping'.[39] Later he developed suspicions that he was being followed and plotted against; later still he ran across his tenth-floor hotel bedroom and threw himself through a window to his death.

LSD was not produced until 1943, two years after Hess's complaints.

Amphetamines, however, had been in medical use since 1938 and they could produce a similar state described as 'paranoid psychosis with ... delusions of persecutions, auditory and visual hallucinations in a setting of clear consciousness'. The major powers were experimenting with so-called 'truth drugs' at this period. The effects of drugs had been brought to international attention by the condition of the victims of Stalin's show trials of 1937 and 1938. These trials had made a great impression on Hess; it is likely, in any case, because of his interest in non-conventional medicines, that he would have kept himself abreast of the latest developments. No doubt he knew that Himmler's doctors used 'Mescalin' on concentration camp inmates; he may have known that the Abwehr used Sodium Thiopental to try to destroy a man's will and make him confess or reveal secrets he was hiding.[40] It is possible, therefore, that when he realised he was in the hands of the secret service – as he assuredly was – he imagined they would administer drugs to break his will and force him to reveal what he knew; and, knowing the effects of such drugs, he imagined suffering them as it were psychosomatically. Alternatively, he may have pretended to believe he was being drugged in the same way he later pretended to lose his memory, either as a subconscious plea for help or as a deliberate step in feigning insanity – although this last does not appear to fit his desperate attempts to convince Lord Simon and the young Guards officers with the momentous importance of his peace mission, nor with his equally desperate attempt at suicide. The other possibilities are, of course, that he was indeed being fed drugs to 'C's' orders or, as the psychiatrists reported, he was a paranoid psychotic.

In his deposition, he specifically denied this:

There is no question of my taking seriously the assertion that I am suffering from a psychosis. I have too much experience behind me for that. If recently I have given the impression that I myself believed in this psychosis it was only because it appeared to me that I should retain more peace ...[41]

This appears to be a confession that there had been at least an element of play-acting in his paranoid behaviour. However, the deposition itself was an apparently logical statement with dates and times, proofs and named witnesses to the incidents he described. While some of the incidents are clearly not attributable to the malevolence of his captors, at this distance in time there is no means of knowing whether the allegations of drugs in his food and medicines constituted a proof of his case or of his psychosis.

The second part of the deposition requested an inquiry into the allegations, to be conducted by persons commissioned by the King, not by the War Office or Prime Minister, further:

that the Duke of Hamilton be given a translation of this statement. That gentleman promised me when I landed that he would do everything to secure my
safety. I know that in consequence the King of England himself has issued appropriate orders ... The Duke of Hamilton may be good enough to ask HM the
King of England to place me in every respect under his protection ...[42]

He concluded by saying that he had come to England trusting in the
fairness of the English people; he would never have thought it possible
he would suffer mental and physical torture, and be 'exposed to the
most terrible experiences of my life'.

After reading the deposition, Major Dicks wrote that his delusion about
his subjective feelings being caused by external agents was 'the hallmark
of the paranoic way of thought'.[43] Dicks had been replaced as resident
doctor some two and a half weeks before, as Hess regarded him as one
of the principal plotters, and only visited on a weekly basis. His successor,
Captain Munro Johnston, agreed with his diagnosis: Hess was exhibiting
a 'marked persecutory delusional system':

He distrusts those in attendance on him, and is convinced poison of a subtle
kind is given in his food and medicine. He claims that this poison affects his
brain and nerves, and is given with the intention of driving him insane. He
explains his attempted suicide by saying it was better to kill himself than become
mad ... On recovery from this [leg] injury, the danger of suicide will again
become imminent, and the present superficial appearance of improvement is
not indicative of any real progress ...[44]

He regarded Hess's 'moody introspection' and the 'bizarre ideas of persecution and torture' evinced in the deposition as indicative of paranoia,
and suggested that he needed the 'care and supervision necessary for
a person of unsound mind with suicidal tendencies'.

If such was the case – and it will be recalled that Karl Haushofer
stated later that his former pupil had shown suicidal tendencies as early
as 1919 – in the matter of his mission he retained a clear mind. This
shows in a forty-five page document he handed to Lieutenant Loftus
on 7 August, asking him to forward it to the Duke of Hamilton. It
began with all his former assertions about the hopelessness of Great
Britain's position due to the U-boats blockade and imminent overwhelming air attack; again he stressed that the picture of the frightful things
to come for England had strengthened him in his decision to fly over,
adding 'We National Socialists regret on hygienic grounds any loss of
blood in the German people but also in the English people.'[45] He meant
'race hygienic' grounds – the loss of the 'valuable' Nordic blood of 'the
two white nations'. And he argued that the longer Britain waited before
the inevitable surrender, the greater her eventual loss of prestige. He

had come, he implied, to allow her to negotiate without loss of prestige:
'My presence in England and the discussions which follow from it can
be the best excuse for a change of course without losing face.'

There was nothing new here. What was fresh and of interest to Foley
and 'Colonel Wallace', who came down to Mytchett Place to read the
exposition, and no doubt to Stewart Menzies, Cadogan and Churchill
when 'Wallace' reported back, was the next section about the Soviet
threat. Hess claimed to have no doubts about Germany's victory, but
posed the hypothesis for the sake of argument that Britain, with the
aid of Russia, finally won:

A victory for England would be equally a victory for the Bolsheviks. The victory
of the Bolsheviks would sooner or later mean their marching into Germany
and into the rest of Europe. The military strength of the Bolsheviks is no doubt
a surprise for the whole world. England is mistaken if she imagines that a German-
Bolshevik war will in any case result in such a weakening of the Bolsheviks
that danger for Europe and the British Empire will be eliminated. Loss of life
plays no part in a country so richly populated. Experience shows that the Bolshevik state can replace losses in manpower in a relatively short time. The Bolshevik
armaments industry must have reached an astonishingly high degree, otherwise
to provide the Army with most modern weapons in such a short time would
not have been possible. But Soviet Russia is no doubt only at the beginning
of her industrial development. Imagine what the military strength of the Bolsheviks will be in the near future if their industries are strongly developed . . .

He supplied the answer: Soviet Russia would become the strongest military power on earth.

Only a strong Germany as a counterweight supported by the whole of Europe
and the confidence of England can avoid the danger. I consider it to be a decision
of fate that Germany has been forced to attack the Bolshevik state at a time
when an understanding of the incipient danger makes it perhaps still possible
to defend civilisation. If this combined defence is not undertaken and if Germany
with the help of her allies is not in a position to stop the danger, the consequences
will be inconceivable, and especially for England . . .

There it was, the long-familiar Nazi appeal to regard Germany as the
European bulwark against Communism and shield of western civilisation.
He was firmly convinced, Hess went on, 'that unless her power is broken
at the last moment Bolshevik Russia will be the world power of the
future which will inherit the world position of the British Empire'.

This warning, which was to be borne out in part – and without the
halt imposed by nuclear weapons might have been borne out in full
– which appealed and was meant to appeal to significant strands of British
imperial thinking, probably reached the ears of Lord Beaverbrook, who

was due to fly to Moscow for talks about war materials with Stalin. On 1 September he wrote to Hess reminding him of their 'last meeting in the Chancellery in Berlin' and suggesting another conversation.[46] Hess replied four days later that, 'in recollection of the meeting in Berlin', he was delighted to be able to see Beaverbrook again.[47]

He had sunk into deep depression after the failure of his latest attempts to break through the secret service to those groups he still felt certain would be sympathetic to his proposals. In view of the fact that his splint would soon be removed and he would be able to get about again, it had been decided to refurbish his suite as a mental hospital ward with armoured glass in the windows,[48] a clear indication that, whatever the cause of his moods, he was regarded as a suicide risk. Nearing the date fixed for Lord Beaverbrook's visit, 9 September, he showed all the signs of agitation he had before his interview with Lord Simon, and busied himself with another long statement of his proposals, headed this time 'Germany-England from the viewpoint of the war against the Soviet Union'.[49]

Beaverbrook, with a pass made out in the name of Dr Livingstone, arrived in the early evening of the 9th and was shown up to Hess's room at 7.30.

'How well your English has improved,' he said after greeting him.[50]

'A little,' Hess replied, 'not very much.'

'A lot. You remember the last time we talked in the Chancellery in Berlin?'

Were these repeated references to the last meeting in Berlin to cover a more recent meeting since Hess's arrival in May, or merely conversational pieces to break the ice?

After some further remarks about Hess's English – which he had to use throughout the talk as there was no interpreter – Beaverbrook lamented that they had come to a bad pass. Hess agreed. Beaverbrook then said he had been very much against the war.

'Me too, I know it,' Hess replied.

'You too, yes – very sorry to see it come about, very sorry indeed. I regretted it greatly. I tried my best for my part to escape ... Now it's become terribly complicated – it's become such an extraordinary combination of complications that it's awfully difficult to see what can be done about it ...'

Beaverbrook rambled on. His aim, like Simon's, was to draw Hess into revealing secrets.[51] Hess warned him that England was playing a very dangerous game with Bolshevism.

'Yes,' Beaverbrook replied, 'I can't myself tell why the Germans attacked Russia, I can't see why.'

'Because we know that one day the Russians will attack us.'

'Will attack Germany ?'

'Yes.'

'It was really the intention to destroy the Russian machine, the Russian war machine ?'

'Yes, Russian machine. And it will be good not only for Germany and the whole of Europe, it will be good for England too if Russia will be defeated.'

Beaverbrook tried to find out how much Hess knew of the Russian armaments industry. Hess said, correctly, that before attacking Russia they had known nothing, it had been 'quite silent'. Beaverbrook returned to the puzzle of the German attack; surely they must have said to themselves, 'First of all we must finish the war with England.'

'But we had been sure that Russia would attack us before that,' Hess replied. 'It's quite logical.'

After more probing about Russian arms production, Beaverbrook said, 'You think Russia will emerge from the war beaten, but in a short time recover and become stronger ?'

'Stronger, I am quite sure,' Hess lied, knowing it was Hitler's intention so to destroy the existing order and 'Germanise' eastern Europe that she could never rise again.

Beaverbrook moved on to another tack. Earlier in the talk Hess had asked him to get permission for the Duke of Hamilton to visit him as he was the only man who was, so to speak, a friend of his here even though, he said, he didn't know him very well; Beaverbrook now asked him if he had other friends in England besides the Duke.

'No, I have no – '

'Except me !'

'No. But you are here.' Hess laughed. 'You will become one.'

Beaverbrook grunted. Shortly afterwards he left with the sheaf of handwritten pages Hess had prepared, promising to come and see him again after his return from Moscow – a promise he was not to fulfil.

He had extracted nothing of value from the talk, as he confessed to Colonel Scott afterwards. But, he said, he found it very hard to believe that 'Z' was insane.[52]

Later Hess managed to have a copy of his deposition about the drugs and poisons he was being subjected to sent to Beaverbrook, who forwarded them to the Foreign Office. Cadogan replied: 'I need hardly say that Hess's accusations that we have been maltreating him are without the slightest foundation . . . some of his delusions have become a complete obsession.'

Beaverbrook did not swallow it. Two years later, in early September 1943, he was to tell Bruce Lockhart he thought Hess had probably been given drugs to make him talk.[53] Years later he told James Leasor he believed Hess was sane.[54] In his talk with Bruce Lockhart he told him he believed Hess had been sent by Hitler to gain a free hand against Russia, with the proviso that he would be disowned if anything went wrong; he thought Hess had meant to land in Scotland unbeknown to anyone, burn his aeroplane and find the Duke of Hamilton. When his plan misfired, he had tried to commit suicide to save his honour. What Beaverbrook did not say, or what Bruce Lockhart omitted to record in his diary, was why Hess and Hitler should have imagined the Duke of Hamilton would help. It is so obvious a question it suggests Beaverbrook was holding something back.

27

DISINFORMATION

As Hess recovered the use of his leg that winter of 1941, his mental state deteriorated alarmingly, or so it appeared; he complained of headaches, eye and stomach pains and was seen by his medical attendants to hallucinate, waving his hands and whispering in the direction of blank walls. His obsession with poison in his food became acute and he wrapped his papers in layer upon layer of tissue, each stuck down and signed, to prevent the secret service prying,[1] so he explained to Foley. Scott recorded in his diary he 'even suggested that the carpenter, poor old Moxham [fitting the armoured glass in his windows], was a secret agent in disguise,[2] and on 4 December he told the surgeon treating his leg that he was losing his memory.[3]

This malaise occurred before 7 December, the date of the Japanese attack on Pearl Harbor which crowned Roosevelt's strategy for bringing the United States into the war, for Hitler immediately fulfilled a pledge to Japan by declaring war on America. This should have marked the end of any lingering hopes Hess retained; it was what his mission had been designed to prevent, full-scale world war in which Germany was sandwiched between the huge space and manpower resources of the Soviet Union and the equally immense economic industrial and naval power of the western democracies.

Certainly Scott recorded that Hess was 'in a very bad state' next day, and on 9 December, although 'a little better' he was 'in an exhausted state and rather tearful'. What his views were on Pearl Harbor is not recorded, but it appears from what he told the Swiss Minister, Walther Thurnheer, three days later that he had not given up hope for his mission.

He had asked to see the Minister, so he told Thurnheer when he called, because he had heard on the wireless that his father had died; he wanted Thurnheer to witness a new will he had made. Then he explained that this was only a pretext. He wanted him to contact the Duke of Hamilton and to deliver an important statement to the King. Thurnheer replied that as he was not an ambassador he had no right of access to the King. Hess nevertheless wrote a long letter to His Majesty while Thurnheer waited, explaining, so he told him, that he had come in the hope of making peace, but had not been given the right opportunities; he was convinced his peace plan could still achieve something if only he could establish contact with the right people. He folded the five-page letter and placed it in an envelope Thurnheer produced bearing the seals of the Swiss Legation and the British Government. The letter concluded by saying he had come to Great Britain unarmed, at the risk of his life to try and end the war, trusting in the fairness of the English people, and he was counting on the fairness of the King. With the letter he enclosed a longer statement of complaint about his treatment. According to Thurnheer's report to his Government, Hess said he would not bother him with details of this; according to Foley, who was of course listening to every word in the recording-room, he 'brought up all the usual poisoning suspicions. He complained that he suffered from intestinal trouble, loss of memory and broken nerves', but, when the Minister asked him if he had any real cause for complaint he said he had not.[4] 'I may say', Foley concluded his report, 'the Minister gained the impression that Jonathan was suffering from delusions.'

By April 1942, when Thurnheer came to see him again, reporting that the Duke of Hamilton had refused to have anything to do with him (Hess), and the best he had been able to do with the letter was hand it to the King's private secretary – he had had no reply from His Majesty – Hess had begun to specify the Jews as the power behind the attempts to poison him.[5] He did not tell Thurnheer this, but he handed him samples of wine and pills which he thought contained this poison – whether it was the well-known Mexican herbal poison he could not say – and asked him to have them analysed and send a report to the German Government so that they could take reprisals on British generals whom they held. Thurnheer left convinced, according to the Army psychologist J. R. Rees, that Hess was deranged.[6]

Hess's memory was working well enough in June for him to send birthday greetings – since the post was taking months – to his 'highly-esteemed and dear friend', Karl Haushofer. Neither in this nor an earlier letter to Haushofer was there a trace of persecutory delusions; indeed, he told Haushofer not to worry about him:

Naturally my present situation is not especially pleasant. But in war people are more often fated to find themselves in not very pleasant situations. That is assuredly not the point! What the point is in the longer term, you know best of all – and in this connection you can certainly be reassured!

You will, I assume, have received from friend Pintsch the letter I left behind for you then [May 1941]. I freely admit it was not very logical to pitch such a letter in a lighter tone – in order somewhat to cushion the shock – and then to enclose a copy of the much more serious letter to the Führer. But meanwhile more than a year has passed and you have all come to terms with that which is!

Often I think of the seminar with the late Bitterauf and the paper I read on Gneisenau. You took an interest in it, as in so much that concerned me.

> Let the waves in thunder roar,
> Life or death may be your lot –
> Whether wrecked or safe to shore,
> Ever stay your own pilot.

It cannot be disputed that I am wrecked. Just as little can it be disputed that I was my own pilot. vvv. In this connection I have nothing to reproach myself about. vvv. At all events I have steered. You certainly know as well as I that the compass we steer by is influenced by forces which, even if we do not understand them work imperturbably.

May they be friendly to you in the coming year!

Ever yours   RH

Please call Harlaching some time to say I am in good health.[7]

In his earlier letter, written the previous September, five days after Beaverbrook's visit, he had recalled Haushofer's astonishing dream in which he had described seeing him striding through tapestried halls bringing peace to the two Nordic nations, and he had been unable to reveal that he was about to attempt just that. 'One day the last part of your dream, so dangerous for my plan [then], will be fulfilled', he had written, 'and I will stand before you again – the only question is when!'[8]

His early letters to his wife equally lacked self-pity or persecutory delusion, were equally philosophical about the wheel of fate.[9] In a statement about his imprisonment which he made towards the end of his time in Great Britain – admittedly sounding as if he had indeed become deranged – he confirmed that his loss of memory, although not his fear of poison, had been assumed: 'The people around me put more and more peculiar questions to me, touching upon my past. My correct answers evidently caused disappointment. However, loss of memory, which I simulated, gradually caused satisfaction . . .'[10]

Hess was undoubtedly odd; whether he was deranged is a different question. It seems as likely from the evidence of his early letters to Ilse, Karl Haushofer and Dr Gerl, and from Beaverbrook's impressions, that he was quite sane and to a large extent play-acting for his British captors. Major Shephard, it will be recalled, had characterised him as 'cunning, shrewd and self-centred . . . very temperamental and will need careful handling if he is to be outwitted . . .' Colonel Scott had described him acting like a spoilt child. There is no doubt he fooled all his interrogators about the extent of his knowledge of Hitler's plans as he fooled them into believing he had come on his own initiative. It seems at least probable that his 'psychosis' was another performance – one which he thoroughly enjoyed. There was little else he could enjoy. Unlike other prisoners of war, he had no fellows to talk to; his 'companions' and attendants were the enemy. By pretending to find poison, by gesturing to blank walls, wrapping his papers in layer upon layer of tissue, stuck down and signed, feigning loss of memory, he could take control of his situation, rather like a precocious child imposing itself on its elders, making them notice him and dance to his tune. It may be imagined he fell into the act gradually after perhaps genuine fears for his safety and a genuine suicidal depression after the humiliating failure of his mission; it would have appealed to his sense of the absurd. It would have been in character. One can imagine the laughter vvvs had he been able to describe his performance in letters home.

From the other side there is the question of what the 'companions' were really probing. Undoubtedly in the early weeks it was anything concerning Hitler's plans to attack Russia or to invade Great Britain, together with general information about war production, bomb damage to German production facilities and morale. It was soon concluded, of course, that he had not been in Hitler's inner circle and knew little. On 19 and 20 June, just before Hitler attacked Russia, 'Colonel Wallace' and 'Captain Barnes' had been withdrawn, but Foley remained. Evidently Cadogan and 'C' still hoped Hess might let something out, otherwise Foley's valuable expertise was wasted. Since Hitler had attacked Russia and Hess had more or less revealed to Simon that the invasion of Britain was not contemplated, they were probably seeking clues about secret weapons. This is virtually confirmed by an entry in Colonel Scott's diary for November 1941 after one of the Guards officers had dined with Hess: ' . . ."Z" on being questioned about Germany's "secret weapons" said that he knew there was one but he had no idea what it was, but that Hitler would not use it except as a last resort.'[11]

It will be recalled that Hoare had reported Ribbentrop's agent, Gardemann, stating that Great Britain would be attacked 'between June 15th and July 15th [1941] with new destruction methods so terrible and deadly that everything done hitherto will seem mere child's play'. Hess had given similar apocalyptic warnings in his interviews with Kirkpatrick and Simon, although without precise dates, indeed with Simon he had said the means was not yet to hand. New 'terrible and deadly' destruction methods suggested an atomic bomb.

The possibility that Hitler's scientists would develop such a weapon before the British or Americans was a nightmare that concerned both Roosevelt and Churchill. German scientists had split the uranium nucleus before the war and had gone into the war with an office for the military application of nuclear fission. Albert Einstein, who had done his seminal work as a German before emigrating to America, had warned Roosevelt even before the outbreak of war of the danger of the Nazis developing an atomic bomb first.[12] Frank Foley had been involved personally in the nightmare insomuch as he had flown twenty-six canisters of heavy water – the moderating agent essential to the German line of nuclear research – from Norway during the invasion and had done the same from France before the fall of Paris.[13] This surely was his concern when he talked to Hess, and the reason he stayed on at Mytchett Place. It was a concern which might have been thought to justify the use of almost any methods and, although MI6 did not have a pharmacological department at the time, they might easily have called in outside experts. Beaverbrook, who probably knew rather more than he ever told, may have been right in his suspicion, as conveyed to Bruce Lockhart, that Hess 'was probably given some kind of drugs by our people to make him talk.'[14]

In fact German scientists were not ahead. When, on 4 June 1942, Albert Speer, Minister of Armaments, chaired a conference on the question in Berlin and offered considerable resources for nuclear development, the spokesman for the scientists, Werner Heisenberg, had to confess he would not know how to use them. Five days later Paul Rosbaud, Frank Foley's pre-war scientific contact in Berlin, flew to Oslo and passed on the news to his sis contact there: German research into nuclear weapons remained at a preliminary stage; minimal resources had been allotted.[15]

On 26 June Hess was moved from Mytchett Place far away to South Wales, into a ground-floor suite in Maindiff Court, formerly the admission clinic for a mental hospital at Abergavenny. The move may have had nothing to do with the intelligence Paul Rosbaud had brought to Norway. Earlier, fears had been expressed that perhaps the Geneva Convention on Prisoners of War was being strained by keeping Hess so near to military targets in and around Aldershot. Alternatively his health and obvious sensitivity to noises from the Army training grounds may have begun to cause serious concern. The precise reason for his move at that time does not appear in the open files. But it is possible he was moved because the reassuring news about German atomic developments meant he was of no further interest to Churchill or 'C'. That is speculation.

The Double-Cross Committee, for which Foley was of course a senior adviser, had not lost interest in Hess – or so it appears from a remarkable report Heydrich had sent Ribbentrop that May. It had come *via* one of his confidential agents from an Englishman who had been brought up in Germany, so Heydrich wrote, who had outstanding connections in influential English circles and who knew Hess personally. This could have referred to a number of English people who had patronised the same natural health clinics as Hess before the war. The Englishman had told Heydrich's agent:

... on the express wish of Hess and with Churchill's permission, he had spent four days in London with him [Hess] the previous December. Hess was lodged in a villa in Scotland, had his personal servants and lacked nothing. Churchill had expressly decreed that Hess, on account of his rank as ss-Gruppenführer, should be accommodated as a General. On the agent's question whether the Englishman had had the impression that Hess was perhaps somewhat confused in his mind, he received the answer that he, the Englishman, had not gained this impression. Hess enjoyed the best of health, was intellectually very lively and was very concerned, for one thing over the destructive fratricidal war between the best white races, for the other over the great losses in valuable human material allegedly caused the Germans by the enemy in the east . . .'[16]

They had roamed London at will, the Englishman had said, both he and Hess in dark glasses, and he had shown Hess everything he wanted to see. On parting Hess had enjoined him to co-operate in bringing about peace as soon as possible.

Heydrich's agent and the Englishman had then discussed several other questions, from which the aims of the Double-Cross Committee – if it was indeed the prime mover – seem to emerge. One point the Englishman stressed as of great concern to his countrymen was the Japanese success in the east, and the danger of a Japanese-Chinese-Indian bloc, rich in raw materials and cheap labour which would be a danger for the white races. Germany and Great Britain needed to unite quickly to save the predominance of the white races in Asia, although he, the Englishman, saw no possibility of that at present. He had gone on to itemise three most damaging things for Germany. Firstly the Jewish question, which would have to be solved internally rather than by allowing the Jews out of the *Reich*, where they would use their money and their connections systematically against Germany. No doubt this was included to establish the Englishman's correct viewpoint. Secondly the bombing of London was a mistake, as it was awakening feelings of hate for Germany not present before. Thirdly, the Englishman had said, the unbelievable corruption in Germany was well-known abroad and damaging to her reputation.

Ribbentrop asked for more details about the source before he laid

the report before Hitler.[17] Heydrich had been assassinated in the meantime, so Schellenberg obliged: the agent had been an Englishman who
had had 'exhaustive discussions with Rudolf Hess, Winston Churchill,
Eden, Greenwood and influential representatives of the Labour Party'.[18]
It is probable Ribbentrop sent the report to the Führer's headquarters,
for it is certain that an Abwehr agent with a high ss rank visited Hess's
elderly aunt, Frau Emma Rothacker, in Zurich that summer saying he
was on a commission from the Führer to photocopy all the letters she
had received from Rudolf Hess.[19]

It is conceivable, although perhaps far-fetched even for Heydrich's
extraordinary mind, that the report on Hess sent to Ribbentrop did not
originate in the Double-Cross Committee, but in Heydrich's own Prinz
Albrechtstrasse headquarters in Berlin, and was intended to leak to the
Russians to cause dissension between Stalin and Churchill. Stalin had
been suspicious about Hess ever since his arrival in Scotland and the
official silence had enveloped him – as indeed Roosevelt had been.

That autumn of 1942 two further stories were spread about Hess, one
certainly from German sources, the other probably. The probable one
was that negotiations were under way for Ilse Hess to join her husband
in Great Britain. Rumours to this effect started at least as early as October;
they appeared so well founded that the Swiss police kept Hess's other
aunt living in Zurich, Helene Hess, under surveillance as a possible link
between the German and British sides in this alleged negotiation[20] –
and no doubt watched Emma Rothacker as well. As developed later,
the story had Ilse making the journey to England and staying with Hess.
This was negotiated, so it was said, by Baron von Schröder – who had
negotiated Hitler's accession to power – representing German heavy
industry worried about the turn the war had taken, and his British and
French colleagues at the Bank of International Settlements in Basle; the
object, to send new peace proposals to England with Ilse Hess, who
was desperate to see her husband.[21] There is no doubt from Ilse's letters
to Himmler that she was indeed desperate to see her husband; but she
wanted the *Reichsführer* to get him home for her. Nor is there much
doubt that British bankers continued to meet their German counterparts
at the Bank of International Settlements. Otherwise there was no truth
in the story.

The other provocation, undoubtedly from German sources, was published in the Swedish paper *Dagsposten* in early October. Announcing
that the time was now ripe to lift the veil of secrecy over Hess, the
Dagsposten stated that his flight to Scotland had not been his own sense-
less idea, but part of Hitler's considered policy to gain peace with Great
Britain and induce her to conclude an alliance with Germany against
the Soviet Union.[22] The anti-Nazi emigré paper, *Die Zeitung*, published

in London, reported this story on 9 October, adding that it agreed 'not only in essentials but also in numerous details with the interpretation given by *Die Zeitung* earlier', and added that well-informed observers in London believed *Dagsposten*'s version was on the whole correct.[23] When Cadogan read the cutting, he minuted that he did not know who the 'well-informed political observers' were, but he was quite sure they were not 'well informed'.[24] Beaverbrook, on the other hand, certainly held the view of Hess's mission given by *Dagsposten*, as he told Bruce Lockhart the following autumn and related to James Leasor long after the war.

Recent disclosure of the Soviet NKVD files on Hess, supposing they are genuine, reveal that Stalin had just received a report from the chief of Czech Intelligence in London, Frantisek Moravetz, stating that Hess's arrival in Scotland had not been the unexpected event depicted, but had been preceded by a correspondence between Hess and Hamilton covering all details of the flight. Hamilton himself had not participated, however: 'All Hess's letters . . . were intercepted by the Intelligence service where the answers to Hess were also elaborated in the name of Hamilton. In this way the Britons managed to lure Hess to come to England.'[25]

Moravetz stated that he had seen this correspondence himself, and Hess's letters 'clearly represented [that] the objectives of the German government were linked with the plans of their attack on the Soviet Union.' This claim appears to invalidate the report. If Hess had not given away Hitler's aim to attack Russia while under interrogation in Britain, why should he have revealed this highest state secret in prior letters liable to interception? Thus Moravetz's story, also to be found, it will be recalled, in the papers of his political chief, Benes, is difficult to believe completely. But of course the Soviets, already deeply suspicious, did believe it.

Stalin reacted on 19 October. *Pravda* published a savage article suggesting that Great Britain had been transformed into an asylum for gangsters, and demanding Hess's immediate trial as a war criminal.[26] The article was repeated on Moscow radio and even published in London in *Soviet War News*. After making a strong protest, the British Ambassador in Moscow, Sir Archibald Clark Kerr, reported back theories about Hess held by the Russian Government. One was that Hess had been in touch with influential Englishmen before his flight who had told him that 'if he came on a special embassy with certain proposals His Majesty's Government would not only make peace but would join in a crusade against Bolshevism'; this group of Englishmen, who had not been exposed by Churchill because they were so powerful, still thought it possible to come to an agreement with Hitler. Another theory was that the British Government foresaw the day when it would suit them to come to an agreement with Hitler, and they were keeping Hess up their sleeve as his plenipotentiary. The Russians were deaf to all the obvious counter-arguments, Clark Kerr reported, and they asked, 'Why, if such ideas are not justified, is there any mystery about Hess?'[27] He assumed, and he was no doubt correct since this was also the view of German intelligence, that Stalin's suspicions were related to his frustration that the western Allies had not launched the so-called 'second front' in west Europe to take the pressure off the Red Army.

Churchill took a firm line, minuting to Eden that 'it would be a great mistake to run after the Russians in their present mood; and still less to run around with them chasing a chimera . . .'[28] He agreed to a proposal that Stafford Cripps, former Ambassador in Moscow, should prepare a report on the whole Hess episode for possible transmission to the Russians. In the meantime, Clark Kerr was instructed to point out to Stalin that Lord Beaverbrook had given him a full account of the affair the previous September and he had seemed satisfied and amused; there had been no change in the British Government's attitude since.

The United States Government supported Churchill by coming out against the Russian demand for Hess's immediate trial, stating publicly that it was impractical to treat the question of trying war criminals piecemeal.[29] This helped Eden to take a strong line in response to questions in Parliament, but, as with former Government replies on Hess, he gave no explanation for the flight or what Hess had said since his arrival. Stafford Cripps's report, completed early in November, gave the officially accepted version – that Hess had come on his own initiative expecting to find a strong anti-war opposition party, and had attempted to reproduce Hitler's mind here – but this was not published; only a summary was sent to Moscow to satisfy Stalin.[30]

Official secrecy was preserved, for Stalin was asked not to publicise the contents of the memorandum. However, on 3 November, the day before it was wired to Clark Kerr, disinformation was leaked in an obviously mendacious interview given by the former Lord Provost of Glasgow, Sir Patrick Dollan, to the *Daily Mail*. Dollan said that Hess had come over bringing Hitler's terms to those in Great Britain who were inclined towards a compromise peace; the terms included the return of all Germany's former colonies, the surrender of part of the fleet and air force – leaving only sufficient to defend the British Isles – the payment of war damages and recognition of Hitler as 'Overlord' of Europe and 'Dictator' of Great Britain, which would become in effect a German colony; Hess himself would be Hitler's 'Protector' in Britain.[31] It was a different story to that which Dollan had given his audiences around Glasgow a few weeks after Hess's arrival. Perhaps it was felt that, if Stalin did not believe Cripps's memorandum, he would at least realise that Great Britain could not submit to such terms. If so, it showed ignorance of the extent to which the British security services had been subverted. Stalin knew more about the affair than the British public or members of parliament.

The following spring, 1943, there was another sensational exposure: 'The Inside Story of the Hess Flight', published in the May edition of the popular monthly journal *American Mercury*, and condensed in July in *Reader's Digest*.[32] The *Mercury's* editor declared 'full faith' in the article's sources and vouched for the anonymous author as a 'highly reputable observer'. The author himself referred to 'reliable information since obtained from German sources and from indications given by Hess himself'. Like Dollan, like the Russian ministers whom Clark Kerr had spoken to in Moscow, the article stated that Hess had flown to Scotland on Hitler's express orders and, far from being a surprise, his arrival was expected by a limited number of people; indeed he had an RAF escort on the final stage of his flight. Dollan made the same claim after the war.[33]

Preliminary negotiations, the article stated, began in January 1941, when an eminent, internationally known diplomat had brought an inquiry from Hitler about the British attitude to negotiations, addressed not to the British Government, but to an influential group including the Duke of Hamilton. This calls to mind Hess's first meeting with Albrecht Haushofer, during which he had suggested finding out the Duke of Hamilton's whereabouts so that 'a neutral acquaintance . . . could seek him out and arrange something . . .' The article went on to state that this initial communication brought by the internationally known diplomat personally had not reached its destination, but had been intercepted by the secret service.

From then on the correspondence was handled entirely by astute British agents. Replies designed to whet the German appetite, replies encouraging the German supposition that Britain was seeking a way out of its military difficulties, were sent to Berlin. The hook was carefully baited . . .

The German side first proposed negotiations on neutral soil, the article went on, but the secret service, using the names and handwriting of the Duke of Hamilton and other former members of the Anglo-German Fellowship Association, rejected that. Berlin then proposed sending a delegate to England and selected Ernst Bohle, chief of Hess's Foreign Organisation. Here, the remarkable fact of the preparations at Lympne aerodrome, Kent, for the reception of Hitler's Condor aircraft flown by Baur, may be recalled – preparations which had been called off at the end of May 1941 – after Hess's arrival. However, according to the article, the British side failed to react positively and Hitler decided Hess should go. There followed, the article stated, a long delay in replying. 'Possibly the imperturbable British required some time to recover from their astonishment.' Finally an acceptance came through, details were arranged, and on 10 May Hess took off on his mission. A reception committee of Military Intelligence officers and secret service agents waited at Dungavel House for Hess to land on the Duke's private strip, but, instead, he parachuted down twelve miles away, and it was this hitch in the plan, the article suggested, which caused the sensational news to be broken to the world; otherwise it might have been kept under cover for a while, if not for the duration.

The article named Ivone Kirkpatrick as the man whom Churchill selected to fly to Scotland to interview Hess – although this was not public knowledge – and described the stenographic record of Hess's peace proposals filling many notebooks. It was also correct in describing Hess as 'optimistic, since he was fully convinced that Britain was licked' and his tone as that of 'a munificent enemy offering a reprieve to a foe whose doom was otherwise sealed'. However, the terms it suggested Hess had brought were not those reported by Kirkpatrick or Hamilton; they were the German evacuation of France except for Alsace-Lorraine, and of Holland, Belgium, Norway, Denmark, Yugoslavia and Greece, in return for which Great Britain was to adopt an attitude of 'benevolent neutrality towards Germany as it unfolded its plans in Eastern Europe'.

Hess, the article stated, had refused to be drawn on Hitler's military plans, but had explained the importance of the eastern mission and pro-mised that Germany would take the full production of British and French war industries until they could be converted to a peacetime basis, thus in effect proposing the use of western arsenals to crush Bolshevism. He had represented Hitler as a humanitarian anxious only to stop the sense-less war with a brother nation.

The article went on to state that Churchill had communicated these proposals to Roosevelt, who agreed with his decision to reject them; both had felt that, as open discussion of such a sensational offer was undesirable, 'the insanity explanation fed to the German people would also suffice for the rest of the world'. They had tried to warn Russia of the coming blow, but the Russian leaders would not believe it and certain Soviet diplomats had insisted the warnings were democratic tricks.

This reference to Stalin's failure virtually rules out a Communist source for the article. The reference to Hitler – not simply Hess – having been fooled by the British secret services rules out a German source. The extraordinarily generous terms Hitler was said to have offered, Churchill and Roosevelt to have rejected, points to British or American sources, the aim obviously to defuse Stalin's suspicions by granting his assump-tions about the secret service trap, but stressing that both the western leaders had resisted Hitler's tempting offer to join a crusade against Bolshevism.

The concluding paragraphs of the article suggest, and it may be thought conclusively, that the inspiration was from British sources – no doubt Churchill's Minister of Information and confidant, Brendan Bracken – for the Duke of Hamilton's honour was upheld in a statement that was factually incorrect – 'neither Hamilton nor any of the others had known anything about the Hess visit until all England knew of it' – and the sis was held up as a paragon:

This was not the first time England reduced a German stronghold by audacious secret service work ... there is no doubt that when the whole story can be told the achievements of that Secret Service will astound the world. And the Hess episode is certain to stand out with a glory of its own among them.

Thus far, although the astounding operation of Masterman's Double-Cross system has been made known, justifying the superlatives in this concluding paragraph, secret service involvement in Hess's flight has not been admitted; there is, therefore, no means of knowing how much truth and how much fiction was seeded in the *American Mercury* account of the preliminary negotiations.

That August Brendan Bracken spoke about the affair in America, admitting both that Hess had flown over 'expecting to find quislings who would help him to throw Mr Churchill out and make peace'[34] and that the Duke of Hamilton had met Hess before the war – in effect contradicting Sinclair's statement in the House of Commons.[35] There followed on 1 September a more sensational disclosure in, once again, the *Daily Mail*: 'The Story all Britain has awaited':

THE DAILY LIFE OF HESS IN PRISON CAMP
How he acts, talks and thinks

The reporter, Guy Ramsey, described Hess living in his wing of Maindiff Court 'set among gracious trees and bright with flower borders that edge the building' as a 'borderline case', indeed 'a borderline case before he left Germany'. Ramsey suggested that, although Hess loved Hitler, he had found the other Nazi leaders too hard, and 'the strain of opposing his waning influence to their growing one set up in him a terror that developed into an obsession'. Medically speaking, Ramsey went on, Hess was a paranoiac, 'hearing voices which do not exist ... fearing poison in his meals'.

From the Foreign Office file on this leak it appears that an officer guarding Hess was arrested for talking to the *Mail* and was to be court-martialled. David Irving has pointed out that one officer's name does indeed disappear from the records at Maindiff Court at this time,

Lieutenant May.[36] It seems more likely, since the newspaper's editor risked printing the story, that it was a deliberate leak, again inspired by Brendan Bracken. The exaggerated account of Hess's loss of nerve before he left Germany points to deliberate disinformation, as does a later almost contradictory passage about why Hess came: 'He maintains that his idea in coming to Britain was entirely his own ... His aim was to find quislings who would make some sort of patched up peace and thus leave Germany free to launch her full weight against Russia.'

After these two partial exposures, one by the Minster of Information himself, the cabinet decided it was time to release the facts, and on 23 September Eden circulated a statement in the House of Commons; this gave the story as it appears in the statements and interrogation reports in the open files today. Eden took care that Hamilton's name was protected: when Hess first announced himself to Hamilton, 'the Wing Commander had no recollection of the prisoner, and was not aware that he had ever seen or met Rudolf Hess'.[37] This, of course, contradicted Brendan Bracken's statement in America. And Eden's statement only listed among Hess's possessions photographs of himself and a small boy, and the visiting cards of the Haushofers, father and son ; 'No other documents or identifications were found on the prisoner.' None the less, for the first time the British public and the world had been given the truth about the peace proposals Hess brought.

The question of why he had believed that the Duke of Hamilton could take him to the leading members of a powerful peace party was glossed over; perhaps Guy Ramsey's report on Hess in the *Daily Mail* as a 'borderline case' and paranoiac, hearing voices which did not exist, disposed of the problem.

Stalin did not think so. When Churchill took this line during a supper at the Kremlin in October 1944, adding that Hess was now 'completely mad' – and for good measure that his relations with Hitler had probably been abnormal – Stalin raised his glass and proposed a toast to the British intelligence service. Churchill looked surprised. 'Which inveigled Hess into coming to England', Stalin went on. 'He could not have landed without being given signals. The intelligence service must have been behind it all.'

Churchill protested that the British Government had known nothing of his flight beforehand. Stalin replied that the Russian intelligence service often did not inform the Soviet Government of its intentions until their work was done.[38]

28
NUREMBERG

By October 1944, when Churchill told Stalin that Hess was completely mad, it had begun to appear he might be. At first, after his move to Maindiff Court, he had seemed to recover. He had liked the doctors in charge of him, describing them to Ilse in recollection as 'especially nice types',[1] cultivated and many-sided in their interests. He had enjoyed walks with the officers guarding him into the surrounding countryside, the beauty of whose hills and peaks and ever-changing colours he had portrayed in letters home. He had become especially friendly with an older lieutenant, Walter Fenton, who replaced Lieutenant May after the 'leak' to the *Daily Mail*. And years later Fenton looked back to the time he spent with Hess as his best months in the war. 'I liked old Hess,' he recalled, 'even though he was a German. He was a very sensible man.' Fenton had a car allotted in which he used to drive Hess to local sites of interest.

We went for long walks and he would talk for hours about the countryside and Britain's ancient monuments. I got to like the old boy very much. I refused to go on leave once because I didn't want to leave him ... He thought Winston Churchill was one of the finest of men and greatly admired some of our military leaders ... he thought a lot of England and thought it was a great shame we ever came to war.[2]

Hess suffered abdominal pains frequently and he still feared poison in his food, or so it appeared. When Fenton dined with him, he was asked to taste the food first or swap the plates around. His moods varied, but he enjoyed listening to good music from Germany on his wireless and he read a great deal, chiefly books sent by Ilse, which soon amounted to a small library. He read the complete works of Goethe during these months together with much British naval history and German biography. He wrote letters to Ilse and 'Buz', and to friends and relations, remembering their birthdays, recalling old times, looking forward to refreshing them in the future. The letters show no trace of the persecution complex he presented to his captors; they were distinguished by that fatalistic or ironic acceptance displayed in his early letters to Karl Haushofer. He was delighted when Ilse wrote with news of his son and their circle at Harlaching, and told her to keep writing about these things. He described the locality, giving geographical hints – mountains, red earth, local dialect – which enabled Karl Haushofer to pinpoint two possible areas, one in Scotland, one in South Wales where he was. To judge by his reading and writing, and Walter Fenton's recollections, he was mentally sharp and as 'normal' as could be expected in the monastic circumstances of his confinement.[3] These were the best days he was to enjoy in captivity. He could still look forward to going home and hiking in the Bavarian Alps.

At the end of August 1943 he received a letter from Ilse about the treatment of his personal staff which shocked him deeply. All except Alfred Leitgen had been released from custody, but they had been expelled from the Party and the males had been posted to punishment battalions on the eastern front.[4] Martin Bormann probably had much to do with this humiliation for his former master. Since Hess's flight, he seems to have done nothing to help Ilse. Hitler had decreed she keep the Harlaching property, a mixed blessing since it proved far too large, and exhausted her physically and financially, but, when she needed help, she turned to Himmler.[5] It took Bormann almost two years to the day Hess left to write to her, and for that she suspected she had to thank the Reichsführer's intercession.[6] Hess raged about his room, as he wrote to her, 'literally foaming with anger' for some days after receiving her letter. When he had collected himself sufficiently to write a considered reply, he pointed out in extenuation of his Führer the huge burden he now had to carry. He was glad to see from all her letters that nothing had changed in her attitude towards this man; nor had his own attitude towards him changed, he told her.[7]

Black moods gripped him that autumn. Whether they were triggered by that first news of what had been done to his people, or whether, as David Irving suspects, they had more to do with a report of a parliamentary debate on the trial of war criminals which he probably read in *The Times* on 21 October,[8] whether perhaps the increasingly sombre war news from Germany contributed, in November he again began to fake amnesia, soon claiming he could remember absolutely nothing. He gave a bravura performance, completely taking in Rees and every other psychiatrist who saw him. By May 1944 his amnesia was so established that he felt obliged, if he were to continue the pretence, to agree to intravenous injections of a drug – Evipan or Pentothal according to different reports – as an experiment to help him recovery his memory.[9] As he told Ilse long afterwards, he recognised the danger that he might give away secrets – which he suspected was the reason they wanted to dope him – or reveal the fraud he was perpetrating. In the event he was able to preserve full consciousness while mimicking unconsciousness: 'In this way I naturally answered all questions "I don't know", with pauses between the words, softly, tonelessly, absent-mindedly. vvv'.[10] He also faked pains; the transcript of the experiment shows much groaning.

'... Pains! In my belly! Oh, if only I were well. Belly ache' (groan) 'Water! Water! Thirst!'

'You will soon have water,' said Dicks, who was conducting the interview. 'Tell us now what you have forgotten.'

'I don't know. Pain! Thirst!...'

'Remember your little son's name –'

'I don't know –'[11]

So it went. Hess groaned and called for water, and said he didn't know, or simply repeated the questions, until suddenly he decided to come to and stare about him with puzzled eyes. 'It was grand theatre', he recalled for Ilse much later, 'and a complete success!'[12]

So it was and, since it required constant alertness, persistence and indeed memory to keep up the act for month after month, it suggests he was far from mad. As he wrote later, he did it all in the hope he would be repatriated.

The war news grew worse: in June the Allies invaded Europe, in July Hitler narrowly escaped with his life when von Stauffenberg attempted to assassinate him with a bomb at the Führer's headquarters; from both east and west the enemy pressed in on the *Reich*, while German cities were reduced to rubble by mass bombing from the air.

Almost as if in his impotence Hess willed himself to suffer with his country and his Führer, his behaviour grew more bizarre, the abdominal pains he complained of more agonising, his hallucinations more graphic; he raged and shouted to himself and to his attendants, wrapped up portions of food and forgot where he put them, forgot what he had been told or people he had seen five minutes before. It was a desperate act to gain repatriation, so he explained later. He suggested that the sight of his family might restore his memory or the sight of familiar surroundings. In October Ilse, who had not received a letter from him since March, when his first shocking accounts of his total loss of memory had reached her, heard *via* British prisoners of war that he had been held for a long time in a sanatorium and wandered about his room talking to himself. She did not draw the same conclusions from this as the English, she wrote to Himmler, since she knew her husband; she knew how in former days after differences with the Führer in which he had to subordinate himself he gave vent to his feelings loudly at home or on the way home. None the less, suspecting that the Reichsführer knew a great deal more about his whereabouts than she, she pleaded with him, could he not bring her husband home?[13]

Accurately seeing into the mind of her distant man, she told Himmler that ever since 20 July – Stauffenberg's bomb attempt – she had felt increasing certainty that her husband was 'more restless' to get home than before, that now in this time of most extreme need for the *Reich* he had more than his own personal reasons for returning. She could imagine Himmler answering her, she wrote, 'Yes, and the events of May 1941 and their consequences?' But, she countered, it required only a wave of the Führer's hand to wipe out all that and all that had happened since. Furthermore she was 'so absolutely convinced that the Führer knows that neither a mad nor a disloyal man flew at that time', that she had not the least anxiety on this score.

She broached a related concern: Karl Haushofer had told her he had been arrested and held in Dachau for three weeks in connection with his son, Albrecht, who had disappeared after the 20 July attempt. She asked Himmler whether Albrecht was still at large and whether he might have escaped from Germany. She feared that he might find his way to her husband in England and trembled to think what dust he might throw in his eyes. 'Dear, best Reichsführer', she appealed, her man had been completely alone for years, unable to mix like all other prisoners of war and, she assumed from his letters, hearing English as well as German radio. While she held his belief unshakable, 'the spiritual burden must gradually become unbearable, above all since the 20th of July!' She implored Himmler to try and bring him home, not simply for his family, but because he remained in the eyes of the *Volk* the symbol of loyalty to the Führer and the embodiment of the original, true National Socialism.

Himmler was, of course, ignorant of Hess's actual whereabouts and powerless to effect his repatriation. In addition he had his own desperate concerns. By January 1945, when his personal secretary replied to Ilse that enquiries about her husband had yielded no result,[14] he had been appointed to command an Army group defending the Upper Rhine against the Allied advance. Shortly afterwards Ilse received two letters Hess had sent on 13 and 18 July 1944; she gained the impression that his loss of memory was a pretence acted out for some purpose hidden to her.[15] That Hess was able to convey this while still pretending loss of memory to his attendants and the censors he knew read his letters is another strong indication he was not deranged.

The news from Germany as the Allied armies squeezed the rump of what was left of Hitler's *Reich* between them affected Hess deeply;

301

it was plain to his medical attendants; he listened avidly to news bulletins; outside he walked through the deepest drifts of snow, kicking it about in frustration.[16] On 4 February he called for a list of people who, he said, must have been hypnotised by the Jews to do certain things. The list included the King of Italy and Marshal Badoglio, who had deposed Mussolini and broken their word to the Führer, von Stauffenberg and others, who had attempted to kill the Führer, even Churchill, who had changed from being an anti-Bolshevik into an ally of Stalin. He asked that the list be sent to Churchill.[17] That evening he borrowed a bread knife, changed into his Luftwaffe uniform, sat in his armchair and stabbed himself twice in the left chest, without, however, penetrating the heart, and screamed out for the attendant.

While convalescing from what appeared to be a suicide attempt, he refused to wash or shave and, on 8 February, announced he had decided to fast to the death. At the same time he appeared deeply suspicious his attendants might poison his water, and sealed his drinking glass with paper and string to prevent it. And he told the doctor the Jews had placed the bread knife near him to tempt him to commit suicide.

Later, after giving up his fast, he started writing a long memoir of his flight to Scotland and subsequent captivity. He did not mention his first suicide attempt at Mytchett Place, stating merely that he had broken his leg, after which the doctor had 'injected brain poison' into his body. He noticed afterwards that Brigadier Rees, whose behaviour had been affable at first, had 'a peculiar glassy and dreamy expression in his eyes', and refused to take his allegations of poison seriously. Later he put his suspicions to 'a certain Lieutenant M' [Malone], who had told him such things were not possible in England. However, he had given Malone one of the pills and he had appeared next morning with the same glassy expression in his eyes as Brigadier Rees. The same thing happened again with the doctor in charge at Maindiff Court. On the first day his eyes had been clear and he had carried himself straight: 'When he came back to see me on the next morning, a change had taken place. Again the slightly absent-minded glass eyes. He carried himself limply and bent, and he walked with soft knees . . . .[18] The eyes, he wrote, were symptoms that these people had been put into an abnormal mental condition by a secret chemical hitherto unknown to the world. He remembered the defendants at the Moscow trials before the war, who made the most astounding confessions, had had the same strange eyes according to reports. The secret chemical had been applied there as well. He suspected that all the crimes and tortures he had suffered whilst in Mytchett Place and Maindiff Court, all the noises, which he listed in detail, all the poisons administered to him had been perpetrated by people made lunatics by the chemical. The worst of the lunatics looking after him had been the doctors, who had employed their scientific knowledge for the most refined tortures.

However, what worry was this to the Jews? They were as little worried about that as the British King and the British people. For the Jews were behind all this ... The British Government had been hypnotised into endeavouring to change me into a lunatic ... to revenge on me the fact that National Socialist Germany had defended itself from the Jews ... revenge on me because I had tried to end the war too early which the Jews had started with so much trouble, whereby they would have been prevented from reaching their war aims ....

It was manifestly the rambling of a deranged mind.

Perhaps not. His letters written at this time give no hint of madness. Taken together with his behaviour, which became increasingly bizarre as the *Reich* went down in disaster, the Russians entered Berlin and his Führer finally committed suicide beneath the rubble of what had been the imperial capital, the exaggerated delusions and manic tone of the document suggest a lover's cry of despair and affirmation, for he believed what he had written about the Jews. Hitler made a similar statement in his last testament before committing suicide on 30 April: the war had been started by finance Jewry, and he enjoined the nation to 'scrupulous observance of the race laws and merciless resistance to the world-poisoner of all peoples, international Jewry'.[19]

On 18 June, six weeks after Hitler's chosen successor, Grand Admiral Dönitz, authorised all German forces unconditionally to lay down their arms, Hess, still acting before his captors like a madman – although several were now convinced he was feigning – wrote the lines to Ilse about his Führer already quoted earlier:

It has been granted to few to take part as we have from the outset in the development of a unique personality, in joy and sorrow, cares and hopes, hates and loves and all the marks of greatness – and also in all the little signs of human weakness which alone make a man wholly lovable.[20]

His thoughts had been much with Ilse when he thought of Hitler he went on, and he quoted a few lines from Nietzsche:

> I love all those, who like heavy
> raindrops, falling one by one
> from dark o'erhanging clouds,
> announce the lightning,
> and drop as harbingers to ground.

On 8 October Hess, dressed in his Luftwaffe uniform with flying boots, was taken from Maindiff Court and flown to Nuremberg to stand trial with the other captured Nazi leaders as a war criminal. He took with him a large number of the statements, depositions and copies of letters he had written in captivity together with samples of food, medicines and chocolate carefully wrapped in tissue, sealed, numbered and signed, for use in his defence to prove how the British had attempted to poison him.[21]

He was placed with the twenty-one others who were to be tried as 'major war criminals' in the prison block attached to the Nuremberg court house. After the comfort and congenial surroundings of his quarters in Great Britain it was a shock. His cell was about nine by thirteen feet, sparsely furnished with a steel cot and straw mattress, a straight wooden chair, flimsy table, wash basin and lavatory without seat or cover. Grey light filtered in through a small, high, barred window set into the stone outer wall. In the oak door opposite a fifteen-inch square aperture at eye level was fitted with a metal grille to protect an electric light bulb and reflector which provided the only illumination outside daylight hours. Guards on duty outside his door around the clock could observe him through the grille at any hour.

His abruptly altered circumstances were made plain immediately on arrival. The prison commandant, the US Colonel B. C. Andrus, told him he would have to hand in everything he had brought. Hess, erect and angular in his high, black flying boots, tried to impress the Colonel with his status as an officer; when this failed, he offered to hand in every-thing save the small parcels of food and medicine samples which he insisted he had brought for impartial chemical analysis. This too failed, and finally he had to give them up.

Not unnaturally after this affront, when the American psychiatrist, Major Douglas M. Kelley, visited him in his cell, he had forgotten every detail of his former life. Kelley told him he had been born in Alexandria; he displayed interest, apparently making a real effort to co-operate. By next morning, when Kelley visited him again, he had only the vaguest recollection of the previous day's journey and his admission to the prison, although he did recall his food samples and asked for assurance they were safe.[22] Afterwards he was taken before the chief US interrogator, Colonel John H. Amen, and played the same game. He could remember nothing; yesterday the doctor even had to tell him where he was born. It was terrible for him, for he would have to defend himself in the trial that was coming soon.

'How do you know that any kind of trial is coming up, as you say?'

'This trial has been talked about all the time. I have seen it in the newspapers . . .'

Hess had been putting on the act so long in Britain it must have become second nature. After an hour and a half stone-walling he was taken back to his cell, then after lunch led out again to Amen's office. Göring was already there. Hess pretended not to notice him.

'Will you look over here to the right to this gentleman?' Amen pointed at Göring.

'At him?'

'Don't you know me?' Göring asked.

'Who are you?'

'You ought to know me. We have been together for years.'

Hess explained he had lost his memory. Göring reminded him of events they had witnessed together, but Hess shook his head dully at each one; he had no recollection at all.

'Hess, remember all the way back to 1923 at that time when I was the leader of the SA, that you led one of my SA troops ... Do you remember that we together made the *putsch* in Munich ... Do you remember that you arrested the Minister?'

'I arrested the Minister?'

'Yes.'

'I seem to have a pretty involved past ...'

'Do you remember that you flew in a plane, you yourself in this war flew to England?'

'No.'

'You used a Messerschmitt plane. Do you remember that you wrote a long letter to the Führer?'

'About what?'

'What you were going to do in England. That you were going to bring about peace.'

'I have no idea of it.'[23]

Göring gave up. Colonel Amen motioned him aside and called in Karl Haushofer, asking Hess if he knew him. Hess repeated his uncomprehending performance.

'Rudolf, don't you know me any more?' Haushofer asked, concerned. 'We have called each other by our first names for twenty years ... I saw your family and your child and they are well ...' He approached Hess and stretched out his hand. 'May I shake your hand? Your boy is wonderfully grown. He is seven years old. I have seen him – '

'In order to calm down an old friend,' Hess said, 'I can only assure you that the doctors tell me my memory will all come back to me. I can't remember you. I just don't know you, but it will all come back to me and then I will recognise an old friend again. I am terribly sorry.'

Haushofer assured him it would all come back; he had known similar cases with old soldiers. 'I can see how these last four years have worried you,' he went on, 'I also see the light in your eyes as in the old days. I remember especially those wonderful letters [from captivity] which took a long time, but whatever you wrote to your wife she also sent to me. Thus we remained in contact with your spiritual life and your feelings . . . .'

Amen allowed Haushofer to speak for a long time, recalling the old days when Hess had flown him over the Fichtelgebirge, circling because the landscape was so beautiful, reminding him of his old mother, his hunting lodge in the mountains, the oak at Hartschimmelhof he had named after him . . .

'I should like to look in your eyes because for twenty-two years I read in your eyes and I am glad to see that a little bit of recognition is coming back into them . . . Don't you remember Albrecht who served you very faithfully ? He is dead now.'

In the final days of the war, Albrecht had been taken from prison where he languished and shot by a special ss Commando, no doubt to Himmler's orders. Haushofer did not tell him this.

'It will all come back,' he went on. 'I see that a lot of it is coming back to you. Your voice is changing and your eyes are changing. Recognition is coming back to you.'

Hess fought down his emotions. 'I am terribly sorry, but at the moment all this doesn't mean a thing to me.'

'But sometimes the old gleam is coming back into your eyes and I think you are recognising. In those twenty-two years I had great worry and pain for you – '[24]

After Haushofer, von Papen was brought in to try his hand at restoring Hess's memory, and after him Ernst Bohle.

Göring told Bohle to remind Hess that he had translated his letter.

'Don't you remember', Bohle said, 'that I translated your letter to the Duke of Hamilton ?'

'No.'

'Don't you remember that you took this letter to the Duke of Hamilton and that it was I who translated it ?'

'I don't remember that. I just don't have the least recollection of that.'

Bohle broke into English. 'This is flabbergasting.'

Haushofer suggested that perhaps he was not called Hamilton then. 'Don't you remember Clydesdale,' he asked Hess, 'the young flyer who flew over the Himalayas ? Don't you remember that he was your guest in Berlin at the time of the Berlin Olympic Games and his name was Clydesdale ? His name was Hamilton later . . . Don't you remember that ? Don't you remember him ?'

'If I don't recognise a person whom I have known for twenty-two years,' Hess countered, 'how do you expect me to know Clydesdale ?'

'If I brought his picture to you,' Haushofer pressed on, 'you would probably recognise him again because we found him very sympathetic at the time. Don't you remember you liked his flying feat when he went over Mount Everest, when he dropped from 2,000 metres and he barely got away? Don't you remember that that made a very strong impression on you?'

'If I don't remember other things that made a much stronger impression on me,' Hess said, somewhat inconsistently, 'how do you expect me to remember that?'

Despite the emotional pounding he received, Hess preserved his expressionless, detached manner and certainly convinced Haushofer, who was devastated.[25] It was the last time Haushofer was to speak to his disciple and old friend and protector. Nazism had taken its toll spiritually, mentally and emotionally. Five months later he was to leave instructions to his surviving son, Heinz, that no identification should ever be placed on or near his grave; afterwards, he set out with his 'non-Aryan' wife, Martha, to a favourite stream near their house there to take poison together.

Hess continued his charade of amnesia throughout the rest of October and November. An extension of the strategy he had employed to resist questioning in Britain, he probably had little idea of why he continued it; no doubt it brought him attention, no doubt he enjoyed the challenge; probably it was his way of striking back at fate and his jailors in the ruins of his world. Psychiatrists were unanimous in ascribing the amnesia to his 'hysterical' tendencies.

Soon he had forgotten, he confessed, that he ever brought documents to the prison. When Colonel Amen gave him one or two of them to read he was amazed.

'It says here "Apart from a medicine which would cause a toothache there was also a strong laxative contained in it, and also a strong poison which would damage the mucous membrane", and it says furthermore, "The last thing caused blood to congeal in the mouth and that the intestines would burn like fire!"'. He shook his head.[26]

Later he was confronted with his former secretaries, Hildegard Fath and Ingeborg Sperr; he could not recollect ever having seen either of them before, a denial which he had on his conscience for some years since it reduced Hildegard to tears.[27] The prison psychiatrist Kelley was present at this arranged meeting. He also continued questioning Hess in his cell and submitted him – and indeed all the prisoners – to various tests, including the 'ink-blot' or Rorschach test. This involved presenting one by one a standard series of ten cards each having an amorphous 'ink-blot' shape depicted on it, and asking what pictures these suggested. By means of the subject's replies Kelley believed a skilled Rorschach worker could deduce 'a complete picture of his personality'. Hess obliged him. On the second card he claimed to see 'two men talking about a crime; blood is on their minds'; on the ninth card he detected 'the cross section of a fountain'.[28]

Kelley deduced from his responses 'a highly schizoid personality with hysterical and obsessive components'. Plainly the Rorschach test was mumbo jumbo, but Kelley was a fascinated and perceptive observer, and noted that Hess's amnesia shifted in a highly suspicious way; he indicated in his official report that possibly Hess had 'suggested an amnesia to himself for so long he partly believes in it'. The conclusions he reached as early as 16 October were robustly unambiguous:

(a) Internee Hess is sane and responsible.

(b) Internee Hess is a profound neurotic of the hysterical type.

(c) His amnesia is of mixed etuology, stemming from auto-suggestion and conscious malingering in a hysterical personality.[29]

To break the amnesia Kelley suggested hypnosis reinforced by the intravenous injection of sodium amytal or Pentothal. Hess, obviously remembering his triumph over Major Dicks, said he was willing to co-operate, but when Kelley told him he had never known this treatment to fail, he changed his mind and refused consent. Without his agreement the experiment was considered too dangerous.[30] None the less his memory or lack of it held the greatest implications for his ability to defend himself at the coming trial, and an international panel of leading psychiatrists was convened to examine him. They failed to make a unanimous report, but agreed that Hess was not insane. Three from Russia reported:

He answers questions rapidly and to the point. His speech is coherent, his thoughts formed with precision and correctness and they are accompanied by sufficiently expressive movements ... intelligence is normal and in some instances above the average. His movements are natural and not forced. He has expressed no delirious fantasies ...[31]

They concluded that his loss of memory represented 'hysterical amnesia, the basis of which is a subconscious inclination towards self-defence as well as a deliberate and conscious tendency towards it ...' His condition did not exonerate him from his responsibility under the indictment.

One French, one British-Canadian and two American psychiatrists signed another report with very similar conclusions:

Rudolf Hess is suffering from hysteria characterised in part by loss of memory ... In addition there is a conscious exaggeration of his loss of memory and a tendency to exploit it to protect himself against examination. We consider that the hysterical behaviour ... was initiated as a defence against the circumstances in which he found himself in England; that it has now become in part habitual and that it will continue for as long as he remains under the threat of imminent punishment.[32]

The British-Canadian member of the panel was Dr D. Ewen Cameron of McGill University, Montreal, a pioneer in drug, electric shock convulsive treatment and mind control, who was later to strike up an infamous partnership with the Director of the CIA, Alan Dulles, to develop 'brainwashing' techniques. Dulles, who had directed the US Intelligence effort inside Germany from Switzerland and was now at Nuremberg, invited Cameron to dine and revealed to him in the strictest secrecy he had reason to believe Hess had been executed secretly to Churchill's orders and the man purporting to be Hess was an imposter. There was a simple test to find out, he continued: the real Hess would have a scar over the left lung where he had been shot in the First World War. Cameron agreed to try to make a physical examination when he interrogated him. He was unable to do so as Hess was handcuffed to his escorting guard during his interrogation and the guard said he had no authority to remove the handcuffs. Cameron did not press the matter.[33]

It is not clear how Dulles came by his suspicion, but Hess's apparent loss of memory and his strange behaviour no doubt contributed. It is possible to infer from the interrogation of other prisoners that Cameron was not the only one in whom Dulles confided his suspicion. Rosenberg was asked repeatedly whether Hess had shown any signs of recognition when he saw him first at Nuremberg and whether his conduct was unusual in view of their previous relationship. However, this might as easily have been to probe whether Hess really had lost his memory.[34]

The trial opened on 20 November. The prisoners were taken one by one from their cells and into a lift to the courtroom above, where two straight-backed benches, one behind the other, had been constructed near the wall opposite the judge's dais and separated from it by the ranks of counsel and officials in the body of the court. Göring occupied the premier position at the right-hand end of the front bench, Hess next to him with Ribbentrop on his left; on the bench immediately behind sat the two Grand Admirals, Dönitz and Raeder.

Hitler and Goebbels had committed suicide below the ruins of the Chancellery, Himmler in a British interrogation centre on Lüneberg Heath and Martin Bormann had disappeared no one knew where. In the weeks and months to come the three defendants at the right end of the dock were to fall naturally into a shadow power play: Göring to assert his right as former heir to the Führer, to dominate and bully the others into an unrepentant stand against their prosecutors; Dönitz, who had served for a brief period as the Führer's successor, to circle him tight-lipped in matters of precedence, while taking an equally unrepentant line in an attempt to uphold the tarnished honour of the armed services; Hess, the Stellvertreter, to nominate himself, as ever, the Führer's loyalest interpreter, refusing to take part in proceedings so self-evidently invalid.

From the outside the picture looked very different. For those who had seen the Nazi leaders strutting in their days of glory the transformation into these men in the dock was astonishing. 'How little and mean and mediocre they look', thought the American William Shirer, formerly a correspondent in Berlin.[35] Göring in faded Luftwaffe uniform without his array of medals reminded him of a genial ship's radio operator, Dönitz very upright behind him in a civilian suit of a grocery clerk, von Ribbentrop was 'bent and beaten and aged beyond belief', and Hess ... how, he wondered, could that broken man have been placed at the pinnacle of a great nation? His face was gaunt like a skeleton, his mouth twitched, 'his once bright eyes [were] staring vacantly and stupidly around the courtroom'.[36]

The drama of the entry of the Judges of the victorious Allied powers and the opening speeches outlining the scale of horror visited on the world and Germany itself by Nazism, appealing to genuine visions of a new world order in which such things could not be, left the principal defendants outwardly unmoved: Göring cockily defiant, Hess exaggerating indifference, apparently cut off by loss of memory in a world of his own. On the afternoon of 29 November they were shocked abruptly out of their attitudes. The President, Lord Justice Lawrence, announced the showing of a documentary film of concentration camps when entered by us troops in the final stages of the war. The court lights went out; only fluorescent lights built into the ledges of the dock cast an eerie glow up over the faces of the defendants. Kelley and another us psychiatrist named G. M. Gilbert, who had joined him at the prison, stationed themselves with notebook and pencil at either end of the double row of prisoners to observe their reactions as they watched the film.

It began with scenes of victims burned alive in a barn. Hess's attention was caught at once; he glared at the screen, as the observers noted, 'looking like a ghoul with sunken eyes over the footlamp'. Others bowed their heads, covered their eyes or looked away as the film unwound; Hans Frank, former Governor of the *General Gouvernement Polen*, swallowed hard, eyes blinking as he tried to fight back tears; Göring kept leaning on the ledge before him, not watching, 'looking droopy'. First to crack was Walther Funk, formerly head of the Reichsbank, whose eyes misted with tears; he wiped them, blew his nose, looked down. 'Hess keeps looking bewildered', the observers noted as piles of dead were shown in a slave labour camp. Dönitz had stopped looking, his head bowed; Funk was crying now. Crematorium ovens appeared on the screen, then a lampshade made from human skin; there were audible gasps from the body of the court, Göring was coughing, Hans Frank saying, 'Horrible'.[37]

There was stunned silence when the film ended and the lights went on again. Hess, who appears from the notes to have shown sustained interest, said, 'I don't believe it.' Göring, his former insouciance quite gone, whispered to him to keep quiet. The Judges rose, Lord Justice Lawrence even forgetting to adjourn the session, and strode out silently.

When the two psychiatrists visited Hess in his cell afterwards, he seemed confused and kept mumbling, 'I don't understand – I don't understand – '.[38]

The following morning, Friday 30 November, General Erwin Lahousen, one of Canaris's confidants in the Abwehr, was called to testify for the prosecution. He gave an account of Canaris's reaction to the massacres of the intelligentsia, nobility, clergy and Jews in the Polish campaign, and quoted his words, 'One day the world will also hold the Wehrmacht, under whose eyes these events occurred, responsible for such methods.'[39] In the afternoon Lahousen described the mass murders committed by Heydrich's Einsatzkommandos in the Russian campaign.

After he stood down, a recess was announced during which the Judges were to consider a submission from Hess's counsel, Dr Günther von Rohrscheidt, that his client was unfit to stand trial. The dock was cleared, apart from Hess himself. Von Rohrscheidt had had an impossible task preparing a defence since Hess had maintained his loss of memory in front of him, but, just before he rose to plead, Hess told him he had decided to say his memory had returned. Von Rohrscheidt, used to his vagaries, told him to do as he pleased; then he rose and began his prepared statement to the effect that Hess's amnesia made it impossible for him to defend himself adequately.[40] Hess listened, in itself a remarkable change in his courtroom behaviour, determined, however, to tell the court, when he was allowed to do so, that his memory was in full working order again. Two people claimed a hand in this conversion, the prison commandant, Colonel Andrus, said he had told Hess to his face that he was feigning and it was not a very manly thing to do.[41] The new psychiatrist, Dr Gilbert, stated in his report that just before the special hearing that afternoon he told Hess – as a challenge – that he might probably be considered incompetent and be excluded from the proceedings. Hess had looked startled and protested he was competent.[42] Probably the fear that he would be disqualified and afterwards suffer the reproach of having sought to evade his responsibility, thus denying his Führer, by faking amnesia caused him to change tactics. At all events after von Rohrscheidt and the Prosecution had exchanged arguments for about an hour Hess was given an opportunity to speak. He pulled a piece of paper from his pocket as he rose.

'Mr President!' He clicked his heels and bowed his head towards Lord Justice Lawrence. 'I should like to say this . . . In order to forestall the possibility of my being pronounced incapable of pleading in spite of my willingness to take part in the proceedings and to hear the verdict alongside my comrades, I would like to make the following declaration before the Tribunal, although originally I intended to make it during a later stage of the trial.

'Henceforth my memory will again respond to the outside world. The reasons for simulating loss of memory were of a tactical nature. Only my ability to concentrate is in fact somewhat reduced, but my capacity to follow the trial, to defend myself, to put questions to witnesses or to answer questions myself is not affected thereby.

'I emphasise that I bear full responsibility for everything that I did, signed or co-signed. My fundamental attitude that the Tribunal is not competent is not affected by the statement I have just made. I also simulated loss of memory in consultations with my officially appointed Defence Counsel. He has, therefore, represented it in good faith.'[43]

A buzz of talk and laughter from the press benches broke the stunned silence after he finished speaking and reporters dashed for the doors. Lord Justice Lawrence called the court to order, then announced the trial adjourned. Von Rohrscheidt turned to Hess; now he would certainly be judged unfit to stand, he said reprovingly.

Afterwards Kelley visited Hess in his cell, according to a diary Hess was keeping, 'bursting with joy' and saying he must congratulate him on this piece of play-acting.[44] According to Kelley's account, it was Hess who was bursting with pride like an actor after a 'first night'. 'How did I do?' he asked him. 'Good wasn't I? I really surprised everyone, don't you think?'[45]

The following morning Lord Justice Lawrence announced that, having heard Hess's statement, the Tribunal was of opinion he was capable of standing his trial; the motion of the counsel for the defence was therefore denied.

Recovering his memory did not affect Hess's attitude to the trial. He continued to feign indifference, not bothering to put on the headphones provided for translation, reading books during the sessions, holding whispered conversations with Göring and others around him, grinning toothily, even laughing out loud. Beneath the act, to judge by letters he smuggled out to Ilse under the guise of notes for his counsel, he was quite aware of the proceedings. Thus the following January he described the trial as in part frightful, in part boring, but at times interesting.[46] He assured her that he had not changed outwardly or inwardly and trusted that the Almighty would give her strength, as He gave him strength. Later, in his closing statement to the Tribunal, he was to say, 'I have no spiritual relationship to the Church, but I am a deeply religious person. I am convinced that my belief in God is greater than that of most people.'[47]

By this time he had replaced von Rohrscheidt, whom, he wrote, he had never trusted, with 'the sharpest, most aggressive [defence] lawyer'[48] in the court, Dr Alfred Seidl, who was representing Wilhelm Frick. At first he had wanted to defend himself, but had been persuaded that his lack of knowledge of legal procedure would make this difficult, if not impossible.[49] Seidl advised him to continue his attitude of indifference to the proceedings.

The Prosecution opened the case against him on 7 February. He was indicted under all four counts: conspiracy against peace and humanity; the planning and initiation of wars of aggression; war crimes including murder and ill-treatment of civilian populations; crimes against humanity, including deliberate and systematic genocide. Since few documents had been found connecting him with specific decisions, the chief thrust of the Prosecution case was that he must have been involved by virtue of his position and offices. The decrees under which his name appeared as co-signatory were adduced as evidence of his participation in the 'Nuremberg' race laws of 1935 and the rape of Poland in October 1939. In view of the race policies pursued in Poland and later in the whole of the occupied east, probably the most damning document produced was an order he had issued demanding support from the Party for recruiting members for the *Waffen-ss*, the fighting units of the ss; it was pointed out that he himself held the rank of ss-Obergruppenführer. Part of his order ran:

The units of the *Waffen-ss* are more suitable than other armed units for the specific tasks to be solved in the occupied eastern territories due to their intensive National Socialist training in regard to questions of race and nationality.[50]

Seidl did not put him on the witness stand. This was no doubt for the same reason he had advised him to continue his play of indifference. It would have been of scant use in any case since Hess had begun to lose his memory again. Dr Gilbert had noticed the first signs at the end of January; they increased through February until by the beginning of March, Gilbert reported, he had 'returned to a state of virtually complete amnesia'.[51] Gilbert believed the amnesia genuine, as did another

313

prison psychiatrist, Colonel W. H. Dunn, who considered it resulted from Hess's exposure to the court proceedings and the mounting evidence of the crimes and cruelties perpetrated by Nazism: 'he took flight into amnesia to escape the dreadful reality presented'.[52]

Here we are at the nub of the problem presented by Hess's reaction to the scale of atrocity carried out in his idol's name. The evidence of hideous tortures, mass sadism, slave labour in unimaginably degrading conditions, the ultimate reduction of human beings to so-called 'Mussel-men' with vacant eyes, lacking the basic will to live, horrific medical experiments on concentration camp inmates, mass shootings, burnings, gassing in mobile vans and purpose-built gas chamber-incinerator plants run as production lines of death – such descriptions day after day, week after week built up a totality of horror numbing the strongest nerves. For a man as sensitive as Hess, who was regarded by his colleagues as 'soft', who knew at one level of his mind that ultimately his Führer was responsible and he was himself since this was the necessary and inevitable result of the *Weltanschauung*, it can be imagined he took flight into unreality. One habitual defence he raised, as in Great Britain, was that it was all the work of the Jews, another, as in Great Britain, was to pretend he had lost all memory. Perhaps, as the psychiatrists believed, he did lose it for a while. This hardly squares with the rationality of his letters home. In Nuremberg that summer his memory duly returned; he wrote to Ilse, the 'miracle has occurred again . . . vvvvv'.[53]

Counsel had made their final speeches by then. On 31 August the defendants themselves were allowed a short statement each, Göring first. The German people had placed their trust in the Führer, he said, and under his authoritarian rule had had no influence on events; they were free of guilt. As for himself, his only motive had been ardent love for his people, their happiness and freedom. After him Lord Justice Lawrence called on Hess. He asked to be allowed to remain seated because of his state of health. 'Certainly,' Lawrence replied.

'Some of my comrades here can confirm the fact that at the beginning of the proceedings I predicted the following,' Hess began. 'One, that witnesses would appear who, under oath, would make untrue statements while, at the same time, these witnesses could create an absolutely reliable impression and enjoy the best possible reputation.

'Two, that it was to be reckoned that the court would receive affidavits containing untrue statements.

'Three, that the defendants would be astonished and surprised at some of the German witnesses.

'Four, that some of the defendants would act rather strangely; they would make shameless utterances about the Führer; they would incriminate their own people; they would partially incriminate each other . . .'

All these predictions had come true, he went on, and then in an allusive way, because the Russians were among the allied powers sitting in judgment, he pointed to the Moscow show trials of 1936 to 1938 and the defendants who had accused themselves in an astonishing manner. A 'mysterious means' had been used to make them speak in this way; the same means could be used to make them act to orders given.

'The latter point is of tremendous importance in connection with the actions, the hitherto inexplicable actions of the personnel in the German concentration camps, including the scientists and physicians who made these frightful and atrocious experiments on the prisoners, actions which normal human beings, especially physicians and scientists could not possibly carry out . . .'

After he had been speaking for twenty minutes the President reminded him that the Tribunal could not allow speeches of great length. Hess replied that in that case he would forego the statement he had wanted to make. Instead he said that he did not defend himself against accusers whom he denied the right to bring charges against him and his fellow countrymen, and he would not discuss accusations concerning purely German matters.

'I was permitted to work for many years of my life', he went on, 'under the greatest son my *Volk* has brought forth in its thousand year history. Even if I could, I would not want to erase this period of time from my existence. I am happy to know that I have done my duty to my *Volk* – my duty as a German, as a National Socialist, as a loyal follower of the Führer. I regret nothing.

'If I were to begin again, I would act as I have acted. Even if I knew that in the end I should meet a fiery death on the pyre. No matter what human beings do, some day I shall stand before the judgement of the Eternal. I shall answer to Him, and I know He will judge me innocent.'[54]

Verdicts were pronounced on 1 October. Hess, who had prepared himself for a sentence of death, continued to play his role of indifference, and did not put his headphones on. He was adjudged to have participated fully and willingly in all the German aggressions which had led to the war, but, while there was evidence showing the participation of the Party Chancellery under him in the distribution of orders connected with the commission of war crimes, the Tribunal did not find the evidence sufficiently connected him with the crimes to sustain a finding of guilt. He was, therefore, judged guilty on counts one and two – conspiracy and crimes against peace – but not guilty of war crimes or crimes against humanity.

Sentences were handed down that afternoon. Again Hess did not bother to put on the headphones.

315

'Defendant Hermann Wilhelm Göring on the Counts of the Indictment on which you have been convicted, the International Military Tribunal sentences you to death by hanging.

'Defendant Rudolf Hess, on the Counts of the Indictment on which you have been convicted, the Tribunal sentences you to imprisonment for life.'

Gilbert was waiting by the cells as the defendants were led down one by one after hearing their sentences. Göring's face was pale, his eyes moist and he was panting, fighting back an emotional breakdown as he asked Gilbert in an unsteady voice to leave him alone for a while. Hess 'strutted in, laughing nervously', and told Gilbert he had not been listening; he didn't know what his sentence was.[55]

29
SPANDAU

Spandau was a fitting jail for the seven sentenced to imprisonment at Nuremberg. Built in the late nineteenth century like a red brick fortress with castellated towers and walls, it had been used during the Nazi period as a collecting point for political prisoners before despatch to concentration camps. It had also served for executions, one of several prisons in Berlin equipped with a newly designed guillotine and sloping, tiled floor to drain blood, and a beam with hooks for the simultaneous strangulation of eight persons by hanging. This apparatus was removed during preparations for accommodating the Nuremberg seven. The small, single cells in which they were to be housed were modified to prevent suicide, and outside a high, barbed wire fence was erected beyond the red brick boundary wall together with an electric fence carrying a 4,000-volt charge. This was designed to prevent rescue attempts. Timber watchtowers were built at intervals atop the wall from which floodlights could be played over the entire perimeter.

The prison was in the British sector of West Berlin, at the extreme western edge of the city near the lakes, but was run jointly by the four victorious powers, the United States, the Soviet Union, Great Britain and France. Each provided a director, a deputy director and thirty-two soldiers for external guard duty ; each took over the prison for one month in four in a regular, unvarying cycle. Besides the external guards there were some eighteen internal guards or warders in control of the prisoners, and a number of ancillary staff.

Arrangements were completed by July 1947 and on Friday 18 July the seven were flown from Nuremberg to Gatow airport, Berlin, and thence, handcuffed individually to guards, bussed at speed through the still ruined city to the jail – the two Grand Admirals, Karl Dönitz and Erich Raeder ; the one-time Foreign Minister, then Protector of Bohemia and Moravia, Konstantin von Neurath ; Hitler's architect and Minister of Armaments, Albert Speer ; the former Minister of Economics and President of the Reichsbank, Walter Funk; the Reich Youth Leader and Gauleiter of Vienna, Baldur von Schirach; and the former Stellvertreter, Rudolf Hess. The handcuffs were removed once the main gates had shut behind them, and they were shepherded over a cobbled yard and up the entrance steps in to the main cell block. There, in the chief warder's room, they were made to strip, leave their clothes and few possessions, and don rough blue-grey convicts' garb procured from a concentration camp and stencilled with the number they had been allotted – by which they would be known for the whole of their time inside. Hess, gaunt and pale, his once luxuriant dark hair now touched with grey, his jaw set in a sullen expression, became 'Number Seven'.

After a medical examination, last of all the prisoners he was escorted through the main iron security door, which shut behind with a resounding clang, to the inner corridor lined with cell doors either side. His was furthest on the right, next to Raeder's. The cell was almost nine feet by seven and a half, and just under twelve feet high to the curved ceiling. To judge by Albert Speer's description, the bare walls were painted a muddy yellow with white above. Opposite the door was a small, high window, its glass replaced by brownish celluloid, barred outside, and below it, against the left wall, stood a narrow black iron bed with grey blankets. The other furnishings consisted of an old, chipped, brown-varnished table less than three feet by nineteen inches, an upright wooden chair, and on the wall above an open cupboard not quite two feet by seventeen inches with a single shelf; in the corner by the door was a flush lavatory bowl with a black seat.[1]

It was early evening by the time Hess entered the cell. Perhaps he was still thinking of his glimpses of the outside and the flight over the free, sunlit countryside of Germany. The steel door was banged shut behind him; he heard the grating as the key turned in the lock and the bolt was shoved to.

Forty years later, on the morning of Monday 17 August 1987, his last, he woke in a different cell. For almost eighteen years, since being rushed into the nearby British Military Hospital at the end of 1969 with a duodenal ulcer, his conditions had been made easier and he had lived in a double cell which had once served as the chapel for the seven. His bed was the one he had had in hospital with head and foot sections which could be raised and lowered. Beside it, to his right, was a hospital bedside cupboard, to his left a table with an electric kettle, his mug and the wherewithal for making tea and coffee, and an anglepoise reading lamp. Behind, on the wall, was a large map of the moon's surface which had been sent to him by NASA in Texas. He had become a lay expert in the exploration of space. In case he needed to get out quickly to visit the lavatory cell, his door was no longer locked or bolted. He was roused at seven instead of six in the mornings, but even this had become rather nominal.

His hair was grey, his back stiffened and bent by arthritis; he could scarcely turn his head to the left, only half way to the right, and, when standing or walking with head thrust forward, he could not look up lest he overbalance; he had little power in his left arm or hand. He was on a variety of drugs for heart and circulatory problems. He was ninety-three years old.[2]

For half his life, less a few months, he had been in captivity. It was forty-six years since his flight to Scotland, 16,901 days. This was his 14,641st day in Spandau, the 7,626th he had spent as the only inmate – but guarded still by the whole Four Power apparatus whose troops changed every month on the month, whose chief warders noted strictly trivial occurrences in the Occurence Book, whose regulations remained scarcely ameliorated from the time they had been drawn up with the horrors of the evidence from Nuremberg fresh in mind. Whether anyone anywhere had ever spent so long in a prison cell, it had not been the intention of the western judges that he should – the Soviet judge had called for death – his punishment had gone far beyond all norms for 'life' sentences in western states. The real refinement of his ordeal had been hope of release.

While still in Nuremberg after the sentences had been handed down, he had escaped into a fantasy in which the western powers released him to lead a new Germany to counteract the 'Bolshevisation' of Europe which he had predicted in Britain; now the danger had become obvious, Churchill had spoken of the 'Iron Curtain' which had fallen across Europe. His fantasy had been so real to him he had spent the months before his transfer to Spandau typing on a typewriter allowed him by the authorities press releases announcing the ministers he had appointed, and the tasks for the people; he had also composed his first speech to his new Reichstag, beginning with a eulogy for the dead, 'and above all of the *one* among the dead; the originator and leader of the National Socialist *Reich*, Adolf Hitler'.[3] The Führer, he was to say, had taken it upon himself to die because he could not submit to undignified treatment. 'He could not submit to the jurisdiction of judges who had no right to try him . . . .'

The state Hess had seen himself heading had been scarcely distinguishable from Hitler's *Führer* State, but without the gross violations; the Jews, for instance, might have asked to go to protective camps 'to save themselves from the rage of the German people' and in these camps conditions were to have been 'as humane as possible'.[4] It should not be thought that his programme was a stronger proof of insanity than his earlier bouts of amnesia, for Dönitz was occupying himself with much the same fantasy of being called to head a new German state.

Spandau had brought Hess, Dönitz and the others down to cold reality for a time. Reduced to the anonymity of numbers, they had not been allowed to speak to one another during their supervised times together in the washing cell, while sweeping the cell block corridor or during their thirty-minute exercise periods around an old linden tree in the prison yard, hands clasped behind their backs, thick, wood-soled prison shoes clomp-clomping the hard ground. The guards had held aloof in those early months, speaking only to give orders, visiting on the seven the hatred accumulated by the Nazi regime. The meals which they ate from tin trays alone in their cells – in order to prevent suicides, without knives or forks – were so meagre they had lost weight steadily ; soon the prison uniforms had hung shapelessly on their bony frames. Albert Speer had found himself bending to recover crumbs of bread which had fallen to the floor and realised it was the first time in his life he had not had enough to eat. 'Constant hunger, weakness'[5] he had noted in the clandestine diary he wrote on lavatory paper and smuggled out.

They had cleaned their cells and washed their underwear, socks and bedlinen by hand in an iron cauldron. At night their sleep had been interrupted constantly by warders turning up the cell lights to 'inspect' them. The Russian warders had made a point of doing this up to four times an hour according to a report on the 'mental torture' of the prisoners made by the French prison chaplain in 1950.[6] The one letter they had been allowed to write home each month had been censored for references to the Third Reich or its personalities, Nuremberg or contemporary politics, as had the one incoming letter allowed each month. Books had been the chief escape from tedium and utter loneliness ; these too had been censored for the forbidden topics. The library Hess had accumulated in Great Britain had formed the basis of a prison collection for whose borrowings Raeder had made himself puntiliously responsible.

Another escape had been the garden. When they arrived, this had consisted chiefly of nut trees and lilac bushes interspersed among a wilderness of weeds and grasses waist high. The first summer they had dug in the weeds and planted vegetables. Von Neurath, the only one who had known anything of gardening, had been given the resounding title 'Chief Garden Construction Director' ; Albert Speer had used his architectural talents to draw plans for landscaping the area. 'How we sweated !' Hess had written home describing their toil.[7] It is doubtful if he meant this to apply to himself. He had refused all work on the twin principles that they had not been sentenced to hard labour and the Nuremberg Trial was invalid in any case. In the winter, when it was no longer possible to work in the garden and they had been set to folding and glueing sheets of paper into envelopes, Hess had refused to come out of his cell; when the warders summoned him, he had moaned and groaned, pretending stomach cramps. Much the same had happened in the garden. 'As always a non-participant, Hess sat on his bench', Speer had recorded during their second year.[8] While the others had worked diligently and complied with the regulations as model prisoners – perhaps hoping for remission – Hess had established a pattern of non-co-operation from the start. At times he had refused to get up and lain abed moaning and groaning until tipped out by the warders; on one occasion, Speer recorded, when it had been raining, he had refused to go outside for the exercise period, again lying on his bed groaning.

'Seven,' the warder had called in to him, 'you'll be put in the punishment cell.'

Hess had got up and, shrugging, walked into the punishment cell himself. He had spent much time in solitary confinement there.[9]

The amount of attention he had succeeded in attracting to himself from the prison staff by his eccentricity and prickliness had kept him apart from the other prisoners. Albert Speer had been similarly cut off, partly on account of his repentance for the sins of the Third Reich during the Nuremberg trial. Dönitz especially had considered Speer's public confessions both self-serving and traitorous, but even Speer had been unable to get close to Hess. To Speer he seemed to play the martyr and buffoon alternately – as it could be said he had in Britain – 'thus', Speer concluded, 'fulfilling the two sides of his personality'.[10] But to Hess it was as if he cut himself off from the others to find peace in his own thoughts. Now, he had written to his mother in July 1949, he was able to understand men who felt impelled to become hermits and withdraw into complete loneliness.[11]

Difficult, pathetic, at times peremptory, as if assuming his former role as Stellvertreter, Hess had yet remained consistently logical in his attitude to the Nuremberg trial and all that resulted from it. Refusing to recognise its legality, he had refused to repent, refused to allow his counsel, Dr Seidl, to enter a plea for mercy[12] desperately though he had wanted to be free to be with his wife and growing son and walk again in the Bavarian mountains. And he had refused to allow his family to visit him in prison. He had considered it dishonourable to give the Allied authorities the satisfaction of forcing him to meet his wife and boy across a prison table with witnesses listening to every word in case the forbidden topics were mentioned. He had rejoiced when Ilse had written to say she understood his reasons, since it showed she too rated their 'own and German honour higher than personal wishes and feelings'.[13]

All the others, even Dönitz, who rejected the trial and his sentence as vehemently as Hess, had been glad to take advantage of the opportunity granted to see their families.

After some two and a half years in Spandau Hess had begun to pretend amnesia again. The rule of silence had been relaxed by this time. He had pointed to the British prison director making his rounds in the garden as he did every day and asked Speer who this stranger was.[14] He had played this trick so often he could hardly have expected to be taken wholly seriously. Nor could he have expected to gain release. No doubt it was a ploy which had become almost habit; it gained attention and broke monotony. He had been in captivity for twice as long as the others and, as Speer recorded later, the days were numbing in their evenness and emptiness; Speer had found it impossible to convey in words the 'forever unchanging sameness', the 'idiot organisation of emptiness'[15] which was the true 'if intangible horror of imprisonment'. Taken together with a gradual thaw in relations with the warders – apart from the Russian month – Hess had no doubt felt the need to inject challenge and emotion into what was becoming almost a good-natured vacuity.

After regaining his memory four months later – and proving it by an outburst of esoteric information on history and literature – Hess had begun suffering crippling stomach cramps and wailing and moaning all night, an eerie sound, which had caused Raeder in the next cell to complain to the French Director that his nerves were being shattered. When after this the Director had ordered Hess's mattress and blankets removed so that he could not lie moaning in bed all morning as well, Hess sat on his chair and wailed.[16]

All the other behaviour patterns he had displayed in captivity in Britain had returned in cycles, the obsession with poisons in his food, the swings of mood down to the blackest depressions when he refused to eat, and the crippling stomach pains; these were deemed to be of hysterical origin since no organic cause had been discovered.[17] Whether real or feigned, like his recurrent periods of amnesia, they had surely been symptoms of despair.

Despair had been fuelled by each glimmer of hope. In November 1954 von Neurath had been released on the grounds of his age and frail health after serving only nine of the fifteen years to which he had been sentenced. In the following months Hess had suffered badly, hardly eating, complaining of unbearable pains and wailing again at night. Speer had noted that Raeder and Dönitz virtually broke off relations with him; he assumed their military background made them intolerant of Hess's lack of bearing and self-control and what he described as his 'whining, self-pitying manner'.[18] Von Schirach and Raeder had begun aping his wails and cries of 'No! No! Ach! Oh! Oh!' Hess invariably won these nocturnal contests. After one such night in April 1955 Speer had visited Hess's cell and found him with a strange, confused look mumuring to himself, beseeching God Almighty to finish him off or let him go mad; later in the garden he had told Speer he could not go on. His weight had dropped to under nine stone by this time.

That autumn Raeder had been freed on the same grounds as von Neurath, age and ill-health, after serving nearly ten years of a 'life' sentence. Dönitz, sentenced to ten years, had followed him outside the next year, and in May 1957 Funk, also serving 'life', had been freed on grounds of health, leaving only the two younger men, Speer and von Schirach, both sentenced to twenty years, in Spandau with Hess. At another psychiatric examination that summer the scenes Hess played out as a matter of routine had been judged once again to be 'hysterical disturbances', not sufficiently serious to merit his transfer to a mental institution.[19]

The cycle of depressions had culminated in the closing months of 1959 with the most severe attacks of stomach cramps. Speer noted the suspicion that Hess had induced them by ingesting small quantities of washing detergent. His weight had fallen to under seven stone and he had become so weak he could not walk unaided even as far as the wash-cell. He had lain, grotesquely emaciated, wailing and groaning all day and night until, on 26 November, while the other two prisoners were in the garden with the duty warder, he had broken a lens of his glasses and used the jagged edge to open a large vein in his wrist. He had bled quietly for some time, beginning to feel very weak and pleasant, and looking forward to being freed from his pain for ever, he had told Speer the following morning, before he was discovered and hastily sewn up by the Russian doctor. Despite the waxy pallor of his face, Speer had been left with the impression of a child who had just carried off a prank. Afterwards Hess had begun to eat heartily again and, as always after an outburst, he became much calmer.[20]

On 10 May 1966, the twenty-fifth anniversary of his flight to Scotland, he had experienced another crisis. He had remained in his cell all day, according to Speer, sitting bolt upright at his table staring at the wall – scarcely surprising since he had by then been in captivity far longer than any normal span for 'life' in western penal systems, sent down by a tribunal whose validity he denied; moreover his two remaining fellows, serving twenty years, were due to be released in less than six months' time. Any spark he had kept alive that he might be allowed out with them had been extinguished two weeks later with the arrival of a motor lawnmower for the warders to use to keep the garden going for him when the working prisoners left.

He had passed that watershed on 1 October. Speer had been astonished by his morale in the last few days; he had watched the preparations for their departure without apparent reaction and made not a single bitter remark.[21] The same philosophical acceptance, so different from his performances before the warders, had been marked in his letters home. They had been full of good sense and advice, relieved by irony or that individual sense of the absurd stressed with the Hess laugh line 'VVV'. He had never complained.

Perhaps the saddest letter he had written had been comparatively early in his confinement, in 1951, after being told his mother had died. It was strange, he had confided to Ilse, despite his physical separation from his mother in the last years, 'the knowledge that she is no longer alive has produced an inconsolable sense of emptiness, the world has changed'.[22]

A little later he had written to his son asking whether he had ever really thought about the laws of nature, how they always presented one with fresh wonders, and telling him of Kant's reply when asked what he considered the greatest miracle: 'The starry heaven above us, the pricking conscience within us.' No science could explain, Hess had written, why one's conscience left one no peace if one had done someone wrong or hurt one's mother perhaps, just as no science, he had continued, could explain the feelings for beauty when listening to Mozart's *Kleine Nachtmusik* or seeing the mountain peaks glowing pink in the early light of dawn . . . .[23]

By 1966, when Hess had become the sole inmate of Spandau, his son had long grown to manhood – without anything but the haziest childish recollection of his father – and had begun publicising his father's plight. A 'Freedom for Rudolf Hess' Association had been formed by the family and had made innumerable appeals to the governments of the Four Powers, to religious leaders and human rights organisations; they had achieved wide international support and western governments had accepted the case for mercy. The Russians had not listened. They remembered the twenty million dead of 'the great patriotic war'; they believed Hess had flown to Scotland specifically to gain British acquiescence in Hitler's attack; besides Hess had been Hitler's right hand and, as the last living symbol of the highest echelons of the Nazi regime, it was unimaginable he could be released.[24] Without Russian agreement the western powers had declared themselves unable to act. His son believed and still believes the Russian veto was an excuse and the western powers, especially Great Britain, had their own reasons for ensuring that his father would never leave Spandau alive.[25] The files remain closed, so there is no evidence either way. It seems more likely, however, that Hess had become a pawn in the Cold War. The western powers had needed to maintain the Four-Power status of Berlin to preserve their rights of access to West Berlin, which lay inside the Soviet-dominated East German State. Since Spandau was one of only two remaining Four-Power institutions, they had feared a quarrel over it; Spandau had also served as a useful point of contact with the Russians – who, for their part, found the prison a useful listening post in the west.

Hess and his lawyer, Dr Seidl, had not helped the case for release. Hess had refused to recant or accept the validity of the Nuremberg trial, and Seidl – when in August 1965 Hess had finally agreed to see him – had spent much of the first interview reinforcing his client's conviction that he had suffered a miscarriage of justice from an illegal tribunal until the Soviet Director had stepped in and cut short his visit.[26] Afterwards he had continued to argue aggressively and, in terms of super-power politics, counter-productively that the Nuremberg trial had no legality. Thus Hess had been held in a three-way bind between the tensions of the Cold War and the purblind refusal of his own supporters to accept the most ancient law of *vae victis*.

In November 1969, the tenth anniversary of Hess's cry of despair by opening a vein in his wrist, he had fallen into a worse decline, staying in bed, refusing to eat, wash or shave, and groaning so loudly with pain that, according to the US Director, Colonel Eugene Bird, he had been heard by the guards on duty on the perimeter wall. 'It was an eerie moan', Bird wrote, 'as loud as a human being could groan without actually screaming.'[27] This time it was not one of his 'campaigns'. When at last the authorities had realised it and rushed him to the special security suite designed for him in the British Military Hospital – the first time he had left Spandau since his arrival twenty-two years before – he had a perforated duodenal ulcer and peritonitis had set in. Eight days later, on the night of 29 November, he had become convinced he was about to die – a point which was to acquire significance for the provenance of a later 'suicide note'. He had demanded the attendance of a British heart specialist, Dr Seidl and a German notary who could witness a statement he wished to sign; he had also asked that his son be informed.[28]

He had survived that night. In the following days, seduced by the comfort and splendour of the hospital room after the stone walls of his cell, and the care from the nurses, finally he had weakened in his resolve not to see his family under the dishonourable conditions of a prisoner and had allowed Colonel Bird to talk him into a Christmas visit from Ilse and his son. They had arrived at the hospital in the afternoon of 24 December – Ilse now grey-haired and Wolf Rüdiger, whom Hess had last seen as the three-and-a-half-year-old 'Buz', now a man of thirty-two. As they had entered the room where he sat waiting tensely he had shot up like a spring from his chair and brought his hand to his forehead, palm inwards in salute.

'I kiss your hand, Ilse!'

They had stared almost unbelievingly at one another before Ilse, restrained by her son from rushing up to him with outstretched hand, replied, 'I kiss your hand, father!'[29]

They had sat at opposite sides of a table set between partitions dividing the room. Hess had put on a cheerful, confident performance, asking about their flight, assuring them he was receiving 'absolutely overwhelming treatment and excellent medical care',[30] talking of his illness, listening to news of relations. They had been allowed thirty minutes, stretched to thirty-four.

Hess had returned to his bed afterwards smiling contentedly. 'I'm so happy I've seen them,' he had told Colonel Bird. 'I'm just sorry I waited so long . . .'[31]

One thing Hess said during that first visit was to acquire equal significance for the provenance of his later 'suicide note' as his certainty the previous month that he had been about to die. It concerned his former secretary Hildegard Fath, known in the close circle as 'Freiburg'. It will be recalled that, while feigning amnesia before the Nuremberg trial, he had pretended not to recognise her, which had caused her obvious distress. He had been unable to explain his reasons in letters home as Nuremberg had been a forbidden topic. This had evidently preyed on his mind, for one of his first remarks during the visit was to ask Ilse to convey his greetings to 'Freiburg' and say he was very sorry he had treated her very badly for over twenty years. There is no question he said words to that effect since they were published by his son in a book about his father which came out in 1984, three years before his death and any question of a suicide note.[32]

That first visit had broken Hess's principled stand against seeing his family while a prisoner. After he had recovered and been returned to Spandau, to the double 'chapel' cell furnished with his hospital bed and chair, he had received visits regularly every month from Ilse, Wolf Rüdiger or other members of his immediate family, apart from his grandchildren, whom he did not want to see in these circumstances.

Whether these visits helped him retain his equilibrium or whether such brief and frustrating reminders of love, family and a forbidden world outside served as exquisite refinements of his ordeal, threatening to crack open the hermit's shell in which he had had to encase himself, is open to debate. However his continued imprisonment had remained, as his son put it, 'unparalleled torture', the faint glimmers of hope of release which had shone from time to time serving as additional twists of the knife.

In February 1977 he had suffered another decline, during which he had tried to sever an artery with a knife. News of this attempt had sparked further appeals for his release from leading figures in the west. Lord Shawcross, formerly chief British prosecutor at Nuremberg, had declared that his continued imprisonment was a scandal: 'In no civilised country in the world is a "life" sentence taken literally. It is still a principle of humanity that a "life prisoner" is released after a suitable period . . . .'[33] The Russians had remained obdurate.

In December 1978 Hess had suffered a stroke which had left his eyesight impaired. In the aftermath, more than forty years after the judgment he had refused to recognise, he had at last been persuaded to appeal, although not against his sentence; he had written to the prison directorate asking them to release him because of his poor health; he wished to see his grandchildren and he was convinced he had only a short time to live. He had pointed to the three other 'life' prisoners, von Neurath, Raeder and Funk, who had been released long ago. His appeal had been rejected – as had another he had made the following year.[34]

By 1984 as he entered his ninetieth year, his health had deteriorated to such an extent that a lift had been installed to ease his twice-daily visits to the garden below. For some years the French prison chaplain, Pastor Charles Gabel, had been accompanying him once a week on these solitary excursions. Gabel had grown very fond of the frail old man and, in April 1986, approaching the forty-fifth anniversary of his original captivity in Great Britain, he had written directly to the British Prime Minister, Margaret Thatcher, on Hess's behalf. Sitting in the garden with Hess on 7 May, he had been able to tell him he had received a cordial reply from Mrs Thatcher; she had said his imprisonment was 'inhumane', but the Soviets refused to release him. Her Government would continue to seek his liberation, she had continued, 'but the matter depended, as before, on the agreement of the Soviets'.[35]

Later that month Hess had written another plea for release addressed to the heads of government of the Four Powers. Since he had left for England in 1941, he had begun, forty-five years had passed; for half his life he had been separated from his family. He was now an old man of ninety-two and he would like to pass what remained of his life with his family and meet his grandchildren, whom he had never seen. If this were not possible, he had added, he asked to be granted a holiday of four weeks with his family, during which time he would undertake no political activity and give no interviews.[36]

Still he was kept inside – with occasional breaks in his special suite in the British Military Hospital when his condition caused grave concern, as it had in March 1987. Still he was kept alive inside with the refinements of modern medicine.

On that morning of Monday 17 August 1987 – his last – his male nurse, an Algerian named Abdallah Melaouhi who had been with him for the past five years, came on duty by his own account at 6.45 and opened up the dispensary.[37] The British chief warder logged his entry to the cell corridor at 7.20.[38] Hess was in the lavatory cell, so Melaouhi waited for him to emerge, then escorted him to the wash-cell and helped him to wash and then to dress. Afterwards he helped him to the dispensary, weighed him and measured his blood-pressure, pulse and temperature, shaved him, trimmed his hair and gave him his daily massage. Then he counted out the pills for his heart and other ailments. It was a normal morning.

Objectively Hess now had more reason to hope for release than at any time in the past. That January Wolf Rüdiger had taken a petition to the Soviet Embassy in Bonn and for the first time received a reply; it had been in the form of an invitation to visit the Soviet Embassy in East Berlin. Contacting the Embassy, he had arranged a meeting at their West Berlin Consulate on 31 March, the date of a scheduled visit to his father. There he had been told that the fundamental attitude of the Soviet Government to his father's case remained unchanged: the war had cost the Soviet Union twenty million dead. The people could not forget it in one or two generations, perhaps not in three or four, and Hess – rightly or wrongly – had become in their minds a symbol for this war.[39]

Disappointing as this had appeared on the surface, Wolf Rüdiger had drawn encouragement from the fact that the Soviets were prepared to discuss the case at all. Meanwhile, the Soviet President, Mikhail Gorbachev, had been signalling his intention of easing the Cold War and, on 13 April, the West German weekly *Der Spiegel* had published a brief story that Gorbachev was considering Hess's release; it was believed, the report went, that he had come to the conclusion that an act of mercy for Hess would be greeted worldwide as a gesture of humanity.[40] When that summer the West German President, Richard von Weizsäcker, had made a state visit to Moscow, he had presented Gorbachev with a dossier on the case for Hess's release and, although this had been accepted noncommitally, von Weizsäcker had interpreted it as a hopeful sign for in the past Russian leaders had simply brushed aside the idea.[41]

Finally, in June, the German-speaking service of Radio Moscow had replied to an appeal from a member of the 'Freedom for Rudolf Hess' Association with a message that President Gorbachev's latest statement allowed the hope that 'your long-standing endeavours for the release of the war criminal, R. Hess, will soon be crowned with success'.[42] Wolf Rüdiger had assumed that Radio Moscow could not have sent such sensational advice unless it had been agreed in the highest quarter in the Kremlin.

It appears from the warders' log that Hess did not pay his usual visit to the garden that morning. It also appears he was not contemplating suicide, for he requested a form for his weekly requisition and ordered thirty packets of paper tissues, three rolls of lavatory paper, a sheet of writing paper and a ruler. This was at 10.20. Of course it was a Monday morning and had he not placed a weekly order it would perhaps have looked odd. Nevertheless, when, according to the log, Melaouhi wheeled in his lunch at 10.40, Hess asked him to buy a replacement for the kettle in his cell which had been defective for some time – a curious request if he were contemplating suicide.

At 12.15 an American warder named Jordan relieved the British warder, Miller, on cell duty. Hess had complained of Jordan to the US Director that April, following it up with a written request for his dismissal: all the other warders were friendly and polite, he had written, whereas Jordan was rude, indeed provoked him and had become a danger to his health.[43]

Probably he was having his usual after-lunch nap on his bed when Jordan took over outside the cell that day. He must have risen at about two, for at ten minutes past he was logged making his way down to the garden with Jordan. What happened thereafter is impossible to determine because the testimony and evidence from the enquiries of the British Military Police Special Investigation Branch and the subsequent review of the evidence by Detective Chief Superintendent Howard Jones of Scotland Yard are closed to the public. It is possible that he and Jordan made their way slowly a short distance to a bench seat on the main path behind the cell block where he liked to rest.

Here he had sat with Speer in those far off days which must by now have seemed another life watching the birds in the trees above, listening to their song; 'Like paradise,' Speer had recorded him saying almost with a touch of embarrassment one spring morning nearly thirty years before.[44] On other occasions he had crouched on the bench doubled in pain and groaning until threatened with the punishment cell if he refused to work with the others.

Here, as the lone prisoner in Spandau, he had sat with the former US Director, Eugene Bird, who had asked him one day whether it were true he had vowed that if he ever got out of prison he would never again keep a bird in a cage, 'Yes,' he had nodded.[45]

Bird had questioned him week after week, dedicated, as he had told him, to getting the first-hand story of his life and righting the inaccuracies put out by authors who had had no way of finding out the truth about his flight. Whether Hess could have told him the whole truth by then may be doubted. He had encased himself in such a shell of half-truth to protect the Führer and no doubt his own wild miscalculation, the realisation perhaps that he had been gulled into a fool's flight, that evasion had become habit and the hard edges of memory must have been chipped away. When Bird had pressed him about whether Hitler had known, he had assured him he had not. If Hitler had known of the plan, he would have had him arrested. He had taken a letter to the Duke of Hamilton, whom he had seen during the Olympic Games, but he could not remember what was in it.[46]

On another occasion he had told Bird it was untrue to say that he had known the Duke of Hamilton. He had never met the man, never dined with him. If he had been in the same room during the Berlin Olympics, they never conversed. Of course, he had continued, he had known about Hamilton's flying exploits.[47]

Bird had been about to play him a tape-recording of a BBC documentary about his flight. Evidently somewhat nervous of what he might hear, Hess had stressed that his mission had been a great one, he was not ashamed of it. He had wanted to end the war and bring about an understanding with England, stop the bloodshed and end the suffering. To Bird's question about whether he had really had high hopes of a settlement when he flew, he had laughed. 'Of course. Otherwise why should I have gone?'[48]

Bird had switched on the tape-recorder. He had not asked him what reasons he had had for his high hopes, nor why he had chosen Hamilton.

Another day they had talked of the Haushofers. They had known nothing about his flight, Hess had insisted; they had been working to find a basis for negotiation, but had not known – and could not have guessed – that he himself would fly to conduct the negotiations.

'We had not heard from the Duke of Hamilton and it was becoming urgent that something had to be done soon or it would be too late. There was the danger that England would make her pact with America before we could get someone over to talk to her on the highest authority ...'[49]

When Bird had pressed him about British claims that he had come over without bringing any specific terms, had demanded a British withdrawal from Iraq and had threatened to blockade England and starve her people, he had replied that these statements were lies; he had never at any time asked for a condition on Iraq and it was against his nature to threaten to starve anybody. Obviously much had been blotted from his memory. He had admitted this on occasion as if acknowledging there were difficult mental blocks: 'In reality I have not told you a lot,' he had said once. None the less, after endless evasions and contradictions, finally he had admitted he had known of 'Barbarossa' before he flew.[50]

On the same bench, some time after Bird had left Spandau and published his book about him, *The Loneliest Man in the World*, Hess had sat with Charles Gabel. The Pastor's weekly visits had always followed the same pattern, first about twenty minutes listening to the records Hess loved, Mozart, Beethoven, Schubert, played on an old record-player in the cell block, then down for a stroll in the garden. It is clear from the records of the conversations which Gabel published later in a book that, despite his age and physical frailty and the interminable years inside, Hess had retained mental acuity and balance. It is clear too that despite his extravagant theatre of distress in the earlier years and his cyclical descents into the ultimate troughs of despair, in the times between he had maintained an iron internal discipline and had made conscious efforts to remain mentally active. He had studied the new science of space exploration and thought creatively about its problems, read widely and deeply in history and philosophy, and always made copious notes on what he read. In addition, until prevented by age and stiffness, he had done daily physical exercises. His main source of strength, so he had told Bird, had been his *strong* belief in God – 'not in the Church, only in God'. He considered his faith in God equivalent to a philosophy of life. His own philosophy, he had said, was based on Schopenhauer's concept that ultimately man was guided by fate, 'but really', he had concluded, 'isn't our fate in God's hands?'[51]

Gabel had had no doubts he was completely sound in mind, and had even been able to discover during their talks in the garden gradually and somewhat to his surprise a wry sense of humour.[52] On the few occasions, though, when he had tried to draw him on his flight – perhaps because of all the previous grillings by Colonel Bird – Hess had remained silent as if it were a matter of complete indifference.

On a number of occasions Gabel had suggested he should make a public declaration of his regret for the war and the sufferings it had brought, particularly for the Jews; the priest had suggested that this would meet the objection of the Russians that he had never shown repentance and it might facilitate his release. On the subject of the extermination of the Jews, Gabel reported later in his book, Hess was always deeply moved, yet he had been fond of repeating that he himself bore no responsibility. He had rejected making a public statement because, he had said, prison was not the ideal place to make a statement which was truly free.[53]

On a later occasion, when Gabel had once more broached the subject, Hess had taken some time to reply, then said he saw no need to put it in writing; he had always regretted the war, its violence and excesses, his commitment to peace had been sufficiently demonstrated on 10 May 1941.[54]

Whether this was a conscious evasion of responsibility, whether he had come to believe it, it was a claim which was made for him by his supporters and repeated in Wolf Rüdiger's books. It sits uneasily with his confession to Colonel Bird that he knew of 'Barbarossa' before his flight; of course he could not have failed to know. It suggests he died unrepentant.

At 2.30 p.m. twenty minutes after he and Jordan had been logged going down to the garden, Jordan returned and told the French duty warder, Audoin, something had happened to his charge – so it appears from the warders' log: The '3' of the '30' obscures another now indecipherable figure. No doubt Jordan was in a state of alarm. He led Audoin down to the garden to a small shed known as the 'summerhouse', where Hess was lying. Exactly how he was lying and in what condition is impossible to know without the reports and testimony from the enquiries, but Audoin at once initiated emergency procedure and, since it was the American month in control of the prison, tried to contact the US Director, with no success.

Melaouhi became aware that something had happened while on the way back to the prison after buying Hess's replacement kettle. It was early afternoon by his account and a guard in one of the watchtowers shouted or made gestures indicating something had happened at the 'summerhouse'. He hurried there to find a scene like the aftermath of a wrestling bout. The ground was torn, the chair in which Hess liked to sit had been hurled aside and the old man himself lay apparently lifeless with no sign of breathing or discernible pulse. Jordan was standing by his feet in a state of shock. There were also two US soldiers whom Melaouhi had not seen before. He knelt by the body and attempted resuscitation, upon which one of the soldiers also knelt and began kneading Hess's chest to try and restart his heartbeat.[55]

The British warder due to relieve Audoin came on duty at 3.35. By this time a military ambulance had arrived, but Hess was still in the garden, thus over an hour since the incident. Medical staff who were attempting to resuscitate him now moved him to the ambulance and he was driven to the British Military Hospital, where he arrived by the British warder's log entry at 3.45 – five minutes later by Audoin's entry. At 4 p.m. Wolf Rüdiger received a phone call at his office from a journalist to say that his father was dying. He hurried home, but it was not until 6.45 by his account that he was rung by the US Director of Spandau and told briefly in English that his father had died at 4.10 that afternoon. He, the Director, was not empowered to give him any further details.[56]

The following morning Wolf Rüdiger took a flight to Berlin with Dr Seidl, thence by taxi to the prison, which they found besieged by a curious crowd held back by police. They identified themselves and were allowed through to the entrance, but the US Director, by Wolf Rüdiger's account extraordinarily nervous and unsure, told them they could neither enter the prison nor view the body. A press announcement was being prepared, he said, and asked them to leave the telephone number of their hotel; they would be given further details at four o'clock. The time went by with no call and Wolf Rüdiger rang the prison. When the US Director eventually came on the line, he regretted he could say nothing yet; the prison directorate was still in conference. The two had no option but to contain their bewilderment and anger, and wait by the telephone. At long last, the call came. The US Director read out a statement about to be given to the press: 'A preliminary investigation indicates that Rudolf Hess attempted to take his own life . . . ' Wolf Rüdiger listened speechless. It was over twenty-four hours since his father died; this brief and unsympathetic announcement was his first intimation of suicide.

'. . . Hess, as he was accustomed to do,' the US Director went on, 'went escorted by a prison warder to sit in a small cottage in the garden of the prison. On looking into the cottage a few minutes later, the warder found Hess with an electrical cord around his neck. Resuscitation measures were taken and Hess was transported to the British Military Hospital. After further attempts to revive Hess, he was pronounced dead at 16.10. Whether this suicide attempt was the actual cause of death is the subject of a continuing investigation . . .'[57]

30
POST-MORTEM

It had been evident for some years that Hess's death would be a political event, consequently a procedure had been laid down by the British authorities and agreed by the Four Powers for post-mortem examination by a leading pathologist. The plan called for Professor J.M. 'Taffy' Cameron, Professor of Forensic Medicine at the University of London and Honorary Civilian Consultant in forensic pathology to the British Army, to perform the autopsy. Should he be unavailable, Lieutenant Colonel 'Bob' Menzies, the only British Army pathologist with a diploma in medical jurisprudence, was to be called. Cameron began the autopsy at 8.15 in the morning of Wednesday 19 August, assisted by Menzies. Other medical and military observers from the Four Powers watched on closed circuit televsion from an adjacent room.

Hess's corpse was still clad in the clothes he had been wearing on his last afternoon in the garden; after these had been removed, Cameron began his external examination of the body, finding:

... signs of recent hospital therapy to the left side of the neck, the thumb side of the left wrist and the back of the right wrist. There were marks on the front side of the chest consistent with resuscitation, particularly over the outer side of the left chest, and over the midline of the chest. There was a circular bruised abrasion over the top of the back of the head and there was a slight swelling (oedema) of the ankles. A fine linear mark, approximately 3 in. (7.5 cms) in length and 0.75 cms in width was noted running across the left side of the neck, being more apparent when the body was viewed with ultra-violet light, as was an old scar on the left side of the chest, 126 cms from the heel, 7 cms from the midline. Apart from a minor abrasion of the upper lip, 1 cm, from the right nostril, there were no other marks of recent injury or violence on the body. Petechiae (haemorrhagic spots) were noted in the conjunctivae of both eyes, particularly on the left side.[1]

Cameron began his internal examination by incising and peeling back

334

the scalp, on the under surface of which he found a faint bruise of the right temporal muscle and 'deep bruising over the top of the back of the head, noted on external examination'. The skull had not been fractured, however. He found the brain intensely congested; in section it revealed haemorrhagic spots. Peeling back the skin of the neck, he found 'deep bruising over the left side of the angle of the jaw and over the left side of the inside of the back of the throat – that within the throat being consistent with resuscitation'. He also found 'excessive bruising' to the upper part of the right side of the thyroid cartilage (voice box) 'consistent with compression of the neck' and deep bruising behind the voice box – particularly over the right side of the neck and to the strap muscles on the left of the neck. He found further deep bruising when he opened the chest, together with a fracture of the breast bone and multiple fractures of the ribs on the left. All fractures he found consistent with attempts at resuscitation and concluded they had no bearing on the cause of death.

He took samples of blood, urine, stomach contents and internal organs which were later sent for analysis. Meanwhile, he had sufficient data to conclude that the primary cause of death was asphixiation, and an official announcement to this effect was put out at 18.00 that evening, together with a statement that a note found on the body clearly implied that Hess had planned to take his own life.

The wording of the note was read out to Wolf Rüdiger Hess on the telephone.[2] He and Dr Seidl were already dubious in the extreme about the idea of suicide. How, they had asked themselves, could a ninety-three-year-old so frail as to be unable to walk to the garden without a stick and a warder's assistance, so stooped and stiff he could not look much above the horizontal without overbalancing, and with very little strength in his hands, have managed to tie a knot in an electric cable and hang himself, as implied by the official statement. Now the content of the 'suicide' note seemed to confirm their suspicion. In translation it ran:

Request to the [Prison] Directorate to send this home.
Written a couple of minutes before my death.
I thank you all, my loved ones, for all you have done for me out of love.
Tell Freiburg that, to my immense sorrow, since the Nuremberg Trial I had to act as if I didn't know her. There was nothing else I could do, otherwise all attempts to gain freedom would have been impossible.
I would have been so happy to see her again – I have received the pictures of her as of you all.
Your big fellow [*Euer Grosser*][3]

The whole tenor and content of this note cried out to Wolf Rüdiger that it was not a suicide note and had not been written recently. Had his father been contemplating suicide he would not have put 'Written a couple of minutes before my death', but something more on the lines of '. . . before I voluntarily depart this life'. The signature *'Euer Grosser'* was a form he had not used since the early 1970s, when he had taken to signing off *'der Eure'* ('Your one'). Above all, the reference to 'Freiburg' and the lack of any reference to his grandchildren convinced Wolf Rüdiger that it must have been written almost twenty years ago, before his first visit to his father in the British Military Hospital on Christmas Eve 1969. It will be recalled that one of the first things Hess had said on that occasion had been to ask Ilse to convey his greetings to 'Freiburg' and say he was very sorry he had treated her so badly for over twenty years.[4] That had salved his conscience with regard to his former secretary and he had not referred to the incident since. Also, since that time he had received visits from his family, not just photographs as the note implied; indeed since beginning to visit him the family had *sent* no photographs at all, but had *taken* pictures for him with them. And none of these had been of 'Freiburg', as was confirmed when the pictures were returned by the prison Directorate. It will also be recalled that Hess had believed himself to be dying on the night of 29 November 1969, and had made various demands. Wolf Rüdiger Hess believes, therefore, that his father probably wrote the note then, but as it mentioned the forbidden topic, the Nuremberg Trial, it had been retained by the prison directorate and not sent on to Ilse.[5]

It had been agreed in October of 1982 that, in the event of Hess's death, his remains would be handed over to his family for private burial in the family plot at Wunsiedel. That evening Wolf Rüdiger and Dr Seidl arranged to take charge of the body at the us Air Force base at Grafenwöhr, and there, on the following day, 20 August, the hand-over took place in an atmosphere which Wolf Rüdiger describes in his book as frosty formality. In view of his doubts about the official verdict of 'suicide', he had decided to commission another post-mortem by German pathologists, and next morning the coffin was driven under police escort to the Forensic Medical Institute of the University of Munich, where Professors W. Spann and W. Eisenmenger were to conduct a second autopsy in the presence of Dr Seidl.

They worked under difficulties. They had no evidence of how the body had been found or what had happened to it subsequently, could not see the video made during Professor Cameron's post-mortem or x-rays taken previously; they did not have Hess's medical records and many of the internal organs were missing, including the larynx and upper throat organs which Cameron had found so damaged. None the less the findings from their initial external examination of the neck were extraordinarily suggestive. Whereas Cameron in his report was to describe nothing in this region save 'A fine linear mark, approximately 3 in. (7.5 cms) in length and 0.75 cms in width ... running across the left side of the neck, being more apparent when the body was viewed with ultra-violet light', the German pathologists saw a 'plainly visible' brownish-reddish marking of variable breadth, 'to the left side up to 6 mm wide, over the middle up to 20mm wide' extending from a high point under the left ear, so far as could be judged, obliquely down to the middle of the throat and around to the right.[6] When they turned the body over, they found a double-track reddish discolouration running almost horizontally around the back of the neck, each of the twin stripes of maximum one centimeter in breadth enclosing a pale line up to six millimetres wide. This was typical of marks left by a single cord around the neck, squeezing the blood either side to form a tram-line effect.[7] Colour photographs were taken.

Their internal examination showed pronounced haemorrhagic spots in the conjunctivae of the eyes, in the neighbourhood of the ears and on the inner surface of the scalp. Their conclusions were that death had been caused by the application of force to the neck by a cord form of instrument.

Meanwhile, in view of the worldwide interest Hess's death had aroused, in particular sensational reports that Right extremists and neo-Nazis were intent on converting his funeral into a festival of remembrance, Wolf Rüdiger and the family had decided that a quiet burial in the family plot as Hess had wished would be impossible. After the autopsy in Munich, therefore, the body was buried secretly in a temporary location.

On 24 August the American Associated Press agency reported further details of the suicide: the electric flex Hess had used to hang himself had been an extension for a reading lamp in the garden hut, which had been fixed to the wall or ceiling; Hess had looped it around his neck while sitting, then raised his legs and fallen sideways off his seat.[8] In what was termed a 'final statement on the death of Rudolf Hess' issued by the Four Powers on 17 September – one month after the event – there was no reference to the extension cable having been fixed already; it stated simply that 'Rudolf Hess hanged himself from a window latch in a small summerhouse in the prison garden, using an electrical extension cord which had been kept in the summerhouse for use in connection with a reading lamp ...'[9] It gave no details of how the old man had contrived to hang himself, the time he had made the attempt, or his condition when found, nor did it suggest why he had been left unattended. It did state 'the routine followed by the staff ... was consistent with normal practice', which could be taken to mean that it had been usual to leave him to his own devices in the 'summerhouse', or that a lapse by the warder, Jordan, was being covered up for international political reasons.

The 'final statement' also referred to the suicide note as having been 'written on the reverse side of a letter from his daughter-in-law dated 20th July 1987'; this proved to be the case when the letter was returned to Wolf Rüdiger's wife by the British Director the following week. Curiously, the note had been sent to the 'senior document examiner from the laboratory of the British Government Chemist', who had concluded there was 'no reason to doubt that it was written by Rudolf Hess'.

By this time Professor Cameron had produced his report. It was as sparse as the Four-Power statement: there was no account of the circumstances in which the body had been found, no discussion of the manner in which Hess had come by his end, only partial differentiation of the damage to the neck which might have resulted from resuscitation and that which might have resulted from the 'suicide' attempt, no suggestion as to how Hess might have acquired the 'circular bruised abrasion' noted 'over the top of the back of the head'. The 'fine linear mark, approximately 3 in. (7.5 cms) in length and 0.75 cms in width', which was noted in the summary of findings as 'consistent with a ligature' – thus the electrical flex Hess had apparently placed around his neck – was described merely as 'running across the left side of the neck'; no indication was given of its angle or precise location. In the conclusions the actual manner of death was described in one word: 'SUSPENSION'. The cause of death was diagnosed as 'ASPHYXIA' produced by 'COMPRESSION OF THE NECK'; as noted, the linear mark on the left side of the neck was referred to as 'consistent with a ligature', thus the inference was that compression was by ligature, but as to how the ligature had been applied and how he had suspended himself or been suspended there was not one word of supporting observation, evidence or argument.

Speculation is no part of the forensic pathologist's task and there is no requirement for a description of how the victim met his end – or might have met his end – nor whether the injuries are consistent with witnesses' testimony – although these things are frequently included. Certainly it would not have been expected that Professor Cameron would confer with Professors Spann and Eisenmenger before drawing up his report; nor, probably, had he either knowledge of or responsibility for what appears to have been disgracefully high-handed, unsympathetic, indeed callous and ungenerous treatment of Hess's family at the end of their long ordeal, which had stretched over decades. None the less the whole purpose of the pre-planning which had resulted in Cameron and Menzies being whisked from their holiday locations to Berlin had been to pre-empt or defuse political repercussions. So far as relations between the Four Powers and West Germany were concerned his report had precisely the opposite effect. Whether it is described as laconic, guarded or simply Anglo-Saxon, it failed to answer the questions raised by the equally laconic, guarded and tardy statements from the prison directorate, or the suggestive findings of Professor Spann's autopsy or the suspicions connected with Hess's extreme frailty and his apparently anachronistic suicide note. Significantly it failed to provide any arguments or observations to support either suicide or murder or indeed misadventure – significantly because the reason for calling in Cameron was essentially political, yet his report left all political questions open.

Wolf Rüdiger Hess and the British surgeon and author Hugh Thomas soon convinced themselves that Hess had been murdered; both wrote books, *Mord an Rudolf Hess? (Murder of Rudolf Hess?)* and *A Tale of Two Murders*, in which they pointed to Margaret Thatcher's Government as prime suspect in a political assassination; both referred to the indications from Moscow that Gorbachev had been about to consent to Hess's freedom; both suggested that the British Government had had him killed to prevent him leaving Spandau alive and talking. Thus far, Wolf Rüdiger wrote, the British had hidden successfully behind the Soviet veto while pretending to urge his father's release; when it appeared the veto would be lifted, they had to silence him. The reasons he discerned in dark secrets for England hidden in those British Government files closed until 2017, possibly also in the Jewish factor. He speculated that his father might have brought over a solution to the Jewish problem by resettlement, the inference being that had his peace efforts been successful, the holocaust would have been avoided.[10] In support of this hypothesis – and it was nothing more – he stated that during the 'Camp David' meeting between the United States President, Jimmy Carter, and the heads of State of Israel and Egypt, Menachem Begin and Muhammad Sadat, in September 1978, Carter and Begin had signed a secret protocol that Hess would never leave Spandau alive.[11] He asserted this without producing evidence of any kind; it explained how the British Government had been able to have his father murdered during the US month in control of the prison.

The murderers were, by his account, two members of the SAS [British Special Air Services] who had entered Spandau on the Saturday night, 15–16 August, before Hess's death. These were the two strangers in US Army uniform whom Melaouhi had come across by the 'summerhouse' that Monday afternoon; their apparent attempt to restart Hess's heart had in reality been designed to finish him off. The information had come to Wolf Rüdiger from a South African lawyer with contacts to western intelligence services, who had learnt it at 8 a.m. on Tuesday 18 August – the morning after the 'murder' – from an officer of the Israeli intelligence service whom he had known personally and professionally

339

for four years. According to the lawyer, Hess's murder had been planned by MI5 to the orders of the British Home Office. The two killers had come from 22 SAS Regiment, Bradbury Lines, Herefordshire, and the US, French and Israeli intelligence services had been initiated into the plot; indeed the final go-ahead had been given by the CIA on the Monday morning.[12]

Hugh Thomas did not go so far as this in his published account; he simply asserted that the British Government was the only party to gain by Hess's death since it had been covering up the truth about him since 1941. What they had been covering up, according to Thomas, was the fact that he was not Rudolf Hess, but a double. Thomas had presented this theory first in an earlier book, *The Murder of Rudolf Hess*, published in 1979. During a period of service in Berlin he had had occasion to see Prisoner No 7 in Spandau without a shirt during a routine medical check, and had noticed that there were no scars on his left upper chest, where the real Hess had been shot in 1917. He had argued not only that the bullet must have left a visible scar but also that an operation to remove the bullet by the German surgeon Sauerbruch would have left even larger scars. Prisoner No 7, however, did not have these marks, and x-rays to his lungs showed no trace of the internal path of the bullet.

It is a mystery how Sauerbruch's operation came to be accepted, because it is plain from Hess's letters in 1917 that his wound had been from a clean through-shot from a small-calibre rifle and no surgery had been involved. When Charles Gabel had told Hess the theory in May 1979, Hess had laughed heartily and it had put him in such good humour that they had discussed substitution theories for some time. Finally Gabel had told him that his wife believed he was himself, and Hess, Gabel wrote, seemed to be thoroughly persuaded of it too. He told Gabel that two English doctors had visited him recently to look for the famous scars – from entry and exit – and had finally found them, although they were not very visible.[13]

Neither Cameron, Spann nor Eisenmenger recorded the scars in their post-mortem reports, but, according to Wolf Rüdiger Hess, in February 1989 Professor Eisenmenger wrote to a colleague to say that during their autopsy they had found on the left chest 'two insipid old scars' from an earlier gunshot wound.[14]

Aside from the practically invisible scars, Hugh Thomas's *Doppelgänger* theory was unconvincing; his hypothesis was that Himmler had had the real Hess shot down over the North Sea, then sent his carefully schooled double over in an identical Me-110 from Norway, but he failed to provide Himmler with a convincing motive, suggesting only that the Reichsführer aimed to displace Hitler, whom the British had refused to do business with. This was a misreading of Himmler's utterly dependant character and devotion to the genius of the Führer. Thomas also misread Hess's character. A large thread of his argument concerned differences between the habits and demeanour of the man who landed in Scotland and the real Hess. However, a study of the real Hess's character provides the strongest case for supposing that the man who landed in Scotland and Prisoner No 7 were indeed Hess; moreover, his letters from captivity reveal a knowledge of the real Hess which a double would not have been able to discover or memorise over such a long period. And after all why should a double keep up the pretence for over forty years of captivity?

Thus neither Thomas nor Wolf Rüdiger Hess have provided a plausible motive for the British and American Governments conspiring – since the 'murder' occurred in the US month on duty – to prevent Hess leaving Spandau alive. There is no evidence for Thomas's assertion that Hess was not Hess – plenty of evidence to indicate he was – and no evidence to support Wolf Rüdiger's hypothesis that included in his father's mission was a plan to solve the Jewish problem by resettlement. There remain only the British Government files closed until 2017. Whether these contain a strong enough motive for murder cannot be known; it is safe to assume that, if they do, the sensitive documents will be 'weeded' or the files themselves will be kept 'closed' long after 2017.

Despite the lack of any provable motive, there are ample grounds for suspicion about Hess's death. Dr Seidl, knowing something of Hess's physical condition, when he first heard the Four-Power statement – issued by three powers only since the Russians refused to agree it – had declared it 'unimaginable' that the ninety-three-year-old could have committed suicide, and had threatened litigation in Britain and the United States to force a 'satisfactory' account of his death.[15] This was before the highly suggestive findings – as will appear – from Professor Spann's post-mortem. The various official announcements, including the 'final statement' do not add up to a satisfactory account. How in the 'few minutes' he was left alone in the 'summerhouse' could Hess with his weak and clumsy grasp have written his suicide note, tied the extension flex to the small window catch, lopped it around his neck, tied it either very tightly or with a slip knot – since the flex acted like a ligature to leave a horizontal mark – and finally have fallen or thrown himself to the ground?

Secondly there is the suicide note. Would Hess have written calmly 'a couple of minutes before my death' if he had meant 'I am about to take my own life'? Would his non-recognition of 'Freiburg' still have been uppermost in his mind more than forty years after Nuremberg? Would he not rather have mentioned why he was about to kill himself? Surely his reason or depression would have filled his mind. How would he have known that Jordan would leave him for sufficiently long to accomplish his end? Why should he mention pictures of his family when he had been seeing his family? Finally, why should he have reverted to a style of signature he had not used for over twenty years? Taken together these points make the 'suicide note' incredible. And why should the note have been passed to the senior document examiner of the British Government Chemist to test its authenticity? Who else would have written such a message in Hess's handwriting on the back of a letter from Wolf Rüdiger's wife and signed it '*Euer Grosser*'? Obviously the note was a forgery copied expertly from a note Hess had written on 29 November 1969, but so misconceived in content and style as to defeat the object, which could only have been to cover up murder or an embarrassing lapse in discipline or efficiency in the prison. Since it is unlikely that such a skilled forger was carried on the prison staff, it suggests the intervention of the security services.

The most positive evidence to support a theory of murder comes from Professor Spann's post-mortem findings. He was at one with Professor Cameron in ascribing Hess's death to asphyxia caused by compression of the neck; the marks he found right round the neck, taken together with the damage to the internal neck organs as described by Professor Cameron and the haemorrhagic spots in the conjunctivae of the eyes, left no doubt whatever that there had been, as he put it in his subsequent 'Opinion' for Wolf Rüdiger Hess, 'an operation of force against the neck by means of a strangulation instrument'; this had interrupted the blood, hence oxygen supply to the brain and brought about central paralysis.[16]

Where Spann and Eisenmenger could not agree with Professor Cameron was in his description of how the strangulation force had been exerted, namely the single word 'suspension', for of the two types of compression of the neck always differentiated in forensic medicine, their findings pointed to strangulation or throttling rather than suspension or hanging. In the British textbook *Gradwohl's Legal Medicine* the ligature mark left by strangulation is described thus: '... usually horizontal and lower than a mark of hanging, being either across or below the thyroid cartilage. There are obviously exceptions to this rule, but they are not common.'[17] The mark left by hanging is described in the same work as following the position of the noose, 'coming to a point at the point of suspension where it is usually interrupted or shows an irregular mark of a knot'. The colour is described as pale at first, but becoming 'brown and parchment like' as the post-mortem period lengthens.[18]

Obviously the marks found by Spann and Eisenmenger corresponded to strangulation or throttling rather than a typical hanging; this is plain from the colour photographs they took, which are reproduced in Wolf Rüdiger's book. The exact course of the mark on the left of the neck running obliquely down from a highest point under the left ear cannot be determined since Professor Cameron's post-mortem cut and subsequent stitching up passes through and possibly distorts the direction; nevertheless the remainder of the mark on the front of the neck runs an almost horizontal course at a height of or below the level of the larynx – Spann and Eisenmenger describe it as 'obviously not above the larynx' – and the double-track marking around the back of the neck is horizontal. As Spann and Eisenmenger put it in their 'Opinion': 'The data pointed rather to a throttling act than a hanging'. They also discussed the internal bruising and injuries to the neck. *Gradwohl's Legal Medicine* states that fractures of the hyoid bone or of the thyroid cartilage (voice box) or both are not uncommon in hanging, and the fractures are usually associated with at least a little haemorrhage. However, Spann and Eisenmenger state in their 'Opinion' that in their experience such massive damage and haemorrhaging in such diverse areas of the neck organs and muscles as described in Cameron's report are not usual in typical hangings and even unusual, 'not to say rare', in atypical hangings or throttlings.

It was no more Spann's and Eisenmenger's task to speculate than it was Cameron's; moreover they lacked the data which would have allowed them to draw conclusions as to whether death had been caused by hanging or throttling; they could only record that their findings did not conform to those of a typical hanging, but they could not exclude 'a special type of atypical hanging'. They did, however, remark on the fact that Professor Cameron had not described the course or height of the 'fine linear mark' he had found on the left side of the neck, nor had he discussed the possibility of throttling.

The present writer put it to Professors Spann and Eisenmenger that the horizontal double mark they had found running horizontally around the back of the neck might perhaps have been caused by 'post-mortem hypostasis' exaggerated by the skin folding as Hess's head was raised and bent back over a stainless steel block during Professor Cameron's post-mortem.[19] 'Hypostasis' is the drainage of blood by gravity after death producing a discoloration of the skin of the lower areas not subject to pressure, that is those areas on which the body is not resting. *Gradwohl* gives the first appearances from twenty to thirty minutes after death as dull red patches 'which deepen, increase in intensity and coalesce to form, within 6–10 hours, an extensive area of reddish-purple colour'.[20]

Spann and Eisenmenger replied that in thousands of autopsies using steel and wooden blocks to support the neck and shoulders they had not observed such marks as they had found [on Hess]; furthermore the marks were on both sides as well as the back of the neck, which argued against this theory. And, of course, the theory could not explain the equally significant marks around the throat; being uppermost when

343

the body was stored, hypostasis would not have shown here.[21]

Spann and Eisenmenger were extremely careful in their reply, but, while stating that they had made no reference to whether Professor Cameron and his colleagues had or had not seen the strangulation marks they had discovered and described, they did not know why the possibility of throttling had not been taken into account in the first post-mortem. They went on: 'We are even of [the] opinion that after our findings the decisive and final diagnosis of hanging without discussion of the other possibilities of an operation of force against the neck was not justifiable.'

They were not saying they were able to decide on the evidence available to them that Hess had been throttled; they were denied practically all the material data on which they might have made a judgement – 'the detailed circumstances of the case, the findings [of the first post-mortem], the witnesses' testimony as well as the video film'. All they could do was repeat that, while it was not a typical hanging, certain forms of atypical hanging could not be excluded.

People can and do kill themselves by hanging from fixtures as low as the handle of a door; Hess could, therefore, have hung himself fatally from the catch of a window. If he had managed to tie a firm enough knot in the flex around the catch – or perhaps the flex was fixed there already – and a tight enough knot in a noose of flex around his neck, he could have thrown himself sideways or backwards – perhaps knocking the top of the back of his head against a table or a part of the door or wall of the summerhouse with sufficient force to cause the bruising noted in Cameron's report, finally hanging half backwards, half right shoulder downwards perhaps, to account for the horizontal mark around the back of his neck and the oblique mark on the left neck rising to its highest point under the left ear, and there lost consciousness as the noose cut the blood supply to his brain. He could have succeeded in 'atypically' hanging himself.

If Hess did so succeed, and if Professor Cameron believed that something of that sort had occurred, and if he knew of the ligature marks discovered by Professors Spann and Eisenmenger which pointed to throttling rather than hanging, why did he not discuss, justify or modify his single word conclusion, 'suspension'? Why, if the aim was to defuse political speculation, was the Four-Power 'final statement' almost equally laconic? And why was it necessary to have a 'suicide note' forged? Had the aim been to incense the Hess family and supporters, and humiliate the West German authorities, it would scarcely have been possible to devise better procedures. The only conclusion to be drawn is that there were strong elements of doubt about how Hess actually died – unless possibly the prison directorate had become so accustomed to arrogant behaviour they knew no other.

Meanwhile the material evidence – the garden shed, flex and furniture, Spandau prison itself – was destroyed; with it went Hess's flying suit and helmet, and his splendid flying boots and all his possessions, taken no doubt as souvenirs. Standing orders required the destruction of a prisoner's belongings on his death in order to prevent their use as Nazi cult objects; there was a danger of this with Hess as he had been built up by his supporters into the 'decent' face of National Socialism and a 'martyr for peace'; it had even been suggested that in other circumstances he would have been a candidate for the Nobel Peace Prize.

On 17 March the following year, seven months after his death, Hess's remains were taken from their secret burial site to Wunsiedel and reinterred in the family plot beside those of his mother and father and his brother Alfred, who had died in 1963. It was the quiet ceremony he had wished. Ilse and his sister Grete were not fit enough to go, and there were barely a dozen mourners including the funeral staff to attend the service afterwards.[22]

His simple headstone bears the legend:

RUDOLF HESS

26.4.1894 – 17.8.1987

ICH HAB'S GEWAGT

'I dared' or 'took the plunge'. That cannot be denied; nor can his son's equally apposite comment that he had, despite spending half his life in cruel and inhuman captivity, 'withstood it mentally and spiritually unbroken'.[23] Nor can it be doubted that the son fulfilled the father's wishes when he concluded his book *Mord an Rudolf Hess?* with the final passages of Hess's address at the end of the Nuremberg trials:

I was permitted to work for many years of my life under the greatest son my *Volk* has brought forth in its thousand year history. Even if I could I would not want to erase this period of time from my existence. I am happy to know that I have done my duty to my *Volk* – my duty as a German, as a National Socialist, as a loyal follower of the Führer. I regret nothing . . ..

POSTSCRIPT

The questions remain about his end as about his flight. Four days before the burial at Wunsiedel, Hugh Thomas made public his belief that prisoner No 7 had been hit on the head and then strangled with a wire by an attacker standing in front of him. Despite the official disdain for his theory that Prisoner No 7 was not Hess, the support he was able to attract after publication of *A Tale of Two Murders* caused the Crown Prosecution Service to commission an investigation into the allegations. The case was given to Detective Chief Superintendent Howard Jones of Scotland Yard's serious crimes squad.[1]

By this time the site had been flattened, the evidence destroyed and witnesses dispersed. Jones's task was confined in practice to studying the testimony and evidence collected during the inquiries by the Special Investigation Branch of the Military Police, the medical evidence from both British and German post-mortem examinations, and weighing up the suspicions and allegations of Hugh Thomas and Wolf Rüdiger Hess. To familiarise himself with the background, he first commissioned a historian to draw up a diagramatic scheme of Nazi leadership and a character profile of the subject of his inquiry.

The following year, 1989, he presented his findings to the Director of Public Prosecutions, whose conclusion, announced in November, was that his report provided 'no cogent evidence' to prompt further investigation into the circumstances.[2] If for 'cogent' the word 'convincing' is substituted, the statement confirms the suspicions aroused by the brevity of Professor Cameron's report and the 'Final Statement', for of course 'no convincing evidence' does not mean 'no evidence'; it is thus clear that elements of doubt exist. Rhodri Morgan, Member of Parliament for Cardiff West, asked that Howard Jones's report be placed in the House of Commons Library; the request was refused.[3] Like the original reports of the Military Police Special Investigation Branch, the Scotland Yard report is closed to the public and will no doubt remain so. Evidently there is something to hide.

Despite the absence of details about the manner of Hess's death, conclusions can be drawn from the failure of the Crown Prosecution Service to take further action. For one thing Wolf Rüdiger's accusations against Mrs Thatcher's Government, the Home Office, M15 and the SAS can be dismissed. Entry to Spandau was checked carefully at all times with numbered passes; the first task of the Special Investigation Branch team would have been to check the entries and exits, and had two SAS men entered the prison, however disguised, their presence would have been noted and accounted for. Had they got themselves up in US Army uniform, they would have been recognised by members of the small *bona fide* US guard detachment as imposters. This would have appeared in the testimony Howard Jones scrutinised. The presence of two such strangers in the prison on the day in question must have provided 'cogent' grounds for further action by the Director of Public Prosecutions, hence it is evident there was no testimony or evidence of this kind whatsoever. In fact, the two 'strangers' in US army uniform Melaouhi reported were US medics.

The obvious and most likely explanation for Wolf Rüdiger's allegations, both about SAS murderers and about successive British Governments intent on keeping his father in Spandau while publicly protesting their desire to release him is Soviet disinformation. The KGB campaign continues to roll, as shown by their recent release of Soviet documents on Hess, filed under his supposed name in homosexual circles, 'Black Bertha'. Wolf Rüdiger, Dr Seidl and the whole 'Free Rudolf Hess' Association were obvious tools for a KGB campaign to foment trouble between West Germany and the NATO allies. To judge by the lamentably strident tone of his book, Wolf Rüdiger fell, no doubt unwittingly, for the Soviet plot. *Mord an Rudolf Hess?* became a best-seller and has gone through several editions; the mostly unsupported political allegations it contains are believed by tens of thousands of Germans, surely an astounding success for the KGB (if this was indeed their doing), a part of which can be put down to the British fetish for official secrecy.

It is also apparent from the Crown Prosecutor's failure to take action that Hugh Thomas's wilder allegations have no basis. Practically the first task in a murder or suicide inquiry is to establish the victim's identity. Howard Jones knew of Thomas's theories; he had met him and discussed his claims at length. Had he found evidence to support the theory that the man in Spandau was not Hess, it must have provided sufficiently 'cogent' grounds for further investigation, for it would have supplied that other essential in a murder enquiry: motive. If Prisoner No 7 had been an imposter, successive British Governments would have had the strongest possible motive for ensuring he never left Spandau alive. It must be concluded, as Hess himself had concluded when Hugh Thomas's first book appeared, that he was indeed himself; there is no question he played the part well.

There remain the questions about his flight. It is doubtful if they will ever be answered satisfactorily, even after 2017. The letter to the Duke of Hamilton which he undoubtedly brought with him must appear when the files are released; if it does not appear, it will be evidence of a serious cover-up. The letter may provide the answer to whether he was lured to Great Britain and, if so, by whom and how. If it does not, it is difficult to account for the lies and continuing secrecy surrounding it.

There are several possible explanations for his flight. The first, held by surviving Foreign Office officials who were directly in charge of his case under Cadogan – Roger Makins (now Lord Sherfield) and (now Sir) Frank Roberts as well as Robert Cecil, who worked for Sir Stewart Menzies and censored Hess's letters – is that Hess was slightly deranged and made the flight entirely on his own initiative out of genuine belief he might persuade the British to oust Churchill and so stop a wasting war between the two white nations – before the attack on Russia – mixed with personal desire to achieve a great feat which would regain for him a position he felt he was losing at the Führer's court.[4] People looked for another, hidden explanation because it seemed such an extraordinary thing to do. In reality there was no secret explanation. It was simply irrational.

The second possibility, held by a number of historians and writers, is that there *was* a powerful opposition in Great Britain who could see no prospect of victory, only the certainty of tremendous waste of lives and treasure leading to the end of the British Empire and the triumph of Soviet Bolshevism or US economic imperialism.[5] Of course there were such people and their diagnosis was quite correct: all three fears were realised. There is no doubt either that such feelings were strong in some of the greatest houses in the land and perhaps strongest in the City of London, nor that there were constant contacts between the City and German financiers through the Bank of International Settlements in Basle. However, no proof has surfaced of a coherent group with plans to oust Churchill and in contact with Hess. If such proof exists in the 'Hess' or 'Peace feelers' files closed until 2017, it is strange that the former Foreign Office men in charge of Hess's case do not remember it. Hess's arrival made such a sensation the antecedent causes are not likely to have been forgotten by those who must have known of them had they been referred to in the official files. The other strong argument against this is Hess's choice of the Duke of Hamilton. If he came to speak to a genuine opposition who had, as it were, invited him over, they would not have suggested a serving officer whom Churchill and the Secretary of State for Air subsequently took great pains to support as completely loyal and honourable.

This leads to the third possibility: that he was lured across by the British secret services, in particular the 'Double-Cross' section. Anyone looking for a rational explanation – as opposed to the irrational 'event' which, it must be stressed, the Foreign Office men actually in charge of the case still believe in – must surely subscribe to this theory. It is known from Dusko Popov's memoirs and at least one German report of the disinformation passed by Popov that the Double-Cross Committee was deliberately exaggerating the extent and power of the 'dissatisfied' elements in Great Britain, and passing names of men supposedly influential who would be prepared for peace at any price. Further, it is known that Tar Robertson of Double-Cross attempted to get the Duke of Hamilton to meet Haushofer. In addition Churchill's, Cadogan's and Jock Colville's responses on the day after Hess's arrival seem explicable only in terms of prior information that Hess – or someone – was coming, and it is known that there are aspects of the affair which are closed to the public until 2017. The probability is that these concern secret service involvement.

Above all, there is the sheer senselessness of Hess risking the success of such a vital mission on the expectation – in the middle of a war it would better be called the off chance – of finding the Duke of Hamilton at Dungavel House. Of course the Duke was not there, nor likely to have been since he had a house at his RAF station. Leaving such a fundamental part of a carefully worked and skilfully executed plan to pure chance suggests something more than carelessness – it would have been idiocy. Hess was obviously odd, fanatic, naive, but it does not appear he was a complete fool; he could not have survived at the top of the Nazi machine had he not been shrewd and crafty. The obvious explanation is that he was set up by the Double-Cross Committee. The details may never be known, but the number of points of communication through Switzerland, Sweden, Spain and Portugal, and over the air waves are legion; many have been mentioned in this book.

It is evident, too, from his repeated appeals in captivity in Scotland and in Mytchett Place that he expected the Duke to introduce him to a substantial 'opposition' group. If such a cohesive grouping existed, Hamilton was obviously not of their number. Instead he informed Churchill, after which the game was up. Thus it is difficult, if not impossible, to believe what may be termed the official version that Hess undertook his hazardous mission on the double off chance that Hamilton was spending that weekend at his country seat and was in close contact with an anti-Churchill cabal, to believe, that is, that he flew from Augsburg literally into the blue without any preparations for after his landing save

349

a commitment to putting his views over to sympathetic and influential Britons. If he did so, he was truly mad.

A minute written by Churchill in April 1945 just before the end of the war in Europe indicates how sensitive he felt Hamilton's position and the rumours of secret service involvement to be. It concerned a visit the Duke intended to make to the United States to attend a conference of airline operators. It was felt he would be badgered by the press about his part in the Hess affair. Churchill instructed the Secretary of State for Air:

... The Russians are very suspicious of the Hess episode and I have had a lengthy argument with Marshal Stalin about it at Moscow, he steadfastly maintaining that Hess had been invited over by our Secret Service. It is not in the public interest that the whole of this affair should be stirred at the present moment. I desire therefore that the Duke should not, repeat not undertake this task.[6]

'Repeat not' suggests an extraordinary degree of sensitivity at that stage of the won war. What might the Duke have said to the US press that he never told his wife or eldest son?

As for Sam Hoare's activities in Spain, the Italian Ambassador's report of his interview with Prince Hohenlowe, and the many closed files concerning German pressure on Spain at this period, these could be used as arguments either for the theory of a powerful opposition in Great Britain waiting to topple Churchill, or to suggest that Hoare was working with the grain of the Double-Cross deception of a powerful opposition – which was of course exactly what Hitler and Hess hoped to hear. Hoare had agreed some plan with Churchill so secret it could not be stated in the diplomatic wires. Moreover Hoare was in contact with Canaris through a director of Transmere in Berlin named Preschel and Dr Otto John, a director of the German airline Lufthansa, among several other go-betweens.[7] This emerged during the Gestapo investigations into the July 1944 plot against Hitler. Otto John, who was a friend of Albrecht Haushofer and took regular strolls with him in the Tiergarten in Berlin, denies any knowledge of Albrecht's attempt to set up a meeting with Hoare.[8] None the less, according to Gestapo investigations, from the conquest of Poland onwards Canaris and Hoare exchanged views through these agents on the removal of the National Socialist regime as a precondition for ending the war. Since none of these contacts appear in the 'peace feeler' files it is evident that Hoare was operating on clandestine as well as official levels. Again the fact that Hess chose the Duke of Hamilton, the very last person to conspire to topple Churchill, suggests that, if Hoare was involved in a double game with Hess, it was deception rather than conspiracy.

The last possibility is that Hitler sent Hess over at least in part as a piece of the grand deception for Stalin before 'Barbarossa'. In support of this there is the evidence of the Nazi disinformation campaign that Hess had quarrelled with both Hitler and Ribbentrop over their policy of close relations with the Soviet Union; Hess was known as the enemy of Bolshevism. He was also known as the most passionate advocate of an alliance with Great Britain. Thus the other edge of this deception was the assumption which was supposed to be made that Hess had flown to make peace with Britain and the corollary that, if he failed, Hitler would not dare attack the Soviet Union and thus open up the dreaded two-front war with the United States supplying the arms for his enemies. Of course Hess failed. Hitler's subsequent onslaught on Russia caught Stalin completely off guard.

It may be that the underlying secret of Hess's mission is that two grand deception plans – Churchill's to persuade Hitler eastwards, Hitler's to persuade Stalin he was going westward to finish off Great Britain – complemented each other at the same point in time; Hess was the very willing, unwitting pawn in both.

AFTERWORD

During 1991 and 1992 the records relating to Hess noted in this book as closed until 2017 were opened;[1] other previously unknown 'Miscellaneous unregistered papers' relating to Hess were also placed on the public record.[2] The expectations raised by this torrent of releases were, however, not met: there were no revelations; almost the only surprise was that such innocuous documents should have been embargoed for so long. A number had evidently been closed beyond the normal term because they contained references to or even memos and reports from MI5 and MI6, but the majority merely duplicated what was known from other records long since in the public domain; the cumulative effect was to authenticate what may be termed the 'official' Foreign Office version of the story, depicting a slightly dotty idealist attempting to retrieve his lost position in the Führer's counsels with a sensational lone bid to bring about peace between the two great Nordic nations. That is a superficial impression; the detailed analysis possible now that all the official papers are available – bar one which is being held indefinitely – reveals unexplained gaps in the record and a fundamental contradiction between the story portrayed in the files and that which has emerged from other equally valid sources. Both versions cannot be correct. The recent releases have in effect compounded the puzzle at the heart of the flight.

More interesting in some respects than the newly opened files is the information that has reached the author from a variety of sources which not only corrects some of the speculation in this book, thus narrowing the focus of enquiry, but provides the key to unlocking the riddle. Unfortunately the documentary proof of this key has not come to light, and the informant is unwilling to allow either his name or credentials to be published. While the existence of the key can be inferred from several documents, without the paper itself it cannot be verified. Hence this too must remain, for the present, speculation.

Before describing the new insights – which reveal the episode as more extraordinary even than the 'official' version and surely one of the greatest secrets of Churchill's conduct of the war – something must be said of the files released: first those Foreign Office files directly relating to Hess[3] which it was suggested on page 254 contained the solution to the discrepancies between official accounts of Hamilton's receipt of a letter from Hess – an important matter in the light of the new information. They do not touch the subject: three consist of speculation, suggestion and second-hand opinion about the reason for Hess's flight,[4] his sanity[5] and the BBC treatment of the story;[6] the fourth contains messages addressed to Hess from around the world after his landing in Scotland, all of which were already available in an open Ministry of Information file.[7] That these meaningless papers, of which only the last could possibly have proved an embarrassment to any living person, should have been embargoed for 75 years is a scandalous example of the British fetish for official secrecy.

Another opened file that fails to match the speculation in this book is the 'B' half of the War Office file on Hess's capture and internment in Scotland.[8] It was suggested on page 207 that this must contain those inventories of Hess's belongings when he landed which had been removed from the reports in the previously open 'A' half of the file. There are no inventories, only medical records, many of which were previously available in open files.[9] Without these inventories there is no documented proof of what Hess brought with him to this country; the suspicion must be that they were removed to conceal the fact that he brought a letter or documents, for it is certain his belongings were listed: thus the officer commanding the 3rd Battalion the Renfrewshire Home Guard reported:

'Captain Barrie took with him the articles which had been taken from the prisoner [Hess] and which were inventoried. Copy of the inventory is attached to this report.'[10]

And Barrie, who signed himself Major, reported after taking Hess to Maryhill Barracks:

'I returned to the Duty Officer and handed over to him all the articles removed from the prisoner and obtained the accompanying receipt.'[11]

One of the files of formerly 'unregistered papers' contains an account of Hess's initial interrogation by the Polish Consul in Glasgow, Roman Battaglia, at the Scout hut in Giffnock before he was taken to Maryhill (see page 208). Battaglia described Hess as 'completely calm throughout. The only slight distress he showed was when he leaned forward at intervals and sank his head on his hands.'[12] He gave a general description of his flight from Augsburg, after which Battaglia asked why he had come.

'I have a message for the Duke of Hamilton.'

'Do you know the Duke of Hamilton?'

'I saw him at the Olympic Games in Berlin, and we have a friend in common.'

'What is this message about?'

'It is in the highest interest of the British Air Force.'[13]

This report appears finally to answer the question about whether Hamilton and Hess had met before; despite many appearances to the contrary, it seems that Hess merely saw the Duke, which probably means a brief introduction, at one of the crowded receptions which they both attended. But the report reinforces the questions about Hamilton's inaction that night. Battaglia claimed to be unaware himself of the prisoner's real identity, but, contrary to Graham Donald's account (see page 208) said that 'several people remarked on his resemblance to Hess'. If, as Graham Donald stated, he (Donald) got through to Hamilton at about 2.00 am – the time Battaglia said he ended his two-hour interrogation – and told him that Hess had flown over to see him with a message, which indeed 'was in the highest interest of the British Air Force', Hamilton's response was at best phlegmatic. It is possible, however, that he reacted more promptly than his report indicates. The Dowager Duchess of Hamilton remembers that he was recalled to the Operations Room that night by a message that something odd had happened with regard to the pilot of the crashed plane; this was no doubt the call from the Controller at Ayr, after he had been told by the Police at Eaglesham that the pilot had a message for the Duke. Afterwards Hamilton returned to the house and went to bed, only to be 'woken in the middle of the night' by another call. He rose and said to her, 'I'll have to go. It's something to do with the crashed plane.' She has no recollection of him coming back. The next time she saw him was the following afternoon.[14] This account at least leaves the question of his movements open. Perhaps he drove to Maryhill barracks that night, although it is difficult to imagine in that case why he should have represented it as later in his report.

Battaglia's report of his interrogation of Hess must surely end the allegations that Fighter Command knew of his intended arrival and deliberately allowed him in. If they did so their follow-up was miserably inept. No attempt was made by any RAF officer to interrogate or bring in this VIP who had flown through their cordon; instead Battaglia, a Pole whose credentials were never checked, was allowed to question him for nearly two hours in conditions which both he and Hess found scarcely credible. Questions were thrown at Battaglia to put to Hess from all corners of the room, some so offensive he did not ask them. 'No accurate report ... was made of the interrogation, and people wandered round the room inspecting the prisoner and his belongings at their leisure'.[15] Battaglia concluded that if the procedure adopted was typical of other interrogations a great deal of valuable information was probably being lost.

Further information on the RAF response to Hess's intrusion reinforces the impression that he was not deliberately allowed in. The plot of his aircraft made by the Royal Observer Corps Centre in Durham City has been preserved.[16] This shows 'Raid 42' coming in due west across the coast at Embleton – rather south of where Hess actually made his landfall – then swinging round out to sea again by the Farne Islands and heading north-easterly, east of Holy Island, while its other or 'split' half '42 J', identified as an Me–110, continued westerly across the country and out of the area. The chart indicates a 'friendly' aircraft over the Farne Islands, which T.N. Dobson, Duty Controller in the ROC Operations room, recalls as a Spitfire travelling north.[17] This confirms the subsequent report on the 'Investigation of Raid 42' (see page 199) which states that 'the filtered track . . . is not that of Raid 42 but a fighter aircraft despatched to intercept Raid 42',[18] and also the Operations Record Book of RAF Ouston, which surmised that the plot of Raid 42 turning east and fading 'may have arisen from plots of 72 White [two Spitfires] who were detailed to raid and were searching off Farne and Holy Islands'.[19] These Spitfires were, it seems, vectored away north-easterly on to the radar plot of themselves, while Hess roared in low under the radar to the southward. That the Operations Record Book of 72 Squadron shows no '72 White' airborne at the time must mean that the officer writing up the record inadvertently omitted this patrol. The mass of evidence and the researches of Squadron Leader R.G. Woodman[20] and Roy Nesbit[21] leave no doubt that altogether four fighters were vectored to intercept Hess: the two Spitfires of 72 White patrolling the Farne Islands, the single Spitfire scrambled from RAF Acklington as Hess crossed inland, and the Defiant – which despite its slow speed was a successful night fighter – scrambled from Ayr as the Controller was advised of a very fast moving 'Bandit' approaching his sector.[22] The Defiant's pilot was instructed 'Angels two five, zero nine degrees!' (Climb to 2,500 feet, steer 009°), and when he had attained height, 'Dive and buster, vector three five zero!' (Dive at full throttle, to attain maximum speed – also to have the enemy above, where it would be visible against the night sky – steering 350°).[23] There is no doubt that the Defiant and Spitfires would have attacked Hess had they seen him.

The only stations in a position to scramble fighters to intercept which did not do so were Turnhouse and Drem, which was controlled by Turnhouse. Notwithstanding a recent letter to a Sunday newspaper, no Spitfires of 603 Squadron, nor Hurricanes of 43 Squadron were sent up. Moreover, as the Me–110 moved into the Clyde (Anti-Aircraft) Gun

Defended Area, also under the control of Turnhouse Operations Room, requests to open fire from the Duty Officer at 42 AA Brigade Headquarters, King's Park, Glasgow, were turned down.[24] A junior NCO in the Brigade office, Joseph Debney, remembers the 'flap' that night. He was in the recreation room some time after 11.00 pm when one of the plotters from the Gun Operations Room (GOR) in the basement came up to collect tea or coffee for his colleagues. 'An unidentified aircraft has been flying around for nearly an hour,' he opened. 'He doesn't respond to challenge and ignores requests to show the colours of the day. At least two heavy AA sites had him sitting on the end of their guns – could they open fire!' Turnhouse had refused permission.[25] Debney's recollection is confirmed by Dennis Rose, an Intelligence officer at Brigade Headquarters on duty that night in the GOR. Request was made to Turnhouse on the lines of 'What do we do about this? Have you got a friendly up?' but permission to fire was refused. Rose asserts this was because Turnhouse rejected the Observer Corps identification of an Me–110 – as indeed they did at Brigade Headquarters – and the aircraft was therefore 'unidentified'.[26] It was the rule not to open fire on unidentified aircraft. Nonetheless Turnhouse's response appears significantly different from Acklington's and Ayr's, both of whom scrambled fighters and vectored them on to a 'Bandit'. In war many anomalies arise to tease the later investigator; while Turnhouse's – thus Hamilton's – inaction may appear another instance of the dog that failed to bark that night (see page 210), it is susceptible to explanation.

That the Observer Corps identification of Hess's aircraft as an Me 110 was greeted with 'hoots of derision' in the Turnhouse Operations Room is well-attested.[27] Further confirmation comes from Nancy Marion Goodall, then a WREN on the naval liaison desk in the Operations Room, whose father, Squadron Leader W. Geoffrey Moore, was Deputy Commandant of the Scottish Command of the Observer Corps. She recalls the lone aircraft being plotted across the table below her and the Observer Corps identification dismissed out of hand; feeling the honour of the Corps at stake, she asked her commander why it could not be an Me–110. 'Because it wouldn't have enough fuel to get home', he replied as if to a child.[28]

Some time afterwards came the report that the plane had crashed, then about half an hour to an hour later the Duke of Hamilton was called to the telephone at the Controller's desk. He appeared to Nancy Marion Moore (Goodall) to be wearing pyjamas under his uniform as if roused from his bed; she retains a distinct image of him, 'standing, hunched over the phone, holding it to his shoulder, looking extremely horrified.' She could not hear what was said, but word went around that 'the CO had been called to speak to the pilot of the crashed plane'.

Everyone, she remembers, remarked on his evident worry. After her watch ended, probably midnight, she drove some twenty minutes in her small car to the house her father rented nearby in Cramond, and finding him still up, told him about the German pilot who had asked to speak to the CO. He replied that he was going to breach confidence, and if she absolutely promised not to tell anyone he would tell her who the pilot was: Rudolf Hess.[29]

Probably the phone call she witnessed was from the Ayr Controller. What time she arrived back at her father's house is uncertain; it depends upon the time her watch ended, which she cannot recall. She does remember, however, that it was night. It seems therefore that the Deputy Commandant of the Observer Corps in Scotland was sufficiently certain of Hess's identity to speak of 'a breach of confidence' when telling her; it is probable, assuming her watch ended at midnight, that he knew before Graham Donald's call at about 2.00 am. Even if it was after Donald's call, would he have been so certain on the unsupported word of one of his officers? Whatever the answer, the news spread fast. When ACW Iris Palmer went on duty in the Orderly Room at Turnhouse at 9.00 am the whole station was buzzing with the story.[30]

It has already been suggested that Churchill was informed by Ernest Bevin on the night of the 10th that Hess was bringing peace proposals to the Duke of Hamilton (see pages 211–12). Testimony that Hess was known to be in the air even earlier that evening comes from James Douglas, then Duty Supervisor in the Mayfair, London, 'Information Bureau' of the BBC Monitoring Service.[31] At some time that evening, probably about 8.00 pm, Douglas received what was termed a 'Flash' message from the BBC Listening Centre at Evesham, who had picked up a south German, he thinks Munich, radio station announcement that the Deputy Führer had taken off on a flight and not returned. He asked Evesham to put it on the teleprinter, which they did, and immediately sent it to the Air Ministry and Fighter Command Headquarters. Subsequently Douglas received two further messages with additional details including the type of plane Hess was flying and the direction he was heading. When Douglas left the Bureau at 11.30 pm Hess was, so far as he knew, still missing in an aeroplane, and on reaching home he told his wife; Mrs Douglas remembers it well.

The difficulty with the story is that there is no trace, either in the BBC Digests of monitored enemy broadcasts, or in the boxes of raw 'Flash' forms retained in the Imperial War Museum archives, of any message about Hess on 10 May; on the other hand both sources have what is regarded as the first announcement of Hess having taken an aeroplane and disappeared put out by the Deutschland Sender, Berlin, at 8.00 pm on 12 May. The obvious inference is that after 50 years

Douglas's memory has slipped by two days. In an attempt to clarify this, the author read the BBC 'Flash' form of 12 May to Douglas without revealing the date, merely asking if this was the message he remembered:

'... Party Member Hess, who had been expressly forbidden by the Fuehrer to use an aeroplane because of a disease which has been progressive for years, has, in contradiction to this order, been able to get hold of a plane recently. Hess started on Saturday 10th May, at about 1800 from Augsburg on a flight from which he has not returned up to now. A letter which he left behind unfortunately showed in its confusion the traces of mental disturbance which justifies the fear that Hess was the victim of hallucinations ...'[32]

On hearing the passage about 'traces of mental confusion' Douglas said this was quite definitely not the 'Flash' he had received. He would have been more vehement had he read the headline on this 12 May 'Flash' form:

'Fuehrer's Deputy mad for years: Victim of Air Accident'.

Why should Douglas have alerted both the Air Ministry and Fighter Command to a message about an aircraft that had taken off two days before, ending with the presumption that it had 'crashed or met with a similar accident'? Douglas, moreover, is quite certain there was no mention of madness or hallucinations in the message he took, and on the other hand there were additional details of aircraft type and course wholly missing from the 12 May broadcast or its repeats, none of which was 'flashed' to London. Also the 12 May communique was reported on the BBC nine o'clock News that night. Had Mrs Douglas listened to the News she would hardly have been surprised by her husband's story about Hess when he arrived home after midnight.

The former head of the London 'Information Bureau', John Keyser, cannot remember these individual messages – not surprising after 50 years since he was not directly involved in them – but states: 'Knowing Jim [Douglas] I would think that his memory was likely to be accurate. More than that I fear I cannot say.'[33]

There are two possible explanations for the lack of documentary evidence to support Douglas's recollection. First the BBC Monitoring Service came under the Ministry of Information, whose Director General was Walter Monckton; it will be recalled that Monckton worked closely with the Security Services and knew more about the Hess affair than his Minister, Duff Cooper (see page 239). In view of the extraordinary sensitivity of Hess's arrival, as will appear, it would be surprising if Monckton did not order the suppression of any mention of these broadcasts in the daily Digests – assuming Douglas's memory correct – and the physical removal of the 'Flash' forms. The alternative is that the messages were not announcements picked up by the BBC Monitoring Service, but radio signals intercepted by 'Y' Service, which monitored enemy signals traffic. It will be recalled that Göring instructed Adolf Galland, commanding a fighter group on the Channel coast, to intercept the Deputy Führer who was flying to England in an Me–110 (see page 220). While Galland recalls this as about sunset, thus about 10.00 pm, it is possible that either he or Douglas is mistaken about the timing, and it was this and subsequent signals about Hess's aircraft that gave rise to the alert in the London 'Information Bureau'. If Galland's timing is correct, however, and the messages were intercepted at about sunset it would have been too late for Fighter Command to take any action; Hess was then making his approach to the Farne Islands and RAF Acklington was attempting to vector the patrolling Spitfires on to him. That is speculation; all that is certain is that Göring was involved in the planning for the mission; Hess could not have passed through so many air defence zones without authority, and the massed air attacks on London that night were not coincidence. It is, therefore, quite possible that Göring's apparently inexplicable message to Galland was a radio signal *en clair* intended to be intercepted by the enemy. It will be recalled that Göring had been involved in many of the recent peace feelers, and he later passed warning of the coming attack on Russia to both the British and Americans (see page 272). Another possibility is that the messages Douglas recalls were intercepted by 'Y' Service from the Messerschmitt works at Augsburg, either from Pintsch to Hess's instructions, or from Professor Willi Messerschmitt himself, who later warned Leigh Mallory of the SS team on its way to assassinate Hess.

From speculation it is a relief to pass to an accurate account of the flight Hess wrote for his son, revealed for the first time in the recently opened papers.[34] Since it was written at Mytchett Place at the time Hess intended suicide after Lord Simon's visit, it has the authority of a dying man's testament about his proudest feat, and as such should end further speculation on the details of the route he took. It follows the chart he drew for his British interrogators and the descriptions he gave them[35] and later his wife, Ilse (see pages 195–8) with the addition of the exact courses flown: 320° to Bonn, thence 335° to 'Zuider Zee-Helder' (the Texel):

'. . . from there first 23 minutes (against the wind) eastwards (65°), then I flew 60 minutes northwards (335°) . . . arrived at the north point I flew 20 minutes (with the wind ∴ at my back some 20 km/hr) on 245° to point B on my chart. It was, however, still so light (I had reckoned with clouds!) that I flew back and forth a long time on 65° and 245°.'

He nowhere mentioned his radio compass, although it seems from his chart that the wsw'ly legs took him down to the latitude of Kalundborg, and thus when 'at sunset' he finally flew west to make his landfall, he arrived 'exactly at Holy Island' on the same latitude. Seeing 'destroyers in line abreast [probably corvettes] and small boats at the island', he avoided it, setting course for the Cheviot (see map on page 197), diving from some 3,000 m (c.10,000 feet) to cross the coast at 10 m (c.30 feet) altitude in order to gain the highest speed and 'offer pursuers no possibility of approaching. There had been a Spitfire 5 km [three miles] behind me.' This was the Spitfire the Duke of Hamilton told him about; he makes no mention of having seen it himself. After 'springing over trees and houses' and climbing similarly up the slope of the Cheviot, he set course 280° to the lake at Broad Law, from thence 300° to Dungavel. 'It was already too dark to recognise this [house]' consequently he flew on to the west coast, seeing a 'fabulous mountain island in full moonlight' before looping back to the neighbourhood of Dungavel and, with much difficulty, jumping out.

He added a rider to the record:

'Buz! Take note, there are higher, fate-shaping forces – which if we want to describe them, we call Divine forces – which intervene, at least if it is necessary in great events. I *had* to come to England and speak here about understanding and peace.

'Often we do not understand the sometimes hard decisions; later one will always recognise their significance.'[36]

In the circumstances of his suicide attempt, this appears to be the definitive account of his flight – apart from his reticence for security reasons about his radio compass – invalidating Helmut Kaden's and the author's own speculation that he might have flown north to the Danish coast before turning west to cross the North Sea on the latitude of Kalundborg. It seems probably therefore that Heydrich escorted him only over the Dutch islands and southern North Sea; this indeed fits Lina Heydrich's account of her husband flying Me–109's on the 'Channel coast' at this time (see page 196).

Hess's mood while he was composing this account for 'Buz' is conveyed by two suicide letters he wrote on 14 June together with duplicates he intended Lieutenant Malone to deliver personally at the end of the war; this was after the lack of response since Simon's visit had convinced him he had failed. One letter was addressed 'Mein Führer':[37] this was his last greeting, he wrote, 'to you who for the past two decades have inspired my life. After the collapse of 1918 you made my life worthwhile again.' 'It had scarcely ever been granted to people to serve a man and his idea with such success as those who had served under him' he went on, and thanked him with all his heart for all he had given him and been to him; after which he quoted five lines from Goethe's poem, *Das Göttliche*:

'Following eternal, implacable, great

Laws

Must we all

Complete the circles

Of our existence.'[38]

He wrote these lines, he continued, in clear recognition that there remained no other way out – hard as *this* end was for him. Entrusting his family and dependants to Hitler's care, and saluting him as the embodiment of 'our great Germany which is drawing toward an undreamed of greatness', he concluded:

'I die in the conviction that my last mission, even though it ends in death, will bear some fruit. Perhaps despite my death or precisely through my death, my flight will bring peace and understanding with England. *Heil mein Führer!*

Your loyal, Rudolf Hess'

The other letter, addressed to Ilse for his whole family, began 'My dear All'; compelled to end his life, he sent them this last greeting and thanks for all they had been to him. This final step was very hard for him, he went on, but there remained no other way out. He had committed himself fully for a great idea, but fate had willed this end. And as in his letter to Hitler, he expressed his hopes for the final success of his mission: 'perhaps despite my death, or indeed through it, there will be peace as a result of my flight.'[39]

The meaning of this delphic utterance becomes clearer from others of the recently opened papers, particularly a letter he addressed to Hamilton – which never reached the Duke – from the Tower of London on 19 May. Evidently already worried that he had fallen into the hands of Churchill's 'clique of warmongers' who might be planning his death, he said that in the letter he had left behind for Hitler he had alluded to the possibility of his death being announced from England as suicide or in suspicious circumstances; but even if there were reason to suspect it had been brought about by 'elements in England opposed to peace' this should not influence the German government against peace. This was his last wish; and, he went on, his death would probably even assist his mission, 'for only after the conclusion of peace could the English themselves settle accounts with those people who would probably also be responsible for my death. My death would play a great part in this from a propaganda point of view.'[40] As is evident from other reports,[41] he had expected the publicity surrounding the drama of his flight to convince the British of the German government's sincere desire for peace and cause them to rise up under those 'opposition' leaders who also desired to end the war. Since this had not yet happened, it seems he hoped publicity attending his death would bring it about.

As for the genesis of his mission, the original of Albrecht Haushofer's letter to Hamilton dated 23 September 1940 is in the recently opened papers,[42] but not the covering letter to Violet Roberts, which remains no doubt in the MI5 registry. A recently opened file of censorship papers contains copies of the original censor's report on the letter and some correspondence to Walter Monckton, Director General of the Ministry of Information[43] explaining 'the web of half truths' in which the letter had become enmeshed by BBC and government statements; all of this material was already in open files.[44] Some further information about the letter is, however, contained in one of the hitherto 'unregistered' papers. Thus MI5 had written on 22 November to the Foreign Office asking if they had taken any action on the copy letter 'written by somebody named "Dr A.H.", obviously a German' which had been forwarded to them, and whether they saw any objection to sending the letter on to the Duke.[45] Henry Hopkinson of the Foreign Office replied on 7 December:

'We have not done anything about it ourselves and we have no objection to the letter being allowed to go on to its destination, if you think this worthwhile in view of the length of time which has elapsed since it was written.'[46]

The lack of urgency shown in this correspondence, and the fact that neither MI5, nor it seems the responsible Foreign Office officials had by December put a name to 'Dr. A.H., obviously a German', bears out information received recently from Colonel T.A. Robertson, then head of MI5 B1A. It was argued in this book that the Double Cross Committee and B1A probably lured Hess to Great Britain with false reports and forged letters purporting to be from the Duke of Hamilton – although it was pointed out that, if so, Albrecht Haushofer himself never received any of these replies. Colonel Robertson states there were no forged replies. The letter to the Duke was not considered especially important, and action was delayed by MI5's move from London to Oxford at this time. When the possibility of following it up was discussed and Hamilton was called down to the Air Ministry and asked if he would go to Lisbon to meet Haushofer (see page 182) Robertson advised against taking up the contact since too much time had elapsed.[47] Thus Hamilton's period of leave from 12 November 1940, a week after Albrecht's letter was sent to MI5, was pure coincidence; and the Czech Intelligence chief Moravetz's assertion that he had actually seen the forged replies purporting to be from the Duke (see page 292) together with similar allegations in the *American Mercury* article of 1943, was disinformation.

That Hess was not specifically targeted and lured over by the Double Cross Committee does not mean that there was no general campaign to indicate disintegrating civilian morale and a strong 'Peace Party' in Britain; undoubtedly there was, and undoubtedly Dusko Popov, one of B1A's star agents, who was as Colonel Robertson confirms, 'friendly with "C" ', took part in it. Nor does it imply that the existence of a British 'Opposition' prepared to reach a settlement with Germany was not disseminated at far higher, Ministerial and Ambassadorial, levels, chiefly it seems by Kelly in Berne and Hoare in Madrid. In England Hess repeatedly asked to see the leaders of this 'Party' which would overthrow the 'Churchill clique'. Hess had good contacts, and he was not insane. Either there was such a powerful group with which he had been in direct communication, or he had been deceived into a firm belief in its existence; it is also possible to conceive a grey area of contingency planning – even perhaps diplomatic blackmail directed at Washington or Moscow – somewhere between truth and deception. For undoubtedly many powerful figures in Britain could see no alternative at that time to a compromise settlement with Hitler.

So far as Hess's own preparations for the flight are concerned, there is in one of the newly opened files of his correspondence in captivity an interesting note he appended to a letter to Ilse of 2 February 1942. This states that in the folder he had given his adjutant, Pintsch, before the flight he had included 'A minute on the relevant dream of the General' (Haushofer), a horoscope drawn up by Schulte-Strathaus and a prophecy given to him at Christmas 1940 by one Grete Sutter. He asked Ilse to copy these and deposit them with a Notary, adding, 'I am interested in the matter from a scientific point of view'.[48] This contradicts the assertion on page 231 that nothing Hess said or wrote suggested an astrological input into his choice of date for flying. His choice of the Duke of Hamilton as intermediary must have been due chiefly to his knowledge that there was a landing strip at Dungavel – although he evidently underestimated the extreme difficulties of landing a high speed modern fighter on a grass runway suitable for the Duke's Tiger Moth, and indeed of finding the house itself at night in the blackout. But there can be no doubt he intended landing, and made no preparations for parachuting. Several documents in the recently opened papers indicate that Professor Karl Haushofer also played a part in his choice of Hamilton – a larger part than Albrecht – although it is probable that Hess talked about 'the General' to deflect attention from the true author of his mission, Hitler. The suspicion finds support in a memorandum by Dr Gibson Graham, who looked after him first in Scotland, then at Mytchett Place. The plan to fly over had been maturing in Hess's mind since August 1940, Graham wrote, 'but he has not mentioned it to a soul' – which was plainly false. The memorandum continued:

'His old friend Professor Karl Haushofer, mentioned to him subsequently that it was terrible for a needless war to continue with prospects of such slaughter. He, the Professor, knew an Englishman [sic] called the Duke of Hamilton who might be a useful link with the King; Hess himself had met the Duke only once or perhaps twice at a dinner party he gave in Berlin. He could not remember exactly because the party was a very big one . . . I imagine that to Hess Professor Haushofer is a prophet whose predictions have always come true. Hess has given several examples. Recently the Professor told Hess that he had seen him, in his dreams, on three separate occasions piloting an aeroplane, but he knew not where . . .'[49]

Hess evidently spun the same line with his 'guardians' at Mytchett Place; here is Frank Foley recording his impressions in August 1941:

' . . . he completely overestimated the importance of the Duke of Hamilton. He has even refused to be enlightened on that subject. It would be incorrect to say he believed the Duke to be a pro-Nazi. He looked upon the Duke as the person appointed by destiny and indicated by his prophet friend, Professor Haushofer, to be the medium through which he could reach those circles which in England he imagined would be receptive of his peace proposals . . .'[50]

This is no doubt true so far as it goes; Hess had indeed discussed the project with 'the General' on 31 August 1940, in such animated mood they had talked until two in the morning (see page 136). It is also true that Hess would never have taken a step of such awesome consequence without express instructions from his Führer. That he had such instructions is indicated in a newspaper article of 30 September 1945, a cutting of which Dr Scott Newton of Cardiff University found recently in a Foreign Office file.[51] This describes how the French war correspondent, André Guerber, found documents in the ruins of the Berlin Chancellery at the end of the war which 'definitely established that it was Hitler himself who decided to send Hess to Britain'.

The documents, which may yet appear from the former Soviet archives, showed that a month before his flight, thus in April 1941, Hitler had sent Hess on a mission to Madrid, 'where through Franco and certain British agents he tried to make contact with the British government', in the process becoming persuaded that Britain was interested in peace. It will be recalled that there is a closed Foreign Office file in the series on German pressure on Spain dated 20 April,[52] and that this date corresponds to what Frank Roberts referred to in a minute of 26 April as 'the scare of last weekend'.[53] Reports of Hess meeting Franco in Madrid began to reach the Foreign Office on 22 April, and on the 25th Hoare replied to their enquiry about these that all the information he had inclined him to discredit the story.[54] From a diplomat of Hoare's subtlety, this was hardly a disclaimer.

Guerber also found a verbatim record of a meeting between Hitler, Göring and Hess at the Berghof on 4 May, at which Hess told Hitler he was convinced England was willing to talk peace. Hitler retorted that he had reached the solemn decision to go to war with Russia before the autumn; he would give Britain a last chance of survival; he wanted the British told to 'get out of the war! Clear out of Germany's war!' This of course accords with the known facts that Hitler had already offered the British peace several times since the fall of France, and on 30 April, four days before, he had set the final date for the attack on Russia, 22 June.

Later the same day, according to the documents Guerber saw, Hitler again summoned Hess, who repeated his belief, founded on Intelligence reports about the results of the bombing and living conditions in England, that the British were ready to settle, concluding, 'We must show the British we are sincere. If we do that the British will rise up and compel Churchill to make peace'. It is clear, particularly from the recently opened files, that this describes Hess's mission precisely. Thus Dr Gibson Graham, in the memo quoted previously, stated that Hess's idea had been to fly over to see the Duke of Hamilton and the King 'in order to be on hand with peace proposals when a new government arose in this country'.[55] Hess had not been able to explain why a new government should arise, but he had been convinced it would.

The date of both these meetings recorded in the documents was 4 May, the day Hitler made his triumphal speech after the Balkan and Greek campaigns to the Reichstag and the Kroll Opera (see page 185). He entered with Hess, Göring, Himmler and Dr Frick at 6.00 pm – allowing ample time for the Berghof conference with Göring and Hess that morning. And both Hitler and Hess stated afterwards that they had talked together after the speech – Hitler when he tried to explain Hess's flight to the top Party men at the Berghof on 13 May,[56] Hess during his first conversation with Kirkpatrick in Scotland the same day.[57] Moreover during his speech Hitler had suggested why a new government should arise in Britain: 'If ever any other politician had met such defeats', he declared, referring to Churchill's responsibility for the debacle in Greece, 'or a soldier had met such catastrophes, he would not have kept his job six months . . .'[58] The sentiments had found echo in the House of Commons three days later (see page 189) and although Churchill had triumphed over his critics, Harold Nicolson noted next day that he feared people would jump at any escape which made cowardice appear respectable.[59] Although the Commons seemed solid behind Churchill,

Hess's sources were by no means as ill-informed as post-war British legend would have it.

The document Guerber found in the Chancellery ruins which clinched his assertion that Hitler sent Hess was a copy of a plan designated 'ABCD [for the four parts into which it was divided] Nr. S 274 K' that Hess was to carry to Scotland. The first part, 'A', was to demonstrate to the British government by means of documents that it was useless to continue the war following the collapse of France; 'B' was to assure Britain that if she withdrew from the war she would preserve both independence and colonies, but would have to undertake not to interfere in the internal or external affairs of any European country; 'C' was an offer of a 25-year alliance with the Reich; and 'D' a stipulation that Britain should maintain an attitude of benevolent neutrality towards Germany during the German–Russian war.

Guerber could not have seen the British Foreign Office files when he wrote this account of the documents, nor the copies of Hamilton's and Kirkpatrick's reports which show that Hess carried out parts 'A' and 'B' of the plan from his first interview on 11 May, for these latter were yet to be produced as exhibits at the Nuremberg trials. But parts 'C' and 'D', the offer of an alliance during which Britain would be required to show benevolent neutrality, while Germany settled accounts with the Soviet Union, are nowhere even hinted at in the reports, nor any other Foreign Office papers. It will be recalled that according to Kirkpatrick's first report, Hess responded to probes about the Soviet Union by saying merely that 'Germany had certain demands to make of Russia which would have to be satisfied either by negotiation or as the result of war', adding that there was no foundation for rumours that Hitler contemplated an early attack on Russia.[60]

This is confirmed in a typed, undated memorandum by Kirkpatrick of 'Reflections' on his talks with Hess in the recently opened files; his first point was that Hess 'does not seem to me to be in the near counsels of the German government as regards operations'; his last point was to repeat Hess's assertion that Germany had demands to make on Russia 'but has no intention of making an immediate attack'.[61] There is no mention of an alliance or of benevolent neutrality. Either Hess did not carry out parts 'C' and 'D' of the plan, or Guerber's account of the document was inaccurate, even fabricated for sensation; the third possibility is that Kirkpatrick deliberately withheld much of what Hess said. Lord Beaverbrook, who was brought into the affair at least as early as Monday morning, 12 May, certainly believed this to be the case. Writing to James Leasor in 1961, he said that Hess must have made it clear – 'or probably made it clear', he moderated it – at his first interview with Hamilton that his object was to negotiate with Britain in respect of

Germany's impending attack on Russia. Beaverbrook added that even if Hess discussed this issue with Kirkpatrick, this part of the talk would have been 'excised from the account Kirkpatrick submitted to the public'.[62]

Beaverbrook was, of course, close to Hoare, Lloyd George, Liddell Hart; he had supported 'Dick' Stokes' 'peace' movement in 1940, and had been described by Vansittart then as 'a buddy of Mr Kennedy and most of the "Money-in-our-time" brigade – a detachment of the Fifth Column'.[63] He had been referred to in a report to the German Foreign Ministry from Lisbon in January 1941 as representing the view in Cabinet that Britain could not take the offensive in the Mediterranean because forces could not be spared from the Motherland; the same report had stated that Lord Halifax had been 'booted out' of the government by Churchill and sent to Washington as Ambassador because he had represented policies of 'Appeasement' in Cabinet. Beaverbrook, Halifax, R.A. Butler, Hoare, and in the background Lloyd George, even the Australian premier, Menzies, were obvious large targets for Hess's mission. And it will be recalled that Kirkpatrick, after his first interview with Hess, had suggested he might open up more freely if he thought he was talking to someone who gave the impression of being tempted with the idea of getting rid of the present administration[64] (see page 227). There is in the recently opened papers a report of another telephone call from Kirkpatrick to the Foreign Office, this time after his third interview with Hess on 15 May, again emphasising that 'if we wanted to get anything more out of Hess we should put someone else in in the role of negotiator who could question him about his proposals, and ask him to justify his assertions . . .'[65] Beaverbrook was an obvious choice for Churchill to send in as a bogus 'negotiator' – providing, of course, he felt he could trust him.

The day after Kirkpatrick's last interview, Hess was taken down to London and lodged in the Tower. On 18 May Kim Philby's Russian controller sent a report of what Philby had learned about Hess from his friend, Tom Dupree, Deputy Head of the Foreign Office Press Department. This stated that, although it was officially denied, Beaverbrook and Eden had visited Hess.[66] The rest of the information Philby relayed from Dupree was accurate: thus 'Hess believed that there is a powerful anti-Churchill party in Britain which stands for peace and which will receive a powerful stimulus . . . from his [Hess's] arrival'. It is quite possible, therefore, that Beaverbrook – and Eden – did visit Hess in the Tower of London; that indeed might explain the repeated references both Beaverbrook and Hess made to their 'last meeting in the Chancellery, Berlin' when Beaverbrook went to Mytchett Place in September (see page 282).

If Beaverbrook had this greater first-hand knowledge of Hess's mission than he ever admitted, his statements acquire added weight; and it becomes of extreme significance that in another of his letters to James Leasor in 1961 he stated he had 'always held the view that Hess was sent, that Hitler knew of his journey, that he intended to negotiate a treaty of peace on most favourable terms [presumably most favourable terms for Great Britain] if Germany could be given a free hand to attack Russia.'[67] This, indeed, is precisely what Beaverbrook told Stalin when he went to Moscow in November 1941: Hess's purpose in coming to Britain had been to enlist British aid in the attack on Russia.[68]

Desmond Morton, Churchill's Intelligence liaison, had said the same to the US Military Attaché, Raymond E. Lee, the previous month: Hess, he said, had told the Duke of Hamilton that Germany was 'about to fight Russia', and Kirkpatrick that he knew 'the Duke would see immediately that this was absurd and awful for England to continue to fight Germany any longer...'[69] It may be argued that this was disinformation; certainly it also found its way to Moscow via the Czech Intelligence chief, Moravetz;[70] certainly it was accompanied by disinformation about Hess living in a mansion near Glasgow reserved for German officers – recalling the story fed to Heydrich's agent in May 1942 that 'Hess was lodged in a villa in Scotland'.[71] But could Beaverbrook, who interviewed Hess at least once during his captivity in England, have been so deceived by Morton's story as to repeat it twenty years later to James Leasor?

Now that all the Foreign Office files have been opened – bar one paper – the contradiction between what may be termed the Hamilton/Kirkpatrick version of Hess's flight emanating from the papers, and the Beaverbrook/Morton version – also transmitted by Philby to Moscow as early as 18 May, and accepted by all the major Intelligence agencies – becomes clear. Either Hamilton and Kirkpatrick deliberately concealed the main thrust of Hess's mission from the Foreign Office, or Beaverbrook and Morton spread deliberate disinformation to the USA – an ally in all but name – and the Soviet Union which was by then a formal ally. For the two versions are mutually incompatible.

The key to this puzzle and the solution to the mystery surrounding the flight has been provided by John Howell,[72] one of whose friends of long standing played a personal part in the affair by virtue of his fluency in German. He does not wish to be known by name or post – and will be referred to only as 'the informant' – but Howell has perfect confidence in his veracity; moreover his story dovetails with André Guerber's discoveries in the ruins of the Chancellery, clarifying the otherwise baffling disagreement between such authoritative sources as the official papers on the one hand and Churchill's confidants, Beaverbrook and Morton, on the other.

The key lies in documents Hess brought with him, and no doubt handed to Hamilton at their first meeting. These comprised proposals for a peace treaty drafted in official language in numbered clauses, typed on Chancellery paper, together with an English translation. They presented Churchill with an historic dilemma, being in the informant's words, 'an offer that could not be refused from a man who could not be trusted'. Had Churchill allowed even a hint of their real content to surface he would inevitably have been driven off the course on which he was determined to steer the country, either by those Tory grandees, City magnates, Service realists and wobbly politicians who at this critical period when Britain was losing the war (and there seemed no prospect of winning, little even of surviving) would have jumped at the terms which offered more than they could have hoped, or from the Labour side of the coalition government and the Communist-inspired Unions in sections of industry, who would have rebelled at making a deal with the Fascists. Nor could Churchill allow any hint of serious peace proposals to reach the new US Ambassador, John G. Winant, or Roosevelt's envoy in England, Averell Harriman.

Beaverbrook conveyed the same idea to James Leasor in 1961, without, however, mentioning documentary proposals: Churchill, he wrote, had no intention of negotiating any peace treaty with Germany, which he was convinced would leave Germany in a position of mastery; 'therefore it was essential there should not be a peace party showing its ugly head . . . he necessarily deprecated the Hess mission and made as much as he could in the way of propaganda against taking it seriously.'[73]

The informant was co-opted into a study of the draft peace treaty shortly after Hess's arrival; he does not remember the date, but it was presumably immediately after Kirkpatrick's return to London from interviewing Hess in Scotland. Kirkpatrick invited a number of German speakers to BBC headquarters, Portland Place, the informant amongst them, and gave them a brief talk on the vital importance of the documents he was about to hand them, and the need for absolute secrecy; nothing whatever could be said. He did not wield the Official Secrets Act, nor need to; these were trusted members of the network based on school and club whose fictional counterparts are familiar from the tales of John Buchan. Afterwards each was given different sections of the draft treaty proposals – which had been re-typed – and asked for a precise translation into English; the translation Hess had brought was stilted as if made with the aid of a dictionary, and the aim was to clarify the terms and the often portmanteau German words, since German does not translate precisely into English. The informant saw the original

369

document once; for the rest he worked on the section assigned to him, as did all the others. He describes the working party as a committee under Kirkpatrick's chairmanship, meeting always at the BBC in Portland Place; from the number of meetings and the detailed discussions it was evident that the proposals were taken very seriously, as indeed they had to be at that stage of the war when Britain fought alone: if Hitler had not struck east and America not come in it would surely have been necessary to sign. One phrase the informant remembers provoking debate was '*wohlwollende Neutralität*' ('benevolent') or as the committee finally rendered it 'well-wishing neutrality'. It will be recalled that part 'D' of the plan André Guerber found called for Britain's benevolent neutrality during the German–Russian war.

The first two pages of the proposals detailed Hitler's aims in Russia, outlining his precise plan for conquest in the east and the destruction of Bolshevism; other sections stipulated that Great Britain keep out of all continental entanglement, in return for which she would retain her independence, her empire and her armed forces. Since the French and other western European nations had colonies which provided potential points of friction with the British empire, detailed provisions were made for the strength of forces in these areas; the informant remembers Clause 12, for instance, dealing in precise terms with forces in the Suez Canal theatre. Surprisingly there was nothing whatever about the Jewish 'problem'. After fifty years the informant cannot recall whether an alliance was proposed as in part 'C' of Guerber's document, but it is evident that 'benevolent neutrality' during the German–Russian war, as in part 'D', was stipulated. As for the date of Hitler's forthcoming attack, the informant is quite clear that Hess did reveal it.

The man entrusted by Churchill to oversee and administer Kirkpatrick's secret committee was 'Jock' Colville; no doubt the typing was done by one or other of Churchill's female secretaries. Colville's involvement perhaps helps to explain the extraordinary muddle he and Hamilton made of their attempt to agree each other's version of events (see pages 214–16).

These treaty proposals Hess brought and the numerous copies and translations typed for Kirkpatrick's 'committee' remain a state secret, buried perhaps in the Registry of MI5 or MI6, perhaps in the Royal archives at Windsor, perhaps destroyed. It is possible, however, knowing what to look for, to observe faint traces between the lines and in the gaps of the official papers and existing testimony.

First, Ernst Bohle and Göring had suggested at Nuremberg, without any prompting, merely in an attempt to revive Hess's memory, that he had carried a 'letter' to Hamilton which Bohle had translated into English for him (see pages 144–5). No trace of this 'letter' has been found. Then, immediately Hess landed the question of whether Hamilton had ever received a letter from him became entangled in official statements with the case of Albrecht Haushofer's September 1940 letter in an extraordinary 'web of half truths'. This would have been explicable as an attempt to clear Hamilton's name of any suspicion of collusion with the enemy had not Lord Swinton, head of the Security Co-ordination Committee, had a leading hand in the tangle.[74] Most significantly in this respect is the absence from the files which should contain them of any inventory of Hess's belongings when he landed. James Leasor's unofficial list from contemporary testimony includes 'a letter addressed to the Duke of Hamilton'.[75]

Passing to Guerber's transcripts of meetings indicating that Hess's confidence was based on Intelligence reports about bombing and living conditions in England, there are numerous examples in the German Foreign Ministry files: from Lisbon on 4 January 1941, an agent reported the German air raids on Britain were working: 'Despite all attempts to deny it, there is such demoralisation amongst the British population that continued resistance appears out of the question.'[76] Towards the end of the month the report which almost certainly emanated from 'C's friend, Dusko Popov (see pages 149–50) spoke of food rationing in Britain and great shortages: 'there are almost no oranges available, butter is very short and bad . . . meat is rationed . . . fresh vegetables are very short, there are almost no eggs . . . sugar is very rationed . . . coffee is poor and still deteriorating . . .'[77] The inner city of Bristol was described as 'completely destroyed and without life. The centre is completely burnt out . . .' The great air raid on London on Sunday, 29 December, was reported as 'the most horrifying' experience of the agent's life, 'a hell of fire, explosions and splinters. The fires after this attack lasted to midday the next day. He [the agent] described the city as destroyed. He could not give details because the destruction was so great and general . . .'[78] Some 100–150,000 people lived in shocking conditions in the Underground, the report went on; 'at night . . . there is a fearful stink, and during the day one steps over people sleeping on the platforms of the stations who have nothing more than the clothes they wear. Since it is feared that epidemics and demoralisation will spread among these people living in the Underground, the first steps have now been taken to provide the simplest necessities for hygiene (ie. toilets) . . .'[79] This, it will be recalled, was the report in which three noble Lords, Brocket, Londonderry and Lymington, were said to be ready to agree to peace on any terms.

On 22 April, soon after Hess returned, it must be presumed, from his mission to Madrid, a report from the Hungarian military attaché in

London described the German air raid on 16 April as exceeding all former raids:

'Although the morale of the population may not be shattered so soon, yet the regular repetition of such destruction of essential services like water and light, whose repair grows ever more difficult in consequence of raw material shortages, must finally cripple the city . . .'[80]

Although a few reports spoke of British morale holding up, Hess undoubtedly had Intelligence to support his view that Britain could not resist indefinitely.

Turning now to his talk with the Duke of Hamilton on the morning after he landed, Sunday, 11 May, the two were alone and the only report of what was said was drawn up by Hamilton. Mrs Pyne, formerly ACW Iris Palmer, one of two female clerks in the Orderly Room at Turnhouse, remembers the Duke returning at some time that afternoon – it will be recalled he made a detour to Eaglesham to see Hess's crashed plane – and telling her to get 'Group' on the line. Normally his invariable first instructions when he first came in were 'Get me Cranwell!', 'Get me Prestwick!', where his two brothers were serving. She describes him as 'shattered, extremely tense' that afternoon, in marked contrast to his normal relaxed manner. She did not hear what he said to 13 Group headquarters since his office was separate from the Orderly Room, nor does she know what calls he made subsequently, but remembers that after a short while he called in the other ACW, Pearl Hyatt, and dictated his report of events to her, which Pearl typed at her desk in the Orderly Room; Mrs Pyne never knew the contents; both girls were aware without being told that this was a matter of extreme gravity – 'the premier Duke of Scotland faced out of the blue with the Deputy Führer!' – and not a subject for gossip.[81]

At some time about 4.00 pm or shortly after he went back to his house near the base. The Dowager Duchess of Hamilton is sure it was this time because they had asked the Squadron Leader Admin., Cyril Longden, and his two children to tea, and they appeared shortly after the Duke, who came straight up to her room above the front door, overlooking the drive – the first time she had seen him since the previous night. He showed her a photograph he had brought back from his interview with the pilot, saying, 'I think it's Hess. I must go to London at once. I haven't told anyone. Don't say a word about it.' His intention, he told her afterwards, was to explain what had happened to her in case he was shot down or crashed on his flight south, but at that moment, seeing her guests through the window, she exclaimed, 'There's Cyril!' It became a joke afterwards that all she could say on being told the Deputy Führer had flown over to see him was, 'There's Cyril!'[82]

It is appropriate here to correct the statement on page 88 that the Duke had been a member of the Anglo-German Fellowship; his son, Lord James Douglas-Hamilton, has checked the membership and found that only his brothers, Malcolm and David were members; Clydesdale was sent an application form but did not return it.[83]

When Hamilton reached Dytchley Hall after dinner that evening and saw Churchill (see pages 216–17) he must have had with him, besides the photographs of Hess and, it may be, Hess's peace proposals, the report of his interview typed by Pearl Hyatt. This report is not in the Prime Minister's or any other open files. No doubt if it contained references to the draft treaty and Hess's remarks on the coming attack on Russia Churchill returned it to him, asking him to redraft it without the sensitive points. That he was asked to re-write it can certainly be inferred from the covering letter enclosing a second report of his interview which he sent to Churchill's private secretary, John Martin, from the Air Ministry on 18 May:

'Dear Private Secretary,

  'As you know the Prime Minister saw some rough notes about my first meeting with Herr Hess.

  'I now enclose a more detailed and accurate report compiled from these notes, which I think the Prime Minister might like to see.'[84]

The report which obviously came with this letter and remains adjacent to it in the Prime Minister's file, is the known, undated 'Report on Interview with Herr Hess by Wing Commander the Duke of Hamilton, Sunday 11th May, 1941',[85] a copy of which was exhibited at Nuremberg. Mrs Pyne remembers Pearl Hyatt taking her typewriter into Hamilton's office – such was the secrecy – to type out this second report after he returned from London. She recalls Pearl exclaiming, 'Oh, I've got to take this darned thing in to the old man's office!' This second or revised report took far longer than the first,[86] but it may be that Pearl was also typing Kirkpatrick's report; certainly Kirkpatrick had returned to Turnhouse with Hamilton after seeing Hess, and in his memoirs refers to an attractive young WAAF at the aerodome typing the reports of his interviews. The original or 'rough notes' report which Pearl had typed on the afternoon of 11 May, before Hamilton flew down to see Church-ill, has, like Bohle's translated letter to Hamilton, disappeared.

As mentioned, when Kirkpatrick telephoned Cadogan with his impressions of his first interview with Hess that morning, he had made the suggestion that 'in view of the reservation that Germany could not negotiate with the present government', it might be possible to persuade Hess to open up freely by putting him in touch with 'some member of the Conservative Party who would give him the impression he was tempted with the idea of getting rid of the present government'.[87] It has been suggested that this might have been tried later by sending Beaverbrook to see him in the Tower of London. A curious story told by retired Squadron Leader Frank Day suggests that Beaverbrook or some other bogus 'negotiator' may have seen him that same evening, Tuesday, 13 May. Day was then a young Pilot Officer learning to fly Spitfires at Grangemouth, near Turnhouse. On 12 May he made his first solo flight in a Spitfire, a proud fact which he recorded in his Flying Log. The following day, thus 13 May, he and five other young pilots on the course were instructed to report to Turnhouse, where they were told they were to stand a guard duty; they were then driven – without being issued with arms – a short distance to a large Victorian house. Inside the front door was a curving flight of stairs. After mounting to the first floor, he and one other Pilot Officer were told to stand outside the middle door of about three on the landing. Presently two men in khaki uniform escorted a tall German officer in uniform with a leather flying jacket up the stairs and through the door Day was guarding; one of the escorts went inside with the German, and Day had a glimpse of an ante room leading into a large living room furnished with easy chairs and a settee. The other escort remained outside holding a paper bag; Day discovered this contained 'pills' the German had brought with him. Some five minutes later a ranking RAF officer came up the stairs with a civilian and both went into the room. Day learned from a manservant that the RAF officer was 'the Duke' – he now supposes the Duke of Hamilton. Later that evening Day was driven back to Turnhouse. Asked in the mess next day, which was buzzing with speculation about Hess, whether he had seen him, Day replied, 'For about thirty seconds'.[88]

Hess is supposed to have been under heavy guard at the Military Hospital, Buchanan Castle, Drymen, north of Glasgow at this time; he had been brought there from Maryhill Barracks in the afternoon of Sunday, 11 May, and remained there until the 16th when he was taken down to London. However, Day is quite certain that the Victorian house he was driven to was neither a castle nor a military hospital, and was a very short distance from Turnhouse – no more than a 20-minute drive. Even allowing for the fallibility of memory after 50 years, common sense indicates that young, unarmed Pilot Officers under training at Grangemouth would not have been driven to a military hospital north of Glasgow to guard a prisoner already cordoned by over 100 soldiers. It also seems certain that he was not taken to Hamilton's house off the base, which was a curious 18th-century tower. Indeed the only certainty is that the tall German officer in a leather flying jacket was Hess since his escort brought his 'pills'; when recounting the story Day was unaware that Hess had pocketfuls of homeopathic medicines with him when he landed, and explained to the doctors examining him that he was undergoing a six-week cure and must keep them with him.[89]

The significance or otherwise of this episode is not known. There are no records of any meeting with Hess on the evening of 13 May, only the interview with Hamilton and Kirkpatrick at the Military Hospital, Drymen, in the early hours of that morning. Possibly the civilian with Hamilton was Lord Beaverbrook, who had flown up to Turnhouse at Churchill's behest, for Kim Philby's report did not state where Beaverbrook met Hess. The civilian could hardly have been Eden, or Day would have recognised him. Possibly it was Kirkpatrick. For the moment the episode remains a matter for speculation.

Whatever occurred that evening, Kirkpatrick's report of his next interview with Hess, which Hamilton also attended, next day, 14 May, does not ring true. At the previous recorded interview in the early hours of Monday morning, 13 May (see pages 225-7) Hess had lectured him interminably on the causes of the war from the German viewpoint, proceeding eventually to the reasons for the inevitability of German victory. When finally he had come to the reason for his flight, his peace proposals as recounted by Kirkpatrick both verbally to Cadogan later that morning and in his written report merely amounted to Great Britain allowing Germany a free hand in Europe, in return for which Germany would allow her a free hand in her empire. Kirkpatrick had attempted to draw him on Russia and Italy, without success, by which time both Hamilton and he had been so exhausted they had returned to Turnhouse. Yet on 14 May, the next recorded interview, Kirkpatrick began by asking Hess how he was, then listened to his complaints and requests – for the loan of books, the return of his camera, homeopathic drugs and a piece of his aeroplane as a souvenir. Next, Hess gave an account of his flight and his difficulties in jumping from the aircraft over Dungavel. When at length he passed to political questions he said only that he had omitted two conditions from his proposals: Germany could not leave Iraq in the lurch, and both German and British nationals would have to be compensated for property appropriated as a result of war; after this he reverted to threats that if Britain did not come to an accommodation Hitler would be forced to starve her into submission.[90] What is missing is any attempt by Kirkpatrick to probe Hess on his extraordinarily woolly proposals for peace – as recorded in his report – or any attempt by Hess to clarify that proposal. Yet Kirkpatrick recorded Hess's parting words as:

' . . . if conversations were initiated as he hoped, he trusted that a qualified interpreter would be provided and that the conversations would not be attended by a large number of persons . . .'[91]

While in Scotland Hess was expecting a negotiation, at the Foreign Office in London Roger Makins minuted that before any directive could be issued to the propaganda agencies about the line to take on Hess, 'It is first necessary to come to some sort of an agreed conclusion as to why Hess made his flight . . .', and he went on to surmise he might perhaps have been affected by the damage and suffering he had seen, and his changed attitude 'may have led others in the Party to judge him queer'; scenting danger, he perhaps staked all on bringing the war to an end.[92] The Foreign Office officials under Cadogan evidently knew no more than Kirkpatrick had told them by phone, and had no inkling of any detailed peace proposals. That same evening Cadogan drafted an insert to replace a part of Churchill's proposed statement to the House; instead of the section beginning 'From his statements it would seem that he [Hess] had the idea that there was a strong peace or defeatist feeling in Great Britain . . .' (see page 235) Cadogan proposed:

'His purpose in coming here is not yet clear and on the information he has so far given it is not yet possible to account for his escapade. We may expect to get an explanation but I am unable to give one now . . .'[93]

Yet it will be recalled (see page 237) there is a hand-written addition in the margin of one draft of this statement that Churchill never made:

'He has also made other statements which it would not be in the public interest to disclose . . .'[94]

Now that all the papers have been opened it is possible to see that there is nothing in Hamilton's or Kirkpatrick's reports to justify this marginal note; the draft statement contains everything from those sources; nothing is omitted. The 'other statements' must either have been reported verbally by Hamilton at Dytchley Hall, or in writing in his first 'rough notes' report – missing from the record – or Beaverbrook or some other 'negotiator' who has left no trace in the records must have talked to Hess before the evening of 14 May; it is perhaps significant that Beaverbrook dined with Churchill that night, backing up Cadogan's and Eden's arguments against Churchill making his statement.

The next day, 15 May, Hamilton flew down to Northolt, London, in a Hurricane bringing Kirkpatrick's first two typed reports of his interviews,[95] and presumably his own revised report, although, as mentioned, he did not send this to Churchill's private secretary, John Martin, until the 18th – perhaps because he wanted to check it with the Air Ministry, perhaps because Churchill asked him to revise it again. Kirkpatrick in Scotland meanwhile paid his third recorded visit to Hess (see page 238). At 4.50 that afternoon he rang the Foreign Office from the hospital at Drymen; the call was taken by Henry Hopkinson:

'Mr Kirkpatrick emphasised that if we wanted to get anything more out of Hess we should have to put someone else in in the role of negotiator who could question him about his proposals, and ask him to justify his assertions and facts etc. He said that Hess now merely regarded him coming there as visits of politeness and that it was difficult to get him on to politics at all. He mainly took the opportunity to ask him for books, complain about the noisiness of the guard and to ask for the return of his [homeopathic] drugs. (I asked Mr Kirkpatrick to make sure this was not done.) Mr Kirkpatrick said that the situation was rather embarrassing for him and that until a negotiator could be put in touch with Hess it would be better to leave him alone and let him think that his proposals were being considered in London . . .'[96]

The question is, what proposals? The only proposal recorded in Hamilton's revised report was that Great Britain should 'give up her policy of always supporting the strongest power in Europe'; the only proposals in Kirkpatrick's reports, apart from support from Iraq and war indemnities for German and British nationals, were that Britain should give Germany a free hand in Europe while Germany gave her a free hand in her empire – save for the return of the former German colonies. These were hardly proposals meriting long consideration. What they needed was detailed elucidation. Moreover they were, according to all reports, not official proposals from Hitler or the German government. Kirkpatrick had said in his first phone call to Cadogan that Hess 'maintained that he had come of his own initiative'; a minute by Makins on propaganda the same day stated '[he] had come entirely on his own and brings no commission from the German government . . .'[97] Next day Churchill's draft statement declared, 'It is abundantly clear . . . that he had no mission to this country from the German government . . .' Kirkpatrick, who was clever and experienced, would not have expected his lone, unauthorised visitor to swallow the line that such vague proposals – as indicated in the files – were being considered in London. His suggestion to Hopkinson scarcely makes sense unless there was a genuine, official and detailed offer on the table, 'an offer that could not be refused'.

There is a note from Churchill to Cadogan the following day, 16 May, which might suggest there was:

'Please make now a fairly full digest of the conversational part of Hess's three interviews, stressing particularly the points mentioned by me in the statement I prepared but did not deliver. I will then send this to President Roosevelt with a covering telegram.'[98]

What can 'conversational parts' of Hess's interviews mean? That there were also 'documentary parts'? If so, the inference is that Hamilton brought Hess's proposed draft treaty down to Churchill at Dytchley Hall, after which it went up to Scotland again in Kirkpatrick's briefcase; Kirkpatrick's task in that case was not so much to make a positive identification – the official communique confirming Hess's identity went out from the Foreign Office at 11.20 pm on 12 May, an hour before Hamilton and Kirkpatrick arrived at the Military Hospital, Drymen[99] – as to probe him on the meaning and authority of his Proposals.

The reason for dissembling is suggested by a plaintive note R.A. Butler addressed to Cadogan on 22 May:

'From time to time odd straws of information reach me about Hess. I see a great many of the foreign diplomats and confess that this is a subject on which I have had great difficulty, since I do not know enough to observe my usual caution, and am somewhat nervous as to how to continue to handle these matters. Could I receive a little more information as to what he has said?'[100]

To which Cadogan replied, 'You are in the happy position of being able to say you don't know! But Mr Hopkinson will show you the Kirkpatrick interviews if you like.' He added that Hess had said little of note since then. 'Thank you', 'RAB' replied on the 26th.[101]

Butler, Eden's Undersecretary at the Foreign Office, was, of course, a known wobbler, close to the previous Foreign Secretary, Halifax, and the 'appeasement' wing of the Conservative Party. It was suggested on pages 276–7 that Churchill had left him in his post after Halifax left for Washington as a deliberate deception; this exchange of minutes supports the view. Butler was an essential part of the lure, but when the ruse worked – no doubt to the immense astonishment of all concerned – he became a threat to Churchill's policy who had to be kept in ignorance.

The deception practised by the inner circle of Churchill's confidants on their own Foreign Office and Service Departments continued. When Lord Simon was due to visit Hess in June, Henry Hopkinson drew up a memorandum for his guidance which stated: 'We have no clear picture of Hitler's aspirations and intentions in Russia'.[102] Kirkpatrick had already written a note for Simon suggesting various lines of enquiry he might pursue with Hess:

'*Russia:* What is the use of our concluding a peace of understanding with Germany if Germany is going to sign up with Russia and bring Bolshevism into the heart of Europe? . . . *Spain and Portugal:* These are not merely European powers. We must know whether Germany has any intention of encroaching on their African possessions . . .'[103]

These and other suggested lines of enquiry were dealt with in detail in the draft proposals Hess had brought over, which according to the informant, were studied by Kirkpatrick's secret committee at the BBC.

They are the obvious questions missing from Kirkpatrick's reports from Scotland. The puzzle is to know why Hess, during his interview with Simon, did not simply refer him to these proposals. Instead, when pressed on his proposed settlement, he handed Simon two half sheets of paper on which he had jotted down the wholly general points about areas of interest conveyed in Kirkpatrick's reports, and headed 'Basis for an understanding'[104] (see page 262). The answer may be that he considered Lord Simon, as a member of the government, was a part of the 'clique' who were preventing him getting in touch with the people he had come to see. This interpretation is leant support by a report Frank Foley wrote at the end of May:

'He [Hess] raised again the question of the Duke of Hamilton and of Mr Kirkpatrick. In his confused way he seems to think that they are outside the political clique or Secret Service ring which is preventing him from meeting the proper peace people and the King. He reiterated that he had come here of his own free will, trusting in the chivalry of the King . . .'[105]

Without the documents which the informant alleges Hess brought with him, without an official inventory to indicate whether he brought documents or not, the case for Kirkpatrick, Hamilton and Churchill's inner ring conspiring to hide this explosive secret even from the Foreign Office remains unproven. Nonetheless, the unexplained, often glaring discrepancies between the stories of all major participants, Churchill, Eden, Colville, Hamilton, Cadogan, Desmond Morton, and the dichotomy between the story contained in the Foreign Office files and that confided by Churchill's closest confidants persuade the author that, until further evidence emerges, a combination of the accounts by André Guerber, the informant and Lord Beaverbrook represents the closest approximation to the truth. It seems probable that the main lines of the proposed settlement were drawn up after the fall of France in conversations with the Duke of Windsor in Madrid and Lisbon, then honed through other intermediaries, no doubt including the Red Cross Commissioner, Carl Burckhardt, and Albrecht Haushofer. Probably Hess went to Madrid in April; possibly while there he intended flying to Gibraltar to see Sam Hoare, as hinted in the House of Commons debate on 19 June (see page 273). Hoare was in Gibraltar for a time and was acting strangely that month. Probably it was Hoare who finally convinced Hess, either directly or indirectly through intermediaries, that Britain wanted peace. That he did so as part of a very 'secret plan' hatched with Churchill and Stewart Menzies (see page 246) seems equally probable, since Menzies' friend, Dusko Popov, spread deliberate disinformation about the 'Peace Party' and the terrible destruction wrought by German air raids. It is possible, however, that 'Slippery

379

Sam' was playing both sides; it is notable that, despite his high ambitions and the excellent job he did for Great Britain in Spain, after the war he disappeared into obscurity with a title. It also seems probable that, much as Churchill and Menzies may have wished to deceive Hitler into turning eastwards, they and all the other participants, not least the Duke of Hamilton, were astounded by Hess's arrival. And if he brought such an offer as the informant alleges, Churchill had no alternative but to confine the secret to a small inner circle while cloaking his arrival in such a fog of evasions and half truths it remains difficult if not impossible to penetrate today.

From the German side it is impossible to know whether Hitler believed in 'Plan ABCD Nr. S 274 K', or whether he sanctioned the mission as the final masterstroke in the deception of Stalin. He expected to conquer the east within months, after which his loyal liege man would be in place in England to negotiate England's surrender. There seems no reason at present to amend the final words of the Postscript.

NOTES & ABBREVIATIONS

Books are referenced by author and, if more than one book by that author is listed in the Select Bibliography, by a number in brackets. Articles are referenced by author, or a key word if anonymous (see list of articles in the Bibliography). The following abbreviations are used in the references:

AA	Politischen Archiv des Auswärtigen Amt, Bonn
Aus. Amt.	Foreign Ministry, Berlin
BA	Bundesarchiv, Koblenz
BDC	Berlin Document Center
CC	Churchill College Archives Centre, Cambridge
D.D.I.	*Documenti Diplomatici Italiani, 1939–1943*, 9th series
D.G.F.P.	*Documents on German Foreign Policy, 1918–1945*, series D
F & C	(captured documents in) Foreign & Colonial Office Library, London
FH	Fritz Hess (father)
F.O.	Foreign Office, London
Fr.	(microfilm) frame number
IfZ	Institut für Zeitgeschichte, Munich
Ilse	Ilse Pröhl/Hess (wife)
IMT	The International Military Tribunal: *Trial of the Major War Criminals*, Nuremberg, 1947 (Engl. language edition)
IWM	Imperial War Museum, London
KH	Klara Hess (mother)
M. of I.	Ministry of Information, London
NA	National Archives, Washington
ORB	Operations Record Book (Royal Air Force)
PM	Prime Minister
PP	Author
P.R.O.	Public Record Office, Kew Gardens, London
RFSS	Reichsführer-SS, Heinrich Himmler
RH	Rudolf Hess
Sec./Sek.	Secretary/Sekretär
St.	State (or Staat); thus Sec. of State
St.G.	Gedenkstätten, Stauffenbergstrasse, Berlin
T-253 etc.	Microfilm of captured German documents, National Archives, Washington
VB	*Völkischer Beobachter*: Nazi newspaper
W.O.	War Office, London
W.R.H.	Wolf Rüdiger Hess (son)

The following abbreviations are used for collections of papers:

BP	Beaverbrook Papers, House of Lords Record Office, London
GS	Geoffrey Shakespeare Papers, Imperial War Museum, London
H/../..	Himmler Papers (captured), Imperial War Museum, London
IS	Ian Sayer's private archive
Monckton	Walter Monckton Papers, Bodleian Library, Oxford
Quinlan	Squadron Leader Hugh Quinlan Papers (box 455), Imperial War Museum, London
Scott	Colonel A.M.Scott 'Camp "Z" Diary' and Papers 69/66/1, Imperial War Museum, London
Simon	Lord Simon Papers, Bodleian Library, Oxford
ZS 262	Alfred Leitgen's testimony, Institut für Zeitgeschichte, Munich

Prologue
1 RH to Ilse, 18. 5.24:
   W.R.Hess (3), 326
2 RH to KH, 16.5.24: ibid.
   323–4
3 RH to Ilse, 29.6.24: ibid. 324
4 ibid.
5 Hafstaengl, 165
6 ibid. 165–6
7 OSS Source Book: Hitler,
   894 (NA)
8 Waite to PP, 29.12.89
9 Monckton, box 3, f.27
10 Fromm, 127
11 Ludecke, 507
12 Hanfstaengl, 165
13 Waite, 284
14 Hanfstaengl, 92
15 19.12.52: ZS 262 f.13
16 v. Krosigk, 239

Chapter One Hess
1 Schwarzwäller, 24
2 RH to KH, 3.7.49: I.Hess
   (1), 208
3 RH to KH, 22.1.51: ibid. 221
4 RH to Ilse, 24.9.24:
   W.R.Hess (3), 352
5 Hanfstaengl, 92
6 Gabel, 241, 262
7 ZS 262 f.100
8 Schwarzäller, 37
9 ibid. 30
10 See E.Grey: *Twenty Five
   Years* (1925), 324 f.
11 1.8.14: Röhl, 669
12 Hitler, 177
13 RH to K & FH, 3.8.14:
   W.R.Hess (3), 88
14 FH to RH, 17.8.14: ibid. 92
15 RH to K & FH, 18.9.14:
   cited Schwarzwäller, 33
16 RH service record: BDC
17 RH to Ilse, Dec. 47: I.Hess
   (1), 164
18 I.Hess (2) 29
19 RH to K & FH, 29.7.17:
   W.R.Hess (3), 202–3
20 RH to K & FH, 10.8.17:
   ibid. 204
21 RH to K & FH, 17.8.17:
   ibid. 205
22 April 43: T-253, Roll 56,
   Fr.1215216
23 RH to K & FH, 7.9.17:
   W.R.Hess (3), 206–7
24 RH to RH, 17.8.17: ibid. 205
25 KH to RH, 26.8.17: ibid. 206
26 RH to K & FH, 22.10.17:
   ibid. 209
27 RH service record: BDC
28 RH to K & FH, 6.10.18:
   W.R.Hess (3), 222
29 RH to K & FH, 11.10.18:
   ibid. 222–3

30 Irving (2), 37

Chapter Two Hitler
1 I.Hess (2), 18–20
2 ibid. 19
3 ibid. 23
4 ZS 262 f.99
5 RH to K & FH, 17.6.20:
   W.R.Hess (3), 261
6 5.10.45, 2–3: IWM FO 645
   box 157
7 Ludecke, 86
8 ibid. 22
9 Waite, 141ff; Cecil, 17f
10 Ludecke, 22
11 I.Hess (2), 25
12 ibid. 24–5
13 RH to K & FH, 24.3.20:
   W.R.Hess (3), 251
14 RH to K & FH, 14.9.20:
   ibid. 264
15 RH to Ilse, 18.6.45: I.Hess
   (1), 102
16 RH to K & FH,
   8.11–4.12.23: W.R.Hess
   (3), 310
17 ibid. 310–11
18 ibid. 311
19 see Waite, 255
20 ibid. 478–9
21 RH to K & FH,
   8.11–4.12.23, W.R.Hess
   (3), 312
22 *The Times*, 12.11.23
23 Schwarzwäller, 69
24 RH to K & FH,
   8.11–4.12.23: W.R.Hess
   (3), 312
25 ibid. 313
26 I.Hess (1), 219
27 W.Schwarzwäller: *The
   Unknown Hitler* (1989), 123
28 Hanfstaengl, 92
29 v. Krosigk, 240
30 RH to Ilse, 29.11.23:
   W.R.Hess (3), 323
31 RH to FH, Jan. 24: ibid. 315

Chapter Three Mein Kampf
1 *The Times*, 2.4.24
2 RH to Ilse, 18.4.24:
   W.R.Hess (3), 321
3 RH to KH, 12.5.24: ibid. 322
4 RH to KH, 16.5.24: ibid. 323
5 ibid.
6 RH to Ilse, 18.5.24: ibid.
   327–8
7 RH to Ilse, 27.5.24: ibid.
   329–30
8 RH to Ilse, 2.6.24: ibid. 331
9 5.10.45, 4–6: IWM FO 645
   box 157
10 RH to K.Haushofer,
   11.6.24: W.R.Hess (3),
   334–5

11 5.10.45, 7: IWM FO 645
   box 157
12 RH to K.Haushofer,
   11.6.24: W.R.Hess (3),
   334–5
13 RH to Ilse, 11.6.24: ibid. 333
14 Cecil, 9, 17–18
15 Waite, 141
16 Ludecke, 86
17 ibid. 87
18 see Cecil, 34
19 see ibid. 45
20 see RH to Ilse, 4.8.24:
   W.R.Hess (3), 347;
   W.R.Hess, cited
   Schwarzwäller, 73
21 Waite, 85
22 ibid.
23 ibid.
24 Hitler 772
25 RH to Ilse, 29.6.24:
   W.R.Hess (3), 342
26 ibid. 343
27 Hitler, 447
28 ibid.
29 see Waite, 25
30 RH to H.Heim, 16.7.24: IS
31 RH to Ilse, 24.7.24:
   W.R.Hess (3), 347
32 RH to Ilse, 23.7.24: ibid. 346
33 see Waite, 70
34 RH to Ilse, 10.9.24:
   W.R.Hess (3), 351–2
35 RH to Ilse, 20.12.24: ibid.
   358

Chapter Four The Secretary
1 H.Frank, cited Waite, 94
2 E.Reichmann: *Hostages of
   Civilisation* (1950), 193:
   cited Waite, 402
3 Ludecke, 257
4 Strasser, 35
5 RH to K & FH, 24.4.25:
   W.R.Hess (3), 367
6 ibid. 368
7 RH to K & FH, 7.7.25: ibid.
   369
8 Ludecke, 97
9 ZS 262 f.100
10 ibid. f.101
11 see ref. 5 above
12 cited E.Mowrer: *Germany
   Puts the Clock Back* (rev'd
   1938), 196
13 RH to Ilse, 14.7.27:
   W.R.Hess (3), 382
14 see Pool, 86ff
15 RH to G.Georg, 15.4.27:
   W.R.Hess (3), 376–7
16 ibid. 377
17 ibid. 378
18 Gossweiler (1), 492; Pool,
   141
19 Pool, 142

20 Gossweiler (1), 502ff
21 Scharzwäller, 78
22 Bird, 276–7
23 Hanfstaengl, 324
24 RH to KH, 14.1.28:
   W.R.Hess (3), 389
25 Thewelweit, 3–18
26 ibid. 61
27 ibid.
28 RH to Ilse, 8.3.28:
   W.R.Hess (3), 391
29 RH to F & KH, 28.6.28:
   ibid.392–3
30 RH to K & FH, 18.12.28:
   ibid. 395

Chapter Five The Brown House
1 cited Pool, 145
2 see Pool, esp. 226;
   Gossweiler (1), 468ff, 624ff
3 RH to K & FH, 10.3.31:
   W.R.Hess (3), 408
4 see Pool, 120
5 Strasser, 63, 67
6 O.Strasser: cited Bullock,
   140–1
7 Strasser, 64
8 C.Duisberg, cited
   V.Berghahn: *The
   Americanisation of West
   German Industry* (1986), 24
9 12.8.30: BDC
10 ibid.
11 28.8.30: BDC
12 Stellungnahme des Leiters
   der Polizei, 20.10.30: BDC
13 see Padfield, 89
14 19.12.52: ZS 262 p2
15 KH to RH, 16.4.31:
   W.R.Hess (3), 409

Chapter Six Power
1 cited Gossweiler (1), 245
2 Abraham, xvii; but see Hayes
3 Gossweiler (1), 347;
   Schweitzer, 102
4 R.L.Koehl: *The Black
   Corps*, (1983), 298
5 RH c.v.: BDC
6 R.Vogelsang: *Der
   Freundeskreis Himmler*
   (1972), 42
7 PS-3337: IfZ: cited
   Gossweiler (2), 295–6
8 ibid.
9 Gossweiler (2), 298

Chapter Seven Night of the Long
Knives
1 Luxemburg, 81
2 see ibid.
3 ibid. 76
4 E.Calic to PP, 17.1.90
5 9.10.45: IWM FO 695 box
   157

6 Ludecke, 519
7 ibid.
8 ibid. 601
9 Fromm, 127
10 ibid.
11 v. Pfeffer to Dr Bennecke,
   21.4.63: IfZ ZS 177 f.69
12 see Irving (2), 144–5
13 19.12.52: ZS 262 f.12
14 see Waite, 49, 460ff
15 1.4.52: ZS 262 f.10
16 Ludecke, 675
17 ibid.
18 Gossweiler (2), 429
19 1.4.52: ZS 262 f.10; see also
   Hanfstaengl, 348
20 Cited Ludecke, 679–80
21 Cited Gossweiler (2), 451
22 VB, 30.6.34
23 19.12.52: ZS 262 f.13
24 1.4.52; ibid. f.10
25 Frank, 143
26 *Das Politische Tagebuch
   Alfred Rosenberg* (1965), 46
27 cited Roberts, 115
28 Schwarzwäller, 102

Chapter Eight The Deputy
1 *N-S Jahrbuch* (1939), 188–9;
   and see Bollmus, 43
2 *N-S Jahrbuch* (1939), 189
3 9.11.45, 14–15; IWM FO
   645 box 155
4 VB, 30.6.34
5 19.12.52: ZS 262 f.13
6 ibid.
7 v. Krosigk, 239–40
8 Hanfstaengl, 324
9 Frank, 157–8
10 Roberts, 31
11 26.9.45: IWM FO 645 box
   155
12 see Bollmus, 48; see J.Fest:
   *Das Gesicht des dritten
   Reiches* (1964), 259, 264
13 19.12.52: ZS 262 f.13
14 1.4.52: ZS 262 f.6
15 ibid. f.9
16 ibid. f.6
17 Frank, 157
18 see RH to Ilse, 29.6.24:
   W.R.Hess (3), 342
19 Broszat, 67
20 RH Personal File: IWM FO
   645 box 151
21 RH to Hitler, 3.9.35: IS
22 RH to K.Haushofer,
   11.6.24: W.R.Hess, 335
23 Hitler, 447
24 Nowak, 35
25 RFSS:*Rassenpolitik*(1934),17
26 Cited Nowak, 35
27 RFSS: *Die Schutzstaffel als
   antibolschewistischen
   Kampforganisation* (1936), 3

28 Lifton, 31
29 ibid. 129
30 ibid.
31 RFSS: *Schutzstaffel* ... (ref.
   27 above), 3
32 Frank, 320–21
33 Waite, 152ff, 442–5
34 ibid. 153
35 ibid. 449
36 ibid. 440
37 Roberts, 265
38 Speer, 353
39 RH to Ilse, 8.3.28:
   W.R.Hess (3), 391
40 9.10.45: IWM FO 645 box
   155
41 see Laack-Michel, 297ff
42 see H.Rauschning:
   *Germany's Revolution of
   Destruction*(1939),241ff,280
43 7.9.33: Laack-Michel, 316
44 Stubbe, 245
45 8.10.33: Laack-Michel, 317
46 27.7.34: ibid. 321
47 ibid.
48 18.8.34: ibid. 322
49 Frank, 157
50 3.12.65: ZS 262 f.18
51 IWM FO 645 box 160
52 Lifton, 21
53 see letters in H/6/261ff.
54 v. Pfeffer to H. Bennecke: IfZ
   ZA 177/1, ZS 177/1
55 A.Leitgen; 19.12.52: ZS 262
   f.13

Chapter Nine The England
Game
1 GS 2, 1–2
2 E.Mann, 'Hess Meeting in
   Spa was Fixed': *Glasgow
   Evening Citizen* (1945)
3 GS 2, 1–2
4 Fromm, 195
5 Duke of Hamilton to PP,
   2.4.91
6 Lord James Douglas-
   Hamilton to PP, 6.4.91
7 Duke of Hamilton to PP,
   3.4.91
8 R.C.Langdon to PP, 13,
   17.5.91; and for
   K.Haushofer's testimony,
   see p. 306 below
9 A.Haushofer to Clydesdale,
   7.1.37, cited Douglas-
   Hamilton, 74
10 Douglas-Hamilton, 74
11 ibid. 74–5
12 ibid. 75–6
13 ibid. 77–81
14 cited Herbst, 66
15 Giordano, 252
16 see Schwarzwäller, 122;
   Ludecke, 679–80

17 A. Leitgen, 3.12.52: ZS 262 f.101
18 cited Schwarzwäller, 105
19 RH speech before Gau- and Kreisleiters, 13.9.37: BDC
20 ibid. 8–9
21 1.4.52: ZS 262 f.6

Chapter Ten War
1 F. Donaldson: *Edward VIII* (1976 ed.), 330
2 Ilse to KH, 20.10.37: PRO FO 371/26566
3 26.9.45, 10–11: IWM FO 645 box 155
4 Ilse to KH, 3.11.37: PRO FO 371/26566
5 RH to KH, 15.1.38: ibid.
6 cited Schwarzwäller, 110
7 Hanfstaengl, 311
8 26.9.45: IWM FO 645 box 155
9 Frank, 158
10 ibid. 159
11 *N.Y. Times*, 21.5.45: cited Irving (3), 25
12 3.12.65: ZS 262 f.18
13 v. Krosigk, 159
14 ibid. 240; Hanfstaengl, 324
15 cited Irving (3), 25
16 Lifton, 40–1, 129–30
17 Ilse to K & FH, 15.12.37: PRO FO 371/26566
18 Duke of Hamilton to PP, 2.4.91
19 3.12.65: ZS 262 f.18
20 v. Hassell, 43
21 IMT vol. 38, 172–3
22 A. Haushofer to Clydesdale, 16.7.39, St.G
23 A.P. Young, 148ff
24 7.8.39: v. Hassell, 67; Hill, 175
25 A.P. Young, 235
26 N. Henderson: *Failure of a Mission* (1940), 310–11
27 Himmler diary, cited Irving (5), 255–6
28 ibid. 256

PART 2 FLIGHT

Chapter Eleven Peace Feelers
1 Karl Brandt testimony, Nuremberg, cited Lifton, 50
2 Bormann scepticism, M. Tregenza to PP, 27.1.90; questionnaires, Nowak, 80–1; Lifton, 69
3 Lifton, 129
4 ibid. 63
5 Scott Newton to PP, 1990
6 A.L. Rowse: *A Man of the Thirties* (1979), 5

7 'C': 'What should we do?' 18.9.39: cited Cave Brown, 190–1
8 Scott Newton, 25ff
9 Colville, 40–1
10 Cave Brown, 214–5; see Dr Frick report, 29.3.40: Mil. Tribunal Case 11, Doc. NG-4672: IWM
11 11–14.5.48, p. 5066: IWM FO 646(213)
12 see Colville, 45
13 Lamb, 126ff
14 DGFP, vol. viii, No. 235, 257ff
15 see Bullock, 509, 512
16 Churchill to Halifax, 1.11.39: cited M. Gilbert, 72–3; MacDonald, 456
17 see Calic, 319ff
18 ibid. 326
19 cited Cave Brown, 219
20 Grantmesnil to PP, 16.4.89
21 ibid.
22 ibid. 26.4.90
23 Deacon, 90
24 v. Hassell, 128–33; and PRO FO 371 26542, C1072/324/18
25 Beaverbrook to Liddell Hart, 13.2.40: BP, C/159
26 PRO FO 371/24363: cited Lamb, 136
27 ibid.

Chapter Twelve Churchill
1 cited Cohen, 5
2 cited ibid. 277
3 cited J.W. Wheeler Bennett: *Action this Day* (1968), 205
4 see Cohen, 44
5 cited Irving (1), 104
6 M. Gilbert, 919f
7 Cohen, 3
8 Cave Brown, 187–8
9 ibid. 177
10 quoted anonymously by Deacon, 32–3
11 For Maxwell Knight, see 'M'
12 Grantmesnil to PP, 26.4.90
13 'Rothschild': *Lobster* 16
14 see D. Cameron-Watt: 'Chronicles of Britain's Secret War', *Sunday Times*, 5.8.90
15 see A. Storr in A.J.P. Taylor & others: *Churchill Revised* (NY 1969), 238ff
16 4.6.40: cited M. Gilbert, 468
17 Gladwyn, 99

Chapter Thirteen Hubris
1 Hill, 204
2 ibid.
3 v. Hassell, 155

4 R 43/11/312 B1.339409; BA: cited Giordano, 227
5 Giordano, 145
6 ibid. 140
7 ibid.
8 24.6.40: Kersten, 88
9 Grantmesnil to PP, 30.11.90
10 Hohenlowe to St. Sek., 23.6.40: F & C 1504 371076
11 ibid.
12 ibid. 371079
13 Prytz told de Courcy the interview *was* arranged: Grantmesnil to PP, 30.11.90
14 M. Gilbert, 598–9; Prytz, 103; v. Weizsäcker to Ribbentrop, 19.6.40, 22.6.40: F & C B15 B002529, B002530
15 Hohenlowe to Hewel, 18.7.40: F & C 1504 371055–60
16 see Armstrong, 54
17 Huene to Aus. Amt., 10.7.40: F & C B15 B002546
18 23.7.40: Hill, 214
19 ibid. 215
20 Irving (1) 369
21 Köcher to Aus. Amt., 18.7.40: F & C B15 B002566
22 Gladwyn, 99; and see Armstrong, 45
23 23.7.40: Hill, 214
24 31.7.40: Halder II, 48
25 Huene to Aus. Amt., 30.7.40: F & C B15 B002609
26 Huene to Aus. Amt., 2.8.40: ibid. B002633

Chapter Fourteen Turn East
1 27.8.40: Halder II, 79
2 H. Höhne: *Canaris* (1979), 361
3 Kiesel, 9
4 Source cannot be revealed
5 Irving (2), 326
6 Grantmesnil to PP, 16.4.89, 8.1.90; Colville, 383
7 see Padfield, 302
8 ibid.
9 *N-S Jahrbuch* (1939), 188–9
10 see IMT vol. 7, 137; and see Padfield, 275
11 St. Sek. M. Luther to E. Calic; Calic to PP, 17.1.90; see Calic, 435ff; Padfield, 302ff
12 see H. Schacht: *76 Jahr meines Lebens* (1955), 481f: cited Calic, 435ff
13 see Padfield, 303
14 Lifton, 14
15 see Klee, 178–9; see also ibid. 316–7
16 Schwarzwäller, 133

17 see v. Hassell, 126–7
18 13.12.39: Laack-Michel, 346
19 see Padfield, 289, 468ff, 484–5

Chapter Fifteen Flight Plan
1 9.6.41: Simon box 88 ff.76–7
2 see Thorne, 54, 71
3 Halder II, 74
4 Köcher to Aus. Amt., 5.8.40: F & C B15 B002646
5 A. to K. Haushofer, 2.8.40: Jacobsen, 402
6 4.8.40: Laack-Michel, 349
7 3.9.40: F & C C109 002185
8 ibid.
9 *F.O. List* vol. 34, 1937–8, 487–8; *Who Was Who* vol. III (1929–40), entry for Herbert Ainslie Roberts
10 10.9.40: F & C C109 002188
11 6.10.39: cited Douglas-Hamilton, 105–6
12 see Huene to Aus. Amt., 29.8.40: F & C B15 613477
13 15.9.40: F & C C109 002193
14 ibid. 002190
15 ibid. 002194
16 10.9.40: F & C C109 002189
17 sworn statement, Nuremberg, 5.3.46: IWM FO 645/31
18 sworn statement, Nuremberg; ibid.
19 9.10.45, p. 4: IWM FO 695 box 157
20 Duke of Hamilton to PP, 2.4.91
21 see v. Weizsäcker Notiz, 23.7.40: Hill 214; see A. to K. Haushofer, 24.7.40: Laack-Michel, 348–9
22 Heberlein to Aus. Amt., 19.8.40: F & C B15 002661
23 Stöhrer to Aus. Amt., 2.9.40: ibid. 002687
24 Huene to Aus. Amt., 10.9.40: F & C 3084D 613498
25 ibid. 613500
26 Huene to Aus. Amt., 17.9.40: ibid. 613511
27 Thomsen to Aus. Amt., 30.9.40: F & C B15 B002794
28 Nicolson, 105–6
29 ibid. 114–5
30 F & C, C109 002197
31 19.9.40: ibid. 002198
32 23.9.40: ibid. 002204
33 ibid. 002201
34 British censor's note: PRO INF 1/912
35 F & C C109 002203
36 ibid. 002204–5
37 26.9.45, p. 6: IWM FO 645 box 155

38 W. R. Hess (2), 59
39 26.9.45, p. 7: IWM FO 645 box 155
40 9.10.45, p. 14: IWM FO 695 box 157
41 26.11.45, p. 8: IWM FO 645 box 155
42 Nesbit, 60
43 4.11.40: I. Hess (1), 81
44 RH to Ilse, 15.1.45: I. Hess (1), 101
45 PRO INF 1/912 150028
46 ibid.
47 ORB RAF Turnhouse: PRO AIR 28 863
48 12.11.40: Laack-Michel, 229

Chapter Sixteen The Double Game
1 Popov, 52ff
2 ibid. 44
3 Masterman, 40
4 ibid. xii
5 Popov, 53
6 ibid. 69–71
7 Huene to Aus. Amt., 4.1.41: F & C 3084D 613659
8 cited Day, 30
9 Colville, 304–5; see BP C/159
10 See Day, 36
11 Howard, 103
12 Huene to Aus. Amt., 23.1.41: F & C 3084D 613659–667
13 Popov, 70
14 ibid. 72
15 Huene to Aus. Amt., 23.1.41: F & C 3084D 613667
16 see his letters to Chamberlain and Halifax: PRO PREM 1/443, PREM 1/331A
17 PRO 371 26542, C1072/324/18
18 Nesbit, 63
19 W. R. Hess (2), 61
20 Leasor, 69ff
21 9.6.41: Simon box 88 f.134
22 ibid. f.133
23 17.11.40: Hill, 226
24 IMT 446-PS
25 Howard, 102
26 8–9.1.41: Halder 2, 244
27 Hohenlowe to Hewel, undated but December '40: F & C 1504 371047
28 Grey's memo on peace feelers, p.8: PRO FO 371 26542, C4216/324/18 f.104
29 Hohenlowe to Hewel, undated: see ref. 27 above
30 K. Bonde to Lady Barlow, 20.1.41: PRO FO 371 26542, C610/324/18

31 20.1.41: ibid. C1426/324/18
32 13.2.41: ibid.
33 ibid. C324/324/18
34 ibid. C610/324/18
35 ibid.
36 28.1.41: ibid.
37 6 & 7.2.41: ibid.
38 Nicolson, 39
39 v. Hassell, 183–4
40 ORB RAF Turnhouse (Appendices): PRO AIR 28/864
41 PRO FO 371 26945 C1052 & C1104/306/41
42 PRO FO 371 26542 C1303, C1687 & C1954/324/18
43 ibid. C2662, C2785, C3156/324/18; FO 371 26945, C3104, C4038, C4456 & C4487/306/41; FO 371 26971, C4411/2117/41 before May 10; FO 371 26945, C5280/306/41; FO 371 26542, C5695, C6974/324/18; FO 371 26565 C5251, C5253, C5589/5188/18 on or after May 10; there may be others.
44 see for instance PRO FO 371 26542, C1322/324/18
45 14.2.41: PRO FO 371 26542, C1322/324/18; 15.2.41 Cadogan minuted 'I agree'.
46 cited Day, 67
47 ibid.
48 P. Rowland: *Lloyd George* (1975), 784–5
49 cited Douglas-Hamilton, 159
50 ibid. 160
51 ibid. 161
52 Sir A. Harris to W. S. Douglas, 21.2.41: PRO AIR 16/619; Crawley, 161
53 Crawley, 161
54 PRO AIR 16/619
55 ibid.
56 10.10.39: DGFP vol. VIII, 262

Chapter Seventeen Sam Hoare
1 cited W. R. Hess (2), 80
2 ibid. 81
3 PRO FO 371 26542, C4216/324/18
4 Colville, 770
5 Eccles, 101
6 ibid.
7 ibid. 158
8 PRO FO 371 26939, C1713/222/41

NOTES AND ABBREVIATIONS

9 ibid.
10 27.2.41: PRO FO 371 26945, C1938/306/41; 1.3.41 FO 371 26966, C2022/1250/41
11 PRO FO 371 26945, C2065/306/41
12 3.3.41: ibid.
13 3.3.41: ibid.
14 4.3.41: ibid.
15 1.3.41: PRO FO 371 26971, C2117/2117/41
16 PRO FO 371 26542, C2505/324/18
17 21.3.41: ibid. f.78
18 ibid. f.76
19 ibid.
20 ibid.
21 v. Lequio to Miny. For. Relations, 14.3.41: D.D.I. vol. V; cited Scott Newton
22 Hoare to F.O., 30.6.40, and M. Palairet to F.O., 30.7.40: PRO FO 371 24407, C7542
23 Eccles, 101–2
24 Hoare to Beaverbrook, 29.5.40: BP
25 Nicolson, 149
26 Mallett to F.O. 6.3.41: PRO FO 371 26542, C2287/324/18
27 13.3.41: PRO FO 26971, C2472/2117/41
28 25.4.41: PRO FO 371 26905, C4161/46/46

Chapter Eighteen The Duke of Hamilton
1 v. Hassell, 187–8
2 ibid.
3 10.3.41: Kersten, 173
4 Halder 2, 419
5 see Padfield, 324
6 Halder 2, 336–7
7 5.10.45, 15: IWM FO 645 box 155
8 v. Hassell, 275
9 v. Krosigk, 241
10 ibid. 242
11 RH to Ilse, 12.2.50: cited Schwarzwäller, 140
12 see I. Hess (1), 67–8
13 v. Hassell, 207
14 Stubbe, 251–2, note 25
15 ibid. 254
16 v. Hassell, 207
17 5.10.45, p. 15: IWM FO 645 box 155
18 See PRO FO 371 26971, C4214/2117/41
19 PRO FO 371 26905, C3890/46/41
20 Maj. Bright memo, 22.4.41: PRO FO 371 26945, C4140/306/41; Campbell to

F.O., 23.4.41: ibid. C4147/306/41
21 Nicolson, 164
22 26.4.41: PRO FO 371 26945, C4245/306/41
23 Colville, 376
24 Eccles, 256
25 PRO FO 371 26945, C4121/306/41
26 29.4.41: ibid. C4431/306/41
27 ibid. C4245/306/41
28 cited Day, 115
29 Lockhart diary, 6.4.41: cited Day, 114
30 see Day, 130
31 Armstrong, 121
32 cited Day, 135–6
33 ibid. 136
34 13.4.41: Nicolson, 162–3
35 Krebs report on return from Moscow, 5.5.41: Halder 2, 396–7
36 Thorne, 73
37 see Cave Brown, 329–30
38 cited Day, 180
39 18.5.41: v. Hassell, 207
40 Stubbe, 253
41 ibid. 255
42 5.10.45, 15: IWM FO 645 box 155
43 E. Mann: 'Hess Meeting in Spain was Fixed', *Glasgow Evening Citizen* (1945): IS
44 see Hoare to Eden, 20.5.41: PRO FO 371 26542, C6049/324/18
45 PRO FO 371 26905, C4802/46/41
46 PRO FO 371 26945, C4456 & C4487/306/41
47 see Irving (3), 58, 73; and see p. 292 below, chap. 27, ref. 25.
48 Stubbe, 254
49 Leasor, 59; Douglas-Hamilton, 161
50 Leasor, 59
51 Douglas-Hamilton, 162
52 ibid. 163
53 Sir R. Fulford to R. Deacon: Deacon, 30
54 Douglas-Hamilton, 164–5

Chapter Nineteen Final Preparations
1 Hess personal file: IWM FO 643/31
2 VB, 2.5.41: ibid.
3 Colville, 383
4 J. Portner to Ilse: cited W. R. Hess (1), 148
5 M. Haushofer diary, 3.5.41: Jacobsen, 508
6 ibid. 5.5.41: ibid. 509

7 12.7.41: cited W. R. Hess (2), 83
8 see Chapter 18, ref. 43
9 5.10.45, p. 15: IWM FO 645 box 155
10 Hoare to Eden, 20.5.41: PRO FO 371 26542, C6049/324/18
11 13.10.44: T-175, Roll 65, ff2581174
12 17.11.40: Hill, 226
13 1.5.41: ibid. 252
14 Notiz von Hewel, 1.5.41: ibid.
15 17.12.40: Halder I, 996
16 No. 185, 12.5.41: Boberach 7, 2287
17 ibid. 2286
18 H-B. Gisevius to E. Calic; L. Heydrich: *Leben mit einem Kriegsverbrecher* (1976), 72: cited Calic, 379f
19 No. 184, 8.5.41: Boberach 7, 2272
20 Nicolson, 164
21 cited M. Gilbert, 1084
22 Fröhlich, 629–31
23 Nicolson, 165
24 see W. R. Hess (2), 344 note 6; Irving (2), 322
25 Bollmus, 120–22; Cecil, 195, 227
26 Bollmus, 120; Cecil, 227
27 W. R. Hess (1), 149; Dr Koeppen to L. Charlton to PP, 22.6.90
28 F. Winterbotham to PP, 26.9.89
29 W. Bechtold statement, 30.4.46: NA RG 238 box 180: cited Irving (3), 64
30 cited W. R. Hess (2), 83; Irving (3), 64, 345 note

Chapter Twenty Flight
1 Leasor, 86
2 I. Hess (1), 78
3 16.11.45, p.12: IWM FO 645 box 160
4 Dr Koeppen to L. Charlton
5 I. Hess (1), 69
6 ibid. 70
7 Leasor, 85
8 ibid. 88–9; I. Hess (1), 70
9 Leasor, 89–90
10 Nesbit, 63–4
11 Bird, 23
12 L. Heydrich: *Leben . . .* (chap. 19, ref. 18), p. 72: cited Calic, 380
13 Calic, 426; Calic to PP, 14.12.89
14 I. Kirkpatrick report: IMT vol. 38, 181; Hamilton add. notes, p.4: PRO INF/912

386

15 I.Hess (1), 82
16 M.Pearson (formerly Ldg. Aircraftwoman on Ottercops Moss line at Fighter Cd. HQ, Stanmore) to PP, 19.4.90; also Operational Research Section (F.C.) RAF: Investigation of Raid 42 on 10.5.41; R.Nesbit papers.
17 Ashbee, 530; F.Ashbee to PP, 14.4.90
18 (Investigation . . .' (ref. 16 above)
19 O.R.B. RAF Ouston, 10.5.41: PRO AIR 28/624
20 O.R.B. 72 Sqdn., 10.5.41: PRO AIR 27/624
21 'Investigation . . .' (ref. 16 above)
22 Wood, 1–2; Observer, 157; (following ROC timings ibid. 157–8)
23 RH to Ilse: I.Hess (1), 83
24 Donald, 282; Observer, 157–8
25 O.R.B. 72 Sqdn., 10.5.41: PRO AIR 27/624; M.Pocock to PP, 16.4.90
26 MacLean, 20; Sqdn. Ldr, R.G.Woodman to PP, 11, 24.6.91; O.R.B. 141 Sqdn., 10.5.41; O.R.B. RAF Ayr, 10.5.41: PRO AIR 27/969 & 28/40
27 RH to Ilse: I.Hess (1), 85
28 ibid. 87

PART THREE CAPTIVITY

Chapter Twenty One Prisoner of War
1 *The Bulletin & Scots Pictorial*, 13.5.41: repro. Douglas-Hamilton
2 I.Hess (1), 88
3 Leasor, 26
4 I.Hess (1), 88
5 *Bulletin* . . . (ref. 1 above)
6 I.Hess (1), 89
7 All times and reports from PRO WO 199/3288A
8 Capt. Brunton report in ibid. (3)
9 00.24 hrs: Lt. W.H.Cowie in ibid. (1)
10 O/C 3rd Batt. Renfrewshire Home Guard in ibid. (1)
11 see Bateman, 8; ORB RAF Ayr: PRO AIR 28/40
12 I.Hess (1), 89; and see Donald, cited Douglas-Hamilton, 284–5
13 I.Hess (1), 89
14 G.Donald to Sir H.Greer, 19.5.41: IWM Misc.

15 Maclean, 20; information from Mrs N.-M.Goodall since this book went to press suggests MacLean's was not the first call. Mrs Goodall was a Wren on duty in the Ops. Rm. RAF Turnhouse that night, and remembers the Duke taking a call about the Me 110 pilot (who wanted to speak to him) at the Controller's desk. 'He looked a very worried man . . . extremely horrified': N.-M. Goodall to PP, 12, 4.6.91
16 Various reports in PRO WO 199/3288A
17 Capt. A.C.White, Duty Offcr. Clyde Area in ibid.
18 Douglas-Hamilton, 172
19 I.Hess (1), 90
20 31.5.41: in PRO WO 199/3288A
21 PRO AIR 25/233
22 M.H.Pocock to PP, 16.4.90
23 4.11.69
24 *The Times*, 12.5.41
25 J.McCowan to PP, 10.6.90; Irving (2), 327
26 IMT vol. 38, 175
27 ibid.; and see Hamilton add. notes in PRO INF/912
28 I.Hess (1), 90
29 Hamilton add. notes in PRO INF 1/912
30 Lt. Col. G.Grahan, 13.5.41: PRO PREM 3 219/7
31 Hamilton add. notes in PRO INF/912
32 Douglas-Hamilton, 178
33 Colville, 386–7
34 Cadogan diary, 11.5.41: CC
35 Douglas-Hamilton, 180

Chapter Twenty Two Peace Plan
1 Hamilton add. notes: PRO INF/912
2 Colville, 387
3 Cadogan diary, 12.5.41: CC
4 Beaverbrook notes for J.Leasor, 20.2.61: BP C/216; Leasor, 159
5 see Halder 2, 414
6 see Leasor, 96ff; see W.R.Hess (2), 343–4 note 1
7 W.R.Hess (2), 343 note 1
8 Galland, 108
9 W.R.Hess (2), 343 note 1
10 see Leasor, 96–7
11 Calic, 380
12 Schwarzwäller, 175
13 see W.R.Hess (2), 344 note 2; Irving (2), 323
14 11.5.41; cited Irving (2), 323

15 11.5.41; Jacobsen, 509
16 Stubbe, 2251; Laack-Michel, 233
17 see Laack-Michel, 233–4
18 Jacobsen, 509–10
19 Jacobsen vol. 1, 403–4; RH to K.Haushofer, 14.9.41: Jacobsen vol. 2, 523–4; W.R.Hess (2), 151; Bird, 225; Irving (3) 61 and ref. note.
20 Karl Haushofer to RH, 9.5.41: Jacobsen, 507–8
21 Stubbe, 252–5
22 British report of the broadcast: PRO INF 1/912
23 Cadogan diary, 12.5.41: CC
24 unsigned, undated ms. note: PRO PREM 3 219/4 ff.26–7
25 PRO PREM 3 219/4, ff.21–2
26 10.5.41: K.Young, 98
27 cited Day, 184
28 12.5.41: cited Day, 184
29 PRO PREM 3 219/4, ff.23–4
30 12.5.41, written 13.5.41:CC
31 Hamilton add. notes: PRO INF/912; Cadogan to Churchill, 13.5.41: PREM 3 219/7 f.171
32 I.Kirkpatrick: 'Record of an interview with Herr Hess': IMT vol. 38, 117f
33 Cadogen report, 13.5.41: PRO PREM 3 219/7 ff.172–3
34 I.Hess (1), 90
35 13.5.41: CC
36 PM's personal minute for For. Sec. M 540/1: PRO PREM 3 219/7 ff.167–8

Chapter Twenty Three The Propaganda War
1 P.Schmidt: *Hitler's Interpreter* (N.Y. 1951), 233: cited Douglas-Hamilton, 218
2 10.30 am., 13.5.41: PRO INF 1/912
3 Frank, 265
4 Fröhlich 4, 639
5 Statement by Nat-Soz. Part Korrespondenz, broadcast German Home stations 14.00, 13.5.41: PRO INF 1/912
6 Frank, 401
7 ibid.
8 R.Cecil to PP, 17.7.89
9 G.Schäfer, W.Darré: cited Irving (3), 83
10 Calic, 381
11 see Halder 2, 413–4

12 Transocean in English, 13.35, 14.5.41: PRO PREM 3 219/4
13 PRO PREM 3 219/7
14 M. Haushofer diary, 13.5.41: Jacobsen, 509
15 ibid. 22.5.41: ibid. 510
16 J. v. Lang: *Der Adjutant* (1985), 282
17 18.5.41: v. Hassell, 206
18 No. 186, 15.5.41: Boberach 7, 2302
19 British radio monitoring resume of foreign sources: PRO INF 1/912
20 see telegrams in ibid.
21 F. Williams memo to Director General M of I, 14.5.41: in ibid.
22 No. 187, 19.5.41: Boberach 7, 2313
23 14.5.41: CC
24 16.5.41: Nicolson, 167
25 undated, unsigned statement, 10 Downing St: PRO PREM 3 219/4 f.14ff
26 ibid. 2, f.15
27 ibid. 3, f.16
28 Cadogan diary, 14.5.41: CC
29 note signed J.M. 14/5 (John Martin, 14.5.41): PRO PREM 3 219/4 f.2
30 undated, unsigned statement, 10 Downing St.: PRO PREM 3 219/4 f.7
31 Col. Duke to Undersec. of St., W.O., 15.5.41: PRO WO 199/3288A
32 I. Kirkpatrick: 'Record of an interview with Herr Hess', 14.5.41: IMT vol. 38, 181f
33 statement (ref. 25 above), 2, f.15
34 President to Former Naval Person, 15.5.41: PRO PREM 3 219/7 f.147
35 I. Kirkpatrick: 'Record of a conversation with Herr Hess', 15.5.41: IMT vol. 38, 183f
36 ORB RAF Turnhouse (Appendices), 15.5.41: PRO AIR 28/864
37 Cadogan note to PM, 15.5.41: PRO PREM 3 219/7 f.160
38 see Armstrong, 123–4; W. Monckton to Duff Cooper, 27.7.41: IS
39 W. Monckton to Duff Cooper, 27.5.41: IS
40 Appointments diary, 1941: Monckton
41 see PRO INF 1/912
42 15.5.41: Armstrong, 129

43 ibid. 130
44 Douglas-Hamilton, 194
45 memo DC to PM, 16.5.41: PRO INF 1/912
46 Cadogan diary, 15.5.41: CC; Cadogan minute, 15.541: PRO FO 371 26565, C5250/5188/18
47 on memo DC to PM, 15.5.41: PRO PREM 3 219/7 f.124
48 see Cadogan diary, 17, 19.5.41: CC
49 17.5.41: PRO FO 371 26565, C5421/5188/18
50 ibid.

Chapter Twenty Four Mytchett Place

1 Maj. J.J. Shephard, 'Report on the conduct of X', 17.5.41: PRO PREM 3 219/7 f.146
2 Col. R.A. Lennie to DDMS, Scottish Cd., 17.5.41: PRO WO 199/3288A
3 'Report on ... X' (ref. 1 above)
4 RH to Ilse, Dec. 47: I. Hess (1), 163
5 Cadogan diary, 19.5.41: CC
6 Gen. A. Hunter; 'Report on the Custody and movements of Hess': PRO PREM 3 219/7; Scott, 20.5.41
7 memo to Gen. Sir A. Hunter, 18.5.41: PRO PREM 3 219/7 f.149
8 Maj. J.J. Shephard, 'My impressions of X', 21.5.41: PRO PREM 3 219/7 f.144
9 ibid. ff.144–5
10 extract from letter, 15.5.41: PRO INF 1/912
11 Hill, 255–6
12 Mallett to F.O., 19.5.41: PRO FO 371 26565, C5397/5188/18
13 PRO FO 371 26542, C6049/324/18
14 Popov, 115
15 memo enclosed in Hoare to Eden, 20.5.41: (ref. 13 above)
16 memo: 'Subsequent note on the candid proposals of DJB', 11.30 pm., 31.5.41, in Hoare to Eden, 4.6.41: PRO FO 371 26542, C 6735/324/18
17 v. Weizsäcker Notiz, 8.6.41: Hill, 258; Ciano diary, 2.6.41: Muggeridge, 352
18 see Lt. W.B. Malone's report, 29.5.41: Scott

19 Translation of Deposition by 'Z': Scott 1.8.41
20 RH to Ilse: 8.1.48: I. Hess (1), 166
21 24.5.41: Scott
22 ibid.
23 Lt. W.B. Malone diary: *The Observer*, London, Sept. 1987: cited Irving (3), 110
24 ibid.
25 'Report on last night's incidents': Scott, 29.5.41
26 Malone diary (ref. 23 above), 113
27 29.5.41: Scott
28 ibid.
29 J. Leasor to *The Times*, 20.8.87
30 E. Calic to author, 25.9.90: no source given; but see S. Bradford: *George VI* (1989), 433, describing Beaverbrook and the Duke of Windsor agreeing in Jan. 1940 that the war ought to be ended at once 'by a peace offer, to Germany'.
31 *Luton Herald*, 10.6.79
32 Col. J. McCowan to PP, 10.6.90

Chapter Twenty Five Lord Simon

1 Parl. questions in PRO FO 371 26565, C5562/5188/18
2 W. Monckton to Duff Cooper, 27.5.41: IS
3 see E.S. Herbert (M. of I.) to Monckton, 22.5.41: PRO INF 1/912; R.H. Melville (Priv. sec. to Sec. St. for Air) note, 29.5.41: PRO AIR 19/564
4 A. Sinclair to Duff Cooper, 21.5.41: ibid.; A. Sinclair to H. Morrison, 21.5.41: ibid.
5 E.S. Herbert to R.H. Melville, 26.5.41: PRO INF 1/912
6 PRO FO 371 26565, C5251, C5253, C5301, C5589/5188/18
7 PRO FO 371 26520, C5300/19/18
8 PRO FO 371 26565, C5537/5188/18
9 see A. Sinclair to H. Morrison, 2.6.41: PRO AIR 19/564; H. Morrison to Churchill, 9.7.41: PRO PREM 3 219/3
10 J. Leasor to PP, 13.2.90, 22.6.90
11 see Kramish, 97, 200–1

12 see correspondence in PRO AIR 19/564; D. Morton to PM, 21.6.41: PRO PREM 3 219/3 f.12
13 4.6.41: Scott
14 Cadogan to Eden, 4.6.41: PRO PREM 3 219/7 f.219
15 5.6.41: Scott
16 8.6.41: Scott
17 PRO PREM 3 219/7 f.117
18 ibid. f.118
19 I. Kirkpatrick to Ld. Simon, 29.5.41: Simon box 88
20 Eden to Simon, 28.5.41: ibid.
21 transcript of Simon interview: ibid. ff.75 ff
22 Kersten, 89
23 Boberach 7, 2272
24 transcript of Simon interview: Simon box 88 f.114
25 9.6.41: Scott
26 E. Mann (see Chapter 18, ref. 43)
27 Ld. Simon: 'R. Hess, preliminary Report', 10.6.41: PRO PREM 3 219/7 ff.103–7
28 ibid. f.103
29 Picker. 169
30 see press cuttings in PRO FO 371 26566, C6773/5188/18
31 P. Dollan: 'Hess No Runaway', *Evening Citizen*, Glasgow, 20.3.53: IS
32 see Padfield, 332
33 Lt. W.B. Malone: 'Statements made by "Z" in the course of conversations, 13/14 July 1941': Scott, 14.7.41
34 14.6.41: PRO PREM 3 219/5

Chapter Twenty Six Psychosis
1 14.6.41: Scott
2 Dicks' report cited Rees, 46
3 Lt. R. Hubbard report, 15.6.41: Scott
4 Lt. the Hon. S.V. Smith to Col. Scott, 15.6.41: ibid.
5 ibid.
6 Malone diary, 15.6.41 (Chapter 24 ref. 23): cited Irving (3), 139
7 Lt. W.B. Malone: 'Report on this morning's interview with "Z"', 15.6.41: Scott
8 Translation of deposition by "Z", 1.8.41: Scott
9 cited Rees, 44
10 Dicks' account in Rees, 47–8: Lt. J. McI. Young's

account: Scott, 16.6.41; Col. Scott to Col. Coates in ibid.
11 Dicks' account: Rees, 48
12 ibid.; Scott to Coates (ref. 10 above)
13 Lt. W.B. Malone: 'Report', 16.6.41: Scott
14 J.R. Rees to Col. Coates, 19.6.41: PRO PREM 3 219/3
15 ibid.
16 see Scott, 20.6.41
17 see D. Morton to PM, 9.6.41: PRO PREM 3 219/7 ff.113–4
18 see Irving (3), 326, 533
19 16.6.41: CC
20 Hansard, 19.6.41, 886
21 ibid. 912
22 ibid. 900–1
23 Dicks: cited Irving (3) 150
24 Lce. Corp. Everatt's report, 22.6.41: cited ibid.
25 Colville diary, 21.6.41: Colville, 404
26 Cohen, 274
27 ibid. 274–5
28 see ibid. 268
29 Howard, 108
30 ibid.
31 diary note, Aug. 41: cited ibid. 109
32 Colville, 122
33 Howard, 80
34 Scott, 20.7.41
35 Lt. W.B. Malone: 'Statements made by "Z" in the course of conversations 13/14th July 1941': Scott, 14.7.41
36 Scott, 26.7.41
37 Lt. M. Loftus: 'Report on conversation with "Z"': Scott, 17.7.41
38 Deposition (ref. 8 above)
39 experiment on Frank Olson, 1957: cited Thomas, 174
40 see Popov, 240
41 Deposition (ref. 8 above)
42 ibid.
43 Scott, 1.8.41
44 'Medical Report', 3.8.41: PRO PREM 3 219/2 f.4
45 2nd report handed to Lt. Loftus: Scott, 7.8.41
46 BP D443
47 4.9.41: ibid.
48 Scott, 22, 28.8.41
49 ms. in BP D/443
50 transcript 'Dr Livingstone and Jonathan' 9.9.41: BP D/443
51 Bruce Lockhart diary, 4.9.43: K. Young, 256
52 Scott, 9.9.41

53 Bruce Lockhart diary (ref. 51 above)
54 Beaverbrook to J. Leasor, 20.2.61: BP C/216

Chapter Twenty Seven
Disinformation
1 Scott, 22.11.41
2 ibid., 20.11.41
3 ibid., 4.12.41
4 Thurnheer report, 12.12.41: E 2200 Bundesarchiv, Berne: cited Irving (3), 200–2; Foley report, 12.12.41: Scott
5 Pte Dawkin's report, 6.4.42; Corp Everatt's report, 7.4.42: both cited Irving (3), 210
6 see ibid. 213
7 20.6.42: T-253, Roll 56, fr.151229ff NA
8 RH to K. Haushofer, 14.9.41: Jacobsen 2, 303–4
9 see W.R. Hess (2), 184
10 RH statement translated at Nuremberg: Rees, 96ff
11 19.11.41: Scott
12 see Thorne, 112; Encyclopedia Br. 29, 575–7, 1022
13 Kramish, 81–7
14 Bruce Lockhart diary, 4.9.43: K. Young, 256
15 Kramish, 126–9
16 Enclosure in Heydrich to Ribbentrop, 4.5.42: F & C 434005
17 Luther (Aus. Amt.) to v. Rintelen, 27.6.42: ibid. 434013
18 Schellenberg to v. Weizsäcker, 10.8.42: ibid. 434016–7
19 see Ilse to RFSS, 16.5.43: T-175, Roll 65, Fr. 2581214–5 NA, together with indecypherable signature (RSHA) to RFSS, 3.8.43: IWM H/28/43
20 Amlegation, Berne to Sec. of. St., Washington, 24.10.42: FBI 4812 NA
21 report, undated: PRO FO 115 3544; Ilse to RFSS: 13.10.44: T-175, roll 65, Fr. 2581173
22 cutting and F.O. minutes in PRO FO 371 30941
23 *Die Zeitung*, 9.10.42: in ibid.
24 ibid.; but see Bruce Lockhart diary, 4.9.43: K. Young, 256; Beaverbrook to J. Leasor, 20.2.61: BP C/216

389

25 L.Beria to Stalin, 24.10.42: NKVD file 20566 'Black Bertha' [RH]; and see Costello, 452–4; and see chap. 18, ref. 47
26 A.Clark Kerr to F.O., 22.10.42: PRO PREM 3 219 ff.39ff; see F.Roberts memo, 19.10.42: PRO FO 371 30941
27 A.Clark Kerr to F.O., 25.10.42: PRO PREM 3 219/6 f.34
28 undated: ibid. f.28
29 *The Times*, 20.10.42
30 in PRO PREM 3 219/6
31 *Daily Mail*, 4.11.42; much fuller account in *Nya Dagligt Allehanda*, Stockholm: see F & C 434022
32 following excerpts from Mercury
33 'The Dollan Story': *The Evening Citizen*, Glasgow, 20.3.53: IS
34 *The Scotsman*, 23.9.43: IS
35 W.R.Hess (2), 186
36 see Irving (3), 242–3, 355
37 *The Times*, 23.9.43
38 Notes of conversation at supper at the Kremlin, by Sir A.Clark Kerr and Mr Birse, 6.11.44: PRO PREM 3 434/7

Chapter Twenty Eight Nuremberg
1 RH to Ilse, 8.1.48: I.Hess (1), 166
2 P.Bloom on Walter Fenton: *Deben Journal*, Suffolk, 5.12.85
3 see I.Hess (1), 93ff.; T-253, Roll 56, Fr.151215 ff.
4 see Irving (3), 241; Pfeffer von Salomon had been expelled from the Party on 24.11.41 and ordered to return his Golden Party Badges – no reason given in the papers: v. Pfeffer file: BDC
5 see correspondence Ilse with H.Himmler and O'gruf K.Wolff: T-175 Roll 65 Fr. 2581142ff (Folder 321) NA
6 see Ilse to RFSS, 16.5.43: ibid. Fr. 2581214
7 RH to Ilse, 4.9.43: cited Irving (3), 242
8 Irving (3), 244
9 see ibid. 355, note 254
10 RH to Ilse, 10.3.47: I.Hess (1), 122
11 Rees, 87ff

12 as ref. 10 above
13 Ilse to RFSS, 13.10.44: T-175 Roll 65 Frs. 2581173–4
14 R.Brandt to Ilse, 18.1.45: ibid. 2581167
15 copy Ilse to RFSS, 26.1.45, sent to Schellenberg, 6.2.45: ibid. 2581160
16 Orderlies' reports, Jan. 45: cited Irving (3), 262–3
17 see Irving (3), 263
18 Rees, 114
19 cited Bullock, 726
20 RH to Ilse, 18.6.45: I.Hess (1), 102
21 see Kelley, 8: Irving (3), 282
22 Kelley, 23
23 9.10.45: IWM FO 695 box 157
24 ibid.
25 K.Haushofer to M.Hofweber, 14.11.45: Jacobsen 2, 442; Prof. Walsh: 'Report on Professor Karl Haushofer ...': cited Irving (3), 357 note 290
26 30.10.45, 10.30–noon, 3–8: IWM FO 695 box 157
27 16.11.45, 14.50–15.50: ibid.
28 Kelley, 24
29 D.Kelley to HQ Int. Sec. Det. US Army, 16.10.45: Quinlan
30 see Kelley, 26–7
31 Prof. Krasnushkin and others, 17.11.45: Prosecution Doc. file, IWM FO 645 box 151
32 Dr J.Delay and others, 20.11.45: ibid.
33 Thomas, 167–8
34 Rosenberg interrogation, 16.11.45, pp. 10–11: IWM FO 645 box 160
35 Shirer, 293
36 ibid. 294, 297
37 G.Gilbert, 29–30
38 ibid. 32
39 IMT, vol. 2, 447
40 30.11.45, pm. session: ibid. 479ff
41 B.C.Andrus: *The Infamous of Nuremberg* (1969), 73, 121–3: cited Douglas-Hamilton, 276
42 G.Gilbert, 36
43 IMT, vol. 2, 496
44 Bird, 53
45 Kelley, 27
46 RH to Ilse, 25.1.46: I.Hess (1), 104
47 RH to Ilse, 15.1.46: ibid. 104
48 RH to Ilse, 5.2.46: ibid. 105
49 see Bird, 55

50 IMT 3245-PS; this quote from IMT vol. 7, 136
51 'Competence of Defendant Rudolf Hess, 17.8.46: Hess pers. file, IWM FO 645 box 151
52 'Report on present mental status of Rudolf Hess', 24.8.46: Quinlan
53 RH to Ilse, 31.8.46: I.Hess (1), 110
54 IMT vol. 22, 368–73
55 G.Gilbert, 272

Chapter Twenty Nine Spandau
1 Speer, 72
2 see W.R.Hess (1)
3 cited Bird, 70
4 cited ibid. 69
5 Speer, 107
6 Pastor Casalis to Prison Directorate, April 50: cited W.R.Hess (2), 158
7 RH to Ilse, 5.10.47: I.Hess (1), 158
8 Speer, 97
9 ibid. 124
10 ibid. 59
11 RH to KH, 3.7.49: I.Hess (2), 130
12 RH to Ilse, 13.10.46: I.Hess (1), 118
13 RH to Ilse, 26.9.46: ibid. 113
14 Speer, 147
15 Speer, 400, 429
16 ibid. 378
17 Psychiatrists' report on RH: cited Speer, 266
18 ibid. 270
19 ibid. 314; see Bird, 138–9
20 Bird, 137
21 Speer, 445–6
22 RH to Ilse, 21.10.51: I.Hess (1), 224
23 RH to WRH, Nov. 51: ibid. 224–5
24 see Gabel, 172; Bird, 237
25 see W.R.Hess (1), 128f; (2), 265; Gabel, 109
26 Bird, 152
27 ibid. 171
28 ibid. 173–4
29 ibid. 194; W.R.Hess (1), 108
30 Bird, 195
31 ibid. 196
32 W.R.Hess (2), 286; and see (1), 108
33 *Bild am Sonntag*, 10.4.77: cited W.R.Hess (2), 402
34 ibid. 326
35 Gabel, 343
36 ibid. 346
37 Melaouhi declaration on oath: cited W.R.Hess (1), 98

38 see photocopy page Warders' Log: *Figaro-Magazin*, Paris, 1.4.89
39 W.R.Hess (1), 136–9
40 *Der Spiegel*, 16, 41 Jahrg., 13.4.87, 151
41 v. Weizsäcker to A.Liddell Hart: A.L-H to PP, 27.1.90
42 21.6.87: cited W.R.Hess (1), 153
43 RH: 'Gesuch an den amerikanischen Direktor, Herrn Keane', 4.4.87: photocopy in *Figaro-Magazin*, Paris, 1.4.89
44 Speer, 348
45 Bird, 278
46 ibid. 225
47 ibid. 232
48 ibid.
49 ibid. 264–5
50 ibid. 275
51 ibid. 223
52 Gabel, 22, 27
53 ibid. 59–60, 254–5
54 ibid. 290–1
55 Melaouhi declaration (ref. 37 above)
56 W.R.Hess (1), 47
57 *Daily Telegraph*, 19.8.87; see W.R.Hess (1), 50

Chapter Thirty Post Mortem
1 Prof. J.M.Cameron: 'Autopsy Report on Allied Prisoner No. 7', undated, 3
2 W.R.Hess (1), 105
3 ibid.
4 W.R.Hess (1), 108; (2), 286
5 W.R.Hess (1), 107–10; and re. photographs WRH to PP, 3.6.91
6 Profs W.Eisenmenger, W.Spann: 'Zussammenfassung der Befunde': cited W.R.Hess (1), 215
7 Profs W. Eisenmenger, W.Spann: 'Gerichtsmedizinisch Untersuchung', 21.8.87: cited ibid. 209, 215
8 cited W.R.Hess (1), 51–2
9 cited Schwarzwäller, 1
10 see W.R.Hess (1), 145f
11 ibid. 142–3
12 ibid. 101–2
13 Gabel, 273
14 see W.R.Hess
15 *Daily Telegraph*, 20.8.87
16 Profs W.Eisenmenger, W.Spann: 'Gutachten', 21.12.88: cited W.R.Hess (1), 225

17 F.E.Camps (Ed.): *Gradwohl's Legal Medicine* (3rd Ed. 1976), 332
18 ibid. 331
19 PP to Prof. W.Spann, 25.7.90
20 *Gradwohl's* (ref. 17 above) 81
21 Profs W.Eisenmenger, W.Spann to PP, 17.9.90
22 W.R.Hess (1), 170
23 ibid.

Postscript
1 *The Times*, 14.3.88
2 *The Guardian*, 7.11.89
3 ibid.
4 Lord Sherfield to PP, 7.3.91; Sir Frank Roberts to PP, 12.2.91; Robert Cecil to PP, 17.7.89, 11.5.90, 10.3.91, and in *Guardian*, 25.6.91
5 John Zametica to PP, 12.5.91; Dr Scott Newton to PP, 12.11.90, 6.12.90; see John Zametica in *The Spectator* (Bibliography)
6 Churchill to Sec. of St. for Air, 6.4.45, Minute M 303/5: PRO PREM 3 219/7 f.167
7 Kiesel, 9
8 Dr. O.John to PP, 27.2.90

AFTERWORD

1 PRO FO 371 26565
2 PRO FO 1093 1–20
3 in PRO FO 371 26565
4 ibid. C5251
5 ibid. C5253
6 ibid. C5301
7 ibid. C5589; & PRO INF 1/912
8 PRO WO 199 3288/B
9 PRO WO 199 3288/A; PREM 3 219/7
10 PRO WO 3288/A f.4
11 ibid. f.9
12 J. Mair: 'Interrogation of Rudolf Hess by Roman Battaglia', 30.5.41; PRO FO 1093 11 ff. 153–5
13 ibid. ff.153–4
14 Dowager Duchess of Hamilton to PP, 12.7.92
15 J. Mair: 'Interrogation . . .' op. cit. ref. 12 above f.155
16 23 Group R.O.C. Historical Archive Committee, Hartlepool
17 T.W. Dobson to PP, 16.5.91

18 Op. Research Section, R.A.F., 18.5.41; Nesbit papers
19 PRO AIR 28 624
20 R.G. Woodman to PP, 11 & 24.6.91
21 R. Nesbit to PP, 25.6 & 4.7.92
22 R.G. Woodman to PP, 24.6.91
23 ibid.
24 D.Rose, Brigade Intell. Offcr., to PP, 16.6.92
25 J.W. Debny to PP, 14.5.91
26 D. Rose to PP. 23.6.92
27 Air V.Marsh. Johnstone: *Where No Angels Dwell*, cited R.G. Woodman to PP, 11.6.91
28 N.M. Goodall to PP, 12 & 14.6.91
29 ibid.
30 I. Pyne to PP, 12.7.92
31 J. Douglas to PP, 13.5–20.10.91
32 BBC Monitoring Service 'Flash', 12.5.41; IWM Box A 216

33 J.Keyser to PP, 20.9.91
34 '*Meinem Sohn*', 10.6.41; PRO FO 1093 1 ff.38–42
35 Noted by a 'guardian' on ibid. f.43
36 ibid. ff.41–2
37 PRO FO 1093 1 ff.47–8
38 PRO FO 1093 10 f.76
39 RH to *Meine Lieben Alle*, 14.6.41; PRO FO 1093 1 f.51
40 RH to *Herzog von Hamilton*, 19.5.41; PRO FO 1093 11 ff.65–6; transl. ff.67–8
41 see for instance Churchill's draft statement; PRO PREM 3 219/4 f.14
42 PRO FO 1093 12 ff.92–4
43 PRO DEFE 1 134
44 see PRO INF 1 912
45 PRO FO 1093 11 f.166
46 ibid. f.163
47 T.A.Robertson to Ld. J.Douglas-Hamilton, & T.A.Robertson to PP, 3.7.92

391

48 PRO FO 1093 3 f.19
49 G.Graham: 'Memorandum on Herr Rudolf Hess', undated, 3; PRO FO 1093 11 f.75
50 Minute signed F.F., 16.8.41; PRO FO 1093 12 f.130
51 *Sunday Despatch*, 30.9.45; in PRO FO 371 46780, C4725
52 PRO FO 371 26945, C4038/306/41
53 ibid., C4147/306/41
54 ibid.
55 G.Graham: 'Memorandum . . .' op.cit. ref. 49 above
56 H.Frank: *Gedächtnis Protokol*, cited Irving (3), 64
57 IMT doc. 117-M
58 cited Irving (3), 64
59 Nicolson, 165; & see pp.175–76 above
60 IMT doc 117-M
61 I.K.: 'Reflections on Conversations with Herr Hess', undated; PRO FO 1093 1 f.36
62 Beaverbrook to J.Leasor, 20.2.61; BP C/216
63 see p.115 above
64 Cadogan to P.M., 13.5.41; PRO PREM 3 219/7 f.171
65 H.Hopkinson memo., 5.5.41 (presumably 15.5.41); PRO FO 1093 1 f.27
66 Vadim to Moscow, Nr.338, 18.5.41; NKVD file 20566
67 Beaverbrook to J.Leasor, 13.2.61; BP C/216

68 Beaverbrook to J.Leasor, 14.9.60; ibid.; & *Evening Standard*, 15.9.59; in BP D 443
69 Capt. R.E.Lee to Brig. Sherman Miles, 5.11.41; NA 'Rudolf Hess' B8026020 IRR files RG 319; cited Costello, 447–50
70 NKVD file 20566 ff.211–14; cited Costello, 447; & see p.292 above
71 see p.290 above
72 J.Howell to PP, letters & conversations 5.2–10.7.92
73 Beaverbrook to J.Leasor, 20.2.61; BP C/216
74 see pp.253–4 above
75 Leasor, 37
76 Huene to Aus.Amt., 4.1.41; F & C D 613641
77 Huene to Aus.Amt., 23.1.41; ibid. D 613660
78 ibid. D 613665
79 ibid. D 613666
80 Huene to Aus.Amt.; ibid. E 080812
81 I.Pyne to PP, 12.7.92
82 Dowager Duchess of Hamilton to PP, 12.7.92
83 Ld. J.Douglas-Hamilton to PP, 15.7.92
84 PRO PREM 3 219/7 f.137
85 ibid. ff.138–9; & IMT doc. 116-M
86 I.Pyne to PP, 12.7.92
87 Cadogan to P.M., 13.5.41; PRO PREM 3 219/7 f.171
88 F.Day to PP, 16.6.92

89 R.A.Lennie, O/C Mil. Hosp., Drymen, 15.5.41; PRO WO 199 3288/B
90 PRO FO 1093 1 ff.32–3; & IMT doc. 118-M
91 PRO FO 1093 1 f.33
92 R.H.Makins minute, 14.5.41; PRO FO 1093 11 f.140
93 insert in Cadogan's hand; PRO FO 1093 11 f.139
94 PRO PREM 3 219/4 f.7
95 see Cadogan to P.M., 15.5.41; PRO PREM 3 219/7 f.160
96 H.Hopkinson memo op.cit. ref 65 above
97 PRO FO 1093 11 f.140
98 P.M.'s personal minute M/550/1, 16.5.41; PRO PREM 3 219/7 f.146
99 see PRO PREM 3 219/ 4 ff.20–23
100 PRO FO 1093 11 f.90; & see ibid. ff.78–81
101 PRO FO 1093 11 f.90
102 10.6.41; PRO FO 1093 10 f.94
103 I.Kirkpatrick to Ld. Simon, 29.5.41; Simon Box 88; see also Service 'Questionnaires for Hess'; PRO FO 1093 10 f.122–6, 149ff
104 translation in PRO FO 1093 1 ff.155–6; & see transcript of interview pp.66ff; Simon Box 88 ff.140ff
105 Report Nr. 16, unsigned, from 'Camp Z', 30.5.41; PRO FO 1093 11 f.85

SELECT BIBLIOGRAPHY

Confined to works referenced in text

ABRAHAM, DAVID: *The Collapse of the Weimar Republic* (2nd ed.), Holmes, & Meier, New York, 1986

ARMSTRONG, W. (Ed.): *With Malice Toward None: a War Diary by Cecil H. King*, Sidgwick & Jackson, 1970

BIRD, EUGENE: *The Loneliest Man in the World*, Secker & Warburg, 1974 (refs from Sphere 1976 ed.)

BOBERACH, HEINZ: *Meldungen aus dem Reich*, Pawlak, Herrsching, 1984

BOLLMUS, REINHARD: *Das Amt Rosenberg und seine Gegner*, Deutsche-Verlags-Anstalt, Stuttgart, 1970

BROSZAT, MARTIN (Ed.): *Kommandant in Auschwitz*, Deutsche Taschenbuch Verlag, Stuttgart, 1963

BULLOCK, ALAN: *Hitler: A Study in Tyranny*, Odhams, 1952

CALIC, EDUARD: *Reinhard Heydrich: Schlüsselfigur des Dritten Reiches*, Droste, Düsseldorf, 1982

CAVE BROWN, ANTHONY: *The Secret Servant: The Life of Sir Stewart Menzies*, Michael Joseph, 1988

CECIL, ROBERT: *The Myth of the Master Race: Rosenberg and Nazi Ideology*, Batsford, 1972

COHEN, MICHAEL: *Churchill and the Jews*, Cass, 1985

COSTELLO, JOHN: *Ten Days that Saved the West*, Bantam, 1991

CRAWLEY, AIDAN: *Leap Before You Look*, Collins, 1988

DAY, DAVID: *Menzies and Churchill at War*, Angus & Robertson, 1986

DEACON, RICHARD: *The Greatest Treason*, Century, 1989

DOUGLAS-HAMILTON: *James: Motive for a Mission*, Macmillan, London, 1971 (refs from Mainstream 1985 ed.)

ECCLES, DAVID: *By Safe Hand: Letters of Sybil & David Eccles, 1939–42*, The Bodley Head, 1983

FRANK, HANS: *Im Angesicht des Galgens*, Brigitte Frank, Neuhaus b. Schliersee, 1955

FRÖHLICH, ELKE (Ed.): *Die Tagebücher von Joseph Goebbels*, Institut für Zeitgeschichte, Munich, 1987

FROMM, BELLA: *Blood and Banquets*, Bles, 1942

GABEL, CHARLES: *Conversations interdites avec Rudolf Hess*, Plon, Paris, 1988

GALLAND, ADOLF: *The First and the Last: The German Fighter Force in World War 2*, Methuen, 1955

GILBERT, G.: *Nuremberg Diary*, Eyre & Spottiswoode, 1948

GILBERT, MARTIN: *Finest Hour: Winston Churchill 1939–41*, Heinemann, 1983 (refs from Minerva 1989 ed.)

GIORDANO, RALPH: *Wenn Hitler den Krieg gewonnen hätte: Die Pläne der Nazis nach dem Endsieg*, Rasch und Röhring, Hamburg, 1989

GLADWYN, LORD: *The Memoirs of Lord Gladwyn*, Weidenfeld, 1972

GOSSWEILER, KURT: *Aufsätze zum Faschismus*, Akademie, Berlin, 1988

——*Die Röhm Affäre*, Rugenstein, Cologne, 1983

HALDER, FRANZ: *Kriegstagebuch*, (Ed. H.-A. Jacobsen) Kohlhammer, Stuttgart, 1963

HANFSTAENGL, ERNST: *15 Jahre mit Hitler*, Piper, Munich, 1980

HASSELL, ULRICH VON: *Vom Andern Deutschland*, Atlantis, Zurich, 1946

HERBST, LUDOLF: *Der Totale Krieg und die Ordnung der Wirtschaft*, Deutsche-Verlags-Anstalt, Stuttgart, 1982

HESS, ILSE: *Ein Schicksal in Briefen*, Druffel, Leoni, 1971

393

SELECT BIBLIOGRAPHY

——*Gefangener des Friedens*, Druffel, Leoni, 1955
HESS, RUDOLF: *Reden*, Zentralverlag der NSDAP, Munich, 1938
HESS, WOLF RÜDIGER: *Mord an Rudolf Hess?* Druffel, Leoni, 1989
——*My Father Rudolf Hess*, W.H. Allen, 1986
——(Ed.) *Rudolf Hess: Briefe, 1908–1933*, Langen Müller, Munich, 1987
HILL, LEONIDAS (Ed.): *Die Weizsäcker Papiere (vol. 2 1933–1950)*, Propyläen, Berlin, 1974
HITLER, ADOLF: *Mein Kampf* (2 vols in one) Zentralverlag der NSDAP, Munich, 1943 ed.
HOWARD, ANTHONY: *Rab: The Life of R.A. Butler*, Cape, 1987
IRVING, DAVID: *Churchill's War*, Veritas, Bullsbrook, Austr., 1987
—— *Göring: A Biography*, Macmillan, London, 1989
—— *Hess: The Missing Years, 1941–1945*, Macmillan, London, 1987
——*Hitler's War*, Hodder & Stoughton, 1977
——*The War Path: Hitler's Germany 1933–1939*, Michael Joseph, 1978 (refs from Papermac ed. 1983)
JACOBSEN, HANS-ADOLF: *Karl Haushofer: Leben und Werk*, Boldt, Boppard/Rhein, 1974
KELLEY, DOUGLAS: *22 Cells in Nuremberg*, W. H. Allen, 1947
KERSTEN, FELIX: *The Kersten Memoirs, 1940–1945*, Hutchinson, 1956
KLEE, ERNST: *'Euthanasie' im NS-Staat*, Fischer Taschenbuch Verlag, Frankfurt/M, 1986
KRAMISH, ARNOLD: *The Griffin*, Macmillan, London, 1986
KROSIGK, SCHWERIN V.: *Es geschah in Deutschland*, Wunderlich, Tübingen, 1951
KUUSISTO, SEPPO: *Alfred Rosenberg in der National-Sozialistischen Aussenpolitik, 1933–1939*, Societas Historica Finlandiae, Helsinki, 1984
LAACK-MICHEL, URSULA: *Albrecht Haushofer und der National-sozialismus*, Ernst Klett, Stuttgart, 1974
LAMB, RICHARD: *The Ghosts of Peace 1939–45*, Michael Russell, Wilton, Wiltshire, 1987
LEASOR, JAMES: *Rudolf Hess: The Uninvited Envoy*, Allen & Unwin, 1962
LIFTON, ROBERT JAY: *The Nazi Doctors*, Macmillan, London, 1986
LUDECKE, KURT: *I Knew Hitler*, Jarrolds, 1938
Luxemburg, Internationales Komitee: *Der Reichstagsbrand: Die Provokation des 20. Jahrhunderts*, Verlag des Freundeskreis, Luxemburg, 1978
MASTERMAN, J.C.: *The Double Cross System*, Yale U.P., New Haven, 1972

MASTERS, ANTHONY: *The Man who was M: The Life of Maxwell Knight*, Blackwell, Oxford, 1984
MUGGERIDGE, MALCOLM (Ed.): *Ciano's Diaries 1939–1943*, Heinemann, 1947
NESBIT, ROY C.: *Failed to Return: Mysteries of the Air 1939–45*, Patrick Stephens, 1988
NICOLSON, HAROLD: *Diaries and Letters 1939–45*, (Ed. Nigel Nicolson), Collins, 1967
NOVAK, KURT: *'Euthanasie' und Sterilisierung im Dritten Reich*, Vanderkoeck & Ruprecht, Göttingen, 1978
PADFIELD, PETER: *Himmler: Reichsführer-SS*, Macmillan, London, 1990
PICKER, HENRY: *Hitlers Tischgespräche im Führerhauptquartier 1941–42*, Seewald, Stuttgart, 1963 (refs from 2nd ed. 1965)
POOL, JAMES & SUZANNE: *Who Financed Hitler*, Macdonald and Janes, 1978
POPOV, DUSKO: *Spy, Counterspy*, Weidenfeld, 1974
REES, J.R. (Ed.): *The Case of Rudolf Hess*, Heinemann, 1947
ROBERTS, S.H.: *The House that Hitler Built*, Methuen, 1939
ROWLAND, PETER: *Lloyd George*, Barrie & Jenkins, 1975
SCHELLENBERG, WALTER: *The Schellenberg Memoirs*, André Deutsch, 1956
SCHWARZWÄLLER, WULF: *Rudolf Hess: The Deputy*, Quartet, 1988
SCHWEITZER, ARTHUR: *Big Business in the Third Reich*, Eyre & Spottiswoode, 1964
SHIRER, WILLIAM: *End of a Berlin Diary*, Hamish Hamilton, 1947
SPEER, ALBERT: *Spandau: The Secret Diaries*, Macmillan, New York, 1976
STRASSER, OTTO: *Mein Kampf*, Heine, Frankfurt/M, 1969
THEWELWEIT, KLAUS: *Male Fantasies*, vol. I, Polity Press, Cambridge, 1987
THOMAS, GORDON: *Journey into Madness: Medical Torture and the Mind Controllers*, Bantam, 1988
THORNE, CHRISTOPHER: *Allies of a Kind*, Oxford University Press, 1978
TREVOR-ROPER, H.R. (Ed.): *Hitler's Table Talk 1941–1944*, Weidenfeld, 1953
WAITE, ROBERT G.L.: *The Psychopathic God: Adolf Hitler*, Basic Books, New York, 1977 (refs from Signet ed. 1978)
WINTERBOTHAM, F.W.: *The Nazi Connection*, Weidenfeld, 1978
WOOD, DEREK: *Attack, Warning, Red: The Royal Observer Corps and The Defence of Britain 1925–1975*, Macdonald & Janes, 1976
YOUNG, A.P.: *The 'X' Documents*, André Deutsch, 1974
YOUNG, KENNETH (Ed.): *The Diaries of Sir Robert Bruce Lockhart*, vol. 2 1939–65, Macmillan, London, 1980

ARTICLES
Anonymous articles are denoted by a key word in brackets in place of the author's name for use in the reference section.

ASHBEE, FELICITY: 'The Thunderstorm that was Hess', *Aeroplane Monthly*, Oct. 1987, pp. 528ff

BATEMAN, DENIS C.: 'Rudolf Hess', *After the Battle*, No. 58, 1987, pp. 1–25

BYRON, ROBERT: 'Nuremberg 1938', *The Spectator*, 22, 29.8.87

DONALD, GRAHAM: 'The Story of Rudolf Hess', *The Journal of the Royal Observer Corps*, Oct. 1942: reprinted in Douglas-Hamilton, pp. 282ff

FRANZ, GEORG: 'Munich: Birthplace and Center of the National-Socialist German Workers' Party', *The Journal of Contemporary History*, XXIX, Dec. 1957, No. 4, pp. 319ff

HAYES, PETER: 'History in an Off Key: David Abraham's Second Collapse', *Business History Review*, 61, Autumn 1987, pp. 452ff

(Kiesel) 'SS-Bericht über den 20 Juli; aus den Papieren des SS-Obersturmbannführers Dr. Georg Kiesel', *Nordwestdeutsche Hefte*, 2 Jahrg., No. 1, Jan. 1947, pp. 5ff

LEUTZE, JAMES: 'The Secret of the Churchill–Roosevelt Correspondence, September 1939–May 1940', *Journal of Contemporary History*, vol. 10/3, July 1975

('M'): 'Was "M" a Soviet Mole?', *World War II Monthly*, April 1988, pp. 9ff

MACDONALD, CALLUM A.: 'The Venlo Affair', *European Studies Review*, vol. 8, IV, 1978, pp. 443ff

MACLEAN, HECTOR: 'Hess Lands in Scotland', *Air Mail*, Winter 1987 pp. 20ff

(Mercury): 'The Inside Story of the Hess Flight', *American Mercury*, May 1943: re-printed in *The Journal of Historical Review*, Autumn 1982, pp. 292 ff

(Observer): 'An Observer's Diary, January 6 1941–May 2 1942: the Hauptmann Alfred Horn story', *Airfix Magazine*, Dec. 1985, pp. 157ff

(Peace): 'Hess, "Hess" and the Peace Party', *Lobster*, 17, Nov. 1988, p. 20ff

(Prytz): 'Prytz-Telegramm', *Der Spiegel*, No. 40, 19. Jahrg., 29.9.65, p. 103

RÖHL, J.: 'Admiral von Müller and the Approach of War, 1911–1914', *Historical Journal*, XLI, 4 (1960)

(Rothschild): 'Rothschild, the Right, the Far-Right and the Fifth Man', *Lobster*, 16, pp. 1ff

SCOTT NEWTON, DR: 'The economic background to appeasement and the search for Anglo-German detente before and during World War 2', *Lobster* 20, pp. 25ff

SIMPSON, AMOS E.: 'The Struggle for Control of the German Economy, 1936–37', *The Journal of Modern History*, March–Dec. 1959, pp. 37ff

(Special Office): 'The Hess story: the Background', *Special Office Brief*, No. 249 (new series), 6.6.84

STUBBE, WALTER: 'In Memoriam Albrecht Haushofer', *Vierteljahreshefte für Zeitgeschichte*, 8 Jahrg., 1960, pp. 236ff

TREVOR-ROPER, HUGH: 'Our Don Quixote', *The Spectator*, 29.8.87, pp. 12–13

TURNER, HENRY A.: 'Big Business & the Rise of Hitler', *The American Historical Review* LXXV, No. 1 (Oct. 1969), pp. 56ff

ZAMETICA, JOHN: 'A Conspiracy to topple Churchill', *The Spectator*, 23.7.88, pp. 23–4

──────SELECT INDEX──────

Many peripheral or observers'/reporters' names and place names have been omitted

Abwehr, 61, 147–9, 255, 279, 291
   (and see Canaris)
Ammann, Max, 47, 69, 184
Amen, John, 304–5, 307
Andrus, B.C., 304, 311
'Appeasers', see Peace party
'Aryans', see Hess, R., attitude,
   to race hygiene
Atomic bomb, 288–9
Auschwitz, 83, 170

'Barbarossa', see Germany, and
   Russia; see Hitler, deceptions
   for/attacks Russia
Barlow, Lady, 154–6
'Barnes, Capt.', 243, 255, 257–9,
   261, 272, 288
Baur, Hans, 145, 158–60, 211,
   233, 294
Beaverbrook, Lord, 115, 118, 142,
   149–50, 156–7, 168, 176, 219,
   235–6, 239–40, 251, 255, 281–4,
   287, 289, 292–3
Beck, Ludwig, 82, 110, 122
'Beerhall Putsch', see Hitler,
   November 1923 Putsch
Beigbeder, Juan, 162, 180, 186,
   223, 246–7
Benes, Eduard. 181, 292
Benson, Flt. Lt., 207, 209–11, 214
Bevin, Ernest, 211–2
Bird, Eugene, 325–6, 329–31
Blackford, D.L., 158, 182–3, 210
Blomberg, Werner v., 65, 94–5,
   100
'Blood purge', see Hess, R. 'Night
   of the Long Knives'
Boa, Don Joachim, 186, 246–7
Bodenschatz, Karl, 103, 221
Bohle, Ernst, 71, 73–4, 77, 82,
   96–8, 139, 144–5, 147, 254, 294,
   306
Bonde, Baron Knut, 154–6, 168,
   234
Bormann, Albert, 73
Bormann, Martin, 71, 73, 75–6,
   98, 107, 131, 190–1, 221,
   229–31, 299, 309

Bouhler, Philipp, 73, 107–8, 132
Boyle, Air Cdre., 182, 211
Brack, Viktor, 108, 132
Bracken, Brendan, 276, 296–7
Brauchitsch, Walter v., 95, 170
Braun, Eva, 70, 221
Brockett, Lord, 114, 150, 182
Brown House, Munich, 45–6
Bruce Lockhart, Robert, 176, 224,
   283–4, 289, 292
Bruckmann, Elsa, 38–9, 41, 101,
   172
Buccleuch, Duke of, 137, 150
Burckhardt, Carl, 124–5, 155–6,
   165, 173–5, 178–82, 186
Bürgerbräukeller, 18–20, 33 (and
   see Hitler, November 1923
   Putsch)
—— bomb attempt on Hitler,
   111–2
Bütefisch, Dr, 55, 57
Butler, R.A., 102, 123–6, 149,
   155, 165, 167, 174, 223, 273,
   276–7

'C', see Menzies, Sir Stewart
Cadogan, Sir Alexander, 115, 150,
   155, 157, 159, 164–5, 169, 182,
   211, 215–6, 218–9, 224, 227–8,
   232, 234–5, 238–44, 254, 256–7,
   272, 281, 283, 288, 292, 349
Calic, Eduard, 60, 196, 220–1
Cameron, Prof. J.M., 334–9, 340,
   342–4
Canaris, Wilhelm, 61, 122,
   129–30, 147–8, 176, 311, 350
Chamberlain, H.Stewart, 26, 38
Chamberlain, Neville, 101–2,
   107–12, 114, 116, 118, 134–5,
   142, 165, 223, 260, 276
Channon, 'Chips', 123–4, 276
Churchill, Winston, 87, 102, 111,
   112–3, 115
—— and Jews, 117–18, 131, 275–6
—— Prime Minister, 116–21,
   123–7, 130, 135, 141, 148–9,
   152, 159, 161–2, 163–4, 167,
   173, 175–8, 181, 185, 189–90,

192, 227, 232, 255, 262, 264–5,
   274–7, 289, 291, 302, 348, 350
—— forbids talks with enemy,
   155, 157, 165
—— reaction to Hess's landing,
   211–12, 215–19, 224–5, 228,
   234–43, 246, 257, 266–7, 272–3,
   281, 289, 295–8, 309, 349–51
Clydesdale, Marquis of, see
   Hamilton, Duke of
Colville, 'Jock', 110, 116, 141,
   162, 185, 190, 215–16, 218, 275,
   349
Concentration camps, wild, 59;
   films of, 310; horrors in, 314–15
   (and see Auschwitz, Treblinka,
   Hitler, extermination of Jews)
Conservative opposition to
   Hitler, 91, 95, 102, 110–13, 122,
   135, 161, 170, 173, 245
Croneiss, Theo, 72, 140, 233

Dahlerus, Birger, 103, 110, 130,
   272
Darré, Walther, 77–8, 191
Death camps, see Hitler,
   extermination of Jews
De Courcy, Kenneth, 113–14, 119,
   123–4, 130
Dicks, Henry, 256, 263–4, 268,
   270–1, 274, 277, 280, 308
Dietrich, Otto, 221, 223
Dollfuss, Engelbert, 82
Dollan, Sir Patrick, 265, 273,
   293–4
Donald, Graham, 207–9
Dönitz, Karl, 303, 309–11, 317,
   320–3
'Double Cross Committee', see
   MI 5
Douglas, Sir W.S. 'Sholto', 159,
   211
Douglas-Hamilton, Lord James,
   158, 182, 209, 214–17
Douglas-Hamilton, Lord
   Malcolm, 88

Eckart, Dietrich, 14, 25–6

Eccles, David, 162, 167, 175
Eden, Anthony, 127, 149, 153, 155–7, 167, 176–7, 180, 215, 218–19, 223–5, 228, 234, 236, 243, 246, 266, 272, 276–7, 291, 293, 297
Eicke, Theodor, 69, 76
Eisenmenger, Prof. W., 336–40, 343–4
England, see Germany, and; and Peace party
Eugenics, see Hitler, attitude, to race hygiene
'Euthanasia' programme, 107, 132

Farben, I.G., 43, 48–9, 53–7, 90, 95, 170
Fath, Hildegard, 99, 139–40, 307, 326, 335–6, 341
Fenton, Walter, 298–9
Foley, Frank, 243, 251, 255–7, 264, 266, 271–2, 277, 281, 285–6, 288–90
Foreign Organisation, see Hess, R., organisation
France, see Germany, and
Franco, Francisco, 162–3, 174–5, 180, 246
Frank, Hans, 68, 74, 76, 79, 83, 98, 229, 231, 310
Freedom for Hess movement, 324, 347
Freikorps, 12–14, 16–17, 20, 41
Freundeskreis RFSS, 53, 57, 90–1, 95, 110, 124
Frick, Dr Wilhelm, 108, 185, 313
Fritsch, Werner v., 65, 94–5, 100
Fromm, Bella, xiv, 61, 63–4, 87, 89
Funk, Walther, 95, 310–11, 318, 323, 327

Gabel, Charles, 327, 330–1, 340
Galland, Adolf, 220
Gardemann, Herr, 180, 186, 223, 246–7, 288
Gas chambers, 108, 132
George VI, King, 191, 214, 219, 238–40, 250–1, 263, 279–80, 285–6, 303
Gerl, Dr Fritz, 9, 85, 287
German opposition, see Conservative opposition
Germany, and England (1914–18), 5–6, 10, 102–4 (1930's), 44, 47, 53–4, 65–6, 73, 85–91, 93–4, 96–7 (1939), 6, 101–3, 108–12 (1940), 122–4, 126–8, 130, 134–5, 139, 144, 149, 151–7, 159 (1941), 162–6, 168, 174–5, 177, 180–1, 186–90, 226–7, 232–5, 237, 244–5, 247, 257, 261–2, 265, 273–4, 280–5, 291, 330, 348
—— and France, 44–5, 65–6, 85–6, 90, 93–4, 108–9, 187, 265; and fall of France, 121–3
—— and Italy, 90–1, 93, 151, 157, 168 (and see Mussolini)
—— and Japan, 91, 94, 134–5,

152–3, 168, 177, 285; anti-Comintern Treaty (1936), 94; Tripartite Pact (1940), 152
—— and Spain, 90, 92–3, 162–4, 174–5, 180–1, 246
—— and U.S.A., 10–11, 43–4, 48, 53–4, 63, 90, 128, 131, 134–5, 139, 149, 152–3, 175, 177, 187–8, 190, 235, 238, 247, 261, 285, 330, 348, 351
—— and U.S.S.R., 53–4, 66, 85, 101–2, 108, 116, 128, 135, 149, 152–3, 166, 168, 170–1, 177, 187–9, 227, 234, 245–7, 257, 262, 265–6, 347–8, 351; Soviet-German Pact (1939), 101–2, 108, 152, 272–4, 281–5, 291; German invasion ('Barbarossa'), 274, 278, 288, 292, 295, 330, 351
Gestapo, 61, 65
Gibraltar, 163–4, 169, 174–5, 246, 273
Gilbert, Dr G.M., 310–11, 313, 316
Graham, Dr Gibson, 244, 248–51, 256, 268
Grantmesnil-Lorraine, Duc de, see De Courcy
Great Britain, see Germany, and England
Grenfell, Russell, 237, 265
Goebbels, Joseph, 36, 47, 55–6, 59, 65, 69, 73, 93, 101, 184, 190, 230–4, 238, 309
Göring, Hermann, 11, 18–20, 55, 59–60, 61–9, 73–4, 87–8, 90, 94–5, 100, 103, 108, 110, 117, 128, 130, 134, 139–40, 144, 150, 154–5, 165–6, 168, 185, 190, 212, 215, 220–1, 234, 249, 252, 266, 272–3, 305–6, 309–11, 314–6

Halder, Franz, 128–9, 132
Halifax, Lord, 102, 109–12, 114, 121, 123–7, 129, 135, 138, 141–2, 149–50, 153, 155–6, 161, 165, 168, 175, 177, 276
Hamilton, Duke of, at 1936 Olympics, 87–9; meeting with Hess (?), 88, 158, 213, 232, 236, 253–4, 273, 296, 306–7, 330; and Albrecht Haushofer, 88–90, 102, 223 (and see letter from); suggested to Hess as middleman, 136–8, 232, 294; Hess decides to fly to, 140, 186, 232, 263, 284, 295; letter from Albrecht Haushofer, 142–3, 145–6, 158, 181–3, 239; letter from Hess, 144–5, 194, 207–8, 213, 239–40, 253–4, 306, 330, 348; takes leave (1940, Nov.), 146, 181 (1941, Jan.), 156, 181 (March), 158, 182 (April), 182 (May), 238; asked to meet Haushofer, 157–9, 182–3, 349; sought by Hess after landing,

206–9, 242, 248, 250, 264–5, 271, 278–80, 283, 285–6, 349; told Hess has a message for him, 209–11; interrogates Hess, 196, 198–9, 212–4, 224–7, 253, 256; informs Churchill, 215–18; tries to clear name, 238, 240, 253–6; defended by Churchill, 236, 254, 297, 348–50; character, 87, 137, 194
Hamilton, Sir Ian, 114, 136
Hanfstaengl, 'Putzi', xiii–xiv, 3–4, 26, 40, 74, 97, 99
Harris, Sir Arthur, 159–60
Hassell, Ulrich v., 82, 100–2, 114, 122, 150, 156, 161, 170, 173–5, 178–82, 223, 233, 245
Haushofer, Albrecht, 14, 81–3, 86, 88–90, 100, 102–3, 122, 133–40, 142–7, 156–7, 159, 161, 170, 173–5 178–83, 186–7, 189, 192, 194, 210, 213, 216, 221–3, 231–2, 239, 245, 247, 254, 265, 294, 301, 306, 330, 350
Haushofer, Heinz, 14, 82–3, 307
Haushofer, Karl, 13–17, 23–7, 33–4, 40–1, 48, 55, 72, 77, 80–3, 85–6, 88–9, 91, 99, 136–9, 142, 147, 154, 171–2, 174–5, 179–80, 186–7, 194, 213, 222, 230, 233, 264, 280, 286–7, 298, 301, 305–7, 330
Haushofer, Martha, 14, 17, 82–3, 86, 186, 221–2, 232–3, 307
Heal, Albert, 211–2, 222
Hess, Alfred, 3, 7, 16, 77, 143–4, 192, 345
Hess, Fritz, 3–4, 7, 13, 22, 32–3, 285, 345
Hess, Helene, 291
Hess, Ilse, hiking companion, xii, 3–4, 21, 39; fellow student, 12–13, 15–17, 31–2; and helper, 23–30, 37, 39; marries Hess, 39–41; wife, 40, 91, 96–7, 145, 173, 192–4, 233, 263, 287, 291, 298–301, 306, 321, 325–6, 336, 345; and Hamilton, 88; and Himmler, 187, 192, 291, 299–301
Hess, Klara, 3, 7, 10, 22, 32–3, 51, 306, 324, 345
Hess, Margarete, 4, 345
Hess, Rudolf, childhood, 3–4; volunteers for WWI, 4–7; WWI, 7–8, 28, 32, 38, 75, 113; decorations/promotions, 7, 10; wounded, 8–10; joins Flying Corps (1918), 10–11, 184; joins Freikorps (1919), 12–13, 16, 58, 61, 75, 82; student Munich Univ'y, 13–14; hears Hitler speak (1920), 15–16; joins NSDAP (1920), 17, 34; Nov. 1923 Putsch, xii, 18–21, 305; outlaw, 21; prisoner, Landsberg (1924–5), xii–xiv, 3, 22–31, 76–7, 97; helps with Mein Kampf, 23–8, 33–4, 37, 77, 79;

Hess, Rudolph (*contd.*)
Hitler's secretary (1925) 33, 41–2, 45–6, 48–9; marries (1927), 39–41; Political Central Commr. NSDAP (1932), 56; SS-Gruppenführer (1932), 56; and Reichstag fire (1933), 59–60; Stellvertreter (1933), 60, 62, 71–7; and Night of Long Knives (1934), 62–70, 72; Min. without Portfolio (1934), 65, 73; and Dollfuss murder (1934), 82; and 1936 Olympics, 87–8; speech to Gauleiters (1937), 91–4; host to Windsors (1937), 96–7; Secret Cabinet Council (1938), 99–100; and *Reichskristallnacht* (1938), 101; Min. Council for Defence (1939), 100; Aug. 1939 speech, 101–2; and 'Euthanasia' progr. (1939), 132 (and see attitudes, to race hygiene below); and assault on Poland (1939), 103; and Bürgerbräu bomb (1939), 112; and fall of France (1940), 123; last meeting with Hitler (1941), 185–6

—— Flight to Britain, peace mission concept (1940), 134, 147–8, 258–9, (1941) 153, 157, 170, 172, 179, 187–9, 192, 213–14, 225–7, 230–2, 259, 261, 265–6, 280–1, 284, 286, 329–30; 351; consults Haushofers, 135–40, 151, 173–5, 186–7, 223; procures plane (1940), 140, 145, 158, 195; decides to fly to Hamilton, 140–1; instructs Haushofer to write to Hamilton, 139, 142–3, 145–6, 181, 216, 292; instructs Bohle to 'English' his letter to Hamilton, 144, 194, 253–4, 292, 306, 330, 348; farewell note (1940), 145, 151; false starts (?), 150–1, 213–4, 261; seeks to contact Hoare, 161, 167, 179–80, 186, 221–2; flies to Madrid (?), 174–5, 247, 273; preparations for flight to Scotland (1941), 172–3, 185–7, 190–3, 219–20, 222, 286–7, 292, 305; takes off from Augsburg (May 10), 183, 192, 194–6, 261; navigation, 173, 194–201; flight, 197–201, 220–1

—— Captivity, held in Scotland, 205–8, 228, 236; interrogated by Hamilton, 213–4, Kirkpatrick, 225–7, 232–3, 235, 237–8, 256–7, Simon, 257–68; Beaverbrook, 282–4; first German b'cast (May 12), 223–5, 234; first BBC b'cast (May 12), 224, 229–30; German explanation (May 13), 230–2, 239; German disinformation, 234, 245, 290–7, 347, 351; Hess's peace terms, 214, 226–7,

237–8, 262, 265, 295, 330; failure, 229–33, 242, 248–9; held in Tower of London, 242, Mytchett Place, 240, 243–4, 248–51, 256–64, 268–72, 277–89, Maindiff Court, 289, 296–303, Nuremberg, 303–16, 319–20, Spandau, 317–33; and fear of drugs/poisons, 248–9, 263–4, 268–70, 278–80, 283, 285–6, 288, 298, 300, 302–4, 307, 322; and depressions, 256, 282, 299, 322–3, 325–6, 331; and abdominal pains, 285–6, 298, 300, 321–2, 325, 329, 331; and amnesia (1941), 64, 279, 285–7, 314 (1943), 299–300 (1945), 14, 60, 81, 140, 144-5, 304–9, 311, 313–14, 341 (1948ff), 322; and responsibility of the Jews, 286, 302–3, 314–5; and suicide attempts (Mytchett), 270–1, 279–80, 282, 284, 302 (Maindiff), 302 (Spandau), 40, 195–6, 249, 323, 326; and psychiatrists, 250–1, 256, 263, 268, 271–2, 277, 280, 282–3, 286, 288, 295–6, 298, 307–9, 323, 331; stands trial Nuremberg, 308–16, 320–1, 325, 327; his final statement, Nuremberg, 314–5; verdict/sentence, 315–16; and freedom attempts, 324, 326–8, 347; and death, 332–3, 338, 342–4; and 'suicide note', 325–6, 335–8, 341–2; and post-mortems, 334–9, 342–4; burials, 337, 345; Scotland Yard Inquiry, 346–7; and closed files on, 156, 207, 254, 324, 339–41, 348–9

—— Character, xii–xiv, 3–4, 9–10, 12–13, 20, 34, 41, 55, 60–1, 64, 68–9, 72–5, 82–3, 85–6, 145, 240, 243–5, 249–50, 264, 268–71, 278, 287–8, 321–2, 331, 341; intelligence, 14, 24, 85; idealism, 16, 34, 36, 38, 41, 50, 55, 73–5, 230, 278, 315, 345; 'Conscience of the Party', 73, 91–2, 132–3, 171–2, 179, 184, 188, 230; reserve, 13, 73, 321; weak/soft, 74–5, 82, 314; unstable, 83, 85, 98, 243, 249, 264, 268, 308 (and see captivity, fears, pains, depressions, amnesia, psychiatrists, above); doubts, 98, 100–1, 133, 313–14; illnesses, 62, 83, 98–100, 123, 133, 145, 230, 232–3 (and see captivity, pains, above); homosexuality (?), xiii–xiv, 37, 40, 60–1, 224, 347; cruelty (?), 20, 58, 61; fatalism, 9, 32, 287; and astrology, 21, 32, 34, 73, 83, 85, 99, 230–3, 287; and fringe medicine, 99, 231–2; and food, 97, 99, 231; love for music, 4,

249, 298, 324, 331; love for flying, 9–11, 12, 37, 48–9, 87–8, 107, 140–1, 145, 172, 306

—— Appearance, 12, 36–7, 60–1, 74, 244, 250, 278, 310, 318–9

—— Attitude, 5–6, 47, 65–6, 73, 85–9, 93, 96–7, 101–3, 107, 114, 123, 188, 190, 193, 226, 231–2, 277–8, 351 (and see Flight to Britain, peace mission concept above); to Communism, 13, 16, 27, 29, 37–9, 48, 58–60, 75–6, 78, 88, 91, 93–4, 120, 171–2, 188, 234, 245, 260, 281, 319, 351; to Jews, 13, 16–17, 25, 27–8, 37, 67, 76–8, 80, 92–4, 101, 117, 222, 260, 266, 286, 302–3, 314, 319, 331–2; to extermination of Jews, 28, 80, 83–4, 107–8, 131–3, 171–2, 260, 266, 331–2, 339, 341; to race hygiene, 13, 28, 72, 77–80, 83–4, 107–8, 123, 131–3, 171–2, 280, 313, 331–2; to Church/belief, 40, 76, 84, 93, 313, 323, 331

—— Relationship to Hamilton, 87–9 (and see Hamilton, meeting with Hess (?), sought by Hess); to Haushofer, Albrecht, 81–3, 89, 187, 301; to Haushofer, Karl, 13–14, 23–5, 80–3, 85, 286–7, 305–7; to Himmler, 49–50, 55–6, 61, 65, 76, 131–2 (and see Hess, Ilse, and Himmler); to Hitler, xii–xiv, 16–17, 21, 22–4, 27–40, 42, 50–1, 55, 58, 64, 66–7, 70, 73–5, 80, 84–5, 91, 94, 97–9, 101–3, 141, 196, 225–6, 229–30, 233, 244–5, 247, 260, 299–301, 303, 314–15, 319, 345; to Röhm, 50, 64, 68–9, 98

—— Organisation, Foreign Organisation, 71–3, 77, 139, 143, 294; intelligence agencies, 49–50, 61–3, 66, 70, 72, 84, 100, 114, 147; *Verbindungsstab*, 60–2, 72, 84, 140, 147; *Volks*-health, 72, 78–9, 84, 99; others, 71–3

—— Liaison to finance/industry, 35–6, 38–9, 41, 44–9, 55–8

Hess, Wolf, 96–7, 99, 144–5, 151, 173, 192–4, 263, 298–9, 306, 321, 324–6, 328, 331–3, 335–6, 338–41, 345–7

Hewel, Walther, 219, 221

Heydrich, Reinhard, 56, 59, 61, 63, 65, 67–8, 76, 78, 82, 108–9, 111, 123, 129, 131–2, 170, 188–9, 195–6, 199, 220–1, 233, 266, 275, 290–1, 311

Himmler, Heinrich, xiv, 13, 19, 32, 49–52, 55–7, 59, 61–9, 71, 73, 76–9, 82, 93–4, 97–100, 103, 110, 112, 123, 129–31, 133, 153, 161, 165, 170–2, 185, 187, 190–2, 221, 279, 300–1, 309, 340

Hindenburg, Paul v., 52, 56–8, 59, 65–6, 70
Hindenburg, Oskar v., 56–7
Hitler, Adolf, war service, xiii, 6–7, 28; post-war agitator, 13–16, 25–6; and Nov. 1923 *Putsch*, 17–22, 35, 111; prisoner, Landsberg, (1924–5), xii–xiv, 22–30, 35, 76; writes *Mein Kampf*, 23–8, 33–4, 37, 77, 79; re-organises NSDAP, 31–6; and 'legal' way to power, 35–9, 41–2, 44–9, 52–8; Chancellor (1933), 58; and Reichstag fire (1933), 59–60; and 'Night of Long Knives' (1934), 62–70; President (1934), 70, 73; course for war (1936), 90–1, 94–5, 101–4; C-in-C Wehrmacht (1937), 95; attacks Poland (1939), 101, 103–4, 107–8; 'peace offensive' (1939), 110–11; conquers France (1940), 121–2; peace offensives (1940–1), 126–7, 165–6, 168, 170 (and see Hess, R., flight to Britain, peace mission concept); turns east (1940), 128–31, 134 (1941, 'Barbarossa'), 152–3, 170–1, 177, 187–8, 190–1; and deceptions for 'Barbarossa', 153, 163, 168, 173, 177, 188–9, 212, 220, 234, 245–7, 350–1; and Hess's mission (1940), 134, 138–9, 141–2, 144, 148 (1941), 158–9, 170, 174, 178–81, 185–90, 192–3, 196, 219–24, 229–34, 247, 256–66, 277, 284, 288, 293–5, 301, 329–30, 350–1; peace terms for GB, 214, 226–7, 247, 262; attacks USSR (1941), 274, 278, 288, 292, 295, 330, 351; declares war on USA (1941), 285; and July 20 1944 plot against, 187, 300–2, 350; suicide (1945), 303
—— Character, xii–xiv, 17, 19, 23–6, 29, 34, 36, 39–40, 42, 54, 75, 97, 116, 249; Führer *Prinzip*, 42–7, 62–3, 73, 75, 98, 103, 245
—— Attitude, to Communism, 13–15, 27, 29, 35, 37, 44–8, 57, 59, 76, 91, 120, 171, 275; to Jews, 15, 17, 25–7, 35, 37, 54, 57, 76–7, 79–80, 117, 171, 266, 275, 303, 314; to extermination of Jews, 28, 79–80, 83, 107–8, 131–3, 171, 266, 275, 310; to race hygiene, 25–8, 47, 54, 78–80, 107–8, 131–3, 171, 266, 303, 311
—— Financial backing for, 14, 34–6, 38–9, 44, 46–7, 54–8
—— Plans to hijack, 158–60, 211
Hoare, Sir Samuel, 112, 129, 138, 143, 155, 161–70, 174–5, 179–81, 185–6, 221–3, 243, 246–7, 251, 254, 265, 277, 288, 350

Hohenlowe, Prinz zu, 110, 124–6, 153–4, 165–7, 169–70, 186, 246, 350
Hoffmann, Heinrich, 61, 64
Höss, Rudolf, 76, 170

Irving, David, 63, 296, 299

Japan, see Germany, and
Jews, see Hess, R. & Hitler, attitude, to Jews, to extermination of Jews
Jones, Howard, 329, 346–7
Jordan, (warder), 329, 332, 338, 342

Kaden, Helmut, 150–1, 195–6
Kahr, Gustav v., 17–20
Kalundborg, radio, 173, 195
Kapp *Putsch*, 12, 16
Kell, Sir Vernon, 118–20
Kelley, Douglas, 304, 307–8, 310–2
Kelly, Sir David, 125–6, 153–5, 165
Kennedy, Joseph, 115, 124, 141
Keppler, Wilhelm, 48, 52–3, 55–7, 90, 95
Kerr, Sir A. Clark, 292–4
Kersten, Felix, 123, 171
King, Cecil, 176, 239–40
Kirdorf, Emil, 38–9, 44, 46
Krafft, Karl, 231–2
Krosigk, Schwerin v., xiv, 21, 74, 98, 133, 172

Landsberg, fortress, see Hess, R. & Hitler
Leasor, James, 151, 158, 182, 194, 210, 219, 251, 254–5, 283
Leigh-Mallory, Trafford, 252
Leitgen, Alfred, xiv, 4, 34, 50, 64, 66, 68–9, 72–3, 75–6, 80, 82, 93, 98–100, 219–20, 299
Ley, Robert, 48, 56, 72–3, 76, 96, 98, 190
Liddell, Guy, 119–20, 239
Liddell-Hart, Basil, 109, 114–6, 149–50, 152, 156, 175–6, 189, 235, 237, 265
Lifton, Robert J., 108, 132
Lindberg, Charles, 37, 87
Lloyd George, David, 115–16, 142, 147, 149, 152, 154–7, 168, 176, 189, 224, 235, 247, 251, 265
Lockhart, see Bruce Lockhart
Loftus, Lt., 277–8, 280
Londonderry, Lord, 86, 137, 150, 273
Lothian, Lord, 126–7, 135, 138, 143, 149
Ludecke, Kurt, xiv, 15, 26, 33, 60–1, 64
Ludendorf, Etich v., 19–20, 22–3, 33
Lympne aerodrome, 159, 211, 294

MacClean, Hector, 208–10
McCowen, John, 252

McClean, David, 205–6
'Madagascar Plan' for Jews, 131–3, 190, 266
Maindiff Court, see Hess, R., captivity
Makins, Roger, 164, 169, 348
Malone, W.B., 249–50, 256, 266, 268–71, 277, 302
Mann, Erika, 85, 179, 186
Mason-MacFarlane, Gen., 164, 169
Masterman, J.C., 148–9, 153, 239, 264–5, 277, 296
Mein Kampf, see Hess, R. & Hitler
Melaouhi, Abdallah, 327–9, 332
Menzies, Robert, 175–6, 189
Menzies, Sir Stewart, 112–14, 118, 130, 138, 147–8, 153–4, 176, 192, 211, 218–9, 224, 228, 234–5, 237, 240, 246, 251, 254–5, 271–2, 279, 281, 288–9, 348
Messerschmitt, Co., 72, 145, 184–6, 195, 212, 220
Messerschmitt, Prof. 'Willi', 140, 145, 184–5, 212, 233, 252, 261
MI 5, 118–20, 146–8, 158, 183, 239, 255, 257
—— 'Double-Cross Committee', 147–8, 150, 153, 157–9, 162, 167, 174, 181–3, 187–9, 192, 222, 237, 246, 255, 264–5, 289–90, 292, 294, 296–7, 348–50
MI 6, 118, 120, 147, 181, 239, 248, 250, 255–6, 289, 296 (and see Menzies, Sir Stewart)
Milch, Erhard, 88
Mitchell, Graham, 119–20
Monckton, Walter, xiv, 238–9, 253–4
Morton, Desmond, 118, 224
Moravetz, Frantisek, 292
Mosley, Sir Oswald, 119
Mussolini, Benito, 35, 90–1, 94, 101, 121, 173, 247, 265, 302
Mytchett Place, see Hess, R., captivity

Nebe, Arthur, 108, 196
Neurath, Konstantin, v., 71, 94–5, 317, 322–3, 327
Nicolson, Harold, 141–2, 155, 168, 175–6, 189–90, 235
Night of Long Knives, see Hitler & Hess, R.
Norman, Montagu, 66, 109, 168
November 1923 *Putsch*, see Hitler & Hess, R.
Nuremberg Laws, 76–7, 79, 83, 313
Nuremberg Trials, 180, 303–4, 308–16

Oberland, Freikorps, 18, 21
Osteria Baveria, 30, 39

Papen, Franz v., 53, 56–7, 306
Payne-Best, Capt., 110–12

'Peace party', British, 109–10, 112–15, 119, 123–6, 128, 135, 141–2, 147–8, 152, 154, 156–7, 159, 162, 165, 167–8, 174–6, 178–9, 181, 188, 214, 224, 230, 232, 235–6, 247, 251, 254, 256, 264–5, 273–4, 292–4, 297, 348–50
Pfeffer von Salomon, see Salomon
Pintsch, Karl-Heinz, 139, 151, 192, 194–5, 219–21, 233, 286
Popov, Dusko, 147–50, 246, 349
Pröhl, Ilse, see Hess, Ilse
Prytz, Bjorn, 125, 135, 276

'Race hygiene', see Hitler & Hess, R., attitude to
radar, see Royal Air Force, reaction
Raeder, Erich, 65, 94–5, 127–8, 309, 317–18, 322–3, 327
'Reaktion', see Conservative opposition
Rees, J.R., 271–2, 277, 286, 299, 302
Reichenau, Walter v., 61, 66, 70
Reichsbanner, 48–9
Reichskristallnacht, 101
Reichstag fire, 59–60, 111
Ribbentrop, Joachim v., 65, 71, 86, 89, 91; as Foreign Minister, 95–7, 101–3, 108, 110, 125, 131, 135, 152–4, 165, 168, 180, 186, 190, 219, 221, 223–4, 245–7, 288, 290–1, 309–10, 351
Roberts, Frank, 157, 175, 348
Roberts, Stephen, 74, 80
Roberts, Violet, 136–7, 139, 142–3, 146, 154
Robertson, T.A., 148, 153, 158, 182–3, 187, 211, 349
Röhm, Ernst, xiv, 13–15, 18–20, 22, 30, 33, 38, 49–51, 53, 55, 61, 63–70, 91
Rohrscheidt, Dr Günther v., 311–13
Rommel, Erwin, 173–4, 189
Roosevelt, Franklin D., 117, 134, 141, 152, 163–4, 177, 179, 190, 238, 266, 274, 285, 289, 291, 295
Ropp, Baron de, 110, 159, 190–1
Rosbaud, Paul, 289
Rosen, Count Eric, 154, 168, 234
Rosenberg, Alfred, 25–6, 33, 66, 69, 73, 77–8, 83, 87, 110, 159–60, 190–1, 193, 219–20, 309
Rothacker, Emma, 214, 221, 229, 291
Rothschild, family, 117

—— Victor, 119–20
Royal Air Force, reaction to Hess's intrusion, 198–200, 210–11, 266, 294
Royal Observer Corps, 199–201, 207–8

SA (Sturm Abteilung), 15, 18–21, 32, 36–7, 48–53, 55, 60–1, 63–8, 91
Salomon, Pfeffer v., xiv, 38, 61, 84, 100, 114, 167
Schacht, Hjalmar, 53, 55–6, 66, 90–1, 95, 168
Schellenberg, Walter, 110–12, 266
Schirach, Baldur v., 318, 322–3
Schleicher, Kurt v., 53, 56–8, 63, 69
Schröder, Kurt v., 53, 56–7, 63, 291
Scott, A. Malcolm, 243, 250–1, 256–7, 264, 268, 277, 283, 285, 288
SD (Sicherheitsdienst – Security Service), 59, 61, 188–9, 233–4, 247, 275
Seidl, Dr Alfred, 313, 321, 325, 332, 335–6, 341, 347
Shakespeare, Geoffrey, 85–6, 265, 278
Shephard, Major, 240, 243–4, 249, 287–8
Simon, Sir John, 86, 112, 134, 150–1, 156, 243, 256–8, 272, 279, 282, 288
Sinclair, Sir Archibald, 142, 213, 217, 225, 253–4, 273, 296, 349
SIS, see MI6
Smith, Hon. S.J., 268–9
Spain, closed files on, 163, 174–5, 181, 246–7, 350 (and see Germany and; and Franco)
Spanish Civil War, 90–3
Spandau, see Hess, R., captivity
Spann, Prof. W., 336–9, 340–2
Speer, Albert, 80, 97, 289, 317–18, 320–3, 329
Sperr, Ingeborg, 139–40, 307
SS (Schutz Staffel), 49–52, 55, 57, 59–60, 65–8, 73, 76, 78, 91, 107–8, 129–30, 132–3, 144, 170–1, 212, 306, 313
—— Attempt to assassinate Hess, 251–2
Stahmer, Heinrich, 161, 167, 180, 186, 221–3, 247
Stalin, Joseph, 37, 116, 120, 171, 177, 188, 245, 272, 279, 281, 291, 297–8, 302, 350–1

Stammers, F.G., 158–9, 182–3
Stennes, Walter, 50–1
Sterilisation laws, 83, 99
Stevens, Major, 110–12
Stokes, R.R., 115, 175, 224, 273
Strasser, Gregor, 32–3, 35–6, 42, 46–9, 53, 55–6, 63, 65, 69, 71
Strasser, Otto, 26, 35, 42, 46–8, 50, 56
Suñer, Serrano, 162–3, 175
Swinton, Lord, 239, 253–4
Synanska, Madame, 129–30

Terboven, Josef, 39, 67
Thomas, Hugh, 339–41, 346–8
Thule Society, 13–14, 16, 18, 25
Thurnheer, Walther, 285–6
Thyssen, Fritz, 45–6, 56
Todt, Fritz, 72, 221
Torr, Brig., 165–7, 169
Treblinka, 83

U-Boat campaign (1917), 10–11, 260 (1940–1), 128, 153, 177, 226, 237, 260, 280
United States, see Germany, and 'Untermensch' (sub-human), 78–9

Vansittart, Sir Robert, 88, 115, 126, 165, 239, 273
Venlo incident, 110–12, 114
Verbindungsstab, see Hess, R., organisation
Verdun, battle of, 7–8
Völkisch movement, 14–15, 18, 28, 30, 32, 38, 42, 44, 47, 77

Wagner, Dr Gerhard, 78–9, 84, 99, 107–8
Waite, Robert, xiv, 19, 64, 79
'Wallace, Col.', 243, 250, 255–6, 272, 281, 288
Weizsäcker, Baron Ernst v., 122, 124, 126–7, 142, 144, 152, 157, 187, 189, 244–5, 247, 265
Widmann, Dr Albert, 108
Wilhelm I, Kaiser, 5–6
Wilson, Horace, 108–9, 115
Windsor, Duke of, 96–7, 126, 128, 138, 167
Winterbotham, Frederick, 66, 85, 89, 110, 159, 191
Wirth, Christian, 132
Wolff, Karl, 67, 233

Zugspitze race, 87–8
Zionism, 117–18, 275–6 (and see Churchill, and the Jews)

SELECT INDEX
AFTERWORD

A. A. Brigade, No. 42, 355–6
'ABCD Nr. S274K', Plan, 366,
370, 380

'Barbarossa', see Germany, and
U.S.S.R.
Barrie, Major, 353
Battaglia, Roman, 353–5
B.B.C. Monitoring Service,
357–9
Beaverbrook, Lord, 366–9,
374–6, 379
Bevin, Ernest, 357
Bohle, Ernst, 370
Burckhardt, Carl, 379
Butler, R. A., 367, 378

'C', see Menzies, Sir Stewart
Cadogan, Sir Alexander, 373,
375–9
Churchill, Winston, 352, 357,
363, 365, 367, 369, 373, 376–80
Clydesdale, Marquis of, 373, and
see Hamilton, Duke of
Colville, 'Jock', 370, 379

Day, Frank, 374–5
Debney, Joseph, 356
Dobson, T. W., 355
Donald, Graham, 354, 357
'Double Cross Committee', see
MI 5
Douglas, James, 357–9
Douglas-Hamilton, Lord James,
373

Eden, Anthony, 367, 375–6,
378–9

Foley, Frank, 364, 379
Franco, Francisco, 364

Galland, Adolf, 359
George VI, King, 364–5, 379
Germany, and England, 366–8,
370, 375, 377, 379
—and U.S.S.R., 365–7, 370, 373,
375, 378, 380
Goodall, Nancy M., 356–7
Göring, Hermann, 359, 365, 370
Graham, Dr. Gibson, 363–5
Guerber, André, 364–6, 368, 370,
371, 379

Halifax, Lord, 367, 378
Hamilton, Dowager Duchess of,
354, 372
Hamilton, Duke of, at 1936
Olympics & meeting with
Hess, 354, 364, letter from
Albrecht Haushofer, 362, 371,
letter from Hess, 353, 361,
370–1, takes leave (Nov. 1940),
362, sought by Hess after
landing, 353–4, 356–7, 379–80,
inaction (?) 354–6, interrogates
Hess, 360, 366, 368, 372–6,
informs Churchill, 373, 376,
378, tries to clear name, 370–1,
379
Haushofer, Albrecht, 354, 362–3,
371, 379
Haushofer, Karl, 363–4
Hess, Ilse, 361, 363
Hess, Rudolf, peace mission
concept, 360–5, 367–70,
379–80, decides to fly to
Hamilton, 362–5, instructs
Haushofer to write to
Hamilton, 362, 371, instructs
Bohle to 'English' his letter to
Hamilton, 353, 370–1, seeks to
contact Hoare, 379, flies to
Madrid (April 1941), 364–5,
379, is convinced English
desire peace, 364–5, 367,
371–2, 379–80, preparations
for flight, 363–4, 366, takes off
from Augsburg, 357–9,
navigation, 359–60, flight,
352–3, 355, 357–64, 375–6,
captivity in Scotland, 353,
374–5, interrogated by
Battaglia, 353–5, interrogated
by Hamilton, 366, 368, 372,
375–6, interrogated by
Kirkpatrick, 365–7, 369, 373,
375–9, interrogated by Ld.
Simon, 378–9, interrogated by
Ld. Beaverbrook, 367–8,
374–5, first German b'cast
(May 10?), 357–9, first official
German b'cast (May 12),
357–8, first BBC b'cast, 358,
peace terms, 369–70, 373,
375–80, suicide attempt,

359–61, 'suicide' letter to
  Hitler, 360–1
— Character, idealism, 352, 360,
  'Conscience of the Party', 376,
  fatalism, 361, 364, astrology,
  360, 363–4, fringe medicine,
  374–5, 377
— Relationship, to Haushofer,
  Karl, 363–4, to Hitler, 352,
  360–1
Hess, Wolf, 359–60
Heydrich, Reinhard, 360, 368
Hitler, Adolf, 352, 358, 360–1,
  363–5, 368, 370, 375, 377, 380
Hoare, Sir Samuel, 363–5, 367,
  379–80
Hopkinson, Henry, 362, 377–8
Howell, John, 368
Hyatt, Pearl, 372–3

'Informant', the, 369–70, 379–80

Kelly, Sir David, 363
Kirkpatrick, Ivone, 365–70, 373,
  375–9

Leasor, James, 366, 368–9, 371
Liddell Hart, Basil, 367
Lloyd George, David, 367

Makins, Roger, 376–7
Martin, John, 373, 376
Menzies, Sir Stewart, 363, 371,
  380
Messerschmitt, Prof. 'Willi', 359
MI5, 352, 362–3, 370–1
MI6, 352, 370–1
Monckton, Walter, 358, 362

Moravetz, Frantisek, 362, 368
Morton, Desmond, 368–9, 379

Nesbit, Roy, 355
Newton, Dr. Scott, 364
Nicolson, Harold, 365

Palmer, Iris, 357, 372–3
'Peace Party', British, 362–3, 367,
  369, 374, 378, 380
Peace proposals, see Hess,
  Rudolf, peace terms; see
  'ABCD . . . ', Plan
Pintsch, Karl-Heinz, 359, 363
Philby, 'Kim', 367–8, 375
Popov, Dusko, 363, 371, 380
Pyne, Mrs, see Palmer, Iris

Roberts, Frank, 364
Roberts, Violet, 362
Robertson, T. A., 362–3
Roosevelt, Franklin D., 369, 378
Rose, Dennis, 356
Royal Air Force, reaction to
  Hess's intrusion, 354–6, 359
Royal Observer Corps, 355–7
Russia, see Germany, and
  U.S.S.R.

Simon, Lord, 359–60, 378–9
SIS, see MI6
Stalin, Joseph, 368, 380
Swinton, Lord, 371

Windsor, Duke of, 379
Woodman, R. G., 355

'Y' Service, 359